Bruce Collins
Chairman

The 350th Anniversary Celebration
of the Town of East Hampton, Inc.

Dear Friends and Neighbors,

In 1948, when I celebrated the 300th Anniversary of East Hampton, I never suspected that I would be serving as the Chair of the Town's next landmark anniversary 50 years later.

The purpose of the celebration to commemorate the Town's 350th Anniversary was to teach the entire ecommunity about the unique heritage which we all share. Our hope was that this knowledge would help us to continue to preserve our Town as we go into the future.

During the year, we had parades and parties, re-enactments and exhibitions, theatrical productions and fireworks; but the centerpiece of our celebration was our twelve-month *Lecture Series*. Local, regional and national historians delivered twenty-seven lectures about East Hampton and its role in the events that formed this great nation. These lectures are now printed in this volume for your reading pleasure.

I hope that you will take this wonderful opportunity to learn about the history of our Town. We need you to join with all of us to help make East Hampton an even better place to live throughout the next 350 years.

Sincerely,

Bruce Collins
Chair

TOWN OF EAST HAMPTON

159 Pantigo Road
East Hampton, New York 11937

CATHERINE H. LESTER
SUPERVISOR

Tel: (516) 324-4140
Fax: (516) 324-2789

Dear Friends:

We are very fortunate to live in and be a part of the Town of East Hampton. From Wainscott to Montauk, ocean to bay, our heritage is apparent in every hamlet and village. Family stories passed down from generation to generation have kept our history alive and have helped us to understand our present.

Throughout 1998, we celebrated 350 years of East Hampton's history.

Our Anniversary Committee planned a year of events to educate residents about the history of our Town. The centerpiece of the celebration was the Lecture Series. I hope you were fascinated by the diverse topics of the lectures - from witch trials, to whaling, fishing, art, pirates and colonial politics.

I encourage everyone to read each of these lectures, now printed in a one-volume book; and in doing so, you will vastly expand your own knowledge of our special Town (and be entertained as well). With this knowledge of our past to guide us, we will help maintain our heritage and make East Hampton become a better place to live in the next millennium.

Sincerely,

Catherine H. Lester

Catherine H. Lester
Supervisor

CHL/bc

VILLAGE OF EAST HAMPTON

Settled 1648 - Incorporated 1920

86 MAIN STREET

EAST HAMPTON, N.Y. 11937-2730

516-324-4150

FAX 516-324-4189

OFFICE OF

Mayor

The 350th Anniversary Celebration's lecture series was a unique opportunity to learn about East Hampton's history. It will lead us, inevitably, to a broader understanding of our community's origins.

The home of Village government, Village Hall, is in the Lyman Beecher House at 86 Main Street. The February lecture, *Leading the Way: Political Force of the Reverends James, Buell and Beecher* was an insightful look into the life of Rev. Lyman Beecher. It is fitting, indeed, that the Village had the foresight to preserve this historical site.

One can argue that as our community has grown and become more diversified, we collectively know less about East Hampton's history. As a community we must never lose sight of our obligation to preserve history and retain as much of our rural character possible.

The 350th Anniversary Lecture Series has made a vital contribution to the ongoing preservation effort. This book will be a source of enjoyment and important research for all of us for years to come.

Sincerely,

Paul F. Rickenbach, Jr.
Mayor

Major Underwriting for the Year-Long
350th Anniversary Lecture Series
Was Provided by the Law Firm
of
TWOMEY, LATHAM, SHEA & KELLEY

BENEFACTORS
Major Underwriting for This Publication Was Provided by
Joan & Joe Cullman
and
William Heppenheimer
in memory of his grandmother
Blanche Miller Heppenheimer

SPONSORS
The following businesses and individuals graciously sponsored
one or more of the twenty-seven lectures in the series:

Alixandra & Stuart Baker
Allan M. Schneider Associates, Inc.
Amagansett Building Materials
Bistrian Gravel Corporation
Bridgehampton National Bank
Bruce & Jane Collins
Cook Pony Farm Real Estate
Dayton & Osborne
Devlin McNiff Real Estate
Dunemere Real Estate
Edward F. Cook Agency
Gosman Restaurant & Bar, Inc.
H.O. Penn Machinery

The Maidstone Arms Inn
  & Restaurant
Harold McMahon
Patricia & Douglas Mercer
The Kenneth & Evelyn Lipper
  Foundation
Manhattan Mortgage Company
Nick & Toni's
Paine Webber of East Hampton
Sabin Metal Company
Sotheby's International Realty
Village Hardware of East Hampton

"Tell ye your children of it, and let your children tell their children and their children and other generations."

—Joel, I: 3.

AWAKENING THE PAST

The East Hampton 350th Anniversary Lecture Series 1998

EDITED BY
TOM TWOMEY

Newmarket Press · New York

FIRST EDITION

10   9   8   7   6   5   4   3   2   1

Library of Congress Cataloging-in-Publication Data:

Awakening the Past: The East Hampton 350th Anniversary Lecture Series/An East Hampton Historical Collection Book, edited by Tom Twomey

    p.   cm.

Includes biographical references and index.

ISBN 1-55704-388-4 (trade edition)

ISBN 1-55704-396-5 (commemorative limited edition)

1. History—New York State.   I. East Hampton   II. Title

F67. W781   1999

972.3'01'081—dc20   99-112796

                                                         CIP

QUANTITY PURCHASES

Companies, professional groups, clubs, and other organizations may qualify for special terms when ordering quantities of this title. For information, write Special Sales, Newmarket Press, 18 East 48th Street, New York, NY 10017, call (212) 832-3575 or fax (212) 832-3629.

Commemorative Custom Edition Limited to 2,000 copies: ISBN 1-55704-396-5
Hardcover Trade Edition: ISBN 1-55704-388-4

ILLUSTRATION CREDITS

Pages xii, 334, 338: Map, illustration, and photograph, courtesy of the East Hampton Library Collection.

Page xiii: Map of the State of New York by Simeon DeWitt, Surveyor General, Albany: 1802, courtesy of the Map Division, The New York Public Library, Astor, Lenox and Tilden Foundations.

Page 10: Photograph, courtesy of the Pharaoh Foundation Collection, Long Island Collection, East Hampton Free Library, and SCAA.

Pages 255, 259, 261: Photographs, courtesy of Noel Gish.

Pages 380, 383: Photographs, courtesy of William J. Madden.

All other photographs or artwork are in the public domain, unless indicated otherwise underneath reproduction.

Designed by M. J. DiMassi

Manufactured in the United States of America.

Contents

ILLUSTRATIONS

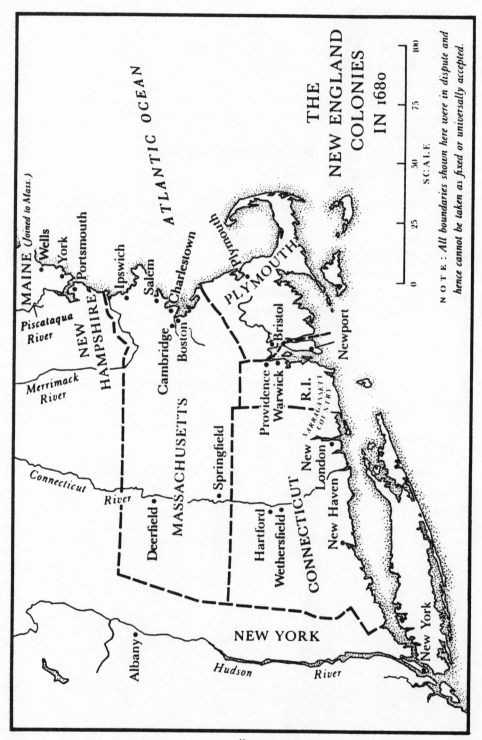

THE
NEW ENGLAND
COLONIES
IN 1680

SCALE

0   25   50   75   100

NOTE: All boundaries shown here were in dispute and
hence cannot be taken as fixed or universally accepted.

MAINE (Joined to Mass.)

Wells
York
Portsmouth

NEW HAMPSHIRE

Piscataqua River

Merrimack River

ATLANTIC OCEAN

Ipswich
Salem
Charlestown
Cambridge
Boston

Plymouth

PLYMOUTH

Bristol

Newport

Providence
Warwick
R.I.

NARRAGANSETT COUNTRY

MASSACHUSETTS

Connecticut River

Deerfield
Springfield

New London

Hartford
Wethersfield

CONNECTICUT

New Haven

NEW YORK

Albany

Hudson River

New York

xii

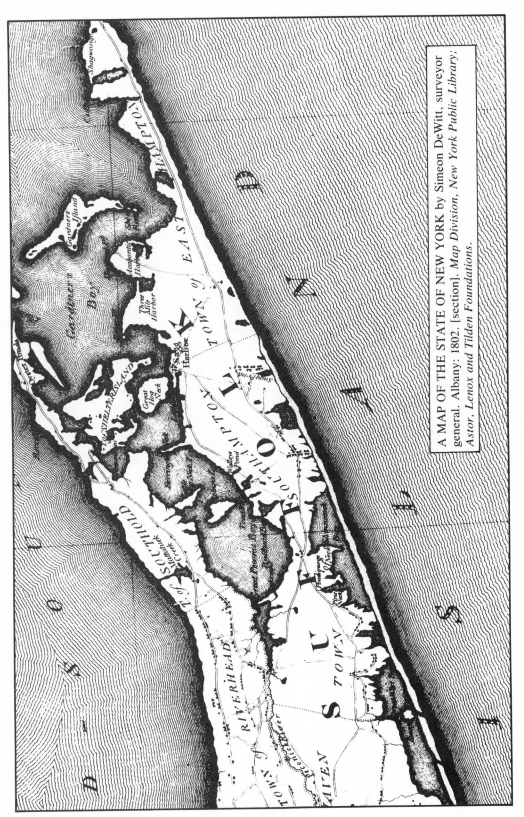

A MAP OF THE STATE OF NEW YORK by Simeon DeWitt, surveyor general. Albany: 1802. [section]. Map Division, *New York Public Library; Astor, Lenox and Tilden Foundations.*

To preserve the records of what came before us promotes that sense of continuity which gives us the faith to continue our own work ...

—Lewis Mumford, 1927

Introduction

L EWIS MUMFORD, who died in 1990 at the age of 95, was one of America's formidable twentieth-century minds. He believed that a community was "a collective work of art" unified through geographic, historic, economic, and cultural ties over a long period of time. He wrote that "our own lives, the lives of our ancestors and neighbors, the events that have taken place in the particular locality where we have settled, are every bit as important as the lives of people who are more remote from us, no matter how numerous these others may be; or how insignificant we may seem along side of them." He believed that since local history is relatively accessible and immediate because it deals with the concrete and commonplace, it vitalizes the teaching of history to the child at school, to say nothing of more mature students. "The things that we can see and touch are those that awaken our imagination," he stated.

In ending his talk before the Dutchess County Historical Society in 1927, Lewis Mumford said, "Every old part of the country is filled with the memorials of our past: tombstones and cottages and churches, names and legends, old roads and trails ... as well as the things we built and used yesterday. All these memorials bring us closer to the past and, so doing, they bring us closer to our present for we are living history as well as recording it and our memories are as necessary as our anticipations.

Mumford would have been proud of the Town of East Hampton. In early 1997, the Town Board of East Hampton created The 350th Anniversary Celebration Committee to commemorate the Town's 350th anniversary. The Committee, led by Chairman Bruce Collins, quickly determined that the purpose of the celebration would be to teach the entire community about East Hampton's unique heritage as a means of preserving the community for future generations.

As Bruce Collins stated at the Opening Ceremony, "In the months ahead, we will have parades and parties, reenactments and exhibitions, theatrical productions, and fireworks, but the centerpiece of our celebration will be a twelve-month lecture series." The Anniversary Committee urged Town residents through a beautiful town wide mailing to participate in the series through the purchase of season tickets to all the lectures.

The excitement about the lecture series grew as local, regional, and national historians agreed to deliver twenty-seven lectures about East Hampton and its role in the events that helped form America. It was quickly decided that at the end of the year, all of the lectures should be printed in one anthology and distributed to our schools, libraries, and book stores for all to enjoy. You have in your hands the end result.

No small town in America has ever celebrated its founding with a lecture series of this scope and depth. Scholars have come from California, Illinois, Delaware, Connecticut, Boston, Princeton, Washington, and Albany to add their insight to why East Hampton has such a unique heritage. Over the year, total attendance reached more than 4,200. Each lecture was broadcast several times on LTV, the East Hampton local community access station. The Lectures were instantly published on the world wide website of the Anniversary Committee sponsored by the East Hampton Library for all to enjoy and print at their home computer. An extensive bibliography of classic East End history books was recommended for further reading by the lecturers and the Town Historian and myself. A painstakingly detailed index was created to make the contents of all of the lectures easily accessible to the scholar and amateur historian alike.

While a majority of the lectures dealt with East Hampton in the seventeenth century, other lectures dealt with living in East Hampton as a craftsman in the eighteenth century. Major developments during the nineteenth century, such as East Hampton's role in the Civil War and the impact on East Hampton of artists, writers, the Long Island Railroad, and Teddy Roosevelt during the latter part of that century were also studied. And to round out the series, lectures were presented about the way art and architecture affected East Hampton in the twentieth century.

What did we learn about the origins of East Hampton from this Lecture Series?

First, the Town was the product of truly global forces at work in the New England region. It was not simply a few utopian men and women deciding for strictly religious reasons to set up camp in the woods of eastern Long Island.

Second, from its earliest days, the East Hampton community had two characteristics: it was fiercely independent and it was relatively affluent. It was not a group of poor downtrodden settlers who labored in agrarian isolation to make ends meet.

What global forces? The men and women who settled in New England were, for the most part, from the upper middle class in England. They owned businesses and property in England before they left. To finance the purchase of boats and supplies for the journey and for the early years of living in the New England, they were able to borrow the necessary funds from London bankers. Property owned in England was used as collateral with interest rates of eight percent or higher. Upon arrival in New England, with gold and silver lacking, timber, fish, and furs were sent back to London to pay back the loans. Each colony appointed an agent in London to assist with the transactions.

For fifteen years or so after the English arrived on the Mayflower in 1620, the English settlers found plenty of natural resources to send back to London to reduce their loans. Timber, fish, and even furs were plentiful. Eventually, these natural resources became relatively scarce. Ships bringing more settlers would also bring cheap blankets, pots, pans, and tools to trade for furs from the Indians. The fur most sought by London merchants was beaverskin since it would hold its shape and remain waterproof when converted into top hats for the London upperclass. Beaverskin was sought then much the way mink is sought today. At first, beavers were plentiful along the southern New England shore where the colonists first settled. But once a family of beavers was caught, others did not replace them since beavers are not roaming animals. They generally stay fixed in a particular neighborhood all of their lives. As the beavers became more and more scarce along the coast, the English settlers looked desperately to other ways of securing this valuable fur to repay their loans.

Let's keep following the money. Indians in Canada and northern New England, for many years before the English arrived, began using wampum in religious ceremonies and for just plain old-fashioned courtship—much the way diamonds, rubies, and other gems are used in our society. Wampum was a small, cylindrical white or purple bead made by our own local Indians from a certain shell found in the Peconic Bay. Because of the uniqueness of the shell and our local Indians' ability to handcraft these special beads many years before East Hampton was founded, the Dutch, shortly after they arrived in what is now New York, referred to the East End of Long Island as the "mine of the New World."

So how does all this fit together? A young engineer, soldier, and pioneer named Lion Gardiner was hired by Saye and Lord Brooke to build a fort at the mouth of the Connecticut River to serve as a trading post and a new settlement. This was done shortly after an expedition to Long Island in 1633 by the English in Massachusetts which confirmed the large quantity of wampum being made on the East End. The fort was placed in a strategic location to keep the Dutch in New York from spreading their trading empire east. Lion Gardiner was commander of this fort at the time of the Pequot War in 1637, which destroyed the ferocious Pequot Tribe in southern Connecticut.

For many years, the Pequots had collected a tax—or a tribute, as it was called back then—from the East End Indians. This tax was willingly paid by the Montauketts for the same reasons we pay taxes today—Indians throughout the East Coast had organized themselves into tribes or what we call today "municipalities." The Pequots and Montauketts were part of the Algonquian nation and, therefore, it was appropriate for the Pequots to collect a tax from the East End Indians for, what I suppose we would call today, "national defense." Since the Indians had no currency, the Pequots collected ten percent of the special little bead called "wampum" produced on the East End as the tribute. The Pequots used this bead to barter with northern Indians for goods. Lion Gardiner, having direct contact with the Pequot Indians, became aware of this tax and also became aware of how valuable this bead was to the Indians from Canada and northern New England.

After the decimation of the Pequot tribe in 1637, Gardiner was contacted by Wyandanch, the chief of the Montaukett Indians.

Gardiner discovered that the Montaukett Indians were very willing to pay the English settlers the tax that Wyandanch had been paying the defeated Pequots. In return, Wyandanch wanted protection against the Indian enemies of the Montauketts and a treaty for direct trade with the English. (Such trading rights are still being negotiated today when undeveloped countries seek most-favored-nation status with the United States.) To Wyandanch, this was a terrific deal since it cost him nothing more than what his tribe was previously paying the Pequots, and it now included direct trading rights with the English. To Lion

Gardiner, this was a great deal since the English settlers could secure for free the valuable wampum bead directly from the Montauketts and use it, in turn, to trade for the beaverskins. By securing a free source of wampum, the English settlers no longer needed to bring from England wool blankets, pots, pans and tools to get the beaver skin sought by the London merchants. By nurturing his relationship with Wyandanch, Lion Gardiner guaranteed peace with the Montaukett Indians, eliminating them as a threat to future settlers of the East End. Best of all, the alliance between Gardiner and Wyandanch produced a free and plentiful source of wampum which, in turn, created fortunes for Gardiner and his allies in New England.

But Gardiner needed to move quickly to consolidate the East End under English control. The Dutch in New York City and Albany had become aware of the value of wampum and its origin on the East End. Lion Gardiner was the first to move to the island right in the middle of Peconic Bay in the middle of the wampum mine. He nurtured the settlement of East Hampton which became the closest English settlement to Montauk, the home of Wyandanch. Lion Gardiner used his considerable political influence to secure the financial and legal support for the origins of East Hampton.

THE DEED TO EAST HAMPTON

On April 29th in 1648, two allies of Gardiner, Edward Hopkins, Governor of the Colony of Connecticut, and Theophilus Eaton, the Governor of New Haven, purchased from Wyandanch and three other Indian sachems the land now known as the Town of East Hampton. Hopkins and Eaton paid twenty coats, twenty-four looking glasses, twenty-four hoes, twenty-four hatchets, twenty-four knives, and 100 muxes or tiny wampum drills. The Indians reserved the right to fish in any convenient places for shells to make wampum.

Two years later, Hopkins and Eaton sold the land to the original English settlers of East Hampton, including Lion Gardiner, for about thirty pounds. An English pound today is worth about $1.60. Back then, it was worth about $1,000. And, thus, the entire Town of East Hampton was purchased for about $30,000. Hopkins and Eaton made a huge profit.

Buy why did two governors in Connecticut purchase the Town of East Hampton from the Indians in the first place? It goes back to William Alexander, who had the title "Lord Sterling." He was a close friend of King James I. James I (who was also the King of Scotland) had already given him the rights to mint all Scottish coins. In 1635, Lord Sterling secured from his friend the king a patent, or the English legal title for all of Long Island. Settlers were flooding New England from England, none of whom had yet settled on Long Island. Two years earlier, Governor Winthrop from Massachusetts had sent an expedition to the East End and discovered it was the source of wampum which fact then became known in England.

But what does this all have to do with Hopkins and Eaton securing the deed from the Indian sachems? Lord Sterling was a shrewd man. With his political connections to the king, he wanted to control the wampum supply and, therefore, the wealth of New England. He wanted to "corner the market" on wampum. He sent his deputy, James Farrett, to New England to begin the process of selling Long Island, reserving to Lord Sterling rights to the wampum. In fact, when Farrett sold Lion Gardiner his island, the deed provided that Lord Sterling would be paid a significant commission on any wampum that Gardiner secured from the Indians in the area.

But Lord Sterling's plan to corner the wampum market was short-lived. Farrett was in the New World for less than two years when he learned that the sixty-eight-year-old Lord Sterling had suddenly died. After quickly selling more land to the settlers at Southampton, Southold, and Fishers Island, Farrett borrowed 110 pounds from Hopkins, Eaton, and others in Connecticut and gave them a mortgage on Long Island just before he left to return to England.

After Farrett borrowed the money and returned to England, three years passed with no word from either Farrett or the family of Lord Sterling. Hopkins, Eaton and their business partners foreclosed the mortgage and began clearing the Indian titles to the land so they could sell the land with no Indian claims to other settlers to get their money back. And that is how the Indian deed of April 29, 1648 came about. Hopkins and his partners had already foreclosed on the Farrett mortgage and were trying in 1648 to eliminate any claim by the local Indians. By the way, the thirty pounds paid to Eaton and Hopkins two years later by the East Hampton settlers was about twenty-five percent of the 110 pounds they previously loaned to Farrett. So it was an important transaction to them. If Lord Sterling had not died in 1640, Farrett would not have borrowed the money from Eaton and Hopkins, and the 1648 deed would not have been executed, and we would not be celebrating the 350th anniversary in 1998.

We will never know what would have happened if Sterling had

lived. But we do know that with Lord Sterling dead and Farrett gone, Lion Gardiner was in control of the wampum mine of the New World.

And so it can be argued that the origin of East Hampton stemmed from the international trade between New England and England in the mid-seventeenth century. East Hampton was born from the political strategy of Lion Gardiner and his partners to thwart Dutch competition, and to secure a monopoly on a precious natural resource that was as valuable as gold or diamonds are today.

INDEPENDENCE AND DEFIANCE

But, why was East Hampton so independent and relatively affluent? As previously mentioned, Lion Gardiner first settled on Gardiner's Island, part of the Town of East Hampton, in 1639, making East Hampton the first continuous English settlement in the State of New York. Lion Gardiner's daughter was the first English child born in the State of New York. She was born in what is now East Hampton.

And during its early formative years, East Hampton remained totally independent of any outside governmental influence. From 1648 to 1655, the town government was answerable to no other government, corporation or person. While a few towns on Long Island and in New England can claim they were technically founded earlier than East Hampton, those townships were all part of a greater entity—either the Massachusetts Bay Colony, the Plymouth Colony, or a part of the United Colonies in Connecticut. On Long Island, Southold was a colony of New Haven and Southampton quickly became attached to Hartford, Connecticut. In these early years East Hampton was not part of Connecticut or New Haven or Massachusetts. Nor was it a corporate entity reporting to English or Dutch stockholders, as was the case with the Bay Colony and New Netherlands. Our sole governing body was its town meetings presided over by the Trustees for the Freeholders of the Commonalty of East Hampton. It was a pure democracy. As a result, it could be argued that East Hampton was a commonwealth, perhaps the first truly independent commonwealth on the North American continent. This independence bred defiance and rebelliousness. East Hampton belligerently rejected New York's attempt to control its future. During the seventeenth century, East Hampton was constantly resisting efforts by European powers to directly or indirectly control, govern, and tax it.

This defiant attitude did not exist in neighboring New England colonies for two reasons: unlike East Hampton, those colonies traced their origins to legal documents and charters initially granted in England and therefore viewed themselves as part of the English extended family. And second, in New England, unlike New York, each town participated in a representative assembly which set the rules and taxes. New York was literally owned by the King's brother and he forbade representative assemblies since he wanted the power to unilaterally set the taxes himself. In other words, there was no need for East Hampton's defiance in New England since the people there were not suffering from the dictatorship of the Duke of York as was the case here. They had a representative assembly. East Hampton did not.

One hundred years before the American Revolution, the people of East Hampton were among the first to establish, articulate, and fight for this nation's basic creed. It was an East Hampton minister who first argued that there shall be no taxation without representation. Of course, the Governor of New York indicted and jailed him for uttering such a seditious remark. This was a harbinger of things to come.

RELATIVE AFFLUENCE

East Hampton was quite affluent compared to its neighbors. It had two rare natural resources, both of which few New England or other Long Island colonies possessed: first, as mentioned earlier, Lion Gardiner's control of the wampum and second, the town's virtual monopoly on whale oil from the whales that beached themselves or were caught very close offshore. The combination of these two resources was unique in New England and on Long Island. They gave East Hampton significant wealth to barter for middle-class luxuries about which other settlements could only dream.

The independence and relative affluence made a lasting, durable, permanent mark on the culture and attitudes, not only of the first settlers in East Hampton, but of the many generations thereafter, right up to the present.

From its origin, East Hampton was unique. It was different. It had wealth. It had political power. Much the same as today.

In the words of Lewis Mumford:

> The value of local history is stimulating the imagination. Once one begins to follow the threads of local history, local manners, local industry, local peoples, one finds that they lead in every

direction....Local history is not a means of exciting false pride in little things or exaggerated pretensions to local virtues that do not exist. On the contrary, it promotes a decent self-respect....To know local history, and to take pleasure in it, is the beginning of that sympathy with remote times and foreign peoples which tends to make one truly a person of the world.

So, sit back and enjoy yourself. Reading this book should be thought-provoking, invigorating, and even fun. The most important thing you can do after you read a few lectures is talk to your neighbors and friends about what you have learned. Think about what makes East Hampton so unique. Share something you found interesting. Pass along our heritage. In doing so, you will be making East Hampton a better community—a better place to live; now and throughout future generations.

TOM TWOMEY
East Hampton Town Historian
President, East Hampton Library
January 6, 1999

THE MATERIAL HISTORY
OF THE MONTAUKETT

Gaynell Stone

IT IS A PRIVILEGE to begin this municipal celebration—East Hampton's observance of its 350th anniversary—which is unprecedented in its depth and breadth of commemoration. After considering area geology and ecology, it is appropriate that this series address the next occurrence—the human peopling of the landscape.

To retrieve that story for our recent volume, *The History & Archaeology of the Montauk*, a variety of documentary records were used—censuses, diaries, histories, public records, and ephemera such as newspaper articles. This is one of the most comprehensive accounts of a Native American group in the Northeast. I believe this was possible due to the uniqueness of the situation here.

East Hampton was the only Long Island area which had a long-term resident Native teacher, Samson Occom of Mohegan, who married Montaukett Mary Fowler. He created a higher level of European "literacy" for the Montaukett, although the Native people had their own form of literacy in individualized marks for signing documents, in their pictographic language carved in stone, wood, etc., and in sign language. But this more "educated" Native group, plus Occom's services as a scribe to transmit their concerns to the British Commissioner for Indian Affairs for the Northern Provinces, Sir William Johnson, created a situation which sets the Montaukett apart from other Island Native groups and created a more extensive documentary record as well.[1]

However, these rich documentary resources produce a limited view of the reality of their life. A more complete ethnohistoric account

1

is possible through the analysis of their material record—visual materials, artifacts, the archaeological record, and oral accounts.

As background, the first known inhabitants of East Hampton were the aboriginal Montaukett, a place name spelled a dozen different ways in early records. It was not a "tribal" name, but a place name which the colonists conferred upon them as they designated them as a "tribe." The meaning of "Montaukett" in William Wallace Tooker's *Indian Place Names on Long Island* is given as either the "high or hilly land" or the "fort country," both of which appear to fit Montauk topography and the presence of two fortified places.[2] The Montauketts are members of the large Algonkian language family and peoples who inhabited the Atlantic Coastal Plain from Canada to the Carolinas; they spoke a variant of the language of the Mohegan-Pequot, across the Long Island Sound from them.[3]

The Native people of the Island and the Montaukett, who inhabited the eastern end of the south fork, appear to have done so at least 9,000 to 12,000 years ago. This could occur after the ca. 18,000-year-ago recedence of the glacier that formed this and the contiguous Manhattan and Staten Islands, as well as the string of islands leading to Cape Cod. These elevations became islands as the water rose about 350 feet with the melting of the glaciers, inundating the continental shelf. The evidence for this early inhabitance are the fifteen known Clovis/Paleo chipped stone points of this period found on the Island, one of them from the Three Mile Harbor area.[4]

Artifacts of the next culture period, the Archaic, ca. 9,000–3,000 years ago, show that the Native people lived around estuaries, harbors, streams and ponds of this beneficent land, as well as made stone tools, hunted, and camped at inland sites. So far no evidence of the Late Archaic Red Paint Burial Cult has been found in East Hampton. Also, there was far more Native use of the land than previously thought; the evidence for this is in the "gray" (unpublished) literature of the contract archaeologists.[5]

The Woodland Period beginning about 3,000 years ago was the lifeway of the Native people when "discovered" by the first European explorers. It was characterized by the development of pottery and first use of the bow and arrow, as well as hunting whales (which could have been possible since Archaic times, when clam and oyster resources became available).[6] There were also trade networks linking Island villages north to the Connecticut River Valley and south to the Delaware Valley and New Jersey; the Hands Creek site in East Hampton was part of it, judging from the New Jersey Abbott-style pottery and argillite blades found there.[7]

These culture periods included the extensive use of the Island's maritime resources—fish, fowl, sea mammals, and shellfish—as well as small mammals, nuts, berries, tubers and extensive vegetal resources. Attesting to the valuable fishing resources, Montauk Point was once known as Fisher's Point, and southern New England as well as local Native people came there to fish; this is how Samson Occom was introduced to the Montaukett. Because of this rich food base, the gardening of domesticates here was late in time—less than 1,000 years ago (not long before the European discovery of the region in the 1600s)—and, apparently, not as extensive as elsewhere.

Maize (corn) horticulture is believed to have traveled to North America from Mesoamerica, but the squash family was indigenous to the midwest and southeast; the corn, beans, and squash cultigens apparently reached Long Island from the midwest, perhaps through extensions of the trade networks mentioned earlier. Archaeological evidence of maize horticulture on the Island is sparse, and I do not know of a "planting field" in East Hampton like that found by the first settlers in Southold, Setauket, Oyster Bay, etc.

However, long before these domesticates were cultivated here, native women are known to have nurtured many plants—mallow, chenopodium, groundnuts (called "sagaponack" locally), Jerusalem artichoke, etc. elsewhere and, presumably, here also. Evidence of the domesticated sunflower has been found in the southeast dating to over 4,000 years, and this is to the east of where domestication probably began, so there is little doubt it was also on Long Island.[8]

Women were the first empirical genetic biologists, as they manipulated the wild plants to produce the characteristics they desired. The women also produced dyes and medicines using their extensive botanical knowledge. What is known of this has been published in the Suffolk County Archaeological Association's Vol. IV, *Languages & Lore of the Long Island Indians*, and Samson Occom's 1761 herbal curative list in Vol. III, 2d ed., *The History and Archaeology of the Montauk*.[9]

Another aspect of Native life is their cosmology; this was described by Samson Occom in the 1760s and printed in the Montauk volume. Visual evidence of the Native belief system throughout the Island exists on gorgets, slate plaques, cobbles, etc. The figure of the thunderbird found at Sebonac in the Shinnecock Hills represents a beneficent figure, as he brings rain, necessary for survival; the figure of the Great Horned Serpent from the Miller Place represents evil forces. The turtle gorget from Nassakeag Swamp in Setauket probably represents the Algonkian origin myth, in which the earth is formed on a turtle's back.

Incised shells, deer ribs, and beaver teeth, which indicate calendri-

cal and other types of record-keeping, were found at Mt. Sinai Harbor
archaeological sites and published in SCAA's Vol. V, *The Second Coastal
Archaeology Reader*.[10] Petroglyphs carved on two boulders were
found at Jericho, and a slate tablet with many images was found at Orient. Those images (whose meaning is obscure) most related to the
Montaukett are clay tablets, in the East Hampton Library Long Island
Collection.[11] Another object which illustrates the cleverness of the Natives is this stone puzzle found at Montauk.[12]

   The Contact Period in Montaukett life began with the european
explorers who bumped into the end of the Island as it juts into the
Atlantic. The first we know of is Verrazano in 1542, who coasted by
but, apparently, did not land; he did leave us with a detailed description
of the life and dress of the Natives of nearby Newport harbor which
may be applicable to the Montaukett. Apparently, their clothing was ex-
quisitely embroidered "like damask" with colored porcupine quills.[13]
The next was Adrian Block in 1614, who may have landed (although
there is no record of it), who named Block Island after himself, and created the first map of the Island, labeling the eastern Natives "Nahicans,"
a name not seen again in succeeding records. The subsequent Bleau
and Visscher maps of 1635 and 1662 note them as "Matouwacks."[14]

   Other early 1600s contacts were the Dutch trader Pieter Barentsen
as well as the English Captain Southack, who wrote on his early 1700s
map of the two forks, "I commaneded ye first ship that ever was at this
place" on the Peconic estuary portion. He also located "Indian Town"
on the Napeague portion of the map. This was the first of a number of
early maps which located Indian Town or Indian Plantation on the
Montauk peninsula—an important visual adjunct to the written
record. The site appeared further east with each deed extracted from
the Montaukett by the settlers taking another portion of their land. The
Montaukett later complained in petitions to the New York State Assembly that they were told they were signing one agreement only to find
later they were lied to, that they were plied with liquor before signing
deeds (Town records reveal payment for the rum, confirming that), and
that the settlers killed their dogs and cut so much of their firewood
that every winter, elderly women froze to death.[15] Besides being documents recording the loss of Montaukett land, this series of 16 deeds
(from 1648 to 1794) is a visual record revealing the "marks," or signa-
tures, which indicate the pictorial literacy of the Montaukett relative to
the literacy of the settlers, many of whom signed with an "X." The
sachem Wyandanch's mark (a figure drawing) on a deed authenticated
it; those deeds without it could be doubtful—and there were many in

the colonists' lust to "buy" Native land with gifts. It was easier to pay Wyandanch than the many heads of bands living across the land. John Strong covers the loss of Montaukett lands extensively in the *Montauk* volume.[16]

The most dramatic material evidence of other contract between the first inhabitants and the colonizing Europeans is the Pantigo burial site, dating from ca. 1650–1750, soon after the 1648 founding of East Hampton. The seventeenth-century contact with explorers and traders had brought diseases, mainly smallpox, against which the Natives had no immunity. This had decimated the population by about ninety percent throughout North and South America within a few generations.[17] In addition, the lack of a hinterland in a linear island setting left nowhere to retreat except the mainland. It is not known how many of the Pantigo burials resulted from the new diseases, but there were other East Hampton Native burial grounds which were not excavated scientifically, as was Pantigo in 1917 by Foster Saville of the Museum of the American Indian.[18]

Although the deceased Montaukett were buried in the traditional flexed position without coffins (with some in the European extended position), most of the 39 recorded graves contained a majority of European trade goods (other graves were dug up by the owner of the site and neighbors and the contents with their information were lost to the public record). The trade items had supplanted those of aboriginal manufacture; only from this archaeological evidence do we know the extent and the timing of European acculturation in the arena of material possessions. Other evidence in the *Montauk* volume indicates the Montaukett retained traditional wigwam housing (1880s), much of the hunting and gathering lifestyle (1870s), the use of herbal medicines, and traditional gatherings into the twentieth century.

One notable category of this mortuary record was trade beads, which had not been analyzed by Saville. Karlin Karklins of Parks Canada, an internationally recognized bead expert, and I analyzed the thousands of beads for the first time. He found that the Pantigo beads were more abundant than on any other northeastern archaeological site. He discovered a few types not previously seen in his research around the world, and that they were mostly from Holland. This does not mean that mostly Dutch traders were here, as English traders used Amsterdam beads extensively as well. Karlin found the trade beads were the most common adornment in the burials; we found fragments of wampum "belts," presumably headbands or belts, and shell and copper alloy beads. Their arrangement gives evidence of the esthetic val-

ues of the Montaukett known in no other way. One burial was that of a
leader, Wobeton, known from the Town Records as well as by this auto-
graphed English spirits bottle.

Another result of the mid-seventeenth-century Contact period was
the construction by the Native people of a series of "fortified places"
due to increasing interaction with the ever-encroaching traders and
settlers. Again, it is mainly the archaeological record that reveals the
shape (based on European models), size, siting, and use of these forts—
some more for trade, others more for defense.[19] The fact that Long Island had more Contact period Native forts than any other area of the
country will be told in detail in SCAA's upcoming Vol. VIII, *The Native
and Historic Forts of Long Island*. The "new" Montauk fort, on Fort
Hill, the only one of the two found so far, will be in the volume; it is the
only one to be shown on a map—John Scott's 1658 map of Long Island, one of the earliest and the best for its time.[20]

As the Contact period became the historic or colonial era, the
Montaukett and other Native people were drawn into the transplanted
European economic sphere in order to buy the new "necessities," such
as gunpowder, flour, sugar, clothing, Dominy furniture, etc. A colonial
economy has an insatiable need for labor for whaling, farming, herding,
dairying, cheese and butter production, textile production, and craft-
ware, hence servants and slaves. Of ninety Suffolk County wills pro-
bated from 1670 to 1688, twenty-four listed English, Negro, and Indian
servants and slaves. Their value was second only to cattle owned. Of
this twenty-four, two percent or eight percent were listed as "Indian
captive servant" or "Indian slave girl." In the *Montauk* volume, Philip
Rabito-Wyppensenwah points out that many of the enslaved Natives
here were from the Carolinas and the Caribbean.[21]

Another form of labor for the Natives was being forced to produce
huge quantities of wampum (shell beads) to pay fines levied upon
them for infractions of local laws (which they often did not understand); the wampum was then used by European traders to purchase
furs from the northern territories. Since the largest amount of whelk
shell for making wampum is found on eastern Long Island beaches, the
area became the "mint" of New Netherland.[22]

Further participation by the Natives in the new economy was service as militiamen in all the provincial campaigns before the French
and Indian Wars and in the American revolution. They served out of
proportion to their numbers in the population and left many Native
settlements with a large number of widows; this led to intermarriage
with Anglos, African-Americans, and other groups. The *Montauk* vol-

ume includes the muster rolls of the local militias in which they served and a painting of how the Natives dressed.

Most of the Montaukett worked for the East Hamptoners and helped make colonial life as comfortable as it was. They were gin (fence) keepers of the livestock pastured at Montauk and laborers for the Gardiners and others. The men used traditional woodworking skills to make piggins, ladles, and bowls for settler homes; they provided fish, oysters, and game for them. Stephen Pharaoh's pay is recorded for "bottoming" (rushing) Dominy chairs. As skilled shore whalers, Montaukett men were fought over by entrepreneurial East Hamptoners to be their crewmen. What today is labor law were rules enacted by the seventeenth century Town officials to control the cutthroat whaling labor practices of that day.[23]

The Native women used the spinning wheel to spin yarn, a necessity for all knitwear and weaving of essential cloth. They became expert makers of butter and cheese, which were major cash "crops" for their masters. Baskets, scrubs, jellies, and fine hand work provided cash for themselves. They cared for the mothers and children of colonial families and were encouraged by the society to be the sex objects of the men; hence, the Montaukett descendants of some of the early settlers.[24]

Besides Native participation in the economic sphere, their souls were sought by the English and Scottish missionary societies to create more tractable workers. The first missionary in the 1740s was Azariah Horton of Southold and a graduate of Yale, who was not very successful. He recommended a successor; this was Samson Occom, a Mohegan who came first as a teacher, then was ordained in the Presbyterian Church after tutelage by the Rev. Samuel Buell. Their diaries are published in the *Montauk* volume; it is astounding that it took 200 years for Occom's "diary" to be in print.

Occom was one of about twenty-seven Native men educated in the European manner by Rev. Eleazer Wheelock and fellow clerics; he was one of the few to survive and the only one to have his portrait painted by the noted colonial limner Nathaniel Smibert. He also was pictured by other paintings, mezzotints, and lithographs; thus we know how this man of genius appeared—an inventor of sensory teaching methods a hundred years before Maria Montessori, a composer of hymns still sung in the Presbyterian church, a skilled craftsman and bookbinder (examples are in the Long Island Collection), an expert gamesman to feed his family, etc. He was the only Native clergyman to keep a diary, a source of so much unknown information on that time.

Recognizing that the Montaukett could not survive in the climate of genocide fostered by East Hampton government, Sam Occom, with leaders of the Mohegan, Pequot, and Narragansett, planned an exodus to the Oneida Territory of upstate New York to establish the Christian town of Brotherton. The first settlement was aborted in 1776 by Revolutionary War hostilities, but was begun again after the war in 1784.

Occom was the minister of the settlement and died there in 1792; his grave is unmarked but is thought to be in or near this Brotherton cemetery on Oriskany Creek behind the house of his brother-in-law, David Fowler. Mary Fowler Occom's brothers, Jacob and David, were also educated by Wheelock and played important roles as translators at the Treaty of Fort Pitt and other colonial parleys. It was David, teaching at Oneida, whose tales of the abuse of the Montaukett moved an Oneida chief to grant them land.

Instead of a haven forever, within a generation, the Brotherton lands were being trespassed upon by settlers from New England. A New York State Assembly commission awarded one-third of their land to the trespassers. The Brotherton were forced to move westward, finally to a spot in Wisconsin they named "Brotherton." They were an "Americanized" group who were highly productive in boat-building, lumbering, milling, and farming. They were the first tribe to become U.S. citizens, and did so to avoid President Andrew Jackson's drive to force all Indians west of the Mississippi. As a consequence of the partition of their reservation, they lost the land which had become their farms. However, the Brotherton continued their gatherings over the years and have recently filed for re-recognition as a tribe under the leadership of June Ezold, an advertising executive and descendant of Samson Occom. A genealogy of eleven generations of Montaukett and Brotherton and several hundred pictures of them is part of the *Montauk* volume.

By the nineteenth century tuberculosis had taken the place of smallpox and other European diseases as the scourge of the Native people. East Hampton church death records, which may be incomplete for the Montaukett, indicate that fourteen of thirty-nine Native deaths between 1825 and 1879 were of consumption, with the deceased ranging from 11 months to 58 years. This documentary record is captured visually in the sketches of the deathbeds of Stephen and David Pharaoh by Tile Club artists which appeared in several national illustrated newspapers of the 1870s.

As well as the usual farm and maritime work, nineteenth-century economic activities of the Montaukett now included work in the developing factories of the area (known through ephemera and oral histories but not public documents); as guides for wealthy hunters and the sportsmen's clubs (known through oral history, ephemera, and the archaeological site of Montaukett Steve Murray's cabin in what is now Connetquot State Park). They delivered, provided livery service for the newly developing tourist industry, and produced wood and textile crafts still in early East End homes. The East Hampton Historical Society has a collection of this material culture (shown in the *Montauk* volume)—the baskets, mortars, pestles, piggins, ladles, bowls, and scrubs which underpinned 18th and nineteenth-century life.

That period of Montaukett lifeways has been retrieved somewhat by the archaeological record of Indian Fields, their last home (now Montauk County Park; soon to be renamed for Theodore Roosevelt's brief stay? Yet one more way to render invisible the original inhabitants?). The artifacts excavated by Edward Johannemann indicate habitation there from 1725 to about 1885. The excavation probably found the home of Charles Fowler (twenty-four feet square of Anglo design with wood floors) and located other houses thirty feet square and eleven by sixteen feet, as well as other structures seven and eight feet in diameter. The site's "Indian barns" showed four variations of storage shelters and a well/cool-storage structure. Faunal remains indicate that they ate a lot of turtle.[25]

Ceramic fragments found (4,539) indicate that more than half of their vessels were redware, the common ware of the early days. About twenty-five percent was pearlware, seventeen percent white ironstone, two percent earthenware, and one and a quarter percent porcelain. When this profile is calculated for other Long Island populations, it would tell us how the Montaukett compared economically and esthetically with other groups.

Maria Pharaoh's "Diary," the only such document about nineteenth-century Native lifeways, describes their self-sufficient, happy homesteading lifestyle-gathering, hunting, fishing, guiding sportsmen and selling crafts. This rare photograph in the Montauk volume shows the Pharaoh and Fowler families living such a life at Indian Fields before 1873.

After David Pharaoh died of tuberculosis, Maria and her children could not maintain the homesteading lifestyle. They were lured to move to Freetown, north of East Hampton Village, by promises by Frank Benson that they could return in summer, would get a yearly annuity, and education for the children. The Benson family, who had bought Montauk peninsula from the Town Trustees, used it as a hunting preserve and planned to develop it. The promises were empty, the Montaukett homes at Indian Field containing their deeds and records were burned, and they were driven away from their ancestral home. Other Montaukett had moved away for better livelihoods to Eastville, a Native/African American settlement on the eastern side of Sag Harbor, while others lived in enclaves in Southold, Greenport, Amityville, and scattered through the Island.

Through the newspaper accounts and censuses scanned by Philip Rabito-Wyppensenwah for the *Montauk* volume, it is apparent that most of the Montaukett women worked as domestics and servants, and most of the men worked at odd jobs, as laborers and as farm hands, although some were skilled carpenters, whalers and seamen, masons, coachmen. However, when they had their pictures taken, they dressed in their best clothes, as everyone did.

A Montaukett family.

By the twentieth century, the Montaukett had disappeared from the Town Records, appearing only in legal records (as in John Strong's account of the loss of their land[26]), in newspaper articles, in oral histories (such as Maria Pharaoh's "diary"), and the visual record shown in the *Montauk* volume. They attended school where star athletes (John Henry Fowler was considered the Knute Rockne of Long Island) rode bicycles, dressed as "dandies," held powwows or gatherings, and wore their regalia as a way of maintaining traditions. Among them was Olivia Ward Bush-Banks, a teacher, journalist, author, and poet whose collected works have been published by Oxford University Press; she was of Montaukett descent, attended powwows, and used her heritage in her work.

The lawsuit begun in the 1870s to regain Indian Fields, which had been taken from them by the developer, Arthur Benson, and his family was lost in 1910 (and the appeals in 1918) when Judge Abel Blackmar pronounced them no longer Indians.

The current generation of Montaukett descendants, numbering in the thousands around the country and in the hundreds on Long Island, are organizing at the request of Robert Pharaoh and Bob Cooper, descendants of Maria Pharaoh, to seek federal recognition and the return of their land. They are collecting genealogies and have sponsored powwows as part of the process to secure their heritage.

In addition, the research of over 30 scholars to provide this compendium of information on one Native group has made a valuable contribution to the multicultural history—the real story—of our most interesting Island.

NOTES

1. Stone, Gaynell. *The History & Archaeology of the Montauk*, Vol. III, 2d ed.; *Readings in Long Island Archaeology & Ethnohistory*, 1993, Suffolk County Archaeological Association, pp. 69-76, 151-154, 227, 284.

2. Tooker, William Wallace. *Indian Place Names on Long Island . . .*, 1911, 1962, Ira J. Friedman Pub., p. 141.

3. Levine, Gaynell Stone & Nancy Bonvillain. *Languages & Lore of the Long Island Indians*, Vol. IV; *Readings . . .*, 1980, SCAA, p. 168.

4. Truex, James & Gaynell Stone. *A Way of Life: Prehistoric Natives of Long Island*, 1985, SCAA, p. 2.

5. Stone, Gaynell. *Montauk*, p. 600.

6. Brennan, Louis. *The Coastal Archaeology Reader*, Vol. II; *Readings . . .*, 1978, p. 55.

7. Silver, Annette. *The Abbott Interaction Sphere: A Consideration of the Middle Woodland Period in Coastal New York and a Proposal for a Middle Woodland Exchange*, 1991, Ph.D. dissertation, New York University, pp. 225-228.

8. Smith, Bruce D. *The Emergency of Agriculture*, 1995, Scientific American Library, New York, N.Y.

9. Levine, Gaynell Stone & N. Bonvillain. *Languages & Lore* . . . , 1980, Vol. IV; *Readings* . . . , pp. 269, 278; Rabito-Wyppensenwah, *Montauk*, 1993, Vol. III, 2d ed., pp. 563, 585; Occom, p. 228.

10. Gramley, Richard. *Second Coastal Archaeology Reader*, 1982, Vol. V; *Readings* . . . , James Truex, ed., pp. 161–172.

11. Strong, John. *The Alginquian Peoples of Long Island From Earliest Times to 1700*, 1997, p. 136.

12. Stone, Gaynell. *Montauk*, 1993, p. 637.

13. Verrazano, Giovanni, in Adams, James T. *History of the Town of Southampton*, 1917, Hampton Press.

14. Stone, Levine & Bonvillain. *Languages & Lore* . . . , 1980, pp. 160, 165.

15. Pharaoh, Benjamin & Stephen, in *Montauk*, 1993, petition, p. 71; maps, p. xxii.

16. Stone, Gaynell. *Montauk*, 1993, Wyandanch deed, p. 89.

17. Denton, Daniel. *A Brief Description of New York* . . . , 1670, London. Weigand, Philip, "The Great Frontier on Long Island: Verrazano and Epidemic Diseases," 1986. Unpublished mss. In the author's possession.

18. Saville, Foster. "A Montauk Cemetery at East Hampton, Long Island" in *Montauk*, 1993, p. 616 ff.

19. Solecki, Ralph. "The Prehistoric Forts of the Long Island Sound Area," 1995, *Northeastern Archaeology*.

20. Stone, Gaynell. *Montauk*, 1993, Scott map, p. xxii.

21. Cooper, Robert. *The Records of the Court of Sessions of Suffolk County in the Province of New York, 1670–1688*, 1995, Heritage Books, New York, N.Y.

22. Ceci, Lynn. "The First Fiscal Crisis in New York" in J. Truex, ed., *Second Coastal Archaeology Reader*, Vol. V; Readings . . . , 1982, p. 306.

23. Strong, John. "Colonial Regulation of Shore Whaling Contracts" in *The Shinnecock: A Culture History*, Gaynell Stone, ed., 1983, Vol. VI; *Readings* . . . , p. 246.

24. Gumbs, Harriet C. "I Remember Montauk" in *Montauk*, G. Stone, ed., 1993, p. 142.

25. Johannemann, Edward. "Indian Fields Site, Montauk, Suffolk County, Part I" in *Montauk*, G. Stone, ed., 1993, p. 643.

26. Strong, John. "How the Montauk Lost Their Land" in *Montauk*, G. Stone, ed., 1993, p. 77 ff.

WYANDANCH, SACHEM OF THE MONTAUKETTS:

An Alliance Sachem on the Middle Ground

—₰₰₰—

John A. Strong

IN THE SPRING OF 1637 the English waged a devastating war against the Pequots and nearly destroyed them. They attacked a Pequot settlement near present-day Mystic, Connecticut and massacred nearly seven hundred men, women, and children (Salisbury 1984 220–25; Jennings 1976, 215–27; Cave 1996, 123–67). The victory opened up the Connecticut Valley to English settlement. Lion Gardiner, a military engineer recruited by Governor John Winthrop, Jr. of Connecticut commanded the Fort Saybrook at the mouth of the Connecticut River.

The English victory also opened up a scramble for control over the Pequots' tributary communities in southern New England and on Long Island. The English, the Dutch, and the Algonquian sachems, such as Ninigret, Miantonomi, and Uncas, now began campaigns of political intrigue to gain influence in the region. Winthrop and the English were particularly anxious to gain a foothold on Long Island before the Dutch expanded their control eastward. The Montauketts and several other Long Island communities, who had established tributary relations with the Pequots, were now thrust into the center of the scramble.

Shortly after the Pequot massacre, Wyandanch, a young Montaukett sachem, came to Fort Saybrook to negotiate an alliance with the English (Gardiner 1980, 137–38). They reached an agreement and Wyandanch joined the English campaign to hunt down the Pequots who were still in arms against the English. One of the reasons that Wyandanch wanted an alliance with the English was because he knew that Ninigret, the Niantic sachem, wanted to bring the former Pequot tributaries on Long island under his control.

The tangle of conflicting interests became evident in the late spring of 1638 when Ninigret led a war party of eighty men across the sound to convince Wyandanch that he should ally himself with the Niantics, a southern branch of the Narragansetts, instead of Massachusetts Bay or Connecticut (WP 1929-1947, 4:43-5). Ninigret was attempting to take advantage of what he believed was a power vacuum on Long Island. He hoped to break the newly formed alliance between the Montauketts and English before it could become firmly established. It was a daring plan which would strengthen his position against his rivals, Uncas and Miantonomi.

Shortly after he landed on Long Island, Ninigret sent a delegation to Wyandanch and urged him to abandon the English and accept a tributary status with the Niantics (WP, 4:43-4). Wyandanch refused and went into hiding to avoid capture, perhaps hoping the English would intervene on his behalf. Ninigret finally did catch the Montaukett sachem and pressed him to reconsider, arguing that Connecticut and Massachusetts Bay would take the Montaukett's wampum, but would not protect them as well as the Niantics could. The Englishmen, said Ninigret, "are liars, they do it but only to get your wampum." The English of Connecticut, he continued, "will speak much but do little" (Ibid.).

Roger Ludlow, one of the founders of Connecticut, reported this incident and the quotes attributed to Ninigret, to John Winthrop, Sr. of Massachusetts Bay. The letter was heavily biased towards Wyandanch and was, no doubt, intended to provoke an angry response against Ninigret from the leaders of the two colonies. There was more at stake here than the question of Wyandanch's security. Ludlow realized that if the Long Island sachems became tributaries of the Niantics, who allied with Roger Williams of Rhode Island, Connecticut would lose an important advantage in future attempts to gain jurisdiction over the area. In spite of Ludlow's own agenda, his report of the raid itself is probably accurate, however much he embellished Ninigret's words.

When Wyandanch refused to abrogate his alliance to the English, Ninigret humiliated him by stripping him in front of his people, seizing thirty fathoms of wampum and other goods, and burning several wigwams (Ibid. 44). The Niantics then attacked several neighboring villages, finally convincing some of the Montaukett elders to accept his terms. Ninigret demanded future payments in corn and wampum as terms of the alliance. Although Ludlow portrays this as a coerced agreement, it is possible that there was some genuine support among the Long Island communities for Ninigret because his agents made several overtures to sachems there over the next three decades. In 1669, for example, a Montaukett faction traveled to Ninigret's village and freely offered to accept him as their sachem (RCRI 1968, 2:269–73).

Ninigret's raid was a strategy commonly used by Indians to establish authority over tributaries (Johnson 1996, 40–43). The purpose was not to seize territory nor to kill many people. Ninigret wanted to assert his dominance over Wyandanch in a dramatic gesture. Uncas, an ambitious Mohegan sachem who had very little power and influence prior to the Pequot War, employed a similar strategy as well as some cleverly adapted European diplomatic tactics to help him become one of the most powerful sachems in New England. Uncas' raid on the Pequot community at Nameag in 1647 was very similar to Ninigret's actions on Long Island. The intent of the raid was to humiliate the Nameag, who were allies of the English. Uncas stripped the people, burned their wigwams and stole their goods (Ibid. 40–41). The English reprimanded Uncas, but left the Nameag under Mohegan control.

Uncas, Ninigret, and Miantonomi were attempting to establish themselves as the primary intermediaries between the English and the smaller Algonquian communities in each of their areas. They wanted to control the flow of information, trade, and tribute between the English and the smaller bands such as the Nameag and the Montaukett. Each sachem also seized any opportunity to gain control of one of their rival's tributaries.

Wyandanch went immediately to Roger Ludlow and demanded that the English recover his wampum. According to Ludlow, the Montaukett sachem made a compelling argument. How can I pay tribute to the English, asked Wyandanch, if they allow Ninigret to come and steal it from me at will? Ludlow agreed and so did John Mason, the commander of the troops who massacred the Pequots. Mason took an armed guard of eight men to confront Ninigret, telling him that unless he made restitution to Wyandanch, the English would send an army against him (WP, 4:45). The Niantic sachem, whose village was only a few miles from the site of the Pequot massacre, reached a peaceful accommodation with Mason.

Wyandanch must have been pleased with the success of his diplomatic efforts, but he also realized how vulnerable he was to such raids in the future. These fears undoubtedly prompted the eastern Long Island sachems to invite Lion Gardiner to establish the first English presence on Long Island the following year. The sachems decided that they would be safer from attack if an English military man took up residence nearby. The English were very receptive because they wanted to obtain a foothold on Long Island before the Dutch expanded eastward from New Amsterdam.

In May of 1639, Gardiner negotiated the first purchase of land from the Indians on eastern Long Island. Whether Gardiner knew about the Stirling patent or not is uncertain. If he was aware of it, he ignored it and negotiated directly with a sachem named Yovawam for the purchase of an island called Manchonat, "the place where they all died," located adjacent to the Montaukett lands. The name may refer to an epidemic which possibly wiped out the inhabitants. Yovawam is probably the sachem identified in a later document as "Youghco," from Shelter Island (RCNP 9:18). Gardiner promptly renamed Manchonat after himself and moved his family there later that year.

Wyandanch's role in the transaction is not recorded, but he undoubtedly was the one who brought the two parties together. He saw the advantages for trade and military security if the English established a presence near his village. Gardiner and Winthrop, of course, were eager for an alliance which would serve to discourage the Dutch from pressing their claims to this area. These common interest served as the primary basis for a close relationship between Gardiner and Wyandanch, which later became celebrated in local folklore.

Although the Earl of Stirling had intended to establish a colony here, his health failed and he decided to sell the patent off in small parcels to companies of settlers who wanted to establish their own towns. On June 7, 1639, he commissioned his agent, James Farrett, to travel to New England and look for customers. Farrett set up a temporary residence on Shelter Island in Peconic Bay in the summer of 1639 and from there explored the shore of Long Island in his small sloop. He had the temerity to take his patent to New Amsterdam where he announced that Lord Stirling's patent included all of Long Island. The Dutch, of course, ridiculed him and ran him out of town (NYCD 1:285-86).

In 1640, however, Gardiner belatedly recognized the authority of the Stirling Patent by agreeing to pay Farrett a yearly fee of five pounds sterling. Farrett then proceeded to sell a parcel of land near what is now Oyster Bay to a company of settlers from Lynn, Massachusetts (Calder 1966, 78-81). When the settlers arrived and began to construct their homes, the Dutch arrested them and sent them back to Massachusetts. Farrett then sent the company to the far eastern end of Long Island, out of reach of the Dutch, where they established the town of Southampton. The episode underscores the fact that claims based solely on the "right of discovery" had no legal standing in international law. Later that fall the settlers completed the dual purchase by negotiating a deed with representatives from the local Indian villages, led by Mandush, the sachem from Shinnecock.

The Earl of Stirling died in 1640 and his family cut off Farrett's funds, leaving him stranded in New England. Farrett sold his sloop and his title to Robin's Island, and mortgaged the remaining land in the patent to a group of entrepreneurs which included Governor Theophilus Eaton of New Haven and Governor Edward Hopkins of Connecticut. Farrett, however, never told the Stirling family that he had mortgaged their patent.

The governors, who were both interested in establishing settlements on Long Island, advanced 110 pounds sterling to Farrett on the condition that he either repay the sum in three years or forfeit all rights to the lands on Long Island. Farrett left for England in 1642 and never returned. When the three-year period ended in July, 1644, the governors claimed possession of the Stirling patent lands. They made no attempt to notify the Stirling family about the foreclosure. By this time the civil war was raging in England and the Stirling family was in no position to protect their interests from Puritans in New England. Although the Stirling family continued to press their claims for several decades, the local colonial authorities on Long Island ignored them (Brodhead 1853–1871, 2:12–12).

A Dutch war against the Indians in New Netherland in 1644 followed the English destruction of the Pequots. Under the administration of Governor Wilhem Kieft, the Dutch troops massacred three Indian settlements in brutal attacks. These defeats made a dramatic impact on all of the Indians in southern New England and on Long Island. Both the English and the Dutch had now demonstrated the effectiveness of their military technology and organization.

Wyandanch, Youghco (Yovawam), Moughmaitow, the sachem from Corchaug on the North Fork of Long Island and Weenagamin, who was probably from Shinnecock, apparently decided that the only way to survive was to accept a tributary relationship with the English. The sachems came to Hartford in the fall of 1644 for a meeting of the commissioners of the United Colonies, which included New Haven, Plymouth, Massachusetts Bay and Connecticut. These colonies had formed the union the year before for mutual protection against Indian attacks and to thwart Dutch encroachment on their lands. Roger Williams' Rhode Island, of course, was not invited to join the union. Williams' theology and his Indian policies remained an anathema to the Puritans.

The commissioners included Governors Eaton and Hopkins, who had foreclosed on the Stirling patent two months earlier. These men may have taken the lead in the negotiations with the sachems. The agreement reached at the Hartford meeting began with a statement affirming that the Stirling Patent had been "passed over to some of the English in these United Colonies" (RCNP 9:19). The sachems agreed to become tributaries to the English, and granted them exclusive purchase rights to eastern Long Island.

The Hartford Treaty reaffirmed an important principle in English colonial law. The crown and its agencies, the colonial governments, held the exclusive right of purchase. During the early years following the arrival of the English in North America, they applied this principle primarily against Dutch rivals, but they soon expanded it to include private individuals within the settler communities as well. Following the English seizure of New Netherland in 1664, all private entrepreneurs had to obtain permission to enter into negotiations with Indian owners for land sales.

This clause in the treaty also reaffirmed the concept of dual purchase. The English were careful to say that the Indians had "engaged their land to them," clearly implying that specific parcels would have to be purchased through negotiation with local sachems later (RCNP 9:19). The commissioners of the United Colonies, although they would have been loath to acknowledge the source, had accepted Roger Williams' thesis that the king's patent was not an absolute title of ownership.

Although the English accepted the principle of dual purchase as a practical compromise, they made few other concessions to Native American sovereignty. From the time of their arrival they assumed de facto jurisdiction over the Indians within their patents. They demanded that all crimes of theft or violence which Indians committed against the English be prosecuted in English courts. The English authorities, however, reserved the right to punish an Englishmen who committed similar offenses against the Indians.

Winthrop defended this principle with the assertion that the concept of jurisdiction was moot in an uncivilized, non-Christian community which had no laws or courts. The English, therefore, required Wyandanch and the four sachems to accept English jurisdiction as a part of their tributary relationship. The sachems promised that any Indians who harmed the English or their goods "upon due notice and proofe they will deliver all such to deserved punishment, or provide due satisfaction for all injuries and offenses donn" (RCNP 9:19).

In the early spring of 1648, Governors Eaton and Hopkins sent Thomas Stanton, a Connecticut merchant to purchase lands for them on the eastern end of Long Island. The English frequently called upon Stanton to negotiate with the Indians because he was one of the few Englishmen who had mastered any of the native languages spoken in southern New England and on eastern Long Island. The governors were anxious to complete the dual purchase of these lands because the Dutch had made an attempt to buy land near the town of Southampton in the fall of 1647 (RCNH 1: 523–24; Ales 1993:20–21). The English met with Wyandanch, his interpreter, Cockenoe,[1] and three other sachems to negotiate the purchase of a 31,000-acre parcel of Montaukett land between the eastern boundary of Southampton and Napeague Bay.

Two provisions of the deed reflect patterns found in many of these early transactions. The English gave the sachems twenty coats, twenty-four mirrors, twenty-four hoes, twenty-four hatchets, twenty-four knives, 100 small metal drills called "muxes" which were used to make wampum (RTEH, 1:3). In spite of the clause in the deed stating that the Indians gave up all rights and interest in the parcel, the sachems probably viewed the transaction as a gift exchange in return for the right of the English to use the land. Certainly there was no connection between the value of these goods, which Governor Hopkins had purchased for thirty pounds, four shillings and eight pence, and the value of the land in the English market.[2]

The second provision in the deed, which allowed for the joint use of the 31,000-acre parcel, could also have been interpreted in terms of Native American concepts of land "ownership." The Indians retained the rights to hunt, fish, collect shells for wampum, and take the fins and tails from beached whales. They agreed, in return, not to molest the English or their goods. It is, of course, impossible to know what was in the minds of the sachems who negotiated the agreement, but the arrangement is certainly closer to the Native American concept of land use than it is to the English view of private property.

Another clause in the deed also suggested a concept of joint usage. The English promised that, "if the Indians, hunting of any deer, they should chase them into the water, and the English should kill them, the English shall have the body, and the sachems the skin" (RTEH 1:3). According to Indian custom, when hunters drove deer or bear into rivers or ponds, the skins were sent to the sachem who controlled the hunting territory (RTSH 1:157). The Montauketts must have assumed, at the time, that they still had a claim to the parcel (Ales 1993, 21).

There is another aspect of the transaction which is significant. In contrast to the Southampton deed, where the proprietors bought their purchase rights from Lord Stirling's agent and then negotiated a deed with the local Indians, the English governors, who owned the patent, purchased the land from the Indians and then sold it to the local proprietors. This process established a precedent for government involvement in such transactions with Indians. Quarrels both between Indians and English and between rival English purchasers over boundaries and terms in the deeds frequently forced public officials to intervene. The extent of public supervision over private purchases of Indian land, however, remained unresolved until the English established the colony of New York in 1664.

The New England governors, who had been primarily concerned with the Dutch, did not show any interest in expanding their own colonies to Long Island at the time. A few families established homesteads in East Hampton over the next three years and finally, in 1651, they purchased title from Governor Hopkins, adding what appears to be an interest payment of eight pounds sterling to the sum paid by Hopkins for the goods given to the Indian sachems in 1648 (Ales 1993, 21; RTEH 1:4).

Wyandanch's growing ties with Lion Gardiner and the East Hampton community increased his status among the sachems on eastern Long Island (Strong 1996). The Montaukett sachem, therefore, was careful to fulfill his obligations under the Hartford Treaty of 1644. In 1649 the English put Wyandanch's commitment to a severe test. They asked him to honor a sensitive clause in the treaty which compromised his sovereignty. The clause stipulated that Indians who injured English people or property be turned over the to the English courts. When the Southampton settlers accused the Shinnecocks of murdering an Englishwoman, Mandush, the Shinnecock sachem, refused to cooperate with the investigation.

The two communities armed themselves and stood ready for a confrontation (RCNP 9:143). The Shinnecocks made a proposal which was in accordance with their custom of providing restitution for the victims and their families rather than punishing the guilty parties. They offered a payment that would be borne by their whole community, but the English rejected this form of restitution.

Lion Gardiner sent Wyandanch to the Shinnecock village and urged him to use his influence to end the impasse. The Montaukett sachem took advantage of the close kinship ties his people had with the Shinnecocks to help him locate and capture the men responsible for the murder. With Mandush's consent, Wyandanch took the accused men to Hartford where they were tried and executed.(Strong 1996, 57-58). Mandush accepted a tributary status under Wyandanch and granted the Montaukett sachem full control over all of the Shinnecock lands. This was a major success for the English policy of indirect rule through alliance sachems. The English had now neutralized a troublesome sachem and strengthened a reliable ally.

The English repaid Wyandanch's loyalty a few years later. In 1653, when Ninigret, his old nemesis from Rhode Island, raided Wyandanch's village, killing about thirty of his men and seizing his daughter, Quashawam, and fourteen other captives, the Montaukett sachem turned to Gardiner and the English for help (Ibid., 59-61).Although the episode is very poorly documented, it appears that Gardiner helped to raise money for Quashawam's ransom.

The kidnapping of Wyandanch's daughter was later celebrated in local folklore. The story was told and retold, and, of course, embellished over the centuries. In 1840, David Gardiner, one of Lion Gardiner's descendants, wrote the earliest account of the incident. "Tradition has it," said Gardiner, "that the raid took place during the festivities celebrating the wedding of the daughter" (Gardiner 1973:23). Other accounts further embellished the tragic event, adding that her intended husband had been killed by the cruel Niantic warriors. Although none of these details are documented, the story of the wedding feast has been repeated many times (Strong and Karabag 1991:192).

Ninigret claimed that Wyandanch and the Montauketts were now his tributaries. Wyandanch and his English allies in East Hampton rejected this assertion. The East Hampton proprietors feared that their exclusive right to the future purchase of Montauk would be jeopardized if Ninigret controlled the Montauketts. The Niantic sachem would not be bound by any agreement between East Hampton and the Montauketts. The United Colonies commissioners were concerned about the shift in the fragile balance of power among the Algonquian sachems. Fearing that the growing power of the Niantics might lead to more violence, they rejected Ninigret's assertion that the Montauketts were his tributaries. The New Haven court voted on August 23, 1654 to send twelve pounds of gunpowder and thirty pounds of shot to Wyandanch (RCNH, 1:117-18).

Wyandanch quickly launched a surprise attack against a party of Niantics who were visiting the Indians on Block Island. The raid was a success, taking the lives of Ninigret's nephew, two Niantic sachems, and sixty of his men (RCNP 10:125). The English aid undoubtedly played a played a significant role in Ninigret's defeat. The military victory also increased Wyandanch's influence with the English and among his own people. This new status, however was soon to bring the Montaukett sachem serious troubles and new challenges at home.

The relations between Wyandanch and the English reflect one of the patterns which emerged following the defeat of the Pequots. Sachems in New England and Long Island sought alliances with the English, who had displaced the Pequot as the dominant power in the area. The English used this opportunity to gain influence in the internal affairs of the Indian communities by providing military and economic support to selected sachems. The English expected the "alliance" sachems to control their own communities, to keep in close touch with their English allies, to help resolve conflicts between their people and the English, to prevent any of their people from harming English settlers or their property, and to negotiate and enforce the terms of land sales. In return the sachems, who in the past governed primarily by persuasion, were now able to use English support to increase their status and their authority over their communities.[3] The system worked well for both parties, but it was clear from the beginning that the English were the dominant partners in the alliances.

Cockenoe, one of the first Long Island Indians to become fluent in English, very likely played an important role in developing Wyandanch's accommodationist policy with the English. He remained one of Wyandanch's closest advisors until the Montaukett sachem's death in 1659. Cockenoe strengthened his relationship with the Montauketts when he married Wyandanch's sister (RTEH 1:261). His familiarity with the English language and customs enabled him to play an important role as a diplomatic liaison between the two cultures. He also benefited materially from his English connections. The colonial documents indicate that Cockenoe was paid for his work as an interpreter, and for such services as marking out the boundaries for deeds and tending the grazing lands on Montauk (Tooker 1980, 183-84; RTEH 2:109-111).

Relations between the Indians and English generally involved such matters as trade, land sales, labor contracts, conflicts involving livestock, and cultural misunderstandings about the nature of "ownership." The latter two concerns played a major role in Algonquian-English relations during the first few decades after the English established settlements on eastern Long Island. The Indians continued to build their wigwams within the boundaries of the deeds. They saw no reason why they should not be able to use any of the unoccupied lands around the

English towns. In English law, however, the proprietors, who had put up the money to purchase the property, owned these "undivided" lands.

The town proprietors in Southampton and East Hampton, for example, allotted to each member of the corporation parcels of land which became their private property. The whole community used the remaining lands for grazing or hunting. Each proprietor held a claim to acreage in the undivided lands which was determined by the amount of money he had contributed to the initial purchase. As the communities grew, the proprietors allotted some parcels of the undivided lands to their children and sold others to new arrivals. It was inevitable that this process would soon force conflicts with the Indians who were living on the undivided lands.

The expansion of these farming communities, of course, caused an increase in the numbers of livestock feeding on the land. The introduction of domestic livestock made a dramatic impact on the ecosystem and was a frequent cause of tensions between the English and the neighboring Algonquian communities (Williams 1995:249–53). The English settlers allowed their hogs to range freely in the woods until harvest time when they brought them in to fatten them for slaughter.[4] Occasionally, when the Indians came upon the hogs they hunted them like wild game and killed them. This was most likely to happen whenever the Indians caught them rooting up shellfish beds. Cattle and horses also created problems. The Indians kept their winter food in storage pits near their wigwams. When they moved to another location, they left the pits open. Grazing livestock sometimes fell into the pits and injured themselves. Another problem arose when the animals invaded the unfenced Indian corn fields and destroyed the crops. Fences, of course, were an alien concept to the Indians.

About the time that the first settlers arrived in East Hampton, a conflict involving these issues arose in Southampton which set a precedent for eastern Long Island. The Shinnecock continued to plant their crops on land which was within the boundaries of the 1640 purchase. The English did not protest until 1649, when they sought to allot some of the undivided lands. The increase in English livestock had also caused friction between the two communities. The Indians complained that English cattle, horses and hogs were getting into their planting grounds.

The Southampton officials called upon Wyandanch to use his growing influence to help them resolve the dispute. Thomas Stanton came from Hartford to serve, once again, as an interpreter. Southampton, anticipating such needs, had placed itself under the jurisdiction of Connecticut in 1644. Stanton and Wyandanch negotiated a settlement with Mandush, the local sachem. The agreement called for the Shinnecock to move their planting ground and fence off their remaining fields. The new agreement allowed the English livestock, except for hogs, to graze in the Shinnecock fields ten days after the harvest so they could graze there all winter. The English were to herd the livestock out of the planting grounds in early spring before planting time.

Apparently the same conflicts which had been resolved at Southampton became an issue in East Hampton about six years after the first settlers arrived there. In the spring of 1655 Wyandanch and two of his advisors, Sassakata and Pauquatoun, met with Lion Gardiner, the Reverend Thomas James, John Mulford, and several representatives from East Hampton. The East Hampton people agreed to build and maintain a fence east of the village which would keep their horses out of the Indian planting grounds from early spring until after the fall harvest. The English also agreed that if their horses got through the fence they would pay for the damages. The presence of Indian planting grounds on the eastern portion of the 1648 purchase indicates that the Indians were still living on the land they had sold.

The East Hampton officials were also concerned about the possibility that the Dutch or rival English investors might purchase the remainder of the Montaukett lands east of Napeague. They pressed Wyandanch and his advisors to give the town exclusive purchase rights. This concession may have been a factor in the English decision to increase their military support to Wyandanch and to bestow upon him a title which greatly overstated his powers at that time. In the text of the 1655 agreement, the English referred to Wyandanch as the "Chief Sachem of Long Island" (Cooper 1993:174). It was an empty title, of course, without English support.

When Ninigret again threatened Wyandanch in the fall of 1655, the English moved quickly to protect their loyal ally. The United Colony commissioners ordered John Youngs, an experienced sailor from Southold, to patrol the Sound and block any attempt by Ninigret to attack the Montauketts. The commissioners instructed Youngs to take, sink or destroy Ninigret's canoes (RCNP 10:151). The action successfully thwarted any plan the Niantic sachem may have had to retaliate for his defeat on Block Island. He did not initiate any further action against the Montauketts until after Wyandanch's death in 1659. Youngs maintained the blockade for over a year and was paid 153 pounds by the United Colonies. In contrast, the missionary, John Eliot, was paid a yearly salary of only fifty pounds by the United Colonies for his "Indian work." Clearly missionary work was far less important to the English than the protection of their alliance sachem. Few Long Island sachems would now openly challenge any leader who could draw on this level of English support.

The importance of a reliable Algonquian ally who had the power to influence the behavior of his fellow sachems was becoming more evident as the scramble for Indian lands continued. English settlers and speculators were purchasing Long Island real estate from any Algonquian sachem who appeared to have some authority over a given tract of land. This inevitably led to conflict because some Indians viewed the transactions as a lease which could be sold again to another buyer, and others purposely misled English buyers into purchasing land which did not belong to them. Wyandanch proved to be most adept at resolving these potentially explosive conflicts.

The Dutch also recognized the importance of cultivating an alliance with a sachem who could guarantee smooth relations with the Indians residing in their territory. They were quick to respond when Tackapousha, the sachem from Massapequa, sought to open negotiations for an alliance with them. The Massapequa sachem had the support of several influential local sachems including Waghtummore, Wogquatis, Uppahanuum, Adam, and Rumegie who represented the villages at Secatogue, Maskinekaug (Matinecock), Merrick, Rockaway, and Canarsie in what is now Brooklyn, Queens, and Nassau County. The negotiations were held at Hempstead on March 12, 1656 (Pelletreau 1903:85; Brodhead 1853-71, 1:519). The Dutch eagerly agreed to an alliance with Tackapousha and anointed him the "Chiefe Sachem" over the Indians of western Long Island (RTNSH, 1:43-44).

Both parties to the treaty agreed, "That all injuries formerly past . . . shall be forgiven and forgotten. . . . That Tackapousha being chosen Chiefe Sachem, ... doth ask the Governor of New Netherland to [be] his and his peoples protector and in consideration of that do put under the said protection, all of their lands and territories upon Long Island, so far as the Dutch line doth run according to the agreement made in Hartford" (DSBD, 2:129-131). They also agreed to consult each other on all negotiations with other Indian groups, and Tackapousha promised not to harbor any enemies of the Dutch (Trelease 1971:146; RTNSH, 1:43-45).

Later, in the fall of 1656, the settlers in Brooklyn, Midwout, and Amsfort complained to Governor Stuyvesant that some clothing had been stolen by Indians from Secatogue, who were under Tackapousha's authority. They told the governor that they had "very gloomy forebodings," and feared that the thefts might be followed by an attack (NYCD 14:368). Tackapousha, realizing that his alliance with Stuyvesant was threatened, moved quickly to assert his authority over the Secatogues. He ordered them to return the goods, "else it might create disharmony and quarrels" and promised the settlers that whenever a theft was reported to him he would provide restitution (Ibid., 369). The settlers rewarded the sachem with a present of gunpowder.

Tackapousha and Wyandanch, supported by their European allies, soon became the two most powerful and influential sachems on Long Island. Both men became the primary liaisons between their people and the new immigrants to Long Island, as well as important players in the international struggle between the English and the Dutch for control over Long Island.

As the East Hampton community grew, the town officials pressed the Montauketts to move from the undivided lands and resettle east of Napeague. They resisted these pressures just as the Shinnecock had done in 1649. In the fall of 1656, the town asserted its right of ownership by ordering that "noe wigwams shall be set up by any Indians whatsoever within our bounds" (RTEH 1:101). This sweeping decree was apparently directed at the dwellings in areas which were desired for new allotments, because a decade later there were many Montauketts still living on the undivided lands near Three Mile Harbor two miles north of the English village.

A year after Tackapousha resolved the difficulties between the Dutch and the Secatogues, the English called upon Wyandanch to resolve a much more serious confrontation. Several Shinnecock men and an African-American woman conspired to burn down several buildings in the settlement. One of the buildings was the home of Eleanor Howell, the widow of Edward Howell, who had helped to found the town in 1640. One or more of the conspirators may have been servants in the Howell household. There had been an unpleasant incident involving the servants of the Howells years before. A young Indian servant woman named Hope had a child by another servant named George Wood. The town court found the couple guilty of "carnal filthiness" and sentenced them to be publicly whipped. The child was given to the Howells to serve as a domestic in their house until he reached the age of thirty (RTSH 1:35). Unfortunately, there is no further mention of Hope or her child in the town records.

According to the sparse court records from the Particular Court of Connecticut, Wigwagub, a Shinnecock, testified that he had been hired to burn the Howell home by two other Shinnecock named Awabag and Agagoneau (RPCC 1928, 22:175-76). Awabag gave him a gun and Agagoneau paid him seven shillings, six pence. Another man, Auwegenum, was present when Wigwagub was hired, but his role in the affair was not mentioned. No motive was mentioned in the records, but it was not simply an act of revenge against the Howells, because several other buildings in the town were also burned. Possibly the attacks were also related to the conflicts over the invasion of Indian planting grounds by English livestock, a common problem during this period. The Shinnecocks had frequently complained to Wyandanch about the English horses that wandered into their corn fields and destroyed their crops (RCNP, 10:180).

The court records did not mention the African-American woman, but Wyandanch later reported that the servant woman was "far deeper in that capital miscarriage than any or all of the Indians" (Ibid.). It is possible that Wyandanch was attempting to shift the blame away from the Indians, but even so his account raises some fascinating questions about the relationship between the small population of African-American servants and slaves and the Indians. Both groups certainly shared common frustrations in their relations with the dominant white settlers. The suggestion that a woman had taken a role of leadership in the small rebellion is also interesting.

When news of the house burnings reached Hartford, the colonial authorities raised a troop of nineteen men, armed them with twenty-five pounds of powder and fifty pounds of shot, and sent them to Southampton under the command of John Mason, the veteran who had commanded the troops at Mystic during the Pequot War (RPCC 1928, 22:176). The mere presence of the man who ordered the massacre of the Pequot must have unsettled the Shinnecock. Mason was ordered to consult with Wyandanch about the matter and to determine whether or not any of the Indians involved in the incident were under Wyandanch's authority.

Mason arrived in Southampton to find that the magistrates had issued gunpowder to the townsmen in preparation for a conflict. The town passed a resolution allowing only four representatives from Shinnecock to enter the English village. The magistrates appointed Wapeacom, Powcowwantuck, Suretrust, and James to carry on all relations between the two communities (RTSH 1:114-115).

There is no record of Mason's activities in the town, but there is a reference in a later document to a Shinnecock man, who killed himself to avoid "just execution" by the English (RCNP 10:180). The man may have been Wigwagub, the only one who confessed to the arson. Mason, apparently not satisfied to leave the matter at that, imposed an exorbitant fine of 700 pounds on the Shinnecock community. The Shinnecock, well aware of Mason's role in the massacre of the Pequot, agreed to accept the fine, which was to be paid over a seven year period (Ibid.). The fine forced them into a debt servitude which could be used both as an instrument of social control by the English and as a means to press for the sale of land to pay the fine. For the Shinnecock, who were not yet engaged in the European economic system, the sum was an impossible burden.

The Montaukett sachem demonstrated that the role of the alliance chief could be more than that of a passive conduit for English governance when he sent a representative with a written petition to the United Colonies session in Boston the following September and appealed the Connecticut court's fine (Ibid.). Wyandanch's decision to go over the head of the Connecticut court and the articulation of his arguments indicate a growing familiarity with English institutions.

When he submitted the petition, Wyandanch also sent seventy-eight fathoms of wampum to the United Colonies' treasurer in New Haven. The wampum was undoubtedly intended to influence the commissioners (Ibid., 194). The sachem began his presentation to the commissioners by reporting that the Shinnecock had already sustained losses from English horses that destroyed their crops. He then argued that Mason had not been fully informed about the arson when he imposed the fine. He told the commissioners that the African-American woman was primarily to blame for the arson and that the Shinnecock involved was dead. Given these circumstances, argued Wyandanch, the fine was excessive. The United Colonies' commissioners agreed with Wyandanch and asked the Connecticut court to reconsider the amount.

While the matter was pending before the Connecticut court, the town of Southampton paid the widow Howell twenty shillings to repair her losses. The damage was apparently not very severe. John Mason received twenty pounds from the town for his role in the affair. The cost of repairing the damage and paying the troops certainly did not justify a fine of 700 pounds. When the Connecticut court reconsidered the matter, they reduced the amount to 500 pounds over a six-year period (RCC, 1:316–17). For the Shinnecock the reduction had little significance because the fine was still far beyond their means.

The Hartford court appointed a group of prominent Southampton men to collect the fine and distribute payment to those who had suffered damages. The committee was empowered to "take from them a certain company of ye Indian men," if the payments were not made (RTSH 2:206-7). The brief reference does not explain what was to be done with the captives, but most likely it was intended that they would be sold as slaves in the West Indies to pay the debt. Although John Ogden, a member of the committee, apparently favored such action, the magistrates refused to take such a drastic measure, knowing full well that it might provoke a much more violent reaction among the local Indians. The Indians were well aware of the fate which befell those shipped out to the West Indies.

Fines of this kind were often used in New England as an effective means of social control. As long as an Algonquian community remained under the shadow of the debt, the English could intervene in their community affairs. The debt was also a strategy used to obtain Indian lands. According to historian Francis Jennings, a favorite strategy of the English was "the imposition of fines for a wide variety of offenses, the Indian's lands becoming forfeit if the fines were not paid by their due date" (Jennings 1976:144-45). As we shall see the English on Long Island were to make equally effective use of this strategy.

In the summer of 1657, Wyandanch was in Setauket to join with Wenecoheage, the local sachem, in the sale of two necks of land on the south shore lying east of the Connetquot River (Bayles 1882:3; Tooker 1962:280). The local sachem acknowledged Wyandanch's right to supervise the negotiations and to receive a share of the payment. The deed clearly indicated that the payment would go to both sachems. The goods given to them included twenty coats, twenty hoes, twenty hatchets, forty needles, forty muxes, ten pounds of powder, ten pounds of lead, six pairs of stockings, six shirts, one well-made trooper's coat, twenty knives, and one gun.

Three days later on July 23, 1657, Jonas Wood of Huntington called Wyandanch to confirm his purchase of a small parcel of meadow land on a neck which bordered on the Massapeaqua lands from Keeossechok, the Secatogue sachem (RTH 1:12-13; Street 1882:10). Wyandanch shared the trade goods which included a new gun, a pistol, and two pounds of powder, with Keeossechok. Wyandanch's role as a certifying agent for the deeds set an important precedent which the English hoped would bring some order to the process of land dispossession. The English settlers were now accepting the endorsement of the "chief sachem" as a requirement for the purchase of Algonquian land.

In 1658 Samuel Andrews, a private entrepreneur, traveled all the

way to Montauk and had Wyandanch endorse his deed to land in what
is now the town of Huntington. When the Huntington town officials,
who claimed the same land, learned of Andrews' mission, they rushed
to Montauk hoping to obtain Wyandanch's endorsement for their own
deed. According to local folklore, Andrews met the Huntington agents
on his way back and mocked them, waving his endorsement in their
faces telling them that they might as well go back home (RTH, 1:15;
Street 1882, 12–13). They did, and promptly brought suit against Andrews. After a long court battle, Andrews' title was upheld, primarily
because he had obtained Wyandanch's endorsement (RTH, 1:16).
Wyandanch endorsed several more transactions in 1658 and 1659, as
Englishmen from all over Long Island sought him out to bolster their
land claims.

Two weeks after his endorsement of Andrews' title, Wyandanch
turned his attention to the Shinnecock land west of Canoe Place
where the Shinnecock Canal is located today. Wyandanch demonstrated his experience as a negotiator and his understanding of English
institutions in these transactions. On May 29, 1658, he leased, for ten
years, a small tract of meadow land near the present-day village of West
Hampton Beach to Thomas Topping. After that time the land was "to be
surrendered peaceably unto the said sachem, his heirs, or successors,
to be disposed of, at his or their discretion" (DSBD 2:152). For the first
and, unfortunately, the last time, the Indian concept of limited use appears in the text of a land transaction. Wyandanch managed, for a brief
moment, to bring the English to terms with the traditional Algonquian
concept of land use.

Less than two weeks later Wyandanch, along with his advisors,
Cockenoe, Sassakata, and Momoweta (Moughmaitow) and his young
son, Wyancombone, sold Lion Gardiner a large tract of beach land in
the same area for an undisclosed sum of money and trade goods (RTSH
1:170–71). Once again, however, Wyandanch insisted on a clause
which would provide him and his family with a regular income. Gardiner agreed to pay the sachem and his heirs twenty-five shillings a
year, each October, forever. The whales which were cast up on the
beach, a major source of wealth on the south shore of Long Island, remained Wyandanch's property. The Indians also retained the right to
cut flag grass and bulrushes, which they used to make mats for the
wigwams. These transactions with Topping and Gardiner were unique
in that they guaranteed a continuing return of income rather than a
final dispossession. Six months later Gardiner granted the right to use
a portion of the tract to a Southampton man named John Cooper on

the condition that he pay Wyandanch the yearly fee (RTSH 1:171).

In August, Wyandanch, Cockenoe, and Sassakata were back in Huntington to sell three more necks of land on the south shore lying to the west of the land purchased by Jonas Wood the year before. Henry Whitney, who made the purchase for the town, paid Wyandanch twelve coats, twenty pounds of powder, twenty Dutch hatchets, twenty Dutch hoes, twenty Dutch knives, ten shirts, two hundred muxes, five pair of "handsome stockings," one good Dutch hat, and a looking glass. Cockenoe, who was paid a separate fee for marking out the boundaries, received one coat, four pounds of powder, six pounds of lead, one Dutch hatchet and seventeen shillings in wampum. The emphasis on Dutch goods suggests that they were considered superior to those produced by the English.

Wyandanch could usually rely on English support against rival sachems. In one instance, however, he overreached his authority. He prohibited the Pequot from coming to Long Island for quahog shells which were used in the manufacture of wampum. The Pequots, realizing that the traditional means of resolving such grievances were no longer possible, brought their case to the United Colonies and asked that their ancient privileges be restored (De Forest 1852:261). The commissioners agreed with them and gave notice to Wyandanch that "the Pequots . . . bee permitted to freely fetch shells there . . . as formerly they had done" (RCNP, 10:199–200).

The English concern for keeping the control of wampum resources and production in their hands is easy to understand. They had established a monopoly over the wampum trade in the Connecticut Valley following their defeat of the Pequot in 1637 and, as a result, soon dominated the lucrative fur trade on the Connecticut River (McBride 1994:41). The English, who were collecting significant amounts of tribute wampum from the Pequots, did not want any limitation on their access to quahog shells.

This minor setback may have prompted Wyandanch to strengthen his alliance with Gardiner and the influential men in the East Hampton community whenever he could. The land titles were, of course, a primary concern of the English, but another important source of wealth on the East End of Long Island was whale oil. The Montauketts took the tales and fins of the whales for their ceremonial feasts, but the English were primarily interested in the oil and baleen because these commodities could be turned into hard currency on the European market (Strong 1990, 17–29). Drift whales were the first cash crop on Long Island.

The question of drift whales came up again in November, 1658 when Wyandanch gave Lion Gardiner and the Reverend Thomas James of East Hampton one half of the whales "or other great fish" which drifted onto the beach between Napeague and the far end of Montauk. This was an important grant because it gave the two men an exclusive right to all of the ocean beaches on Montaukett lands. The town of East Hampton owned the whale rights from Napeague on west to the Southampton border and held them in common trust. Wyandanch did require a small percentage of their profit, but left it to James and Gardiner to pay "what they shall judge meete and according as they find profit by them" (RTEH 1:150).

Wyandanch's generosity to the two influential East Hampton men may have served him well two months later when he brought suit in the town courts against a young townsman named Jeremy Vaile for damages to his large canoe. The vessel, probably one used for trips across the sound, may have been thirty or forty feet long. The suit is significant because it is one of the earliest recorded instances of an Indian plaintiff seeking damages from an Englishman in an English court.

Lion Gardiner testified for Wyandanch against Vaile, and charged him with negligence. Vaile and Anthony Waters, another East Hampton man, borrowed the canoe to carry some goods over to Gardiner's Island and ran into some bad weather. They landed the canoe on the island, but failed to secure it properly. Gardiner ordered them to return and make sure it was safe, but by the time they got back, the canoe was damaged and full of water. The court ruled for the plaintiff and awarded Wyandanch ten shillings (RTSH, 1:152)

As Wyandanch's influence grew, proprietors from all over Long Island sought him out to bolster their land claims. The Southold magistrates, led by Barnabas Horton, met with Wyandanch, Cockenoe and the Corchaug Indians in January 1659 to clear up some questions about who had the right to sell the land on the North Fork of eastern Long Island (Pelletreau 1882:9). Unfortunately we have no record of the specific issues involved in the dispute, but later documents indicate that Plum Island was one of the areas in contention. The Southold settlers on the north fork of Long Island English raised some questions about the property on Plum Island, which had been purchased by Governor Eaton from two Corchaug sachems, Momoweta and Paummis, in 1648. Southold officials, William Wells and Richard Woodhall, bought the island from Eaton for the use of the town, but they never established a settlement there. Later, John Youngs bought the land, but he never occupied it either (DSBD, 1:15). The Corchaug, acting on their traditional view of ownership, apparently reasserted their control over the island by default. The Southold men called upon Wyandanch to resolve this matter and other questions about the rest of the North Fork as well.

Wyandanch asserted that the Corchaug were not now, nor had they ever been, the owners of the North Fork or Plum Island. These lands, said the Montaukett sachem, were inherited from his ancestors, and had been sold to Richard Woodhall and William Wells "diverse years since" (RTS, 1:194). The Corchaug did not protest this claim by Wyandanch and "remained wholly silent not in the least contradicting what the sachem said." Their silence may have been a commentary on Wyandanch's growing power and influence rather than a sign of their agreement with his assertion of hegemony over their lands.

Later, in the spring of 1659, Wyandanch and his young son, Wyancombone, gave a large tract of land from what is now the Shinnecock Canal to the village of Westhampton Beach to John Ogden as a partial payment on the fine for arson in 1657 (RTSH 2:354). Ogden had apparently purchased the debt from the Southampton officials, who were unsuccessful in forcing payment from the Shinnecock. The boundaries included some meadow land which had previously been leased to Thomas Halsey, probably under the same terms as Wyandanch had negotiated with Topping for meadow land on the western border of this deed. When Halsey's lease ran out, the land went to Ogden, but the small parcel of meadow along the south beach which Gardiner had leased from Wyandanch in 1658 and turned over to John Cooper was excluded from Ogden's deed. Wyandanch was careful to include a clause which protected the Indians' right to fishing, hunting and the gathering of wild plants in the area. Lion Gardiner and his son, David, witnessed the lease.

That same day, Wyandanch, Gardiner and their sons confirmed the purchase of a half neck of land by Jonas Wood in 1657 (RTH, 1:21–22). Apparently Tackapousha and the Massapequa sachems challenged that purchase of Secatogue land from Keeossechok (RTH, 1:21n). Wyandanch asserted his authority over Tackapousha and, at the same time, served the English interests by helping to avoid another expensive and disruptive legal battle in the colonial courts.

The following month Gardiner leased the whale rights to a section of Atlantic beach west of the area he had purchased from Wyandanch the year before (DSBD, 2:85–86). The lease ran for twenty-one years, and Wyandanch was promised five pounds sterling or an equivalent amount of goods for each whole whale carcass. The sachem reserved

the tails and fins for himself. Gardiner then turned over the whale
rights to John Cooper, who was beginning to develop a whaling enterprise, which would soon become a major industry on the south shore
of eastern Long Island.

On July 14, 1659, shortly before his death, Wyandanch signed a
most unusual document. It reads almost like a last will and testament.
Written in the first person as if dictated by Wyandanch, it acknowledged Lion Gardiner's friendship, counsel, and material aid over a
twenty-four year period. Gardiner, said Wyandanch, "appeared to us not
only as a friend but as a father" (RTSM 1:3–4). In return for this friendship Wyandanch made him a gift of 30,000 acres of land between
Huntington and Setauket which included most of what is now the
Town of Smithtown in the middle of Long Island. The Nissequogue
River, which runs through the center of the tract was the home
Nesseconsett, the Nissequogue sachem.

A close examination of the document raises a number of questions
about its authenticity. The relationship between Wyandanch and Gardiner was certainly close, but it seems unlikely that Wyandanch, who
had previously sold land and whale rights to Gardiner, would now give
him a tract of land as big as the one he sold to East Hampton in 1648.

Another question concerned Wyandanch's claim to ownership of
the land. Nesseconsett had sold the eastern half of the tract to Ed-
mond, Jonas and Jeremy Wood, and Daniel Whitehead in 1650 (Smith
1882, 1–2). The Englishmen, however, never attempted to occupy the
site and Nesseconsett later transferred it to Wyandanch, who apparently inherited an interest in the land from his grandmother. In 1656,
Asharoken, a Matinicock sachem had sold the land in the tract lying to
the west of the Nissequogue to Jonas Wood, William Rogers, and
Thomas Wilkes (RTH 1:6–7).

One of the witnesses to Wyandanch's most generous gift to Lion
Gardiner was Richard Smith, who later purchased a large portion of
the tract. In a conversation with Gardiner's widow, Sarah, sometime
later, Smith said that he had expected that "he should meete a great
deal of trouble about the land." Sarah Gardiner confided to Smith that
she believed the title was so vulnerable to challenge that she had considered abandoning the claim (RTEH, 1:336).

The challenges came quickly. Nesseconsett took the matter to
court, protesting that Richard Smith had taken away his land on the
east bank of the Nissequogue. Smith finally paid the sachem a gun, a
kettle, ten coats, a blanket, and some powder and lead (RTSM 1:8–9).
Settlers in Setauket and Huntington both engaged Smith in a long se-

ries of lawsuits which went on for several decades. (Smith 1882, 2–8; Street 1882, 22–23; NYCD 14:640–43).

Wyandanch died some time during the fall of 1659. According to Lion Gardiner, the Montaukett sachem was poisoned, but this is not corroborated in any of the colonial records. It also possible that he died in the plague which took the lives of an estimated two-thirds of the Algonquian people on Long Island between 1659 and 1664 (Gardiner 1980, 146; Strong 1996).

Wyandanch's passing was one of the events which marked the end of an era in Indian-white relations on Long Island. The era was characterized by the scramble of imperial powers at one level and aggressive individual entrepreneurs at another, to grab as much land as possible. The other markers were the death of Lion Gardiner in 1663, the English conquest of New Netherland in 1664 and the great plague.

There was no longer a need for a "Grand Sachem." The growth of the English settlements and the declining Indian population shifted the demographics heavily in favor of the whites. The English were now in a position to dominate the Algonquian people. The need for a single Indian leader, who could arbitrate disputes and control local sachems, however, was now over. In 1665, Richard Nicolls, the first governor of the newly established colony of New York, officially declared that there was no longer any "grand sachem" of Long Island. "Every sachem," said the governor, "shall keep his particular property over his people as formerly" (DSBD, 2:127). The English, who had created the position, had now abolished it.

NOTES

1. This is the first time Cockenoe's name appears in the Colonial records. His skill as an interpreter was well known throughout Long Island. He was frequently called in to help negotiate deeds and boundary disputes. In his brief biography of Cockenoe, William Wallace Tooker suggested that he may have learned English while in the service of the missionary, John Eliot (Tooker 1980, 176–79). Eliot mentioned an Indian youth from Long Island who had quickly mastered English. The young man then helped Eliot in his study of Indian languages. Unfortunately there is no way to corroborate Tooker's speculation.

2. It is difficult to determine the value of a specific parcel of land in the English market at this time. In 1659 good meadow land in East Hampton cost I pound per acre and woodland was valued at 6 shillings per acre (RTEH 2: 168–170). Later in the seventeenth century land averaged from

one to three pounds sterling per acre, unless it was swamp or wetland.

3. Richard White (1991, 36-40) used the term "alliance sachems" to describe the Algonquian leaders who formed alliances with the French in the seventeenth century on the "middle ground" between the two cultures in the Great Lakes area. His analytical model works very well for the middle ground on Long Island in the same period.

4. As the English settlements grew, the problems caused by free ranging hogs worsened. Finally, in 1683 the colonial government passed a law requiring people to keep their hogs confined (Kavenagh 1973, 2:1288-89). Anyone finding a stray hog could kill it. One third of the meat went to the individual who found the hog and the rest went to the town.

SOURCES

Ales, Marion Fisher. 1993. "A History of the Indians on Montauk. Long Island." In *The History and Archaeology of the Montauk Indians*, edited by Gaynell Stone, 5-67. Stony Brook: Suffolk County Archeological Association (hereafter SCAA).

Axtell, James. 1985. *The Invasion Within: The Contest of Cultures in Colonial North America*. New York; Oxford University Press.

———.1992. *Beyond 1492: Encounters in Colonial North America*. New York: Oxford University Press.

Bayles, Richard. 1882. "The Town of Brookhaven." In *The History of Suffolk county, New York*, edited by W.W. Munsell, 1-101, New York: W.W. Munsell.

Black, Robert C. 1996. *The Younger John Winthrop*. New York: Columbia University Press.

Bradford, William. 1981. *Of Plymouth Plantation 1620-1647*. New York: McGraw Hill.

Brodhead, John Romeyn. 1853-71. *History of the State of New York*. 2 vols. New York: Harper Brothers.

Calder, Isabel. 1966. "The Earl of Sterling and the Colonization of Long Island." In *Essays in Colonial History Presented to Charles Mclean Andrews*, edited by Isabel Calder, 74-95. Freeport, NY: Books for Libraries Press.

Cave, Alfred. 1996. *The Pequot War*, Amherst: University of Massachusetts Press.

Cook, Sherburne F. 1973. "The Significance of Disease in the Extinction of the New England Indians." *Human Biology 45*, no. 3:485-508.

Cooper, Thomas, ed. 1993. *The Records of the Court of Session of Suffolk County in the Province of New York, 1670-1688*. Bowie, MD: Heritage Books.

CSAIP Connecticut State Archives, *Indian Papers 1647-1789*, Documents I:10-23, Connecticut State Library, Hartford CT.

De Forrest, John. 1852. *History of the Indians of Connecticut From Earliest Known Period to 1850*. Hartford: W.J. Hammersley.

Denton, Daniel. 1968. "A Brief Description of New York, 1670." In *Historical Chronicles of New Amsterdam, Colonial New York, and Early Long Island*, edited by Sidney Pomerantz, 1-22. New York: Empire State Historical Publications.

Dixon, C.W. 1962. *Smallpox*. New York: Little, Brown, and company.

DSBD. *Department of State Book of Deeds*. Unpublished Documents Office of the Secretary of State, Albany, NY. (NY State Archives Series 453 volumes 1-9.)

Gardiner, Curtis. 1890. *Lion Gardiner and his Descendants*. St. Louis: A. Whipple (available in East Hampton Library, Long Island Collection).

Gardiner, David. 1973. [1840] *Chronicles of the Town of East Hampton*. Sag Harbor, NY: Isabel Gardiner Mairs.

Gardiner, John Lyon. 1980. "Montauk Vocabulary, Recorded From George Pharaoh, March 25, 1798." In *Languages and Lore of the Long Island Indians*, edited by Gaynell Stone Levine and Nancy Bonvillain, 15-16. Stony Brook, NY: SCAA.

————. 1798. *The Journal and Farm Book of John Lion Gardiner*. East Hampton Public Library Collections. East Hampton, NY.

Gardiner, Lion. 1980. [1897] "Relation of the Pequot Wars," in *The History of the Pequot War*, edited by Charles Orr, 11-149. New York: AMS Press.

Hedges, Henry. 1897. *A History of the Town of East Hampton*. Sag Harbor, NY: J.H. Hunt.

Jennings, Francis. 1976. *The Invasion of America: Indians, Colonialism and the Cant of Conquest*. NY: W.W. Norton.

JEHT. 1926-27. *Journal of the East Hampton Trustees*, edited by H.D. Sleight, 7 vols. East Hampton, NY: Town of East Hampton.

Johnson, Eric. 1996. "Uncas and the Politics of Contact." *Northeast Indian Lives, 1632-1816*, edited by Robert S. Grumet, 29-47, Amherst: University of Massachusetts Press.

Kavenagh, W. Keith, ed. 1973. *Foundations of Colonial America*. 3 vols., New York: Chelsea House.

McBride, Kevin. 1994. "The Source and Mother of the Fur Trade: Native-Dutch Relations in Eastern New Netherland." In *Enduring Traditions*, edited by Laurie Weinstein, 31-51. Westport, CT: Bergin and Garvey.

Moynihan, Ruth. 1977. "The Patent And The Indians: The Problem of Jurisdiction in Seventh Century New England." *American Indian Culture and Research Journal*. 2, no. 1: 8-19.

NYCD. 1856-87. *Documents Relative to the Colonial History of the State of New York*. 15 vols., edited by Edmund Bailey O'Callaghan and Berthold Fernow. Albany: Weed, Parsons and Company

O'Callaghan, Edmund Bailey. 1966 [1845-48]. *History of New Netherland*. 2 vols. Spartanburg, NC: The Reprint Company.

Pelletreau, William. 1882. "The Town of Southampton." In *The History of Suffolk County*, edited by W.W. Munsell, 1–54. New York: W.W. Munsell.

RCC. 1850-1890. *The Public Records of the Colony of Connecticut*, 15 vols. edited by J. Hammond Trumbull. Hartford: F.A. Brown (AMS Reprint, 1968)

RCNH. 1857. *Records of the Colony and Plantation of New Haven From 1638-1649.* 2 vols. edited by Charles J. Hoadly. Hartford: Case Tiffany.

RCNP. 1968. [1859] *Records of the Colony of New Plymouth*, edited by David Pulsifer, 10 vols. New York: AMS Press.

RCRI. 1968.[1850–65] *Records of the Colony of Rhode Island and Providence Plantations in New England*, edited by John R. Bartlett. 10 vols. New York: AMS Press.

RPCC. 1928. *Records of the Particular Court of Connecticut, 1639-1663.* Connecticut Historical Society Collections, Volume 22.

RTEH. 1887. *Records of the Town of East Hampton*. 5 Vols. edited by Joseph Osborne. Sag Harbor, NY: Hunt.

RTH. 1887-9. *Huntington Town Records*. 3 vols. edited by Charles R. Street, Huntington, NY: Town of Huntington.

RTNSH. 1896-1904. *Records of the Town of North And South Hempstead*, edited by Benjamin Hicks, 8 vols. Jamaica, NY: Long Island Farmer Print.

RTSH. 1874-77 *Records of the Town of Southampton*. 8 vols. edited by William Pelletreau. Sag Harbor: Hunt.

Sainsbury, John. 1971. "Miantonomo's Death and New England Politics, 1630-1645." *Rhode Island History 30*, no.4:111-23.

Salisbury, Neal. 1984. *Manitou and Providence, Indians, Europeans, and the Making of New England, 1500-1643*. New York: Oxford University Press.

Salwen. Burt. 1978. "Indians of Southern New England and Long Island." In *Handbook of the North American Indians*. vol. 15, The Northeast, edited by Bruce Trigger, 160-89. Washington D.C.: Smithsonian Institution Press.

Smith, John Lawrence. 1882. "The Town of Smithtown." In *The History of Suffolk County*, edited by W.W. Munsell, 1-42, New York: W.W. Munsell.

Street, Charles R. 1882. "The Town of Huntington." In *The History of Suffolk County*, edited by W.W. Munsell, 1-90 (The book is not paginated sequentially. Each town history is paginated independently). New York: W.W. Munsell.

Strong, Lara, M. and Selcuk Karabag. 1991. "Quashawam: Sunksquaw of the Montauk." *The Long Island Historical Journal* 3(2):189-204.

Strong, John A. 1990. "The Pigskin Book: Records of Native American Whalemen." *The Long Island Historical Journal* 3, no.1:29-40.

———. 1996. "Wyandanch, Sachem of the Montaukett." In *Northeastern Indian Lives*. edited by Robert Grumet, 48-73. Amherst. MA: University of Massachusetts Press.

Tooker, William Wallace. 1980. "John Eliot's First Indian Teacher and Interpreter, Cockenoe de Long Island." In *Languages and Lore of the Long Island Indians*, edited by Gaynell Stone Levine and Nancy Bonvillain, 176–89. Stony Brook, NY: SCAA.

———. 1980a. "Cockenoe-de-Long Island." In *Languages and Lore of the Long Island Indians*. ed., Gaynell Levine and Nancy Bonvillain, 176–89. Stony Brook, NY: SCAA.

White, Richard. 1991. *The Middle Ground, Indians, Empires, and Republics in the Great Lakes Region, 1650–1815*. New York: Cambridge University Press.

Williams, James Homer. 1995. "Great Doggs and Mischievous Cattle: Domesticated Animals and Indian-European Relations in New Netherland and New York." *New York History*. 76, no. 3:245–64.

Williams, Roger. 1963. *Complete Writings of Roger Williams*. 7 vols. New York: Russell and Russell.

———. 1973. *A Key to the Language of America*, 1643, with notes by John J. Teunissen and Evelyn J. Hinz, Detroit: Wayne State University Press.

WP. 1929–47. *The Winthrop Papers*. Edited by Allyn B. Forbes, 5 vols., Boston: Massachusetts Historical Society.

LION GARDINER,

Long Island's Founding Father

Roger Wunderlich

In the year of our Lord, 1635, the tenth of July, came I, Lion Gardiner and Mary my wife from Woerden a towne in Holland, where my wife was born to London and from thence to New England and dwelt at Saybrooke forte four years of which I was commander: and there was borne to me a son named David, 1636 ... the first born in that place, ... Then I went to an island of mine owne which I had bought and purchased of the Indians, called by them Manchonake by us the Isle of Wight, and there was born another daughter named Elizabeth ... in 1641, she being the first child of English parents that was born there.
—Lion Gardiner, lines in a family Bible[1]

LONG ISLAND AS AMERICA is the premise that the history of this Island reflects as well as contributes to most major phases of national life from colonial times to the present. One may examine the Long Island story through the prism of national history, or view the nation's history in terms of events on Long Island—the subjects are interchangeable.[2]

The Long Island as America thesis applies equally to the impact of European settlement on the Native American people: the pattern of colonial growth; Long Island in the Revolution and then in the early Republic; slavery; whaling; the building of the Long Island Railroad; farming, fishing, and shipbuilding; the Civil War and the Gilded Age; the Gold Coast estates; the rise of the suburbs; the Roaring Twenties, replete with the Jazz Age, Prohibition, and the revival of the Ku Klux Klan; Long Island as cradle of aviation; the Great Depression; Robert

Moses, the controversial master builder; Long Island as arsenal of fighter planes and producer of the Lunar Module; the post-World War II population boom, exemplified by Levittown; the social upheavals of the sixties; the change at the end of the Cold War from a manufacturing to a service economy; and current, postsuburban Long Island, where most of its people work as well as live, beset by the high cost of taxes, housing and energy. There is no better example of this concept than the career of Lion Gardiner, with whom the search for Long Island's founding father begins and ends. Lion Gardiner, who lived from 1599 until 1663, was the original English settler not only of Long Island but also the future state of New York. This robust pioneer stands as the first as well as the prototype of the colonists, who, in the words of Silas Wood, Long Island's first major historian, "had forsaken the scenes of civilization, broken asunder the ties that bound them to their native soil, . . . encountered the dangers of the ocean, and . . . submitted to the hazards and privations of a new and savage country." [3]

Gardiner's lifework exemplified the transition from the old to the modern world. He took part in three of the principal movements that marked the emergence of popular government from the bonds of absolute monarchy: the winning of Holland's independence from Spain, the English Revolution, and the Puritan colonization of New England and Long Island. As a young man, he served as an engineer in an English regiment stationed in the Netherlands in support of the northern provinces' battle to break away from the Spanish empire. While engaged in this early war of national liberation, he was hired by leading opponents of the state and church of England to build a fort at Saybrook, at the mouth of the Connecticut River. In 1639, at the end of his four-year contract, he crossed the Sound to become lord of the manor of Gardiner's Island, a fertile sliver of land between the forks of Paumanok. In 1650 he purchased land in the recently founded town of East Hampton; three years later he left Gardiner's Island in the hands of retainers and moved to the fledgling village to assume a leading role in its civil and religious affairs. His cordial relations with Native Americans saved eastern Long Island from the bloody interracial warfare that plagued New England. Toward the end of his life, he became the catalyst for the creation of Smithtown, conveying to William Smith the 30,000 acres given to him by the Montauk sachem, Wyandanch, whose daughter Gardiner helped to ransom when she was kidnapped by mainland Indians. [4]

Gardiner exerted a major influence on the development of East Hampton, which, together with Southold, Southampton, Shelter Island,

Huntington, Brookhaven, and Smithtown, comprised the scale-model city-states that distinguished eastern Long Island. Although they restricted first-class citizenship only to Puritan co-religionists, these self-governing Bible commonwealths endowed future generations with two of the building blocks of liberty, the town meeting and the independent church, wholly owned and managed by its congregation. As Silas Wood described them, "each town of the first settlement was a pure democracy: the people of each town exercised the sovereign power. All questions were determined by the voice of the major part of the people, assembled in town meeting."[5] These eastern towns found themselves outside the orbit of domination, so distant were they from the centers of Dutch and British power. In the words of another of Long Island's nineteenth-century historians, Nathaniel S. Prime, they were "absolutely in a state of nature, possessing all the personal rights and privileges which the God of nature gave them, but without the semblance of authority one over another." When they found it expedient to ally themselves with New England, it was not because of doubt that they could manage their internal affairs, "but solely for defence from foreign aggression. And the nature of the union was rather that of an alliance than subjection."[6] When parting from Great Britain took center stage a century later, the descendants of Puritan pioneers were ready for a republic.

As a townsman of East Hampton, Gardiner helped to shape a new and American social design, which enabled ordinary folk to own property and enjoy the freedoms restricted to the privileged gentry across the sea. However, though he was our founding father he was not our patron saint. While his statesmanship cemented peaceful relations between the settlers and the Indians, he also presided over the peaceable but permanent transfer of Long Island real estate from its Native American owners to himself and his fellow settlers. As the symbol of two phenomena—the formation of the model Puritan township and the nonviolent displacement of Indians—Lion Gardiner personified the dual and sometimes ambivalent mission of the colonists of Long Island.

Necessity compelled Gardiner and his compatriots to cope with the basic conditions of life in completely new surroundings. This involved the providing, from a standing start, of food, shelter, and artifacts, and a safe and harmonious social order attuned to the New World, not the Old. Above all, as they dealt with these elementary needs, the uninvited settlers grappled with the question of their legal right to the land that was now their only home. It was glaringly apparent that every acre was the possession of the indigenous Native Americans.

It is easy to judge the past by present standards. A moralist can argue that the 6,000 Long Island Indians were entitled to hold their land forever, thus changing the English influx from a settlement to an invasion. Or, that because there was so much room to coexist on this lush and sparsely settled island, Lion Gardiner et al cannot be excused for basing their system of land acquisition on dispossessing the Indians. In particular, why did the English not pay a fair price instead of trading trifles for treasure?

We may beg the question by reminding ourselves that in many ways it is moot: by the end of the seventeenth century, Long Island's Indian population was almost wiped out by the germs of smallpox, measles, and other diseases inadvertently spread by their almost immune English carriers. In his memoir, written in 1660, Gardiner mentioned a recent "time of a great mortality," during which "two thirds of the Indians upon Long-Island died." Ten years later, in the first English account of New York, Daniel Denton observed how few Indians remained on Long Island, a state of affairs he welcomed as God's serendipitous bonus to British colonists: "It hath been generally observed, that where the English come to settle, a Divine Hand makes way for them, by removing or cutting off the Indians either by Wars one with the other, or by some raging mortal Disease."[7]

Although death by disease played the largest part, the issue of how the Indians lost their land still goads our historical conscience, and we seek acceptable motives for the policies of the colonists. The blunt reality is that the tide of English immigration, swelled by the prospect of land for the taking, proved far too strong for deterrence by legal niceties. Lion Gardiner, the intrepid pioneer and archetype of English homesteaders, was also a business man obsessed with acquiring real estate from its present, ancestral owners. Many of his contemporaries held that the Indians were primitive simpletons, whose collective holding of tribal grounds made real estate dealing impossible. According to the conventional wisdom, the aborigines were too uncivilized to conceive of buying and selling land they naively believed belonged to all who lived on it.

Lion Gardiner, to his credit, exhibited none of this pervasive prejudice. He accepted Indians as friends and not inferiors: his cordial relations with Yovawam and Wyandanch, the successive sachems with whom he dealt, exempted eastern Long Island from the interracial bloodshed that afflicted Connecticut and Massachusetts. In the process, however, Gardiner amassed a fortune in land by "buying" it for trinkets, and expediting sales by promoting the Native American seller, especially Wyandanch, to the fictitious but handy rubber-stamp rank of

"Sachem of all Long Island." One way to obtain the land was by force: the Long Island way, perfected, if not invented, by Lion Gardiner, was to "purchase" deeds from a super-sachem and have them confirmed by colonial writ. As contended by John A. Strong, a current authority on Long Island's Indian legacy, Lion Gardiner crowned Wyandanch with the title of Grand Sachem "to legitimize his purchase of lands all over Long Island." The Montauks' lack of military power "made a mockery of this presumptuous title," the sham enabling "Gardiner and his associates to avoid the difficulties of negotiating with the numerous small bands living on the lands in question."[8]

Lion Gardiner's lineage has not been traced, but according to Curtiss C. Gardiner, who wrote the history of his famous ancestor on the 250th anniversary of Lion's arrival on his island, "He was probably a gentleman without title, of the middle rank, between the nobility and the yeomanry, yet he might have been a yeoman." Granted that seventeenth-century spelling was on a do-it-yourself basis, Lion generally signed himself as "Gardener," a name which Curtiss C. Gardiner pointed out "may be derived from an occupation, the keeper of a garden," and subsequently "may have been changed . . . to Gardiner, that the occupation and the name of a person might be the more readily distinguishable." His unusual first name "was Lion, as he invariably wrote it so": there is no reason to speculate that his baptismal name was Lionel. His army grade was sergeant, as evidenced by letters to John Winthrop Jr., the governor of the Saybrook colony and Gardiner's only superior there, in which one correspondent referred to "Seriant Gardener," another to "Sergiant Gardiner." Gardiner's later rank of "Leiftenant" was a promotion for his service at Saybrook.[9]

Nothing is known of Gardiner's life before 1635, the starting point of his memoir, "Leift. Lion Gardener his Relation of the Pequot Warres." While serving as "an Engineer and Master of Works of Fortification in the legers of the Prince of Orange, in the Low Countries," he was recruited by Hugh Peter and John Davenport, the exiled Puritan ministers of the English church of Rotterdam, and "some other well-affected Englishmen of Rotterdam," to build and command a fort in New England. The project was sponsored by upper-class dissenters from the government of Charles 1, who, during the 1630s, suspended Parliament, demanded Anglican orthodoxy, and levied unacceptable taxes. In addition to Davenport, who became a founder of New Haven, and Peter, a firebrand chaplain-to-be of Oliver Cromwell's army and Protectorate, its supporters included Viscount Saye and Sele (William Fiennes) and Baron Brooke (Robert Greville), the spokesmen in the

House of Lords of the Puritan opposition; Sir Arthur Haselrig, a prominent rebel in the House of Commons; and George Fenwick, another member of Parliament who defied the royal authority. Of these, only Fenwick came to live at the fort—it was he who named the place Saybrook to honor its two main sponsors. Once the Long Parliament convened in 1640, and especially after war with the Crown erupted two years later, the organizers lost interest in Saybrook; Fenwick sold it to the colony of Connecticut in 1644, before returning to England to resume his seat in Parliament and command a militia regiment.[10]

A third nineteenth-century Long Island historian, Benjamin Franklin Thompson, assessed Lion Gardiner as "one of the many young men of Britain of bold and adventurous spirit, who, seeking fame or sympathizing with the oppressed," joined the ranks of English nonconformists, "both of the church and the laity," fighting to liberate Holland. Lion's commander in the lowlands was Sir Thomas Fairfax, the future general of Cromwell's army. His Saybrook employers were ringleaders of the movement that eventually overthrew the British monarchy, beheaded the king, and instituted a short-lived republic: it seems unlikely that this band of dissidents would hire Gardiner had he not sided with their cause. According to Curtiss C. Gardiner, "he adhered to the Parliamentary party, and was a Dissenter and a friend of the Puritans." However, Lion Gardiner's memoir expresses no political viewpoint in connection with Holland or Saybrook. While in Holland, Thompson noted, he married "Mary Willemson, a native of [the small city of Woerden], and a lady of prominent connections." It is tempting to assume that Gardiner sympathized with his rebel employers, but it is also possible that this unblinking realist took the Saybrook job for the hundred pounds a year it paid, and the chance to begin married life as the leader of a bold and prestigious venture.[11]

As it turned out, Saybrook was a disaster. "According to promise," wrote Lion, "we expected that there would have come from England 300 able men, 50 to till the ground, and 50 to build houses. But our great expectation at the River's mouth, came only two men, Mr. Fenwick, and his man." A recent historian of the Winthrops found that after five discouraging months, John Winthrop Jr., Gardiner's superior, "quit Saybrook . . . before the end of his term as governor, and left Lion Gardiner in charge of the thinly manned outpost, to spend a miserable winter [1636-37] behind the palisades, beleaguered by Pequots." Somehow, Lion managed to shepherd his small flock of settlers through the hardships of that bitter season, when he "had but twenty-four in all, men, women, and boys and girls, and not food for two months, unless we saved our cornfield, which could not possibly be if they came to war, for it is two miles from our home." [12]

The war he dreaded was with the Pequots, the intractable local Indians with whom traders had been skirmishing, and whose extermination was held necessary by many New England settlers. As a harbinger of impending conflict, twenty Massachusetts Bay men raided the Pequots and marched home again, to Lion Gardiner's "great grief, for, said I, you come hither to raise these wasps about my ears, and then you will take wing and flee away." He was a pragmatist, not a pacifist. He disapproved of small sorties that resulted in counterattacks on his vulnerable fort, in one of which he was shot in the thigh by a Pequot arrow. But in 1637, when Captains John Mason and John Underhill led a large force of colonists and Indian allies against the Pequot stronghold, Lion rejoiced in the "Victory to the glory of God, and honor of our nation, having slain three hundred, burnt their fort, and taken many prisoners." Although he praised the outcome of the Pequot War, he criticized the carnage as the avoidable result of violence and counter-violence that began with the murder of a Pequot by an Indian friendly to Massachusetts:

> Thus far I have written in a book, that all men and posterity might know how and why so many honest men had their blood shed, yea, and some flayed alive, others cut in pieces, and some roasted alive, only because . . . a Bay Indian killed one Pequit. [13]

The Pequot's defeat led to Gardiner's meeting with Wyandanch, the Montauk leader, who visited Saybrook three days after the battle. Although Gardiner referred to Wyandanch as the "next brother to the old Sachem of Long Island," it is more likely that they were colleagues, with Wyandanch next in line to succeed the "old Sachem," Yovawan, whom the English called Poggatucut. [14]

According to Gardiner, the purpose of Wyandanch's call was to "know if we were angry with all Indians," or only with Pequots. In his typically forthright manner, Lion answered "No, but only with such as had killed Englishmen." When Wyandanch asked if the English would trade with "they that lived on Long Island," Gardiner gave him a conditional yes: "If you will kill all the Pequits that come to you, and send me their heads, then . . . you shall have trade with us." Wyandanch said he would bring this news to "his brother . . . and if we may have peace and trade with you, we will give you tribute, as we did the Pequits." Gardiner sealed his bargain with a grisly demand with which Wyandanch complied:

If you have any Indians that have killed English, you must bring
their heads also . . . so he went away and did as I had said, and
sent me five heads, three and four heads for which I paid them
that brought them as they had promised.[15]

It was not a squeamish age on either side of the ocean. Settlers captured by Native Americans sometimes suffered deaths as horrible as
that inflicted by fellow Englishmen on one of Gardiner's former employers, the Reverend Hugh Peter, who, shortly after the Restoration,
was hung, drawn, and quartered after being forced to witness the similar fate of a friend.[16] The price of peace on Long Island was harsh, but
the pact between Gardiner and Wyandanch, and the lasting friendship
that followed, relieved eastern Long Island of the English-Indian carnage that persisted for forty years in New England, from the Pequot
War in Connecticut through King Philip's War in Massachusetts.

Soon after Winthrop left Saybrook, Lion wrote to him that those
who remained would be loyal and work hard for the colony, but "it
seemed wee have neither masters nor owners." If not provided for, he
continued, "then I must be forced to shift as the Lord may direct."[17]

To shift as the Lord may direct was something Lion did incredibly
well. At the end of his Saybrook contract, in 1639, he crossed the Sound
with his family and some farmer-soldiers from the fort to become the
first of an unbroken line of lords of the manor of Gardiner's Island,
seven and a half miles long and three miles across at the widest point,
a few miles off-shore from East Hampton. Lion called it the Isle of
Wight because of its contour; the Indian name, "Manchonake," meant a
place where many had died, perhaps from some great sickness that
swept the east end of Long Island before the coming of the English.
The description of Gardiner's Island in 1798 by its seventh-generation
proprietor might well have applied to the island in Lion's time:

> The soil . . . is good & is very natural for Wheat and White
> clover. The timber is of various kinds, mostly large White oak . . .
> The land is well watered with brooks, springs & ponds . . . Beef,
> Cheese, Wheat, and Wool are the staple articles . . . Fish of vari-
> ous kinds may be procured at almost any time. For fertility of
> soil & for various advantages it is not perhaps exceeded by
> many farms in the United States.[18]

In the opinion of Curtiss G. Gardiner, the traditional consideration
of "one large black dog, one gun, a quantity of powder and shot, some
rum and a few Dutch blankets [is] not well founded." The real price,
recorded in a lawyer's notebook, was "ten coates of trading cloath,"

paid to "Yovawam Sachem of Pommanocc and Aswaw Sachem his wife," for Lion Gardiner and his heirs "to have and to hold . . . forever (as of) the third day of the moneth, called, by the English May in the yeare by them of their Lord . . . 1639." Ten months later, Lion obtained a confirming grant from the agent of the Earl of Stirling, then the king's grantee for Long Island and its adjacent islands. The consideration of five pounds a year empowered Gardiner:

> to enjoy that Island . . . he hath now in possession, Called . . . by the English the Isle of Wight . . . forever . . . And also to make Execute & put in practice such Laws for Church & Civil Government as are according to God the King and the practice of the Country without giving any account thereof to any whomsoever.[19]

Even before he moved from Gardiner's Island, Lion Gardiner took an active part in the affairs of East Hampton and its church. He was instrumental in the selection of the first minister, Thomas James, a young man about whom he wrote to John Winthrop Jr. in 1650, the year the church was gathered. The letter began, characteristically, with a proposal to sell ten cows "for fiftie pound, in good marchantabl wampem, bever, or silver." As for the newly formed church, declared Gardiner in keeping with Puritan striving for a congregation of visible saints, it aimed for quality, not quantity: it would rather part with some of its members than "resave more without good testimonies." East Hampton was willing to pay "the young man . . . 20li a year, with such that as I myself eat, til we see what the Lord will do with us." In a passage illustrative of Gardiner's erudition at a time of widespread illiteracy—his history of the Pequot War was peppered with biblical quotations—he asked Winthrop to tell the "yung man (who) hapily hath not manie books . . . that I have . . . the 3 Books of Martyrs, Erasmus, moste of Perkins, Wilsons Dixtionare, a large Concordiance, Mayor on the New T(e)stement."[20]

In contrast to many of his peers, Gardiner did not clutter his mind with superstition, as proven by his reaction to an accusation of witchcraft. The defendant, Goody Garlick, was charged with causing the death in childbirth of none other than Lion's young daughter, Elizabeth Howell, in 1657. Perhaps because Goody and Joshua Garlick, her husband, worked for him for many years, or perhaps because he had too much common sense to believe in "black cats and harlequin devils . . . Lion seems to have exerted himself in behalf of this unfortunate woman," wrote Alexander Gardiner. Lion's influence aborted a trial at Hartford and saved Goody "from an awful fate."[21]

Lion Gardiner and Thomas James became bosom friends, a relationship that expanded from ecclesiastical to business matters. A 1658 entry in the East Hampton Town Record reported that "Wyandanch, Sachem of Long Island," gave half of all whales cast up on the beach from "Nepeake eastward to the end of the Island" to Leiftenant Lion Gardiner, and the other half to Thomas James. The "first good whale" was given "freely and for nothing," after which the grantees would pay "what they shall Judge meete, and according as they find profit by them." However, it is likely that this windfall was prompted by the Montauks' by-now complete reliance on the armed power of the settlers. The Pequots, before their defeat, and the Narragansetts after that had staged predatory raids on the Montauks, extorting payments of wampum in exchange for refraining from violent reprisals. Following Gardiner's pact with Wyandanch, the Indians, decimated by sickness and unable to compete in war, transferred their allegiance and annual payment of tribute from mainland Native American to English "protectors." In his 1983 study of East Hampton, T. H. Breen concluded that the Montauks lost their gamble that "their alliance with Gardiner and the other settlers would translate into power over the Narragansetts." When this "strategy backfired, they found themselves even more dependant upon the English."[22]

When New England Indians tried, without success, to foment armed resistance to English rule of Long Island, Wyandanch not only refused to join the conspiracy but reported the plot to Gardiner, for which Nathaniel S. Prime commended him:

> Though often cajoled and threatened by the N. E. Indians to induce him to conspire against his new neighbors, he not only rejected their overtures but even delivered their agents into the hands of the English. He reposed unbounded confidence in Lion Gardiner; and communicated to him, without reserve, every thing that involved his own interests, or the safety of the whites.[23]

Prime's impression of Wyandanch as a statesman who crossed racial lines to preserve the peace is not shared by Gaynell Stone, a current scholar of Long Island's Indian heritage. According to Stone, the militarily

> weak Wyandanch was a figurehead supported by the English ... to consummate their continuing land purchases ... Perhaps he had no choice, caught as he was between two aggressive forces, the Narragansetts and the English.[24]

East End English settlers and Native Americans never met on the field of battle, but the Montauks and Narragansetts did. In a 1654 raid the Narragansett/Niantic warlord Ninigret is said to have pillaged the camp of Wyandanch on the night of his daughter's wedding, killed the groom, and kidnapped the bride. On behalf of the grief-stricken father, Thomas James begged John Winthrop Jr. to help to speed delivery of the wampum raised for ransom, "which he [Wyandanch] hears was intercepted by Thomas Stanton [a colonist]." "At last," wrote Curtiss C. Gardiner, "through the exertions of [Lion] Gardiner . . . (the young woman) was redeemed and restored to her afflicted parents."[25]

To express his gratitude, Wyandanch, with his wife and son, made a free gift to Lion Gardiner, "his heirs, executors and assigns forever," of land that "lyeth on Long Island . . . between Huntington and Setauket . . . [and] more than half way through the island southerly." Dated East Hampton, July 14, 1659, the deed acknowledged twenty-four years of Lion's "kindness . . . counscell and advice in our prosperity," with special remembrance that:

> in our great extremity, when we were almost swallowed up of our enemies . . . he appeared to us not only as a friend, but as a father in giving us money and goods, whereby we defended ourselves, and ransomed my daughter.

Above the marks of his son Wyancombone, and "The Sachem's Wife" (Wicchiaubit), the signature of Wyandanch is a drawing of two stick figures shaking hands, an unusual gesture of affection and equality. Yet a skeptic will wonder who worded the document, which states that now that the sachem and his wife are old, "we have nothing left that is worth his [Lion's] acceptance but a small tract of land left us, [which] we desire him to accept," a strangely modest description of 30,000 choice acres.[26]

If Lion used his friendship with Indians to his advantage, his trust in them was genuine. When Wyandanch was ordered to testify before the magistrates of Southampton, and his people feared for their sachem's safety, Lion, who happened to be at the Montauk camp, presented himself as a hostage. "I will stay here till you all know it is well with your Sachem," he declared, in his strong, terse, style, "if they bind him, bind me, and if they kill him, kill me." All's well that ends well, albeit somewhat grimly; Wyandanch found the four Indians who committed the murder in question "and brought them to Southampton, and they were all hanged at Hartford." In 1659, Wyandanch met his death, perhaps from sickness, perhaps at the hands of hostile Indians because of his English collaboration. In his memoir, Gardiner stated that although Wyandanch perished during the "great mortality (epidemic) among them (the Indians) . . . it was by poison." He mourned the passing of the sachem: "My friend and brother is gone, who will now do the like?" a lament with ambiguous overtones.[27]

In 1660, the governor of Barbados, who was a friend of John Winthrop Jr.'s, expressed interest in buying Gardiner's Island. Oh no, wrote Lion to Winthrop, "I having children and children's children, am not minded to sell it at present." Not "at present" or ever would this island leave possession of the Gardiners (although it nearly changed hands several times in the present century). "Butt I have another plac," went on Lion, "(I suppose) more convenient for the gentleman that would buy, liinge upon Long Iland, between Huntington and Setokett."[28]

When this sale fell through, Lion and his son David conveyed to Richard Smith (then known as Smythe) the land that would be the principal part of the future town of Smithtown. Smith, a friend of Lion's, was one of the three English witnesses to Wyandanch's deed; it is said that Wyandanch's daughter was returned to her father at Smith's home in Setauket, where the grateful sachem presented his gift of land to Gardiner. Lion died soon after this, and his son consummated the sale to Smith, of which no record remains.[29]

Lion Gardiner died in 1663, at the age of sixty-four, one year before the English conquest of New Netherland from the Dutch: the creator of its first settlement never heard the words "New York." Although he had to dilute his fortune in order to redeem the debts run up by David, his extravagant son, he left a considerable estate. In his will he apologized to his wife, his sole beneficiary, for not leaving more, because David, "after hee was at liberty to provide for himself, by his own engagement hath forced me to part with a great part of my estate to save his credit, soe that I cannot at present give to my daughter and grandchild that which is fitting for them to have."[30]

In 1665, one year after the English ousted the Dutch from New Netherland, Mary Gardiner died and, contrary to Lion's wishes, left Gardiner's Island to their son. Richard Nicolls, the governor of the newly formed New York Province, gave David Gardiner a grant for the Isle of Wight at an annual quit rent of five pounds. Five years later, the rent was commuted to one lamb yearly, upon demand, by Governor Francis Lovelace. In 1686, David received a new patent from Governor Thomas Dongan, who erected the Isle of Wight "a lordship and manor to be henceforth called the lordship and manor of Gardiner's Island." The rent of one lamb a year was renewed, as was the Gardiners' sovereignty. In the judgment of Benjamin F. Thompson, the fees for these parchments were "perquisites of the governors ... to fill their pockets at the people's expense." Power to hold court-leet (criminal) and court-baron (civil), as well as the advowson (the naming of clergy), and other ancient rights issued to David Gardiner were never exercised—they were given in anticipation of the manor's "becoming a numerously tenanted estate," which it did not. Their ownership remained uncontested, but the Gardiners' unlimited powers were curtailed in 1788, when the state legislature annexed the island to the town of Easthampton (then one word).[31]

The life of Lion Gardiner, Long Island's first English settler and founding father, illumines our understanding of Long Island as America. To begin with, his experience contradicts the assumption that Long Island was cloned from New England. Gardiner and fellow settlers were not New Englanders who came to Long Island, but English emigrants who sojourned in New England before choosing to make the Island their permanent home. He embodied the old and new system of ownership: he was the lord of his own manor who also served as a townsman of the Puritan commonwealth of East Hampton. There, in the words of the historian Peter Ross, "he filled the office of magistrate and in all respects was regarded as the representative citizen of that section of the island." His rejection of charges of witchcraft shows that even widely held superstition did not corrupt the clarity of his mind, even though the case pertained to the death of his own daughter.[32]

Gardiner learned the language and gained the trust of his Indian neighbors, whom he treated without condescension. When a Southampton court summoned Wyandanch to testify, he unflinchingly offered himself as a hostage pending the safe return of the sachem. Largely due to his diplomacy, the interracial wars of the mainland did not erupt on eastern Long Island. In the process, Gardiner acquired a handsome fortune in Long Island land by inducing his Indian friends to sell him large tracts at small prices, confirmed by English deeds.

Three hundred and fifty-nine years have passed since Lion Gardiner, freedom fighter and pioneer, set foot on eastern Long Island. He and his hardy wife, Mary, who left her comfortable home in Holland to cross the ocean with her husband and suffer the rigors of frontier life, are symbols of the transition from the Old World to the New by the first generation of emigrants. They were Americans long before the word was coined.

NOTES

1. Curtiss C. Gardiner, *Lion Gardiner and His Descendants* (St. Louis: A. Whipple, 1890), 3. These lines, in Gardiner's hand, were written in a Geneva *Bible* found many years after his death. First published in 1560, the unauthorized, pocket-size Geneva *Bible*, with Calvinistic marginal notes, was the pre-King James version favored by the English laity. Gardiner's inscribed copy, published in 1599, the year of his birth, is in the exhibit case of the East Hampton Free Library's Long Island Room, open from 1 to 4:30 P.M., Monday through Saturday, under the supervision of Dorothy King.

2. James E. Bunce and Richard P. Harmond, eds., *Long Island as America: A Documentary History to 1896* (Port Washington: Kennikat Press, 1977); the Long Island Historical Journal, published semiannually by the Department of History, SUNY at Stony Brook, is devoted to the study of Long Island as America.

3. Silas Wood, *A Sketch of the First Settlement of the Several Towns of Long Island, with their Political Condition, to the End of the American Revolution* (1824; reprint, *Historical Chronicles of New Amsterdam, Colonial New York and Early Long Island*, Cornell Jaray, ed. 1865, reprint, Port Washington: Ira J. Friedman, 1968), 19.

4. Lion Gardiner is his own best source, in "Leift. Lion Gardener his Relation of the Pequot Warres," *Collections of the Massachusetts Historical Society* (hereafter cited as CMHS), vol. 3, 3d series (Cambridge, 1833), 131-60; the manuscript, written at East Hampton in 1660, was found in 1809 among the papers of Gov. Jonathan Trumbull of Connecticut; see also his letters to John Winthrop Jr. in the "Winthrop Papers" (hereafter cited as "WP") CMHS, vols. 10, 3d Series, 6 and 7, 4th series, and 1 and 8, 5th series, and Records of the Town of East Hampton (hereafter cited as EHTR), 5 vols. (Sag Harbor: James H. Hunt, 1887) 1: passim. For secondary sources for Lion and later Gardiners (written mainly by descendants), in addition to Curtiss C. Gardiner, cited above; see John Lyon (most later Gardiners with this name were Lion, but some were Lyon) Gardiner, "Notes and Memorandums Concerning Gardiners Island, Written in May 1798 by John Lyon Gardiner the Present Proprietor of That Island .... *Collections of the New York Historical Society for the Year 1859* (New York, 1970), 260-72; Alexander Gardiner, "History of the Gardiner Family," CMHS, vol. 10, 3d series (Boston, 1846), 173-85; Sarah Diodati Gardiner, *Early Memories of Gardiner's Island* (The Isle of Wight, New York) East Hampton: East Hampton Star, 1947; William S. Pelletreau, "East Hampton," in *History of Suffolk County* (New York: W. W. Munsell. 1882), especially 5, 25, 30; Robert Payne, *The Island* (New York: Harcourt, Brace, 1958); Jason Epstein and Elizabeth Barlow, *East Hampton; A History and Guide*, rev. 3d ed. (New York: Random House, 1985); Roger Wunderlich, "An Island of Mine Owne": *The Life and Times of Lion Gardiner, 1599-1663*," LIHJ 2 (Fall 1989): 1-14.

For Smithtown, see J. Lawrence Smith, "Smithtown," in *History of Suffolk County,* New York: W. W. Munsell, 1882).

5. Wood, 19.

6. Nathaniel S. Prime, *History of Long Island, from Its First Settlement by Europeans. to the Year 1845, with Special Reference to Its Ecclesiastical Concerns Part I* (New York: Robert Carter, 1845), 77–78.

7. Lion Gardiner, "Pequot Warres," 157–68; Daniel Denton, *A Brief Description of New-York: formerly Called New Netherlands* (London, 1670, reprinted in Cornell Jaray, ed. 1865, reprint, Port Washington: Ira J. Friedman, 1968), 6–7.

8. John A. Strong, "How the Montauk Lost Their Land," in Gaynell Stone, ed., Readings in *Long Island Archaeology and Ethnic History,* vol 3, *The History & Archaeology of the Montauk,* 2d. ed. (Stony Brook: Suffolk County Archaeological Association, Nassau County Archaeological Committee, 1993), 79; for Gardiner and Wyandanch, see also Strong, *The Algonquian Peoples of Long Island: From Earliest Times to 1700* (Interlaken, N.Y.: Empire State Books, 1997, prepared under the auspices of Hofstra University, 1997), passim.

9. Curtiss C. Gardiner, 46. xvii; Edward Hopkins to John Winthrop Jr., 28 October 1635, "WP," CMHS, vol. 6, 4th series (Boston, 1863), 326, 329, announcing the departure from London of the Batcheler, the twenty-five-ton North Sea bark bearing "Serieant Gardener, his wife and her maid, and his workmaster to New England"; Sir Richard Saltonstall to John Winthrop Jr., 27 February 1635 (new style 1636), ibid., 579–91, asking to be commended to "Sergieant Gardiner . . . whom I purpose, God willing, to visit this summer, if he will provide a house to receiue me & mine at my landing." Two letters signed "Lion Gardener," in 1652 and 1660, were endorsed "Leift. Gardiner" by John Winthrop Jr. ("WP," CMHS, Vol 7, 4th Series, 64–65); in the "Pequot Warres" and most of his letters in the "WP," Lion spelled his last name "Gardener."

10. Lion Gardiner, "Pequot Warres," 136. English units in the Netherlands defended the Dutch Republic, a loose federation of provinces under the stadholdership of the prince of Orange, which waged a long and successful struggle for independence from Spain (see Pieter Geyl, *The Netherlands in the Seventeenth Century,* rev. and enl. ed. (New York: Barnes & Noble, 1961 [first pub. 1936 as *The Netherlands Divided*]); for a guide to modern interpretations of the English Revolution, including those of Christopher Hill, R. H. Tawney, H. R. Trevor- Roper, Lawrence Stone, Perez Zagorin, and many other historians, and the roles of Viscount Saye and Sele, Baron Brooke, Sir Arthur Haselrig, George Fenwick, Hugh Peter, John Davenport, Sir Richard Saltonstall, Sir Thomas Fairfax, and others encountered by Gardiner, see R. C. Richardson, *The Debate on the English Revolution* (London: Methuen, 1977), and Derek Hirst, *Authority and Conflict: England 1603–1658* (Cambridge: Harvard Univ. Press, 1986).

11. Benjamin F. Thompson, *History of Long Island from Its Discovery*

and Settlement to the Present Time, 3rd. ed., revised and greatly enlarged with additions and a biography of the author by Charles Werner (New York: Robert H. Dodd, 1918) 3:313-14; Curtiss C. Gardiner, 46.

12. Lion Gardiner, "Pequot Warres," 137-39; Richard S. Dun, *Puritans and Yankees: The Winthrop Dynasty of New England 1630-1717* (New York: W. W. Norton, 1962), 69.

13. Lion Gardiner, "Pequot Warres," 140, 150, 151. Like Gardiner, Mason and Underhill were soldiers in the Netherlands before coming to New England; see Major John Mason, "A Brief History of the Pequot War," CMHS, vol. 8, 2d series (Boston, 1836):120-53; Louis B. Mason, *The Life and Times of Major John Mason, 1600-1672* (New York: G. P. Putnam's Sons, 1935); Captain John Underhill, *Nerves from America* . . . (London, 1638; facsimile reprint ed. New York: Da Capo Press, 1971), an account of the Pequot War that justified the slaughter because sometimes "Scripture declareth women and children must perish with their parents" (40).

14. Lion Gardiner, "Pequot Warres," 150. Yovawan, the Manhansett sachem, and Wyandanch, the Montauk sachem, resided in present-day eastern Suffolk County, the region the Indians called Paumanok.

15. Ibid.

16. Prime, 93.

17. Curtiss C. Gardiner, 65.

18. John Lyon Gardiner, "Gardiners Island," 270-71, 261-62.

19. For the terms of the original deed for Gardiner's Island, copied in the records of a Boston lawyer, Thomas Lechford, see Curtiss G. Gardiner, 58-61; EHTR, 2-3.

20. Lion Gardiner to John Winthrop Jr., 27 April 1650, "WP," CMHS, Vol 7, 4th Series, 59; for William Perkins (1558-1602) and other Puritan theologians, see Perry Miller, *Orthodoxy in New England* (Boston, 1933), *The New England Mind: From Colony to Province* (1953; reprint, Boston: Beacon Press, 1961), and *Errand Into the Wilderness* (Cambridge, Mass.: Belknap Press, 1956).

21. Alexander Gardiner, "Gardiner Family," 183-84; for the charges against Goody Garlick, see EHTR 1: 132-36, and 139-40.

22. EHTR 1:150, 13 November 1658; T. H. Breen, *Imagining the Past*, East Hampton Histories (Boston: Addison, Wesley, 1989), 112.

23. Prime, 93.

24. Gaynell Stone, "Long Island as America: A New Look at the First Inhabitants," *Long Island Historical Journal I* (Spring 1989): 166.

25. Curtiss C. Gardiner, 65; *Thomas James to John Winthrop Jr.,* 6 September 1654, "WP," CMHS, vol. 7, 4th series, 482.

26. J. Lawrence Smith, "Smithtown," 2. The deed is recorded in the *Book of Deeds*, office of the Secretary of State, Albany, NY, 11: 118-19; a copy is in the collection of the Brooklyn Historical Society.

27. Curtiss C. Gardiner, 65; Lion Gardiner, "Pequot Warres," 157-58; for Wyandanch's death, his appointment of Lion and David Gardiner as

guardians of his son, the challenging of this by John Ogden, a rival of the Gardiners, and the purchase of 9,000 acres of Montauk land by the Gardiners and others from Wyancombone and his mother Wicchiaubit, known as the Sunk Squaw after her husband's death, see Strong, "How the Montauk Lost Their Land," 35, 79-80.

28. Lion Gardiner to John Winthrop Jr., 5 November 1660, "WP," CMHS, vol. 7, 4th series, 64-65; the governor of Barbados was called "Mr. Serie" by Winthrop, and "Daniell Searle" by Lion.

29. For the founding of Smithtown, without any bull, see J. Lawrence Smith, "Smithtown," 2-3.

30. Gardiner's estate was inventoried at £256, his property on Gardiner's Island at £511, as enumerated in Pelletreau, "East Hampton," 26.

31. Thompson, 1:198, 209, 3:318.

32. Peter Ross, *A History of Long Island, from Its Earliest Settlement to the Present Time*, 3 vols (New York: Lewis Historical Publishing, 1902) 1:80.

LEADING THE WAY

The Political Force of
the First Four Ministers:
Thomas James, Nathanael Huntting,
Samuel Buell, and Lyman Beecher

———◦◦◦———

Rev. John Turner Ames

MY FIRST VISIT TO East Hampton came almost exactly three years ago this week, in early March, 1995. That is quite possibly a disqualification for participating in this distinguished lecture series, for I am in no sense an expert in East Hampton history. And I am very aware that many of you are. A third of this afternoon's audience probably knows more than I do about the Trustees' records, about the sites and locations of the old buildings, and about the quirks, foibles, and eccentricities of the early ministers. You'd think that at my age I would have more sense than to get involved in a subject about which so many others know so much—and care so much.

But maybe I've been bitten by the bug, the bug of East Hampton history that seems more omnipresent than the deer ticks which nobody can see, but which everybody knows about.

And maybe the bite came on that first visit, sponsored, as you can guess, by the Pastor Nominating Committee of the First Presbyterian Church. As I was being shown through the church sanctuary, the portrait of Nathanael Huntting was pointed out to me; and the person leading the tour told me that the first three ministers in East Hampton served about fifty years each. I made appropriate noises—actually I think I said: "I'm afraid I don't have fifty years left"—but, as a matter of fact, I simply believed that my guide was mistaken.

Presbyterians—like the ancient Hebrews, and, it must be said, like many in East Hampton—are inclined to allow their faith to shape their history. I assumed that this was simply an example of that kind of hyperbole. I was wrong, of course. The story is true.

East Hampton was served in the first century and a half of its existence by a remarkable trio of ministers: Thomas James, the feisty Puritan pioneer; Nathanael Huntting, the scholarly frontier pastor; and Samuel Buell, the revivalist, the educator, the political conciliator who would have been on the winning side whoever won the Revolutionary War. Lyman Beecher, who served only here eleven years, is included because there are lots of good stories about him and because he is the only East Hampton minister who ever had a national reputation. Only I must tell you at the outset that it was established after he left here.

East Hampton was settled by Puritans originally from Connecticut, augmented later by immigrants who came directly from England. It remained Puritan throughout the period under discussion today. That is the most important single thing that one needs to know about these people in order to understand how they lived; how they organized their community and conducted its affairs; how they related to each other and to the indigenous inhabitants who lived here before them; and, of course, how they understood their relationship to their God.

Puritanism was a theology. It was a particular way of understanding the Christian faith. That is of critical importance, but that is not the only thing we need to know about Puritanism in order to understand it.

For although Puritanism was a theological movement, it was also a political movement and a social movement. It regulated the relationships between persons of various social and economic classes. It determined how political decisions would be made and how the economy of the community would be organized.

Puritanism has gotten a very bad reputation in the modern age, because it is almost totally misunderstood. Our ancestors are believed—even by us—to be censorious busybodies, preaching a legalistic religion which we equate with modern fundamentalism. H. L. Mencken—more of a wit than a historian—is famous for describing Puritanism as the "horror that someone, somewhere, may be enjoying themselves." Nothing could be further from the truth. You cannot understand seventeenth or eighteenth century Puritanism by reference to any modern religious movement or to nineteenth century prohibitionists or blue-nosed prudes. That simply is not who they were.

Puritanism in New England also cannot be understood by reference to the Mayflower settlers who founded the Plymouth Colony. They were Puritans, to be sure, but they were Separatists—radicals—

political and religious extremists—who did come to these shores to find freedom in the wilderness. Because they have captured the popular imagination of American folklore, they have become better known than the much larger, and much more important, settlements that began ten years later with the establishment of the Massachusetts Bay Colony.

Puritanism was a third-generation development of the Protestant Reformation in England which established the Church of England as independent from Rome. Unlike the Continent, in which the reformation was a religious revival, in England it was an act of state. Henry VIII, who was given the title "Defender of the Faith" by the Pope in gratitude for a tract he wrote against Martin Luther, established a church which was simply independent—not necessarily Protestant.

Under Henry's three children: the Protestant Edward, the Catholic Mary, and the politically astute Elizabeth—the circumstances of whose birth required that she be a Protestant—the Church of England was buffeted by theological and liturgical change for a generation until it reached a compromise accommodation, called the Elizabethan settlement. The original Puritans were those who flocked back to England at Elizabeth's accession—having breathed the heady wind of Calvinism during the Marian exile—determined to continue the religious reform in England in a more protestant direction.

Under Elizabeth's Stuart successors in the next century, these Puritans rose to increasing prominence in both church and state. They dominated the commercial and business life of the nation, especially in the city of London. They controlled one of the two universities, Cambridge. Many were middle-class farmers, especially in East Anglia and Southwest England. They were opposed by the large rural landowners, the aristocracy, and the peasants who were beholden to them.

And as the foolishness of the Stuart kings required more and more money, which could be raised only by Parliament, the economic interests of the aristocratic landowners and the urban merchants naturally clashed. Throughout the early seventeenth century Puritanism dominated the political life of England; and by 1640, despite a very unfair electoral system that gave disproportionate political influence to the large landowners and the aristocracy, it controlled the government. This, of course, gave them control of the established church.

The English Puritans were thus not an oppressed and harassed underclass; many were artisans, farmers, merchants, university graduates. Beginning with John Winthrop and the establishment of Massachusetts Bay in 1630, many hundreds of Puritans flocked to these shores during the decades preceding the English Civil War. They established here a society based on a Calvinistic understanding of Christianity. This included a political theory in which governmental authority is given—by God—to "the people"—not to the king.

Exactly who comprised "the people" has been a subject of continuing dialogue in American history. Originally, of course, it did mean "white males," and our history has been the sometimes uneven story of the expansion of that definition. Sometimes other restrictions, such as land ownership or church membership, were included. But at least it did not mean that power came from the top down, but from the bottom up. The bedrock political principle of Puritanism was that governmental power belonged to "the people;" that free people had a right—a right given them by God—to self-government.

Thus the "Holy Commonwealth" that the Puritans established in New England was—at least according to the definition of the time—democratic, anti-aristocratic. Because the Bishops in England were their enemies, the religious equivalent of aristocracy, they established independent churches, knowing no authority higher than those persons elected by each congregation—lay elders and a minister.

But they were not inherently opposed to church organization and to a system of religious connectionalism. Nor were they inherently opposed to established state churches. They were simply opposed to the kind of church organization and church establishment with which they were familiar in England. They wanted to establish their own, more to their liking.

As they spread through southern New England, they perhaps inevitably came to eastern Long Island and established a community here. And the church was as integral a part of their community as was any other part. They also started a school, dug a pond and fenced in a sheep fold, established procedures for sharing common grazing land and conducting whale watches, built windmills which were shared communally, and did a great many other things. The church was simply a normal and essential part of the community's life.

The first individual in East Hampton to be paid out of communal funds was the minister, Thomas James. He came here in 1651 at a salary of forty five pounds a year, plus a house. This sum was promised by the General Court and paid by an assessment on all freeholders; what we would call a property tax. The first church building was also erected by the General Court and paid for by public funds. This situation lasted in East Hampton until the 1840s—as late as the ministry of Samuel Ely, ministers were called and paid by the Town Trustees.

The church was called simply "the meeting house." They were not conscious of being affiliated with any denomination, and for us to attribute any denominational label to them is incorrect. Later, in the eighteenth century as America became much more religiously pluralistic, the Puritan movement became denominational. In fact it divided into two denominations, Presbyterian and Congregational and the churches in Long Island became Presbyterian, but that is another story. It is incorrect to describe the church in East Hampton in its early days as "Congregationalist." It was simply "the meeting house."

In April of 1649, Lion Gardiner wrote to Governor Winthrop of Connecticut asking him to assist in finding a "suitable minister" for East Hampton. As concerning the young Man you writ of, this is our determination, not to have above twelve families, and we know that we can pay as much as twenty-four in other places .... At present we are able to give this man your writ of Twenty Pounds a year, with such diet as I myself eat, till we see what the Lord will do with us; and being he is but a young man, happily he hath not many books, therefore let him know what I have. And Gardiner proceeded to include a list of his small, but select, theological library, some of which are still to be found in our marvelous library [across the street] with Thomas James' notes in the margins. Thus the Proprietor and the minister were immediately established as soul-mates—supporting, encouraging, and befriending each other to the very end.

It was, in fact, not until August, 1651 that Thomas James arrived in East Hampton—at a salary more than twice what Gardiner had first offered. In addition to forty-five pounds a year, James was given twelve acres, including enough woodland to provide for his fuel needs, and the first grain to be ground at the mill each Monday.

The villagers were still worshiping in Thomas Baker's "ordinary" but in the fall of 1651 they decided to build a meeting house. It was built on a site in what is now the South Burying Ground. Lion Gardiner's home was directly across the street, and Thomas James lived next to Gardiner.

East Hampton was isolated, but it maintained economic, social and political connections with Connecticut. The Connecticut Colony had been established in 1634 under the leadership of Thomas Hooker who rebelled against the extreme theological rigidity of John Cotton and the Boston establishment. From the beginning the New England Puritans were less monolithic theologically than is commonly assumed, and Hooker was more evangelical, less legalistic, than the Bostonians.

Although the desire for more land was also a reason for their exo-

dus, Hooker put more reliance on God's grace and less on the uncon-
ditional nature of God's election than Cotton did, and he had a much
less restrictive conception of church membership. The precise issue at
controversy here was whether a child could be baptized whose parents could not—or did not wish to—testify to an "experience of grace."

A more important issue was that this "experience" was, in Boston, a
qualification for church membership; and church membership was a
qualification for eligibility to vote. Thus this extremely scholastic version of Calvinism also gave the ministers and elders in Boston the right
to control the voting franchise for the first two generations. That was
not true in the Connecticut Colony—though it was in the New Haven
Colony —and it was never true in East Hampton.

Thomas James immediately became an indispensable member of
the tiny village of East Hampton. It was normal for the minister, as one
of the few educated members of the community, to be the teacher, to
be everybody's secretary, to witness wills and arbitrate minor disputes.
James repeatedly served as a trustee of the town, and often as secretary
of the board. He also watched over and defended their political rights.
He learned the Algonquin language of the Montauketts and was frequently called upon to be an interpreter between the settlers and the
indigenous inhabitants of this peninsula.

For the first several years the villagers had no sort of written laws;
they simply lived together under the tacit and implied common law
with which they were familiar. In 1654 however, Thomas James wrote
Governor Winthrop and secured a copy of the Connecticut Combination—or Charter—and in October of that year they adopted a version
of that document as the charter of the town. It was their minister,
Thomas James, who drafted the document and wrote the copy which
the thirty male freeholders in East Hampton signed.

It is a stereotypic statement of Puritan political theory:

> For asmuch as it hath Pleased the Almighty God by the wise
> dispensation of his providence, so to Order and Dispose of
> things that we, the Inhabitants of East Hampton are now
> dwelling together; the word of God requires that to maintain
> the Peace and Union of such a people ther should be an Or-
> derly and Decent Government established according to God. . .
> to maintain and preserve the Purity of the Gospel of our Lord
> Jesus Christ, which, according to the Truth of such Gospel, as
> now practiced among us. As also in our civil affairs to be
> guided and Governed by such Laws and Order as shall be made
> according to God, and which by vote of the Major Part shall be
> in force among us.

You will note that there is no reference to the authority of the King. Like the Mayflower Compact, divine authority is given to the people to govern themselves—in this case "the major part" meaning majority.

In 1660 the Puritan experiment in government failed in England, owing to its radical excesses, and the Stuart Charles II was restored to the throne. Governor Winthrop hastened to London to pledge loyalty to the new government and came back with a Charter for the Connecticut Colony—including the "island adjacent"—which among other things guaranteed freedom of worship to protestant dissenters. This was the legal basis on which the East Hampton Church continued to practice its Puritan theology and liturgy, even after it was forcibly incorporated into the Royal Colony of New York a few years later when the English expelled the Dutch from New Amsterdam.

The Puritans of the East End strenuously protested against becoming part of New York, but to no avail. There then began constant problems with royal governors and their representatives and streams of petitions and protests over taxes and other matters. An "Address" to the Governor, written October 1, 1685 protests that a representative assembly which had formerly met at Hempstead had been abrogated. The letter, which was written by Thomas James, claimed that such representation was "a fundamental privilege of our English nation." It goes on to express the fear that "by denial of such privilege, our freedom should be turned into bondage and our ancient privileges so infringed yet they will never arrive at our posterity." The next year a much more serious incident occurred involving a land dispute. Skipping the details of this controversy, which are well documented and not particularly relevant, eleven prominent citizens of East Hampton were ordered arrested on the grounds that a petition they had presented to the governor was libelous.

The next Sunday, October 17, 1686, Thomas James preached a fiery sermon supporting his parishioners. His text, wrenched absolutely out of its context, was from the Book of Job, "some remove the landmark." Josiah Hubbert, the Sheriff of Suffolk Country, described the sermon in a letter to the Royal Council:

> ... the whole subject of his sermon was to show the evill and pronounce the Curses against those who removed their Neighbor's Land Markers and in his applicacon he brought it to the present Matter of this Towne ... / He said that / this order for it was noe excuse through it were an Edict from the King himself.

The next morning a warrant for James' arrest was issued, and he was taken to jail where he spent the next three weeks until he petitioned the Governor to release him on the grounds that he was a loyal subject of King James II.

As Henry Hedges, the first historian of East Hampton, wrote in 1849:

> East Hampton was happy in its choice of minister. For nearly half a century he had been an able and devout minister to his people, intelligent in the understanding of their rights as free-born Englishmen, fearless in their defence. Only with his last breath went out his watchful regard as their minister. In attestation of his conscious discharge of duty, his intrepid soul prompted the desire to be so buried as to rise facing his people on the resurrection morn.

The same tradition also assumes—with perhaps more dubious validity—that the congregation, or at least a quorum of it, will be in place to rise, facing the minister.

One of the interim supplies engaged during James' last years was Nathanael Huntting, then a twenty-one-year-old Harvard graduate, who came to East Hampton in 1696 to "assist" Mr. James, though he was not ordained and installed as pastor until three years later.

Huntting had graduated from Harvard College in 1693 and received an M.A. degree, which was extremely unusual in the seventeenth century, in 1696. He was secured for East Hampton by the redoubtable Samuel Mulford who journeyed to Massachusetts to make the choice and present the call. Huntting came to East Hampton with his bride, Mary, and occupied the house which the Town: "by unanimous vote: Doe freely give and grant unto him ... and his heirs ... forever." This house, as you know, was operated after his death by the Huntting family as "a common publick house," as it was derisively called, until quite recent times. Huntting's salary was sixty pounds a year, plus firewood. According to the records the salary and the firewood were granted "by a Major vote" while the house grant unanimous. Does this mean that there was controversy over the salary? I do not know.

By the beginning of the eighteenth century, the Puritan movement was running out of steam, especially in Boston and at Harvard College. The idea of a Holy Commonwealth, standing in a national covenant with its Lord, was fading. By the third generation, Puritan theology had frequently degenerated into scholasticism and the national covenant, once a mainstay of Puritan thought, was yielding to moralistic individualism.

Cotton Mather, the grandson of the great Boston divine John Cotton and Nathanael Huntting's teacher at Harvard, documents this decline in his *Magnalia Christi Americana*, published in 1702, a vast biographical and historical record which purports to be a history of "Christ's great deeds in America." It is generally thought to be the high-water mark of Puritan scholasticism; but because it is so tedious and so difficult, no one has, in fact, ever read it. Here as Mather surveys the religious scene in southern New England—which is what he thought American consisted of—he finds little to praise.

Religio peperit Divitias, Filia devoravit Matrem. Religion brought forth prosperity, and the daughter has destroyed the mother.

The so-called "Half Way Covenant," which permitted baptized persons who had not themselves become church members to present their children for baptism, increased the numbers, but not the zeal, of the church. The best known stories of the third and fourth generation concern witchcraft trials, fanatical intolerance of dissent, and a static quality to religion. Though the records do not say this, of course, the absence of any evidence to the contrary suggests that the same thing was happening in East Hampton.

Certainly by the beginning of Huntting's ministry the "Half Way Covenant" was in effect here, though whether it was instituted by James or Huntting cannot be determined. Skipping the theological details, it is simply a liberalization of Puritan theology, a watering down of the previous zeal. It is both a recognition of and a cause of the decline of vital religion among the New England Puritans around the turn of the eighteenth century.

East Hampton genealogists and historians can, however, be eternally grateful to Nathanael Huntting for his meticulous habits of record-keeping. His book of baptisms, marriages and deaths is an invaluable source, and the oldest such record in the town. Huntting's scholarship is also impressive. He copied a theological textbook, Willard's *Body of Divinity* and there are hundreds and hundreds of his sermon manuscripts in the East Hampton library. Anyone who reads these—and I have, at least, glanced at a few of them—would be impressed with the accuracy of Huntting's reputation as a man of profound scholarship.

Controversy with the royal governors continued and increased, and though the right of dissenters to worship legally was no longer contested, East Hampton residents objected vociferously to the requirement that they pay taxes to support the established Anglican Church. In fact, in the long series of controversies between Samuel Mulford, whom East Hampton regularly elected to the General Assembly of the colony, and Lord Cornbury, the fanatically High Church royal governor, the payment of church taxes was routinely included among Mulford's protests against "encroachments of our Liberties."

In 1728 the East Hampton Trustees voted that "right or wrong, the town money shall go to ye payment of Mr. Huntting's taxes," meaning his support, though whether this protest was successful is not recorded.

Toward the end of Huntting's active career in East Hampton, the malaise which had affected religion in this country came to a more or less sudden end with what is called the "Great Awakening." It began as early as 1734 when a revival of religion occurred under the preaching of Jonathan Edwards in Northampton, Massachusetts. The revival itself, however, should be neither surprising nor accidental. Puritanism was itself, by expressed intent, a religious reform movement which carried the seeds of its own reform within it.

Led by a remarkable series of ministers, the revival spread quickly throughout western Massachusetts and Connecticut. Yale College, founded in 1701, became a center of revival influence; while Harvard, which opposed it, gradually drifted into liberal Unitarianism. It is interesting to note in passing that evangelicalism and Unitarianism are the twin children of Puritanism—equal heirs.

The revival occurred simultaneously throughout the English colonies, from Georgia to New Hampshire. In 1740 George Whitefield, the English disciple of John Wesley though Calvinist in his theology, came to New England on his second visit to America. Whitefield attracted thousands of people wherever he preached—8,000 in Boston Commons, for example, in 1740. Whitefield took a dim view of the religious situation in New England:

> I am verily persuaded the Generality of Preachers talk of an unknown, unfelt, Christ. And the Reason why Congregations have been so dead, is because dead Men preach to them.

One of Whitefield's followers was John Davenport, a young Yale graduate, in fact the grandson of Yale's founder, who became minister of the church in Southhold in 1738. After spending a summer with Whitefield in New England, he came to East Hampton. According to the historian, "everywhere he aroused resentment and opposition by his fanatical harangues and his arrogant attacks on 'unconverted' ministers."

The local historians simply record that there was a great religious revival in the winter of 1740–41 and mention that owing to Huntting's advanced age and infirmity "the controversial Mr. Davenport" was the preacher. What undoubtedly happened was that the itinerant revivalist came to town and the minister was torn between a wish to prevent the unseemly excesses which had accompanied Davenport's preaching elsewhere and the fact that the fiery young preacher was both very popular and very effective.

My guess is that Huntting would have tried, unsuccessfully, it turned out, to prevent Davenport from preaching in the East Hampton Church. It is apparent that at least some of the congregation liked the radicalism of the itinerant revivalist and began to attend the services he conducted rather than those conducted by Mr. Huntting. The records of both church and town are silent as to how this irregular situation was dealt with, but it must certainly have caused grief for the elderly and somewhat old-fashioned minister. One of Huntting's successors, and my predecessors, Earnest Eels, quotes Davenport as calling Huntting "a carnal old Pharisee," "a blind guide" and saying that the venerable old man, who had been a faithful pastor here for forty-four years, was "unconverted." This kind of thing, especially as it was apparently supported by at least some of the congregation, must have torn the church apart.

After leaving East Hampton in the spring of 1741, Davenport began an assault on the southern coast of Connecticut and Rhode Island. He was arrested in Stamford under Connecticut's law against itinerant preaching, tried by the General Assembly at Hartford, judged mentally disturbed, and deported under guard to Long Island. His excesses continued unabated, however, and he was arrested at least twice more in Connecticut and Massachusetts, where he was declared by the court to be non compos mentis and expelled; but he apparently continued to be the pastor in Southhold, and preach occasionally in East Hampton throughout the remainder of Huntting's tenure here.

In 1745, with the congregation seriously divided, some in East Hampton began to look around for another minister to assist Mr. Huntting and to succeed him after his death. An invitation was extended to the Rev. David Brainard, a very famous missionary to the Indians in Massachusetts and Long Island whose diary, which I have in my possession, is a wonderful account of that work. There was opposition in the congregation to this invitation, however, and Brainard declined it.

Just at that time, as the Town Council was lamenting the cost of searching for another minister, Samuel Buell appeared in East Hampton with a letter of introduction from the Rev. Aaron Burr, Sr., a Presbyterian minister in Newark, New Jersey:

> Dear Sir,
> These come by Mr. Buell whom we have prevailed with to make you a visit. It seems a very kind Providence yt sent him into these parts at this time.
> He appears to me to be the most likely person to unite your people. He is a pious, judicious, and ingenuous young man, and an excellent preacher.
> You will be pleased with him, and find occasion to bless God yet he is sent among you. Mr. Tennent joins with me in recommending him to you, in ye fullness of ye blessings of the Gospel of Peace. We should not have stopped his designed journey to Virginia for any other place . . .

All the available local records indicate that Mr. Huntting retired voluntarily, owing to his advanced age and infirmity. But I cannot help but wonder if the old gentleman was perhaps eased into retirement by the controversy in the church stirred up by John Davenport and by the availability of a much younger and more dynamic successor. In any case, Huntting did retire in 1746, at the age of seventy-one, after serving as the minister in East Hampton for forty-nine years. He lived in retirement for seven years and died in 1753.

Samuel Buell was, in fact, an excellent choice as the third minister in East Hampton, a worthy advocate of the revival who exhibited none of the excessive emotionalism which had characterized the extremists such as Davenport. During Buell's early ministry there were several periods of revival in the church, in which large numbers of new members were received, but the controversy seems to have dissipated. Buell published several accounts of these revivals, and it is evident that the church did experience a significant renewal and revitalization in his early ministry.

Buell was ordained in East Hampton on September 19, 1746. His ordination sermon was preached by the greatest and most renowned minister in America, Jonathan Edwards. Edwards, like Buell, is typical of the best of the revival ministers. These are not ranting TV preachers or sawdust hucksterers who in this century have demeaned the name revivalist; these were fervent, effective, and scholarly evangelical ministers who were always dignified and sober in demeanor. Edward's ordination sermon, "The Church's Marriage to her Sons and to her God," which is in our library, amply demonstrates this. It is a scholarly work of thirty-seven octavo pages, with carefully crafted arguments and skilled use of language:

> You have now heard, Reverend Sir, the great Importance, and high Ends of the Office of evangelical Pastor, and the glorious Priviledges of such as are faithful to this Office, . . . May God grant that your Union with this People, this Day, as their Pastor, may be such that God's People here may have the great Promise God makes to the Church in this Text, now fulfilled unto them. . . .

He concludes, thirty-five pages later:

> Let me take Occasion, dear Brethren, from what has been said, to exhort you, not forgetting the Respect, Honour, and Reverence, that will ever be due from you to your former Pastor, that has served you so long in that Work, but by Reason of Age and growing Infirmities, and the Prospects of his Place being so happily supplied by a Successor, has seen met to relinquish this Burden of the Pastoral Charge over you.

One of the characteristics of the revival was the establishment of schools, and New England is still peppered by academies and colleges which were begun under the auspices of the "New Light" ministers. The names Dartmouth, Brown, Amherst, Andover and Hamilton are familiar. To them can be added "Clinton Academy," which is one of Buell's most enduring legacies. In 1753 Buell established the first library in East Hampton when he wrote in the front of his own books, "This book belongs to the Philogrammatican Library in East Hampton, 1753." Many of these books are still available to you this afternoon—or Monday morning.

At about the same time as Buell became its minister, the East Hampton Church became Presbyterian. Buell was, in fact, one of the charter members of Suffolk Presbytery which was organized in April, 1747 in Southampton. Seven ministers were present: Buell, and the pastors from Southampton, Bridgehampton, Brookhaven, Mattituck, Cutchogue, and Huntington.

Suffolk Presbytery affiliated itself with the Synod of New York which was the "New Side" branch of the Presbyterian Church—the church having divided in 1745 over the revival. The New Side, which was pro-revival, was attractive to the Puritan churches in New York and

New Jersey. They brought a dimension of theological and liturgical freedom into a Presbyterian denomination, then largely Scottish and Scot-Irish and mostly confined to the Middle Colonies. Suffolk Presbytery, which became Long Island Presbytery a few years later, was only very loosely Presbyterian in the early days. The local congregations continued to order their affairs much as they always had. When the two branches of the Presbyterian Church reunited in 1757, this Puritan influence became a permanent feature of American Presbyterianism—causing it to be significantly different, in some ways, from the established church in Scotland.

Like both his predecessors, Buell was actively involved in the public affairs of this community. In May of 1756 a large contingent of Suffolk County men assembled in East Hampton before leaving for Lake George to fight in the French and Indian war. The day before they left, the church service was devoted to their send-off. Buell preached from I Chronicles 19:13:

> Be of good courage, and let us behave ourselves valiantly for our people, and for the cities of our God, and let the Lord do that which is good in his sight.

His sermon is a classic exposition of the "just war" theory which was first articulated by St. Augustine in the fifth century. Making the point that a defensive war is frequently necessary as well as lawful and an offensive war sometimes so, he then asserted that:

> 'tis so notorious a cause that we wage in war at this time, none need scruple the lawfulness of it—'tis in defence of our own people, and the cities of our God—'tis for a land that is ours by the first discovery and priority of possession, which is allow'd to give title among civilized nations . . . 'tis . . . for the good of prosperity as well as our own that we now wage in war.
>
> We learn by experience 'tis impossible to live by such blood thirsty neighbors as the French and their allies in America. They have broken the most solemn traties, made most injust encroachments and committed the most horrid barbarities in a time of professed peace. By their line of forts, surrounding our frontiers by land, they design we shall have but a garden spot in America—and as soon as possibly strong enough, to drive us all into sea—or, subject us to popish tyranny and superstition worse than death . . . while villainy secures all—our lives, our liberties, our religion.

The growing controversy with the Royal Governors, and resentment against British colonial policies affected East Hampton, of course, as they did all of British North America. These controversies, and the story of East Hampton during the Revolutionary War are well documented. One cannot support Judge Hedges' comment, however, made in 1849, that there was not a single Tory in East Hampton. While hundreds of supporters of the revolutionary cause—including scores from East Hampton—fled eastern Long Island for Connecticut in the fall of 1776, after the British victory at the Battle of Long Island, most of the residents remained here and acquiesced to the British occupation of the area as best they could.

During the war and the British occupation of Long Island, Buell conducted a regular correspondence with leaders of both sides, especially the Patriot Governor Trumbull of Connecticut, and the Royal Governor, Lord Tryon, who for at least part of the war maintained his headquarters in Southampton. He complained to each about the other, especially the depredations which the armies of both sides wrought on the livestock of East Hampton. Though he protested to each his loyalty to their cause, he also fearlessly condemned soldiers of both sides who came here to steal cattle—as evidently both sides did.

Throughout the war—with General William Erskine headquartered in the Brown House on Main Street and British warships often anchored in Gardiner Bay—Buell, along with the townspeople who had not fled to Connecticut, maintained cordial relations with their military occupiers. He, along with most of the residents of East Hampton who remained here, took the oath of allegiance to George the Third which Colonial Abraham Gardiner required, and he routinely assured the Royal Governor of his loyalty to the British.

Tryon was not deceived, and described Buell to Lord Germain, the Secretary of State for the Colonies, by saying:

> Rev'd Mr. Buell, Presbyterian Minister of East Hampton . . . a favorer of the Rebel Rank until converted by the victory of the 27th August . . .

referring to the British victory at the Battle of Long Island.

In the third year of the war, Buell worked out a barter arrangement between Trumbull and Tryon by which commodities—"rum, sugar, molasses, tea—whatever may please the ladies . . . except salt and military goods . . ."could be exchanged between Long Island and Connecticut. As a minister he was perhaps better able than others to maintain a relationship with both sides in the war, to the benefit of the people of the town.

Buell summed up his own credo in a letter written to Governor Trumbull in 1778:

> I cannot afford oil to those springs which seem to move and accelerate or retard the Wheels of State as on one Side or the Other . . . at whatever Bar of the Public I may stand—and perhaps stand impeached, for my conduct in the present Day—I am not anxiously concerned—if Wisdom sits at the helm of government and Justice tempered with clemency, holds the Balance of retribution . . .secure within myself . . . am incomparably more concerned for the Weal and Prosperity of my Native Country and the Public.

There is no doubt that under a military occupation, Buell, as a faithful pastor, did the best he could to preserve as much of normal life as was possible under extremely difficult circumstances. There is also no doubt that no matter who won the war, the minister would have been on the winning side. Perhaps those of us who have never lived under military occupation should refrain from criticizing the conduct of those who do.

In 1783, with the ratification of the Treaty of Paris, the British evacuated New York City and Long Island, and the people of East Hampton proceeded to elect representatives to the New York State Assembly. Almost immediately Buell turned his attention to the establishment of a school in East Hampton, and on December 28, 1784 the "East Hampton Academy" was incorporated. Five days later the school opened in the Presbyterian Church, where it met until the building now known as Clinton Academy was constructed at a cost of $5,000. Buell died on July 19, 1798.

For the third time in a row East Hampton called a very young minister, straight from the university, to succeed its elderly, venerable, but perhaps tired and feeble pastor. This time they may well have gotten more than they bargained for, for although the people of East Hampton must by now have become tolerant of ministerial eccentricities, pecularities and outspoken involvement in public affairs, they were probably not prepared for Lyman Beecher. One writer comments that Beecher's five feet, seven inch statue "in no way indicated his strength when he battled for the Lord, and even less betrayed the formidable character of the resistance he could offer to the minions of hell."

The stories about Beecher's eccentricities, and the controversies with the Trustees over his salary are well known and well documented. He did, after all, write an autobiography and there are numerous books and articles by and about the man who was without doubt the most famous minister in America in the 1830s and '40s. The best and most recent of them is by my professor at Duke, Stuart Henry, entitled *Unvanquished Puritan*. Beecher, called "the father of half the brains in America," had eleven children who survived infancy. The first five were born in East Hampton, including Catherine, an educator, feminist, and author of eighteen books. Harriet and Henry Ward, the most renowned of the children, were born in Litchfield.

Beecher graduated from Yale where he studied theology under Timothy Dwight, the great defender of orthodoxy against the depredations of deism and French rationalism. He tells in his autobiography of reading the obituary for Samuel Buell and of discussing with a friend the possibility that he might be called to succeed to what was quite a prestigious pulpit. His friend, Tudor Davis, came to East Hampton, where he apparently had connections, and returned to New Haven to report that the orthodox faction of the church were looking for a minister who could "stand his ground in argument and break the heads of the infidels." Beecher found here a church that was to some degree at least, divided by the "Age of Enlightenment" and influenced by deism. He blamed two faculty members at Clinton Academy for introducing "infidelity and French rationalism" into East Hampton. It is difficult to know at this remove how serious a threat this was, but there was a group in town called the "Infidel Club"—more of a drinking club than a theological discussion group would be my guess.

Beecher immediately became controversial. He was nicknamed the "snow bird" not because he went to Florida in the winter, but because neither storm nor season stopped his ceaseless movement. His attack on "The Infidel Club" can best be told—at least from his own perspective—in his own words:

> I did not attack infidelity directly. Not at all. That would have
> been cracking a whip behind a runaway team . . . make them
> run faster. I always preached right to the conscience. Every ser-
> mon with my eye on the gun to hit somebody. Went through
> the doctrines; showed what they didn't mean; what they did;
> then the argument; knocked away objections, and drive home
> on the conscience. . . . At first there was winking and blinking
> from below to gallery, forty or fifty exchanging glances, smiling
> and watching. But when it was over, infidelity was ended.

It is obvious that Beecher appealed to at least some of the younger, more zealous members of the congregation. Equally obvious, he was an embarrassment to the older, more established, perhaps more dignified—shall we say stuffy?—parishioners. The controversy with the town authorities over his salary, therefore, conceals a larger controversy over the style of his ministry.

Beecher was one of the first persons to interest himself in East Hampton history. On New Year's Day, 1806, he delivered a sermon on the history of the church and town. Acknowledging the outstanding collection of records of which East Hampton is justly proud—at least I hope you are sufficiently proud of it—Beecher said about the early settlers:

> They would have abhorred the infidel maxim, that religion and politics have no connection. . . . They considered that the precepts of their religion as extending to the regulation of their civil as well as to the regulation of their moral conduct. . . .

The seeds for Beecher's national reputation—which centered around his controversy with the Unitarians in Boston, with the fundamentalists in Cincinnati, and over abolition everywhere—may have been laid in East Hampton by a sermon he preached here in 1804. Two of the most famous statesmen in America—Alexander Hamilton and Aaron Burr—met in a dual that was fatal to both. Hamilton lost his life, and Burr his reputation. Shocked over the death of Hamilton, the nation was scandalized by the behavior of Burr, who, under indictment for murder, appeared as Vice President to preside over the United States Senate.

In the midst of this intense national uproar, Beecher preached a sermon which, because of its wide circulation, became sensational. Blaming "infidelty" which many took to be a thinly veiled reference to Jeffersonian deism, Beecher said:

> There is no way to deal with these men . . . but to take the punishment of their crimes into our own hands. Our conscience must be the judge, and we must ourselves convict, and fine, and disgrace them at the polls.

The anti-dueling movement became a national crusade, with Beecher as one of its main leaders; and a few years later, in Henry Clay's presidential campaign against Andrew Jackson, an alleged duelist, it was said that 40,000 copies of Beecher's sermon were distributed around the country by the Whigs.

You may be interested in a brief summary of Beecher's career after he left East Hampton. Ordained in Connecticut as a Congregationalist, he became a Presbyterian in East Hampton. He then served Congregational Churches in Litchfield, Connecticut and Boston, where he became nationally known as the main opponent of the Unitarians. In 1832 he became a Presbyterian again when he accepted the presidency of Lane Theological Seminary in Cincinnati, Ohio. Immediately he became embroiled in the national controversy over abolition and at the same time he became the victim of attacks by Presbyterian fundamentalists—a breed he had never met in Long Island or New England. In 1835, in a sensational and nationally famous trial, he was narrowly acquitted of heresy charges by the Presbytery of Cincinnati.

Beecher, seven of whose sons became ministers, returned to East Hampton in 1843 with two of them—William and Edward—and all three preached here the same day. Judge Hedges, who was in the congregation, describes the marvelous event in great detail.

These four ministers were a truly remarkable quartet; the first three by virtue of their long tenure, and all four by the fervor and vigor of their ministry here. All four were brilliant, all four were eccentric, all four were men of tireless energy. All four engaged the issues of the day and thus stand in the best and most noble tradition of the Reformed branch of Christianity.

Thomas James was the clerk of the Town Trustees for many years and wrote—presumably he also drafted—petition after petition to the Royal Governors asserting the right of a free people to govern themselves: to levy taxes on themselves for the support of causes they favored, to meet in representative assemblies to make decisions about the community's affairs, and to support only those religious institutions which were in accord with their understanding of the Word of God. When he believed these rights were imperiled, he was willing to go to jail on a charge of sedition in defense of them.

Nathanael Huntting, though more of a scholar than any of the others, was often thought a suitable choice, frequently along with Samuel Mulford, to represent East Hampton before the Royal Governors when petitions of grievances were to be presented.

Samuel Buell was a patriotic supporter of the colonists' grievances against the colonial government and in the difficult days of the military occupation he was the principal spokesperson for the community in dealing with authorities on both sides. He thought that starting a school and a public library was an appropriate concern for a minister.

Lyman Beecher, though a bit of a gadabout, was absolutely fearless in attacking evil wherever he saw it—including the prominent members of the congregation he served. An unashamed partisan, he had no problem with his famous sermon being widely circulated as an anti-Jefferson tract.

So these were remarkable men. I must say also, in passing, that they served a remarkable congregation. The members of the local church seem to be incredibly long-suffering in their willingness to endure the eccentricities, the pecularities, the very human frailties of their ministers. They tolerated theological and political hobby-horses; supported protest, revival, revolution; and though they didn't pay them much, they built beautiful church sanctuaries and gave the ministers fine homes in which to live—two of which, Huntting's and Beecher's, still grace Main Street.

These men were parsons—in the old fashioned sense, meaning "chief person of the community." Whether they were the chief citizen of East Hampton, they were certainly among the leading citizens in the days when the minister was not only the spiritual leader of the community, but also its conscience, its teacher, its advocate. It is a humbling honor to be the nineteenth minister of the East Hampton Church.

SOURCES

Autobiography and Correspondence of Lyman Beecher, 1866.

Black, III, Robert C. *The Younger John Winthrop*. Columbia University Press, N.Y., 1966.

Black, Robert C. *The Younger John Winthrop*. 1966.

Boxer, C.R. *The Dutch Seaborne Empire 1600–1800*. London, 1965.

Breen, T.H. *Imagining the Past; East Hampton Histories*. Addison-Wesley Publishing Co., N.Y., 1989.

Bridenbaugh, Carl. *The Colonial Craftsman*, 1950.

Bushman, Richard L. *The Refinement of America; Persons, Houses, Cities*. Alfred A. Knopf, 1992.

Collections for the Year 1809 from the New York State Historical Society, 1811.

Curtis C. Gardiner. *Lion Gardiner and His Descendants*. St. Louis, A. Whipple, 1890.

Daniels, Bruce C. *The Connecticut Town* (1979).

de Waard, C (ed.). *De Zeeuwsche Expeditie Naar de West onder Cornelis Evertsen den Jonge 1672–1674* (Gravenhage, 1928).

DeForest, Bartholomew S. *Random Sketches . . . With a Historical Sketch of the Second Oswego Regiment*. Albany: Avery Herrick, 1866.

Demos, John Putnam. *Entertaining Satan: Witchcraft and the Culture of New England*. Oxford University Press, 1982.

Documents Relative to the History of the State of New York Procured in Holland, England, and France, 11 Vols., 1853-1861, compiled by John Romeyn Broadhead.

Dunn, Richard S. i. 1962.

Edward, E. & Rattray, J. *Whale Off—Story of American Whaling, 1932.*

"En Plein Air," exhibition catalogue, Guild Hall Museum, 1989.

Fernow, Berthold (ed.). *The Records of New Netherlands: From 1653 to 1674 Anno Domini*. New York, 1898.

Foster, Stephen. *Their Solitary Way: The Puritan Social Ethic in the First Century of Settlement in New England*. New Haven: Yale University Press, 1971.

Foy, Jessica H. and Schlereth, Thomas J. (eds.) *American Home Life, 1880-1930; A Social History of Spaces and Services*. University of Tennessee Press, 1992.

Gabriel, R.H. *The Evolution of Long Island.*

Gardiner, David. *Chronicles of the Town of Easthampton*, County of Suffolk, New York (1840, 1871).

Gardiner, Jonathan T. *The Gardiners of Gardiner's Island.*

Gardiner, Jonathan T.; Baker, Jonathan; Osborn, Jonathan S. *Records of the Town of East Hampton, Long Island, Suffolk County, New York—With Other Documents of Historic Value*, Volumes I and III. Sag Harbor, N.Y., John H. Hunt, printer, 1887.

Gardiner, Lion. *Lion Gardiner, His Relation of the Pequot Warres*, Collections of the Massachusetts Historical Society, Vol. 3, 3rd Series (Cambrdige, 1833), 131-60.

Gaynor, Jay and Hagedorn, Nancy. *Tools, Working Wood in Eighteenth Century America,* 1993.

Godbeer, Richard. *The Devil's Dominion; Magic and Religion in Early New England*. Cambridge University Press, 1992.

Heatley, Jeff. *Colonel Theodore Roosevelt, The Rough Riders & Camp Wikoff, Montauk Point, New York—1898*; to be published in May, 1998.

Heyrman, Christine Leigh. *Commerce and Culture.*

History and Archaeology of the Montauk Indians, Vol. 3. Gaynell Stone (ed.).

History of the Town of East Hampton, by Henry P. Hedges, 1897.

Housley, Kathleen. *The Letter Kills But the Spirit Gives Life; The Smiths-Abolitionists, Suffragists and Bible Translators*. Historical Society of Glastonbury, Ct., 1993.

Hummel, Charles. "The Business of Woodworking, 1700-1840" in *Tools and Technologies: America's Wooden Age*, Kebabian, Paul and Lipke, William (eds.), 1979.

Hummel, Charles. *With Hammer in Hand: The Dominy Craftsmen of East Hampton*, New York (1968-1982).

Innes, Stephen (ed.). *Work and Labor in Early America*, 1988.

Innes, Stephen. *Creating the Commonwealth: The Economic Culture of Puritan New England.*

Jennings, Francis. *The Invation of America: Indians, Colonialism and the Cant of Conquest*, 1975.

Jones, Mary J. A. *Congregational Commonwealth* (1968).

Journals of the Trustees of the Town of East Hampton (starting in 1725).

Karlsen, Carol F. *The Devil in the Shape of A Woman; Withcraft in Colonial New England.* Vintage Books, N.Y., 1987.

Kennedy, John H. *Thomas Dongan, Governor of New York*, 1930.

Kupperman, Karen O. *Providence Island, 1630-1640: The Other Puritan Colony.*

Lockridge, Kenneth A. *A New England Town; The First Hundred Years.*

Long Island Landscape Painting 1820-1920, Ronald G. Pisano (Little Brown, Boston, 1985)

Long Island Landscape Painting/Volume II: The Twentieth Century, Ronald G. Pisano (Little Brown, Boston, 1990)

Marhoefer, B. *Witches, Whales, Petticoats and Sails*, 1971.

Matthiessen, Peter. *Men's Lives*, 1986.

McGrath, Franklin (ed.). *The History of the 127th New York Volunteers.* n.p.: ca. 1898.

McMurry, Sally. *Families and Farmhouses in 19th Century America.* Oxford University Press, 1988.

Miller, Perry and Johnson, Thomas H. (eds.) *The Puritans: A Sourcebook of Writings.* 2 vols. New York: Harper & Row, 1963.

Miller, Perry. *Errand into the Wilderness.* Cambridge: Harvard University Press, 1956.

Miller, Perry. *Nature's Nation.* Harvard University Press, 1967.

Miller, Perry. *The New England Mind: From Colony to Province.* Cambridge, Harvard University Press, 1953.

Mowier, L.T. *The Indomitable John Scott.*

Novak, Barbara. *American Painting of the 19th Century—Realism, Idealism and the American Experience*, New York, 1969.

Nylander, Jane C. *Our Own Snug Fireside: Images of the New England Home, 1760-1860.* Yale University Press, 1993.

O'Callaghan, E.B. (ed.). *Documents Relative to the Colonial History of the State of New York.* 15 Vols., Albany, 1853-1887.

Phelan, Thomas P. *Thomas Dongan, Colonial Governor of New York, 1683-1688*, 1933.

Pisano, Ronald. *Long Island Landscape Painting 1820-1920*, Brown and Co., Boston, 1985.

Prince, Helen Wright (comp.). *Civil War letters and Diary of Henry W. Prince.* n.p.: 1979.

Rattray, J. *Ship Ashore*, 1955.

Rattray, Jeannette Edwards. *East Hampton History, Including Ge-*

neaologies of Early Families. Country Life Press, Garden City, N.Y., 1953.

Ritchie, Robert C. *The Duke's Province: A Study of New York Politics and Society, 1664-1691.* 1977.

Roosevelt, Theodore. *The Rough Riders.*

Shammas, Carole. *The Pre-Industrial Consumer in England and America.*

Stone & Bonvillain. *Languages & Lore of the Long Island Indians,* 1981.

Stone & McKay. "Long Island Before the Europeans," *Between Ocean & Empire: An Illustrated History of Long Island,* 1985.

Stone, Gaynell (ed). *The History and Archaeology of the Montauk,* Suffolk Co. Archaeological Association, Stony Brook, 1993.

Stone, Gaynell. "Long Island as America: A New Look at the First Inhabitants," *Long Island Historical Journal,* 1:2, 1989.

Stone, Gaynell. *The History & Archaeology of the Montauk,* 1995.

Stone, Gaynell. *The Montauk: Native Americans of Eastern Long Island,* 1991.

Stone, Gaynell. *The Shinnecock: A Culture History,* 1984.

Strong, John A. *The Algonquian Peoples of Long Island From Earliest Times to 1700,* 1997.

Taylor, Robert J. *Colonial Connecticut* (1979).

The American Archives, 11 Volumes, 1837-1853, compiled by A.A. Force.

Thompson, B. *History of Long Island,* 1918.

Trelease, Allen. *Indian Affairs in Colonial New York: The Seventeenth Century,* 1960, reprinted 1997 with introduction by William Starna.

Underhill, Lois Beachy. *The Woman Who Ran for President.* Bridge Work, Md., 1995.

Van Wyck, Frederick. *Select Patents of New York Towns,* 1938.

van der Zee, Henry and Barbara. *The Story of Dutch New York.* New York, 1978.

van Rensselaer, Mrs. Schuyler. *History of the City of New York in the Seventeenth Century.* New York, 1901.

Ziel. *Steel Rails to Sunrise.*

THE CAPTAIN AND THE KING

The Life of Captain Samuel Mulford

(1644-1725)

—⟲⟲⟲—

Dr. David E. Mulford

ONE EVENING—I think it was in January of 1995—the phone rang in our home in the mountains of Western North Carolina. It was a reporter from *Newsday*, the Long Island daily. Said the reporter, "I'm doing an article on your ancestor, Captain Samuel Mulford. I was told that you have written a number of articles about him, and I wanted to ask you some questions."

You may wonder why the interest in a man named Samuel Mulford, who lived from 1644-1725. Why have I been so fascinated with his life? Why have academic theses at Fordham, the University of Virginia, and other universities as well been written about him? Why was his life story depicted in both radio and television on the old "Cavalcade of America" program? Why did historian Timothy Breen make him the central figure of his book, *Imagining The Past*? Why would a news reporter call me, Samuel Mulford's fifth great-grandson, on a winter's evening in 1995 to talk about him?

The reporter went on to explain why he was given this particular assignment. Captain Samuel Mulford is remembered as one who fought against a tax the British crown imposed on whale oil, at a time when whaling was a major industry of eastern Long Island, and he was successful. "The mood of the country now," said the reporter (and remember this was shortly after the 1994 Congressional elections), "is anti-tax. Maybe Speaker Newt Gingrich and Governor George Pataki can learn something from Samuel Mulford." Well, maybe we all can, because, as a history buff, I am convinced we can learn from history, and if Samuel Mulford has something to teach us today, all the better. So, the

reporter and I talked from some time about this fascinating but still relatively unknown hero of pre-Revolutionary America.

I explained that I had grown up only a few hundred yards from the
house in which Samuel Mulford lived, and I still own property which
Samuel Mulford owned.

Furthermore, this early American hero is buried no more than a
few yards from the graves of my parents in East Hampton's Old South
End Cemetery. Asked the reporter, "Were stories of Samuel Mulford
passed down in the family?" "Yes." "What did it feel like to grow up in a
community where your roots went so deep?" I tried to tell him. This reporter, may I add, did write an article about Captain Mulford which appeared in Newsday under the title, "The Captain and The King," the title
I have borrowed for my presentation today. But now, let me tell you a
little bit about Samuel Mulford. I won't try to cover all of the details. I
wrote a much fuller account of Samuel Mulford's life in an unpublished
book, *Puritan Profile*, a copy of which is in the Long Island Collection
at the East Hampton Library. But I want to convey to you why Samuel
Mulford has been remembered, and what I think he has to teach us
today.

His father, John Mulford, came from England to Massachusetts in
the 1630s. In 1643, he and his wife came to the newly-settled
Southampton, on the eastern end of Long Island. In 1648, John Mulford
was one of the first settlers of East Hampton, located some twelve
miles further east, a rich agricultural area, bordered on the south by the
Atlantic and on the north by what is now Gardiner's Bay. Active and
interested in law and politics, John Mulford became Commissioner of
Indian Affairs, Justice of the Peace for the County of Suffolk, Deputy to
the General Court at Hartford, and a Representative for Suffolk County
in the first Assembly of New York in 1683.

Soon after his coming to East Hampton, John Mulford held an office which gives clear indication of the esteem in which he was held
by his peers. Jeannette Edwards Rattray in *East Hampton History and
Genealogies* tells us about it in these words:

> When the eastern end of Long Island was first settled, a patent
> on certain lands was issued to the colonists direct by the reign-
> ing King of England; and under that charter the colonists insti-
> tuted a government; the first Republic on American soil, it
> might be called. The chief magistrate was constituted a com-
> mon court. A second court was constituted by a jury of twelve
> freeholders, and a third, the highest judiciary, was a general
> court, presided over by the magistrate, but in which the whole

body of freeholders was constituted a jury. From 1650 to 1654, the name of John Mulford, and his only, appears as chief magistrate of this little republic, which had full treaty power with the Indians.

While some have pointed out the weaknesses inherent in this particular arrangement, it nevertheless did set a pattern of service which Samuel was to emulate.

Samuel, John's oldest son, was born, probably in Southampton, in 1644. When he was four years old, the family came to East Hampton, which was destined to be Samuel's lifelong home. If we let our imaginations go, we can picture this boy, growing up in a new settlement, hewn out of the woods, bordering the restless sea. The houses, such as they were, encircled the village pond, with a meeting house and the beginnings of a cemetery on a knoll close-by. The boy grew strong under the influence of hard work and salt air. From his father he learned the rules of whaling and politics, both of which were to play such an important part in his later life. On summer days he made his way across fields and through woods to the windswept dunes guarding the ocean. There he gazed across blue waters that, years later, he was destined to cross on a mission which took him to the Royal Court of London.

From his father, Samuel Mulford inherited a keen mind, high principles, unyielding determination—yes, even stubbornness. And all these qualities became increasingly evident as he grew into manhood and took his place in the life of the community. Early in life he was made a Captain of the Militia, and was known until his death as "Captain" Samuel Mulford. For a long time he was a "Recorder of the Town" as well as a Town Trustee.

In most family records, Samuel's wife is listed simply as Esther, who died November 24, 1717, aged 64. Research has led me to the conclusion that she was Esther Conkling, a daughter of Ananias Conkling. For this, however, there is no proof. Six children, so the records tell us, were born and lived to maturity: Mary, Elizabeth, Samuel, Timothy, Elias and Matthew, the ancestor of the present-day East Hampton Mulfords.

Amazing as it may seem, Samuel Mulford's real political career began when he was past sixty years of age. A lifetime of turbulence, disappointment and gratifying success were packed into his final twenty years. But let's look at his "first sixty years." They were certainly not years of idleness.

Documents pinpoint certain events in his life. In 1683, when his father, Judge John, was chosen Representative for Suffolk County to the first Assembly of New York, Samuel is listed, with others, as a delegate to "select such representative." In 1686, we read that certain parties obtained an order from the Governor and Council that land be laid out for them in the town of East Hampton. A strong protest against this order was drawn up and signed by Samuel Mulford, Recorder of the Town, and nailed to the wall of the meeting house. In 1689, Captain Mulford was appointed by Lieutenant Governor Leisler Justice of the Peace for Suffolk County, and continued in this position until 1712.

As early as 1702, Captain Mulford, who is reported to have had a whaling company of twenty-four men, erected a wharf and warehouse at Northwest, at that time the harbor of the town. In 1702, when the Northwest storehouse was built, tradition is that thirteen whales were killed and brought ashore at one time between East Hampton and Bridgehampton.

A neat, yellow-covered volume, now preserved in the Long Island Collection, was Captain Mulford's diary, and is inscribed, "Samuel Mulford, my book." It was kept by Mulford from 1702 to 1706 and was taken up by another member of the family in 1772. Among the many interesting but cryptic notations recorded in this journal are lists of furs exported from Northwest in 1706. A typical list, one of several mentioned is as follows: "159 muskrats, 70 foxes, 32 racoons, 2 catts, 3 otters, 1 mink."

Seventy years after Captain Mulford put in his wharf at Northwest the shipping had so increased that better and deeper landing was sought. In this enterprise, East Hampton and Southampton men combined. The Town Trustees of East Hampton, in 1770, granted liberty at Sag Harbor to build a wharf where channels led close to the shore and vessels could be easily loaded.

After 1770 the wharves of Samuel Mulford were no longer used, and as the years went by, the farms were deserted, and the fields reclaimed by woods. However, I'm getting ahead of my story. In 1705, when he was 61 years old, Samuel Mulford was elected to represent Suffolk County in the General Assembly in New York. During the time he was in the Assembly, he fought for several things particularly needed by his people:

1. A fair representation for Suffolk County in the Assembly, and a just tax quota.

2. A port of entry close at hand, so that the residents of Long Island could trade with New England and the mother country without first journeying one hundred miles to New York.

3. Freedom from the law that put a five percent tax on whale
oil and forced whalemen to take out a license.

But it was his protest against the tax on whale oil and bone that is
most remembered. Let me give you the highlights of what happened.

To protest this tax, Captain Mulford made his first trip to London in
1706. The trip, from all indications, was successful, for nothing more
was demanded or paid during the remaining years of Lord Cornbury's
administration as Governor of New York.

However, upon the accession of Governor Hunter, the tax was revived. Hunter decreed that a whaleman should pay one-twentieth of all
whale oil and bone gathered from either drift whales or those captured in boats, and furthermore, that this share should be taken to New
York City. Fishing was among the rights granted to the people in the
patent to their lands, and for that patent they paid a yearly tax of forty
shillings. Samuel Mulford, with his two sons, Timothy and Matthew, and
enough Indians to complete the crew of a boat, went to sea whenever
the lookout reported a whale, and they disposed of the catch according to the ancient custom under which the captors had all they killed.
As a result, Samuel Mulford was arrested and a long court battle ensued.

Captain Mulford's defense against Governor Hunter's charge is a
masterpiece. Mulford mentions the privileges granted to the people of
East Hampton concerning the use of "rivers, riverlets, lakes, ponds,
brooks, streams, and harbors." His knowledge of the Bible is illustrated
in the following passage from his defense:

> "We have Water and Lakes, which is Sea granted to us. In the
> 8th Chapter of St. Matthew, verse 32, it is said, 'The Herd of
> Swine ran into the Sea;' And St. Mark, Chapter 5, verse 13 saith
> 'They ran into the Sea;' St. Luke, Chapter 8, Verse 33 saith, 'They
> ran into the Lake and were choaked.' So that by the most Infal-
> lable Rule, the Lake is Sea and the Sea adjacent to the Land is
> Lake, which is granted to us ... "

The court battle went on for some time, without resolution.

Captain Mulford then decided that he would go once again to London to lay his grievances openly before the British government. To con-
ceal his departure, Samuel Mulford, who was then 72 years of age, went
to Newport, Rhode Island, and proceeded on foot through the wilderness to Boston, and from there sailed for England. We can easily picture
him. The history books describe him: "Dressed in homely garb, of the
type made on the farm; his head held high, proud of his Puritan back-

ground; his manner simple, but polite; a man self taught, but with great intelligence and firmness."

And here is where we come to the one story about Samuel Mulford which made the history books. It is said that while he stood outside the gates of the King's palace, unable to get in, his pockets were picked. That night he sewed fishhooks in his pockets, and the next day again took his place outside the palace. Again, someone tried to pick his pockets, but found a surprise waiting for him. Mulford immediately turned the thief over to the police, and the incident received so much publicity that King George I granted Mulford an audience. Eventually, the whale oil tax was repealed.

Now, did all this really happen? Some scholars think not. Todd Savitt in his master's thesis, "Samuel Mulford of East Hampton," inserts this in a footnote: "No evidence was found to corroborate the legend that Mulford had an audience with the King as a result of the disturbance created when he caught a pick-pocket outside the Royal Palace by lining his pockets with fishhooks." Timothy Breen has come to a similar conclusion.

Did George Washington chop down the cherry tree and then confess, claiming he could not tell a lie? Did he throw a silver coin across the Rappahannock River? Probably not, but those are the kinds of things he might have done and could have done, and they tell us a lot more about Washington's character and strength than many factual stories. Sewing fishhooks in his pockets and then using the resulting publicity as an opportunity to secure an audience with the King might have happened or might not have happened, but it is perfectly in character with the kind of man Samuel Mulford was.

John Lyon Gardiner characterized Mulford in 1798 as "a man of an original genius, of good judgment, but of an odd turn." Whether or not the episode can be proven does not bother me in the least. The fishhook episode captures the very essence of Samuel Mulford, and I will continue to repeat that story as long as I live!

In any event, Captain Mulford pleaded his case before the House of Commons by reading a "Memorial" which contained a bold denunciation of the misrule of the governor in New York, and a charge of burdensome taxes. We can well imagine the reaction of the governor when he heard this, especially when he received a letter from the Lord Justices in London saying: "We must observe to you that we hope you will give all the due encouragement" to the whalers. To this Governor Hunter was forced to reply, very humbly, that he had remitted the tax on whale fishing.

An interesting exchange of letters between the governor and a Mr.

William Popple in England reveals the governor's true feelings. In one letter, dated June 3, 1718, he mentions that the continuing complaints of "that poor cracked man Mulford" are tiring him greatly. In another letter, dated July 7, he writes: "I assure you that I want nothing but a conveyance to bring me to you . . . after the encouragement Mr. Mulford and some others have lately met with from some great men . . ." He complains bitterly that ". . . the voice of a whole Province is not judged of force sufficient to disprove the simple allegations of one crazed old man . . ."

But the battle was not over. Subsequently, Captain Mulford was expelled twice from the Assembly. The first time he was promptly reelected, but the second time, at the age of 76, he decided that the time for his retirement had arrived. Having been widowed in 1717, he had remarried, and he returned to a life of comparative quiet in East Hampton.

When death came to Samuel Mulford, it was mercifully quick. On August 21, 1725, he went for his usual early morning walk, was taken ill, and within eight hours was dead, probably from what we would call a heart attack or stroke. He was 81 years old.

Now, back to the question I raised at the beginning of my talk. Why has the life of this man fascinated me since I was a teenager? Why was a newspaper reporter assigned to write a feature article on Samuel Mulford in 1995?

No one who studies the life of Samuel Mulford can doubt that he was intelligent and courageous, yet at the same time stubborn and, on more than one occasion, unnecessarily blunt. Also, there is no doubt that part of his motivation was to protect and advance his own and Long Island's mercantile interests. He was a shrewd businessman as well as an astute politician—and there's nothing wrong with either of these traits. But what has really endeared him to me, and to many others, is that in addition to what I have just said, Samuel Mulford was a man who fought the tyranny of a government which took advantage of the little person; a man who said unfair taxation cannot continue; a man of integrity and courage who said, "I can make a difference" and then proceeded to do just that; a man who was willing to forego personal ease and comfort for a greater cause.

But perhaps most significant of all, as we evaluate the life of Samuel Mulford, is the fact that in the course of a few years, almost all of the goals for which Samuel Mulford worked were obtained by the demand of the people and the concession of the crown.

In his address at the 250th anniversary of the settlement of East

Hampton, Judge Henry P. Hedges glanced backward to the early days of American history, and wondered what the early patriots would think of the present generation. He said, "If Samuel Mulford lives in the spirit land, does his thought go to the locality where as a patriot and hero he suffered and wrought that future generations might be free? Does he there see a spirit nobler, loftier, grander than his own?"

Today a modest brown stone in the Old South End Cemetery marks the final resting place of Samuel Mulford. Back-to-back with this is the tombstone of his first wife, Esther, while a few yards away is that of his second wife, Sarah Howell Mulford.

I wonder what Samuel Mulford would think if he returned to East Hampton today; walked along the streets; talked with its citizens; or tramped the Northwest woods to view the site of his wharf? Or what he would say if he knew his story had been told to millions through the media of radio and television, through academic theses, books, articles and talks? We can be sure his comments would be swift and to the point, but said with a twinkle in his eye. May East Hampton and America never forget Samuel Mulford, champion of freedom.

SOURCES

Breen, Timothy H. *Imagining the Past.* Addison Wesley Publishing Co. 1989

Brodhead, John. *Colonial History.* 1855

"Diary of Samuel Mulford," preserved in the Pennypacker Long Island Collection, East Hampton Library.

Flint, Martha B. *Early Long Island.* G.P. Putnam, New York, 1896

Fussman, Cal. "The Captain And The King," *Newsday,* February 8, 1995

Gardiner, David. *Chronicles of the Town of East Hampton.*

Hazelton, Henry. *The Boroughs of Brooklyn and Queens, Counties of Nassau and Suffolk, Vol. 3.*

Hedges, Henry P. *A History of East Hampton.* J. H. Hunt, Sag Harbor, 1897

Mulford, David Eugene. *Puritan Profile.* Unpublished manuscript, 1974.

Mulford, William R. *Genealogy of the Family of Mulford.* David Clapp and Son, Boston, 1880.

O'Callaghan, E.B. *The Voyage of The Sloop Mary.*

Pryor, Donald J. "Samuel Mulford's Place in New York Constitutional History," Thesis, Fordham University, 1961.

Rattray, Jeannette E. *East Hampton History and Genealogies.* Country Life Press, Garden City, N.Y., 1953

Savitt, Todd Lee. "Samuel Mulford of East Hampton." Master's thesis, University of Virginia, 1970.

Spears, John R. *The Story of New England Whalers*. Macmillan, New York, 1908.

Various papers of Samuel Mulford, preserved in the Pennypacker Long Island Collection, East Hampton Library.

JOHN WINTHROP, JR., OF CONNECTICUT

The First Governor of the East End

Richard S. Dunn

IF THE MAN I'M GOING to tell you about this afternoon had had his way 325 years ago, East Hampton would now be a town in the state of Connecticut rather than in New York. Whether that would have been a good thing or a bad thing, I leave to you. But John Winthrop, Jr.'s repeated efforts to annex the East End of Long Island to Connecticut are well worth examining. Obviously he failed. But the East Enders in the 1650s, 1660s, and 1670s wanted him to succeed. And the struggle that he led for about twenty years for control of eastern Long Island reveals a lot about the political situation in English America at that time.

John Winthrop, Jr. was one of the most attractive, intelligent, and interesting men in seventeenth-century New England. He has always been overshadowed by his famous father, John Winthrop (who was governor of Massachusetts from 1630 to 1649), and indeed the father was a more creative and influential leader than the son. But John Winthrop, Jr. was a highly creative and influential leader in his own right. He was born in England in 1606, came to America one year after his father in 1631, and had a strikingly diversified career until he died in 1676. Winthrop was good at many different things. He was the premier scientist in early America, and a founding member of the Royal Society in England. He was a skilled physician who treated hundreds of patients. He conducted experiments in alchemy. He extracted salt from sea water. He discovered a deposit of black lead or graphite near Sturbridge, Massachusetts from which he tried to extract silver. And he built and operated the first iron works in New England at Braintree, south of Boston.

But Winthrop's most enduring accomplishments were political. He was a town builder and a colony builder. He founded three towns: Ipswich in Massachusetts, and Saybrook and New London in Connecticut. He moved permanently from Massachusetts to Connecticut in 1645, and was elected Governor of Connecticut eighteen times between 1657 and his death in 1676.

Winthrop was endlessly exploratory, trying new scientific experiments or finding new places to live. He moved around a lot in the 1630s and 1640s—in large part I think because he wanted to keep some physical and psychic distance from his authoritative and imposing father. We know a quite a lot about the relationship between these two men because they wrote to each other frequently, and many of their letters are preserved in the magnificent collection of Winthrop Papers in the Massachusetts Historical Society in Boston. The father's handwriting is execrable, and the son's hand is also pretty hard to decipher. But it is worth the challenge to figure out what they had to say to each other, and then to read between the lines. On the surface father and son got along swimmingly, and the younger Winthrop was always scrupulously deferential to his revered parent. But I'm sure that he disagreed with him on many many occasions. The son was a much less rigid Puritan than the father, and he had a much more diplomatic temperament. For example, the younger Winthrop remained on cordial terms with Roger Williams after Williams had been banished to Rhode Island in 1635 for his radical religious opinions. He avoided attending the Massachusetts Court session in 1637 where Mistress Anne Hutchinson and about eighty of her fellow Antinomians were banished or disfranchised or disarmed for challenging the elder Winthrop's religious beliefs and practices. A decade later the son continued his friendship with his fellow scientist Robert Child, after Child was imprisoned in Boston in 1646 for daring to criticize the Massachusetts government. And the younger Winthrop even showed some tolerance toward Quakers, the most radical religious sect of the time. In 1658, nine years after the elder Winthrop's death, the leaders of Massachusetts, Plymouth, Connecticut and New Haven colonies approved a drastic course of action toward Quaker missionaries. Any Quaker who reappeared in one of these four colonies after having being punished and expelled twice before was to be put to death. Winthrop refused to endorse this policy. And he tried to persuade his fellow magistrates not to enforce it. But he failed. Between 1659 and 1661, four Quakers were executed in Massachusetts.

I don't wish to exaggerate Winthrop's benevolence. He was never completely altruistic. He always had a healthy interest in acquiring real estate for himself and his children. His biggest tract was 50,000 acres of wilderness land surrounding his lead mine at Sturbridge. He never developed this land, nor did he cultivate the farm land he acquired in the 1630s at Ipswich, Massachusetts. But he did operate a large farm on the Mystic River near Boston, and when he moved to New London he opened up further extensive farm land. He was also one of seven partners in a land company that claimed Indian title to a huge tract within the territorial limits of Rhode Island on the western shore of Narragansett Bay. And in 1641 he acquired possession of Fishers Island off the Connecticut coast in Long Island Sound. He used Fishers Island as his stock pen. By the 1660s he had 100 head of cattle, 400 sheep, and 400 goats as well as some horses and deer on this island, and he regarded Fishers Island as one of his most valuable assets. Winthrop's acquisition of Fishers Island gave him a personal interest in the future development of Long Island Sound—and by extension, a personal interest in the future development of Long Island.

As you know, the western end of Long Island had been initially settled by the Dutch and the eastern end by the English. Southampton and Southold were the first towns on the East End; Southampton was started in 1640, and Southold soon after. East Hampton was the third town, started in 1648. All three towns can be seen as off-shoots of the mass migration of 20,000 Englishmen to New England between 1630 and 1640. The East End towns were principally settled by people who had tried living in Massachusetts or in one of the other New England colonies and then moved on to Long Island in search of better opportunities or more freedom. The most important early planter in East Hampton, Lion Gardiner, had lived in Saybrook, Connecticut, before he moved to Gardiners Island and East Hampton. And as often happened when new towns were started in New England, many of the original Long Island settlers knew each other previously because they came from the same towns or villages in England. In East Hampton's case, about a third of them came from Maidstone in Kent. The three East End villages were very isolated geographically, and East Hampton was the most isolated of all. The first settlers bought their land from the local Indians, but they did not have English patents and so their titles were insecure. They lived simply, in a virtual state of nature, with minimalist local self-government and no external supervision. And they wished to keep it that way.

However, the East End towns did need protection from Dutch or Indian attack, so they were willing to consider continuing some sort of

loose affiliation with the New England governments that they had
withdrawn from. The two closest of these colonies were Connecticut
and New Haven, on the northern side of Long Island Sound. Both Connecticut and New Haven had been founded in the 1630s by migrants
from Massachusetts who acted entirely on their own without any
sponsorship from England. Neither colony had an English patent, let
alone a royal charter. But this did not matter in the 1640s, because King
Charles I and Parliament were fighting a civil war, which allowed the
New England colonies to manage their affairs as they wished. In 1643,
Connecticut and New Haven formed a military alliance with Massachusetts and Plymouth to protect themselves against the Indians and
the Dutch and the French. Thus they were able to offer some measure
of protection to the East Enders. The people in Connecticut and New
Haven lived in small self-governing towns that were similar in structure
and character to the three English towns in eastern Long Island. Connecticut incorporated a dozen towns on the Connecticut River and
along the Sound. New Haven colony was smaller and more rigidly
Puritanical; it incorporated six towns along the western end of Long
Island Sound. In the mid-1640s, the town of Southampton decided to
join Connecticut, and the town of Southold decided to join New
Haven. From 1647 to 1664—a period of eighteen years—Southampton
regularly sent representatives to the meetings of the Connecticut General Court at Hartford. Usually one or two Southampton men were
chosen as magistrates, or members of the colony council, in the annual
Hartford elections, as a way of legitimating Connecticut's jurisdiction
over the town. But in most respects Southampton operated as an au-
tonomous unit: the townsmen chose their own leaders and conducted
their own local court. Meanwhile, the people in East Hampton hesi-
tated to accept even this degree of union. In 1649, they finally did ask
to join Connecticut, and the Connecticut General Court ordered that
"East Hampton, of Long Island, shall be accepted and entertained
under this Government according to their importunate desire." The
town adopted Connecticut's law code, but continued to dicker over
the terms of union and to complain about the difficult "passage by sea"
from East Hampton to Hartford. When the people of East Hampton
discovered that they were expected to pay taxes to support the Connecticut government, they balked again and told the Hartford authorities that they wished to discontinue their union. In 1655, the
Connecticut General Court sent a stiff letter to East Hampton telling
the townspeople that they were in a "divided, shattered condition" and
that they needed to submit to some settled jurisdiction, and that they

ought to "pay what is their just dues to this Commonwealth." This letter did not work, however, and for several more years East Hampton continued to cling to its independent status.

In 1650, the Dutch governor of New Netherland and the English leaders of Connecticut, New Haven, Massachusetts, and Plymouth had agreed to a Long Island boundary line running from Oyster Bay to the vicinity of Jones Beach that gave the western quarter of the island to the Dutch and the thinly occupied eastern three-quarters of the island to the English. But this treaty did not resolve the Dutch-English tensions on Long Island. The English population was growing faster than the Dutch population, and as English settlers moved into the Dutch towns at the western end of the island, they demanded New England-style local self-government. Back home in England, where Parliament had defeated the King and executed Charles I in 1649, the aggressive Puritan commander Oliver Cromwell took charge of the government and went to war with the Dutch in 1652. There was fear among the English colonists in 1653 that Governor Peter Stuyvesant of New Netherland was preparing to invade New England. And in 1654, Cromwell sent an expeditionary force to New England to attack New Netherland. The town of East Hampton mobilized to join this war. No actual fighting took place, because the English and the Dutch negotiated a peace treaty in 1654. But the situation remained tense and unstable.

It was against this background that John Winthrop, Jr. was elected governor of Connecticut in 1657. One year later, at the close of his first year in office, the town of East Hampton finally accepted the jurisdiction of Connecticut—which is why I can speak of John Winthrop, Jr. as the first governor of the East End. In 1658, East Hampton was a small community; some thirty-two families lived here, and the total population was less than 200. In negotiating with Connecticut, the town asked to have the same terms of union that Southampton already had. Articles of agreement were drawn up and signed, and representatives from East Hampton attended the Connecticut General Court session in Hartford. John Mulford of East Hampton was elected as a member of the Connecticut Council in May 1658 as a way of confirming East Hampton's incorporation into the colony.

Why did the East Hamptonites finally decide to join Connecticut in 1658? One reason, I think, is that they were drawn by John Winthrop, Jr.'s election as governor. Winthrop lived in New London, the closest Connecticut town to the East End, and he was known and admired in East Hampton. In the 1650s, Lion Gardiner corresponded frequently with him about buying and selling and exchanging livestock and grain. Another East Hampton correspondent was Robert Bond—also a leading settler—who wrote to Winthrop in 1652 to thank him for giving medical treatment to three members of his family. Then Bond wrote again to ask if Winthrop could help the children in a neighboring East Hampton family who had white scabs all over their heads. Unfortunately Winthrop's answer has not survived. But Bond's grateful letters suggest that he had great confidence in Winthrop. Gardiner addressed him as "Honored Sir." Bond addressed him as "Worshipful Sir."

There was a second reason why East Hampton decided to join Connecticut in 1658. The town was bitterly divided over the behavior of Elizabeth Garlick. Goodwife Garlick had been accused of witchcraft and arrested in March 1658. Some of her neighbors were certain of her guilt, and others were certain of her innocence. Witchcraft was a capital offence according to the law codes in all of the New England colonies, and the people of East Hampton concluded that they did not have the authority to try capital cases. So they turned to the Connecticut courts. Elizabeth Garlick was brought to Hartford, along with the witnesses against her. And Governor Winthrop presided over Garlick's witchcraft trial.

Seven people had been tried for witchcraft in Connecticut courts between 1647 and 1654. All seven had been found guilty and executed. Elizabeth Garlick was thus the eighth Connecticut witch suspect to be brought to trial in a dozen years, and her chances looked bleak. However, the Hartford jury returned a verdict of not guilty. Subsequently, three other witch suspects were indicted in Connecticut between 1659 and 1661, and they also escaped hanging. Then in 1662-1663, when Winthrop was in England, witchcraft accusations reached a crescendo in Connecticut. During these two years, ten suspects were indicted or tried, four were executed, and two others escaped before they could be judged guilty. When Winthrop returned, the accusations continued but the outcomes were different. Seven more suspects were brought to trial during the closing years of his governorship, but none was executed. Clearly Winthrop's moderating temper helped to effect this change of policy.

During the next few years, East Hampton settled into the same relationship with Connecticut as Southampton. Both towns elected their local officers and conducted their local courts and impaneled their local juries. It was agreed in 1659 that no disputes could be referred from the East End of Long Island to Hartford unless one of the litigants appealed the local decision. Thomas Baker of East Hampton was elected a Connecticut councilor for five years in a row, from 1659 to 1663. In addition, his neighbor Robert Bond was elected a councilor in 1660 and 1661, so that during these two years two of the twelve seats on the Connecticut Council were occupied by East Hampton men. In 1661, the Connecticut General Court fixed the boundary line between East Hampton and Southampton, and declared that it was set "forever." However, there seems to have been considerable friction between the two towns. In 1664, the Connecticut General Court reproved East Hampton for shooting a stray Southampton horse and impounding stray Southampton cattle, and directed the town to construct adequate fencing to protect its fields from intruding Southampton livestock.

Meanwhile, momentous changes were taking place in England—changes that quickly affected East Hampton. Puritan control fizzled out after Oliver Cromwell's death in 1658, and Charles II—son of the martyred Charles I who had been executed by the Puritans in 1649—was restored to the throne in 1660. Most New Englanders were distressed by this turn of events, but John Winthrop, Jr. was not among them. He saw the need for settled constitutional government at home, and he saw the opportunity to gain royal recognition and political sovereignty for Connecticut. None of the New England colonies except Massachusetts had royal charters in 1660, so their title to self-government was highly suspect in the eyes of royal officials. Winthrop set out to remedy this situation. The Connecticut General Court proclaimed its allegiance to Charles II, and empowered Winthrop to go to England and obtain a royal charter. The Court was thinking big: it instructed Winthrop to petition for chartered boundaries that extended east to the Plymouth line, north to the Massachusetts line, and south to Delaware Bay. In other words, the new Connecticut would incorporate Rhode Island, New Haven, and Dutch New Netherland—presumably including Long Island.

Winthrop revealed none of his plans to the governments of Rhode Island, New Haven, or New Netherland, and in July 1661 he set sail from New Amsterdam rather than Boston in order to avoid requests for assistance in England from Massachusetts and Plymouth. Reaching London in September 1661, he mixed with scientific friends and was elected a member of the brand-new Royal Society. He gave advice to the Society for the Propagation of the Gospel in New England on how to work with the Narragansett and Pequot Indians. But chiefly he assessed the government's colonial policy and sought the patronage of influential courtiers who could help him get a royal charter for Connecticut. He found that the King and his ministers had no clear idea of what was happening in English America, and that Charles II was quite willing to make large territorial grants in America and to charter colony governments as long as he didn't have to pay for their upkeep.

Winthrop petitioned the King for a charter that would give Connecticut large privileges and generous territorial bounds. His application was quickly approved. The Connecticut charter was drawn up and dated April 23, 1662, and enrolled and sealed on May 10, 1662. The charter granted the colonists complete self-government, and permitted them to continue their exisiting political structure unchanged. Connecticut officials were to swear allegiance to the King, and Connecticut law must conform to English law, but there was no requirement that the colony report to the home authorities, nor any mechanism for enforcing royal instructions. The colony boundaries were defined in an *extraordinarily* loose way. The King granted Connecticut:

> all that part of our Dominions in New England in America bounded on the East by Narragansett River commonly called Narragansett Bay where the said River falleth into the Sea, and on the North by the Line of the Massachusetts Plantation, and on the South by the Sea, and in longitude as the Line of the Massachusetts Colony running from East to West, that is to say from the said Narragansett Bay on the East to the South Sea on the West part, with the Islands thereunto adjoining.

Interpreted liberally, Connecticut was granted jurisdiction over a huge ribbon of territory approximately 100 miles wide north to south and 3,000 miles wide east to west across the North American continent, though no one in Charles II's government had any idea that the South Sea or Pacific Ocean was so far distant from the Atlantic Ocean.

In negotiating his charter, Winthrop revised the boundaries requested by the Connecticut General Court. He set the eastern boundary of Connecticut at Narragansett Bay instead of the Plymouth line, and thus laid claim to the western half of Rhode Island where the land company that he shared in was situated, but left the eastern half of Rhode island—where Providence and Newport were located—outside of his jurisdiction. He omitted reference to Delaware Bay, and thus avoided laying explicit claim to all of Dutch New Netherland. But his charter definitely incorporated New Haven Colony, and Winthrop evidently intended to annex Long Island as well. To be sure, Long Island was not mentioned by name in the charter. But the charter did refer to the islands adjoining Connecticut—which seemed to include Long Island. When the Connecticut magistrates received the royal charter in September 1662, they immediately concluded that it embraced Long Island. Councilor Samuel Willys told Winthrop that "those of Long Island that I have spoken with all like well that our patent should include them, as the words seem fully to do."

As it turned out, Winthrop was too clever for his own good. In 1662, Rhode Island also had an agent in London, one Dr. John Clarke, who was trying to obtain a royal charter for his colony. When Clarke learned that Winthrop's charter had passed the seals, he got the Lord Chancellor to call it in so that he could examine it, and then complained that "Mr. Wintrup hath injuriously swallowed up the one half of our Colony." Clarke insisted that the Connecticut charter be redrawn to exclude the western half of Rhode Island. Winthrop stayed on in England an additional year in order to negotiate with Clarke. In the end, he signed an agreement that the Connecticut-Rhode Island boundary was at Pawcatuck River (as it is today) rather than at Narragansett Bay, and he solicited the crown to issue a charter to Rhode Island, dated in July 1663, which fixed that colony's western bounds at the Pawcatuck River. However, the Connecticut General Court ignored Winthrop's 1663 boundary adjustment with Rhode Island, and kept trying to expand east to Narragansett Bay well into the eighteenth century.

Winthrop's charter also initiated a bitter struggle with New Haven Colony, which rejected union with Connecticut. While still in England, Winthrop had done his best to block any effort by New Haven agents to petition for a separate royal charter, but he found on returning to Connecticut that his Hartford colleagues had adopted strong-arm tactics in his absence. The Connecticut government had received four defecting New Haven towns into her jurisdiction, and ordered the remaining towns to surrender. This only stiffened resistance. New Haven appealed to Massachusetts and Plymouth, and they told Connecticut to stop trespassing. By the end of 1663, the two colonies were nearly at war. Finally in December 1664, the remaining New Haven Colony towns voted to join Connecticut, but some New Havenites never surrendered. The Reverend Abraham Pierson, pastor of the Branford church in New Haven Colony, condemned Connecticut's ecclesiastical system as far too loose, and in 1667 he led most of his Branford flock to a wilderness site not far beyond Manhattan where they founded a town called New Ark—the town we know today as Newark, New Jersey.

Meanwhile, Winthrop's efforts to annex Long Island also ran into trouble. When he was negotiating for his charter in England, he encountered a certain Captain John Scott, a real estate speculator who was trying to obtain a proprietary patent for Long Island for himself. When Scott discovered that Winthrop had gotten ahead of him, he paid a quick visit to America in the fall of 1662 while Winthrop was still in England to stir up opposition to Winthrop's plans. He told everyone who would listen to him on Long Island that they were excluded from the Connecticut charter. And he assured the people of New Haven Colony that the King had explicitly excluded them from the Connecticut charter. When Scott reappeared in England in 1663, Winthrop made a bargain with him in which Winthrop wrote a letter telling the Connecticut General Court to stop trying to annex New Haven Colony. In return, Scott promised not to petition for a royal charter for New Haven. But Scott continued to scheme for personal control of Long Island.

By the time Winthrop got home in June 1663, the Connecticut General Court was claiming authority over all the English villages on Long Island—on the West End as well as the East End. Governor Peter Stuyvesant asked Winthrop if the Dutch-English boundary agreement of 1650 was still in force, and Winthrop equivocated. He told a Dutch delegation that the Connecticut patent comprehended land in New England, not New Netherland, but when the Dutchmen asked to have this statement in writing, he declined, "saying it was sufficiently plain from the patent itself." In November 1663, a troop of 100 Englishmen marched through the five English towns in western Long Island, and Stuyvesant felt forced to surrender his claim to these towns in the hope that he would be allowed to keep control of the Dutch towns adjacent to New Amsterdam.

At this point, Captain John Scott returned from England. He had learned what Winthrop didn't yet know, that Charles II was planning a new war against the Netherlands. He was sending an expeditionary force to capture New Netherland, and he was going to give the Dutch colony to his brother, the Duke of York, the future James II. New Netherland would become New York. Scott hoped that if he posed as the Duke's agent and chased the Dutch officials out of their remaining Long Island villages before the arrival of the invasion fleet, he might be given title to the island as a reward for his services. This was not an altogether foolish hope, because the Duke of York took very little interest in America, and after the Dutch colony was captured he did in fact give away the southern part of his territory to two of his friends who established the colonies of East Jersey and West Jersey. Scott offered to help Connecticut secure full possession of Long Island, marched into the West End at the head of an armed band, and proclaimed that Long Island was the King's territory. Stuyvesant recognized him as "President of the English on Long Island" and the Connecticut government belatedly discovered that Scott was appointing his own officials in some of the English towns, and that he was establishing his own private state on Long Island.

In March 1664, Scott was seized, taken to Hartford for trial, and found guilty of usurping the King's authority. In May, the Connecticut General Court declared that Long Island was within her charter limits. However, at this same court, when two East Hampton men—John Mulford and Robert Bond—were nominated for election to the Connecticut Council, neither was chosen. For the first time in seven years East Hampton had no representative on the colony council. Why Mulford and Bond were passed over, I do not know. Perhaps they were considered to be too friendly to Captain John Scott. In June 1664, Governor Winthrop visited the English towns in Long Island and replaced Scott's officers with new ones.

In July 1664—one month after Winthrop's visit to Long Island—a small royal fleet sailed into Boston harbor. Colonel Richard Nicolls was in charge. He had four frigates and 400 men, and orders from Charles II to take New Netherland. Then he was to govern the captured territory for the Duke of York. Nicolls asked for additional troops from the New England colonies and proceeded to western Long Island, where he established headquarters near Coney Island. Winthrop joined him there in mid August 1664 to support the English invasion force. When Stuyvesant tried to stall for time, Winthrop rowed over to Manhattan under a white flag, and delivered a letter to Stuyvesant and his Dutch Council, urging them to accept Nicolls' generous terms of surrender. Stuyvesant tore up the letter, but the outcry from the Dutch burghers was so great that he feared they would mutiny. So he pieced the letter together and let everyone see it. On August 27, Stuyvesant surrendered without a shot being fired. Winthrop was one of the six Englishmen to sign the articles of capitulation. New Netherland became New York.

Winthrop discovered to his dismay that Charles II had granted a royal charter to the Duke of York, dated March 1664, that conflicted head on with the Connecticut charter issued two years earlier. The Duke was given, in addition to Dutch territory, all of Long Island, Martha's Vineyard, Nantucket, a large section of Maine, and everything on the New England mainland west of the Connecticut River! And the charter declared that the Duke's grant superceded any previous English grant which might conflict with it. Thus not only was Long Island taken from Connecticut, but the western half of the colony, containing every significant town except New London.

After assisting with the Dutch surrender, Winthrop's next task was to secure Connecticut's boundary with New York on as favorable terms as possible. Winthrop and his son FitzJohn Winthrop returned to New York in November 1664 to congratulate Governor Nicolls on his victory and to negotiate the New York-Connecticut boundary. They argued their right not only to the western half of Connecticut but to the eastern two-thirds of Long Island, where they had been exercising authority for twenty years. Winthrop sweetened his argument by presenting a gift horse to Nicolls from his Fisher's Island stud farm. Nicolls liked and respected Winthrop, and he dropped the Duke's claim to the Connecticut River. In fact he was misled by the Connecticut delegation into drawing the boundary between the two colonies at Mamaroneck River, further west than it had been before. But otherwise Connecticut lost out. Long Island was to be part of New York "as is expressed by plain words" in the Duke's patent, and all other offshore islands in Long Island Sound were assigned to New York, even Fisher's Island, which was only two miles from the Connecticut coast. However, Nicolls confirmed Winthrop's title to Fisher's Island in return for a quitrent of one lamb per annum. It was perhaps some consolation to Winthrop that Captain John Scott's pretensions to the presidency of Long Island were also dismissed. Nicolls decided that the Captain was a knave, and Scott skipped off to the West Indies.

Nicolls quickly promulgated a special law code known as the Duke's Laws, modeled largely on New England codes, for use in the English towns on Long Island. And he announced that the civil administration and property titles previously settled by Connecticut would continue unaltered. In 1666, he granted a patent to the town of East Hampton confirming all purchases and privileges. However, the people of East Hampton and the other East End towns were discontented with life under the Duke of York. They complained that there was no legislative assembly in New York. The Duke was no friend of representative government, and he instructed Nicolls not to call a popularly elected legislature. The East Enders had never paid much attention to the Connecticut General Court because of their distance from Hartford, but now that they had no legislature they wanted to have one. Furthermore, the New York government seems to have kept closer watch on them than the Connecticut government, and made them pay taxes. The East Enders had never been enthusiastic taxpayers, and they vociferously objected to taxation without representation.

Winthrop and Nicolls kept on close personal terms. In 1665, Nicolls urged Winthrop to retire from the Connecticut governorship and move to New York, and in 1668, when Nicolls was himself replaced as governor of New York, Winthrop wrote him a sorrowful farewell letter. The new governor of New York was Francis Lovelace. He kept in amicable correspondence with Winthrop, but was not a real friend as Nicolls had been. Probably he suspected that Winthrop was encouraging rebellion among the English towns on Long Island, particularly the three East End towns of East Hampton, Southampton, and Southold. When Lovelace burned their "seditious" protests, the people of East Hampton, Southampton, and Southold sent an appeal to the King, "praying that they might be continued under the Government and Patent of Mr. Winthrop," or else be granted independence. This appeal was referred to the King's Council for Foreign Plantations in July 1672.

Before the Council could reach a decision, the situation in America had dramatically altered once again. As we have just heard in the previous lecture, a new Anglo-Dutch war broke out in 1672. Governor Winthrop called a special session of the Connecticut Court to ready the colony's defenses against the Dutch. In midsummer 1673, a Dutch squadron several times more powerful than Nicolls' fleet of 1664 was plundering Virginia and heading north. Governor Lovelace of New York chose this moment to visit Winthrop at Hartford. While he was off in Connecticut, the Dutch fleet sailed into New York harbor and besieged Fort James. The outmanned English garrison surrendered after putting up token resistance, the Dutch took Lovelace into custody, and resumed control of New Netherland. Rumors flew that they would soon move on to New England with an army of 3,000 men. Ironically, only the Duke of York's most dissatisfied subjects on eastern Long Island offered any resistance to the Dutch. On August 7, 1673 the people of East Hampton and Southampton appealed to Hartford for protection. The Connecticut Court warned the Dutch commander to stay away from the East End, which had never been in Dutch hands, and in October 1673, the three towns refused point blank to take an oath of allegiance to the Dutch governor, Anthony Colve. Fortunately for them, the Dutch fleet had sailed away in September, greatly reducing the enemy's potency, and Colve was afraid of inciting a New England attack on New Netherland. Winthrop for his part was eager to protect the East End, figuring that this would strengthen Connecticut's claim against the Duke of York for jurisdiction over the three towns.

From October 1673 to April 1674, Long Island was a battlefield.

The East Enders would raid the Dutch farmers at the West End, and force them to retire with their grain and livestock to the fort on Manhattan. Repeatedly Colve sent countersorties against the East End towns, and Winthrop's son FitzJohn would race across the Sound from New London with Connecticut volunteers. In February 1674 a pitched battle of sorts took place at Southold. A Dutch ketch and two sloops drew up before the town, the commander demanded surrender, and prepared to land his men. As FitzJohn Winthrop described the scene in a letter to Hartford, the Dutch commander

> fired one of his great guns upon us, but the shot grazing by the disadvantage of the ground did no hurt to our men. I gave order to return him thanks by firing a piece of ordinance upon him, but the shot falling at his fore foot did him no hurt. Whereupon he fired two more great guns, and his small shot, which fell thick but did us no hurt. We then presently answered; many of our small shot hitting the ship as we could perceive, but know not of any hurt done him. Whereupon he presently weighed and set sail.

Although the Dutch had been driven off, further attacks were anticipated, and FitzJohn Winthrop and his men remained on the East End until mid-April 1674. They finally came home when Connecticut learned that the two home governments had signed a peace treaty in February.

Governor Winthrop was happy to hear that the Dutch were handing New Netherland back to the English, and that the Duke had appointed a new governor, one Major Edmund Andros, to manage New York. He set out once again to detach the East End from the Duke's province. East Hampton, Southampton, and Southold asked to join Connecticut, and their application was accepted "as far as shall be in our lawful power from His Majesty's gracious grant in his charter." The three towns voted in June 1674 to petition the King, and raised £150 to cover the cost of petitioning. Winthrop started to draft a narrative of the Dutch attack for presentation to the King's Privy Council. In this narrative he emphasized the heroism of "those famous towns of the East end of Long Island, by whose loyalty, pruidence, and valor the honor of the English hath been maintained in these parts of the world."

But once again Winthrop's plans for annexing eastern Long Island were checkmated by the Duke of York. Governor Andros arrived at New York in November 1674, and received the colony from the Dutch. He learned that the people of the three East End towns—led by John

Mulford of East Hampton, John Howell of Southampton, and John Younge of Southold—had declared that they were under the government of Connecticut "and are desirous to use all good and lawful means so to continue." Andros told Winthrop that if there was "any pretended Engagement between you (which cannot now be valid) I do hereby desire that you will send to disabuse any such persons at the East End of Long Island." And he immediately went out to the East End and told the three towns that they were within New York jurisdiction and must accept his authority. The three local leaders—Mulford, Howell, and Younge—were forced to submit. The Duke was pleased with his governor's decisive behavior, and complimented him in April 1675 for "reducing to obedience those three factious towns at the East end of Long Island."

The Duke also urged Andros to revive New York's claim to the western half of Connecticut. Andros had already done so. He wrote to the Connecticut General Court to state that New York's eastern boundary was the Connecticut River. "I do therefore desire," said Andros, "and will not doubt from so worthy an assembly, that you will give present and effectual orders for my receiving, in his Royal Highness's behalf, that part of his territories as yet under your jurisdiction." The Connecticut government protested that the New York-Connecticut boundary had been settled in 1664, but Andros reiterated his demand that western Connecticut be surrendered. In June 1675, at the height of King Philip's War, Andros sailed into the Connecticut River with two sloops full of soldiers. He found the militia of Saybrook and the other neighboring towns standing in arms. Evidence from Andros's memoranda indicate that he intended to take possession of Saybrook Fort, but when the Connecticut militia began unlimbering the cannon in the fort, he kept to his ship. The local militia captain handed him a letter from the Connecticut General Court stating that the militia would forbid Andros from landing his men. Outbluffed at last, Andros came ashore without his troops and read the Duke of York's charter to the hostile crowd. They in turn made him listen to the Connecticut Court's proclamation against him. Connecticut ordered all subjects of the colony government "utterly to refuse to attend, countenance, or obey the said Major Edmund Andros or any under him. God save the King!"

Andros sailed away, and the crisis faded when the Duke of York ordered him to drop the fight over western Connecticut. So the net result of two years' agitation was to leave everything as it had been in 1664: the Duke kept Long Island and Connecticut kept her mainland territory. By this time Winthrop himself was an old man, in poor health.

The first governor of the East End died in 1676 at age seventy. But this isn't quite the end of my story. In 1739, more than sixty years after Winthrop's death, a new town was founded in Connecticut. A band of settlers migrated from the village of Eastham on Cape Cod to a site in central Connecticut about ten miles east of Middletown. Apparently these migrants didn't want to call their new Connecticut town by the same name as their old Massachusetts town, but they did want to come close. So—you guessed it—they named the place East Hampton.

"IT WERE AS WELL TO PLEASE THE DEVIL AS ANGER HIM"

Witchcraft in the Founding
Days of East Hampton[1]

Hugh King & Loretta Orion

Iɴ 1657 Eʟɪᴢᴀʙᴇᴛʜ Howᴇʟʟ, the daughter of Lion Gardiner, East Hampton's most prominent citizen, died screaming she was killed by a witch. According to legend, Lion Gardiner protected the woman his daughter believed killed her with witchcraft, and offered her asylum for the rest of her life on his island. The legend gives the impression that the founders of the town were somehow immune from the prevalent superstitions of their time. The court records tell us that they managed to resolve the crisis without sacrificing the witch, despite the fact that the founders were as susceptible as others living at that time to beliefs in witchcraft. To appreciate this rare peaceful resolution of a witchcraft crisis, we need to understand the mentality of the seventeenth century. The witnesses at the inquest concerning the charges of witchcraft told us how they felt, thought, and acted when confronted with matters of life and death, fortune and misfortune. The records also show us how the newly devised legal system served them in this and other types of crises. If we acquaint ourselves with the religious and magical beliefs that helped them to understand the crisis, we have a more complete picture of just how remarkable it was that they never hung a witch in this town.

In the seventeenth century, even in civilized Europe, the supernatural was very much part of everyday experience. Protestant Reformers felt especially vulnerable because they cut themselves loose from the safety net of the soul-saving rites of the Catholic church. They chose instead to face the uncertainty of life in this world and the next without the comforts of the intercession of the saints, or rites of extreme unction, exorcism, or confession and forgiveness of sins.

Because most Protestants believed that nature lacked an inherent, self-sufficient order, they felt the world was precariously poised on the brink of chaos. Without God's restraining hand the waters—which were by nature heavier than earth—would inundate the land, all substances, all bodies, stars, earth, and seas, in short, the whole structure of the world would collapse in an instant and be reduced to nothing.[2]

Furthermore, chaos was exactly what humans deserved, because Adam had destroyed the original perfection of the world.[3] Because of Adam's sin, the world and humans became so hopelessly corrupt and depraved that humans were incapable of redeeming themselves or nature by their own efforts. To make matters worse, God allowed Satan to have his way in the sinful world. Satan worked diligently, with the help of witches, to disrupt the precarious order of the world. And with religious reformations in progress in the seventeenth century, each of the contending churches and sects saw the power of Satan behind the efforts of their adversaries.

The fact that God maintained order from moment to moment was testament to God's love for undeserving sinners. John Calvin thought that was reassuring proof of God's reliability. Puritans were supposed to see it that way, but not all could.

Although all humans deserved eternal damnation in hell, God, in his mercy, had decided to forgive a select few. These, despite their sinful natures, were predestined for eternal life with him. The rest would reap their deserved eternal punishment in hell. God had made this selection before he created the world, and he would not change his mind. Because humans were incapable of understanding God's will, it was impossible to know who was among the elect.

However, with so much at stake, the Puritans were always on the lookout for clues. The world was pregnant with supernatural meaning and signs of God's intention. Any unusual event—lightning, hailstorms, even the appearance of a very large cabbage in the garden—was as a sign of God's approval or anger, usually the latter. Although it was impious to presume to interpret natural occurences, such as meteor showers, as signs of God's intentions, Puritans recorded them and pondered their significance in their diaries.

Puritan orthodoxy shaped all facets of life in the colonies. Statements of the laws included quotations of the relevant passages from the Bible on which they were based. Although everyone was not a member of a congregation, member or not, all were expected to contribute to the maintenance of the church and pastor, and to believe and behave according to Puritan ideals.

All around the world people believe some extraordinary individuals have an inherent, supernatural capacity to harm others that normal, good people do not. This may be because the belief is useful. It explains the cause of misfortune, and at the same time it absolves the accuser of personal responsibility, justifies both contempt for the witch and the most extreme measure to be rid of them, including murder. The person accused of being a witch became the embodiment of evil, a useful antithesis against which the righteous defined their own goodness. The witch acquired the hideous features of the accusers' projected fear and disgust. In the seventeenth century fear and disgust bore the features of deformed femininity, old age, and familiarity with animals rather than civilized humans.

In the sixteenth and seventeenth centuries there were two distinct species of witch, each bearing the characteristics of one of two sets of fears. The oldest image of the witch represented the fears of common people. This witch harmed her neighbors' health and property by causing unfavorable weather, destroying crops and livestock and subverting the efficiency of housewives. These harmful magics were known as *maleficium*. A new species of witch evolved in the context of contending religious reformations and the instability of governments. This witch made a pact with Satan. He, or more often she, agreed to assist Satan in his campaign to destroy the church and orderly society. In exchange, Satan provided these witches with privileges and protection against poverty, sickness, and other misfortunes that the state either could not, or would not, provide.

Together these two images of the witch could account for all misfortune, personal and social. Theologians and scholars controlled the media, so theirs was the definitive portrayal of the witch. Laws against witchcraft reflected this anxiety about Satanic conspiracy. Demonology scholars, churchmen and lawyers established the features of Satanic witchcraft as objective facts. Their treatises explain that witches flew through the night to Sabbath gatherings where they conspired with Satan. Witches collaborated with familiar spirits— often animals—and could turn themselves into animals. During the sixteenth and seventeenth centuries it was heretical to doubt the reality of Satanic witchcraft.

There was plenty of misfortune to explain in those troubled times. The collection of religious wars, plagues, syphilis, enormous inequalities in wealth and faltering monarchies would have seemed uncanny.

A witch with her familiar animal spirit.
(Radio Times Hudson Picture Library, in *Encyclopedia of Magic
and Superstition*, New York; Crescent Books, division of
Crown Publishers)

Authorities knew it was a Satanic conspiracy. When individuals suffered sickness, starvation, and other effects of these collective disasters, they accused one another of maleficium. The latter gladly resorted to the legal mechanisms in place to be rid of the witch, but they couldn't expect much help from the courts unless they were able to modify their stories of maleficium to accommodate the judges' concern with Satanic conspiracy. The colonialists brought these two versions of the witch with them, along with the laws relating to this capital crime. Witchcraft served them as a ready explanation for both the familiar and the novel misfortunes they encountered in the wilderness of the new world.

The earliest evidence we have for suspicion that Goody Elizabeth Garlick, wife of Joshua Garlick, was a witch comes from Goody Simon's memory of a strange thing that happened one day when she was having her fits.[4] You will notice that most of the women were called "Goody" or "goodwife," except those of more elevated status who were called "Mrs." On the day of Goody Simon's fits, Goody Bishop hurried down the main street of the town of East Hampton with some dockweed that she got from Goody Garlick. Goody Bishop was hoping the herbs would ease Goody Simon's fits. When Goody Bishop arrived at Goody Simon's house the ailing woman recoiled in horror and threw the herbs in the fire. While she and Goody Davis burned the herbs, Simons explained that it had been like this on another day when she and several of the people who came to East Hampton were living in Lynn, Massachusetts. On that occasion, also, a friend brought healing herbs to ease her fits. Then a strange black thing had entered the house. While Goody Simons was in the throes of a strong fit a neighbor asked "Who has a black cat?" Another answered, "Goody Garlick."

The women were able to organize the diffuse black thing into the form of Goody Garlick's cat because of the common belief that witches sent familiar animal spirits, or turned themselves into animals, to do their mischief. It was not unusual for the colonialists to see spectres. One example hits pretty close to home. In July of 1665, the inhabitants of several towns on Long Island witnessed an apparition. They heard the sound of guns and drums coming from the sea. In the clear light of morning they saw "companies of armed men in the air clothed in light-colored garments, and the commanders in red."[5]

Why didn't the women realize that Goody Simons' fits and strange visions were symptoms of her pathology? They probably did; however, that was an inadequate explanation. Because for Puritans, reason, science, philosophy and other knowledge were products of the deceptive senses.[6] These were only useful as indicators of the ultimate cause behind superficial appearances. Ultimately all disharmony was the result of Man's sin. It would be important then, to know "whose sin?"

Was Goody Garlick the only person who owned a black cat? Probably not, but she knew something about healing. It was she who gave Goody Bishop the herbs that ended up in the fire. Many healers were accused of witchcraft, particularly if their cures failed. After all, what was to prevent them from using the same power to harm rather than heal? Possession of valuable knowledge and skill also made Goody Gar-

lick different and more powerful than other women. It is also likely
that Goody Garlick was French.[7] Being one of few foreigners among
the English would have made her suspect.

Goody Simons commented while burning Goody Garlick's herbs
that she would have neither Goody Garlick nor Goody Edwards near
her. The two women had something in common and it wasn't a fond-
ness for black cats. Their insults were taken seriously. Women seldom
came to the attention of the magistrates, unless their words or actions
threatened the status or property of men. Lion Gardiner sued Goody
Garlick—along with her husband and Goody Simons—for "uttering
slanderous speeches."[8]

As far back as 1643 in Lynn Massachusetts, Goody Edwards was described as "an ignorant, sottish and imperious woman," after she struck
a man and "scoffed at his membership."[9] In East Hampton she was ordered to pay a fine or stand with her tongue in a cleft stick.[10] A few
years later, the constable came to fetch her to court. Goody Edwards
threatened to burn the warrant and kicked the constable. When the
constable's assistant, the eminent Mr. Thomas Talmage, came to his
friend's defense, Goody Edwards kicked him hard enough to break his
shin. When her husband urged her to keep her peace, Goody Edwards
berated him for bringing her to live among heathens and promised
that when she got home she would hang him.[11]

On another occasion Goody Edwards came to the attention of the
court. Goody Price called Goody Edwards a liar when she bragged
about a petticoat she brought from England. It was not Goody Edwards, but her husband who brought the suit for defamation. This apparently trivial female conflict might have remained a private squabble
had it not endangered Mr. Edwards' posterity. He complained to the
magistrates that people would say as his son walked by, "There goes
the son of a base liar!"[12]

But Goody Edwards was never brought to court for accusations
of witchcraft; Goody Garlick was. Goody Edwards' hostility came
under the jurisdiction of the public court because she was a liability
to men as well as women. The overwhelming evidence against Goody
Garlick consisted of offenses against women. These festered outside
the court.

Soon after the Garlicks moved to Gardiner's Island with the Gardiner family uncanny events followed in the tracks of Goody Garlick.
Soon after Lion Gardiner sued both the Garlicks for slanderous
speeches, Gardiner's ox broke its leg. Then a black child was taken
away strangely. Next, a man died under suspicious circumstances. Then

a perfectly normal pig gave birth to piglets in some anomalous fashion and died. According to Goody Davis these events happened one after another, all of a sudden, and all in connection with Goody Garlick.

Goody Davis and other women confirmed their suspicion that Goody Garlick was responsible for these uncanny events with some countermagic. The ritual was based on the belief that when witches harm a person or an animal, they open a channel of communication. The afflicted can exploit this link to discover the identity of the witch or effect revenge by returning the harm to its source. If they burned some hair, urine, or flesh of the witch's victim, the witch would experience pain and be compelled to come forth. The women burned the tail of the sow that died strangely. Goody Garlick showed up. We may wonder just how soon after the burning of the tail she showed up, and how many other people passed by unnoticed while they waited, but to their satisfaction, Goody Garlick proved her guilt.

Goody Davis was very interested in proving that Goody Garlick was a witch because she was convinced that Goody Garlick killed her baby with the evil-eye. Goody Davis was no stranger to misfortune. She had been widowed twice, and her present husband, Faulk, was a philanderer. Then, one day, Goody Davis dressed her baby in clean linen. Goody Garlick came by and complimented the mother on how pretty the baby looked. Then she said, "the child is not well for it groaneth." On hearing these words Davis felt her heart rise within her. Goody Davis saw death in her baby's face. The child fell ill and never opened its eyes or cried until it died five days later.[13] Goody Davis told her friends that Goody Garlick killed her baby with the evil eye.

Why did Goody Davis believe Goody Garlick gave her the evil eye? Her words were benign enough. However, believers in the evil eye attribute equal danger to the hostile and the overly appreciative gaze. The lethal gaze is believed by the jealous to express envy. The difference between jealousy and envy is this: the jealous wish to protect what belongs to them; the envious wish to destroy or expropriate what belongs to others.[14] Goody Garlick said the child looked pretty; Goody Davis heard envy. Goody Davis was understandably jealous, or shall we say, defensive and protective of her baby. The infant mortality rate was high; all new mothers were anxious. Goody Davis was a new mother. Goody Garlick was beyond her child-bearing years. Goody Garlick commented that the child might be ill. Goody Davis heard a prophetic threat. Witchcraft trial records reveal that many older women were accused by young ones. For these young mothers the witch is the anti-mother. The good mother sees to it that her children thrive; the anti-mother turns mother's milk to poison and makes children sicken and die.[15]

The Garlicks moved from Gardiner's Island into the town. Their fortune was on the rise. They acquired land allotments in the town that would eventually elevate them from the lowest to the middle status group. This may have provoked some envy. When the Garlicks were planning to move to East Hampton, Goody Davis warned the people in town that they would regret having Goody Garlick as a neighbor because of all the uncanny misfortunes that followed in her wake.[16] As she predicted—or perhaps because she predicted—the anti-mother image of Goody Garlick grew stronger as more new mothers and their babies were added to Goody Garlick's list of casualties.

One day Goody Garlick came by to ask Goody Edwards' daughter for some breast milk. The young mother complied and soon thereafter, her breast milk dried up and her child sickened. Goody Davis, informed Goody Edwards' daughter that the same sequence of events followed after Goody Garlick asked for breast milk from two other women, Goody Stratton and Goody Davis' daughter. Goody Davis' grandchild recovered, but Mary Stratton's baby died, just as Goody Davis' baby had died from Garlick's evil eye.[17]

Men had just as much, or possibly more, difficulty getting along with one another.

Men redressed their grievances with that good old staple of East Hampton history: the lawsuit. Between 1650 and 1656 the magistrates recorded more than thirty-four court cases dealing with matters such as trespass, damage to crops, ownership disputes, overcharging in business transactions, and disagreements over land boundaries. Nearly half of the cases involved slander and defamation.

Highlights of these cases include the accusation that a servant stood behind Mrs. Gardiner and made "bow-wow noises." The Reverend Thomas James accused a man of attempting to seduce both his daughter and his maid. Four men, including Goody Davis' husband, were accused of being "notorious masturbators." This was a capitol offense, punishable by death. For the first time the East Hampton magistrates called on the expertise of an external court. Only after extended examination of witnesses and serious debate and consultation with authorities in Connecticut did the townsmen decide the offense was not worthy of loss of life or limb.[18]

In the year preceding our story these public interpersonal conflicts escalated to the point of overburdening the court. The townsmen passed a series of ordinances to discourage the contentious behavior.

These have the tone of Old Testament justice: "an eye for an eye." Anyone who brought charges against another must be prepared to suffer the same loss of life, limb, or goods, that he would have done to his neighbor if the charges were proven false. Any man who struck another in anger would pay a fine to the court, and pay for his victim's cure as well as the productive labor lost as a result of the injury. A fine of up to five pounds would be imposed for slander.[19]

In the year preceding the Goody Garlick witchcraft case fifteen cases came before the magistrates; that is, one case for every twelve people in the town. If you think the magistrates were overburdened with court cases in the founding days of our town, listen to these statistics! In 1997 there were more court cases than there were people in the town, if we include vehicle, traffic and parking violations—problems that the town fathers didn't have to worry about. In 1997 the East Hampton court adjudicated 19,584 cases for a population of 16,779 people. If we exclude traffic violations, there is a ratio of approximately one case for every five people living in the town.[20]

In the midst of this whirlwind of contention a sudden illness came upon Elizabeth Howell, Lion Gardiner's daughter, one evening in February of 1657. Elizabeth, who was then sixteen years old, had recently given birth to her first child. She was alone in her home until a friend, Samuel Parsons, came to visit her husband, Arthur Howell. He was not at home, she told him. However, Elizabeth invited her guest to warm himself at the fire. She confided that she was suffering from a headache and that she thought she had caught a chill. Samuel left for a short while, then returned to find her worse. Elizabeth bound a cloth around her head to ease her pain. Presently, Elizabeth's husband, Arthur Howell, returned home with a friend, William Russell. They found Elizabeth huddled by the fire. She said, "Love, I am very ill of my head, and I fear I shall have the fever." Arthur took her to bed. "Lord have mercy upon me," she sobbed, then asked her friends to pray for her.

No doubt Elizabeth prayed for relief of her pain. But, for Puritans, the spiritual significance of suffering was of the utmost importance. In sickness they felt themselves hovering precariously between heaven and hell. For those who were not certain that they were among those elected for eternal life suffering was an opportunity to repent, and receive faith in one's election. Those who had received the conviction that they were among the elect might be tempted to doubt its authenticity. For those whom God had not chosen, no such conviction—at least no genuine one—could ever come. In that case, suffering was nothing more than a preview of eternal damnation. The conversion experiences generally didn't happen before the age of mid-twenties.[21] Elizabeth was only sixteen. Judging from surviving records, most of the second generation Puritans either never received it, or didn't demonstrate it in the customary way.

Elizabeth prayed, herself, that she would not lose her senses. Shortly thereafter she said, as she suckled her baby, "My poor child it pitties me more for thee than for myself for if I be ill, to be sure thou wilt be ill too."

After the baby was taken from her, Elizabeth sang the words of a psalm, then terrified her friends by shrieking, "A witch! A witch! Now you are come to torture me because I spoke 2 or 3 words against you! In the morning you will come fawning . . ." Samuel said, "The lord be merciful to her . . . It is well if she bee not bewitcht."

The men were reluctant to disturb Lion Gardiner with this new problem because he was attending his wife who was also quite ill. Finally, they sent Samuel Parsons to inform Lion Gardiner of his daughter's condition. Lion found his daughter peering fixedly at the foot of her bed shrieking, "A witch! A witch!" He asked her, "What do you see?" "A black thing at the bed's feet," she answered, sobbing and flailing to fight an adversary that she alone could see. Her struggle became more frenzied. Elizabeth's husband tried to restrain her, but she resisted him with uncharacteristic strength. At last she exhausted herself.

The next morning Lion Gardiner found that his daughter's condition was deteriorating. He decided to inform his wife. After several failed attempts to rise from her own sickbed, Mary Gardiner struggled across the village green to the bed of her daughter. Daughter and mother wept in each other's arms until Elizabeth said, "Oh, mother, I am bewitched." Mary, now startled, said, "No, no, you are asleep or dreaming."

But Elizabeth insisted, "I am not asleep. I am not dreaming. Truly, I am bewitched." Mary asked her "Whom do you see?" After some hesitation, at last Elizabeth shrieked, "Goody Garlick! Goody Garlick! I see her at the far corner of the bed, and a black thing of hers at the other corner."

This is the first time that Elizabeth named the witch. She was delirious with fever, perhaps from an infection following childbirth. Mary Gardiner said, in her deposition, that Elizabeth named the witch, but it is possible that the two women arrived at the conclusion collaboratively. This seems to have been the case in the Salem trials some thirty years later. Adolescent girls became delirious. When asked what ailed them, at first they said they didn't know. When adults suggested the names of certain women who might be bewitching them, the girls obediently confirmed the adults' suspicions.[22]

Again, Elizabeth struggled with an adversary, who was invisible to everyone except herself. "Hush, child," Mary said, "This is a terrible thing you say. You must never say it again, not to your husband, not to any living soul. For your husband, if he heard you speak so, would surely tell . . ."

Mary Gardiner's testimony ends with that dangling sentence. Who might Elizabeth's husband tell? Perhaps the mother was afraid that the Garlicks would find out and retaliate. Mary told her daughter explicitly not to tell her husband because he might tell. He might tell his father. Arthur Howell's father, Edward, was one of the devout Puritan founders of Southampton. While Puritans acknowledged that Satan was empowered by God to create disorder through witches, he would think it blasphemous to believe any human could independently wield supernatural power that belongs only to God. The pious response to suffering was repentance, not blaming others. In any case, it seems Mary feared an accusation of witchcraft might boomerang and bring shame on Elizabeth or the Gardiner family.

Mary was obliged to return to her own home and bed. That day, three neighbors—Goody Birdsall, Ann Edwards, and Goody Simons—stood by as Elizabeth's afflictions intensified. She alternated between long periods of incoherence and clear and violent outcries. "She is a double-tongued woman . . . She pricks me with pins . . . Oh! She torments me . . ."

"Who torments you," the women asked. At first Elizabeth was reluctant to reply. Finally she screamed, "Ah, Garlick, you jeered me when I came to your house to call my husband home. You laughed and jeered me, and I went crying away."

If sticks and stones don't break your bones, why were so many men suing each other for slander and defamation in the East Hampton court? Insults damage not only one's public image, but the personal estimation of the self. The Garlicks derided Elizabeth Howell's competence as a housewife. We do not see women defending their honor in court as men did. This personal humiliation would not interest the court because it cast no shame on Elizabeth's husband or the family's honor. Women negotiated their individual reputations privately among themselves. Lawsuits and witchcraft accusations were two separate, gender-specific defenses against insults. Most witchcraft accusations followed an argument or confrontation of this kind.

Elizabeth continued to rant "Oh, you are a pretty one."

"Send for Garlick and his wife," [23] she cried out, "I would tear her in pieces and leave the birds to pick her bones." She answered the women who wondered why she would do such a thing, "Did you not see her last night stand by my bedside, ready to pull me to pieces? She pricked me with pins, and she brought a black thing to the foot of my bed."

Then, clutching her throat, Elizabeth gagged and choked. Ann Edwards forced Elizabeth's mouth open with the handle of a knife. Finding no obstruction there, Ann next gave her some oil and sugar. (This was a common remedy against witchcraft.) After a brief calm, Elizabeth coughed and her attendants saw a pin fall from her mouth. Simons retrieved the pin and held it to the light. [24] There had been no such pin in the house before.

Many pins were produced at the bedsides of the alleged victims of witchcraft. These are exhibited in museums in Salem Massachusetts and in Europe. Where did they all come from?

It was Goody Simons who retrieved the pin, allegedly from Elizabeth's mouth. [25] She had something at stake in providing clear physical evidence of Goody Garlick's witchcraft. She was convinced that Goody Garlick tried to harm her by intruding her herbs into her house. Goody Simons may have seen this as an opportunity to exchange her terror of Goody Garlick for effective aggression. This time the witch was endangering the life of a prominent woman. If Goody Simons could confirm Elizabeth's suspicions with objective evidence, maybe this time, Goody Simons could persuade others who were more influential than herself to confront the witch. With slight of hand, Goody Simons might have provided that concrete evidence.

Goody Simons remained and slept in the bed with Elizabeth after the other women went home. Arthur, and William Russell and a female slave, Boose, stationed themselves around the bed. Somewhat past midnight everyone except Elizabeth and Simons, who were sleeping, were frightened by a strange sound, as if someone were scratching near the bed. The men searched around the bed and were mystified when they found no source of the sound. (Perhaps Simons was tampering with the evidence again.)

Later the two men were startled by a rumbling and grating on the inside of the fireplace, for which they could find no cause. To Arthur it sounded like "a great rock were thrown down on a heap of stones, but found no place to rest." Neither Simons nor Elizabeth awakened to hear these strange disturbances, although at other times during the night Elizabeth woke Simons to ask her if she didn't see someone at the foot of the bed. Elizabeth complained repeatedly "ye prick me with pins."

The next day, Sunday, neighbors visited, including the pastor, Thomas James, to lead prayers for her soul.

Puritans were supposed to welcome death. The angels were at the bedside, ready to convey the souls of those whom God had elected to heaven where they would be embraced by Christ and know joy and pleasure, and at last, complete understanding. However, Satan, and his demons, were also there, ready to convey the forsaken soul to the eternal fires of hell. The deathbed was the battleground where Satan and the angels fought over the dying person's soul. The bravado must have been difficult to maintain considering no one could know with absolute certainty that they were among the elect and that the angels would win. Puritans prayed and fasted to console the tortured soul of the dying, but there was nothing any human could do to persuade God to redeem those he had not already chosen.[26]

Puritans and other Protestants denied themselves the comforts of last rites when they condemned such rituals as blasphemous Catholic practices. Although Pastor James left us very few records of his thoughts, it is likely that he responded as other pastors of the time did, by reading this crisis as a signs of God's impatience with the contentious people of the Town of East Hampton.

Elizabeth, parched by fever, coughed and sobbed, clutched her head and her throat, as she descended deeper and deeper into delirium, surfacing now and then to give voice to her torment: "Garlick . . . double-tongued . . . ugly thing . . . pins . . . ," And, she called out for her mother, until she finally grew quiet and her torment ended with death.

The Puritans searched for signs of how the battle between Satan and the angels was going. This description of the manner of Elizabeth's death does not make it seem that the final saving grace ever came to Elizabeth Howell.

After the burial of Elizabeth Howell, the magistrates conducted an inquest to investigate the dead woman's claim that Goody Garlick had killed her with witchcraft. You have just heard the story the witnesses told in their depositions. Judges in East Hampton had more experience than they wished with the rational conflicts of men over property, status, unseemly conduct and their rights and obligations. They had no experience with the capital crime of witchcraft, or with the secret world of womens' anxieties over the borrowing of breast milk and the uncanny causes they saw behind uncanny sicknesses and deaths and injuries to humans and animals.

All of the witnesses to Elizabeth's strange death testified, except for one. There is no record of a single word spoken by Lion Gardiner before the court.

Soon after the charge of witchcraft was made, Joshua Garlick filed a suit against Goody Davis for slandering his wife. Goody Davis was her most prolific accuser, although she never told her stories in court. The magistrates heard her stories secondhand in the testimonies of other women.[27] It is curious that Goody Davis was absent from Elizabeth Howell's deathbed, as she seemed to be present every other time there was an uncanny misfortune that could be attributed to Goody Garlick's maleficium. In fact, it seems that after the Davises moved into town, Goody Davis made her peace with Goody Garlick. The women remembered that Goody Davis had warned them that they would regret having Goody Garlick as a neighbor. When they asked about this new familiarity with her former enemy, Goody Davis said, Goody Garlick "brought many things to me . . . and is very kind to me," and, after all, "she were as good please the devil as anger him."[28]

Few men other than those who witnessed Elizabeth's strange death spoke at the inquest. These few testified after Joshua Garlick sued Goody Davis for slandering his wife. These men all said they had heard Goody Davis say that Goody Garlick had killed her baby with her evil eye, or that she believed Goody Garlick was a witch. One of these statements came from Lion Gardiner's employee, Goodman Vaile. He told the court that he heard Lion Gardiner comment that Goody Davis had killed her own baby. For the sake of a little wampum she had sold her breast milk and starved her baby to death. This secondhand description of Lion Gardiner's opinion is the likely source of the legend that Lion Gardiner defended Goody Garlick. We must consider, however, that discrediting Goody Davis is not the same as defending Goody Garlick, and that Gardiner did not offer the evidence himself. Because Vaile and the other men testified after Joshua Garlick filed his suit against Goody Davis, it is likely that they were offering evidence to support the Garlicks' charge of slander. Lion Gardiner's secondhand comment may have been offered by Vaile to support his own opinion that Goody Davis was a slanderer.

The motives of the women were clear. Apparently without prompting or guidance from the magistrates, they offered evidence of the harm, sickness and death of humans and animals that the alleged witch caused with her malevolent power. We have no record of the questions the magistrates might have asked, but we find no evidence that they attempted to coerce the witnesses to make their stories of maleficium conform to the theological and legal definition of witchcraft as Satanic conspiracy. This is probably the product of their lack of experience with the legal procedures relating to the crime of witchcraft.

What kind of evidence was sufficient to prove that Goody Garlick tormented Elizabeth Howell to death while she was not physically present? The magistrates were baffled. They wasted no time in asking the more experienced court in Connecticut to try the case. The town of East Hampton was obliged by a prior agreement to defer to the jurisdiction of the Connecticut Court in cases of capital crimes, but the magistrates seem to have forgotten in their panic, because they sent Lion Gardiner specifically to make these arrangements along with the two magistrates, John Hand and Thomas Baker, who were also responsible for accompanying the accused to Connecticut.[29]

In the Particular Court of Connecticut Goody Garlick was indicted with these words:

> Elizabeth Garlick, thou art indicted by the name of Elizabeth Garlick the wife of Joshua Garlick of East Hampton, that not having the fear of God before thine eyes thou hast entertained Satan, the Great enemy of God and mankind, and by his help since the year 1650 hath done works above the course of nature to the loss of lives of several persons (with several other sorceries), and in particular the wife of Arthur Howell . . . for which, according to the laws of God and the established law of this Commonwealth, thou deservest to die.[30]

Goody Garlick must have been terrified. Colonial laws against witchcraft called for the death penalty by hanging. The Connecticut court had already tried at least eight prior cases of witchcraft since 1647. It is likely that there were many more accusations than those for which records survive because the officials of the court complained that many who were charged with capital crimes fled to Rhode Island to escape prosecution.[31] In only two of the known cases did defendants escape death by hanging. One woman was released; the other may have escaped.[32] All of the accused were women, except one man who was accused along with his wife.

Goody Garlick was probably imprisoned for the intervening time, between her inquest in East Hampton and her trial in Connecticut.[33] We may assume there were some witnesses from East Hampton, but we do not know who they were or what they said as the records of the trial are lost.

Voluntary confession was the most conclusive evidence. Although the New England legal code expressly rejected the use of torture, defendants were subjected to considerable psychological pressure to confess. In the later trials in Salem, defendants were able to save their lives by confessing; only the recalcitrant and unrepentant were hanged. No such deal was struck in the other colonial courts. Still, most of the accused provided the judges and juries with the hard evidence they needed to make a conviction by confessing. It is tempting to condemn legal officials for pressuring defendants to confess. But, how else were they to prove that spectres harm people, or that the misfortunes they were asked to prosecute were related in any demonstrable way to the intangible malevolence of witches? They would, of course, wish to base their life or death decision on some hard fact. They may also have had the noble motive of giving the accused the opportunity to redeem their souls by confessing their crime.

The second most reliable evidence—after confession—was evidence of a distinctive mark on the body of the accused. "Witchmarks" were believed to be of two types. The witch's familiar spirits were believed to come to a teat on the witch's body, generally in some secret place, to suckle. The court would also post a guard to watch for the appearance of the familiar when it came to the witch to be fed. Also, the Devil was believed to distinguish his witches with other marks on their bodies. These were described as being "entirely bloodless and insensitive, so that even if a needle be deeply thrust in, no pain is felt and not a drop of blood is shed." [34] These, too, were expected to be in the secret parts. The examination for these marks would amount to torture. We know that a committee of women was assigned to examine another accused witch, Goody Knapp, in Connecticut. Goody Knapp was convicted and hanged largely because of the evidence of the witchmarks the women were able to produce. [35]

Then, there was the ordeal of the trial. Rather than explicit torture, New England judges preferred the more gentle—though insidious—persuasion. They interrogated accused witches in such a way as to put them into a state of confusion to elicit a confession. Defendants in criminal cases were not entitled to legal counsel. The only guidance available to the accused was that of the very judges who would attempt to confuse them to elicit a confession.

The case was heard in the Particular Court of Connecticut in Hartford, probably on May 5, 1658 by seven magistrates including the governor, John Winthrop, Jr., along with a jury of twelve men. This was Winthrop's first witchcraft trial. It is unlikely that Goody Garlick confessed, and we have no records to let us know if a witch's mark was found on her body. Failing that, the courts relied on legal treatises to

The frontispiece to Matthew Hopkins' The Discovery of
Witches, *1647. A "witch-finder" appears with two
witches and their familiars.*

establish proof. It is likely that the Connecticut court relied on one
written by Michael Dalton.[36] Imagine that you are members of the jury.
Would you have found Goody Garlick guilty of witchcraft according to
these standards of proof?

First, it was necessary to establish that witchcraft was the cause of
death, rather than natural causes. If the following conditions were present, it indicated the presence of witchcraft:

1. When a healthful body shall be suddenly taken without
probable reason, or apparent natural cause.

2. When two or more are similarly taken in strange fits. *The
depositions of the inquest would have informed the judges
and jury that during Goody Simons' fits black spectres—presumably Goody Garlick's cat—had similarly appeared and
her fits worsened.*

3. When the afflicted party in his fits tells truly what the witch, or other absent parties are doing or saying or the like. *This evidence was provided also.*

4. When the parties shall do strange things, or say strange things, and yet when out of their fits know nothing of what they did or said.

5. When there is a supernatural strength such that a strong man or two shall not be able to keep down a child, or weak person upon a bed. *Arthur Howell apparently had this difficulty restraining Elizabeth.*

6. When the party doeth vomit up crooked Pins, Needles, Nails, Coals, Lead, Straw, Hair, or the like.

7. When the party shall see visibly some Apparition, and shortly after some mischief shall befall him.[37]

If the judges were satisfied that Elizabeth died of witchcraft rather than natural causes they would consider the evidence to decide if the accused was responsible for the witchcraft.

The criteria included testimony that the accused had appeared to the sick party in his or her fits; and that the afflicted was able to name the suspected witch, and to describe their actions.[38]

As it turned out, the Connecticut court did not find sufficient evidence to deprive Goody Garlick of her life. But, they didn't acquit her either. In fact John Winthrop, Jr. commended "the Christian care and prudence of those in authority with you in search into ye case according to such just suspicions as appeared."[39] The court required that Joshua Garlick post a hefty bond to assure his wife's good behavior, and Goody Garlick was required to appear periodically before either the East Hampton court or that in Connecticut.

Why didn't the court convict Goody Garlick? The officials of the court and the witch's accusers were speaking two different languages. For her accusers witchcraft is maleficium, that is, "harmful magic," like the uncanny harms and deaths they attributed to Goody Garlick. However, according to Puritan orthodoxy, and the laws based on it, no human was capable of such supernatural harm without Satan's help. The legal definition of witchcraft as Satanic conspiracy is explicit in the text of the indictment, "thou hast entertained Satan, the Great enemy of God and mankind."[40] But the fine points of Puritan theology were the business of learned gentlemen, not tenant farmer's wives.

Although the witnesses failed to mention Sabbath gatherings or pacts with the devil, they did provide some suggestive evidence that the court chose to ignore. Goody Simons and her friends said they had seen the strange black thing that made them think of Goody Garlick's cat. That might have qualified as evidence that the witch had a familiar spirit. Goody Simons found the pin in Elizabeth's mouth.[41] Others testified that they saw it and that no such pin had been in the house before. Goody Davis had made that suggestive remark that "it were as good to please the devil" in reference to Goody Garlick. But the court didn't consider that sufficient evidence; in fact they appear to have followed Goody Davis' lead.

Although they agreed that the suspicions of witchcraft were just, they chose the conservative course. They preferred not to risk angering the devil—not to mention, God—for killing a person whom they could neither adequately prove guilty or innocent. Instead, John Winthrop, Jr. advised that the people of East Hampton should deal with Goody Garlick and her husband as best they could. Winthrop wrote: "We think good to certify that it is desired and expected by this court that you should carry neighborly and peaceably without just offence to [Joshua] Garlick and his wife and that they should do the like to you."[42]

This could have done nothing to reassure Goody Garlick's accusers back in East Hampton. The court had confirmed the suspicions then sent the accused witch back to them—vindicated! That Goody Garlick got off with what they must have considered a technicality must have made her appear invincible.

According to the legend, Goody Garlick was saved by Lion Gardiner, the father of her alleged victim. Although he was a powerful and influential man, we must be reluctant to assume he would attempt to subvert the legal process in Connecticut. It is possible that he did not want his opinion to be on the record. On another occasion the East Hampton court agreed to destroy the records of the case involving charges that Joshua Garlick had slandered him in exchange for payment.[43] Would he ask the Connecticut court to protect his privacy in the same way?

Gardiner was well acquainted with the judge of Goody Garlick's trial, John Winthrop, Jr. It was Winthrop who brought Gardiner to Connecticut to build a fort at Saybrook. They maintained a cordial and productive relationship throughout their lives.

If Gardiner attempted to protect his privacy in the public records of the Connecticut court, his efforts were wasted. All of the records of the case were lost, leaving us with no idea of what he might have thought, said or wanted. We have nothing except his servants' report of his opinion on the death of Goody Davis' baby. Gardiner was probably skeptical of the women's belief in maleficium, as all pious educated men should be. However it would have been heretical to deny the reality of Satanic conspiracy, the night-flight of witches, or the reality of their animal familiars.

Puritans read the manner of death as a sign of the status of the soul. A difficult death was not necessarily proof of unworthiness, because grace could come at the final hour to the elect. However, the description of Elizabeth's death that we find in the court records gives us little hope that a blazing epiphany of saving grace ever came. This may have interested Lion Gardiner much more than witchcraft. If God had allowed Satan to use Goody Garlick to torment his daughter to the very last moment of her life, Gardiner would have had to consider the possibility that his daughter was not among the elect, and that her soul was not welcome in heaven. He had a lot at stake in believing that this was not so. Perhaps this accounts for his silence on the issue of witchcraft.

In fact the Connecticut court's response to the charges against Goody Garlick was consistent with their treatment of a similar case. The only other witch who escaped conviction in that court prior to Goody Garlick's trial was Katherine Palmer. The wife of John Robins accused Katherine Palmer of tormenting her with witchcraft. Robin's husband entered this complaint on his wife's behalf.[44] Women didn't bring their own complaints to the court in Connecticut, either. Evidence of complicity with Satan was absent from the accuser's complaints, just as it was absent from the complaints of Goody Garlick's accusers.

Katherine Palmer's case was a very early witchcraft trial in Connecticut. Perhaps this inexperienced court, like that of East Hampton, was not yet adept at persuading witnesses to modify their stories of maleficium to conform to the charges of Satanic conspiracy that the court required for conviction. Katherine Palmer's husband was also required to post a bond for his wife's good behavior, just as Joshua Garlick was. The court's only justification for usurping a man's control over his own wife's behavior was proof of her complicity with Satan. Evidence that women harmed others by supernatural means was not sufficient.

Some scholars believe the witch hunts were a conspiracy against women.[45] Most of the accused were women. We believe this is because it is more difficult to believe monstrous accusations about others who resemble ourselves. In many ways males and females are inscrutable to one another. The gentlemen of the court treated men differently on those rare occasions when they were accused of witchcraft. Men were not subject to the same pressures to confess, and when they did confess, they were almost all rebuked as liars. Their penalties were generally a whipping or a fine for telling a lie. Apparently the gentleman of the court found difficult to believe a person of their own gender was capable of being a witch.[46]

Why might the gentlemen of the Connecticut court find it difficult to believe that Goody Garlick was such a monster? Most of the women who were condemned to death by the gentlemen of the Connecticut court were servants, poor women, or widows who inherited more wealth than it was then deemed appropriate for a woman to command. Many of them confessed to making a pact with Satan because he gave them, in exchange, the easing of the burdens of their labor, or gifts of such comforts as they could not hope to acquire otherwise.[47] Goody Garlick didn't conform to this pattern, which probably made it harder for the gentlemen of the court to believe she was the kind of woman who could be guilty of witchcraft.

It requires an impressive act of the imagination to feel empathy for a stranger, or someone who does not resemble oneself. It is also difficult to imagine that someone one know personally can be capable of the uncanny powers of the witch. Unless the misfortune in question is one's own. One's own misfortune almost always seems uncanny. In that case, it is tempting to suspect someone who knows us well enough to have jealous motives and exaggerate the power of their malevolent intent. Such was the case with Goody Garlick's accusers. Unaffected persons—including the magistrates, judges and jury— were either not interested, or found it difficult to understand or believe the womens' complaints or their explanations for them.

This appears to be the way the witch hunts ended in Europe and the colonies. When individuals who resembled the judges and members of the jury in status or religious affiliation came before them, they suddenly became incapable of believing in witchcraft and the trials ground to a halt. It didn't stop people from accusing their neighbors of maleficium. After the courts refused to investigate such claims, the accusers took the punishment of the witches into their own hands.

This has been explained as an issue of class. We think it is more personal and intimate than that. It is easier to be empathetic to those we know and who resemble ourselves, so long as they do us no personal harm. To the extent that we are able to think of others as different from ourselves, it is easier to believe the most uncanny things about them, particularly if we have something to gain by believing it.

Goody Garlick's judge, John Winthrop, Jr., was well acquainted with her husband, Joshua. We have no evidence of his opinion of either of the Garlicks. However, we know that Gardiner provided Winthrop with valuable goods, including livestock and wampum. The intermediary in these exchanges of goods and payments was Joshua Garlick. The fact that Winthrop relied on Joshua Garlick's honesty in these exchanges would have made it difficult to believe that his wife was capable of the uncanny powers attributed to witches.

Not many women showed up for their trials as Goody Garlick had, flanked by some of East Hampton's most eminent townsmen, Thomas Baker, John Hand, and Lion Gardiner. These men may not have been supportive of her; they had come to establish a relationship between East Hampton and the Connecticut court. But the fact that they all showed up with Goody Garlick could hardly fail to make her humanity recognizable to the gentlemen who served as her judges and jury.

The coincidence of Goody Garlick's trial with John Winthrop, Jr.'s first appearance on the bench was sublime good fortune. Winthrop was a Puritan whose profession of saving grace is on record.[48] He was also a philosopher, natural scientist, and a member of the Royal Society in London. He was a physician who often treated the poor for free. He was described by his friends in these ways: he is "a gentleman in everyway lovely and full of love;"[49] "You are a man most curious and able, and of a nature prone to pardon."[50]

Winthrop's intervention in another witchcraft case provides further evidence of his forgiving nature. Several years after Goody Garlick's trial, Elizabeth Seager went so far in conforming to the legal definition of Satanic conspiracy as to tell the court she sent Satan to tell them she was no witch. She was found guilty of complicity with Satan in 1665. A year later John Winthrop, Jr. called a special session of the Court of Assistants, to review her case. The court, over which Winthrop presided, reversed the conviction and ordered her "set . . . free from further suffering and imprisonment."[51] She was, however, advised to leave town.

Winthrop was notoriously patient, even with the Quakers who met the most extreme oppression in the colonies. The law required that their hands be cut off for merely entering a settlement. Winthrop had an unusual capacity to recognize the humanity not only in those who resembled him in gender, status and religious beliefs, but all humans. After Winthrop's brief tenure on the bench, convictions for witchcraft resumed in the Connecticut court.

We believe that Goody Garlick was the only person ever accused of witchcraft in East Hampton, and one of the few who escaped the death penalty because the fledgling court of East Hampton knew its limitations. They had no established preconceptions about what evidence was admissible for the crime of witchcraft. They did not encourage the witnesses to modify their story of maleficium to conform to the legal definition of witchcraft as satanic conspiracy. With few exceptions the witnesses were women and their complaints related directly to female concerns with their responsibilities as wives and mothers. These were alien to the male business of the court. Without hesitation the court honored its prior agreement to refer capital cases to the more experienced Connecticut court.

Goody Garlick was fortunate that her humanity was recognizable to the men who judged her, and that her judge was an exceptionally forgiving man. However, the women back home must have realized, after the Connecticut court sent the problem back home to them, that they could hope for no help from the legal system for their very different anxieties and conflicts and that it was best to try to resolve them in the same way they defined them, among themselves. They must have come to better understand Goody Davis' comment, "it is better to please the devil than anger him." Goody Davis made her peace with Goody Garlick, and never bothered to try to explain her distinctly female problems to the men of the court.

Did they really go peaceably with the Garlicks as the Connecticut court recommended? We find no evidence in the court records that they had serious problems with the Garlicks. But we have seen that women's business is mostly invisible to the courts. And when they did bring their complaints they didn't translate well to the male language of the law. Perhaps if the women brought their problems to the court, as women do now, the ratio of court cases to the size of the population might have more closely resembled those of 1997.

Both of the Garlicks lived long and prospered. One of them lived to be 100 years old, and the other nearly as long. Goody Davis died within a year of her former enemy's trial. Goody Simons moved away. Goody Edwards persisted in her arrogant, sottish, and aggressive ways. But no one thought to accuse her of witchcraft. After the failed attempt to convict Goody Garlick, the men, as well as the women in East Hampton seem to have decided that with Goody Edwards, too, it was better to follow Goody Davis' advice: it is better to please some people than anger them, even if they seem like the devil.

NOTES

1. We wish to thank the East Hampton Historical Society for their support of the initial research, the members of the 350th Anniversary Committee who chose to include this paper in the lecture series, and the Maidstone Arms for underwriting this presentation.

2. Zwingli, De Providentia, CR 93:99, in Susan E. Schreiner, *The Theater of His Glory; Nature and the Natural Order in the Thought of John Calvin*, Michigan; Baker Books, 1991: 118.

3. The following summary of the Puritan world view is based on the following sources. Karl Barth, *The Theology of John Calvin*, (transl. Geoffrey W. Bromiley), Grand Rapids, Michigan; William B. Eerdmans Publishing Company, 1995 (orig. 1922); Edmund S. Morgan, *Visible Saints; The History of a Puritan Idea*, New York; NYU Press, 1963; Perry Miller, *The New England Mind; The Seventeenth Century*. Cambridge; Harvard University Press, 1967.

4. All details of the story come from the records of the inquest regarding the charges of witchcraft against Goody Garlick unless otherwise indicated. Most of the depositions were taken between February 24, 1657 and March 11, 1657. *Records of the Town of East Hampton*, Volume 1, Sag Harbor, New York; John H. Hunt, Printer, 1887: pp. 128–155.

5. This vision was recorded by the Puritan diarist, John Hull. He was a merchant, silversmith, mint-master, who also served as the treasurer of the Massachusetts colony. "Diary," *Transactions of the American Antiquarian Society*, 3 (1857), p. 218.

6. Perry Miller, *The New England Mind*, pp. 25–30.

7. It is possible that Goody Elizabeth Garlick was the descendant mentioned in the will of William Blanchard, a French Huguenot. The will mentions "sister Garlick's children." That Blanchard's "sister Garlick" was Elizabeth Garlick, wife of Joshua, cannot be proven, however, Demos' exhaustive archival research uncovered no other person bearing that name. John Putnam Demos, *Entertaining Satan: Witchcraft and the Culture of Early New England*, New York; Oxford University Press, 1983 (orig. 1982), p. 233, n. 51 p. 470.

8. The action for defamation is entered jointly by Lion Gardiner and William Mulford. The court record explicitly states that Gardiner entered the action against Simons; Mulford entered complaints against both of the Garlicks for "scandalous speeches against the wife of the said plt. [plaintiff]" It appears that the case ultimately involved offenses against Gardiner, or his wife, because the case was settled by an agreement between Gardiner and Joshua Garlick. The two men posted a bond of ten pounds to assure that neither of them would "stirr in this Accon [action]" again. The court them agreed to "cross" the action; it is crossed out in the original. This may indicate that the case was closed, as many entries are crossed out in the original. Because the intention to "cross" was mentioned in the record, and because the details of the case are, in fact, missing, it may mean

the records were deleted at the parties' request. The entry is made July 3, 1654. RTEH, Vol. 1, pp. 58-59.

9. Entry dated 1653. *Records and Files of the Quarterly Courts of Essex County, Massachusetts*, 9 vols., Salem, Massachusetts, 1911-78, Vol. I, p. 58.

10. EHTR Vol. I, 1651, pp 21, 1653, pp. 35-36.

11. EHTR Vol. I, 1653, pp. 35-36.

12. Ibid.

13. Davis' story of the evil eye was given in testimony by Goody Birdsall.

14. Tobin Siebers, *The Mirror of Medusa*, Berkeley; The University of California Press, 1983.

15. Diane Purkiss, "Women's Stories of Witchcraft in Early Modern England: The House, the Body, the Child," in *Gender and History*, Vol. 7 No. 3 November 1995, pp. 408-432.

16. Goody Hand's testimony at the inquest of Elizabeth Howell's death. RTEH Vol. I, p. 135.

17. Goody Edwards testimony at the inquest of Elizabeth Howell's death, RTEH Vol. I, 134.

18. Among the notorious masturbators was the unfortunate Goody Davis' husband, Faulk Davis. He was punished with both the pillory and a public whipping. Two of the other men were also publicly whipping. For John Hand Jr., who was the son of one of the magistrates who decided the case, no punishment is mentioned. The proceedings are recorded for 1654, RTEH Vol. I, p. 57.

19. RTEH Vol. I, February 12, 1656, pp. 104-105.

20. Personal communication, The Honorable Catherine Cahill, Justice of The East Hampton Town Court, May 1998.

21. It was common practice to baptize the children of Puritan parents who had demonstrated saving grace with the expectation that by the time the children reached maturity they would demonstrate their own elect status. Most of the baptized children never received saving grace by the time they were mature. Judging from surviving records, Edmund S. Morgan says it was uncommon for second generation Puritans to have the requisite religious experience before they were in their twenties. Often it came much later and many never received it. *Visible Saints, History of a Puritan Idea*, New York; New York University Press, 1963, pp. 126-27.

22. Paul Boyer and Stephen Nissenbaum, *Salem Possessed*. Cambridge: Harvard University Press, 1974.

23. Simons deposed that Elizabeth demanded that they send for Goody Garlick three times. EHTR Vol. I, p. 130.

24. The retrieval of the pin was mentioned in the testimonies of two of the women who were present (Goodys Birdsall and Edwards), but not by Simons.

25. It is interesting that Simons never testified that she saw or found the pin in her depositions. The appearance of the pin is described in the

testimonies of both of the other attendants at the bedside, Goodys Birdsall and Edwards. Edwards also testified that to "her best Rememberance," Mary Gardiner said that there was no such pin in the house [before]. RTEH Vol. I, p. 139–40.

26. Gordon E. Geddes, *Welcome Joy; Death in Puritan New England,* Ann Arbor Michigan; UMI Research Press, 1981 (orig. 1976), pp. 21–34.

27. Goody Davis was Goody Garlick's most prolific accuser, although she never appeared at the inquest. Her tales appeared secondhand in the depositions of six of the fourteen witnesses: Goodys Brooks, Hand, Edwards; Thomas Talmage, Richard Stratton, and Goodman Vaile and his wife. Most of her stories were reported by Goody Hand. Edwards, Bishop, Birdsall, Talmage and Richard Stratton also deposed to hearing this story from Davis. The latter two deposed the information four days after all the others had deposed and Joshua Garlick had entered an action of defamation against Davis. The men may have been offering support of the action taken against Davis for defamation by Elizabeth Garlick's husband Joshua, rather than for the purpose of offering evidence against Elizabeth Garlick. Joshua entered his action of defamation on behalf of his wife on March 15, 1657, four days before the town inhabitants voted to send Elizabeth to Connecticut for trial. No other evidence is recorded about the case in the intervening year. EHTR, pp. 152, 154.

28. Goody Hand's testimony at the inquest concerning Elizabeth Howell's death, RTEH, Vol. I, p. 135.

29. At a Session of the General Court in Connecticut, November 7, 1649 it was recorded that East Hampton "shall be accepted and entertained under this government according to their importunate desire," (p. 200) It appears the people of East Hampton wavered in their enthusiasm over this arrangement, or the obligation to pay their fees to the court, because the General Court of Election in Hartford recorded the intention to send a letter to the people of East Hampton advising them that "it can be no advantage, but rather the contrary, to their divided shattered condition, not to have dependence upon or be under some settled jurisdiction, and therefore advise them so to do, and to pay what is their just dues to this commonwealth." (May 17, p. 274) J. Hammond Trumbull, *The Public Records of the Colony of Connecticut, Prior to the Union With New Haven Colony, May 1665,* Hartford, Connecticut; Brown and Parsons, 1850. The East Hampton magistrates instructed Thomas Baker and John Hand to Connecticut along with Lion Gardiner to "to bringe under their Government acordinge vnto the termes as Southampton is and alsoe to carie vpp Goodwife Garlick yt she may be delivered vp unto the Authoritie . . ." RTEH, Vol. I, March 19, 1657, p. 140.

30. *Records of the Particular Court of Connecticut, 1639–1663,* Hartford Connecticut, 1928, p. 188.

31. R.G. Tomlinson, *Witchcraft Trials of Connecticut; First Comprehensive Documented History,* Hartford Connecticut; The Bond Press, 1878, p. 6.

32. Louis J. Kern, "Eros, the Devil, and the Cunning Woman: Sexuality and the Supernatural in European Antecedents and in the Seventeenth Century Salem Witchcraft Cases," in *Perspectives on Witchcraft; Rethinking the Seventeenth-Century New England Experience* (A Selection of Papers From the Tenth Salem Conference), The Essex Institute Historical Collections, Vol. 129 No. 1, January 1993.

33. Joshua Garlick was charged by the Connecticut court for their transportation to and from Connecticut. Letter from John Winthrop Jr., IN J. Hammond Trumbull, *The Public Records of the Colony of Connecticut,* pp. 572-73.

34. Nicholas Remy, *Demonolatry,* ed. Montague Summers (1595; reprint, London; John Rodker, 1930), p. 9; C. Tomlinson, *Witchcraft Trials of Connecticut,* p. 6.

35. Tomlinson, *Witchcraft Trials of Connecticut,* p. 6-9; Demos, *Entertaining Satan,* p. 191.

36. Michael Dalton, *The Countrey Justice,* first published in 1618 and reprinted several times in the next 100 years. Kern, "Eros, the Devil, and the Cunning Woman," p. 67, see especially n. 13.

37. Dalton, *The Countrey Justice,* p. 385.

38. Ibid.

39. John Winthrop, Jr., In J. Hammond Trumbull, *The Public Records of the Colony of Connecticut,* pp. 572-73.

40. See above, n. 30.

41. See above, n. 25.

42. See above, n. 33.

43. See above n. 8.

44. Tomlinson, *Witchcraft Trials,* p. 4.

45. See, especially, Barbara Ehrenreich and Deirdre English, *Witches, Midwives, and Nurses; A History of Women Healers,* Westbury N.Y.: The Feminist Press, SUNY, 1973 (Second Edition, Fifth Printing).

46. Carol F. Karlsen, *The Devil in the Shape of a Woman; Witchcraft in Colonial New England.* New York; Vintage Books, 1989 (orig. 1987), pp. 51-52.

47. Ibid. P. 127, n. 34.

48. John Winthrop, Jr.'s conversion experience occured in the context of John Cotton's religious revival in Boston in 1634. John Winthrop, Sr. recorded it in his diary. Morgan, *Visible Saints,* n. 61 p. 98.

49. Winthrop's surviving commissioners' eulogy. U.C. commissioners to Leete and the Connecticut council, April 5, 1676, ms. copy inserted in Pulsifer, ed. *Colonial Records, Plymouth Colony,* X, blank page 468, copy in The Connecticut Historical Society.

50. Henry Oldenburg, in a letter of March 10, 1672/2, *Manuscripts of the Winthrop Papers,* 16.40, Massachusetts Historical Society.

51. *Connecticut Colonial Probate Records, vol. III: County Court 1663-1677* (Connecticut State Library, Hartford Connecticut), leaves 35-36, 52.

THE EMPIRE STRIKES BACK ON THE EAST END IN 1674

The Military and Political Contest for
Dominion of the East Riding Townships
during the Third Anglo-Dutch War

Donald G. Shomette

FRANCIS LOVELACE was an affable fellow, noble of mind and tolerant of most religious creeds. As the governor of New York, however, he was, as one chronicler aptly put it, "a follower in beaten paths, rather than a trail blazer." And as a military commander, he was totally incompetent. By the summer of 1673, Lovelace had been chief executive of the former Dutch city of New Amsterdam, and the colony it dominated, for five years, but during that time his accomplishments were as limited as his leadership was insipid. When major issues of substance arose, he was but a shuffler content to fall back on established political protocol and the tactics of procrastination.

In 1669, his first crisis in office erupted, incredibly enough not among the predominantly Dutch population of New York City, but among the English towns of Long Island. The most serious problem arose when various townships asserted in unison that they possessed the right to annually elect their own legislators. Some even challenged the very commission by which Lovelace held his office. The issues of taxation, representation, and land ownership formed the core of conflict. In 1670, that contention was nearly brought to a head by a tax levied to pay for needed repairs to Fort James, the main defense works for New York City. Lovelace was soon fending off serious opposition from such towns as Jamaica, Flushing, and Hempstead, which had declared the assizes to be in direct conflict with British law and the citizenry's right to elected representation. By 1672, and the outbreak of war with the United Provinces of the Netherlands, the fort still lacked

132

the necessary repairs. The governor, who had begged off meeting the dissension head on, was again moved to secure funds. This time, however, he compromised and requested not a tax, but a voluntary contribution from each town to pay for the needed work. The English settlers of Long Island were disgruntled that their moneys were to be used almost entirely for the improvement of the defenses for the city of New York, whose population was primarily Dutch and who did little to support the war effort. Predictably, their response was negative.

The towns of Long Island complained that they were taxed more heavily than those of their New England neighbors—and without benefit of representation in court by deputies. Many claimed that they were forced to comply with unfair laws imposed by haughty officials who insulted and threatened them. Some towns even indicated they would rather be transferred to the jurisdiction of neighboring Connecticut or to be made free corporations rather than continue in their present harness. And throughout the maelstrom of discontent, Francis Lovelace and the English citizenry of the colony of New York, wrapped up in their own bickering, failed to tend to their defenses.

The Declaration of War against the United Provinces was not published in English America until May 26, 1672, and Governor Lovelace, fearing upheaval amongst the Dutch citizenry of New York, would delay publishing the proclamation until June 27. Yet, for the next six months the colony continued on as normal: no Dutch army or navy appeared to wrest control of the colony from England, and a false sense of security enveloped the office of the chief executive.

Then, on January 22, 1673, Lovelace informed Governor John Winthrop of Connecticut that reports from Virginia had come in stating that the Dutch had dispatched upwards of forty well fitted ships to the West Indies. If such information was to be relied on, he suggested, "it will be high time for us to buckle on our armor." Despite his manful talk, however, Lovelace still did little to improve defenses.

Throughout the early months of 1673, the colony suffered from frequent invasion scares. Though he displayed little fear of the Dutch, Lovelace prudently summoned to New York 350 English troops stationed at outposts on both the North River and on the Delaware—only to dispose of them when the purported crisis was over. Fort James was now garrisoned with only eighty soldiers. Yet, Lovelace's confidence in the colony's safety was apparently total. Indeed, he saw no harm in leaving New York to visit with his neighboring governor of Connecticut, John Winthrop. In late July 1673, he set off for Hartford to confer with Winthrop on business related to a recently established postal route between New York and Massachusetts Bay. He could not have picked a more inappropriate time to leave the colony, for it was precisely at that moment, when New York was militarily defenseless and without its chief executive, that Commanders Cornelis Evertsen the Youngest of Zeeland and Jacob Benckes of Amsterdam appeared off Sandy Hook with a strong fleet, and a desire for reconquest of the former Dutch colony of New Netherlands.

The Evertsen expedition had its origin in a plan conceived by the hard-pressed government of Zeeland, nearly bankrupt by the war in late 1672. According to the plan, a small squadron of warships would sortie with the secret mission of seizing the island of St. Helena, off the coast of Africa, as a base from which to attack ships of the English East India Company as they returned from India around the Cape of Good Hope. The purpose of the expedition was to obtain as much profit with the least cost to Zeeland, and at England's expense. As a secondary alternative, should the first objective become impossible to achieve, the squadron was to inflict as much damage as possible upon the English and French colonies in the Western Hemisphere as possible, commencing with the Guianas in northern South America and extending through the Caribbean and along the North American coast to Newfoundland. Evertsen sailed with six ships on December 5, 1672, but unexpectedly encountered a British squadron, coincidentally sent out to intercept the homeward bound Dutch East India Company fleet. After a short battle off the Cape Verde Islands, Evertsen elected to pursue his secondary mission. After bringing his fleet to Fort Zeelandia at Paramaribo, Dutch Surinam for refitting, by May 1673 he was ready for his raid on the Americas. As Dame Fortune would have it, off the island of Martinique, the Zeelanders encountered another Dutch squadron, this one under the command of Captain Jacob Benckes, from Amsterdam, that had been preparing to conduct its own sortie against the enemy colonies. Joining forces, the two commanders were soon raging through the Windward Islands, attacking English and French forts, settlements, and merchant fleets as they went. With varying success, they attacked Montserrat, St. Christophers, Nevis, and St. Eustatius before turning their prows northward. In early July, they entered the Chesapeake Bay, defeated a British Navy squadron, captured seven rich tobacco ships and destroyed ten more. Among the prisoners taken had been Captain James Carteret and Samuel Hopkins of New Jersey, who had been connected in quarrels with the Lords Proprietors of New Jersey. The dissident Carteret and Hopkins, expelled from the colony, readily divulged information regarding the weak state of New York and the poor condition of Fort James and its garrison. Evertsen and Benckes acted swiftly. New York would become the next target of their terrible swift swords.

The approach of the Dutch fleet was discovered on July 28, well before it had come to anchor off Staten Island. Indeed, it was Thomas Lovelace, the governor's brother, who had scurried "against tide, through a swelling sea" in a log canoe to bring the terrible news to Fort James. There he found, in his brother's absence, one Captain John Manning in charge as acting governor. Half a dozen large ships, it was reported, had been sighted from Sandy Hook. And there was every reason to suspect that more were coming up.

The arrival of the enemy caught Manning at a particularly bad moment: the fort was without sufficient manpower, tools, or arms. Many of the heavy guns mounted on the walls were pointed toward land, not the sea, and the platforms and carriages of most were broke or beyond repair. Beyond perhaps half a dozen guns, effective firepower was almost nonexistent.

All available troops in New York City, approximately ninety in number, were ordered into the fort. All seamen in port were directed to board their ships in the harbor. Provisions, beer, liquor, and "other necessarys" to withstand a siege were brought in. Warrants were issued to the officers of the various militia units on Long Island, primarily among the English towns, "to get their companies together and immediately repair to the garrison." At the same time another order was issued "to press Horse and man to go to Hartford" to inform Governor Lovelace of the situation. If the governor could be warned and the neighboring province of Connecticut stirred to come to New York's assistance there might be a fair chance of holding out. By the morning of July 29, a total of twenty-one sail could be counted in the lower bay. Morale in the tiny garrison plummeted.

In the afternoon, when several giant frigates glided through the Narrows and came to anchor under Staten Island, the entire town stood enthralled "in a strange hurly-burly" by the waterside. Some townsfolk spent the time in moving their goods out of the city, while many English citizens thought "no place so safe for their storage as the fort." Beacons were fired to warn those still unaware of the impending danger. Apparently, Manning failed to attend to the protection of other areas of the city defenses, preferring to reserve his limited manpower for the walls of Fort James. That night, a party of Dutch saboteurs from the city spiked the guns in a battery known as the rondeel near City Hall.

On the following morning, the garrison at Fort James prepared to meet the enemy, though the fleet spread before them under the red, white, and blue flag of the United Provinces of the Netherlands was the largest ever seen in the harbor. Rumors had been freely circulating about the fort, but by far the most chilling story was that there were as many as 3,000 men aboard the warships.

Across the waters, the Dutch fleet awaited the flood tide to carry it within firing range of the fort. Six hundred troopers were selected for the landing, a mixture of Dutch and expatriate English marines well-seasoned and capable of working efficiently together. Their commander was Captain of Marines Anthony Colve, a most competent soldier of considerable experience on both land and sea.

The delay caused by the tides provided the expedition commanders with an appropriate moment to formally extend the official demand for surrender to the governor of Fort James or suffer the consequences of "immediate action on both water and on land."

Within a short time, a flag of truce had boarded the Dutch flagship *Swaenenburgh*.

"What ship are you and by whose order have you come into the river that belongs to the Duke of York?" the English envoys demanded.

"You can see very well from the flags and ships who we are," replied the Dutch commander with severity. "We have come to bring the country back under obedience to their High Mightinesses the Lords States General, and his Serene Highness the lord Prince of Orange under whose government this once was." Evertsen then informed the envoys stiffly that his commission "was stuck in the muzzle of the cannon, which they would quickly learn if the fort was not handed over." If surrender was not forthcoming within a half hour, the fort would face a violent assault by land and sea.

Then, even as the envoys departed, the Dutch cleared their decks for action and began the disembarkation of the 600 marines for the final assault. Ashore, the five-score defenders of Fort James locked the gates and stood to their defenses. Theirs was a forlorn hope at best.

The halfhour passed without incident. Then two guns were fired to leeward as warning shots to announce that the grace period was over. Suddenly, the flagship opened with a broadside, an action soon imitated by every ship in the fleet. The cannonade was instantly returned in kind by the fort. Amid the choking smoke of gunfire, Colve's landing boats picked their way across the river like so many bugs upon the water.

As the exchange of fire continued, it became apparent that the fort's guns were not well-served, even though after the initial broad-side they had managed, by one report, to shoot *Swaenenburgh* "through and through." For an hour, however, both sides continued the fight, though one by one Manning's guns collapsed on their platforms. Many of the defenders began to consider their position hopeless, al-though a few maintained a staunch determination to resist to the end. One brave soldier, flourishing his sword in defiance, leaped upon the wall by the English flag, fully exposing himself to the heavy Dutch fire, promptly had his head shot off, and collapsed into a bloody heap. Out-gunned, outmanned, and fearful of an uprising of the Dutch burghers of New York, Manning ordered up the flag of truce and "beat a parley" even as Colve's hardened veterans bumped ashore on the banks of the North River, just above Governor Lovelace's gardens and orchards near the site of present Trinity Church. The town's Dutch citizenry flocked to the river's edge "to welcome them with all the demonstrations of joy they could make." As the troops marched down the Broad Way, they were encouraged to storm the fort by no less than 400 ebullient burghers, many of whom were themselves armed and eager to join in the fray.

At the appearance of the powerful enemy land force beneath his battlements on one side, and with the already proven devastating power of the Dutch fleet on the other, Manning had little choice. The fort was surrendered with the full honors of war.

Evertsen and Benckes had soon taken control of the works, which were renamed Fort Willem Hendrick, and in so doing had secured the keys to the colony of New York. The two Dutch commanders moved quickly to consolidate their military control over New York, which was promptly renamed New Orange on July 31.

Even as the garrisoning of the fort was carried out, Evertsen moved to prepare for another operation-an attack on the great English New-foundland [Terre Neuf] fishing fleet, which Zeeland authorities had in-cluded in the secret instructions months before. Four ships, were immediately provisioned for the operation.

As the days and weeks that followed would attest, Cornelis Evert-sen and Jacob Benckes were increasingly viewed by the majority of Dutch inhabitants of New York, and even those in New Jersey and Delaware, as liberating heroes. Yet most Dutch citizens, true to their oaths of nine years earlier that they would bear no arms against any na-tion, had awaited the outcome of battle before making their true senti-ments known. That their oath of loyalty to England contained the clause "whilst I live in any of his Majesty's territories," however, permitted all to absolve themselves of charges of violations of good faith. New York, and soon New Jersey and Delaware, could no longer count themselves as belonging to his majesty's territories. Evertsen and Benckes were well aware that the Dutch citizenry's support would be imperative in the days to come if their victory was to take hold and particularly if it were to be implemented over the strategic towns of eastern Long Island.

The weeks following the surrender of Fort James and New York were filled with hectic activity for the Dutch victors who moved quickly and resolutely to consolidate their immediate gains. They were well aware that if they were to secure their flanks to the north, east, and west, they would be obliged to extend their activities and influence well beyond the confines of the city. The initial step would have to be political, beginning with the total dismemberment of the English administration of Francis Lovelace. To accomplish this, they required the allegiance—or at least the tacit neutrality—of the citizenry, first of New York and then of the surrounding areas.

The two Dutch commanders, their confidence soaring, now boldly resolved to restore not only New York to its founding masters, but indeed all of the Netherlands' former dominions on the Mid-Atlantic coast, and more. A seventy-man expedition was dispatched up the Hudson to Fort Albany to retake the settlement there (Beverswyck during the former Dutch administration), and the so-called "colony" of Rensselaerswyck as well.

Despite its originally limited objectives, Evertsen's raid on America had become something far greater than anticipated. It had become, almost overnight with the recapture of New York, a mission of liberation of all former Dutch American dominions from English rule.

The establishment of a provisional Dutch government became the paramount goal of Evertsen's and Benckes' agenda during the first days of August. If New Orange were to remain in Dutch hands, it would require a stable Dutch government. Thus, on August 2, the able Captain Anthony Colve was appointed military governor-general pro tem of the province and commander of Fort Willem Hendrick. A Council of War moved quickly to re-establish the province's mainland boundaries as they had been defined by the English's Hartford Treaty of 1670 between Connecticut and New York. But now they boldly added to that claim all of Long Island as well as the proprietary of New Jersey and Delaware, which had formerly been part of the Netherlands' American holdings.

The Council was methodical in its institution of a Dutch form of civil government in New Orange and the dismantling of the former regime. The old city magistrates and municipal officers were formally released from their oaths of allegiance to King Charles II and the Duke of York taken nine years earlier under duress of conquest. The city seal, mace, and magistrates' gowns were duly surrendered by Mayor John Lawrence. An election was scheduled to select candidates for the offices of burgomasters (magistrates), schout (sheriff), and schepen (aldermen).

There were still the many towns surrounding Manhattan to the south, to the east on Long Island, across the North River to the west, and on the mainland to the north to be dealt with. Staten Island, the settlements of New Jersey, and those on the Delaware had to be attended to as well, lest a nucleus of opposition be formed to challenge the renewed Dutch presence on the North American mainland. The five Dutch towns on Long Island—New Utrecht, Brooklyn, Bushwick Inlet, Amersfoort, and Midwout—and the single English town of Gravesend had welcomed the conquerors of New York almost from the moment of their arrival. The English towns of Easthampton, Flushing, Hempstead, Jamaica, Newtown, Oyster Bay, Southampton, Setauket, Huntington, and Southold on Long Island, West Chester and East Chester on the mainland to the north, and Staten Island to the southwest, were another matter. The Council of War ordered these places to send two deputies each to tender formal submission to the Netherlands. Each of the deputations from these enclaves of potential resistance, particularly from the towns to the east of Oyster Bay, such as Easthampton, were then directed to nominate by general election candidates for schout, secretary, and schepen, from which the Council would make the final selection. By August 29, even the most recalcitrant English village, Southampton, which had pleaded in vain with New England for help, had delivered up its constables' staves and English flag and submitted nominations for the prescribed offices.

Dutch authority was easily imposed over the flanking English colony of New Jersey with equal aplomb and remarkable celerity. The rights and privileges guaranteed to New Jersey were also accorded Flushing, Hempstead, Jamaica, Middleboro, and Oyster Bay on Long Island and West Chester on the mainland, and eventually all of the towns, including Easthampton, lying within the now substantial Dutch orbit. They too were obliged to accept allegiance to the Netherlands and to nominate a slate of schouts, schepen, and burgomasters. On August 19, the Council learned that all of the towns along the Hudson Valley as far as New Albany, including the vast wilderness establishment of Rensselaerswyck, had submitted to Dutch rule. Two weeks later, on September 2, a deputation from the Delaware, or South River, region presented its credentials to the Council and readily offered submission. It was an almost flawless and orderly transition from English civil government to a traditional Dutch form, and without a drop of blood being shed.

The Council of War, of course, refused to extend its good will or largess to the Netherlands' foes, the kings of England and France, or to their subjects who continued to "injure, spoil, damage and inflict all possible loss and obstructions" upon the subjects of the Prince of Orange and the Lords States General. They were to be treated with an iron fist and, from the Dutch point of view, justifiably so. Reparations and satisfaction for losses incurred in the transfer of government from the Stuyvesant administration nine years before, had long been sought, but in vain. Now that would all be rectified.

Needless to say, the nearly bloodless conquest of New York, and the submission of the surrounding territories, created considerable consternation in the neighboring colonies to the north. But in nearby Connecticut, the concern was borne not so much out of fear of attack as for the loss of territory that Governor Winthrop had been laboring to annex to his own colony. For quite some time he had nurtured hopes of securing a toehold on the eastern end of Long Island, where long smoldering dissension against the Lovelace administration had all but exploded in open rebellion even before the Dutch invasion. Winthrop had gone so far as to conduct discussions on the matter with numerous key figures, and towns such as Southampton were inclined to support his efforts. Now, he realized, if the invaders successfully extended their authority over the whole of Long Island, under treaty terms at the end of the war it might revert back to the crown and the Duke of York. With the weak Lovelace regime certain to be replaced, any hopes of annexing, or receiving the region through intercolonial or proprietary treaty, would likely evaporate.

On August 17, Winthrop summoned his government into an emergency session at Hartford. The governor's best intelligence estimates, supplied by his son FitzJohn Winthrop, suggested that "the Dutch had landed 3000 men upon Manhatas Island." Such estimates, although far from accurate, nevertheless greatly influenced Connecticut's attitude in dealing with the foe. As all were probably aware that the colony could not hope singlehandedly to confront such a powerful enemy on such short notice. Connecticut needed time to organize and time to secure assistance from her more powerful and populous neighbor to the northeast, the Massachusetts Bay Colony. Thus, Winthrop's strategy was one of preparing for war while winning time in the name of peace. A Grand Committee was appointed with powers to recruit troops and requisition ships, animals, or other means of transport. Simultaneously, the Assembly dispatched two deputies, James Richards and William Roswell, to New Orange to lodge official protests with the invaders on behalf of the "united colonyes of New Englant," and to assure the invaders that peace was their only desire.

Significantly, one of the major thrusts of the unilateral protest—though it was not couched as such—did not concern the conquest of New York at all, since "the chiefe trust of those parts reside in other hands," but the submission of the lands east of Oyster Bay, including Easthampton. The principal occasion for discussion was provided by a minor protest concerning the Dutch seizure of a vessel belonging to a Connecticut citizen close to one of that colony's harbors. It was intended, however, only as an excuse for Connecticut to assume the mantle of an injured party in the negotiations that followed.

Richards and Roswell had arrived late on August 13 at Fort Willem Hendrick and dutifully presented Connecticut's formal letter of protest drafted by colony Secretary John Allyn. They informed

> the Commanders that, as they [Connecticut] had remained at peace in the time of the previous Dutch government, even in a season of war, they, on their side were equally disposed thus to continue without molesting this Province, or making use of any act of hostility against it. On condition that nothing be undertaken to the prejudice of their Colony from this side [New Orange], it certainly will not first attempt anything hostile; in case such should be committed against them by this Province, they thus protest themselves guiltless of the blood that may be shed in consequence.

Incredible as it may have seemed, the colony of Connecticut appeared to be offering the peace of a neutral state, unilaterally and without consulting the crown, with the Netherlands. New Jersey and Delaware, were one thing, but Connecticut was another matter, though it now appeared on the surface of it all that she wished only to be left alone. When the envoys were requested to provide the proposals in writing, however, they refused, claiming they lacked the authority. The negotiations were almost instantly terminated.

On the following day, the delegates were given a short and uncompromising reply drafted by Secretary Nicholas Bayard to be carried to Hartford. Evertsen and Benckes, the terse note read, were authorized by the States General of the United Netherlands and the Prince of Orange "to doe all manner of damage" to their enemies on land and sea. Long Island, formerly an English dominion, now belonged to the Netherlands and would thus revert to Dutch administration. As for the matter of the villages of that island, which lay east of Oyster Bay, they had been directed to take a loyalty oath "to prevent certain unpleas- antries." Those failing to do so would be subjected to force of arms, as would those (such as Connecticut it was implied) who "urged" them to do so.

The warning to Connecticut was clear: hands off the East Riding townships.

Evertsen and Benckes worked tirelessly to bring New Orange into a state of military readiness and to strengthen the backbone of de- fense, Fort Willem Hendrick. With the departure of the Newfoundland squadron, there were four warships, a fireship, and a snaauw left at New Orange. Only after the fort was in an advanced state of readiness would the two commanders sail to rendezvous with the Newfound- land squadron at Fayal in the Azores and return home. On August 22, the small pinnace *St. Joseph*, a prize taken in the West Indies, was dis- patched for Europe with Evertsen's report and a list of arms and mate- rials needed for the fort and the defense of the colony. But it was imperative that the fleet soon follow before the winter gales threat- ened the completion of their missions.

By late August, as word leaked that the fleet was preparing to leave, many in the city became disturbed over the prospect of aban- donment. On August 27, a city delegation met with the two comman- ders at Fort Willem Hendrick to plead with them to remain. The two commanders agreed to leave Captain Colve behind as commander, and the twenty-five-gun ship *Suriname* and the *snaauw Zeehond* until help arrived. The citizenry nevertheless, penned a petition to the gov- ernment of Zeeland, outlining the commercial value and virtues of the colony to the fatherland, and requesting assistance for the loyal Dutch citizens. Evertsen reinforced their plea with a letter of his own. Both letters were sent home aboard a prize bus called *Expectation*, under the command of Captain Maerten Jansse Vonck, a former privateers- man. Unfortunately, neither *St. Joseph*, which had been sent home a few days earlier with news of the capture of New York, New Jersey, and Delaware, or *Expectation* would ever reach the Netherlands.

Then, on September 11, the combined Dutch fleet finally de- parted, much to the sadness and considerable anxiety of the loyal citi- zenry of New Orange.

Colve's situation was one of some discomfort, and certainly one filled with uncertainty. The possibility of attack from New England or even England was undoubtedly uppermost in his mind. Fort Willem Hendrick and the harbor batteries were in a forward state of repair thanks to the efforts of Evertsen and Benckes. However, he could not long concentrate solely upon the improvement of the defenses of New Orange, for the governmental house of cards established with such ease by Evertsen and Benckes, backed by the big guns of their ships, had already started to wobble. Upon the departure of the fleet, several of the villages on the eastern end of Long Island, or the East Riding of Yorkshire as the region was then called, had begun to vigorously reassert their disdain for Dutch rule. Several, such as Easthampton, displayed a marked disaffection for the New Orange administration, nurtured in no small measure by Connecticut in their increasingly rebellious attitudes. In late September, Colve received the first of a series of unwelcome intelligence reports concerning the East Riding towns, and several even closer to the central Dutch orbit. An agent provocateur sent from Connecticut with orders from that government "to raise men for theire accts in the sd towne, etz, and the Like Seditious Words tending to Meuteny," was discovered in Hempstead. As a consequence, the town's inhabitants were refusing to take the oath of allegiance.

The failure, in fact, of many of the inhabitants of the East Riding towns to swear allegiance, and the proclivity of some to temporize, posed considerable danger to the Dutch administration. Disaffection and incitement to rebellion, sowed by Connecticut, might well result in appeals for intervention. Immediate address was imperative. On September 21, the governor commissioned Captain Willem Knijff (Knyff), Lieutenant Antonij Malepart, and clerk Abraham Varlett to travel to the villages east of Oyster Bay, call town meetings at each place visited, and administer oaths of fidelity to the inhabitants. That there be no grounds for contention, provisional instructions were dispatched to the schout of the East Riding district and to each town's magistrates. The instructions were to be posted and detailed the manner in which civil government was to be carried out.

On October 9, a dejected delegation returned to New Orange from the East Riding towns. For Colve, their report was depressing, if not unexpected. The commissioners visited all of the towns east of Oyster Bay as ordered, including Easthampton, called for town meetings, and tried to administer the oaths of allegiance. But with the exception of Oyster Bay, where the oath was taken, and Huntington, where the inhabitants requested to be exempted from the oath but promised fidelity in writing, all of the towns refused to cooperate. Southampton, the seat of opposition, outright refused Colve's instructions.

The inhabitants now refused to acknowledge any sovereign but the king of England, but promised to live in peace "Soe long as wee are not Molested by them [the Dutch] nor any other from or vnder them Vnlesse Called thereunto by his Ma[jes]ties Power of England." Southampton's stance was at least consistent in its vigorous opposition. Soon after having been summoned by Evertsen and Benckes to submit to the new Dutch government, the town had appealed to Hartford for aid. While Connecticut listened, Southampton "received no Incouragement to stand out of our-selves although they favored us so farr as to consider our Condition." The town had then appealed to the Boston General Court in a message delivered by one John Cooper, "a resolute man," who proposed that with but 100 armed men, all of the towns of Long Island could be brought back into the English fold. The New Englanders "wholly refused to engage the country in the undertaking." Failing to garner support, the town issued a declaration, addressed to all of the English colonies, explaining their situation and why they were being forced to acquiesce to the Dutch. Now, with a breath of support from Connecticut, Southampton had gained new resolve.

The citizens of Southold also refused to follow Colve's directives, claiming that they thought the oath was only intended for the schout of the East Riding and the magistrates of every town, and that for each of the inhabitants to be required to take it would deny them freedom of conscience. They were upset by the orders to seize all debts belonging to the subjects of the king of England. But of equal import, the town had been obliged to dismantle its former government as they had initially agreed to after the conquest, yet in the interval had not instituted a replacement and was without any form of protection. The town, claimed the inhabitants, was vulnerable "to the Invasion of those who threaten dayly wth ye spoiling our goods." They informed the commissioners that Southold was willing to submit "during the prevelince of your Power over us" only if a firm and peaceful government was permitted, which would provide protection from "ye Invasion of those wch Dayly threaten us." Though the inhabitants of Southold did not identify just who might conduct such an invasion, it was undoubtedly apparent to Colve that they feared reprisals from Connecticut or their neighboring bastion of anti-Dutch sentiments, the town of Southampton.

Easthampton refused outright to accept Dutch authority, preferring to be "regulated by our fformer Lawes and that authority is resident amongst us." Though unwilling to recognize Dutch sovereignty over itself, this town too, requested to live only in peace. Like Southold,

Easthampton feared English reprisals should it enter the Dutch fold. The inhabitants informed the commissioners that they could not "but bee Sensable of the great danger wee are in boath from those that are neere home So well as those abroad of Our owne Nation." Indeed, the town's own security depended upon maintaining its former allegiance. Significantly, Colve learned soon after the receipt of Easthampton's official response that it had been sent to New Orange by a messenger who had passed through Southampton. There, the letter was intercepted, opened, and examined by opponents to the Dutch regime. The document was then read "wth severall Railing Expressions," whereupon the messenger suggested that another be sent in its place, which was done, and which Colve had accepted as the authentic reply. Late on the evening of September 23, having learned of the interception, Easthampton constable Thomas Dyment and Recorder Thomas Tallmage dispatched a second letter, informing the New Orange government that it was "not the first time wee have had our letters opened & stopt at Southampton and many threatening Expressions have proceeded from severall disaffected persons there wt Respect to our Submission to your governmt that we have yeilded Unto."

Setauket also claimed only a strong desire to live in peace, but was equally intimidated and could not "bear eup alone against the prevaling sense of Neighbouring Townes." Thus, at a town meeting held on September 27, the inhabitants voted to preserve their allegiance to the king of England.

Huntington's citizens requested that they be excused from taking the oath on the grounds that they had never been under the Duke of York's authority in the first place, had never sworn an oath to him, or, for that matter and with few exceptions, to the king of England. The Netherlanders had but two enemies, they said, England and France, "& against ye Frensch wee are Resolved . . . to defend our Selves against there tirrany." But if the English arrived, they would remain neutral "till forced to doe other waijes." The town asked for a trial period of one year of independence under their own laws. If in that time Colve saw "Cause and Cleer foult" in their peaceful relations, they would swear allegiance. They wished neither allegiance with their neighbors of the East Riding country, they stated, nor with the Dutch to the west, but sought only to "Stand of our Selves."

Perceiving that the attitude of English Long Island ultimately could readily degenerate into military confrontation, Colve sought to determine exactly where the government of New Netherlands stood with the Dutch population there, most of whom lived quite close to his base of power. He summoned the schepens from Midwout, Bushwick Inlet, New Utrecht, Amersfoort, Brooklyn, and Gravesend. Would they observe the oath of allegiance which they had taken, asked the governor? Would their patriots be willing to come to Manhattan in case of attack to resist the common enemy? "They had no doubt," replied the schepens, "but it will be done by the entire people."

Colve, reinforced by the support of the Dutch citizenry, now ordered that another delegation be sent to call upon the Long Island towns of Huntington and Setauket to try and secure the oath of allegiance from the inhabitants. Three days later the envoys returned to New Orange in triumph, for both towns had reconsidered their positions and complied. Distant Easthampton, Southampton, and Southold, the triumvirate of dissension, would be far more difficult. On October 20, Colve commissioned Councilor Cornelis Steenwyck, Captain of Marines Carel Epesteijn, and Lieutenant Carel Quirinssen to travel to the three towns and secure their obedience and allegiance, "to the End I may not be forced to use such meanes as would tend to the ruine & greatest Damage of some of them."

This time the commissioners employed the warship *Zeehond* to make the trip swiftly, and to remind the settlers of the military force available to the Dutch at New Orange. On the issue of allegiance, Colve was now prepared to bend slightly. If "great objections were made to the oath" the inhabitants of the three towns were to be permitted to merely promise obedience, although magistrates would be required to swear allegiance. In the event that there was obstinate refusal to both oath of allegiance or promise of obedience, the inhabitants were to be publicly informed that "they will be the cause of their own ruin." The commissioners were advised to collect the names of the chief mutineers in writing and return without delay to New Orange.

In the meantime, across Long Island Sound, Connecticut prepared to contest the Dutch efforts head on.

On October 21, the governor and General Court of Connecticut wrote Colve a scathing and accusatory letter. It was not, the Connecticut government haughtily wrote, "the manner of Christian and Civill nations to disturb ye poore people in Cottages & open Villages in times of warr or to impose oaths upon them." Having heard of late efforts in the East Riding country urging his majesty's subjects to take an oath contrary to their allegiance to their actual sovereign, and "to use many threatning Expressions towards them in case of the Refusall of such an oath," Connecticut expressed disbelief that Colve could have commissioned such actions. He could only have done so, they assumed, "to attaine some plausible pretence for Plundering & pillaging." If such were indeed to occur, they warned, it would be the Dutch farms and villages that would suffer. If Colve continued to pursue the issue of forcing allegiance on the Englishmen of Long Island, they threatened, the English colonies would "not make it their worke to tamper wth your peasants about sweareing but deale wth your head quarters."

Colve indignantly replied that the Long Island towns had first submitted to the new Dutch regime upon favorable conditions, surrendered the English colors and constable staves, and selected new magistrates. Had "evilly disposed" persons from Winthrop's colony not interceded, they would have peaceably taken the oath of allegiance. It was well known to everyone, he added scornfully, how much more gently the Dutch treated vanquished enemies than the English.

Undismayed, the Steenwyck Commission set off on their perilous mission to Southold, Southampton, and Easthampton aboard Captain Eewoutsen's *Zeehond* on October 21. Their voyage would be fraught with many disappointments, storms, and dangers. Finally, at daybreak on October 27th, after having survived a hurricane at sea, a near shipwreck, and repeated delays, Plum Gut, on the eastern end of Long Island, was sighted as was a sail to leeward. Supposing it to be a West Indiaman, and thus fair game, Captain Eewoutsen raised English colors to mislead her, set his courses, and hoisted his topsails. The tide being against the unidentified ship, she quickly came to anchor near Shelter Island. *Zeehond* came to also, having cornered her prey in shoal water, lowered the English flag and hoisted the Prince's colors, whereupon the second vessel instantly lowered her own in submission.

It was soon discovered that the vessel had come from New London bearing none other than Governor Winthrop's own son, Captain FitzJohn Winthrop, and one Samuel Willys. It was then learned that they bore commissions from the government of Connecticut, which they promised to later show the Dutch, and a letter addressed to Governor Colve. Steenwyck, Epesteijn, and Quirinssen displayed their own commissions, together with evidence of the initial petition and agreement between the East Riding towns and the Dutch government of New Orange.

During this unexpected parlay, Winthrop and Willys argued that because a single article in the surrender agreements, regarding the freedom of the East Riding towns to procure weapons for the whaling industry, had been refused, all articles of the agreement between the Dutch provisional government and the Long Island towns "had been rendered null & void."

The following morning, October 29, Winthrop and Willys dispatched a copy of their commission, as promised, to the Dutch. It could not have failed to excite concern among the members of the Steenwyck Commission. The commissioners had been ordered to go over to Long Island or Shelter Island to treat with whatever forces they might meet there, and endeavor to divert the Dutch from any hostilities against the inhabitants. They were authorized to warn the Dutch that if they continued to proceed, "it will provide us to a due Consideration what wee are Nextly obliged to doe."

The letter for Colve was also delivered to the Dutch commissioners. In it, Connecticut requested that the Dutch abandon their voyage and all efforts to persuade the English of Easthampton, Southold, and Southampton to take the oath. The Dutch commissioners responded that they were duty bound to carry out their commission. Both Dutch and English commissioners would now vie directly for the support of the inhabitants of Southold.

The Steenwyck Commission set off for Southold late in the morning, somewhat behind their English counterparts. About 2:00 P.M. both boats neared the town about the same time. The Dutch commissioners, however, were dismayed to hear drum beats and a trumpet sound, and to observe a salute with muskets fired when Winthrop and Willys passed. Fearful of landing, but obliged to go ashore owing to low water and the turn of the tide, the Dutch discovered a troop of cavalry riding back and forth along the beach in front of them. As their boat bumped ashore, four of the horsemen rode toward them and offered them mounts. The commissioners accepted and were soon met by Willys and Winthrop and a troop of twenty-six to twenty-eight men on horseback. Together they rode toward Southold, passing, en route, a company of sixty menacingly armed men. Entering the village, they proceeded to the house of one Thomas Moore. Steenwyck quickly called for a town meeting to inform the citizens of the reason for his visit and to present the commission from the Dutch government.

Winthrop and Willys presented their case first, stating that the citizens of Southold were subjects of the king of England and had nothing to do with any orders or commissions of the Dutch. "Whosoever among you will not be faithful to his Majesty of England," they challenged, "your lawful Lord and King let him now speake."

The Connecticut commissioner's challenge was answered by a wall of silence.

Steenwyck then spoke, reminding the citizens that they were the subjects of the Lords States General and the Prince of Orange, as evidenced by their colors and constable staves, by the nomination of their magistrates presented to the governor, and the election of said magistrates afterwards. The elected officials from Southold were called, but only one appeared, but only to resign from office. The schout for the East Riding district was then summoned, but also resigned his commission, "having been already threatened by the inhabitants that they would plunder his house." Dismayed, Steenwyck turned to the assemblage and asked them directly if they would remain faithful to the States General and take the oath. Again, a dead silence pervaded the meeting.

The commissioners now directed that Colve's orders be read, that there be no mistaking the potential consequences of the course they were taking. Winthrop and Willys interceded, loudly stating that the inhabitants were subjects of the king and had nothing to do with a commission from the Dutch. The Steenwyck Commission, it was quite clear, was faced with overwhelming and intractable opposition, skillfully led by the Connecticut Commissioners, and enforced by the fear of reprisals against those who dared support the Dutch. Nothing further could be done. The Dutchmen resolved to leave Southold and visit Southampton the next morning.

As the Dutchmen prepared to depart, they were verbally accosted by a group of English inhabitants of the East Riding country led by a firebrand named John Cooper (the same that had served as Southampton's emissary to Boston). Cooper warned Steenwyck, in no uncertain terms, that he "take care and not appear with that thing at Southampton."

What was meant by the word "Thing?" questioned Steenwyck.

"The Prince's Flag," spat Cooper.

Did he speak for himself, or on behalf of the authority of the inhabitants of Southampton, asked the Dutchman.

"Rest satisfied," retorted the Englishman, "that I warn you and take care that you come not with that Flag within range of shot of our village."

What village *did* they intend to visit the next morning, queried the Connecticut Commissioners? It mattered little what answer was given, however, for Governor Winthrop's men quickly informed the Dutchmen that they would also be in attendance, "as they intended to be present at every place the Commissioners should visit."

Intimidated, rejected, and dismayed by the obvious influence of the Connecticut men over the Long Islanders, the Steenwyck Commission, perhaps wisely, resolved that a visit to either Easthampton or

Southampton would prove fruitless, if not dangerous, and returned to New Orange.

The atmosphere of crisis in New Orange was all pervasive, but kept in check only by the stern leadership of Governor Colve and the hope that reinforcements might soon arrive from the Fatherland. Unfortunately, the crises was destined to degenerate even further before it got better. The most serious news was that of the stranding in enemy territory of *Expectation*, one of the two vessels sent out for home in the fall of 1673 with dispatches and appeals for help. Indeed, the wreck of the ship not only caused Dutch morale in New Netherlands to plummet, but also set in motion a chain of events that further threatened the security of New Orange.

The seeds of the new crisis were planted in early November 1673, when the city learned that the little vessel that had departed for the Fatherland on September 2, lay dismasted and helpless near Nantucket, Massachusetts. Colve immediately sent Captain Eewoutsen in *Zeehond* to aid the crippled bus. He returned with disheartening news but also with four English prizes in hand. The stranded *Expectation* had been captured on November 3 by a Boston privateer brigantine commanded by one Captain Thomas Dudson. Captain Vonck and his crew were safe but being held prisoner in Boston. In reprisal, Eewoutsen seized the first New England vessels that crossed his path and returned with them to New Orange.

The capture of *Expectation* and the enemy's interdiction of the letters and the emissary she carried meant much to the potential survival or collapse of the colony. And unbeknownst to Colve, the second vessel sent out to the fatherland, the *St. Joseph*, had also been taken by an English privateer. The English colonies, and the home government in England were now informed of the state of Dutch morale, strength, and the condition of the colony, but the Fatherland was still blissfully unaware that New Netherlands was even in Dutch hands.

Boston was stung by the ship seizures. The New Englanders had long been jealous of the successful Dutch burghers in New York, and after the fall of the city had feared an attack on their own colony. Yet, the New Englanders, to avoid reprisals while a powerful Dutch fleet was on the coast, cautiously refrained from entering the fray when the town of Southampton requested armed assistance soon after the conquest. Some prominent Bostonians, such as Richard Wharton, however, were well aware of the danger if the Dutch were permitted to remain unmolested and to flourish. He urged, early on, that an "expedition to unkennel the enemy" be undertaken.

Boston had refrained from acting against the Dutch regime as much from hatred of the former Lovelace government as from fear, even when offered support by His Majesty's man-of-war *Garland*, to attack and reduce New York to submission. the New England magistrates replied that they would contribute to the expedition only if the province could be annexed to their government. Otherwise, they would rather the possession of New York remain with the Netherlanders "than to come under such a person as Colonel Lovelace who might prove a worse neighbor."

Massachusetts appeared content to let sleeping dogs lie. Now, with the *Expectation* incident, the situation changed radically. The seizure of the four New England ketches, they felt, demanded redress. The Boston government dispatched a protest and to demanded the release of the vessels. If the vessels were not released, the government threatened, "We doe declare our Selves bound & Resolved by ye help and assistance of god to Endeavour a full Reparation by force of Armes."

The gauntlet had been tossed, but the unwavering Colve refused to blink. New Netherlands would not yield.

Following the New Englander's ultimatum, Colve's administration of New Orange grew more strict with every passing day. With resolve, he authorized another effort to inform the States General, Zeeland, and Amsterdam of the situation. On January 1, 1674, the ketch *Hope* was dispatched with orders to sail for home as soon as wind and weather permitted. The governor then attempted to turn his full attentions to the dissident towns of the East Riding of Yorkshire.

Throughout the winter Massachusetts blustered mightily about action against New Netherlands, but could not decide upon a course. It was, in fact, Connecticut, spurred by the prospect of finally securing the East Riding country, that caused Colve the greatest discomfort. During the winter, FitzJohn Winthrop had finally been directed by his father to raise a force to physically secure and occupy the East Riding towns for Connecticut. Accompanied by several Massachusetts observers, Major Winthrop secured ready assistance at New London and Stonington for his mission across the Sound. Finally, in late February 1674, he sailed for Long Island, which was now fully prepared to accept Connecticut's dominion with open arms.

With a fair wind behind him, the major soon arrived at Shelter Island and then pressed on to Southold. He had no sooner landed there than a breathless post rider from Setauket arrived with an urgent dispatch intended for the local militia commander. The major was immediately informed that *Zeehond*, a ketch, and two sloops, then anchored near White Stone, were waiting the first fair wind to sail for Southold "to reduce or destroy" the towns on the East end of Long Island. Colve, it appeared to the English, was at long last going to attempt to make good his threat to punish the towns of the East Riding with fire and sword.

Winthrop quickly dispatched an express to the chief officer at Easthampton and to Captain Howell, the commander of the Southampton militia, to inform them of the impending danger, and to convene a council of war at Southold "for the preservation of these towns." Within hours, the three officers and the several observers from Boston were immersed in conference, discussing the best way to defend the provisions, which, it was learned, the Dutch intended to take on at Shelter Island. After due consideration, the Bostonians suggested that the officers totally ignore the provisions and concentrate their attention on the defense of Southold.

Howell was ordered to raise forty soldiers from Southampton. This force was to be ready to march at an hour's warning. The lieutenant at Easthampton was to raise an additional twenty men. With these mobile forces, Winthrop hoped to be in a condition to give the Dutch a warm welcome wherever they might land.

At 7:00 A.M., Sunday, February 23, FitzJohn Winthrop was informed that the snaauw, a ketch, and two sloops were within gun shot of Plum Gut, with a fair wind and tide to bring them in. The sudden appearance of the Dutch warships managed to startle everyone, especially the local inhabitants. They soon recovered their composure and the major immediately summoned the sixty militiamen from Southampton and Easthampton to Southold. The diminutive Dutch squadron did not press toward the town, but came to anchor off Shelter Island, landed fifty men and demanded provisions from Captain Sylvester, the proprietor of the island.

Captain Eewoutsen's flotilla remained anchored off Shelter Island throughout the night. The next morning, the fleet hove to off Southold. Eewoutsen anchored his flotilla in "an handsome order," and brought all of his great guns to bear, while preparing his men for a landing in force. Fearful of the bloodletting that appeared imminent, Sylvester beseeched Eewoutsen for permission to personally deliver the Dutch surrender terms to Winthrop. The captain agreed. Winthrop was soon informed that the enemy had come to demand "subjection" of the East Riding towns to the States General and the Prince of Orange. Upon surrender, it was promised, Southold would enjoy the same privileges that had been conferred upon the other towns of New Netherlands. Refusal would only bring swift and total destruction.

Upon receipt of the terms, the major quickly drafted a tart reply refusing surrender. Immediately, Eewoutsen began filling his sloops with men for the landing. Watching the Dutch motions, the major prepared to meet the enemy with an advance guard of fifty men. As the sloops prepared to press for shore, *Zeehond* opened the engagement with cannonfire. The English quickly replied in kind, the ball splashing harmlessly in the water near the snaauw's bow. Then commenced a flurry of small arms fire from both sides, accentuated now and then by cannon. The Dutch fire, "which fell thick" upon the English, however, did no damage, and the English fire accomplished little more than to splinter the sides of the warship. But for troops in open boats, Eewoutsen considered, the defender's fire was all too hot. Thinking better of conducting a costly assault on a town that would only continue to refuse subjugation, he called off the attack. Soon afterwards, he ordered anchors raised and all sail made for New Orange.

The Battle of Southold was to be the high water mark of Dutch efforts over the East Riding towns of Long Island, indeed, of the last days of Dutch empire on the American continent.

The battle at Southold, though preserving, perhaps strengthening, Connecticut's hold on east Long Island, had been for Major Winthrop a harrowing experience. But his dispatch, telling of the successful repulse of the Dutch, reached Hartford on March 1, giving his father and the Council much more about which to rejoice. The major was ordered to remain on Long Island "till at least these present motions of the Dutch be over." Reinforcements, he was told, were on the way. In fact, Connecticut had recently requested that the Massachusetts Bay colony send a man-of-war to clear the coast of the enemy's ships once and for all.

The governor of Connecticut's appeal to the Massachusetts Bay Colony for once did not fall on deaf ears. Unlike some in his government, Governor John Leverett had, from the outset, been a strong advocate of action to secure the East Riding towns. Yet the colony he governed was still mixed in its sympathies. Even after word of the skirmish at Southold arrived in Boston, Leverett was obliged to apologize to Winthrop for his colony's indecisiveness. On March 14, however, he informed Winthrop that help was on the way. The General Court had ordered two vessels to be outfitted as men-of-war. They were to secure the passage through Long Island Sound and "repress the present insolency of the Dutch." The court had further resolved that the ships would transport 200 soldiers for the defense of navigation and "to Joyne with our Confederates as matters may present." Two weeks later, Massachusetts was ready to field the two vessels, both fully outfitted and furnished with ammunition and provisions. The first of these vessels was the sixty-ton ketch *Swallow*, of Salem, with twelve guns and sixty men, and commanded by Captain Richard Sprague. The eight-gun, forty-man ketch *Salisbury*, similar in burthen to *Swallow*, was commanded by Captain Samuel Mosely. Massachusetts eventually surpassed its own objectives, for within a short time, a force of 560 foot soldiers and two troop of horse had also been raised. The Plymouth settlement followed with an additional 100 men for the cause of country and king.

The failure of the Southold expedition and the preparations of Massachusetts and Connecticut only added to the siege mentality of the Dutch. Colve no longer suffered any illusions as to which side the English of Long Island would take, even among those villages that had declared their allegiance. The walls of Willem Hendrick now bristled with 180 great guns, and by English accounts, the garrison numbered nearly 800 regulars and militiamen. New Orange would not be easily subdued. Colve informed the Dutch "out people" from the surrounding towns that they were to retire to the city on notice of the enemy's approach, but this time they were directed to come "provided with proper hand and side arms." Those who failed to come in at the first alarm would be considered traitors and enemies, and would be punished by death and the confiscation of their property. Departure from the city during such an emergency was to be punished in a like manner.

Colve labored tirelessly. But even as rumors circulated, the long feared attack on New Orange failed to materialize. Though many said Charles II was determined to retake the province by force, there were also whispers of a different kind in the air—whispers of peace. By the spring of 1674, however, few public officials placed any credence in the recurrent rumors of peace that filtered in from New England and Virginia, including Colve.

In an effort to keep the New Englanders, who were moving to dispatch their own naval force, off balance, Colve continued to field Eewoutsen's *Zeehond* as frequently as possible, sending her on patrols in Long Island Sound and along the coast of New England. In May the snaauw was sent into the sound specifically to raid enemy shipping. Sailing eastward along the north coast of Long Island, Captain Eewoutsen descended on the unsuspecting English like a fury taking many New England ships within sight of land, much to the dismay of Connecticut, Rhode Island, and Massachusetts.

While the Colve administration pressed on with defensive preparations and aggressive naval patrols, New England was beset and confused by contradictory rumors. On March 30, Governor Leverett informed Winthrop of the most recent account to reach his colony directly from London, which was a letter dated October 28, 1673—five months previously. By mid-April, hopes for the arrival of a naval reinforcement from England to retake New York had begun to falter, and New England's aggressive stance was noticeably calmed by mutterings that peace was in the offing.

Then, on May 7, a vessel arriving at Boston after a month's passage from Scotland, delivered the first positive news and a copy of the peace treaty between England and the United Provinces. New Netherlands was to be returned to English authority. Long Island and its myriad towns were to remain under the old regime. Furthermore, it was said that a frigate and four ships would shortly bring a new governor to New York. Colve was obliged to learn secondhand of the peace when he inspected a packet of seized letters. Yet, by mid-June, news of unquestionable veracity concerning the peace arrived in New Orange from New England. Coolly and methodically, the Governor General of New Netherlands prepared for the inevitable transition. On July I, the same day that Governor Anthony Colve read the Treaty of Westminster in New Orange, James, Duke of York, an ocean away, officially commissioned Major Edmund Andros "to bee my Lieut and Governour" of New York.

On October 9, 1674, Captain Hendrick van Tholl came to anchor before the austere walls of Fort Willem Hendrick, with instructions direct from the Raden of the Netherlands for Colve to surrender and vacate New Netherlands. On October 22, Edmund Andros arrived. Eight days later, on October 31, Anthony Colve formally relinquished the province of New Netherlands to Governor Major Edmund Andros in behalf of His Majesty of Great Britain, Charles II.

New York would remain under English dominion for the next 109 years. And the East Riding towns of Long Island would continue in their independent-minded ways forever after.

EAST HAMPTON
VERSUS NEW YORK

A Very Old Story

———⁓⁓⁓———

Robert C. Ritchie

IT IS NOT VERY OFTEN that a Californian is invited to tell New Yorkers about anything, especially their history.

Let me begin by wishing many happy returns to the community of East Hampton on the occasion of this notable birthday. Where I come from things are a little bit younger. Spanish explorers made few inroads into California and true settlement came during the eighteenth-century. As for the English, other than Sir Francis Drake, California lays no claim to an English settlement of this antiquity and there is much to suggest that Sir Francis Drake never made it further north than Baja California, but please do not report my heresy back to the Golden State. But 150 years ago the European intrusion began and the world would soon rush in. I hope that you can come to the Huntington and see our exhibit celebrating our notable birthday.

My topic today is the long struggle East Hampton waged to retain its autonomy from New York and while the title is not specific to the city of New York my intention is to discuss New York and New York City in part because during the colonial period they were hard to distinguish from one another, as New York City was the seat of government. Let me also add that I use the subtitle "a very old story" because I am an Early Americanist and there are other far more competent scholars who can chart the continuing need for the community to defend its interest in and against the state and the city after 1800, although as you will see I will verge into the nineteenth century at the end of my talk.

156

The communities of eastern Long Island and especially East Hampton fought long and hard to retain their independence—they were the community equivalent of the famous Greta Garbo line—"I want to be alone." Or at least alone with Connecticut. Yet there was always a degree of ambivalence in the plea for while asserting their independence the community knew that it also needed a relationship with a larger entity, nor were they intent on abandoning a relationship with their home country in England. These needs would keep them from truly trying to become independent; the goal was really the maximum leeway for the community and the ability to participate in making the laws that related to them. They also wanted a relationship with a larger entity of their choosing. As a small town at the edge of the wilderness they had a limited ability to maneuver, but that would not keep them from the struggle. In fact, if they had the knowledge of contemporary geographers who use central place theory they would not even have tried to fight against the inevitable as this theory makes it clear that any city that grew on Manhattan Island would dominate the area around it both economically and politically. We know of course that New York City has an extraordinary hinterland and if its greatest boosters are to be believed the whole of the country is in New York City's orbit. Well, what was the nature of the struggle between David and Goliath? Let me review the long contest.

East Hampton came to life as a result of the constant hiving out of New England. As colonist poured into Massachusetts Bay and decided that better opportunities lay further afield it meant that the islands south of New England would sooner or later attract their attention. Long Island beckoned and out of that movement would come the cluster of small, struggling communities that would include East Hampton by 1648. From the beginning they were not quite alone, as they had Native American neighbors, and more importantly a strong Dutch presence at the other end of the island. Of course they did not see themselves as being quite alone, for it was not their intention to reject their compatriots in New England. Their problem was that they had moved into a zone of contention between England and the Netherlands and between New Netherlands and Massachusetts Bay and Connecticut. Without going into detail, the towns could do little to affect this struggle as diplomatic and military wrangling between the European powers and their local representatives swirled around them. They could and did make their private arrangements with New Netherlands leaving them more or less alone, but beyond this they were pawns and had the additional problem of adventurers such as John Scot and John

Underhill playing on the international stage, to their detriment. In the end, in 1664, England would settle the matter by conquering New Netherlands and introducing a new era for the towns. By this time East Hampton was happy to be in Connecticut's orbit. Connected by a strong geographic, religious and economic relationship, East Hampton and the other towns sought and obtained a relationship with their near neighbor. This happy relationship would come to an end with the arrival of an English invasion force which conquered the Dutch and set out to put New England in its place. Richards Nicolls, the new governor of what was now New York, was commissioned with others to investigate many practices in New England and to assert the rights of the Duke of York who now claimed a colony that started in Maine, dodged around parts of New England, and then claimed everything between the Connecticut and the Delaware rivers. Long Island was in the dominion of the new proprietor and no matter how the towns pleaded their case and how Connecticut might bluster the elemental fact was that East Hampton was part of New York. The towns would fight against this and lay claim to rights, liberties and privileges in the new province. The struggle they fought was continuous. Rather than set it out in great detail, let me summarize the issues that came up with nearly every governor with whom they fought, up to Governor Robert Hunter.

With Richard Nicolls, the first governor of the new colony, the issues were immediate and visceral. He came representing a proprietor who cared little for participatory government and who ordered his new governor to create a highly centralized administration. For towns used to a New England pattern of town autonomy inside a system of representative government, this would hardly do. The towns would immediately appeal to Governor John Winthrop, Jr. of Connecticut for help, and while Winthrop was willing he could not defy Nicolls and the English government so the boundaries between the colonies were drawn up and Long Island fell to New York just as the Duke desired. The Long Island representatives involved in discussions with Nicolls, John Young and John Howell, refused to agree to this division and so they went home.

Nicolls agreed to meet the colonists, especially those from Long Island, at a meeting in Hempstead. This would be an unhappy occasion. He planned to attend with a frame of government and a set of laws; the townsmen expected to have a full consultation and for them if the best of all possible worlds transpired they would be returned to Connecticut. If this did not occur, they had a set of proposals—their lands to be

held in free and common soccage, elections for town officials, election
of the militia officers, no militia training outside the town, three court
sessions each year on their own grounds to try small cases, no rate, tax,
or levy without the approval of the "General Court," and so it went. Little of this figured in Nicolls' plans and as he reported "he mett with
great tryalls and exercises of Patience and some very disobliging persons whom I sought to satisfy both with reason and Civility." Civility
would not do it and there was no satisfying the men of Long Island.
While Nicolls might try to placate them in small ways there was no
hope of agreement on the basic nature of the government. In Nicolls'
plan there would be no representative government, taxes would be set
at the center by the governor and the council, they could elect their
own town officers but they were subject to the oversight of the governor's appointees in a new body, the Court of Sessions, they could only
nominate men as officers in the militia, nor were they given guarantees
as to their land. They were free, however, to return home and grumble—not too loudly—as much as they liked.

Taxes soon brought them back into conflict with Nicolls as he
sought to assert the rights of the Duke of York in order to gain the
funds needed for his government. In 1666 the protests from the pulpits
and by magistrates led him to complained to an officer that:

> "(you report that they say) they are inslav'd under an Arbitrary
> Power, and that I do exercize mor than the King himslefe can
> do, which is so high an imputation, that I can not suffer my
> selfe to be reputed or Blasted in the hearts, or by the Tongues
> of such false and malicious men therefore instead of writing to
> mee under the notion of some people say thus and thus, be
> think yourself of some particular Persons who do thus slander
> mee with a charge of no less weight than High Treason."

Nicolls was pained mightily but there was a limit to how far he
could go. What in the end could he do to East Hampton—quarter
troops there and in every other town on eastern Long Island? Hardly
likely, as they were needed to watch the Dutch who were still a large
majority of the population, so he had to swallow his bile and push as
far as he could go and learn to live with the feisty, independence
minded Islanders just as much as they had to accept the reality of their
situation. No matter how much they protested, petitioned, and complained New York was the proprietary colony of the Duke of York. Thus
an unhappy truce prevailed. Nicolls wanted order and they wanted
democracy. As Nicolls wrote to Lord Clarendon, "Democracy hath

taken so deepe a Roote in these parts, that the very name of a Justice of the Peace in an Abomination," but he at least had laid the foundations of "Kingly Government in these parts."

Nicolls did have some power to assert. When he arrived he had not guaranteed the land grants of any of the towns and so they had to apply for new patents. East Hampton complained, but submitted its patent for approval only because security of their lands was too important and they would deal with the devil to make certain of their claims. But when Nicolls granted salaries to the hated Justices of the Peace, East Hampton immediately led the protest. In the end the Justices lost their new salaries and the privilege of not paying taxes in their towns, keeping only a nice schedule of fees for their activities. Each side won something. And so it went. Nicolls would leave in 1668, licking his wounds and having accomplished much; the towns could jeer him off but with no hope of immediate change.

For four years Governor Nicolls struggled, rather successfully, to create a government for New York. His successor Francis Lovelace did not have to bear the burdens of imposing a new regime on the English towns, yet his administration was not free of conflict. His disputes with the towns were mostly over economic affairs rather than systems of government, although East Hampton and the other English towns never gave up the positions they had adopted—they merely bided their time.

Lovelace had to deal with many problems; perhaps the most bothersome was that of finance. He needed money to support the English garrison in New York City besides meet all the other costs of running the government. Slowly but surely he fell under the sway of the city merchants who could provide the wherewithal and the credit to keep affairs running. For their generosity the merchants demanded that they get something in return—nothing less than control over the colony's economy. Their little mercantile system centered on New York City which would be the main entrepôt for all goods leaving and entering New York. Whether it was wheat or pork or horses, they had to pass through Manhattan. To make things worse, prices were also set for goods of all sorts in a way that clearly favored the merchants, who were left to charge what they wanted for imported goods. But for East Hampton the most egregious sin of all was the attempt to control the whale oil trade. By this time the towns at the east end of the island had developed a successful whale fishery. Adapting Native American technique, hiring the natives, and adapting their own skills had allowed them to increase the industry significantly since the days when they could only claim the right whales that washed up on beaches. Now the numbers caught every year was increasing; the amount of whale product going off to Boston climbed year by year. The governors and the merchants were very much aware of this and wanted their share of the revenue. The result was a more aggressive policy. New customs agents were posted to the east end of the island with the intent to redirect the trade away from Boston and Connecticut toward New York City. Nothing could have created a more direct challenge to the town and its sister towns of Southold and Southampton.

Their protests boiled over in 1669. Prior to the Court of Assize that year the towns complained through a petition about the set prices, controls on the prices of imports, while advocating free trade in all ports, standardized English weights and measurements for the whole colony, and other matters, including the fact that there was no assembly. Lovelace more or less ignored them only conceding the standardized English weights. At the same time he posted an order that all wills had to be proved in New York City—the better for merchants to collect their debts. Tension remained high until the Assize of 1670 when the Court imposed even more controls on trade—hogs, for instance, could only be butchered at New York City—and a new tax was to be levied to repair the fort in the city. The new tax became the symbolic issue for most of the towns who sent representatives to a protest meeting that produced a petition representing the opinions of most of the towns on Long Island. Lovelace had the document condemned and burned in front of city hall.

East Hampton and its sister towns went much further than the other towns and had good cause to do so for Lovelace, enraged by the vehemence of their protests, had burned their petition and went on to invalidate their patents imperiling their control over town lands. Lovelace did agree to send a commission to treat with them although their instructions gave them little leeway to negotiate and they were empowered, if the towns were too recalcitrant, to call out the militia. No records survive this meeting but shortly thereafter the towns sent delegates to a meeting of their own where they were to discuss obtaining a new charter for the three towns. Rather audacious (one would think) but the towns were serious and followed through with a petition to King Charles that was referred to the Council for Foreign Plantations. The petition asserted that the three towns had:

> Spent much time and pains and the greatest part of their Estates in settling the trade of whale fishing in the adjacent seas, having endeavoured it above these twenty yeares, but could

not bring it to any perfection til within 2 or 3 years, last past, and it now being a hopeful trade at New York in America the Governor and the Dutch there do require ye petitioners to come under their patent, and lay very heavy taxes upon them beyond any of his (majesty's) subjects in New England, and will not permit the petitioners to have any deputys in Court, but being chiefe, do impose what Laws they please upon them, and insulting very much over the Petitioners threaten to cut down their timber, which is but little they have for casks for oyle.

The petition concluded by requesting that the towns be returned to Connecticut as it was closer or be given their own charter. The petition is a shrewd indictment of the government, particularly the sharp dig at the Dutch which they probable hoped would arouse sympathy for their cause. It was not very good politics. James, the Duke of York and brother to King Charles, sat as a member of the Council for Foreign Plantations and so nothing was ever heard of the petition again. The petition does reveal how tenuous was the relationship between New York and East Hampton and the other towns. They detested the new economic controls that were added to the other issues they already had such as no assembly and did not accept that the government of New York was a valid one. Nearly ten years of English administration had not reconciled them to rule from New York City so they would suffer on while beneath the surface tensions lingered ready to erupt.

Suddenly, in July 1673, a great opportunity befell East Hampton when out of nowhere a Dutch fleet appeared and reconquered New York for the Netherlands. What calamities might befall New York were just opportunities in eastern Long Island. The Dutch could have New York and threaten them, but this was just an opportunity to once again reach out to Connecticut and return to the New England fold. Their presumption was noted in New Amsterdam. The Dutch administrator Anthony Colve was not about to allow the towns to leave his control. Connecticut warned the Dutch to leave the towns alone, but Colve insisted that they take an oath of allegiance which the towns refused to do. By the time a second set of envoys was sent out to insist the towns take the oath they were confronted by Sergeant Major FitzJohn Winthrop and the Connecticut militia who repelled them in a haze of gun smoke that produced no injuries. The Dutch party retreated while the English celebrated their victory in the battle of Long Island. Connecticut became more brazen by warning off the Dutch from interfering with the towns while the Dutch could do more than turn up the heat of the rhetoric.

Unfortunately for East Hampton reestablished New Netherlands was a mere pawn in a much larger international chessboard and one that was easy for the Dutch government to surrender, so in 1674 by treaty they gave up all rights to the colony and it would never again be an issue between them and the English. The Duke of York reestablished his position as proprietor and sent over Sir Edmund Andros to carry on his government. Long Island came back into the orbit of New York. Not that this deterred the doughty townspeople. Having returned to their beloved Connecticut they were not about to accept the "tyranny" of New York. Some Long Island towns banded together with Jamaica and sent Andros a petition in December, 1674, informing him that as he did not know what they were thinking he should call an assembly that Nicolls had promised them—long and incorrect memories—where they could give him a piece of their mind. East Hampton, Southampton and Southold wanted a tougher response. They had returned to their true home where they desired to remain and they told Andros that they had fought off the enemy with Connecticut's aid when the New York had left them naked to their enemies so they were happy where they were. Governor John Winthrop, Jr. of Connecticut gave his blessings to their entreaty and this claim was also sent to England. Andros was not about to suffer this insult so he ordered the town leaders including John Mulford to submit or be declared rebels. After warning Winthrop not to interfere, which Winthrop acquiesced to, Andros personally descended on East Hampton and the other towns and brought them into his jurisdiction. Abandoned by their beloved Connecticut, the towns faced west to fight the next round.

Under Andros the same tensions between the government and the eastern towns remained in place. The governors asserted a right to one sixteenth of the product of the whales that washed up on the beach. Beached whales were the right of the monarch, who had many odd rights to the foreshore of the kingdom. The whaling towns, who by now had developed a whaling fishery, caught more and more whales at sea where the king had no rights. If the government wanted to collect its share of the whale oil and bone it would have to have officials on the beach or on the docks of the towns if they had any hope whatsoever in getting a part of the whale. On occasion customs agents were provided for on the out of the way ports but this rarely worked to benefit the government as the men rarely stayed in place long. The other issue for the government was the fact that the whale oil was shipped through Boston to England and not New York City. That meant lost

trade and, of course, lost opportunity to sell goods to the eastern townships who were increasingly prosperous. The loss of both transactions
also meant lost revenues for the government. Altogether an unhappy
situation for the central government and for the merchants on Manhattan.

The first change in the institutions of government that would
bring some pleasure to the townspeople came in 1683 with the arrival
of Thomas Dongan as governor. Dongan was deeply suspect by the ar-
dent Protestants of the towns as he was a Catholic and a creature of
the Duke of York, but he was to create a change in government that the
Duke felt he had to concede mostly due to his weakened political position in England rather than by the press of events in New York. Dongan was told to create a more democratic frame of government in the
colony by creating an assembly to participate in government. When
this was announced, and after the writs were issued by the High Sheriff, East Hampton decided to go along but in doing so they tested Dongan's "patience and moderation" for while electing representatives to
the conference that would create the new frame of government they
announced they did so not because the sheriff had issued writs but
because they did not want to miss an opportunity to assert their
rights. In an address carried by the town representatives they informed Dongan that they regarded him as an instrument of God who
was there to restore their freedom and privileges and that their representative would stand up for "our priviledges and English liberties."
And so they did. The representatives of the colony wrote 15 laws and
created a "Charter of Libertyes and Priviledges." The charter was a very
important document as it asserted the liberties closes to the hearts of
the people and those acceptable in some degree by the authorities. As
citizens of a republic that guarantees our rights in the constitution we
have an automatic reaction whenever we see words such as liberties,
privileges and equate them with our current rights. What was being
asserted in this seventeenth-century context is different from what
exists for us today. Let me discuss two documents that were dear to
the hearts of the people of East Hampton in the seventeenth century.
One is the New York Charter of 1673 and the other the Massachusetts
Body of Liberties of 1641.

This latter document is divided into ninety-five chapters that
illuminate rights while creating a body of laws for Massachusetts Bay.
The first seventeen laws draw out rights of persons—no punishment
without legal process; economic rights—no monopolies, right to make
a will; rules of service—no military service out of the plantation, no
punishment for nonattendance at court. Most of these laws are specific

to men and a number of them could be overruled by the General Court or legislature if there is an emergency. Chapters 18–57 relate to judicial matters: allowances for bail; no property seizures; no more than forty stripes of the lash regardless of the crime and none at all for "true gentlemen"; death sentences carried out after only four days had passed from the conviction; eyewitnesses needed for a crime where the death sentences could be imposed; no torture; free access to all records; and that men found offensive to a town meeting could be fined by the other freemen (thus limiting free speech). The rules for free men (Chapters 58–78) relate mostly to keeping the peace in church affairs, permitting freemen of town to make laws but no punishment over twenty shillings, the right to choose their own delegates to General Court, and all votes should be by conscience only. The liberties for women are exactly two—if not left enough in a will to support a wife the General Court must give relief in the form of a competence and a husband cannot beat his wife unless he hits her in defense against her assaults. Children had four liberties, the most important dealing with inheritance; if there was no appropriate will the oldest child was to get a double share and daughters to get equal share of the rest. Servants also had four liberties including the right to sue to free themselves from a cruel master; if maimed or defaced they got freedom and after seven years must get their freedom. Foreigners and strangers had specified rights; they were allowed to participate in most town affairs and could not be enslaved unless they were lawful captives taken in war, or if they willingly sold themselves while in colony or are sold to "us." Laws punishable by the death penalty were limited to murder whether by guile or anger, treason, witchcraft, bestiality, blasphemy, homosexuality, and in adultery for both offenders. Finally, for churches the rules of order and rights were promulgated, giving them great latitude to choose and discipline members but churches could only be founded by those "orthodox" in judgment and if error was suspected local churches could assemble at the suspect church and examine its people.

So it is hardly a testament of rights so much as it is a law code. It has to be noted that at critical points it gives either the General Court or the majority of a town the ability to take away rights in the name of the whole.

The New York charter is similar. Much of the first third of its chapters is taken up with organizing an assembly and asserting its rights as against the government most importantly giving the right to pass laws while recognizing the Duke could veto them. It also gave the individual rights to control their person and be treated by the law only through proper means such as trial by jury and that they could hold property without illegal interference. Women had only one specified right and that was as widows they could continue to live in their home for at least forty days on the death of their spouse. The last third of the Charter speaks to the issue of freedom of religion. It asserts that right only for Christians; no doubt the many Dutch and English Calvinists would have happily excluded Catholics but Dongan, a Catholic, had to approve this document and it was unlikely he would do so unless there was a broad definition. The charter did give the towns the right to control religious belief within their borders by allowing the community to choose the minister and taxing everyone to support the majority church—the better to protect themselves from the dreaded Quakers. So these "Liberties and Privileges" are much more concerned with the assertion of practical rights of assembly and taxation, wills and trials and less with abstract rights of speech and the press. In other words they supported the political and legal aspirations of the struggling colonists who needed practical ideas rather than the abstract thinking of the enlightenment that would come with the Revolution.

The heady feeling that the townspeople had in finally asserting their rights to assembly and make laws for themselves did not last long. While the Duke's advisors were ready after some amendments to accept the new laws and the Charter of Lyberties they were never allowed to go into operation as King Charles died and James came to the throne committed to the idea of creating a super colony in the north, the Dominion of New England. It is unfortunate that this happened. The two sessions of the assembly created a body of laws that responded to popular needs and showed a degree of sophistication in what was needed in the colony. But instead of this building a new political body the successes of the assembly were swept away and the old system of a governor and a council made up of a few favorites, mostly from Manhattan, were left to govern while the remainder of the colony went on feeling abused.

Dongan also gave them reasons to feel abused as he set out to enrich himself. Like his predecessors who looked at whaling and its revenues he lusted after the royal share. Unlike his predecessors he was more forward in collecting his due by sending commissioners to scour the beaches and watch the ports and as a result a nice little revenue ensued. His need for money and his venality led him on to more serious efforts to squeeze the people. Quitrents were a common taxing device at the time in that they were taxes on land. In New York they had been attached to large grants of land, especially the grants to the townships, so they were assessed on the community and not directly on the individual. In fact they were small and yielded very little.

Dongan seized on this and created a new group of collectors and a court of exchequer where land tax disputes would be held, as he rightfully suspected the local courts would always see the government's case. Then he challenged all prior land grants. In March, 1684 the council issued an order to the townships on Long Island to produce their patents. Some towns complied but most dragged their feet refusing to submit their patents as they feared what they might get back. Dongan kept up the pressure through threats and to make sure of his legal ground sent representative patents to England for review. No doubt he was unsettled by the result, for the legal officers of the Duke said they could find no problem except in those where large tracts of unused lands were still being held—true for most Long Island towns. Dongan used the latter to go after the towns and one by one they gave in and in some cases even paid back quitrents. East Hampton refused to surrender; neither did Dongan. When all else failed to convince the righteous he decided to grant the application by a group of ten individuals who said they were being denied land in the town even though they were made to pay taxes. So in July, 1686 each of them received 30 acres by order of the council. Samuel Mulford and other town leaders marched through town with the beat of a drum and nailed a protest to the meeting house door followed by an intemperate sermon by the Reverend Thomas James. Dongan was not amused. An information was filed against the town's leaders leading to a warrant for their arrest. As the door to jail yawned open before them Mulford, James, and the others decided things had gone far enough and while they protested that the ten land claimants had never paid taxes they sued for a pardon. It was granted and East Hampton's patent was renewed with a higher quitrent and a special £200 tax was levied on them.

Dongan was venal and often collected land or money under the table for his deeds and East Hampton hated him, but the fact remains that this episode tells us much about the one-sided nature of the struggle between the town and the central government. East Hampton could protest, shake its fist, beat its drum, and write wonderful petitions, yet in the end the real power lay in the hands of the governor. They was always a legal means at hand that could be used to demand obedience and the governors such as Andros and Dongan could bring them to heel. East Hampton was left to grumble and look longingly toward Connecticut dreaming of what might have been while living with the reality of their nightmare 120 miles away.

The name of Samuel Mulford has already emerged and until he died in 1725 the next period could be called the age of Mulford. Samuel, or "Old Fishhook" was an extraordinary man, a human sore thumb, the splinter in your finger, the stubbed toe—he simply could not be ignored and he certainly refused to be ignored by anyone, governor or king. The owner of a whaling company, landowner, cattleman, and merchant, he came to be the embodiment of East Hampton's desires to keep at arm's length from New York. He came into his own in the eighteenth century. From Dongan on the town carried on its trade in whale products. When Jacob Leisler and his friends seized control of New York in 1689 East Hampton was the only town not to recognize his government. Leisler left the whale trade alone and one would have thought he could have won the grudging support on the townspeople when he called for an assembly. Not so; the town refused to participate in elections because to do so meant complying with a regime similar to that which had imposed the "old bondage." Instead they sought once again to be returned to Connecticut. When the government in England reimposed its authority the old whaling and trading rules were reimposed if not vigorously asserted. Governor Benjamin Fletcher, an old friend of the pirates who flourished in the 1690s, worked with William (Tangier) Smith to grab as many beached whales as possible and with Fletcher you could be sure of one thing, anything seized would end up in his pockets. By this time New York did have an assembly in which East Hampton participated to better watch over its interests. When Governor Bellomont tried to get it to pass a statute against fraudulent trade in whale products nothing was heard of the statute in the assembly and we can guess why.

Samuel Mulford with his rasping personality and in-your-face style came into his own as he struggled against Edward Hyde, Lord Cornbury, governor from 1702 to 1708. Like most governors Cornbury looked upon his stint in America as an opportunity for personal enrichment while defending the royal interest and the whale trade beckoned him.

As Cornbury put it "there has been for some time no Trade between the City of New York and the East End of Long Island, from whence the greatest quantity of whale oil comes. And indeed, the people of the East End of Long Island are not very willing to be persuaded to believe that they belong to this province. They are full of New England principles."

To correct this situation Cornbury went beyond the normal claims of the crown in regard to beached whales, an old right, to stating that the whale was a royal fish and therefore could not be so easily fished as before. He decreed that whaling adventurers would have to obtain a license to do so, and then yield one fourteenth of value of oil and bone. To make sure all of this worked the licenses had to be obtained in New York City and the taxes also yielded there. He obviously hoped that this would tie the whale fishery to New York City and make collection very much easier, for now if you did not have a license there would be trouble, and when you came to get your license there would be opportunities to ensure you were taxed before you received a new license. And when you traveled to New York City there were ample opportunities for speculation, fraud and delay as the whalers had to sail there and await there licenses at considerable expense. When the assembly provided no relief, it was more and more under the control of landowners who preferred taxes on trade than taxes on land and its products, so the whalers could expect little relief.

Mulford was not about to let this go so he did something quite remarkable: he went to London. A rather audacious thing to do. He was after all the representative of a prosperous but little-known town in New York. His opponent was a royal governor, the cousin of the Queen and whose father and uncle sat in the privy council. Undeterred, he pled his case and as one could predict he got nowhere. The government was not in the business of discouraging a governor from making his colony pay for its administration. Mulford learned from this lesson and one hopes used the opportunity of being in London to make trading contacts. He, of course, like most of his fellows did the minimum business in New York City and continued to drive a trade to Boston and through Boston to London.

Mulford's next opponent was Robert Hunter, one of the savviest governors colonial New York ever had. He wanted to bring an end to the ongoing and by now old clash of the pro and anti-Leislerians in the colony and to redo its politics. By now the political balance was falling in the direction of the great landowners of the Hudson River Valley and it was to them that Hunter turned for support in and out of the Assembly. This meant that the merchants and traders of New York would have a much tougher time, for Hunter would turn to them first as a revenue source. However, he also wanted to increase trade in New York which was now emerging from the shadow of Boston and wanted to further expand its trade. Besides reinvigorating the licensing system, he imposed a new ten percent tax on all goods imported from another colony where the origin of the goods was not that place itself. In other words you could ship tobacco from Virginia but you could not import English goods from Boston without paying the duty. The target could not have been more obvious. He also set out again to collect that old hated tax in the townships, the quitrent, and transferred jurisdiction over the cases of non-payment to the court of chancery where an ambitious new collector started to sue the towns, especially East Hampton.

In 1712, two years after Hunter arrived in the colony, Hunter was after Mulford in court. Mulford maintained that Hunter had no right to do what he did and that it contravened the law—with Mulford there was always a higher law. Needless to say he lost in the court of Chancery and in the Supreme Court on appeal. That left him the floor of the assembly in which to make his case against Hunter, as he did in 1714 in a fiery speech attacking Hunter for attempting to make them his "tenants at will," in other words servants with no rights. He outlined the many calamities that had befallen individuals under this governor and expanded his plea into a more universal idiom:

> We have an Undoubted Right and Property by the Law of God and Nature, settled upon the Subject by Act of Parliament; which is not be taken from them by the Supreme Power, without due Course of Law. The End of Law is to secure Persons and Estates; the End of Government to put the same in Execution, to the purpose that Justice by done.

As a member of the assembly Mulford could get away with this blazing rhetoric and an attack on the governor if his fellow members were willing to let him, and they did until he did an extraordinary thing by publishing his speech, compelling the governor and the assembly to take action. Mulford was expelled from the assembly in 1714 and later charged and arrested for seditious behavior. Undeterred by his bail he left for London in 1716 when he was seventy-one—a true patriarch to his people—to make his plea there. Once there he continued his assault on Hunter and had published an "Information and Defense of His Whale Fishery," laying out his case against him. This time with the new Whig government firmly in control Mulford received a more open hearing, for as Tim Breen has pointed out he had carefully crafted his appeal to the language of the Glorious Revolution, a language appreciated by the Whigs and not by the former Tory government. Hunter was forced to defend himself when Mulford won a surprisingly, for Hunter, warm hearing from the Board of Trade, who told Hunter to cease all legal matters against him. Hunter and the Assembly mounted a major campaign against Mulford, charging that he was trying to stop the legitimate actions of the assembly to raise taxes with which to fight the Indians on the frontier, he was prone to telling great lies about the whaling industry to suit his own purposes, he only wanted "to promote his beloved Connecticut," he was a bail jumper in the province for publishing sedition, and if such men could run to England and get relief from their crimes, then all criminals would soon be fleeing to London. Against these charges the Board of Trade was not about to side with Mulford and he could only afford to remain in London and press his case for a limited amount of time, so while he brought some degree of discomfort to Hunter, Mulford did not triumph. He had one last moment of protest. When Governor Burnet arrived in 1720 he decided that rather than following a custom of holding an election for the assembly on the arrival of a new governor he would keep the compliant one then in existence that Hunter had so carefully nurtured. Mulford would have none of it and launched another protest, and for his troubles he was kicked out of the assembly once again. He would die in 1724 and East Hampton would not see his like again.

East Hampton fought to retain its ties to Connecticut or at the very least keep New York out of its affairs for about 100 years. Tied to New England economically and religiously, they fought to retain their ties to the Puritan colonies. They also needed a higher power to whom they could take judicial matters that threatened the town such as the early witchcraft trial of Goody Garlick and for them the best place was nearby Connecticut. The fact that New York had a government that denied them the right to meet with their fellow colonists and make the laws, especially those on taxes, made it an abomination. It was also very far away and seemed intent on many things that were of no interest to East Hampton such as fighting wars against the French and Indians in the far north. Still one would have thought that would have let matters slip by. They were largely left alone to manage their own affairs and their chief trade was carried on with Boston, regardless of what the New York government did. All too often, however, there was enough interference to remind them of New York and even after representative government arrived they still did not like New York. And while Mulford represented their spirit he was to be the last great tribune of the town, for dreadful things would happen.

As the glory years of the whale trade faded into memory and the town became an isolated agrarian community like so many other towns in New York a gradual transition took place—one that would have horrified men such as Samuel Mulgrave. Like it or not, the people of East Hampton became New Yorkers: if not by the middle of the eighteenth century, certainly around the time of the American Revolution, when Long Island was occupied by the British and when the colonists sought new identities that kept them from being anything but

British—and for the people of Long Island that would be New Yorkers. This would be a slow process but the results were inevitable. Identity was one thing, physical incorporation another that would come later with the railway.

The attraction was not just the natural beauty of East Hampton, it was especially her beaches. During the 1730s in England a new beach culture was created as physicians touted the therapeutic effect of salt water. The upper classes flocked Scarborough, Brighton, Ramsgate, and Weighmouth and other bathing resorts to enjoy the effects of the sea water. A whole new beach culture emerged as men and women climbed into bathing machines to enter the water for a brief immersion. On leaving the water they would promenade, shop, ride, attend the theater and a myriad of activities that filled in the time between their dips. While the new culture flourished first in England it traveled at the end of the eighteenth century to Germany and then to France and by the beginning of the nineteenth to the United States. Until this time beaches were places where people went to work. No better illustration of this exists than the beaches of East Hampton where the whale industry was carried out first with the beached whales and then with those that were hauled ashore. Recreation or therapeutic purposes did not loom large with these men. There are records for the middle of the eighteenth century of young people going to the beach in large groups to enjoy a "frolic." This is an intriguing term. In Britain people swam nude in the eighteenth century and one wonders about the Puritan traditions in eastern Long Island and comes to the conclusion that they were not nude—but if they were clothed did they go in the water? And what was the nature of the frolic? Who knows? By the middle of the nineteenth century swimming was introduced to the culture of the beach and people started to spend more time in the water and seek out beaches away from the resorts. The coming of the railway after 1844 on Long Island made this possible. As the lines traveled across the island they brought about the colonization of the townships. Nothing would be the same, especially after 1918, when the prosperity of the country made it possible for many to find recreation and pleasure at the eastern end of the island. East Hampton was still an independent township but now much involved with a modern lifestyle beloved of city dwellers, especially those in New York City. As someone who only views this from afar I understand that this has revived a sense of combat with the invaders, but I will leave that topic for others.

THOMAS DONGAN
AND THE CHARTER OF
EAST HAMPTON

Peter R. Christoph

IWAS ASKED TO TALK about Thomas Dongan and the charter he granted to East Hampton, hence the title of my talk. Actually, what he granted was a patent, not a charter, and please don't ask me to explain the difference. It is sufficient to know that what a town is granted is called a patent, and what a city receives is called a charter.

In 1686 there were serious differences between New York governor Thomas Dongan and the town of East Hampton, leading to the type of patent that East Hampton received in December of that year. The first question for us to deal with is: who was Thomas Dongan? The second is: what was the area of conflict between him and East Hampton? I think the best way to handle this is to begin by describing the career of Thomas Dongan, including his administration of New York, to the end of 1686, and then review what had been going on in East Hampton, especially in relation to land title, up to the same point, so that we can see why East Hampton received the sort of patent that it did. And I will conclude with a view of Thomas Dongan's career after 1686. I'm sure that the further history of East Hampton has already been well covered by the other speakers in this series.

Thomas Dongan, like all of New York's colonial governors, came from a military background. Unlike his predecessors, Dongan was Irish, and, alone among New York's colonial governors, Roman Catholic. This is important to any understanding of the ups and downs of his career and of the times in which Dongan lived.

Thomas Dongan was born in 1634 at Castletown, County Kildare, the second surviving son of Baronet Sir John Dongan and Mary Talbot Dongan. Thomas's father was a member of the Irish Parliament. His mother's brother was the Earl of Tyrconnell. In short, Thomas Dongan was "castle Irish," not "lace curtain Irish"; more than an officer and gentleman, he was an officer and nobleman. And one of his uncles was the Archbishop of Dublin. This was a practicing Catholic family.

In the 1640s, the English had their Civil War, which ended with the deposing and beheading of King Charles I and the establishment of a commonwealth government, led by Puritans. This was not good news for Catholic Ireland, which, in fact, was invaded by English Protestant troops in 1649. However, the Dongans, including fifteen-year-old Thomas, had already joined the exodus of Stuart supporters from Ireland and England to France. In that same year, the dead king's teenaged sons, Charles the heir apparent and James, Duke of York, had also escaped to the continent, first to Holland and later to France.

The teenaged Dongan enrolled in the Irish Regiment serving with the French army. It is possible that at this time he first met the Duke of York, who served in the French army until 1656. The Duke returned to England in 1660 with his brother, now King Charles II, but Dongan remained in the French army for another eighteen years, and in 1674 attained the rank of colonel.

Then in 1678, when it appeared that England might go to war against France, King Charles ordered all British troops serving in the pay of France to return to England. Dongan resigned his commission and went to England, at great personal financial sacrifice, and despite attractive offers from the king of France to remain.

Charles II made some partial compensation to Dongan, granting him a life pension of 500 pounds a year and a commission as general of an army being raised for an invasion of Flanders. However, the king almost immediately changed Dongan's assignment, appointing him lieutenant-governor of the British colony of Tangier in North Africa. It was not a lucrative appointment.

Dongan complained that he lost money during his two years at the post but he apparently demonstrated qualities of leadership and administration that recommended him to the King and the Duke of York.

A year later the Popish Plot occurred in England. This was a supposed plot by Catholics to infiltrate the government and corrupt or kill the king. In fact, it was a total fiction, created by corrupt Protestant politicians as a way to destroy opponents. A number of innocent persons were convicted with perjured testimony and tortured to death. During this period, it was noticed that the three top officials at Tangier, including the governor and lieutenant-governor, were all Roman Catholic, and of course came under suspicion, with the result that Dongan was recalled in February 1680 and the governor soon after.

Dongan did nothing of note after his return to London, it was a good time for a Catholic not to do anything that would draw attention to himself. Eventually the Popish Plot hysteria ran its course; the king finally put an end to it when charges were made against his brother. But Dongan was in the right place when King Charles and the Duke of York were seeking a governor for New York. On September 30, 1682, he was commissioned governor of New York and her dependencies, and a few days later was also commissioned vice-admiral of the Duke of York's territories in America. The Duke handed Dongan his instructions in January 1683, including authority to establish a popularly elected general assembly.

Thomas Dongan sailed for his new post in America on the frigate Constant Warwick, arriving at Manhattan on August 25, 1683. He was to serve as governor of New York and its dependencies, which still included Pemaquid (in Maine), and Nantucket and Martha's Vineyard (off Massachusetts). Dongan also held a commission as admiral with jurisdiction in maritime cases for New York, Connecticut, and New Jersey.

Religious Issues

Accompanying Dongan on his voyage to America were two chaplains, the Anglican Dr. John Gordon and the Jesuit Thomas Harvey. They illustrate the Duke of York's intention to have freedom of religion in his colony, and served as a reminder to all that he was working for the same in England. The Duke was openly Catholic, the king secretly so, and although the Duke favored religious freedom in England for both Protestant dissenters and Catholics, the dissenters did not trust him and opposed his policies. However, the next six years would be a golden age for New York's large Roman Catholic minority, which for the first time would be served openly by three English Jesuits and two lay brothers, and would even have a parochial school on Manhattan. Their arrival would be viewed nervously by New York's Dutch Calvinists. Anthony Brockholls, carried over from the previous administration, continued to serve as deputy governor and commander-in-chief of Fort James in New York; with the arrival of Jarvis Baxter as commandant at Fort Albany, the colony's two forts and the governorship itself were all in the hands of Catholics. Some saw it as evidence of religious freedom, others as first steps on the road toward enforced Catholicism. It is important to keep the religious situation in mind, because there would be serious consequences a few years later.

People were even suspicious as to Dongan's motives when he began the liberal dispensing of trading licenses to fur traders. Some sixty French traders, frustrated by the regulations imposed by their own government in Canada, moved to New York to set up shop, most of them settling at Saratoga, on the Albany-Montreal trading route. Suddenly, New York had a community of foreign Catholics located at a point that was of strategic importance, both economically and militarily.

In October 1685 Louis XIII revoked the Edict of Nantes, and persecution of France's Protestants began. Dozens of them found their way to New York. With French Catholics settling at Saratoga and a considerable number of French Protestants arriving in New York City, fears of a French takeover began to trouble New Yorkers. Even the colony's English Catholics came under suspicion, as Protestants wondered if they were potential traitors who would hand New York over to Catholic France.

A GENERAL ASSEMBLY

Not everything about Dongan's arrival was viewed negatively by colonists. More readily accepted by the general populace was the Duke of York's decision to have Dongan establish a general assembly, for which the king granted an enabling act, the Charter of Liberties, to the inhabitants of New York and its dependencies. This was a move which the colonists, particularly those on Long Island with ties to New England, had long advocated.

Some have seen the establishment of an elected assembly and the assembly's adoption of the Charter of Liberties as important steps toward democracy. But in fact, the General Assembly would exist only at the pleasure of the king, and only as long as it did not strain his tolerance. All the acts passed by the Assembly were subject to review by the Duke of York and ultimately by the king, whose vetoes could not be overridden.

What the colonists had sought, especially those on eastern Long Island, was to imitate the New England model. But even that was a cautious democracy. In New England the ballot was restricted to persons of means within the established (Puritan) church. Although New York's model had no religious restriction, it was otherwise little different. The general assembly was to be popularly elected by "every freeholder and freeman," which limited the franchise to males in possession of real estate with a value of at least forty pounds. This left a lot of people, including many owners of small holdings, disenfranchised. From the government's standpoint, voting should be restricted to holders of large properties who thereby had a major stake in the success of government: why on earth would you give the vote to the rabble? Both the king and the town proprietors were agreed that democracy needed to be restricted; they differed as to what those restrictions should be and whose rights needed to be restricted.

The elected representatives of the whole colony first gathered in General Assembly on October 17, 1683. They chose as speaker Matthias Nicolls, whose service in New York government began two decades earlier, and as clerk they chose John Spragg, the provincial secretary.

The Duke of York had once said he saw no need for an elected assembly, as he thought it would involve the same men that were already in government. In that, he appears to have been right.

The Assembly was granted the rights to levy taxes and make laws, and at its first meeting it passed fourteen laws, all approved by the governor and council and submitted to the Duke for ratification. One of the acts was to form twelve counties. This, taken together with other acts of Dongan to charter the city of Albany and recharter New York City, and the establishing of circuit courts in which local justices participated, could be seen as advancing local government and popular participation in the political process. Or, one could interpret it as part of a pattern to increase the role of central government in local affairs, especially since the principal officers of the cities continued to be appointed, not elected. In fact, both views are correct: the people were given a platform to voice their concerns and vote on issues that affected them, but the king's appointed officials could end those freedoms anytime.

COUNCIL AND COURTS

Balancing the democratically inclined General Assembly was the government council. The council, whose members were appointed by the king, functioned as governor's cabinet, as upper house of the legislature, and, together with the governor, as court of appeals. In the governor's absence, one or more councilors collectively would administer the colony. At this point in time, the Council was comprised almost entirely of officeholders from England and New York City merchants.

They included two holdovers from the preceding administration, Dutchmen Frederick Phillipse and Stephanus van Cortlandt, who would serve throughout Dongan's administration, as did Anthony Brockholls, who served also as commander-in-chief of the military and deputy governor. Others who served off and on during the administration were primarily career government officials: among them Jarvis Baxter, like Brockholls a military commander and a Catholic. Among the colonists on the council was Nicholas Bayard, a nephew of Peter Stuyvesant. Bayard was being rehabilitated after having been jailed in 1674 for resistance to English government. Another long-term colonist was the even pricklier John Youngs from South Hampton, who had once been threatened with charges of treason for trying to place Long Island under Connecticut rule. However, Youngs was not a factor on the council: he seldom made the long trip to New York City to attend council meetings. The members of the council, for the most part, were Dongan's closest advisors. Dongan had to answer to the king and the Duke, both of whom wanted to see some profit from the colony, and Dongan himself was not adverse to turning a personal profit on the job. It is not surprising that the three wealthy Dutch merchants on the council had more influence with successive governors than Englishmen on the council with no business connections.

Dongan made changes in the courts. The court of assizes, which met once a year at New York, was abolished. It had been virtually inaccessible for poor people at the farther reaches of the colony. It was replaced by circuit courts which met twice a year in each county. The circuit judges, who would sit with the county's justices of the peace as a judicial panel, were chosen by the governor. The judges throughout Dongan's administration were the venerable Matthias Nicolls, officeholder for twenty years, and Captain John Palmer, holder of numerous Staten Island offices.

While the establishment of circuit courts on the one hand eased people's recourse to the courts, on the other hand it enabled the governor to send in his own judges to oversee local hearings. Cities were granted charters and the aldermen were popularly elected, but mayor, clerk and other major officers were appointed by governor or king. The general assembly was popularly elected, but the laws it enacted could be rejected by the king. Governor Dongan on behalf of the Duke of York offered unprecedented local authority in several ways, but always the governor was enabled to strongly influence local affairs, and the duke could always negate them.

CHARTERS AND GRANTS

During his administration, Dongan cemented a number of political alliances within the colony by granting new patents to various communities, in addition to the charters to the two cities. He also erected a number of manors, about half of all those ever granted in New York. A number of large land patents were granted, usually to companies of investors who rewarded Dongan generously with gifts. The large number of manors erected and large patents granted by Dongan could be viewed as rewarding faithful servants of the government, or as means to tie important men more closely to the government, or as providing large fees (and bribes) to enrich Dongan personally. These various motives are not mutually exclusive. Rich men got land, Dongan got paid, and the government won friends among its important citizens.

Today, we consider it a serious offense for a public official to accept bribes or large gifts from those doing business with the government. In the seventeenth century, the salaries of colonial governors and other public officials were never large enough to cover the expenses of office. That is one reason why wealthy men were given such positions; they were expected to pay many of the expenses out of their own pockets. But the only people willing to accept positions in far-off, primitive colonies were those gentlemen and noblemen who were caught in a cash-flow problem and needed a position where they could replenish their personal coffers. As a result, gift-giving and bribery were normal and expected, and while they were illegal, the chances of conviction were remote, unless one had done something to really displease the king.

Besides issuing patents to new communities, Dongan in 1686 granted New York City a new charter, and Albany received its first English charter. In that same year, Dongan began enforcing an order of council for the existing towns to renew their patents, which gave the king and himself much needed revenue. Some towns resisted, and it is at that point that we must turn our attention to the history of East Hampton's relations with the government of New York.

EAST HAMPTON AND ITS PATENT

After the conquest of New Netherland in 1664, Governor Richard Nicolls sought to bring together the various regional interests of the colony under the proprietorship of the Duke of York. In a gathering at

Hempstead of representatives from throughout the colony, a new set of rules was worked out, called the Duke's Laws. Neither the Dutch at Albany nor the Puritans on eastern Long Island were happy about the new laws, nor about the Royalist government which would rule over them. It was the decision of Nicolls, and his successor, Francis Lovelace, to leave Albany pretty much to its own devices for the time being, but to bring all the English speaking parts of the colony under the Duke's regulations immediately.

There was much resistance on Long Island, where the towns sought to secede and join with either Massachusetts or Connecticut. To stop the grumbling, a law was passed in 1666 to stop talk against the deputies who passed the Duke's laws. But when eastern Long Islanders decided to stop paying taxes to New York, Nicolls' patience reached its limits and he informed the leaders of the eastern towns that they would pay their taxes or be charged with treason. The punishment for treason was a particularly unpleasant form of death, and no one doubted that Richard Nicolls was a man of his word, so the resistance collapsed. But no one was happy.

Since none of the existing land patents in the colony had been issued under the proprietorship of the Duke of York, all patents had to be reissued with the proper wording. The recipients of the new patents did not get them for free; they had to pay fees to the governor, the colonial secretary, and the clerk who actually wrote the new patents, so the renewal of all the patents in the colony provided a goodly source of income to those officers for the next few years.

Richard Nicolls granted a new patent to East Hampton on the thirteenth of March 1666-7. It granted "all the privileges belonging to a town within this government. The patentees and associates, their heirs, successors and assigns shall pay such duties as now are or hereafter shall be established by the laws of this government." In other words, the same people are still in charge, and don't forget to pay your taxes.

As far as the East Hampton men were concerned, the promised rights were not forthcoming. In June 1682, East Hampton men on military training day drew up a petition to acting Gov. Brockholls, complaining that, although they paid their taxes, nowhere on Long Island did citizens have free representative government. Brockholls, who had neither the authority nor the inclination to help, offered no sympathy.

In 1683, Dongan proclaimed the establishing of the long awaited General Assembly. The eastern towns of Long Island were to send two representatives. East Hampton asked that the representatives stand up in the assembly for the maintenance "of our privileges and English liberties." They wanted all writs to run in the king's name and not the Duke's: they were willing to be the king's subjects, but they did not want to recognize the Duke's title to their territory. They also noted that they participated in the elections, not in answer to the writ of the sheriff, which was issued in the Duke's name, but because they refused to miss any opportunity to assert their liberties.

The issue of who controlled land and land-title in the colony was about to be given a thorough hearing, as governor and East Hampton men engaged in a series of encounters. In March 1684–5, Dongan ordered the county sheriffs to investigate all titles in their jurisdictions. The reason he gave was that "Several inhabitants in the province request liberty and license to purchase land. It is uncertain what land are disposed of, since several persons possess land to which they have no legal title or at least have neglected to record the same." Therefore the sheriff was ordered "to inquire of Suffolk inhabitants by what title they enjoy their possessions and return the same to me to find out if they be recorded." While they were at it, the sheriffs should also collect all quitrents and arrears of quitrents due the Duke of York.

The reaction in East Hampton was typical of most towns: they didn't like the new order, both because they were not inclined to pay taxes if they could help it, and because the implication of quitrents was that the land belonged to the Duke, who allowed them to own it at his pleasure. Threatened with a hearing before the court of exchequer, where Dongan was almost certain to win, most towns gave up the struggle, but East Hampton continued to press its case.

In July of 1685, the Rev. Thomas James and Capt. Josiah Hobart were dispatched by East Hampton to treat with the Governor about the quitrent. Their instructions stated that they were to surrender no existing rights or privileges, but only to seek an agreement whereby East Hampton's quitrent would be no more than that of neighboring towns. While they were at it, they should seek confirmation of the town's rights as granted by former governors. That effort went exactly noplace, so in August, Lt. John Wheeler and Ens. Samuel Mulford were sent off to try and gain from the governor "better security and confirmation for our lands, and also to agree upon a quit rent upon as easy terms as they can." That also went noplace. The town planned to submit its annual protest at the General Assembly, but Dongan dissolved the Assembly in August 1685. Before it could meet again, King Charles died, and the Duke of York became King James II.

The General Assembly had been James's creation, but as king he thought it a bad idea, and abolished it. He also revoked the charter of liberties and all the other laws the assembly had passed, except of course those for raising taxes.

At the beginning of October, therefore, East Hampton sent a petition to the governor, noting that the government of New York had been established under the king by Col. Richard Nicolls, "By word and writing we were promised and engaged the enjoyment of all privileges and liberties which other of his majesties subjects doe enjoy. Since that time we are deprived and prohibited of our birthright freedoms and privileges to which both wee and our ancestors were born. Laws and orders have been imposed upon us from time to time without our consent and therein we are totally deprived of a fundamental privilege of our English nation." All of this smacked of insubordination, and would not have been well received by Dongan.

It was at this point that the governor received a petition from nine men who had long lived in East Hampton, but were not proprietors of the town, seeking to be granted title to land. The town had been operating under the assumption that undivided land in the town belonged to the original proprietors. Dongan decided that it belonged to all freemen of the town, and he instructed the sheriff to have a surveyor lay out thirty acres for each of the nine petitioners, from any land not already claimed.

East Hampton saw Dongan's land grants to the nine men as an infringement of its privileges. Dongan ordered them to send "four men to appear at New York to answer" what charges might be made against the proprietors. The proprietors instructed the delegates to be well-prepared to present the town's case, and sent another two men to Connecticut for advice and help. The instructions show that East Hampton intended to revive an old argument, that because the east end of the island had not been protected by New York at the time of the Dutch invasion of 1673, the towns at that time had placed themselves under the care and supervision of Connecticut, and should therefore still be considered part of that colony. This was a dangerous argument: Dongan could charge the proprietors with treason.

Finally, on October 6, a meeting was called to protest the governor's actions, leading to the posting of the town's complaints without bothering to seek the necessary permission from a justice of the peace. That brought a charge from New York that seven men "did confederate together to bring his Majesty's authority into contempt and scorn," that they "did riotously, contemptuously and unlawfully assemble themselves together with diverse others unknown ... without any warrant or authority and did publish and affix on the wall of the meeting house a certain scandalous and libelous paper." Dongan had the seven protesters arrested on charges of sedition, as well as five men who had sided with them. A week later the Rev. Thomas James lent his support to the accused, and preached a sermon criticizing the colony's council for awarding land in East Hampton to the nine petitioners. He was arrested on charges of sedition.

Let us consider the situation at this point. The town of East Hampton opposed the authority of the Duke of York and his agents, and after he had become king, which made New York a crown colony, the townsmen continued their insubordination to the point of violating the laws against riot. The governor is furious, and claps a baker's dozen in jail, among them the town's clergyman. It hardly seems a propitious time to seek a new patent with added rights favorable to the interests of the town's proprietors.

At this point, nonetheless, the town on November 18, 1686, instructed John Wheeler and Samuel Mulford once again to seek a town patent from the governor. Not only are they to see if a patent can be procured from the governor, but it should exclude the nine men who had been granted thirty acres each, the quitrent should be low, and payment should be made in East Hampton, not way off in New York. And the proprietors should be able to hold town meetings without a warrant from a justice.

Under these circumstances, we are not surprised that the patent Governor Dongan granted to East Hampton was on terms other than the town's own choosing. The ruling body of the town was no longer to be the proprietors, but a board of trustees representing all the freeholders and commonality: that would make the votes of the thirty-acre men equal to that of the greatest proprietor. It was the trustees, now, who owned the undivided land, not the proprietors. Two constables, two assessors, and the twelve trustees were to be chosen yearly, but to hold an election, the trustees had to request a warrant from one of the justices of the peace, all of whom were appointed by the governor. The town had sought permission to buy Montauk from the local Indians, and the patent granted them the right to bargain with the Indians, but if they bought the land they were to pay a yearly quitrent, and at New York, not East Hampton. That would be in addition to the forty shillings a year quitrent for their present bounds. And we should note that now that New York was a crown colony, refusal to pay taxes to New York or any attempt to join Connecticut would be treason against the king.

The patent was signed by Dongan on December 9, 1686, and approved by the Council the same day. It was the same council whose actions the town had so long opposed, and all of whose members the town probably detested: four Royalists, three of them Catholic, and two of New York City's Dutch merchants. The council was now particularly resented because, with the General Assembly abolished, the Council had adopted the function of the assembly, passing acts for the governor's signature. And worst of all, most of the council's acts were for the purpose of increasing taxes. Typical was the decision to grant pardons to the thirteen townsmen charged with riot. The men were free, but the town was charged with a special tax of 200 pounds to pay for the patent and legal fees.

INDIAN AND FRENCH RELATIONS

While all this was of major importance to East Hampton, it was just another nuisance to the governor, who had inter-colonial issues to deal with. When Dongan arrived in the colony in 1683, he had a number of long-standing problems awaiting him. Territory in dispute included the land between the Connecticut and Hudson rivers, claimed also by Connecticut. Pennsylvania had designs on Iroquois lands on the upper Susquehanna, and Dongan's first order of business upon his arrival was a trip to Albany, to encourage that community's leaders to use their influence among the Iroquois to prevent any land sales to Pennsylvania. Meanwhile, Massachusetts had an interest in Pemaquid and the offshore islands. Massachusetts officials were issuing licenses to trade at Pemaquid, which Dongan declared invalid.

All these were problems with other Englishmen, and, like the problems within the colony, would eventually be worked out at some level of government. Problems with other neighbors were more complicated, and even dangerous. England and France had been edging toward war for several years, there were constant rumors throughout Dongan's years of administration that war was finally about to break out, but it did not actually begin until 1689. New York's interest was not in far-off wars but in the threat that French Canada posed to its northern frontier if war between England and France did break out. Complicating the problem for the two colonies was their jealousy over trade with the Iroquois.

New York had long claimed sovereignty over the Five Nations of the Iroquois, which the Iroquois acknowledged when it was to their advantage, and ignored when it was not. This ambiguity led New York into constant diplomatic difficulties with other colonies. Iroquois raids on Virginia and Maryland were an embarrassment, and Dongan arranged conferences in two successive years at Albany. The Iroquois leaders apologized for their young hotheads and blamed the French in Canada for arming them. Agreements were reached, gifts were exchanged, but raiding parties continued southward. The Iroquois promised not to make any treaties without checking first with Dongan, then went ahead and made a formal treaty with the French anyway, and almost immediately broke it. Their understanding of power politics and the nature of treaties was virtually European.

The French had their own problems with the Iroquois five nations, who were raiding French trading parties returning from Sioux territory, and had assaulted a French fort on the Illinois River. The French planned to retaliate and sought assurance of neutrality from New York. Dongan, of course, restated New York's claim to sovereignty over all the five nations and their territory, and forbade any French incursions south of the Great Lakes. In June 1687, Dongan warned the Seneca of French intentions against them, and Albany sent them powder and lead. The men of the nation went on war alert, and sent the women and children to Cayuga villages and to Albany for safety.

The French invited the Iroquois nations to send representatives to a conference. However, when the Iroquois ambassadors arrived at Montreal they were seized and sent to France, where they were put to work as galley-slaves. French troops then attacked Indian villages along Irondequoit Bay, and went through Seneca country burning fields and villages. The Seneca called for a meeting with Dongan at Albany, where they filled him in on what had been happening. He urged caution and recommended releasing French prisoners.

Dongan took the military situation seriously enough that he spent the winter of 1687–88 in Albany overseeing the palisading of that town and Schenectady, leaving Brockholls and the council in charge at New York. He had Albany send scouts to Lake Champlain, and sentries were posted at Albany and Schenectady. The Long Island militia was called upon to send up one man in ten to help with the frontier defenses, and Dongan called on the Iroquois for reinforcements.

The Mohawks and Mahicans now began to attack small forts and villages near Montreal and the area of present-day Kingston, Ontario. A party of Jesuits sent by the French governor came to Albany in February 1688 to discuss peace with Dongan, the French being convinced that the Iroquois were not acting on their own. While good intentions were expressed by both sides, the conference really did not accomplish anything. The Iroquois harassed the Canadians all that winter.

Most of the French at Niagara were either killed or died of disease. Fort Frontenac was invested. By spring the Iroquois controlled Canada from the Richelieu River to Montreal. Finally the French asked them to come parlay, but remembering what had happened to their ambassadors the last time, the Iroquois took the sensible and intimidating step of sending 1,200 warriors as representatives to Montreal. The French governor agreed to peace and solicited from France the return of the Indians serving in French galleys. However, no one expected that the troubles were over, and in May Dongan went to Albany again for further defensive preparations and discussions with local officials. This time he left the three Dutch counselors Phillipse, van Cortlandt, and Bayard in charge at New York, since Brockholls was in charge of a military force along the border.

New York in the Dominion of New England

Meanwhile, King James was advancing a plan begun two years earlier to cancel the charters and abolish the elected assemblies of his northern colonies, which he could then unite into one dominion under one governor and one council. The Dominion of New England was formed in 1686 from Massachusetts Bay, New Hampshire, and Plymouth colonies, and Pemaquid was annexed to Massachusetts. Dongan in fact had long campaigned for just such a move, pointing out that Pemaquid was more properly a dependency of its neighbor, Massachusetts, than of distant New York.

On December 19, 1686, former New York governor Sir Edmund Andros arrived at Boston as the new governor-general of the "Territory and Dominion of New England in America." Almost at once a tug-of-war broke out between Andros and Dongan for Connecticut, with Dongan sending off agents to woo the unresponsive Yankees, who did not want to be part of anything else, certainly not any colony led by either the long distrusted Andros or the Catholic Dongan with his Dutch confederates.

East Hampton was more receptive to the idea of the dominion. In July 1688, the trustees voted to send delegates to meet with Andros, and instructed them to take John Youngs along as advisor. East Hampton still wanted to be out of New York: if they couldn't join Connecticut, they were glad to settle for Massachusetts. However, the king had his own ideas; on All Hallow's Eve, Andros forced Connecticut into the dominion, and the next day Rhode Island. The dominion was looking even more attractive.

But the king wasn't finished. New York and New Jersey were added to the dominion on March 23, 1688. Governor Dongan found himself laid off from his job, or in modern terms, downsized. To make his being superseded more palatable, Dongan received an offer from the king of a regiment and a commission as major general of artillery. He opted instead to retire and by July 28 he was ready to give up his government.

That winter, Anthony Brockholls would oversee a garrison at Pemaquid, while Patrick MacGregorie and other regular officers from New York were assigned to other forts on the Maine frontier. Thomas Dongan, the most experienced soldier of them all, retired to his farm at Hempstead, and to his 25,000-acre Staten Island estate, Cassiltowne, named for his birthplace.

Ex-Governor Dongan

The year 1688 ended with the colonists caught up in their own concerns, unaware of events in Europe. The Netherlands had been at war with France for several years. Now a Dutch army led by King James's Dutch nephew, William of Orange, had landed in England. James II had found himself virtually without friends among his own subjects and fled to France. William and Mary had begun their reign in England. Now that France's enemy, William of Orange, was not only commander-in-chief of the Dutch armies but king of England as well, France declared war on England. But the Americans would only learn of all this the next spring.

When word arrived, the governments established by James collapsed. The unpopular Dominion of New England vanished like a puff of smoke and Governor-General Andros was thrown in jail by Boston's citizens. In New York, the news that there was a new king brought down the government. A period of anarchy ensued until New York militia captain Jacob Leisler assumed the role of acting governor.

With an unstable and makeshift government, Leisler, and many ordinary citizens of the colony, feared not only the French military threat to the north, but the possibility that some groups in New York might be less than enthusiastic in their support of King William. Leisler even imagined that disaffected groups in the colony, which he supposed would include those who had grown rich under James's rule, and Frenchmen, and Roman Catholics, might conspire with the French colonial government to the north. In particular, Leisler saw Thomas Dongan as a menace to Protestants, and accused him of organizing a Catholic army on Staten Island to overthrow the government.

With Leisler in control of provincial headquarters at Fort James, Dongan left the colony in August 1689 for Connecticut, and then moved on to Rhode Island. By November he had quietly returned to his farm at Hempstead, but when Leisler issued an arrest warrant in February 1690, accusing Dongan of advancing the interests of James II in violation of his oaths to King William, Dongan renewed his wandering, first to New Jersey and then to Massachusetts. In 1691 he made his way across the ocean to London, and there he stayed, for there was no longer anything for him in Ireland. His brother William, Earl of Limerick, had gone into exile in France, along with James II, and the family estates were confiscated by the crown.

James made one attempt to regain his throne, leading an army into the friendly confines of Catholic Ireland, from where he proposed launching an assault on England herself. But King William, William of Orange, took an army to Ireland and met James at the battle of the Boyne. James's army sustained heavy losses; James panicked and fled the battlefield and continued on, eventually all the way back to France. On that day, Ireland's Protestants became Orangemen.

In 1698 Thomas Dongan's brother the earl of Limerick died, leaving no male descendants (his only son having been killed at the Battle of the Boyne). Thomas then became the fifth earl of Limerick. He had been petitioning since 1692 for recompense for his services in America, and for the arrears on his pension granted by Charles II, to which he now added a request for the return of his ancestral estates. In none of this was he successful. He eventually sold some of his American properties, which enabled him to spend his last years in genteel poverty. He died on December 14, 1715, at the age of eighty-one, in London where he had lived for twenty-five years, and was buried there in St. Pancras churchyard. A lifelong bachelor, he left his estate on Staten Island to three nephews who emigrated to America.

These were momentous times, and I fear that it is all a bit much to put into a speech and expect anyone to comprehend it all. But perhaps we can summarize and give some general impressions of what this all means.

Thomas Dongan was sent as governor to New York because he had what were considered the requisite qualities for public administration in those days: he was a nobleman, and had served thirty years in the military. A year or so as lieutenant-governor of Tangier was sufficient practical experience. But, in fact, he did a good job as New York's governor during a very difficult period.

Within the colony, there was still plenty of resentment against English government by the overwhelmingly Dutch population. This was not just ethnic bias: the Dutch did not have the contacts in England necessary for success as merchants, and the Dutch were first and foremost merchants. Of the English in the colony, the vast majority on Long Island and at Westchester were Puritans Congregationalists and Presbyterians and they had come over here to escape from Anglicans and Royalists.

That Dongan was a Royalist we know; from the standpoint of Dutch and English Calvinists, his being Catholic was even worse than being Anglican. That he had served thirty years in the French army hardly endeared him to people in a colony whose northern neighbor was still called New France. The New England colonies were suspicious of a neighbor colony that was a Royal possession. New Jersey chafed under New York's influence and was unhappy that as long as the governor of New York held the title of admiral, New York still controlled their shipping. The reliability of the Iroquois as allies extended only as far as they saw the alliance as in their self-interest, but Dongan did a good job of holding their loyalty. Relations were certainly prickly at times, but overall, the Iroquois were New York's firmest allies.

Against this background, Thomas Dongan tried to administer one of the most internally combustible of colonies. There was animosity between Dutch and English, between Royalists and Puritans, between Protestants and Catholics. These were not simple dislikes: people were forced into exile for belonging to the wrong party. People were killed for belonging to the wrong party.

Dongan was placed in a particularly difficult situation in that the Duke of York, later King James, expected him to bring about freedom of public worship for most of the religions in the colony.

Lutherans and Quakers and Catholics liked that idea—they had been repressed under the Dutch—but many Protestants were more than a little upset with a Catholic chapel and chaplain in the fort at Manhattan, a Jesuit parochial school in the midst of New York City, and Jesuit missionaries roaming through the colony cementing the far-flung Catholic community. In the end, Dongan's strongest supporters in the colony were those who most benefited from his position. Other than his religious allies, they would be the owners of large, landed estates and wealthy merchants who did business with the government. During the Leisler regime, they would all be tarred with the same brush: even Dutch Calvinists like Stephanus van Cortlandt and Nicholas Bayard were accused of being soft on Catholicism and disloyal to King William. It was not a time when tolerance was viewed as a positive quality.

It is difficult to evaluate the measures adopted during Thomas Dongan's governorship. Dongan's reorganization of the legislature, the courts, and local government extended a measure of popular participation in government, but also expanded the influence of central government throughout the colony. City aldermen and town officials were popularly elected, but county officials and the principal city officers were appointed, not elected. It was more democracy than King James was comfortable with, less than the colonists desired.

One of Dongan's most difficult problems was the long-standing feud between the towns of eastern Long Island and the government of New York. He sought to make peace with them, tried to accommodate them as much as he could, and overlooked many of their affronts. But in the end they had to understand that Long Island was part of New York and they would have to submit to its government.

What was the purpose of granting a patent to East Hampton? It was hardly intended as a favor to the residents here. For one thing, issuing the patent put some money in Dongan's pocket, although that is not why we are interested in it. More importantly, it made all land title here dependent upon the royal colony of New York. The annual quitrent was a reminder that refusal to pay tribute could result in loss of property title. The proprietors lost their title to any unassigned land, and government in the town henceforth would represent all the landholding freemen and other residents: a proprietor's vote carried no more weight than anyone else's. Other places had manor lords; the east end of Long Island had equality, or at least something approaching it the vote was, after all, limited to the more successful residents. If there was democracy here, it was very local and very limited, but it was a start. It would be another three centuries before every adult in this country would have the right to vote, only in the 1960s that we eliminated the last of the poll tax laws that disenfranchised the poor. But the movement toward universal voting, together with clear land title without quitrents began here in that most difficult and uncompromising of towns, East Hampton.

THE PERSISTENT EAST HAMPTON
TOWN TRUSTEES

Stuart B. Vorpahl, Jr.

L ONG ISLAND TOWNS have a form of government, in part, peculiarly their own. It differs greatly from that of localities in other sections of the state and nation. This has a bearing on titles and fee of the land. Much of the Trustee Journals have to do with titles and land conveyances. The land tenure in East Hampton is bewildering to newcomers, often puzzling to natives. For nearly 150 years before New York State adopted its State Constitution, after the Revolutionary war, East Hampton Town had been settled."[1]

East Hampton's government was well-established before Governor Dongan demanded his patent of December 6, 1686, which renamed the "patentees," created by the Nicholls Patent of March 13, 1666, as the Trustees of the Freeholders Commonalty of the Town of East Hampton, one body corporate and politic.

I wish to map out how our Town Trustee form of municipal government evolved, being that its roots go back 350 years.

Within a year of the settlement of Maidstone in 1648, the thirty-four families had established a government partly democratic and partly representative in the most simple form: "Being without the jurisdiction of any chartered colonies, it became necessary for them to establish regulations of their own formation or to adopt those of a system already devised."[2]

They now ordained a general court composed of the whole assembled people. Three men at first were selected at the general court and four to a special court.

All Laws were enacted and all the general affairs were regulated at

191

a town meeting, at which every inhabitant was bound under penalty to be present. "No person was allowed to sell or buy lands without the permission of the Town."[3]

The Settlers had purchased Maidstone from Governor Eaton of New Haven and Governor Hopkins of Hartford, Connecticut, without prior conveyance or any acquittance for the payment. The general court sent Ralph Dayton and Robert Bond several times to Connecticut over a period of years before they were furnished with evidence of their title and payment.

The Town contained a government under their own voluntary unwritten compact subject to the supervision of the general court, appointed by the assemblage of people, independent of the other settlements for eight or nine years. In 1655, they wrote a more formal social compact. In 1655, a committee of two persons—and, again, in 1657, a committee of three persons—was sent to Connecticut to treat with the magistracy concerning placing the Settlement under the protection of that colony.

Because of the hostility of the Dutch and foreign Indians warring with the English, East Hampton in 1657 submitted themselves to Connecticut's jurisdiction so far as to be entitled to its protection. The union continued until 1662 when a charter was granted to Connecticut by the Second Charles.

As Connecticut was procuring a patent or charter from the King, East Hampton was encouraged to do the same. They sent a committee to Southampton upon the subject as both towns held their possessions by virtue only of Indian deeds and prior settlement. They became uneasy with regard to their title. The Earl of Sterling had relinquished his claim to the Island and it was then open to future grant from the crown.

In 1663, the residents of East Hampton encouraged a construction of the patent of Connecticut embracing Long Island within its jurisdiction. The legal jurisdiction being now assumed and admitted, a code of civil government was received from the General Assembly convened at Hartford. The inhabitants of East Hampton proceeded to organize courts and establish rules relative to the management of their general affairs. At the same time, a code of civil government was received from the general assembly convened at Hartford. Before these arrangements could be carried into effect, an expedition fitted out by the Duke of York arrived in New York. Charles II had granted Long Island to the Duke upon its surrender by the Earl of Stirling, together with the country occupied by the Dutch. Upon a demand of Colonel Nicolls, the Dutch Governor, after some preliminary arrangements, surrendered the country. Governor Winthrop, after seeing the letters patent to the Duke of York, relinquished the intended jurisdiction of Connecticut over East Hampton.

Long Island was incorporated with the Colony of New York under the Duke of York. The deputy governor Richard Nicolls in March 1665 convened a meeting at Hempstead of two deputies from each town on Long Island and two from Westchester for the purpose of organizing the government. These towns were erected into a shire by the name of Yorkshire, which was divided into three ridings. The Towns in Suffolk County formed the East Riding. A body of laws called the Duke's Laws were promulgated. They superseded those under which the Towns had previously acted and were continued until 1683. The several towns were recognized and were required to take out patents from the governor for the lands within their acknowledged limits.

East Hampton purchased the Nicholls Patent on March 13, 1666, the land bounds being from the Southampton Town line to Fort Pond at Montauk on still east to the utmost extent of the Island.[4] Seven were named as patentees, which constituted the complete government for East Hampton Town.

This is the reason that the Town Trustees' official corporate seal is dated 1666.

The townspeople's feeling of security with the Nicholls Patent confirming their purchase and legally establishing their government was short-lived.

The increase in population and adherence to their worship independent of the established Church of England now made them fit subject for the rapacity of governors commissioned for the very purpose of subverting representative government and repairing their ruined fortunes by extortion from the colonists. In swift succession, governor succeeded governor, each in the main baffled by the sturdy resistance of the people, nowhere more persistent than in East Hampton Town.

The three eastern towns of this county—Southampton, Southold and East Hampton—were the backbone of the country, if not of the whole colony of New York, in advocating representative government and resisting encroachment upon their liberties.

On June 19, 1682, at a Town meeting, an address or petition was read to the inhabitants wherein was declared

> some agrievances yt did lie uppon ye spirits of ye people in respect of ye present government and it was by a major vote concluded and granted yt this foresaid petition should be signed yt it might be in areadines to be sent upp to ye Honorable Governor when wee heare of His arrivall at York.

It was signed on June 21st, 1682.

This was East Hampton's greeting to Governor Thomas Dongan when he arrived in the colonies.

In 1683, the newly appointed Gov. Dongan was instructed to call a general assembly of all the Freeholders. In October, 1684, the assembly met and claimed in a Bill of Rights as Englishment that, "Every Freeholder and Freeman should vote trial by jury, no tax to be levied but by consent of the assembly" etc.[5]

In 1685, less than a month after James the Second ascended the throne, he prepared to overturn the institutions he had conceded. By ordinance, a direct tax was decreed, titles to real estate were questioned, that larger fees and quitrents might be extorted and of the farmers of East Hampton who protested against the tyranny, six were arraigned before the council.

On October 1st, 1685, the overseers (patentees) addressed Governor Dongan about the Town's grievances. It is 3-1/2 pages long in Volume II, Town Records. "This expression of 1685 would develop into the Declaration of 1776."[6]

In May 1686, Governor Dongan was endeavoring to compel the people of East Hampton to purchase a new patent at an exorbitant price and they were resisting the attempt at extortion. In June 1686, the Townspeople voted two committees to defend the rights of those arrested and the Town's rights.

On July 29, 1686, ten persons complained to the Governor that the Town would lay out no land to newcomers to the Town. Governor Dongan ordered the High Sheriff to lay out each thirty acres. The townspeople objected by written protest on October 6, 1686. It was deemed libel and the governors council arrested twelve East Hampton men, including their minister, Thomas James.

The arbitrary power of Dongan prevailed; a patent was procured dated December 9, 1686 which

> secured individually to the Holder, all Lands then taken up and appropriated to the purchasers all lands unappropriated in proporcian to their severall and respective purchasers thereof and gave to the Trustees of the corporation the preemption of first purchase right as to the than unpurchased part of Montauk.

The Dongan Patent changed the prior existing patentees to Trustees of The Freeholders and Commonalty of the Town of East Hampton, body corporate and politic, increasing their numbers to twelve, to be elected annually.[7] It gave the Town Trustees rights over the Town's area and made the Town a State in all but name.[8]

The Town Trustees levied a tax to pay the £200 cost of the Patent; £120 came from the purchasers and proprietors of the Home Town and £80 charged at Montauk.[9] An extra amount was assessed to pay the costs "arising about men's protest."

On March 10, 1689–90, the Town Trustees directed a letter be sent to Governor Jacob Lesler reciting that

> We have agreed to send over to his Majesty both a true narra-
> tion of ye grievance we have suffered this many years under an
> arbitrary power and petition to their majesties yt we might be
> rejoined with Connecticut government as formerly agreeably
> to the act of parliament yt all places....shall have the same priv-
> ileges they enjoyed in ye year 1660 restored unto them."[10]

Obviously, the inhabitants of East Hampton were not pleased to be bound to the colony of New York by the Dongan Patent.

The close of the American Revolution had no imapct upon the widespread authority of our Town Trustees and their patents, as the patents' validity were fully recognized by both state and federal con-stitutions.[11] These constitutional provisions remain to this day in spite of a fraudulent attempt by the New York State Legislature to remove said provisions in 1962.

The Town Trustees made the final land allotments in 1748 (three-acre division). Almost all private title to lands in East Hampton origi-nated with the overseers or Trustees by allotments or sale. The last major land sale of commons by the Town Trustees was in the early 1950s.

Much of the Town Trustees' business involved selling or exchang-ing of land. They conducted all town affairs, they established the schools, they regulated use of the commons, managed the great herds of cattle, sheep and horses annually turned out at Montauk, protected the Indians hired for the "whaling designe." They passed many laws and ordinances and enforced the same by appointing trustee committees or directing the constables to carry out their orders. Most penalties in-volved fines or impounding, "offending stock." Yet in 1727, Recom-pence Squier was chosen common whipper, allowing three shillings for each person he shall whip.[12]

Severe offenses would result in banishment from town, ordered by the Town Trustees.

The Trustees levied three different Tax Rates: Town Rate, Montauk Rate and Sheep Rate.[13] They represented the proprietors,[14] the Free-holders and Commonalty and the Montauk proprietors.

They directed the assessors how to proceed in their assessments and ordered the disbursement of tax money so raised for the use of the Town. The Clerk of the Trustees exercised practically the duties and functions of the modern supervisor in town affairs.[15] The Trustees really ran the town.[16] They held all of the powers and even more than the present day Town Board.[17]

As the Town's lands became more "freeholder" than "proprietary" ownership the Town Rates were decided at the annual Town meeting and funds were voted upon for Town Trustee use. This lasted until 1919 when the annual town meetings ended and the Town Board assumed many duties formally administered by the Town Trustees.

Of all the lawsuits the Trustees were involved with over a long period, the most important was the Montauk case whereby the Town Trustees lost their right to manage the Montauk commons in 1851.[18]

The Trustees, in turn, then claimed complete ownership and control of all the remaining common land and waters in East Hampton Town.

Since the beginnings of the Town, the Trustees, undertakers, townsmen, etc. would charge fees for any usage of the commons, be it cutting wood (even for a pump stick), harvesting cranberries, beachplums, seaweed, cutting of hay, grazing rights, fishing and hunting rights, any use whatsoever could only be done upon permission of the Town Trustees.[19]

Since 1852, the Town Trustees have sold several thousand acres of "Commons," mostly to pay for "lawyering," such as the long-running seaweed suits and the Fort Pond Bay case.

Besides laying out of many roads, Merchants Path to Northwest Harbor being one of importance, the Trustees created all of the Sag Harbor waterfront properties[20] by selling underwater lots[21] in Northwest Harbor starting with the permit[22] to build Long Wharf in 1770. Each lot was required to be filled in as terms of sale. Northwest Harbor was the only harbor suitable for commerce and fishing ventures (codfishing and whaling) for all the east end Towns. The only underwater land New York state can claim in Northwest Harbor are the two parcels they bought from the Town Trustees in 1803–08 and 1821 for extensions of Long Wharf. Northwest has always been a harbor of The Town according to the language of The Patents. The Fort Pond Bay case, rightfully lost by the Trustees, confirms their ownership of Northwest Harbor.

They still administer the Rysam Fund for poor school children established by Captain Rysam's Will in 1809.[23]

The Trustees controlled all hunting and fishing, both within the

patented bounds and in the adjoining bays and sea as one of the fran-
chises and attachments to the land bounds of The Nicholls and Dongan
Patents.[24] Trustees' Reservations on commons sold would include the
inhabitants' continued right to hunt and shoot.[25] Until recently, the bay
constables were under the jurisdiction of the Trustees; also, at times, a
game constable served the Trustees.

The Town Trustees historically have always taken a dim view of any
attempts by New York State to infringe upon their patented rights.

On June 21, 1882, they vowed to challenge the constitutionality of
a state act to prohibit animals running at large on public highways. East
Hampton and Amagansett Main Streets were laid out very wide so as to
"yardup" the livestock to be driven on or off Montauk. Cattle were still
driven on Montauk roads in the 1950s.[26]

In November 1935, baymen protested to the Trustees concerning
attempts by New York State conservation officers to enforce a State
Law on escalloping in Three Mile Harbor. The Town Trustees voted
unanimously to control the products of the waters within the bounds
of the Town of East Hampton by the set of ordinances adopted by the
Trustees in 1932.[27]

On April 10, 1945, the Town Trustees voted to defend any and all
persons who were to be arrested by a state conservation officer for
shellfishing in Town waters without the state shellfish license.[28]

In March 1952, William Lester and Stuart Vorpahl requested to
place eel pots in Hook Pond without paying license fees to New York
State. The Trustees referred the matter to counsel.[29]

On November 11, 1980 a motion by Jim McCourt was seconded
and approved that the Trustees would fill out an Environmental Assessment Form for the starfish liming project but let it be known that as a
separate organization preceding all other governments, they did not
have to, but would like to, cooperate with the Town Government.[30]

As a courtesy, the Trustees invited New York State's Department of
Environmental Conservation to observe the liming project if they
wished.

The Town Trustees have never transferred or abandoned their
patented authority to manage and control their holdings, free from the
"lett or hinderance" of any person or persons whatsoever.[31]

Our Town Trustees went from being the Government for East
Hampton in all aspects, to literally "begging for their bread" because of
a hostile Town Board in 1934.

No other form of government has any legal authority to interfere
with Town Trustee matters. The Trustees, because of the "Iron Bound"

language of the Patents, cannot be legislated against.[32] The relationship today between the Town Trustees and all other forms of Government is best described in the court documents pertaining to the "Hassan Case" in May, 1980:

> The Town Trustees are elected by the voters of the Town and regulations for the trusteed lands are established through formal legislation by the Town Board enacted only on request of the Trustees.[33]

Originally, the Town Trustees legislated the Town affairs but, all too often, they have agreed to let someone else steer the boat; however, they never have relinquished ownership of the vessel to anyone. The Trustees of the Freeholders and Commonalty of the Town of East Hampton are one of the oldest continually elected forms of government in this country. The language of their patents will insure that the Town Trustees will be an integral part of East Hampton Town Government far into the future.

NOTES

NOTE: From 1650-1725, Town and Trustee Records were the same.

1. Town Trustee Records, 1870-1897, *Introduction, Long Island Towns*, State, also "Reservations", pp. 1 and 11.

2. Gardiner, David. *Chronicles of Town of East Hampton, 1840*, printed in 1871, pp. 10-37.

3. Gardiner, *David. Chronicles of Town of East Hampton, 1840*, printed in 1871, pp. 10-37.

4. Town Trustee Record, 1807-1826, *What Trustees did; Introduction*, pp. 1-65.

5. Town Records, Vol. VI, *Convey Common Land*, pp. 666-677.

6. Town Records, Vol. II, 1685 *Petition to Gov. Dongan*, pp. 6, 7, 169-172.

7. Town Records, Vol. II, *Account of Suffolk County*, pp. 2-12, & Dongan Patent, pp. 194-203.

8. Town Trustee Records, 1870-1897, *Introduction, Long Island Towns, State*, also "Reservations", pp. 1 and 11.

9. Town Records, Vol. IX, *Osborne Shaw Brookhaven Town Historian*, pp. 13-16 and Vol. II, p. 6.

10. Town Records, Vol. II, *Petition of 1689-90 to Rejoin with Connecticut*, pp. 6-250.

11. N.Y. Senate Bill Introduction 1384, Senator Bronston, January 17, 1961.

12. Town Records, Vol. III, *Tanner Warned*, pp. 155 & *Common Whiper*, p. 429.

13. Town Trustee Records, 1725-1772, *Introduction & Town Rates*, p. 43.

14. Town Records, Vol. VI, *Trustees Threefold*, pp. 626-27.

15. Town Trustee Records, 1725-1772, *Introduction & Town Rates*, p. 43.

16. Town Records, Vol. IX, *Osborne Shaw Brookhaven Town Historian*, pp. 13-16 and Vol. II, p. 6.

17. Trustee Records, 1926-1939, *Osborne Shaw*, page 9.

18. Trustee Records, 1807-1826, *Sag Harbor*, pp. 31-37, and Town Records, Vol. VI, pp. 357-358.

19. Trustee Records 1772-1807, State land office, no jurisdiction in patented Towns; what Trustees did & Sag Harbor, pp. 30-37.

20. Samuel Mulford Papers, Long Island Collection, East Hampton Library; Trustee Records 1845-1870, *Hunting,* pp. 53, 64, 70, 77, 78, 83, 113. 1822-1845, p. 284, 161-162, *Charles Mott.*

21. Samuel Mulford Papers, Long Island Collection, East Hampton Library; Trustee Records 1845-1870, *Hunting,* pp. 53, 64, 70, 77, 78, 83, 113. 1822-1845, p. 284, 161-162, *Charles Mott.*

22. Trustee Records, 1870-1897, *Northwest Harbor*, 1678 *Letter Horses from Shelter Island on Hogg Neck*, pp. 300-303.

23. Trustee Records, 1940-1955, *Rysam Fund*, pp. 27-29.

24. Samuel Mulford Papers, Long Island Collection, East Hampton Library; Trustee Records 1845-1870, *Hunting,* pp. 53, 64, 70, 77, 78, 83, 113. 1822-1845, p. 284, 161-162, Charles Mott.

25. Town Trustee Records, 1870-1897, *Introduction, Long Island Towns, State*, also "Reservations", pp. 1 and 11.

26. Trustee Records, 1870-1897, *One State Prohibits Cattle on Roads*, p. 131.

27. Trustee Records, 1926-1939, *Escalloping Law*, p. 245; *State Laws not Valid in Township*, p. 258.

28. Trustee Records, 1940-1955, April 10, 1945. *Trustee Vow to Defend*, pp. 141-42.

29. Trustee Records, 1940-1955, *Hook Pond*, p. 233.

30. Trustee Records, *Current Minutes* November 11, 1980, p. 2 & Starfish File.

31. Town Records, Vol. II, *Account of Suffolk County*, pp. 2-12, & *Dongan Patent*, pp. 194-203.

32. Trustees' Current Records, *Hassan Case*, 78 c. 1432, pp. 4-5.

33. Trustee Records, 1926-1939, *Dredge Three Mile Harbor*, p. 261.

FOR THE ORDERING OF THE AFFAIRES OF THE TOWNE

The Origins of Government
in East Hampton

—⟶—

Langdon G. Wright

JUST AS EAST HAMPTON residents carefully parceled out their land, the organizers of this ambitious lecture series have divided the topics. My assignment is to talk about the origins, development, and functions of East Hampton's government in the first fifty years or so of its existence.

In June, 1653, William Edwards sued Benjamin Price and his wife for defamation, claiming that Mrs. Price had called Mrs. Edwards a "base lying woman." This, Edwards lamented, was "a deep wound that is laid upon his wife.... Hereafter it may be spoken here go the brats of a base liar." But the case quickly turned against Edwards, as witnesses testified that Goody Edwards had kicked the constable and threatened to kill him; that when a man went to the constable's aid, she kicked him and broke his shins; and that when her husband told her to take her punishment patiently, she threatened to kill him as well. "It was also affirmed that Goodwife Edwards said that her husband had brought her to a place where there was neither magistrates nor ministers. Also she said that he had brought her to live among a company of heathen and that she would hang him when she came home."

Was East Hampton really that bad? Probably not. But we have had a tendency to romanticize the communities Englishmen sought to establish. It's hard not to, when you read John Winthrop's hopes for Boston as a City on a Hill in his "Model of Christian Charity":

> We must be knit together in this work as one man. We must entertain each other in brotherly affection. We must be willing to

200

abridge ourselves of our superfluities for the supply of others'
necessities. We must uphold a familiar commerce together in
all meekness, gentleness, patience, and liberality. We must delight in each other; make others' conditions our own, rejoice
together, mourn together, labor and suffer together, always having before our eyes our commission and community in the
work, our community as members of the same body. . . .

It's hard not to romanticize the communities when you read some
of their covenants, a document which all adult male residents were
supposed to sign. It usually stated the ideals of the settlers and outlined
key policies. In Artickells of Agreement drawn up in Eastchester in
1665, for example, the settlers pledged to endeavor to keep and maintain Christian love and civil honesty; to faithfully console what may be
of infirmity in any one of us; and plainly to deal with one another in
Christian love. They all agreed to pay for the support of a minister; stipulated that no man was to receive more than fifteen acres of land until
all men had that quantity; required men who wished to sell land to tender it to the town or to a man approved by the town; required that
men attempt to settle disputes by arbitration; that all men make and
maintain good fences; that they cooperate in building bridges and
roads, guarding cattle, educating their children, and—in a later adden-
dum—improve one day each spring in hunting rattlesnakes.

No wonder, then, that Kenneth Lockridge has described Dedham,
Massachusetts as a "Christian utopian closed corporate community."

Early East Hampton probably lies somewhere between utopia and
Goody Edwards's version. Where can we locate it? These are the ques-
tions I would like to address: What was the structure of government in
East Hampton? What did it attempt to do? How well did it succeed?
Who participated in it, and who did not? Given the opportunity pre-
sented by being a new town in a "new" world, how did they proceed?
Did they innovate, or did they try to reproduce forms which were fa-
miliar to them? And, lastly, what social values did they express?

As I read the records, certain themes emerge.

First, I find no evidence that East Hampton residents had any grand
social vision—no covenant, no expressed desire to create a city on a
hill. Instead, they worked out the frame of their government in a series
of ad hoc decisions made over the years; voluntarily borrowed from
Connecticut, and less voluntarily from the Duke's Laws established in
New York in 1665; and showed indecision about the responsibilities of
the town and its elected officials, and even about the titles of those officials.

Second, they were sometimes torn between what T. H. Breen has called "persistent localism," the jealous protection of what they felt was theirs—their land, their rights—and the inescapable and sometimes necessary fact that they had to be part of a larger whole, whether Connecticut or New York.

Third, they often experienced tensions between participation and exclusion, between communalism and individualism. And by the end of the period I have studied, around 1710, there is evidence that individualism was gaining the upper hand.

I will develop these themes.

It was no great surprise to me that East Hampton never drew up a covenant. Of the English towns in New York I have studied, only Southampton (in its "Abstract of the Laws of Judgment as given by Moses to the Commonwealth of Israel" and the "Disposall of the Vessell" in 1647) and Eastchester (in its "Articles of Agreement" in 1665) produced covenants or similar documents. And in the sixty-three New England towns John Martin examined in his book *Profits in the Wilderness*, only about half ever had one.

It was something of a surprise to me that the town government developed in an ad hoc fashion over time. Many towns were careful to specify what elected officials could do, and what powers were reserved to the town meeting. East Hampton did not. The decisions of the magistrates and the town meetings are intermingled, and it is often difficult to tell whether an order was made by the town as a whole or by its elected officials. Many begin with "It is ordered" or a similar phrase—a passive construction that obscures who made the order (and a grammatical construction that is still the bane of teachers today).

There even seems to have been some indecision about what to call the elected officials. The "constable" appears early on and regularly. But the others were referred to in the early years as "the men that are in authority" or the men chosen "for the ordering of the town's affairs" or the men elected "to make orders for the good of the town." Only in the 1650s does the more standard title "townsmen" begin to appear. And thereafter, titles change in accordance with dictates from higher authority: the "townsmen" become "constables" in accordance with the Duke's Laws; "selectmen" in 1684; and "trustees" in 1686 with the charter granted by Governor Thomas Dongan.

BORROWING

The form of government and even some of the nomenclature they borrowed from Massachusetts and New England. They called their town meetings "General Courts" or "Courts of Election," terms which appear in both the charter of the Massachusetts Bay Company (1629) and the Fundamental Orders of Connecticut (1639).

In April, 1651, the town directed Robert Bond to go to Connecticut not only to secure evidence of their title to the land, but also to procure a copy of that colony's "body of laws." Two years later, they agreed that Connecticut's laws "shall stand in force among us." Subsequently, they adopted "the order in Connecticut laws for paying of rates" and copied into the town's records the colony's definition of freemen; regulations concerning the appointment of packers of meat and innkeepers; and punishments for those who took up abode with Indians. The records of court cases used the English terms "trespass upon the case" or "action of the case" to describe tort claims.

FRAMEWORK OF GOVERNMENT

Whatever their name and number—which varied from three to four to seven to twelve—the men in authority/townsmen/constable/selectmen combined legislative and judicial functions. In the first recorded "Court of Election" held in October, 1650, the settlers decided that the four men chosen "for ordering the affairs of the town" plus the constable were to constitute a court to try cases under forty shillings. (Cases above that amount were to be heard by a seven-man jury). Any two of the officers could issue a warrant for arrest. Any citizen could "purchase a court" by paying 1s 6d to each person employed and 2s for entering an action. A "General Court "held a year later, elected three men "for the execution of those orders committed to their trust" and in addition to trying cases, empowered them "to consider of those things that may concern the public good of this place." In 1652, the General Court voted that any one "aggrieved" by an action of "the men that are in authority" could appeal to the next General Court "or when the freemen are assembled together for their public occasions." Not until 1653 does there appear some indication of the relative power and responsibilities of the magistrates and the people. In that year, the seven men (four had been added, in reaction to a perceived threat from Indians) were instructed "to make all orders and do what they see to be good for the town, only giving out of lots excepted." In 1661, three men were elected "to make orders for the good of the town." Those orders included levying taxes "and doing or cause do be done any public work that they or the major part of them apprehend to be for the good of the whole." And that is as far as the records go in indicating the powers and responsibilities of elected officials.

What about the town meeting itself? Who participated? How frequently were they held? What did they do? How well did they work?

I can't really tell who "belonged." Some towns distinguished between "freemen" (those who owned a certain amount of property or were entitled to a share of the common lands, and who, therefore, were entitled to vote) and those who merely lived in the community. Other towns made full membership in the church a prerequisite for membership. East Hampton records contain no such distinctions. In 1662, Connecticut's laws regarding freemen were copied into the records. These required a person who wished to be admitted to present a certificate signed by a majority of their townsmen attesting that they were "of a civil, peaceable, and honest conversation"; that they were twenty-one years old or older; and that they had an estate of £20. Any freeman who committed a "scandalous offense" could be disfranchised by a civil court. I'm not sure whether these rules were intended to apply to East Hampton's town meetings, or to remind them who was qualified to vote in Connecticut elections. There is no evidence that the town excluded any Englishman from a town meeting (women and Indians, of course, could not participate), and if they had a property requirement, it was easily met: in a 1675 tax list, all but one of the fifty-seven people enumerated had an estate valued at more than £20. In 1683, all seventy-one people rated were worth more than that amount. Nor is there evidence that church membership was a prerequisite—certainly not by 1698, when Nathaniel Huntting's list of all who were communicants when he was ordained contained the names of only six men, in addition to twenty-two women.

Indeed, the emphasis was on participation, rather than exclusion. If East Hampton had no particular utopian vision of itself, it, like other contemporary towns, at least recognized that consensus and cooperation were essential—in maintaining fences in the common fields, in defending the town, in watching for whales—and that men who participated in making decisions were more apt to abide by them. So one of the orders made during that first Court of Elections in 1650 was that failure to attend a town meeting would bring a twelve-shilling fine. In May, 1651, they actually levied fines ranging from sixpence to one shilling against "the delinquents who did not appear at the town

meeting according to warning." Later that year, they agreed to fine anyone who left a meeting early.

Adult males not only had to attend the town meetings; they had to
vote. In November, 1652, the town decreed that every man shall vote
by holding up his hands "either with or against in all matters, upon
penalty of paying 6d, the thing being before deliberately debated."

How frequently did they meet?

Town rules required only two meetings a year: a General Court to
be held in April (later changed to March), and a Court of Elections in
October. But the men in authority could call for additional meetings
when the need arose. The wording of the records, as I said, makes it difficult to tell what was a town meeting and what was not, and there are
some evident omissions. (There is no evidence of any meeting between November 5, 1689 and February 13, 1691, during Leisler's Rebellion, for example.) So trying to count the meetings is an uncertain,
and perhaps futile proposition. But it appears that the town actually
met as seldom as once a year for elections only, and at least as much as
seven times. The pattern seems to have been to meet in the early
spring before planting, and in the late fall after harvest, though meetings could be called at any favorable time. In 1651, for example, the
General Court adjourned itself "for three weeks or else the first wet
day and all to appear at the beat of the drum."

What did they do?

Certainly "foreign relations" and protection of the town's lands
were top priorities. Any perceived threat to their title was always the
occasion for a special meeting, as Robert Ritchie has already described.
Early on, in January, 1651, they deputized three men "for the settling of
a firm peace" with Southampton by agreeing to provisions concerning
trespass and damages caused by livestock. (One article of the agreement was that no one from either town was to place hogs or cattle
within a half mile of the boundary unless he attended them daily.) Negotiations with Southampton continued on occasion for the rest of the
century.

East Hampton adopted the common field system of agriculture, in
which inhabitants had a home lot, plus parcels of land in scattered locations. For example, when Benjamin Hand sold a portion of his land
to John Kerle in 1668, the sale included: six acres in a "second home
lot" north of the town; four acres in the two-mile hollow by the Plains;
two and a half acres in the eastern plains; four acres in the Indian well
plains; three acres in the meadow at Nepeague; and two and a half
acres in the meadow at Accoboneck great neck.

With each freeholder owing seven or more parcels of land, and with the need to keep livestock out of planting fields, it should not be surprising that more town meeting decisions regarded land and fences than any other subject. Next, perhaps, was laying out roads and paths to reach those fields, a subject that was handled both by the town as a whole and by its elected officials.

The town was also responsible for hiring and paying a minister and building a meeting house. Because of the longevity of Thomas James, the minister they hired in 1651, this wasn't a frequent item on the agenda, though it took two meetings that year to agree to pay him a £50 salary, to build a meeting house (the location of which was to be determined by a committee of three), and to pay Thomas Backer 18 pence for every Lord's Day the meeting was held in his house. In 1678, the town proactively agreed to reserve land for a new minister when Mr. James should die. James did not die for another sixteen years, in 1696, but in 1691 the town began a serious search for an assistant and eventual replacement, inviting Mr. Davenport (and offering him £60, £20 more than James was then making). Three years later, in 1694, it took three meetings to agree on a salary for another assistant, Mr. Jones; to vote to provide his firewood in addition to his salary; and to appoint Enoch Fithian to go to New Haven to escort him. In 1695, the town agreed to give him the same salary if he would stay another year, but we find them in the following year directing the trustees to search for another minister, a search which didn't end until 1699 when both the town and the trustees reached agreements with Nathaniel Huntting.

There is only one other entry in the records during the period concerning the actual practice of religion: In 1688 the constable and overseers expressed their concern about "the great disorder that is at the meeting house" on the Sabbath "by many persons staying abroad in time of public worship and spending their time in sleeping or talking, not being able to profit by the word preached." (Was this a criticism of the people, or of the declining faculties of the Rev. James?) The officials resolved to present the offenders at the next town meeting, and in the meantime demanded that masters of families supervise their children and servants to see that they didn't play during the service.

More frequent than religious matters were the variety of decisions dealing with the town's economy. Regulating livestock and protecting them from predators was a major activity. In 1652, for example, the town required every man who owned six cows to keep a bull as well, and set a six-penny stud fee to be paid for every cow belonging to others which the bulls served. In 1668, in an attempt to improve the breed, the constable and overseers decreed that no bulls were to be kept unless they approved of them, and reduced the stud fee to 4 pence for every calf. The second recorded General Court, in March 1651, permitted any man to set a gun to kill wolves, but not within a half mile of the town. The guns had to be set at night and picked up by sunrise, but any cattle killed by the guns were to be paid for by the town as a whole. On January 13, 1654, in one of the examples of communal activity, a meeting agreed that every man was to go to the swamp the next day and see if wolves could be killed. Failure to participate in the hunt earned a four-shilling fine.

Raising sheep became a major economic activity. The 1683 tax list recorded 1,044 sheep owned by fifty-three of the seventy-one people rated, with 39 owning ten or more. Along with the sheep came numerous regulations concerning herding and fencing, and an ingenious way to raise money. In 1678, the constable and overseers directed that individuals could have them herded into their yards or enclosures at night "for the benefit of the dung" if they paid the shepherd two shillings sixpence for his efforts and agreed to compensate the owners for any sheep lost or damaged. In 1689, the trustees decided to rent the flock to the highest bidder twice a week, and to apply the income for public purposes.

Like other English towns, East Hampton sought to attract millers and other artisans. In November, 1653, the town agreed with Vinson Meigs that if he would build a mill, they would pay him £50, give him forty acres of land, and transport lumber and millstones for him. In 1654, the town invited Goodman Mechem of Southold to come and weave for the town, promising him a £5 bonus and two acres of plowed land. In 1670, the town granted "Abraham the Dutchman" some land, providing that he agree to live on it for three years and follow his trade of weaving.

Finding a smith proved troublesome. In 1668, the town voted to give Edward Avery a three-acre home lot and ten other acres of land providing he stay in town for three years. That agreement apparently fell through, because in February, 1669, the town promised Thomas Skidmore, a smith from Huntington, a home lot, house and fence, and 20 acres of upland for six years' service. That agreement apparently fell through: A year later, the town offered a similar deal to Jeremyah Velle, Jr. provided he serve for six years "upon reasonable terms." That deal, too, apparently fell through. In 1671, we find an offer to Thomas Smith, who stayed for only a little more than a year. (An entry in the records dated September 24, 1672 notes Smith's intention to leave). In addition to millers and smiths, agreements were sought with a cooper, Andrew Miller, and a shoemaker, James Loper.

The town also regulated dealings with Indians, and at times assumed sovereignty over them. That first recorded Court of Elections, in October 1650, established a £5 fine for selling powder, lead, shot, or sword to Indians, and a £10 fine and the censure of the court for selling them guns or pistols. In 1653, a meeting agreed that no Indian was to come into town, except on a "special occasion," and none were to come armed, "because the Dutch hath hired Indians against the English and we not knowing Indians by face." Three years later, the town forbade any Englishman from renting land to Indians, and prohibited Indians from setting traps or erecting wigwams within the town bounds without permission. Nor were Native Americans to travel up and down or carry any burdens in or through town on the Sabbath. An intriguing but unamplified entry from a town court in 1673 notes that "The Meantacut Indians having declared who was their sachem, we do approve of him." And, lastly, a decade later, the town meeting ordered all Indians to kill their dogs, "unless one to a wigwam." If this were not done within a fortnight, it would be legal for any Englishman to kill any Indian dog they encountered.

The town dealt with a variety of other matters, too. Fire prevention was an early concern. In October, 1651, the General Court ruled that within six weeks, every house owner was to procure a ladder sufficient to reach the roof, and that anyone carrying fire must keep it closely covered. In February, 1657 the town appointed Mr. Gardiner and Goodman Concline to view chimneys once a month, levying a two-shilling fine if any hadn't been daubed or swept.

How well did government work?

There is only a little evidence of disagreement in meetings or disrespect for men in authority. In February, 1652, perhaps in a prelude to the defamation suit, Goody Edwards was ordered to pay a £3 fine or have her tongue put in a cleft stick for expressing her contempt for a warrant and desiring that the warrant be burned. In 1655 William Simons was fined "for his provoking speeches to the three men in authority being a disturbance to them in their proceedings." The fine, ominously, was to be used to make a pair of stocks.

Opposition sometimes forced the town meeting to reverse itself. In April, 1655, the General Court voted to send two men to Connecticut "concerning coming under their government." But a month later, "after long debate by the town at several times...it is at last determined to repeal the foregoing order." (The union with Connecticut wasn't achieved for another three years).

Two meetings in 1698 document another disagreement and also show the town's inability to cope with dissent. In the first, perhaps sensing they were broaching a contentious subject, the town "unanimously agreed that they would lay themselves down and rest satisfied with what the major part of said town would agree upon" in the matter of whether to build a new meeting house or repair the old one. The majority voted to build a new one, but Richard Stretton and John Hoppin protested, vowing not to pay taxes for a new meeting house as long as the old one could be made serviceable. In this instance, a small but persistent minority was able to triumph: in June, the town meeting reversed itself and decided to repair the old one.

And sometimes, the town needed to resort to higher authority to resolve an issue it couldn't settle. In 1679, for example, a meeting failed to reach a consensus on how to pay a schoolmaster, and could only agree to refer the matter to the Governor and Court of Assizes for their determination "which way is the most just and equallest to be carried on."

The scanty evidence of disagreement is to be expected, given the purpose for which the records were created. They were intended to be a permanent record of decisions that had been made, not the arguments advanced or the process by which the agreements were reached. But there are several indications that meetings could be disorderly or inefficient. In 1654, for the "comfortable and speedy dispatch of public business" the town decided that anyone uttering "provoking speeches" would pay a fine of five shillings or more. In 1657, "for the prevention of disorder in courts or meetings of the town by propounding many things which may tend to confusion" the town decided that no man could bring up any matter himself, but had to get the townsmen to put it on the agenda. There are a few other references to "long debate" and in 1652, the recorder (Benjamin Price) wrote in exasperation that "upon serious consideration and tedious debate, it is at last agreed" that John and Stephen Osburne will be paid £8 for keeping the two old hounds for a year." (The town kept the hounds, it appears, for use in hunting.)

It is not surprising, then, that the town was often content to let elected officials manage most of their routine affairs.

What were their social values?

Order and harmony were probably their primary values. Division of land was done with an eye to preventing controversy. When three men were appointed to lay out Occaboneck Meadow in July, 1651, they were urged to use "their best light and discretion." In the same year, an order for adding to house lots provided that land was to be laid out so that "every man may go from his house lot to his other division without trespassing upon any other."Assignment of plots to individuals was done by drawing lots, in an effort to eliminate any hint of favoritism.

In 1657, the town meeting enacted rules against bearing false witness and striking a neighbor.The offender, if he wounded a person, had to pay for the cure and for the time the victim was disabled. Also in 1657, the townsmen, "for preventing contention about grinding" directed that it was to be done on a first-come first-served basis and that a person could have no more than three bushels ground if others were waiting. Exceptions to the rules were later granted to Rev. James and to people who lived at a considerable distance from the mill.

Working together was another way of affirming communal values. The first town meeting divided the town into two parts, each half to take turns cutting whales. Anyone who didn't take his turn was to be fined five shillings. All men fit to bear arms were also expected to participate in the militia. Each was to provide himself, or be provided with, a gun, two pounds of powder, and four pounds of shot. In June 1653, it was ordered that a pond was to be dug for watering cows. Ralph Daiton and Thomas Baker were chosen to supervise the work, and all men who owned cows were to bring sufficient tools and do the digging.

EXCLUSION

Town or town officials reserved the right to determine who could settle and who must leave, though they exercised that right sparingly and occasionally ignored their own decisions.The first such instance came in October, 1651, when the general court gave Daniel Turner two weeks to join a family, become a servant, or leave town. In 1656, after Daniel Fairfield, a servant to Goodwife Mulford, became involved in a scuffle at school and was convicted in a suit brought by the minister "for acting filthiness with his maid and attempting a dalliance with his daughter," the town ordered that whoever hired Fairfield was to post a £20 bond for his good behavior. This order was canceled a month later, though, "for a trial of his behavior and with respect for Goody Mulford's necessity of help." I have found only four more instances of warning out in the records, and the warning out was not always carried out. In 1697, for example, a town meeting instructed the trustees not to accept one Sarah Whitehair as an inhabitant. Yet in 1694, we find the trustees making provisions to take her to Oyster Bay for medical treatment, and in 1699 agreeing that the town would pay her bills.

In 1665, the constable and overseers directed that "no man shall presume to make sale of his accommodation or give entertainment to any scandalous person or persons or any that may prove prejudicial to the town without the town's consent." A decade later, they ruled that no one was to entertain any English "stranger" for more than a week, unless the stranger could produce a certificate from the place he came from attesting to his good character; or unless his host posted bond for him or obtained the consent of a Justice of the Peace, constable, or overseer. They added in an aside "that word Englishman encludeth any nation except Indians." This was not the last such order, indicating that they may not always have been duly followed. In May, 1670, a town meeting agreed "that no more land shall be given or granted by the town to any stranger," but the records show that they did, in fact, continue to accept new inhabitants.

The town also acted to protect its resources. In March, 1670, part of an agreement with the cooper Andrew Miller was that if he made more casks than the town could use, he couldn't use the town's timber for ones he sold to "strangers." In June, 1676, the town got the Court of Sessions to make laws preventing non-residents from cutting wood without the permission of the constable or overseers, and preventing residents from selling wood to outsiders. In April, 1697, the town agreed to support the trustees in suing people who had not been granted land but who were enclosing and plowing lands belonging to the town.

There are indications that communal values were in conflict with, and were to some degree replaced by, individualistic values. One such indication is the refusal to serve when elected to office. In 1676, the town elected Stephen Hedges as Constable. Rather than serve, he appointed John Osborne "in his room." In 1678 and 1679, Samuel Parsons was twice elected overseer, and twice refused the office. In 1684, when James Dyament was elected constable, he hired John Parsons to serve in his stead, with the explicit approval of the town. In 1679, Benjamin Conckling struck a deal: in return from being excused from muster and watch and ward, he bought a set of colors for the militia.

Another indication of individualistic values is the evidence that some people demarcated their portions of the common land as private property. In 1668, a meeting reached a "general agreement" that every man would maintain his share of the common fence, even though he had already fenced his portion of the common field. In June, 1682, the constable and overseers learned that "sundry persons" had laid claim to, and had staked out the cow pasture. They appointed two men to pluck up the stakes.

In 1678, twenty-five inhabitants of the south part of town agreed to build a horse mill to grind corn for their own families, but for no one else.This may have resulted from the town's problems in attracting and keeping a miller, but it is also, I think, evidence of a growing sense of separation.

And in March, 1683, the inhabitants explicitly recognized that communal values had eroded: "there being not a full meeting as was desired" those in attendance felt obliged to appoint a committee to deal with a controversy over land, and pledged to abide by the committee's decision.They complained they were forced to this expedient, "seeing it is so hard a matter to get the town together."

In 1699, renting sheep for the benefit of their dung, which must have seemed like a good idea initially, became the center of a controversy which pointed out a growing sense of difference between the proprietors and other residents. In the preceding year, the trustees had decided that money received from the dung would go to the proprietors.Apparently hearing some dissatisfaction, they decided to put the matter to a vote, and the town chose to use the income to pay the shepherds and general expenses. But Benjamin Osborne and Thomas Hopping protested this decision, "saying they did expect to have their parts of the said money according to their propriety in common pasturing."The issue—whether this income was to be applied for the general good of the town as a whole, or for the benefit for a portion of the town—continued. In 1706, the trustees began using it to pay the town's quitrent, a practice which appears to have continued for several years.

But I don't want to preach another sermon on the decline of community. Such lamentations began with William Bradford's chronicle *Of Plymouth Plantation*, written in the 1640s, and have been kept up by Cotton Mather and other, more recent, historians. Indeed, Charles Adams, in *The Language of Cities* (1971), was driven to define "community" as "that mythical state of social wholeness" which has had "brief and intermittent flowerings through history, but always seems to be in decline at any given historical present," that is, vanishing in the moment the historian chooses to examine.

I do want to suggest that balancing the public good with private interests was becoming something more of a problem in East Hampton as the seventeenth century wore on, and that perhaps it is still a problem today.

EAST HAMPTON:

A Strategic Outpost of
Connecticut in the 1660s

Christopher Collier

I T FITS THE YANKEE IMAGE that Connecticut gained jurisdiction and control over East Hampton by foreclosing a mortgage. Land engrossment and speculation became the field upon which Puritan settlers in New England did God's work. Never have the spikes of Mammon and heaven nailed a people so painfully to cross-purposes as in seventeenth-century New England. The story of how eastern Long Island fell into the thrall of Connecticut is the most complicated of some very complicated colonial sagas I have encountered. I will simplify. But I will hope to be both clear and correct.

We begin in England. In 1622, Charles I granted a charter to a group of "adventures" under the name of the Council for New England. The Council was given permission by the king to exploit the whole territory—from the Atlantic to the Pacific—lying between the fortieth and forty-eighth parallels, that is, a line running through Philadelphia, Columbus, Ohio, and west along the line separating Nebraska and Kansas on the south and, on the north, including Price Edward Island and Nova Scotia through a point in Quebec Province about sixty miles north of the northern-most tip of Maine, all the way to the Pacific Ocean. Obviously, Long Island is to be found somewhere in there. The Council for New England broke up in 1635 and parcelled out its territorial holdings among its principal members. At the same time, probably at the suggestion of Charles I, who owed him a large chunk of land, the Council granted to one William Alexander, Earl of Stirling, much of present-day Maine and Nova Scotia, and all of Long Island. Stirling authorized agents to establish settlements on the Island, effectively only the eastern portion since the Dutch held the western end.The principal agent, James Forrett, arrived in New England in 1639, a year after the founding of New Haven, and the same year as the settlement of the New Haven satellites, Milford and Branford. Forrett encouraged some recent Massachusetts immigrants to migrate further and settle first in today's Southampton and then East Hampton. Meanwhile, Stirling died. Some of the Earl's heirs died at about the same time; others had no interest in the Long Island venture. Forrett was left stranded, but with full authority to dispose of the lands there. He needed cash to pay off his obligations and to get back to England.Thus, the mortgage.

At this point, it is time for me to exercise my Connecticut expertise and provide some context for the East Hampton history that follows. Connecticut was settled by migrants from Massachusetts—as was Southampton—and for, in part, the same reasons: a need (or desire) for more land for cornfields and cow pasture.There were some political reasons, as well, that motivated these Connecticut migrants, principally the limitation of the suffrage to church members; a similar complaint probably motivated the Long Islanders, too. Unlike Lord Stirling's settlers, the folks just below the rapids in the Connecticut River had no legitimizing charter, grant, or license.They were squatters. But they were imaginative squatters and innovators. They legitimized themselves by first establishing governmental machinery in 1636, and three years later, by writing a constitution and setting up a government according to its terms. The first such happenstance known to the western world—and the original at Connecticut's official sobriquet: "The Constitution State."

In 1641, when James Forrett was attempting to liquidate the Stirling lands, the chief political figures in Connecticut were John Haynes, governor; George Wyllys, deputy governor; and Edward Hopkins, member of the Council.Along with George Fenwick, major-domo of the separate plantation of Saybrook, at the mouth of the Connecticut River, these were four of the mortgagees who bailed Forrett out in 1641.The three other mortgagees were Theosophilius Eaton, governor of New Haven (a separate and independent—but equally illegitimate—colony, remember); Stephen Goodyear, deputy governor; and Thomas Gregson, magistrate. Clearly, they were acting in an official capacity for their respective governments.At the end of the three-year mortgage, the lands involved fell into the possession of the two colonies.This joint action is unique in the annals of the two often antagonistic colonies' separate existence, which continued until 1662.

Meanwhile, New Haven had bought Southold and taken under its jurisdiction Stamford, a detached settlement separated from New Haven by the Connecticut towns of Fairfield and Stratford, both settled in 1639. I mention Southold and Stamford to make the point that New Haveners could get to Southold quicker than they could get to Stamford and, of course, much quicker than they could get to Hartford. Indeed, on a clear day, they could almost see Southold. It's only about twenty-one miles across the water in a straight line from New Haven to Southold.

Southampton was settled by migrants from Massachusetts and New Haven at about the same time as were the New Haven satellites of Milford, Guilford, Branford, and Stamford. These places voluntarily put themselves under the jurisdiction of New Haven. Why would they do this? One reason—perhaps the principal one—is that New Haven, though without a legitimate charter or appropriately grounded grant, had a government up and running.

Another reason why these communities would surrender their de jure independence is that they needed more protection from threatening Indians than the settlers' small numbers could provide. New Haven troops allied with those of other English colonies and the Narragansett Indians had only four years before being annihilated by the formerly powerful Pequots located then just south of Foxwoods Casino, the place where today they take back much more property than they lost in 1636. But now the Narragansetts—victorious with the English in the Pequot War—threatened. A third reason for putting themselves under New Haven jurisdiction was that much of the entrepreneurial energy and capital for eastern Long Island settlement came from the leaders of the New Haven enterprise and, as we have seen, from the New Haven government as well as the colony's governors personally. The settlement of Long Island, in fact, according to Isabel Calder, was part of the overall vision of New Haven's founders, Theosophilius Eaton, John Davenport, and later, Stephen Goodyear. These men had hoped to establish a larger colony extending from the Earl of Warwick's claim on the east—where Branford is—to the Delaware Bay on the west, including Long Island. Efforts to settle on the Delaware, effectuated between 1640 and 1643, were quickly squashed by Dutch and Swedish officials. On again-off again jurisdiction over Huntington, Hempstead, Oyster Bay, and some places in Westchester County was finally resolved not by the Dutch, who had military control of those areas through most of the two-and-a-half decades under discussion, but by Charles II. But I get ahead of my story.

For various reasons then, these settlements along Long Island Sound—both both shores of it—came under the de jure jurisdiction of New Haven. But let me qualify that thought. We should keep in mind that the New Haven Colony (as distinct from the Town of New Haven) was not compact. It was broken up by the Connecticut towns of Stratford and Fairfield. The New Haven Colony records lump Guilford, Stamford, and Yennicock (Southold) together as having "upon the same foundations and ingagements entered into combination with us." That "combination" was evinced, for instance, in 1644, when the court at New Haven adjudicated a case originating in Southold. Thus, New Haven Colony consisted of the contiguous towns of Guilford, Branford, New Haven, and Milford; and on the mainland down the cost separated from Milford by about thirty miles, Stamford; and across the Sound, Southold and Southampton. Thus, the organization into towns of the settlements on the eastern end of Long Island was part of the establishment of New Haven Colony, a union of seven towns settled in three years (1638 to 1641). A second qualification to this picture (the first, remember, is that the towns were not contiguous), is that jurisdiction did not carry with it control. The legal relationship was de jure—not de facto. In fact, the towns maintained a high degree of local autonomy. Since New Haven itself had no legal standing and, of course, would not want to call attention to itself to any official body in England, its ability to control events in the offshoot towns was greatly limited. The efforts of the New Haven founders to establish a great—as it turned out— sprawling empire, then, constitute the context for the institutional beginnings of East Hampton.

The local history of the early years of East Hampton is well known to this audience. The imperial history—if I may call it that—is much less well known; indeed, if I may indulge an appropriate oxymoron, it is widely unknown. I say this after a fairly thorough search through the Connecticut literature where the topic of the eastern Long Island towns might be discussed.

Up to now, I have focused on the New Haven branch of the Long Island towns' connection to the mainland. I must now turn your attention to the independent colony of Connecticut, consisting in the 1640s of the original three River Towns—Windsor, Hartford, and Wethersfield; the contiguous Farmington; and the distant Fairfield and Stratford. To complicate matters, Connecticut, in 1644, bought the Warwick Patent that underlay the establishment of Saybrook, so that distant, noncontiguous town also became part of Connecticut. Recall that Forrett's mortgage was held jointly by the governors, deputy governors, and other magistrates of the two colonies. Thus, Connecticut had as much claim to rule Southampton (and, by extention, East Hampton) as did New Haven. In 1643, thus, we find that Southampton had come under the jurisdiction not of New Haven, but of Connecticut. In 1644, Southampton sent a deputy—that is, a representative—to the General Court at Hartford. This, in spite of the fact that it was New Haven that had gained permission from the New England Confederation, in 1643, to extend its jurisdiction over Southampton.

In general, towns preferred Connecticut jurisdiction to New Haven because New Haven's laws were both stricter in their biblical transformation into civil ordinances and more strictly enforced. Additionally, church membership—hard to gain in any Puritan community—was a prerequisite to the suffrage in civil as well as church matters in New Haven, but not in Connecticut. Thus, when East Hampton established itself as a separate town in 1649 or 1649, it naturally fell under the nominal jursidiction of Connecticut. I cannot find, however, that it was ever fully integrated. No deputies from East Hampton ever took their place at the semiannual meetings of Connecticut's governing body, the General Court, and in keeping with a tradition that provided for no taxation if no representation, Connecticut at first levied no taxes on East Hampton. Nevertheless, the General Court voted in November, 1649 that "East Hampton, of Long Island, shall bee accepted and enterteined under this Government according to their importunate desire."

American colonists of the seventeenth and eighteenth centuries were interested more than anything in gaining possession of land. In New England, such a concern ran a very close second—perhaps neck-and-neck—with heaven, hell, and God's will. Thus, in 1650, the voters of East Hampton sent for a "boddie of laws"—that is, Connecticut's Code of civil law adopted that year—and ordered, also, "that Ralph Dayton is to go to Keneticut for to procure the Evidence of our Lands, and for an acquittance for the payment of our lands. . . ." Apparently, East Hampton landholders were attempting to buy the lands claimed by Connecticut. These negotiations were resolved in 1650, when East Hampton inhabitants bought out their share of the mortgage. Some question about this financial arrangement remains, however, because in 1663, East Hampton settlers again offered to pay the mortgagees for the land. In 1657, as I have noted, East Hampton's nominal subservience to the Connecticut General Court was reconfirmed, and the next year, the Court authorized magistrates either on "the maine" or the Island to hear disputes and carry appeals to the courts in New

London. Nevertheless, East Hampton settlers continued to govern themselves de facto as though they were wholly independent. They sent no deputies to the Connecticut General Court nor, apparently, did they send in their lists of taxables to be "rated" and assessed. In 1655, the General Court wrote to the East Hampton townsmen that "it can bee no advantage, but rather to the contrary, to theire devided, shattered condition, not to have dependance uppon or bee under some settled Jurissd: &c. and therefore advise you so to doe, &c. and pay wtt is theire just dues to this Commonwealth." A "shattered" condition might very well be in the eye of beholder; what looked shattered to the Connecticut General Court might have looked normal to East Hampton farmers. Continued recalcitrance on the part of the independent-minded East Hampton settlers brought further admonition from the Connecticut Court. In 1657 and 1658, that Court cracked down; magistrates and constables were appointed for East Hampton, and these officials were authorized to carry cases to courts in New London. Despite their continued lack of participation in Connecticut government—or, perhaps, because of it—the General Court granted to the magistrates elected in Southampton and East Hampton authority to impanel juries and hold courts there. That East Hampton ultimately accepted Connecticut authority is demonstrated by its voluntary submission of the Garlick witchcraft case of 1657-58 when the Town voted that "Thomas Baker and John Hand go into Keniticut for to bring us under their government." Yet, still, East Hampton sent no deputies or tax lists to Hartford.

In Connecticut, in the mid-seventeenth-century, just as today, towns had no original powers, no local autonomy; they are municipal corporations created for the administrative convenience of the Colony/State. That, at least, is the historical and constitutional situation, despite many towns' efforts to assert otherwise. East Hampton's remoteness made real control by the distant General Court difficult—nearly impossible. We have seen that the town, for the most part (especially in representation and taxation), avoided participation in Connecticut government. That situation was to be profoundly threatened by events of 1660-1665. In 1660, the Crown was restored to the line of Stuarts in the person of Charles II. Puritan rule in England was over. In Connecticut, the ruling figures counted this as an opportunity to achieve the legitimization of the little colony's government. They sought a royal charter, and in 1662, got what they wanted.

The Royal Charter confirmed Connecticut's form of local self-government and for the first time defined the geographic bounds of the

Colony. It was to extend from Narragansett Bay on the east to the Pacific Ocean on the west with a northern limit at the Massachusetts line. And, most contentiously, it was to incorporate all of New Haven and its satellite towns. It is the southern boundary, however, that is of interest to the East Hampton story. The Charter gave bounds of Connecticut as" on the south by the Sea. . . . with the Islands there unto adjyneinge." In 1662, the Connecticut General Assembly welcomed Southold under the new Charter and extended the jurisdiction of the Southold magistrates—Captain John Young, in particular—to cover Southampton and East Hampton. The Court also ordered that all the Long Island towns be rated for taxes just as all the mainland towns were. All freemen on the Island were to take the oath which began I, so-and-so, "being by the Prvidence of God an Inhabitant within the Jurisdiction of Connectecott, doe acknowledge myselfe to be subject to the Government thereof."

One can only wonder what the reaction in aggressively independent East Hampton was. That the Court really meant business became clear when it stipulated that East Hampton's taxes might be paid in wheat or peas—an indication that they meant to collect it. Mr. Mulford and Mr. Bond were appointed magistrates for East Hampton. I do not find, however, that any taxes were ever paid to the Connecticut General Court. It was at this point that East Hampton tried to buy its way out from under Connecticut. But ownership of the land did not bring escape from governmental jurisdiction. Connecticut jursdiction at the eastern end of Long Island seemed clear enough until Charles, after beating the Dutch and driving them out of New Netherland, gave that colony to his brother, the Duke of York. The Duke's patent not only extended way into what Charles had included in the Connecticut bounds—and that which Connecticut had been effectively governing for over twenty-five years—but also appeared to include Long Island. The patent covered "all that island or islands commonly called by the general name or names of Meitowax, or Long Island." This was a wake-up call to Connecticut officials. The General Court passed a resolved declaring "that they claim Long Island for one of those adjoining islands expressed in the Charter," but added an escape clause, "except [if] a precedent right doth appear, approved by his Majesty." Governor Winthrop and four other magistrates were dispatched to New York to congratulate his Majesty's Commissioners there and to take the opportunity to get a favorable adjustment of the boundary. Though it was the mainland encroachment east to the Connecticut River that was of most concern, evidence that Long Island was also at issue lies in the presence of "Captain Young" of Southold among the Connecticut commissioners.

Up to this point, as I have pointed out, the Long Island towns had not been represented nor listed for taxes at the General Court. That body now took action. In October 1664, Southold—now incorporated into Connecticut as part of the New Haven absorption—was ordered to pay its taxes, and the farmers in East Hampton were ordered to fence in their tilled lands. But the struggle to subdue the Hamptons was only a minor sideshow to the battle with New Haven under the big tent and the even more problematic dispute with the Duke of York over the lands between the Hudson and the Connecticut Rivers. The effort to get New Haven to acquiesce in Connecticut's jurisdiction is an internal matter and need not concern us here. It is enough to point out that the resolution of the matter entailed two years of bitter acrimony and the actual flight of the whole town of Branford (to New Jersey where they established Newark). We are more interested in what happened to East Hampton. It is not—much to its disadvantage—a Connecticut town today. Why not?

As I noted earlier, Charles I had given Long Island to both the Connecticut Patentees and to his brother, James. An additional complication—a very major one—was the overlap in the two charters of what is today western Connecticut, including the panhandle that reaches into Westchester County. The quick story is that a series of compromises gave Greenwich to Connecticut, and Hastings, Rye and Bedford to New York, as well as all the Long Island towns at both ends, from Flushing to East Hampton. Your town, you see, was bartered away so that Connecticut could keep Fairfield and Litchfield Counties, and the Duke of York—soon James II—could keep Westchester County and Long Island. I leave it to you to decide who got the best of that deal.

BY CHOICE OR BY CHANCE

Single Women's Lives in

Nineteenth-Century Suffolk County, N.Y.

Sherrill Foster

> *Whistling girls and crowing hens*
> *Always come to some bad ends!*
> —Nineteenth-century saying

BY CHOICE OR BY CHANCE, six women of nineteenth-century East Hampton lived single lives either because they never married or because they became widowed or separated in mid-life.

How did they fare in the changing social and economic times of nineteenth-century Suffolk County? They were well-educated; most of them attended Clinton Academy. They kept diaries, ran a farm or a business, educated their children. They were daughters of well-to-do families whose uncles and brothers "went west" in search of better land, perhaps more land. The sandy soil of East Hampton had become depleted after 200 years of intensive use. Even the demand for the products of the livestock herded onto Montauk was lessening as modern machinery, banking systems and communications became ever more prevalent.

I will be discussing these six women: Phebe van Scoy, Polly Hicks, Cornelia Huntington, Abbie Parsons, Delia Sherrill, and Eliza Glover. The first three were single women. Phebe van Scoy lived in Northwest and ran a farm "by herself," so tradition says. Polly Hicks of Amagansett also ran a farm by herself, and Cornelia Huntington, the doctor's daughter, was a poet and author, neither financially rewarding.[1]

The next two were in their mid-thirties when they became widows and did not remarry: Delia Sherrill of East Hampton and Abbie Parsons of The Springs. Eliza Glover, at age fifty-five, was legally separated in New York City in 1890 from her husband after having eleven children.

These six women lived long lives: Polly Hicks lived to age ninety-one; Cornelia, eighty-seven; Phebe Scoy, eighty-one; Delia, seventy-seven; and Eliza, seventy-five. Only Abbie died at age fifty-four, her life cut short by cancer.[2] Each of these women had a well-developed sense of her own worth.

As well as their own diaries and references in others, each of these women can be found in the New York State Census of 1855 and 1865 which lists the crops raised, livestock, worth of farm, and what each family sold. This was chiefly cordwood, shipped to New York City for fuel, and, in turn, New York City shipped out horse manure to be sold for fertilizer.

The northeastern United States generally enjoyed a good economy during the mid-eighteenth century, the two decades before the War of 1812, and the latter part of the nineteenth century.

During the nineteenth century, middle-class families valued intimacy and family privacy. Home was not simply a place of residence—it was a focus for social life, a central element in class consciousness.[3] Houses had separate spaces—sewing, music, breakfast, dining, and most important, sleeping where each had his own room. Servants came down the back stairs next to the kitchen. This same century saw canned food, ready-made clothes, laundries, bakeries, indoor plumbing, cooking stoves, and ice boxes. There were brimstone matches, rubber overshoes, the steam press for newspapers, and the daguerreotype.[4] As clothing and furniture styles changed as well as eating habits, these women were alert to these changes and embraced them all in the name of respectability.[5] When Polly Hicks and her younger sister, Rebecca, were creating their cross-stitch sampler in the early 1800s, they were being prepared for living a "refined life." These women's lives were overlaid with this change from pre-Revolutionary "gentility" to nineteenth-century "respectability."

Legends in their own time, Phebe van Scoy and Polly Hicks were noted as farm managers—"running a farm by themselves" as contemporaries said. Diary keepers Eliza Glover and Delia Sherrill lived in families of other diary keepers.

Housing is indicative of wealth and social standing, then as today. Two of the women lived in large, stylish houses built for their marriages: Abbie (Kimble) Parsons in The Springs and Delia (Parsons) Sherrill in East Hampton.

In 1848, the New York State Legislature passed a law granting legal ownership of property to women, married or not. This law would prove a boon to these women. Divorce laws became more liberal.

Fewer than half of free white males in the U.S. owned real estate at mid-century.[6] Yet all of these women did. These legal, economic and social changes impinged on the lives of these six nineteenth-century women.

PHEBE VAN SCOY

Phebe van Scoy (1787–1868) is the only one of the six who lived her entire life in the same house. She assumed complete control of her father's farm in 1846 when she was fifty-nine. The farm raised grains for the market, butter was made. Polly Hicks (1790–1881), too, became the owner of a similar farm when her father died in 1833. She was forty-three. Her capable brothers and sisters had left home.

Cornelia Huntington also inherited her father's house on Main Street.[7] Although Cornelia is known as a diary keeper, only one ("book 5") has survived.[8] One of her sisters and her only brother married. She and her younger sister, Abbey, lived in their father's house where they remained after his death. She was then fifty-five; she was sixty-one when Abbey died.

Adelia Anna (Parsons) Sherrill (1838–1915) became a widow in 1874 at age thirty-six. She had married when she was twenty-one, in 1859, moving into the newly constructed Greek Revival-style house, the Sherrill family home which was a short distance from her parents' and grandparents' homes. She continued to live with her father-in-law, bringing up her children in the house and the farm her only son would inherit.

Abigail Jane (Kimble) Parsons (1848–1901) was thirty-seven when her husband died in 1885. She, too, lived in a newly constructed Italianate-style house with a cupola, built near her husband's retail store and post office in The Springs. Abbie continued his business.

Eliza Jane (Fisk) Glover (1835–1913), at age fifty-five, was legally separated in 1890 from her husband of thirty-five years. Of their eleven children, only nine grew to maturity.

Northwest's first buildings were the warehouses of the East Hampton merchants. By mid-eighteenth century, the Town Trustees, probably pressured by descendants of the first settlers, decided on a special division or sale of the acreage. Phebe Scoy's grandfather, an early purchaser, was the first to move there shortly after his marriage in 1757.

From 1760, for about a hundred years, Northwest was a thriving community. At first, "lop" fences were created to enclose the livestock, cattle and sheep. Barley, oats and Indian corn were harvested. These grains were taken to the many wind-powered grist mills in the area.[9] The livestock was transformed into hides, tallow, meat, and wool—all very marketable products in the seventeenth and early eighteenth centuries. Isaac van Scoy, Phebe's grandfather, had moved to Northwest in 1757, purchasing 300 acres of land on which he built his dwelling house, barns and other outbuildings. In 1771, he built a larger house for his eight children—a new two-story, thirty-four-foot-by-thirty-foot frame house.[10] When his wife, Mercy Edwards, died in 1782, a Connecticut sandstone marker was erected in the family's burial plot on the farm.[11]

Although Phebe van Scoy (1786–1868) is known to posterity as a woman who "ran a farm by herself," she was not living in isolation. The nine families who "farmed" in Northwest became a close-knit group; the original settlers' children married and even some of their grandchildren married each other.

In 1792, a school house was built in Northwest on the van Scoy property. In that year, there were thirty scholars; children of the other families were Bennett, Edwards, Miller, Parsons, Payne, Ranger, Terry.[12]

After the Civil War, the families moved away, the land reverted to woodland, and the houses disappeared through fires or dismemberment. Today, much of the land is publicly owned parkland.[13]

Isaac, Jr., Phebe's father, began oyster harvesting along the creeks and in the harbor at Northwest.[14] When he married about 1783, after the British occupation of Long Island, he continued to live in the family house. When his son was born in 1790, after two daughters, Isaac, Jr. planted a yellow bark oak tree near the front door. This male chauvinistic emblem lasted 140 years until the tree was blown down in the disastrous 1938 hurricane.

Phebe's family included her parents, Isaac and Temperance, her older sister, Mercy, then Phebe, then the two brothers and baby sister, Betsey, all born within ten years. Her sister, Mercy, married at age twenty in 1805 and moved to Southold. This mother may have died about this time, and Phebe, as oldest daughter at home, may have been in charge of the house. Little sister Betsey also may have died at this time as there are no further records of her. Phebe was twenty-four years old in 1810.

In 1815, brother Arnold married and moved to Sag Harbor where he became a daguerreotypist.[15] Brother Isaac Sylvester remained to work on the farm. In 1820, he married Charlotte Parsons, daughter of the nearby Parsons Family. Their only child, Charlotte, born in 1831, was seven years old when her mother died. Perhaps Isaac Sylvester and little Charlotte lived in the house with Phebe and her father.[16]

Isaac Sylvester caught the gold fever in 1849 and invested $500 as a stockholder in the Sabina, a former whaling ship (with a total of sixty shares), going as a passenger to the west coast with many friends and a cousin. Perhaps Phebe put some money into this venture.[17]

At the time of the 1850 Federal Census, Phebe had been managing the farm for four years. This census indicates that Phebe's only resident help on the farm was a black woman, Phebe Horne, age twenty-six, who lived in the house with Phebe. As noted, canned goods, brimstone matches, rubber overshoes, and ready-made clothing eased the house-wife's lot. For the heavy work, plowing and such, Phebe was depen-dent upon her neighbors but, more likely, hired day laborers.

In 1865, according to the New York State Agricultural Census, the population of Northwest was sixty-six people. Wainscott had eighty-nine persons and East Hampton, 775.[18] Phebe van Scoy's ninety-acre farm had a cash value of $1,200 and livestock, $120. Cash came in by selling five cords of wood in 1864 for which she got $25. In 1864, she also made seventy pounds of butter and cured 200 pounds of pork, in-dicating that she had some livestock as well as fields of grain.[19]

When Phebe died in 1868, at age seventy-six, her unusual lifestyle had made her a legend in her own time. The road to her house was known as the "Road to Phebe Scoy's."

After her death, the farm became the property of her cousin's son, George E. Van Scoy (1844–1911) who married in 1872. About ten years later, George's wife's father purchased the property and took the two ells off, removing them to his own farm. "The rest of the house was soon dismantled by anyone needing a little lumber."[20]

POLLY HICKS

The Hicks Family Farm of forty to fifty acres was near the heart of Am-agansett. The family lived near present-day Indian Wells Highway in a three-bay, side-entrance, two-story, gable-roof house with a two-story ell to the rear, vernacular Federal in style.

A label on a lovely slat bonnet in the collections of the East Hamp-ton Historical Society reads "Worn by Miss Polly Hicks." What kind of a woman was Miss Polly Hicks?

Miss Polly Hicks began life in the middle—a middle child who gets to look at both ends. Polly was the fifth child of nine, with three older brothers, an older sister, and three younger sisters. In 1800, as noted

The house in Amagansett owned by Polly Hicks. She sold the farm in 1855 for $1500, her nest egg.

above, she and her sister, Rebecca, each worked on a cross-stitch sampler.[21] Polly was ten and Rebecca, six.

In 1833, when her father, Zachariah Hicks, died, only two of the eight surviving Hicks children—Polly and Joseph—were living at home. Their mother died the next year. Polly, now age forty-four, and Joseph, her older brother (by a year and a half) ran the farm for the next twenty years. The 1850 census gives us a clue: unmarried, Joseph is listed as insane. Polly not only had to manage the daily work on the farm, but had to see that Joseph, probably mentally retarded, was doing useful work within his mental capacity. Joseph died in July of 1853, and Polly was able to sell the Amagansett farm in March of 1855 for $1,500.

With the money from the sale of the farm, Polly moved in with her sister, Rebecca, and her family.

Rebecca had married in 1815 and had seven children before she became a widow in 1839. The family lived on the east side of Three Mile Harbor in East Hampton on a farm called "Duck Creek." They also owned and farmed adjacent farmland called "Franklin Farm." Each farm had a large old house. Franklin Farm was run by Rebecca's oldest son, Daniel, with help from his siblings and later, his wife, Mary Edwards.

In the 1860 census, Polly is listed as an occupant of Daniel and Mary's household along with their two daughters, ages seven and one (there was also a thirteen-year-old live-in "boy" helper). By 1870, Polly, age eighty, is listed as a "boarder" in the same household of Mary (Edwards) Edwards, now a widow, and her daughters, Hannah, seventeen, and Mary, eleven.

The various mid-nineteenth-century epidemics had decimated the Hicks/Edwards family. Three of her nieces and her brother-in-law, Joseph Edwards, had died. In 1865, the dysentery epidemic took four more members of the family including nephew Daniel Edwards, the major breadwinner.

As noted, in 1870, Polly, age eighty, is listed as boarding with the widow Mary E. Edwards and her two daughters. In 1880, Polly, age ninety, listed as "aunt," is living with her surviving niece and nephew, Samuel Edwards, age forty-five, and his sister, Rebecca, a household of single persons. They had a twenty-three-year-old farm laborer living with them, Henry Talmage. The following year, Miss Polly died.

Polly had the advantage of commercially canned food and ready-made clothing. Her life span incorporates the timeframe of this change of attitude. Although her management ability enabled her to keep solvent, a farm as a viable source of income and lifestyle was fast disappearing in the last decades of the nineteenth century. In the twentieth century, males from this farm family had turned to fishing.

CORNELIA HUNTINGTON

An entirely different lifestyle, centered in the village, was that of Cornelia Huntington. Highly intelligent, she exercised her faculties in writing poems, many celebrating life events of her friends.

Daughter of a medical doctor and sister of another M.D., she was the second child of four of Dr. Abel Huntington, a sixth-generation New Englander.

She was never called "Miss Cornelia"; apparently, her intimate family name was "Corneal" as quoted in some of her poems. Born in 1803, she lived the whole of her life in the nineteenth century. Her one novel, a melodramatic tragedy, was situated in the East Hampton of the 1840s. The novel, *Sea Spray*, was published under a pseudonym, Martha Wickham, in 1857.[22] Catherine Beecher, a childhood acquaintance of Cornelia, was establishing female educational institutions. Cornelia was three years younger than Catherine, who lived her first ten years in East Hampton. In 1846, Catherine published her first book, *Miss Beecher's Domestic Receipt-Book*; copies have survived in East Hampton households.

An old, handwritten note on the library copy of Cornelia's novel says "written in 1852." About sixty percent of all fiction volumes published in American between 1830 and 1860 were highly wrought, adventurous or satirical, while just over twenty percent were domestic or religious. In the 1840s, many were sensational "blood-and-thunder" novels; 705 of these were written by men, twenty-three percent by women, and seven percent published anonymously.[23] *Sea Spray* seems to fit all categories.

Cornelia Huntington (1803–1897), in her novel written by 1852, describes East Hampton as it was during the lives of these six women.

The opening paragraphs of her book, written in the typically florid style of the period, carry the feel of the place which, even today, many believe still to be true:

> The last rosy flush of a surpassingly bland and beautiful day in December fell over the little village of Sea-spray. The sun had set, but the western sky was yet glowing with floods of golden light, and the whole clear expanse, above and around, was bright in the softly fading gleam.
>
> It was a pleasant hour—that quiet interval between daylight and darkness; and it was a pleasant village, too, that now lay dozing in its soothing glimmer. There was nothing remarkable in the simple, unpretending village of Sea-spray, which stretched itself about a mile from the Atlantic shore, on the eastern extremity of Long Island: the main street lying in a little miniature valley, the rise on either side being so slight as to be scarcely perceptible. There was nothing picturesque in the surrounding scenery; the fields lay on one flat, unbroken level, and there was neither a brook nor a rock within an hour's travel of the street; but the dash of the eternal wave was always sounding amid its solitudes, and the solemn and monotonous road . . .
>
> Stretched far away into the ocean . . . the villagers pursued quietly and contently their own usual avocations, . . . dwelling soberly where their fathers had dwelt, treading patiently the paths their fathers' steps had beaten, tilling the same fields, sheltered by the same roofs, believing in the same stern creed . . .
>
> There was fear now, however, that the spirit of innovation had begun to creep stealthily among them; the 'brushing up' mania had broken out here and there, and in several places along the street, snug little edifices might been seen in all the glows and glory of fresh paint and side-lights . . . turning up

their puggish little portico noses in defiant scorn of the long, low, rickety roofs that confronted them; barns had marched sullenly back from the front line, and wood-piles had retired indignantly to the rear, to give place to painted pickets and ornamental shrubbery.[24]

Such was the romantic description of the village that was the center of these women's lives, the "refined" village of these six women.

Cornelia's novel, *Sea Spray*, was published before any of Harriet Beecher Stowe's books on life in late colonial America.[25] In her own posthumous book, *Odes & Poems*, the editor, her nephew, Dr. Abel Huntington, noted that she did not want her poems published during her lifetime.[26] However, she wrote for the Spooner publications, *Long Island Star*, in 1864 under her name, adding "Author of *Sea Spray*."

There were several houses on Main Street, East Hampton that remained vacant after the British occupation of Long Island during the Revolutionary War.

The young Rev. Lyman Beecher had purchased one. He spent time and money repairing the house. Captain Thomas Wickham, in 1776, was appointed Auditor of Refugees' Claims with an office in Middletown, Connecticut. He did not return to East Hampton. In 1797, Dr. Abel Huntington (1777–1858) purchased the large house, now at 136 Main Street, across the street from Clinton Academy.

The Huntington children attended Clinton Academy, the esteemed school. At Clinton Academy, the alert Cornelia absorbed much in the open-style classrooms of the school. She closely observed her fellow students. In this, she followed the male Huntingtons in their medical notes. It would be her nephew, Dr. George Huntington, who would present a paper in 1872, based on these earlier doctor's records, that would identify and define a hereditary disease known as Huntington's Chorea.[27]

Clinton Academy was much loved by its students, as many of them who have written about their education can attest. Judge Henry P. Hedges, chronicler of East Hampton, enjoyed his school days. Cornelia, he notes, was a brilliant student.

It is unfortunate that so few records of this important school have survived. As noted above, the Huntington children probably attended Roxana Foote Beecher's "preschool" classes before going on to Clinton Academy. Cornelia was seven years old when the Beechers left East Hampton for Litchfield, Connecticut. She was already enrolled in Clinton Academy.

In 1813, her mother died; Cornelia was then ten. In later life, she writes about her parents at this time in an undated poem/letter in rhyme to Mrs. M.D.R.:

The twilight in my early home in vivid tints I view,
where in the spring-time of my life its first great grief I knew.
I see my Father pace the room with measured tread and slow,
With folded hands across his back and whistling soft and low ...
I see my Mother's fragile form and clear mild eyes of blue,
with that fixed, far off, dreamy gaze so well my childhood new.
...And Mariette, sedate and grave, though but a child in age,
...And that "black headed witch"—Corneal ...
And Abby—fair as moonlight mist—flitting like fairy slight,
With flossy locks of flaxen hair and forehead marble white.[28]

When Cornelia was about fourteen, the widowed Mrs. John Lyon Gardiner moved her five children into the East Hampton house, leasing the island to David and Juliana Gardiner, second cousins, of New York City. Their four children were born on the island including the to-be-famous Julia, "The Rose of Long Island." In 1825, the lease ended. Mrs. John Lyon Gardiner returned to the Island with her son, David, now twenty-one, and Eighth Proprietor, the two girls, Sarah, eighteen, and Mary, sixteen, and the two younger sons, John and Samuel Buell Gardiner, thirteen and ten, respectively.

Cornelia and younger sister Abby were invited to spend several weeks on the Island with their former classmates.

Starting a new diary, Cornelia wrote,

I have been on the Island more than a week during which time the weather has been rainy and unpleasant. Yet has my time passed delightfully away and I shall never forget the happiness I have enjoyed in this little week of my existence ... I have looked across the bay a great many times today, for it is the first day ... that I could discern the low level shore and scarcely perceptible hills of my own native abode, but as the sun set tonight (mist-mantled as it was) behind that dear isle which looked so lovely and sublime ... Tuesday afternoon we have taken a ride about the Island this afternoon and I have been very well pleased with the excursion—the day is cloudy and the wind very boisterous and chilly ... If at this early season the scenery does not appear to the best advantage especially to those who admire to see the earth smiling in her summer attire—but to me who love to contemplate nature in her most desolate state ...[29]

Cornelia Huntington, from her book of poems.

In the 1826 diary, Cornelia writes under 23 December, "I have had a party this week and heaven deliver me from ever being doomed to linger through another such a miserable evening. I had rather reap an acre of barley than to be condemned to be 'Lady Hostess' to people, who will neither afford nor receive entertainment, and I am now fully resolved never to give another party until I am married." Marriage was an alternative that Cornelia kept in the back of her mind. In the 1859 poem-letter to Jerry Mulford, she implies she thought his letter a long-distance proposal.

Cornelia in her diary decries the custom of "calling":

> We spent the morning in receiving calls which in my opinion a foolish custom—but it is the fashion and we must all bow to the all prevailing name of fashion ... (diary).[30]

One fashion Cornelia did not disparage was that of creating poetry. Her friends enjoyed her poetry, much of it with the lilting rhythm. From 1815, in Hartford, Connecticut, Lydia Sigourney published this saccharine verse.[31] Whether Mrs. Sigourney was an influence on Cornelia cannot now be determined; Cornelia was interested in the work of Mary Wollstonecroft who advocated education for women.

Cornelia Huntington's novel, *Sea Spray*, is replete with English-ness. The main characters' names are so British—Mr. & Mrs. Evelyn, Mr.

Atherton. Cornelia may have envied her brother Dr. George Lee Huntington's star boarder, John Wallace, the mystery man of East Hampton.
John Wallace was a Scotsman who had come to East Hampton in 1846
at the age of fifty-seven, funded by checks from a New York bank. He
was soon boarding with Dr. George Lee Huntington.

Wallace was Church of England. By 1855, Wallace began to conduct, as a lay reader, Episcopal services in Clinton Academy. Within four
years, there were enough communicants to consider a special meeting
place. A chapel was constructed for summer services near Sophie
Jones house, now the Home Sweet Home Museum.[32] Cornelia, fascinated by this aura of British life, became an early communicant. Fifty
years later, John Wallace's real identity was found. His name was John
Wood and he was an Edinburgh lawyer who had had a dispute with his
family and left.

In her writings, Cornelia mentions knowledge of the work of Mary
Wollstonecraft (1759–1797) who is best known for her book of 1792,
A Vindication of the Rights of Woman, which John Wallace would
have known and perhaps brought a copy with him from Scotland.
How much her novel was influenced by conservation with John Wal-
lace about his homeland and its social customs will never be known.

In her poems, Corneal divulges herself. In a poetic answer to a letter of 1859 from Jerry Mulford, an East Hampton "boy" now living in
Ross Grove, Illinois, Cornelia says, "My path has lain in sunshine, few
sorrows I recall/and I've only known such changes as time must bring
to all:/My brown abundant tresses, with their wavy wealth of curls,/I
wear stuck up behind my ears, in awkward, knotted quirls/ . . . My face
is brown and wrinkled, my eyes are growing dim,/My figure, never
graceful, is anything but slim. . . ." In this same poem, she describes her
younger sister (by three years), "Abby who was lithe and light as a
seagull on the wing,/sits reading by the ingleside, an invalid, poor
thing."[33]

In 1858, at age eighty-two, her father died. Still living in that house
with her sister, Abby, Cornelia was able to have long discussions with
John Wallace at her brother's house. Her missing diaries may have included her thoughts during these years. Cornelia sold the house on
Main Street after Abby's death and is recorded in the 1865 New York
State Census with her brother in his much newer house on Newtown
Lane. George Lee, his wife and two children, who in 1865 were fifteen-
year-old George (who, as a graduate student, would present the paper
on Huntington's Chorea to a scholarly medical audience), Mary C.,
twelve, and the star boarder, John Wallace, age seventy-nine.

In the 1880s, life was closing in on these long-lived Huntingtons. Her sister, Mariette, recently widowed, lived in the castle-like house in the hills of Bridgehampton. Dr. George Lee Huntington would die in 1881 and Mariette, herself, at age eighty-two, in 1882. George's widow would die just two months before Cornelia.

Against the background of the two managerial women discussed above, Cornelia Huntington appears as a little princess. When she died in 1890, at age eighty-seven, she was perhaps an object of awe in the town. An era had passed. The next three women typify the post-Civil War American woman. Each had a say in the setting up of the household, two of whom moved into new houses built for them; the third, Eliza Jane Glover lived in New York City on East Fourth Street perhaps in a rowhouse, before she and her husband and children moved in 1863 to Southold to a purchased home on several acres of land, where the Glovers had a vegetable garden as well as livestock.

ADELIA ANNA SHERRILL

Adelia Anna (Parsons) Sherrill became a widow in June of 1874 at the age of thirty-six. Delia grew up in East Hampton with her parents in their family home opposite the Dominy-built "Hook" Mill. Further north, into the "Hook", were other "old family" homes—Talmage, the Dominys themselves, and just beyond, one branch of the Sherrill Family. This family had four boys, just Delia's age. She settled on Nat—tall, slim Nat—who was just six years older.

Her husband, Nathaniel Sherrill, died from pneumonia at age forty-two. He was out haying in early June with his crew when a sudden rainstorm came. This thorough soaking soon turned into pneumonia.

Delia continued to live comfortably in the Sherrill family's new house, occupied by eight people. Six of these were Delia's own children, twelve-year-old Abbie, the infant Willie (who would soon die, probably from childhood diabetes), and the four daughters ranging in age from three years to fourteen. Her father-in-law, Stephen Sherrill, ran the farm aided by an able crew. Some of the men ate noontime dinner in the ample kitchen of the Sherrill House, supervised by a cook-housekeeper who may have also lived in the house. As her father-in-law continued to manage the farm—the livestock and the growing of grains—Delia could devote her whole attention to her children and her unique "domestic role" as a nineteenth-century woman of the house.

In her diaries, Delia notes the novels she is reading. In March, 1870, "It is a severe snowstorm tonight—been sleet all day—have been reading *The Changed Bride's* by Mrs. Southworth. Wrote to Uncle Nat and Mary Cartwright tonight."[34] She finished the book at the end of the week. Another book of hers, *The Lamplighter* (published anonymously in Boston in 1857), is inscribed in beautiful Spencerian hand "Miss Adelia A. Parsons, Sea Spray, L.I.," the immediate influence of Cornelia! On a further text page in not such an elegant hand is written "Miss Anna M. Sherrill, East Hampton, L.I.," Delia's eldest daughter.

The 1880 Federal Census lists the occupants of the house as being Stephen Sherrill, age seventy-nine, farmer; his daughter-in-law; and the five children. Also listed as occupants of the house are Lois Talmage, age twenty-three, unmarried servant, and Allen Smith, age seventeen, unmarried farm laborer, all born in New York State. Delia undoubtedly let Lois have a pretty free hand in the management of the kitchen. This would give Delia the free time to visit relatives, have tea with friends, go shopping in Sag Harbor and all the other things she did. There is no indication in her diaries of any conflicts with the cook-housekeeper.

Living as one of two adults in a household was unusual for Delia. Her own family, who lived about a quarter-mile up the street, had contained five people when she married—her grandmother, mother, brother and sister. Delia had moved into a very full household. In addition to her husband's parents, there were Nat's three brothers. During her fifteen years of married life, the composition of this household was recast.

The Civil War soldier brother was killed, her mother-in-law and the oldest brother died in the 1865 dysentery epidemic, and the youngest brother moved to Derby, Connecticut to operate a store. Nat and Delia became the "head" couple in the house, although Nat's father, sixty-four-year-old Stephen, remained in control of the farm.

Delia wrote in her diary for January 1, 1875, "This morning was awakened by the children's calling 'A Happy New Year, Mama.' I trust it will be a happier year than the last has been, in that I have lost both my husband and baby, dear little Willie, a sick child from the time he was ten weeks old, until he died, age eight months. . . ."[35]

Delia's life continues. Her father-in-law manages the farm with all the same help as before. Delia has tea with her friends and relatives; the children grow up.

In May, 1875, Delia notes "Phebe Baker came to work for me today and I expect her to stay all summer." In the back of her diary is recorded "Phebe Baker commenced work May 10th 1875. Wages $2. Pr week."

Delia continues to do the washing on Monday, the ironing on Tuesday with Wednesday to finish if need be. Phebe would be helping in all these chores. Note that Phebe "came to work for me." Friday and Saturday, Delia baked. Other days, she sewed clothes for herself and the children. She cuts rags and then has a "rag party" with her friends who sew the ends of the rags together to be rolled up into a ball. This is then taken to a weaver who will weave a rag rug.[36]

When Delia does her baking, she moves into the kitchen which is ruled by the cook-housekeeper, who has prepared all the meals for both family and the farmhands who eat at the house. Delia can spend a day shopping in Sag Harbor and come home to find the meal ready to eat. She has some income from stock and notes which she occasionally sells to buy luxuries such as a set of chairs for the dining room. In her diary, she notes the day the cattle are driven to Montauk and the day they return. Her son, Abbie, was with the group driving on May 11, 1875. "Abbie has been to drive the cattle to Montauk, the first time he has ever been, he went away at four o'clock this morning and arrived home at seven tonight." Abbie was thirteen years old.[37]

Her own mother died in April, 1875. Her brother, William Lewis Parsons, had come from Yates Center, Kansas to be with their mother, arriving about a week before she died. Her younger sister, Juliet, could not make it from the upper mid-west. "April 29 [1875] I went up home this morning—home no longer now Mother is not there...."[38]

Living in her mother's house was her brother, Abraham S. Parsons, his wife, and their five daughters, making eight people.

Early in 1878, Abraham Parsons decided to buy the mill in Amagansett, moving his family there. Delia was able to give her brother a note for $200 on the purchase of the mill.[39]

Aware of the strong influence of culture, Delia records in her diary (21 March 1878) "Abbie and May commenced to take singing lessons of Miss Libbie Dayton today." Abbie was 16; May, 13.

In 1890, Abbie married moving his bride into the house. Stephen, Delia's father-in-law, died two years later.

Delia continued her extensive correspondence with her siblings, keeping them aware of events in East Hampton. The local paper of December 1901 noted that the Ladies Village Improvement Society's new cookbook (with some recipes by Delia) "had a wide circulation, going to Minnesota and Kansas."[40] Delia had sent copies to her sister and brother.

ABIGAIL JANE KIMBLE

Abigail Jane Kimble was born and grew up in Dyberry, Pennsylvania, a small hamlet in the Delaware River Valley just north of Honesdale. In the late eighteenth century, the Kimbles, with many of their neighbors, had moved from eastern Connecticut to this part of Pennsylvania, known as the "Connecticut Town of Westmoreland."[41] This Kimbles owned and lived at a stage stop which grew into a general store, post office and small hotel.[42] This public service background would be a strong help to Abbie.

How did Abbie of Dyberry meet Joseph Parsons of The Springs? Well, their great-grandmothers were sisters.[43] Married in 1869, Abbie and Joseph moved into the new house in The Springs, set well back from the road; it encompassed the natural environment with a good view of Accabonac Creek and Gardiner's Bay beyond.[44] Just down the street, at the corner and past The Springs Chapel, was the grocery store that Joseph owned. He would soon be appointed postmaster.

Abbie was a helpmate in the store as well as living a well-ordered life at home. For Abbie and Joseph, children came at four-year intervals. They were given the fashionable double names, the boys getting more romantic first names: Walton Grant, Phebe Jane, Lena Kimble, and Raymond Schoonover. Abbie herself was Abigail Jane, and her husband, Joseph Dudley.

After sixteen years of married life, tragedy struck. Joseph contracted the measles at age forty-three and died from its complications in 1885. But thirty-seven-year-old Abbie had previously looked for added sources of income. The 1880 census reveals that in that year, Abbie and Joseph had two boarders—one a thirty-eight-year-old fisherman, the other a seventeen-year-old clerk in the grocery store.

When Joseph died, his children were fifteen, eleven, seven and three. Fifteen-year-old Walton was helping in the store and in the yard. Eleven-year-old Phebe could help in the house. Abbie took over the management of the retail grocery store. However, she was not appointed postmistress until some years later in 1895, a position she held until she died in 1901.

Both Abbie and Delia were able to continue their lifestyles in their "new" houses as well as provide an inheritance for their sons.

In the very open proto-big-business environment such as East Hampton, like so many small towns across America, new and exciting ways to make money developed. In East Hampton in 1884, a future business leader wrote to his brother, homesteading in Kansas, who apparently had asked about returning home to the East Hampton farm.

The letter details the costs of each item of farm life; the value of crops—wheat, oats, potatoes, straw hay—and the value of the animal products: pork, butter, eggs, milk. He then adds that renting their house in the summer makes up the farm deficit.[45]

Ten years earlier, in 1873, this thirty-two-year-old man had become the Town Clerk, a position he held for twenty-nine years. With this meager salary, he progressed to being a private banker. He was on the organizing boards of such modern businesses as the Home Water Co., East Hampton Electric Light Co., East Hampton Lumber Co. and East Hampton Telephone Company.[46]

Such opportunities would have been available to Nathaniel Sherrill and Joseph Parsons if they had not died prematurely. Their aware siblings had moved to other towns to avail themselves of these typical nineteenth-century opportunities.[47]

ELIZA JANE FISK GLOVER

In Southold, another midlife man was trying to accomplish similar objectives. William Henry Hobart Glover was thirty-two years old in 1863 when he and his family moved to Southold from East Fourth Street in Manhattan.[48]

Already the father of five children, he and his wife, Eliza Jane Fisk, would have six more in Southold. The old Glover family were early settlers of Southold. William's father, Thaddeus Glover, had moved to New York City about 1800 to take part in the building boom as a carpenter, possibly supervising such work. These Glovers loved the East Fourth Street neighborhood, his widow remaining there the rest of her life.

Eliza Jane Fisk was a New Yorker whose husband, William, had been a builder in lower Manhattan during the building boom of the early years of the nineteenth century. Eliza's brother, John A. P. Fisk, was noted in a *New York Times* story as being a "third generation chop house keeper" in the Wall Street area. The Glover diaries are all from after their move to Southold in 1863. Eliza's father had died that year, but her mother remained in the house on Fourth Street living with her youngest daughter, the New York City school teacher, Henrietta Fisk ("Aunt Tetts").

Most of Eliza's relatives stayed in the city although not on Fourth Street. Some sisters lived in Harlem, others in Brooklyn. Henrietta's connection with the public schools was used by the Southold Glovers extensively. All nine of their surviving children lived with Aunt Tetts while they attended high school in the city.

Aunt Tetts visited in Southold over school vacations and in the summer. WHHG's 1870 diary mentions Aunt Tetts more than he mentions Eliza. He painted and wallpapered Aunt Tetts' room in his Southold house and he stayed in her house on East Fourth Street whenever he had business in the city, which was often. He was trying to set up a fish oil factory in Southold.[49]

W. H. H. Glover's 1877 diary gives many details of the social life, especially with his cousin, Israel Peck, and his family on their large estate, "Oak Lawn" in Southold. County trotting races were held on this extensive acreage on the south side of the main road. The Glovers' house in Southold seemed to be part of a farm with barns and animals. The soil must have been good as the older boys would be planting vegetables and picking and selling them. They built brick walkways in the yard. WHHG repapered many rooms. He also used modern conveniences. "Sunday 25 March . . . took a wash in little Bath tub in forenoon. . . ." On November 1, "Joe built new drain for Bath tub" ("Bath" was always capitalized). Taking the train to the city, WHHG almost always wrote to Eliza upon arrival even though he often went home the next day (mails were much faster then than today).[50]

Of their nine surviving children, five were married in the 1880s before their parents' legal separation. As Eliza looked around the partially empty house, she realized that her marriage had not brought complete faithfulness from her husband nor the happiness she had expected. She found that WHHG was paying a great deal of attention to her sister, Henrietta. Therein lies the problem. By 1890, Eliza Jane (Fisk) Glover had gotten a legal separation from W. H. H. Glover.[51] He had been paying too much attention to Aunt Tetts.[52] Details of the separation are not known; possibly Eliza received a meager amount of money. She lived by extensive visits to her married children.[53]

The repercussions of this legal separation were difficult for some of her children. Charles, the fifth child, sided with his father; thus, Eliza never visited him. Ida, her oldest daughter, seems to have been very calm about it. Eliza stayed long periods at Ida's house in East Hampton. Lill, the seventh child, had severe emotional problems whenever her mother came to visit the couple of weeks.

In June 1906, Eliza left daughter Ida and her family in East Hampton and "took the cars" to Southold where she was met by her son-in-law, Lill's husband, and the two young grandsons. Waiting in the house was Lill's oldest child, eighteen-year-old Florence, and Lill. Lill became sick. The diary: "Lill was sick all afternoon, vomiting and headache. She was not able to eat supper with us." Lill's daughter, Florence, was recently married to Orville Beebe. The family would attend Orville's Southold High School graduation later in the week.

It had been sixteen years since Eliza's legal separation. Forty-year-old Lill was still emotionally upset and retreated into sickness.

The eldest son, fifty-one-year-old Harry, takes over much of the "entertaining" of his mother, as does forty-five-year-old Willie, both of whom lived in Southold. They take her visiting and on rides. Possibly the reason Eliza does not stay with either of these sons is because her former husband is residing there. (Aunt Tetts died in 1899.)

The younger sons—Mort, Lou and Fred—had married in the late 1890s and lived in Queens. They are more hospitable and Eliza spent time at their homes.

Eliza takes part in the life of each community. While visiting Ida, Eliza notes all who come to call; she follows the activities of her grandchildren. When her teenaged granddaughter comes from distant Kansas to visit her Aunt Ida, she has the ideal East Hampton vacation—boating, picnics, rides in the "new" automobile, parties with lots of boyfriends.[54]

> "July 22, 1907 . . . Hester Glover came on noon train. Herbert took her to the dance in Eve . . . [Herbert was seventeen-year-old Hester's cousin]. July 23 . . . Hester out for a drive . . . July 24 . . . A lovely day, Hester went to the beach with a party of Young Girls to take dinner & tea. Alice Dayton called to see Hester . . . Hester at the Beach all day. Got back just before dark." Each day, a note on Hester. "July 29. A cloudy morn, rain in Aft. Hester went sailing with Edith & Mary & Frank Eldredge, got home about 7 P.M. Had a fun time although it rained in Aft. They all came home in bus . . . July 31 . . . A beautiful morn, quite warm. Hester off to Montauk with a party of young folks, got home on the 8 PM train, said she had a lovely time . . ."

Eliza gets older; her diary entries became sparse, then stop. Somehow, she has a flat in Brooklyn, where she dies in 1912, a year before her husband. He had tried to be a leading businessman; Eliza had helped him, but he missed his goal.

This is a glimpse into how these very different women lived, how they continued to thrive even though the more easily mobile males in their families sought their fortunes elsewhere. Such are the various records of these six middle-class women. Some recorded their lives by writing diaries or poems. A calmness pervades their singular, well-ordered lives.

THE WOMEN'S FAMILIES

PHEBE VAN SCOY (1787-1868), Northwest, East Hampton. Daughter of Isaac van Scoy (1758-1846) and Temperance Payne. Siblings: Mercy (1783-1830?), Isaac Sylvester (1790-post-1860), Arnold (1793-1857), Betsey (1796?-?).

POLLY HICKS (1790-1881), Amagansett and Duck Creek. Daughter of Zachariah Hicks (1749-1833) and Rebecca Sherrill (1758-1834). Siblings: Jacob (1782-?), Samuel (1783-?), Elizabeth (1786-1874), Joseph (1789-1853), Rebecca (1793-1865), twin son (d.y.), Hannah (twin) (1795-1826), Lydia (1798-1873).

CORNELIA HUNTINGTON (1803-1890), East Hampton. Daughter of Dr. Abel Huntington and Frances Lee. Siblings: Mariette (1800-1882), Abby (1806-1864), George Lee (1811-1881).

ADELIA ANNA (PARSONS) SHERRILL (1838-1915), East Hampton. Married 1859 to Nathaniel Huntting Sherrill (1832-1874). Children: Anna M. (1860-1918), Abram Elisha (1862-1924), Mary Jerusha (1865-1940), Julia Parsons (1868-1939), Amy Blanche (1871-1949), William N. (b.&d. 1874).

ABIGAIL JANE (KIMBLE) PARSONS (1848-1901), The Springs. Married 1870 to Joseph Dudley Parsons (1842-1885). Children: Walton Grant (1870-1929), Phebe Jane (Jennie) (1874-1945), Lena (1878-1950?), Raymond Schoonover (1882-1940).

ELIZA JANE (FISK) GLOVER (1835-1913), East Fourth St., NYC, and Southold. Married 1855 to William Henry Hobart Glover (1831-1912). Children: Harry Warren (1856-1929), Ida Frances (1857-1909), William Hobart (1859-1940s?), Edwin Fisk (1862-1864), Charles Mortimer (1863-1943?), Nettie Irene (1864-1919), Gertrude Lillian (1867-1940s?), Elmore Livingston (1869-post-1880), Morton LeRoy (1871-1940s?), Lorraine Linwood (1873-1940s?), Arlington Frederick Clayton (1875-1940s?).

NOTES

For the notes pertaining to this lecture, see pages 451-454.

EAST HAMPTON IN
THE SEVENTEENTH CENTURY

John M. Murrin

L ET'S TRY TO DISCOVER, if we can, what was distinctive about East
Hampton in the seventeenth century. In many respects it was a typical New England town. It was settled by families (not unmarried servants), and they took seriously what one New Jersey diarist of the
eighteenth century called the First Commandment—that is, God's first
injunction to Adam and Eve: "Be fruitful and multiply."

They were and they did. The thirty-eight householders who participated in the first land divisions probably spoke for a total of 120 to
150 settlers in the early 1650s. A tabulation for 1687, less than half a
century later, shows that the population had grown to 502: 223 free
white men and boys, 219 free white women and girls, twenty-six male
servants and nine female, and eleven male slaves plus fourteen females.
The record does not indicate how many of the slaves were Africans or
Indians.

We also learn that 98 of the 223 free white men were able to bear
arms (forty-four percent), which fits well with the rule of thumb that
about half the male population of a well-settled community was under
age sixteen. That estimate leaves only six percent as elderly or disabled.
The record also tells us that 116 infants had been born in the previous
seven years, of whom 108 had been baptized. Had the other eight
(seven percent) died, or did they belong to dissenting families? We
shall probably never know. We are told that fifty-seven deaths had occurred over the same period (did this total include the eight infants?),
which means that live births outnumbered deaths by about two to
one, an explosive rate of population growth. Only two men called

241

themselves merchants, and we can probably guess who they were—
John Mulford, an original settler (or his son Samuel), and Abraham
Schellinger, a Dutch immigrant.

The settlers weren't the only ones to increase and multiply. The
town's herds and flocks were reproducing at a fantastic rate. In a detailed tax list for 1683—four years before the population survey I've
been using—the town had 137 horses, almost 1,000 cows, 151 oxen
(nearly a team for every household), and just over 1,000 sheep. According to T. H. Breen in his East Hampton Histories, the number of
sheep would multiply to more than 16,000 during the 1690s.

What have we learned so far? East Hampton was a community, not
yet very stratified, in which a large majority (seventy-one of ninety-
seven) men on the tax list owned their own farms and participated in
the local Congregational church under the long and quite successful
pastorate of Reverend Thomas James, who served his people for about
half a century. Almost every household had at least one horse and one
cow, and most had more. Sheep thrived on eastern Long Island, but not
on the mainland where they were easy prey to wolves. The total assessed wealth of the town had increased by a third in just eight years,
a rate of growth which, if sustained, would reach over 130 percent in a
single generation. But the twenty-six men on the rate list who did not
own land suggest the beginnings of a class of dependent people. And
the huge number of sheep probably tells us that much of the wealth of
this town was generated by women putting in long hours of diligent
labor at their spinning wheels. This description does not take any account of the whale industry, which thrived in the town for about forty
years after 1670 and probably generated more capital than any other
economic activity.

Life expectancy was probably comparable to what it was in the
rest of rural New England, where it was among the highest in the
world. Compared with the rest of the early modern world, colonial
New England sometimes looks like an organized movement for "Im-
mortality Now!" I doubt that any local resident could brag, as another
Long Island woman did to the governor in the 1680s, that she had
more than 360 living descendants, or an average of a birthday every
day of the year. But I found only two estate inventories in the first volume of town records (one included quite a few books) and only two
coroner's inquests, one for young John Talmadge who drowned swimming after helping to bathe some sheep in a pond. Did the town have
higher standards of hygiene than most of us attribute to other New
England villages at the same time?

In a few respects, as most of East Hampton's historians have emphasized, the town did rather better than most other New England villages. I'm not aware of any homicides in the town. Despite occasional alarms caused by mainland Indians or the Dutch, the town never waged war against anybody in the seventeenth century, although the Montauk Indians did go to war against the Narragansetts across Long Island Sound. The town's relations with the Montauks, while probably overromanticized, were more cordial than the norm. In purchasing the land, the founders offered valuable trading goods, including small drills useful in converting sea shells into wampum, and—a big surprise!—twenty-four looking glasses or mirrors. Thomas James, the minister, learned Algonquian, preached to the Montauks, and apparently converted some of them. The rise of whaling after 1670 provided regular employment, and frequently a form of debt bondage, for many Indian men, often (I suspect) as skilled harpoonists. This pattern was unusual but not distinctive. Something quite similar also took hold on Martha's Vineyard and Nantucket.

Yet in still other respects, East Hampton appears more contentious and, yes, cruder or coarser than the typical New England town. Backbiting and slander suits frequently disrupted the town. Several sexual scandals alarmed the residents. Daniel Fairfield was accused of seducing both the daughter and the maid of the Reverend James. Four men, two married and perhaps in their forties, and two unmarried young men of about twenty, shocked the community in the summer of 1654 by engaging in what seems to have been competitive masturbation. One was put in the pillory, two were whipped, and the fourth scolded. But when continuing rumors implicated a teenager, the magistrates treated the accuser as a slanderer rather than the boy as a probable malefactor. The court specifically decided this sexual offense was not a crime that extended to life and limb. Coming just a few years after New Haven Colony had hanged a Guilford man for public masturbation, the justices were doing their best not to overreact, even though these trials involved behavior that certainly qualified as lewd and notorious by seventeenth-century Puritan standards.

We see pretty much the same pattern in East Hampton's locally famous witch scare, an event that also places East Hampton well within New England traditions. Although nearly everyone still believed in the devil and probably in witches, nearly all of the actual trials in North America occurred in New England. Two accusations have survived for Pennsylvania, one for Westchester, and one actual trial (an acquittal) for Virginia. At a minimum, a witch trial does show us neighbors willing to

entertain deeply unflattering thoughts about one another—that someone had become so vile that she was an explicit servant of Satan. Salem
Village, the site of North America's largest and most famous witch
hunt, was also a fiercely divided community.

The East Hampton case began in the winter of 1658 when Elizabeth Howell (daughter of Lion Gardiner, probably the most famous
man in town), went to bed with what seemed a routine illness, suddenly got worse, and then cried out while delirious that she had been
bewitched. She died the next day. Although her mother tried to prevent
her accusation from spreading, Goody Simons, a notorious gossip, revealed the name of Elizabeth, wife of a contentious settler named
Joshua Garlick. The wife of Foulk Davis (he was one of the public masturbators) then encouraged everyone to dredge up old memories of
every hostile encounter with Elizabeth Garlick. Over the previous ten
years, several mothers had asked Goody Garlick to nurse their infants,
and several of the babies had died not long after. She had also been associated with the nocturnal appearance of a terrifying black cat on
Gardiner's Island. Because Elizabeth Howell had also seen a black cat in
her delirium before dying, the coincidence looked ominous.

The local justices, who lacked the power to try a capital crime,
sent Goody Garlick to Hartford for trial, where she was acquitted on
grounds of insufficient evidence. The costs were apportioned among
the Garlick family, East Hampton, and the colony government. T. H.
Breen thinks the magistrates had little choice but to send her to Hartford for trial but that they probably believed, after hearing all of the testimony, that the real menace to local harmony was Foulke Davis's wife,
the gossip, and not Goody Garlick. The court sometimes imposed enormous fines for slander.

I don't know of any judicial proceedings in Connecticut involving
East Hampton people prior to this case. The town had submitted to
Connecticut rule in 1649 and then tried to back out in 1655. But the
Connecticut General Court told them that "it can bee no advantage,
but rather the contrary, to theire devided, shattered condition, not to
have dependance uppon or bee under some settled Jurissd." Obviously
Hartford had heard about East Hampton's quarrels. The colony also or-
dered the town to pay its taxes.

In the Garlick case, the town—for the first time that I know of—
surrendered the final power of determination to an outside authority. It
recognized a real limit to its own autonomy. A few years later, as Breen
notes, the town fathers for the first time called their village "a little
commonwealth." East Hampton was coming together as a community,

a town with a collective identity, not just a gathering of quarrelsome householders trying to share the same space. Slander trials fell off sharply in the 1660s. Disputes over property took their place in the town court.

If East Hampton was better off than some towns and also more contentious during the first two decades, it also became—politically— quite outspoken, even precocious, in its dedication to the rights and liberties of Englishmen. Its marginal place as a Puritan island perilously adrift within a larger, non-Puritan colony helps tell us why.

I classify East Hampton as one of the last in a second phase of New England town founding from 1636 through the 1640s. The first phase, which included Salem, Boston, Dorchester, Roxbury, Braintree, Charlestown, Lynn, and Ipswich, consisted of towns settled directly by people arriving from England. The second phase was composed of towns founded by settlers dissatisfied with their first choice and eager to find something better. In some cases they were driven out, as when Roger Williams fled to Narragansett Bay and established Providence, or when Anne Hutchinson and her admirers settled on Rhode Island and founded both Portsmouth and Newport. Thomas Hooker led a voluntary exodus to the Connecticut Valley, while Theosophilius Eaton and John Davenport left Massachusetts to create New Haven. Most of these migrants moved, quite deliberately, beyond the charter boundaries of Massachusetts in quest of greater religious, political, or economic autonomy. They did not bother to get royal patents for their new communities. Many of them drafted "covenants" instead.

Among East Hampton's near neighbors, Southampton and Southold were settled around 1640 by congregations that had formed themselves and chosen a minister on the mainland before migrating to Long Island. Southold's settlers came from New Haven, already the most severely Puritan society in the world, and agreed to govern themselves according to the law of God (the Bible). Only male church members could vote. Southampton attached itself to Connecticut, which never restricted voting to church members and which showed much greater respect for English customs. East Hampton followed the Southampton pattern, although its church was formed after the settlers reached Long Island. The town never had a formal covenant or statement of purpose. New Haven and Southold abolished trial by jury, which has no biblical precedent. East Hampton used juries regularly and allowed lots of men to participate in public life. Yet the town's link with Connecticut remained tenuous until the witch scare. East Hampton and Southampton seldom appear in the public records of colonial

Connecticut. In sum, East Hampton, one of the last towns to be established in this second phase, placed a high value on its autonomy even though the settlers faced severe difficulties in maintaining internal harmony and cohesion.

Why, then, did the town pull together more successfully after the mid-1660s? T. H. Breen gives a great deal of credit to the whaling industry and the prosperity it stimulated. No doubt his point is valid. But I would like to suggest another powerful catalyst to internal cohesion. The town faced a new threat to its emerging traditions after the English conquered New Netherland in 1664 and then asserted control over all of Long Island in 1665. The Duke of York's patent also gave him the land west of the Connecticut River, that is, nearly every settled town in the colony of Connecticut, including Hartford and New Haven. But Connecticut's governor, John Winthrop, Jr., met with his New York counterpart in 1665 and conceded Long Island to New York in exchange for recognition of his colony's authority over its mainland towns. In effect, East Hampton now paid a high price for its earlier autonomy. It had never contributed much to Connecticut. Connecticut lost little by ceding it to New York.

Yet the three eastern towns clearly preferred to be governed by Connecticut, not New York. They protested against the Duke's Laws of 1665 and against the taxation without representation that had been established under that autocratic code. They engaged agents in England to try to acquire their own royal charter from the Crown. When the Dutch returned in 1673, retook New York (they renamed it New Orange in honor of William of Orange), and held it for fifteen months, the English towns of central Long Island and East New Jersey accepted Dutch rule, but the three eastern towns submitted to Connecticut instead.

The reimposition of rule under the Duke of York and his new governor, Edmund Andros, again made the islanders uneasy after 1674. When Andros returned to England in 1680, he neglected to renew the colony's expiring revenue act. In 1681 the English merchants of New York City, strongly supported by the English (but not the Dutch) towns on Long Island, launched a tax strike by refusing to pay port duties. The Duke's Court of Assize, which was supposed to be a major instrument of his autocratic control, then met, but instead of arresting the protesting merchants, it tried and convicted the customs collector for usurping power. It also urged the Long Islanders to shut up while it petitioned the Duke to grant the colony an elective assembly. The Duke, under terrible pressure at home during the so-called Popish Plot and Exclusion Crisis, at last gave in and conceded an elective assembly.

It met in New York City in the fall of 1683. East Hampton chose delegates "to Joyne with the rest of the [East Riding towns] to give ye Representatives Instructions to stand upp in ye assemblie for ye Maintenance of our priveledges & English liberties." The assembly passed the New York Charter of Liberties of 1683, a document that tried to guarantee representative government to the colony forever. Most Long Island and East Hampton historians give the major credit for this achievement to the English towns on Long Island. They certainly supported the change, but in my opinion the strongest momentum behind the Charter came from New York City. The Quaker migration to the Delaware Valley had terrified the English merchants of the city, who were afraid William Penn's new colony would drain their own of English settlers and leave them to be swamped by the Dutch. Penn and his first assembly had agreed on their own Charter of Liberties in March 1683. The New York Charter of Liberties was the northern colony's answer seven months later.

This eternal achievement lasted all of two years. In 1685 Charles II died and was succeeded by his Catholic brother, the Duke of York, who became King James II. For twenty years the English settlers of New York had been agitating for the liberties that would make them as happy as New Englanders. James now declared, in effect, that he had found a new way to accomplish this objective. He would make New Englanders as miserable as the English settlers of New York.

James disallowed the Charter of Liberties and restored autocratic government in New York. Because the law courts had recently annulled the Massachusetts charter, he united all of the New England colonies into what he called the Dominion of New England, and he sent Sir Edmund Andros to America to govern this enormous province autocratically—without an elective assembly. In 1688 Andros added New York and the Jerseys to the Dominion.

England's Glorious Revolution finally resolved this crisis. William of Orange invaded England in November 1688, most of the English army defected to him, James fled to France, and Parliament declared William and Mary joint sovereigns of the kingdom. Boston overthrew Andros in April, and this disaffection soon spread to—you guessed it—the eastern towns of Long Island. But once again the decisive action came from New York City. This time the Dutch settlers took the lead. They rose at the end of May, took possession of Fort James, renamed it Fort William, and put Jacob Leisler, a militia captain, in charge of the colony. The eastern towns supported him at first, but then—as during the

Dutch reconquest of 1673—they again explored the possibility of reuniting with Connecticut. In East Hampton, Samuel Mulford—who was becoming the town's most prominent spokesman—remained a strong advocate of Leisler, however.

New York's uprising ended tragically. In 1691 William sent New York a new governor who tried and executed Leisler for treason, an act that poisoned the colony's politics for the next ten or twelve years. During these struggles, Samuel Mulford became an active participant in provincial politics. Between the Glorious Revolution and 1720, he spoke out often and eloquently on behalf of his town and the liberties of Englishmen.

To sum up, East Hampton's early history was distinctive but not quite unique. In most respects the community was a typical New England town, a little more prosperous than many, more accommodating than most toward the Indians, but also more fractious and fragile than most, at least during the first two decades. East Hampton also provides an interesting case study of what could happen when a non-Puritan province tried to absorb a strongly Puritan village. Its absorption into New York made the town far more articulate and outspoken in defense of English liberties than most mainland towns.

The town also became absorbed into the Atlantic economy, especially through whaling but also through piracy, an activity that has left only fascinating hints in the surviving records. The town had considerable success in resisting the formal demands of empire. Despite constant pressure from New York City and the government of New York, it did most of its trading with Boston and Connecticut. During the Revolution, when most of Long Island went loyalist, East Hampton stood firmly for the American cause. This pattern leads me to my final point. When did the people of East Hampton at last feel comfortable being New Yorkers rather than Yankees? You tell me. Long after the Revolution, I suspect, and maybe not until the twentieth century.

PIRATES

—◦◦◦—

Noel Gish

Long Island is a place surrounded by water. This island was shaped by the frozen water from the continental glaciers 20,000 years ago. Since the glaciers retreated the rising tide and the ravages of the wind and rain have molded this small sand encrusted island even more. The island and the water are one.

I have always told young people to think of this island as a fish newly caught lying on the beach. The head is pressed against the great mainland to the west, its body stretches eastward with two flukes playfully extending into the Atlantic, that this fish calls home. The island fish is huge stretching almost 120 miles, bigger than any striper that I have caught or even lied about catching. And, it is the water that surrounds and nourishes this place the Natives called Paumanauk. The water comforts us and seems to draw us near. It may be the salt water, the composition of which is so similar to the salinity of the embryonic sac, that makes it all seem so familiar. Maybe, we as people, are drawn somehow unknowingly to the comfort of the womb.

It was the sea that brought life to the Algonquins, who were the first of the island's inhabitants. It was the sea that brought the first Englishmen to the township of what would become East Hampton. Lion Gardiner came across the Atlantic to work in Connecticut, but it was here on the island that he chose to make his home. East Hampton history begins with the purchase of Gardiner's Island in 1639. The first English child born in Suffolk County, even in New York State, was Elizabeth. Even though Gardiner's Island was his island, Lion Gardiner is buried in East Hampton. Even today, the sixteenth Lord of the Manor has residence here. The link of the town to Gardiner's Island is strong indeed.

The ocean brought life to the island and it was the sea that has been both a blessing and curse to those who live along that boundary between earth and water. The sea moderates the climate, it provided the breezes to turn the early windmills and power the earliest sailing ships. It is that wonderful marine climate that made agriculture possible. It is a climate of long springs, mild summers and cool autumns. One can always depend on an "Indian summer" in East Hampton. Even after the summer season is over and all of the city people have departed, any islander will tell you that the best weather is at hand. Cool nights, warm days, and the harvest of the earth and the sea are still coming. The bounty of Peconic Bay scallops or striped bass rounding Montauk, heading south are part of this magical time called fall. It is the nearness to the water, the ocean, that makes this all possible.

The earliest of settlers to East Hampton numbered a mere nine, nomads from England, from an area around Maidstone, some ten miles up river from the North Sea and the port of Kent. This small English lot first settled in Lynn, Massachusetts, then wised up and continued to the south fork of Long Island. These English farmers who lived near the sea must have found this place quite suitable and probably surprisingly milder than the land they left in either England or Lynn, Massachusetts.

The first important maritime industry in this town was whaling. Whaling on the eastern shore of Long Island began with the Native Americans. We don't have to go back to the Old Testament and Jonah to find a good whaling story. The tales of whaling always seem to get my heart pumping, and my mind racing.

Captain George Waymouth, an English explorer, reported that he observed Indians pursuing and killing whales along the coast in 1620. In the work *The History of the American Whaling Fishery*, written by Alexander Starbuck in 1876, the author states "Whales were first taken off Long Island in 1644 by Southampton Indians." The Native Americans probably didn't take them; it was probably easy to say they waited for the whales to come to them. Drift whales were common and coastal storms, disease, and simple misdirection would often strand the leviathan along the sandbars.

The native islanders would boil the blubber and mix the oil with their corn and beans, or they would rub the oil into animal hides as a preservative.

If whaling started in Southampton, it wasn't long before it was an active industry in East Hampton. In the original deed of 1648, the native indians were promised "to have fynnes and tayles of all such whales as shall be cast upp, and desire that they may be friendly dealt with in other parts." The deed for Montauk and the point divides all whales with equal shares going between whites and Native Americans.

Early East Hamptonites found that whaling was of great concern according to town records, November 6, 1651. "It was ordered that Goodman Mulford shall call out ye town by succession to look out for whale." The whale was a valuable creature, probably more of value than any fur bearing animal. The whale oil was an important source of illumination. The whale oil lamp was more reliable than reed lamps or lard lamps. Whale oil was the fuel of choice. The oil could be a lubricant. Farm tools that were put away for the season could be protected from rust with a rubbing of oil. East Hampton recipes tell of mince pies made with whale meat. If the town was lucky to find a sperm whale, the waxy spermacetti from the cavity of the head made an excellent candle. When mixed with the oil from the bayberry, the candles not only glowed, but filled the home with a perfumed scent. The bone of the whale could be used to make buttons, collar stays, corset stays, and handles. The baleen became chair springs, hair brushes, and even buggy whips.

The whale's importance seems to have even divided families. In 1653, East Hampton "orders that the share of whale now in contro-versy between widow Talmadge and Thomas Talmadge shall be divided among them as the lot is." There is no truth to the rumor that this is the legal precedent for community property settlements.

The early prosperity of East Hampton and other villages was largely based on the onshore whaling industry. This onshore whaling was not expensive, for no large boats were built and long voyages were not necessary. Tools and implements could be made by local black-smiths. Small boats might be kept along the shore, always ready for use. The time for shore whaling spanned December through May. This made it a perfect match for agricultural pursuits which lasted from May through November.

Whaling became an all-town task. The area in and around East Hampton was politically divided to insure orderly division of beached whales. There was a finders fee paid to the person who took note of a beached whale. Native Americans were paid at the rate of five shillings, while an East Hamptonite discovering the whale was given a piece of the whale three feet broad.

Whale watchers were set up to make whale sightings less a form of chance. Small huts, similar to wigwams, were erected as beach shelters. When a whale was sighted, the watcher would scamper up a pole or tree waving his shirt or coat.

Making a weft, as it was called, set in motion an exciting chain re-action of activity. Soon horns would be sounded, then the cry "whale off" would be heard as citizens hurried to their appointed tasks.

The small boats were run into the surf. The harpooner, tiller and rowers, all in unison, were set on the same goal. The whale was pur-sued, chased and struck with a harpoon. The crew held on while the wounded whale took them for what would later be known as a Nan-tucket sleigh ride. (I'd like to refer to it as the Hampton Jitney even though it has no basis in history). The chase was not fun or sport, it was exhausting for both the hunter and the hunted. Closer and closer the crew would row toward the whale. Now a lance was driven deep, turned in the wound, hopefully hitting the heart or lung. The ordeal would be over soon if the whale spouted blood. Now with the whale in tow the boat would row back to the shore. Sometimes, the small boats were driven far and the way home was even more difficult and dangerous as winter or spring storms appeared quickly. Small boats would be no match for the dreadful Atlantic.

The whale was returned to the beach where it was met by others ready to cut into the mammal. Huge try pots were now burning on the beach, sometimes lighting the way home for the whalers. The entire male population of East Hampton was divided into two whale-cutting teams. The job was to render the whale blubber into oil, rescue the baleen, bone and all the other parts that were useful. The women ar-rived on the beach to bring food and warm clothing if the weather warranted it.

By 1680, Amagansett was the most profitable point for whaling on the east coast, not New Bedford, not Nantucket, not Sag Harbor, but Amagansett. In 1687, there were seven companies engaged in whaling on the south fork. So intense was the competition for whales that a boundary had to be set between East Hampton and its neighbor, Southampton. Drift whales and day long whaling expeditions were now big business and the profit from those whales could fuel not only lamps, but fuel the economy of the town.

Jacobus Schellinger owned one of the East Hampton whaling com-panies. He along with his wife and family had come from Staten Island. Many say he was the first city resident to work his way out to East Hampton, but definitely not the last. So well known and respected was Schellinger for his whaling expertise that the village of Nantucket of-fered him royalties on every catch a Nantucket fisherman would make if only he would come and teach them his whaling methods. Jacobus could not be moved by promises of money, he remained in East Hampton content with his life, his work and the people around him.

It's hard to imagine that there once was a day when whales were a regular sight on the shores of Long Island. I remember vividly the stranding of a whale in 1980 on the south shore of Long Island at Fire Island. Sick and disoriented, it was helped into the old ferry slip. Feisty, they called the small sperm whale. Over the next few days before its release, tens of thousands of people came to gaze at the black mass that moved ever so slowly. Smiles greeted each move of the tail, and a wheeze from the blowhole brought almost uncontrolled cheers. There has yet to be another close encounters with the big kind since.

However, those encounters were once very common. In Frederick P. Schmitt's book *Mark Well the Whale* he writes:

> Whales were so numerous offshore in 1700 that a woman walking the dunes for a few miles from East Hampton to Bridgehampton counted thirteen stranded animals and saw countless others spouting nearby.

It wasn't long before the government got involved in the all too profitable whaling industry. Robert Hunter, the Royal Governor of New York, passed a tax on half the oil and bone from all drift whales. The King of England called the whale the "Royal fish" and asked officials to license all takers of the "big fish." There were no cries from the citizens of Kingston, Syracuse, Albany or Utica, but the people of Long Island and those of East Hampton became incensed at the tax. To surrender fifty percent of the catch after all the effort, labor and even the potential loss of life was unthinkable.

Samuel Mulford was a seventy-year-old member of the General Assembly of New York and an East Hamptonite who was not going to take this government abuse. He first took action against the governor, but when authorities led him through a legal maze of English law, the homespun whaler went over the governor's head, way over his head. Samuel Mulford boarded a ship for London to take his case right to the top—King George I. In England, this country whaler was truly a fish out of water. His informal dress, New World language, and unsophisticated air gave him little chance with the aristocrats in London.

Day after day Mulford worked his way through the crowded London streets, across the common to petition the government just to hear him. Each time he failed and each time his pockets were picked. No matter how careful he was the precious little money he had was quickly draining away. Mulford could not afford the losses any longer. He went back to his rented flat and sewed fishhooks into the lining of his pockets. The next day as he began his pilgrimage once more through London an unsuspecting Oliver attempted to separate Samuel from his money. But to the thief's dismay he became firmly and painfully attached to the old man's trousers. The authorities had their pickpocket and a rather amusing story. Word spread quickly among the London thieves about an old man with a gimpy walk whose pockets had nothing but fishhooks. Soon almost everyone in London seemed to resemble Samuel Mulford. Pickpockets took a holiday rather than mess with the man from the colonies. Mulford became an instant celebrity, the man who had singlehandedly fooled the London thieves. So quickly did his notoriety spread that he not only got to address the members of the House of Common, but he met with King George himself.

Within a year the whale tax was revoked. Governor Hunter was furious at Mulford for his impetuous behavior. The governor had him expelled from the New York Assembly, whereupon East Hampton reelected him again the following year.

Samuel Mulford died at the age of eighty in 1725. His tombstone reads "Honest Sam Mulford" but his legend reads Fishhooks Mulford. The East Hampton whaler had defended the principle of "No taxation without representation" almost fifty years before the revolution.

It wasn't long before the whaling industry moved from onshore whaling to offshore whaling expeditions. Voyages became longer and longer, the whaling ships bigger and bigger. There were no ports on the south shore, so Sag Harbor became the home port for many an East Hampton whaler. The whaling voyages brought personal wealth back to the East Hampton town. There were men from town who sailed with Captain Mercator Cooper in 1845 when his ship, the *Manhattan*, first sailed into Tokyo Bay almost eight years before Commodore Matthew Perry in 1853. Although Long Islanders were first to Japan, we are not first in the history books. Men like Jeremiah Mulford sailed out of Cold Spring Harbor. He was captain of the *Nathaniel P. Talmadge* during several cruises around the Horn and into Alaskan waters. His final cruise in 1848 was difficult. He had to survive a mutiny before returning to East Hampton four years later.

The offshore whaling trips were difficult at best. Conditions were grim, filled with long periods of boredom separated by short periods of incredible excitement and danger. Families were apart for long periods and sometimes forever. Rennseleer Conkling of Amagansett de-

Whaling was difficult and dangerous at best.

parted this world similar to Gregory Peck in the film *Moby Dick*. Con-kling was last seen heading straight out to sea lashed to the back of a wounded whale. Herman Melville's classic had nothing on the stories from East Hampton.

There are still traces of those off shore whaling days hiding in East Hampton trunks and attics. Log books and diaries tell stories, but so does the art of the whaler, scrimshaw. The teeth of the sperm whale, pieces of baleen and bone were shaped and etched with stories and memories. Pie crimpers, ditty boxes, sewing implements and swifts were accomplished during the long periods at sea when they were just looking for whales. This Yankee folk art once considered to be dispos-able junk is now highly prized by those who understand the brief era of Yankee whaling. So search out those old trunks of Auntie Tuthill, Stanley Miller and Cheryl Foster, for there are gems yet to be found.

One of my favorite trips as a small boy growing up in Hicksville was a journey to the Museum of Natural History in New York City. There amid the towering frozen skeletons of the dinosaurs I played out my own *Jurassic Park*. I remember how the museum smelled to me, old, stale; it seemed huge and disjointed. I remember the fish house and the massive whale that hung overhead. Little did I know that the Mu-seum of Natural History and East Hampton's whaling past were so firmly linked.

It was February 1907, and Roy Chapman Andrews, a naturalist and explorer was journeying out to Amagansett on his very first assignment for the American Museum of Natural History. Dr. H. C. Bumpers, director of the museum, had read about a whale that had been killed on the east end by Captain Joshua B. Edwards. The seventy-eight-year-old whaler was at the end of his whaling career, but not at the end of his fame. He had sailed around the world numerous times, but nearing eighty he chose to spend these days in and around East Hampton.

Mr. Bumpers wanted to acquire from Edwards the whale skeleton for study and exhibition at the museum. By the time Mr. Andrews arrived the crew at Amagansett had removed the blubber from the whale. The carcass, all fifty-four feet of it, sat slowly sinking into the sand. The whale was the largest right whale ever recorded at that time. The skeleton would be of great importance, but how could they get it back to New York with the temperature at twenty degrees and a tough wind tearing across the beach? The carcass, even with the blubber removed, still weighed almost fifty tons. The museum hired six local men to hack carefully at the remaining carcass, removing the bones, as Mr. Andrews checked each piece against a huge blueprint of a whale's skeleton

The incoming tide meant the men worked waist deep in water. Then, without warning, a storm came out of the west. The waves crashed into the carcass. The workmen furiously anchored the beast to the beach, hoping it would not be washed away. The storm lasted three long days, and when it was over the whale was gone. The anchoring ropes were there, but no whale. The ropes were still taut; the whale was now buried beneath the sand. The temperature that day was only 12 degrees as the work crew labored to remove the remaining bones out of the freezing water.

Missing from the survey of the whale skeleton were two pelvic bones, essential to a total restoration. The bones were only a mere twelve inches long and a further search of the remaining sand and carcass did not reveal them. Mr. Andrews had an idea. Racing down to the try works where Captain Josh had sent the blubber, Andrews fished a long handled wire net into the 250-gallon cast iron cauldron. Triumphantly, two pelvic bones emerged from the oily soup. For many years the skeleton of Captain Edwards' whale was exhibited at the museum to educate and enthrall visitors. It was the American Museum's exhibit, but it was an East Hampton whale.

It was not only whalers that traveled our shores in search of profit, but other men who sought profit by questionable means. As early as

1689, French pirates had raided Block Island, off Montauk Point, and attempted to hit New London. People along the beach not only watched for whales, but sails. There were those familiar ships and some not so. And, there were those ships that flew no colors at all.

Captain William Kidd was a man who was a legend in his own time. In June of 1697, the sloop *Antonio* anchored off Gardiner's Island. The lord of the manor was then John Gardiner, who came out to meet the famous adventurer. Kidd proceeded to bury twenty four chests of gold, silver, silk and precious gems in a hollow on the island.

Gardiner was informed that should Kidd return and not find the treasure he (Kidd) would have his head or that of his sons. Captain Kidd had started out as a privateer, which was perfectly legal in those days. As a privateer he worked for England with permission to seize the bounty of other nations specifically the French and Spanish. But Kidd had run into trouble with the English who thought him more pirate than privateer. The treasure was buried as a bargaining chip in negotiations with Governor Bellomont who ruled New York and Massachusetts. But the negotiations soured and Kidd was sent back to England in chains.

Kidd was tried not for piracy but murder. It seems that in a slight altercation he hit one of his crew members over the head with a bucket and killed him. Kidd was hung in 1701; his treasure was removed by Gardiner and sent along to Governor Bellomont who returned it to London. But somewhere along the way, between Gardiner's Island and London, some of the treasure was misplaced.

Rumors have persisted for centuries that Kidd's ship buried more treasure, from Plum Island to Oyster Bay and from East Hampton to Coney Island. I can tell you that no one since John Gardiner has ever admitted to finding any treasure in the sand dunes of East Hampton town. I can also tell you that William Kidd's name did appear in documents during my research in Smithtown. Captain Kidd was hired in 1697 to act an an "agent of protection" for ships sailing out of the Long Island Sound. It seems that Smithtown found it easier to pay Kidd a protection fee than to lose all their cargo and ships to "them pirates."

Other pirate tales tell of Joseph Bradish who sailed the *Adventure Galley* out of London in 1698. He was spotted off Sagaponack by Henry Pierson who sailed out when he saw the strange ship off shore. Reverend Ebenezer White, Pierson's neighbor, joined the pirate and Henry on a ride to East Hampton where they met with John Mulford and Nathaniel Huntting, a young East Hampton minister. We now have two government officials, two ministers and a pirate engaged in a series of discussions. What a wonderful combination of characters.

Later Bradish returned to this ship bringing ashore four sealed bags containing 2,805 pieces of eight and a bag of jewels. He asked Colonel Pierson to take care of them. The *Adventure Galley* lay off Sagaponack for a few more days before ships were hired to unload the Galley's cargo. One ship was from Southampton and two from Southold. No ships were from East Hampton so obviously suspicions grew.

The *Adventure Galley* weighed anchor and sailed to Block Island where the unloading continued; after which, the pirates fired guns into the bottom of the ship causing it to sink. The crew and cargo ships scattered. On April 27, 1699, one of Colonel Pierson's neighbors told the authorities of the treasure left him by Bradish. Lord Bellomont ordered the holdings turned over to him. The rest of the treasure was never found. I suggest we start with the Sagaponack minister, because the East Hampton minister, Reverend Nathaniel Huntting, gave a sermon about the evils of piracy a week later!

There are other stories of money ships, slave ships who ran Black ivory after the whaling trade had faded. The stories of rum runners and smugglers of the 1920s may be too fresh for anything other than a discussion of current events in East Hampton.

Nathaniel Prime wrote *The History of Long Island* in 1845 and said:

> Although the bays on the south side of the island are numerous and large and completely defended from the rage of the ocean by the great barrier of sand, more durable than stone; yet the inlets are so few and difficult of access, even for small craft , that it is impracticable to enter them when the refuge is most desirable. In the whole length of the island, there are but ten openings in the Great Beach, and these are constantly varying by violence of the waves, so that after a single storm, the channel which is never deep may be materially obstructed or changed. This necessarily renders the coasting business on the whole south side exceedingly uncertain and precarious.

What was Nathaniel Prime speaking of, this place of shifting sand and ever changing shoreline? The first coast zone survey of Long Island had been done only ten years before Prime wrote his work. In the one hundred and fifty years since Prime's work, the beaches and outer bars have accounted for precarious coastal business and awful disasters. The movement of sand along the shore, the treacherous rocks that loom under the waves have terrorized ships since the earliest times.

The first beacon constructed on Long Island was on the eastern tip of the south fork. Montauk light was one of the first federally funded marine projects approved by George Washington in 1796. The original construction was made on Turtle Hill some 300 feet from the raging Atlantic. Now, in less than 200 years, the 300-foot distance has been considerably shortened. Engineers of the time thought the Montauk light would last 200 years; their estimate may not be that far off the mark.

Additional lights were constructed at Fire Island in 1826; Shinnecock or Ponquogue light was established in 1858 and had to alter its

The first beacon, at Montauk Point.

signal characteristics to distinguish it from the Montauk light. That initial error probably resulted in some wrecks from unwary mariners. Other lights were constructed on Plum Island in 1857 and Gardiner's Island in 1855. Even though there were more naval aids, the coastal fogs and frequent storms made landmarks and lighthouse identification difficult.

Shipwrecks have occurred on Long Island ever since 1656 when the Dutch vessel *Prins Maurits* carrying colonists to the New World went aground on the barrier beach near Saltaire, across from present day West Islip. Then as now, the native population came to the rescue. But in 1656 the rescuers were a band of Algonquins known as the Secatogues. They helped the stranded passengers and even sent runners to New Amsterdam to advise Governor Peter Stuyvesant of the incident. The passengers, crew, and treasured Old World possessions were brought back to New Amsterdam.

Here on the East End ships stumbled ashore for the next three hundred years, and, sadly, not all the passengers, crew, and cargo would return safely. One of the more infamous shipwrecks of the eighteenth century was the *H.M.S. Culloden*. This seventy-four gun British ship of the line was part of the fleet that patrolled the Long Island Sound from New York City to Newport, Rhode Island during the Revolutionary War. Since the Battle of Long Island, August, 1776, the entire island from Brooklyn to Montauk Point was occupied by British forces. It was on January 23, 1871, that the *Culloden*, loaded with a contingent of marines and crew numbering 650, went aground on the west side of Lake Montauk. The ship had been trying to make the open water as a heavy winter storm with strong winds and freezing rain struck the Long Island Sound. All efforts to free the ship were fruitless. The guns were turned overboard, the cargo removed and the vessel burned to the water line. However, there was no loss of life.

Over the years the name Culloden Point became less an historical landmark and more of a landmark for fishing expeditions. The ship's timbers rose and sank with every nor'easter that blew through, but little was left to really mark the exact location of the wreck. In the 1970s attempts to find the ship's remains were successful and several artifacts including a cannon were recovered from the sight. The *H.M.S. Culloden* was made one of the first underwater archeological sites designated by New York State.

The number of wrecks and strandings in and around the south fork increased. In 1828, the brig *Mars* came ashore near Georgica in remarkably fine weather. Some of the load of molasses the ship was carrying was removed. Molasses cookies and cakes became the rage for the next few months in East Hampton and the surrounding towns. The real sticky subject was the talk that the molasses had been only ballast for a cargo of slaves. The *Amistad*, off Montauk in 1839, was not the first ship with a cargo of "Black Ivory" to pass the East Hampton shore.

In 1836 the wreck of the *Bristol* and the ship *Mexico* took the lives of some 206 passengers and crew. Although the wrecks took place to the west, the agonized frozen corpses washed up on the south shore from mid-October until January of 1837. These gruesome scenes along the beaches were burned into many a south shore diary. Walt Whitman in his new work *Leaves of Grass* immortalized the wreck of the *Mexico* in his poem *Sleepers*, so that even the people of East Hampton could connect with the tragedy.

Two men with the cannon from the H.M.S. Culloden.

In May, 1839, the *Edward Quesnel* came ashore at Napeague. Seven men were drowned as the vessel along with its cargo of whale oil was thrown upon the shore. The precious whale oil was quickly recovered, and the lights on the south fork burned a little longer and a little brighter that year. Henry P. Hedges of East Hampton recalls the other details, the bodies drawn up on the beach, pale, motionless and ghastly; it became a haunting memory for many.

In 1851, the *St. Catherine* out of Ireland went aground at Amagansett. She was carrying 270 immigrants on their way to Castle Garden. All of the passengers were rescued with the help of T. Mulford and Nathaniel Hand.

In 1842, the *Louis Philippe* came ashore near Mecox. Bound for New York from Bordeaux, France, the cargo of trees, shrubs, and European varieties of plants and roses were thrown overboard to lighten the grip on the sandbar. The beachcombers had a field day recovering the agricultural specimens all along the beach. It has always been rumored that some of the elm trees along East Hampton's main street were rescued from the *Louis Philippe*. Even if it's not true, it makes a great story.

The wreck of the *John Milton* on February 19, 1857 is one of the most often repeated episodes in East Hampton history. The vessel, weighing some 1445 tons, was heading eastward along the south shore looking for its home port in Massachusetts. The ship seems to have mistaken the Shinnecock light for the Montauk light and made her turn north too soon impaling the vessel on the rocks off the point. The ship broke up and there were no survivors among the thirty-three persons on board. The bodies that washed ashore were buried in the burying ground at East Hampton. The *Sag Harbor Express* in 1890 had the recollections of a young Doctor A. Huntington:

> My father was coroner and I recollect how a messenger came on horseback the next morning bringing from Montauk news of the fearful wreck and loss of life; and later, just as the dusk of twilight gathered around, how two farm wagons rolled slowly through the snow up to our home and fourteen frozen corpses were lifted out and laid side by side in the carriage house. I remember also what feelings of awe, I went with my father later in the evening and gazed by the light of a dimly burning lantern on the ghostly spectacle.

Weeks later Mr. Aleck Gould was walking the beach only to find the arm of a sailor's peacoat in the sand. The coat was heavily laden with more than $400.00 in gold coins. The coat belonged to the Captain of the *John Milton*, an Ephraim Harding.

The money was turned over to the captain's widow who sadly lost her twenty-year-old son in the wreck along with her husband.

There was an increasing incidence of shipwrecks and groundings. The early attempts of aid for the *Louis Philippe* and the *Edward Quesnel* were all voluntary. It was the duty of every south shore family to use the spy glass and frequently scan the sea. If anything looked unusual neighbor would signal neighbor and everyone would make for the beach. It was not only men, but women and children as well.

Housewives built fires and made food and volumes of warm drink. Clothing and blankets were ferried to the beach for both the rescued and the rescuers. The early lifesaving efforts were made by men and women with simple values: life and property were important. These East Enders, the fishermen and whalers, who responded to a marine crisis were true to the principle of "helping thy fellow man."

The first organized efforts to protect the loss of life did not start on Long Island. The Massachusetts Humane Society of 1780, as part of their work, set up unmanned "relief huts" along the vast stretches of their beaches. The huts were stocked with provisions and instructions of how to get help. Those sailors lucky enough to find the beach and find the huts might survive.

The federal government took action in the 1840s at the behest of Dr. William A. Newell, a congressman from New Jersey. The doctor succeeded in passing legislation to help deal with the ever increasing maritime incidents and the loss of life. As the "golden door" beckoned the Old World, millions of Europeans sought our shore. The commercial status of New York as the economic capital meant that ships from all over the world would be coming in greater and greater numbers. Between 1839 and 1848, Newell estimated 338 shipwrecks in the New York–New Jersey area, 122 of them on Long Island, an average of one major wreck each month for almost ten years.

The first federal appropriation of some $20,000 in 1849 was made to set up eight unmanned relief stations mainly on Long Island. In the first year of operation over 300 lives were saved. Soon a Life-Saving Benevolent Association was established with better equipment, more stations and a body of paid men organized to patrol the beaches. By 1872 the Treasury Department reorganized the Life Saving Unit again. There was the hiring of qualified surf men and new permanent facilities were created. It had become the United States Life Saving Service.

The Life Saving Service improved methods of sea rescue. When launching rescue boats into the ocean was not possible, a mortar might be used to shoot a lifeline out to the floundering vessel. A 24-pound ball could be launched almost 400 yards. Various types of mortars were employed, including the Manby and the Parrott, until the Lyle Gun was introduced in 1877. The Lyle Gun was much lighter and easier to manage than the old mortars. The bronze construction made it less prone to corrosion from the salt water. It could also throw a projectile with lifeline over 470 yards. Small amounts of powder on the Lyle Gun were enough to make it work well; too much powder by an inexperienced volunteer and the gun might travel as far back as the projectile went forward.

The successful deployment of the lifeline was only the first part of any rescue.

After a larger, strong line was played out to the ship, a clothesline pulley system was set up from ship to shore. Next passengers and crew would enter life rings with canvas pants attached, called the breeches buoy. One by one the rescue of passengers and crew would continue, as the rescued hung above the crashing surf, swinging precariously from side to side, jerking forward with each and every tug given by the men on the beach.

There was the life car, which was a metal lifeboat that, unlike the breeches buoy, could carry several people. A small metal boat with a metal cover could travel the same harness system used by the breeches buoy. The life car was dark and cramped, coupled with a few panic-stricken passengers; it did not always meet with a high degree of confidence. Even though it worked very well, the 225-pound life car fell out of favor and the lighter breeches buoy, although it only moved one individual at a time, was quicker. By the turn of the century the life car was rarely used.

Lifeboats were the mainstay of the rescue effort. At first the boats were made of wood, approximately twenty-seven feet long. They were designed to not only be self-righting but self-bailing as well. Later, metal boats were experimented with at some stations.

These boats were strong and light, they would dent but not leak. Unlike the wooden boats, they did not require the constant maintenance to prevent them from drying out and leaking.

The cry of "ship ashore" was like the fire alarm of today. A remarkable group of men that served the U. S. Life Saving Service were stationed all along the beach from Montauk Point station, Ditch Plain, Hither Plain, Napeague, Amagansett and Georgica. The keepers and the surf men carry names that drive deep into East Hampton's history. These include Conkling, Dominy, Gould, Edwards, King, Mulford, Parsons, Hedges, Stratton, Miller and Hobart just to name a few.

By the time the *George Appold* wrecked on January 9, 1889, the U.S. Life Saving Service was in full operation. The wreck occurred a mile and a half west of the point. The weather that day was clear, calm, but cold when the *Appold* ran some rocks in the minutes just past midnight. The ship seemed fine and one lifeboat was launched, easily making it to the shore. There was plenty of time for preparation which at first seemed unnecessary until a storm erupted, badly damaging the ship's wooden hull. As the storm increased in intensity the crew was ferried one by one to shore. The ship broke up on the rocks and its cargo floated ashore over the next few days. Bolts of calico cloth, New England rum, shoes, boots, stockings, hats and underwear were devoured by eager beachcombers. Quilts of similar calico seemed to magically appear on clothes lines throughout town, as if purchased through the Sears catalog. Sometimes parties were held after a wreck and participants were told to bring all unmated shoes with the hopes of finding their "sole mates." "Wreck shoes" were worn by school children who were most easily identified by the copper toes that seemed to indicate some mysterious fashion trend. Although East Hampton history speaks of the ugly calico, or the wreck shoes, very few negative comments have been found concerning the 100 barrels of rum. Just two months later on March 14, 1889, Charles Raynor Bennet of the

Georgica station saw a distress flag on a ship offshore. Then he noticed a lifeboat had been lowered. The crew of the mystery ship touched the beach and headed single file up the dunes, then stopped in their tracks when they saw the Life Saving Station. Mr. Bennet saw a ragged crew of men suffering from scurvy, who had been without food or water for days. Their ship, the *Wingate*, was of British registry, had lost its rudder and had been adrift for almost a week. They had delayed coming ashore because they feared that the island was inhabited by cannibal Indians. They became desperate and decided to give one leap for the shore then run (the crew of the *Wingate* was saved—they were however later eaten by a sightseeing group from New Jersey).

Not all rescues ended in disaster. Like the wreck of the *Appold*, the wreck of the *Elise Fay* on February 17, 1893, caused the people of East Hampton to go nuts, literally. The schooner went down off Ditch plain station, but her crew of seven were all rescued. Her entire cargo of coconuts made it to shore. Local residents found every conceivable way to use coconuts over the next year. In 1893, it was expected that one invited for dinner would arrive with a coconut cake.

Did the elements of these marine mishaps have any effect on the artists of East Hampton? Two prominent artists who journeyed to the south fork were Winslow Homer and Thomas Moran. Both men painted typical rural scenes. Many involved a beach on a sunny day, the sea and tranquility. The period for both in East Hampton is marked by the arrival of the U.S. Life Saving Service and various important shipwrecks. They both had to be aware of the lifesaving operations. Homer spent five years on the shore of Long Branch, New Jersey before coming to East Hampton in 1874. His painting entitled "East Hampton" is very refined. Although the beach is crowded, Homer focuses on a few elegantly dressed women relaxing on the beach. The rest of the crowd fades into that typical south shore summer haze.

In Homer's next work "The Tent," again, we see women and children in a relaxed mode, enjoying the fresh sea breeze sheltered from the blazing sun. I wonder how much of his experiences and stories from East Hampton played into his work ten years later. There are still women and the water remains a key ingredient but the mood and tone are much different.

Thomas Moran came to East Hampton on the suggestion of some artist friends in 1878. He returned over several summers until he took up permanent residence in 1884. Moran, like Homer, was aware of the importance of the sea in his work. His was a calm sea, inviting and comforting. Moran had to have been aware of the *Bengal* that ran aground off Amagansett in April of 1878 and Captain Joshua Edwards' efforts to rescue the crew. He must have heard of the ship *Daylight* that ran aground at Georgica in 1882 or the *John D. Buckalew* in February of the same year that lost all its crew save one off Hither Plain. These incidents are summarized in one of Moran's less known engravings done in 1886, "The Much Resounding Sea."

The U.S. Life Saving Service saw gradual improvement over the years. In 1899 all Long Island stations were telephone-connected. Now help was only a phone call away. Wrecking tugs and revenue cutters could be summoned if needed.

By 1915 the Life Saving Service had proven its worth. The nation needed to develop an even more effective and efficient branch of coastal service. Existing station keepers and hands were offered positions in the newly ordained United States Coast Guard. The birthplace of the Coast Guard, you might say, was in part right here in East Hampton and Long Island. And can you imagine what may have happened had not Coast Guard Seaman Second Class John C. Cullen been on patrol on June 12, 1942 at the Amaganesett station the night the German saboteurs came ashore from *U-202*?

There is just one more East Hampton marine story that I believe is worth telling. I have not found it listed in any account of the Life Saving Service or exploits of the Coast Guard. It does not involve a great whaling event, or the rescue of hundreds in a stormy sea.

It begins on a summer's day, July 7, 1883. A young man was beginning to lower the sail of his catboat in Gardiner's Bay. It was only three days since the Fourth of July and the island was still in a holiday mood. The young man, known only as Irvine, was an inexperienced sailor but wise enough to see an approaching storm. He headed himself and his seven-year-old passenger Anna Miller back to the shore. The wind was beginning to shift quickly as the front neared and a strong gust of wind caused a jib in the boom. The boom struck young Anna, knocking her overboard. Irvine dove after her and managed to keep her head above the increasingly choppy water. The frightened girl clung tight to her rescuer who himself now needed to be rescued. He was quickly becoming exhausted by the effort, as the boat drifted further and further away. That innocent summer day of sailing could have ended tragically.

Fortunately for Irvine and Anna, a young East Hampton girl named Maria D. Parsons had witnessed the accident from shore. Quickly she launched a skiff and rowed nearly a quarter of a mile to reach the pair now barely afloat. With the storm still bearing down, Maria managed to lift Anna into the boat and helped Irvine slowly climb aboard. Exhausted, he could barely help Maria row the boat back to shore.

On February 7, 1888, after several witnesses gave accounts of Maria's extraordinary feat of courage and daring, the United States Life Saving Service awarded Maria D. Parsons a silver medal with the accompanying citation:

> With great presence of mind and bravery she rescued the man and child from drowning. It was fortunate that Maria Parsons was skilled in the use of oars, otherwise her noble efforts would have proved fruitless, the courage and self possession she displayed considering her years deserves the highest commendation.

How could young Maria not have been a good oarswoman? She was a Parsons, a member of one of East Hampton's oldest families. She grew up around the bays and oceans, the land and sea were one to her. Without her effort, two people may have perished. Who knows how those two people changed the world? Maria D. Parsons was the real life George Bailey of East Hampton. By the way, Maria was only ten years old when she performed her gallant rescue; that's a fifth-grade elementary student.

Since 1874 the U.S. Life Saving Service and the U.S. Coast Guard have awarded just 1,800 medals. President Ronald Wilson Reagan made over seventy saves as a young lifeguard and never got a medal, but Maria D. Parsons of East Hampton did!

The marine heritage of this island community is long and rich. The part played by the people of the south fork and the town of East Hampton has been significant. Take pride in the 350th anniversary of this town. Be proud of the place where you live, take pride in its past and take care of its future.

TRADE AND COMMUNITY:

East Hampton's Curious

Commercial Origins

―◦◦◦―

T.H. Breen

IN *INVISIBLE CITIES*, the twentieth-century Italian novelist Italo
Calvino recounts how Marco Polo once informed Kublai Khan about
all the places Polo visited on his fabulous journey to the East. For his
aging patron, the traveler painted word pictures of splendid cities,
each possessing a distinct character, so that in the telling of his stories
they became cities of inordinate beauty, or brilliant color, or subtle
light, or incalculable treasure. In the gathering dusk of his life, the
Great Khan finally grew impatient, reminding the inventive Polo that
although he had declaimed at length about distant cities of exotic
splendor, he had failed even once to mention Venice. To this, Polo responded politely, "What else do you believe I have been talking about?"
At the end of the day, Calvino's Venice was not an objective historical
fact, but rather, a fertile site of imagination, indeed, a sum of human perceptions, some complementary, others conflicting, no one of them
alone quite adequate to capture the many facets of the city's rich interpretive possibilities.

No less than Venice, East Hampton invites imaginative engagement. For a very long time residents and travelers have constructed
stories about the history of the town, spinning out local narratives that
inevitably revealed more about the interpreters than about the object
of their analysis. And, of all the accounts that have been advanced to explain East Hampton to itself over the centuries, none have enjoyed
greater acclaim than what might be called the tale of the original self-
sufficient community.

In the beginning, we learn, East Hampton was a little common-wealth, peopled by strong-willed, independent men and women, children of the Protestant Reformation who had sailed to the New World to create in Governor John Winthrop's Old Testament rhetoric "a Citty upon a Hill." According to this compelling narrative of settlement, the first colonists placed the general good before personal profit, and as an homogeneous community went about the business of taming the wilderness, it established impressively egalitarian institutions such as the open town meeting and common field system. To be sure, the seventeenth-century migrants and their children understood the need to trade—with each other and with the local Native Americans—but they surely were not capitalists in any contemporary sense of the term.

The myth of the founding generation—and labeling it a myth does not mean that it was untrue—acquired even greater credibility because other historic New England towns told themselves precisely the same story. Like Dorchester and Amherst in the Massachusetts Bay Colony, like the Puritan villages of Connecticut and New Haven, early East Hampton came to represent a pre-modern, pre-capitalist, and pre-industrial moment, an appealing world we had somehow lost. Not surprisingly, for more recent critics of American society, the possibility of documenting a simpler life unsullied by economic greed and wage oppression sparked deep nostalgia. Consider, for example, a jeremiad penned by one of the finest professional historians of the late nineteenth century. J. Franklin Jameson concluded his careful study of East Hampton's common lands published in 1883 with a sober reflection:

> One hears rumors of fine clubhouses and summer cottages, of iron piers and fast New York trains and European steamship lines; but surely one sees with some regret the breaking-up of an institution [the common fields of Montauk] which has lasted two centuries, and which carries the mind back far beyond the time of Wyandance or the coming of the Mayflower, far even beyond the coming of Hengist and Cerdic, to the days of our German forefathers and of the greatest Romans, who first described the customs which they followed in cultivating their half-cleared fields at the edge of the solemn forests.

Just as eighteenth-century European reformers once employed imagined "primitive American savages" to expose the corruption of so-called civilized urban life, evocations of pastoral seventeenth-century towns provided a convincing device for flaying material progress.

The tale of the original self-sufficient community that echoes through the pages of East Hampton histories is not wrong. Like Marco Polo's stories of various cities, it registers a particular, sometimes partisan perspective on how the community developed in the flow of time. It reflects an interpretive position often put forward by those who have come to imagine early East Hampton as a self-contained society or as a narrow stage on which the members of the first families did those things which endear them to modern genealogists.

The splendidly preserved records of early East Hampton also sustain an alternative historical narrative. This one imagines a different community, one that from the moment of initial planting sought ties with a vast Atlantic world and exploited local resources with an eye to commercial opportunities in distant markets. Perhaps at the beginning the settlers of East Hampton anticipated selling only livestock and hides to traders in New England. The goals of the town's farmers were probably modest. But whatever their expectations may have been when they initially confronted F. Scott Fitzgerald's "fresh, green breast of the new world," they soon discovered a source of personal wealth swimming offshore in the form of right whales. These oil-rich mammals did not introduce the spirit of enterprise into East Hampton—that had been present from the very first—but the whales did present some local families with sudden prosperity, a development that had a profound impact on the lives of people of three races and on the physical environment of this little community.

The white migrants who at mid-century claimed East Hampton as their own most likely came from the southern counties of England. Family historians dispute whether particular founders originated in Devon, Kent, or Sussex. Probably not a few of the people whose names appear in the early town records had lived at least briefly in London. But however interesting such speculations may be, it is not necessary for our purposes to establish precisely where in southeast England the first East Hampton settlers had lived. The history of the entire area is well documented. On the eve of colonization, two forces dramatically transformed the ecclesiastical and economic character of these counties. First, the area experienced a remarkable burst of commercial activity. In the early seventeenth century, for example, County Kent contained a disproportionally high percentage of England's town dwellers and industrial workers. The chief industry in Kent was cloth working, particularly the production of lighter worsteds and "new draperies" introduced into England during the previous century by Protestant refugees from the Low Countries. Second, the southern counties which sent so many people to the New World were centers of Reformed Protestantism, better known as Puritanism.

The point is not that the East Hampton colonists had been industrial artisans or weavers before moving to America. On such matters
the records are silent. Nor, in fact, do we know much about their religious experiences at the moment of transferring to the New World.
What is certain, however, is that the lives of most Kentish men and
women during this period were shaped profoundly by participation in
a vibrant market economy and by a growing popular conviction that
the Lord expected true believers to cleanse the Church of England of
corruption and error. Even small Kentish farmers sold surplus grain
and livestock to London buyers. Indeed, according to historian Jack P.
Greene, many years before the outbreak of civil war in England, ordinary yeomen had developed "a highly competitive, individualistic, and
acquisitive 'modern' mentality." Greene may exaggerate, but no one
doubts that the first New Englanders understood the workings of a
complex commercial system.

And, of course, the East Hampton migrants were also Puritans. Had
their only concern been with material prosperity, they could have easily moved to Holland, then the most advanced industrial economy in
Europe. Many English men and women did just that, taking the safer
route across the English Channel. But those drawn to New England
wanted more; they pledged—again in the words of Winthrop—"to love
the Lord our God, and to love one another to walke in his wayes and to
keepe his Commaundements and his Ordinance, and his lawes, and the
Articles of our Covenant with him that wee may live and be multiplied,
and that the Lord our God may blesse us in the land whether wee goe
to possesse it." It was not that they sacrificed dreams of the good life by
migrating to Massachusetts Bay. Rather, they thought that economic
prosperity and true religion were fully compatible, for as Winthrop reminded the first Puritan settlers, "The whole earth is the Lord's garden
and he hath given it to the sons of men, with a general condition, Gen-
esis I:28, increase and multiply, replenish the earth and subdue it,
which was again renewed to Noah."

These two concerns—establishing a reformed Protestant church
pleasing to a Calvinist God and carving independent, prosperous family farms out of a "howling wilderness"—were major themes in the
promotional literature circulating among English Puritans during the
1630s. The Reverend Francis Higginson, a founder of Salem, Massachusetts, seems to have been carried away by the rich economic potential
of New England. In a short account sent back to his co-religionists in
England, Higginson protested that unlike other writers of the day, he
had sedulously avoided "frothy bumbasting words" in the interest of
telling curious readers "the naked truth" about the rich opportunities

to be found in the northern colonies. The minister testified that the
"fertilitie of the Soyle is to be admired at," for with remarkably little
labor it produced an abundance of grain and grass, roots and fruit,
vines and firewood. In fact, he reported that "A poore servant here that
is to possesse but 50 Acres of Land, may afford to give more wood for
Timber & Fire as good as the world yeelds, then many Noble men in
England can afford to do." How much of this hyperbolic rhetoric ordinary men and women still living in Kent believed is impossible to as-
sess. The prospect of "poore" families so quickly acquiring fifty acres of
land must have made a powerful impression, however, as did the arresting observation, "It is scarce to be beleeved how our Kine and
Goats, Horses and Hogges doe thrive and prosper here and like well of
this Countrey."

Assurances that "stockmen"—farmers who raised livestock for
market—could do well in America resonated powerfully among the
Puritans of Kent and neighboring English counties. By the mid-1630s
the religious situation in this region had deteriorated, and the perse-
cuting allies of Archbishop William Laud were furiously driving reform-
minded ministers from their pulpits throughout the land. It was in this
threatening atmosphere that people such as John and William Mulford
decided to take their chances on New England. They journeyed first to
Massachusetts Bay, where by the time of their arrival, the thousands of
men and women who had followed Winthrop's fleet across the Atlantic
Ocean had already created a scores of small agricultural communities.

Although these villages did not yield the easy abundance promised
by promoters such as Higginson, they provided impressive amounts of
land to their inhabitants, land for home lots, land for tillage, land for
wood, and land for livestock. The only problem for latecomers was
what they perceived immediately as overcrowding. Even at the dawn
of European settlement, it seemed as if an earlier wave of colonists had
claimed all the best acreage. Adequate grazing rights were increasingly
hard to acquire. According to Winthrop, late arriving migrants grumbled publicly about the "want of accommodation." And rather than
compromise their expectations of economic prosperity and independence in the New World, they moved again, this time to the Connecticut Valley and Eastern Long Island. Although Winthrop lamented the
dispersal of so many Puritans, he understood the force of their argument. "The occasion of their desire to remove," the governor explained,
"was for that all towns in the Bay began to be much straitened by their
own nearness to one another, and their cattle being so much increased."

Relocation within New England did not, of course, indicate slippage of religious commitment. The Reverend John Davenport and Theosophilius Eaton, founders of the New Haven Colony, were if anything more scrupulous than were the leaders of Massachusetts Bay about the finer points of Calvinist theology. So too were the people who followed John Winthrop, Jr. and the Reverend Thomas Hooker to Hartford. To be sure, the men and women who made their way first to Southampton, and then to East Hampton, may have complained loudly about being "stinted," but they never lost touch with the religious impulse that had originally brought them to America. The first settlers persuaded the Reverend Thomas James to serve as their minister, paying him by the standards of the day a generous salary, and although few early church records have survived, we have no reason to doubt that James agreed on most ecclesiastical matters with John Cotton, John Davenport, and Thomas Hooker—the major spokesmen for reformed Protestantism in New England.

And in addition to their church, the East Hampton colonists acted swiftly to create civil institutions in character much like those they would have known in Massachusetts Bay, and perhaps in some places in rural Kent. They distributed land, formed an effective governing body, and established a rule of law. The first magistrates confronted several complex, potentially explosive disputes—a case of alleged witchcraft, for example—but as in other agricultural communities, most of their time was taken up with questions about adequate fencing, grazing rights, and "unruly swine."

If by some trick of time we could freeze East Hampton at mid-century, viewing the community as a single image rather than as a process, we would readily discern the outlines of a classic New England town. It seems to possess in this imagined frame all the attributes of what historian Kenneth A. Lockridge called a "Christian Utopian Closed Corporate Community." The founding families of East Hampton practiced mixed husbandry, and finding themselves in a broad, open environment, rich in native grasses, they expanded their herds of livestock. No one became fabulously wealthy on the eastern end of Long Island, but then, that was not their goal. Most original settlers did well enough. With the exception of Lion Gardiner, who fancied himself as a sort of lord of the manor, the settlers of East Hampton experienced a kind of rough economic equality.

Military security does not seem to have been a source of serious concern. Indeed, the local Native Americans presented no real threat to the the safety of the white community. The Montauks were an Algonquian people, who had recently taken a terrible beating at the hands of the Narragansetts and who in their hour of need turned to the East Hampton colonists—especially to the indomitable old soldier Lion Gardiner—for protection. The whites viewed the Montauks largely as obstructions to the expansion of grazing rather than as potential economic partners. Since the Native Americans offered no organized resistance to the town's development, the settlers probably mistook resignation for accommodation and thus, credited the desperate Montauks with friendliness.

However inoffensive the Indians may have seemed during the early days, they were most definitely not welcome in the village center. In 1653, the East Hampton government decreed that "no Indian shall come to town unless it be upon special occasion, and not to come armed because.the Dutch hath hired Indians against the English and we not knowing Indians by face." As we shall discover, within a decade the colonists would miraculously learn not only how to identify individual Indians by face, but also by name. That was not something that one could have predicted at the start, for in the beginning a homogeneous, egalitarian community of Puritan farmers insisted on maintaining a clear separation of races.

In East Hampton, whales deflected a predictable course of local history. They help explain—at least in this commercial narrative—why at the end of the seventeenth century the town did not look much like Andover or Dorchester, Farmington or Springfield. During the cold winter months, these slow-swimming, oil-rich mammals migrated to the waters off Long Island. No doubt, they had followed the same annual route time out of mind. What transformed East Hampton during 1650s and 1660s was not the unexpected arrival of the right whales, but rather a growing appreciation among entrepreneurial white colonists that oil and bone might be shipped to distant English and Dutch markets at a great profit.

At first, the little Puritan commonwealth struggled to control the temptation to turn this natural resource into private gain. The records of East Hampton chronicle the efforts of the town government to organize "whale watches." Much like militia duty in other New England towns, this shared civic responsibility involved all able-bodied men. During the long winter months they took turns scouring the beaches of East Hampton for "drift whales." As everyone understood, if these animals were not quickly processed, the carcasses would rot, losing all commercial value. In 1650, local officials divided the households of East Hampton into two groups, much like the celebrated fire companies that later appeared in colonial American cities.

As soon as someone spotted a beached whale, one of the two teams of men was supposed to turn out immediately. Harvesting the whale involved nasty, malodorous work. The men were probably cold and wet, and the town magistrates set fines for those who failed to appear. In 1653, the town passed what might be termed a "whale code," a series of ordinances laying out exactly which of the community's residents might legally share the return on oil and bone. We note that while every inhabitant was assigned to a whale company, only those who owned a home lot and thirteen acres of land could expect to profit from the oil. This law probably represented only a minor breach in the town's sense of fair play. After all, it was the members of an entire class within East Hampton—the village householders—and not a few privileged individuals who stood to make extra income from the whales so fortuitously washed ashore.

No doubt, even in the early days of settlement far-sighted men in East Hampton appreciated that killing whales at sea would be much more efficient than waiting for the animals to beach themselves. Harvesting whales in open water seems such an obvious improvement that one wonders why it took so long for the villagers to take this step. The question, however, only betrays a profound ignorance of the complexity of the challenge. Not until James Loper arrived in East Hampton in 1666 did the local farmers learn the difficulties posed by what they came to call the "Whale Design." First, one required a substantial amount of capital, more money certainly than an ordinary stockman would possess. A whaler not only needed a small boat—usually described in contemporary records as a "canoe"—but also an expensive iron kettle in which to turn the blubber into marketable oil. These investments represented only the start. The task demanded harpoons, special knives, an array of tools, and access to tightly-fitted barrels capable of carrying the liquid product to New York or Boston, London or Amsterdam.

Second, each step in the process demanded patience and knowledge. The slightest misjudgment during the preparation of the oil could ruin the entire batch. No wonder that a 1672 petition drawn up by various towns on the eastern end of Long Island confessed to having "spent much time, pains, and expense for the settling of a trade of whale-fishing in the adjacent seas, having endeavoured it above 20 years, but could not bring it to any perfection till within the past two or three years."

Although the East Hampton whalers never achieved perfection, they did quite well for themselves. The returns on capital investment were impressive. As Edward Hyde, Lord Cornbury, a royal governor of

New York explained, "a Yearling [whale] will make about forty Barrils of Oyl, a Stunt or Whale two years old will make sometimes fifty, sometimes sixty Barrils of Oyl; and the largest whale that I have heard of in these parts, yielded one hundred and ten barrils." With high quality oil selling on the open market for between one and two pounds sterling, a skilled East Hampton entrepreneur could hope to make a tidy sum from the "Whale Design." The good economic fortune of the Long Island whalers caught the attention of commentators in Massachusetts, and one informed New England readers in 1678 that the inhabitants of East Hampton "of late have fallen upon killing of whales, that frequent the south side of the Island in the latter part of the winter, wherein they have a notable kind of dexterity; and the trade that ariseth therefrom hath been very beneficial to all at that end of the Island."

What seems so striking in this early description of East Hampton's economic transformation is the word "all." It gives the impression that everyone in the community somehow shared in the profits of the Whale Design. The town records, however, tell another story. After the 1660s we still encounter discussions of local whale companies, but unlike those of an earlier period—those which involved every able-bodied man in East Hampton—these companies are private endeavors. The rising demands of capital investment coupled with the pressure of quality control—a function of specialized skills in the work place—meant that only a few well-positioned families could hold their own in a highly competitive international market. The companies of this period associated with such familiar names as Gardiner, Mulford, Loper, and Schellinger were *private* concerns.

However one characterizes the economic transformation of East Hampton, one much recognize that it had the effect of creating a new set of relationships within the community. In plain terms, some inhabitants became partners in the Whale Design; others did not. A natural resource once defined as a shared or common opportunity had generated a level of economic inequality that none of the founders had anticipated when they first moved to East Hampton in search of open grazing lands. In his eighteenth-century history of this community, John Lyon Gardiner commented on the shift from common to private exploitation of natural resources, and although Gardiner's syntax leaves much to be desired, his account shows that this was a critical moment in the town's development:

> It appears from the records that the business of killing Whales
> at the South side of the town in the Atlantic Ocean was regu-

larly followed by the town & profitts of the Whale divided among the Inhabitants in proportion of their rights in the town as Original Purchasers. But as soon as their lands & stock required much attention; this business was carried on with profitt by Individuals.

The town's good fortune created a sudden demand for laborers. Chasing right whales in the frigid waters of the open Atlantic was dangerous work. Rowers had to pull furiously just to keep up with the prey, and it was not uncommon for an injured animal to surface suddenly, overturning a boat and leaving the crew of four or five men to survive as best they could. Since the leading members of the private whale companies had no desire to put their lives at risk, they recruited men who would, and it was during this period in the town's history that the local Indians who had so recently been excluded from the affairs of East Hampton made a dramatic reappearance as whalers.

Because the Montauks proved so adept at hunting whales, white people assumed that the Native Americans must have harvested whales at sea long before the Europeans conquered New England. But a moment's reflection reveals the weaknesses of this kind of argument. Commercial whaling represented a response to the development of an international market for oil. North Atlantic trading networks were a function of European colonization. Without these economic structures, it would have made no sense to harvest whales in the open ocean. In any case, the Montauks could easily have satisfied their own needs by processing an occasional drift whale. It is more persuasive to declare that the local Indians excelled at hunting whales at sea because in East Hampton, they had no other viable means to make money and after the 1650s were fearful for their own future.

During this period of rapid commercial expansion, Europeans and Indians defined the character of race relations through an annual cycle of labor negotiations. Some months before the commencement of the whale season, representatives of the private companies approached individual Montauks with formal, legally binding work contracts, many of which were duly entered into the town records. The whale companies agreed to provide the basic equipment that the Indians would need for the hunt—a boat and harpoons, for example—and on their part, the Indians promised to "go to sea a whale killing" and to give a "true and faithful performance." The contracts often promised the Indians a portion of any whale they managed to catch. Within a few years, the language of these documents took on a formulaic quality, varying only in minor details. In one standard East Hampton whale contract—one signed on March 5, 1681—five local Indians pledged "each man for himself to go upon a whaling design for Benjamin Conkling or his assignees the next whaling season which will be in the year 1681 upon half share as is usuall between the English and the Indians."

The rigorous concern for legality in these matters seems to reveal an extraordinary commitment to equitable relations between the races. After all, the East Hampton whale companies might have taken a different course. As they well knew, the English planters who cultivated tobacco and rice in the southern colonies had no use for such contractual niceties. They simply enslaved their workers. But before we congratulate the owners of the whale companies for their sense of fair play, we might look a little more closely at the contracts themselves. The English settlers came from a society defined by common law; they understood the meaning of due process, especially in matters related to property. By contrast, the Montauk whalers had no written language. They defined the law within their own cultural traditions. And so, when we examine the town records, noting that the contracts were negotiated between "we, the English" and "you, the Indians," and take into account that the English signed their names to these documents while the Indians scratched personal marks, we wonder just how much the Indian whalers actually understood about the agreements.

The legal vocabulary suggests a striking imbalance in these negotiations. A contract recorded on April 14, 1675—a typical document from this period—declared that "we the aforesaid Indians do engage ourselves to go to sea from year to year at all seasonable times for these our Copartners a whale killing till we have discharged to their satisfaction all former arrears or debt we stand engaged to them." And in March 1683, Hector, a Montauk, promised that "if I do not get so much by my half share this next season as will pay the said Robert Kedy what I shall be indebted to him, then I do hereby engage to go for him the next season ensuing until such time as I have paid him whatsoever I shall be indebted unto him." Over and over we encounter the phrase "from year to year." Even to enter a whaling contract the Indian had to post a bond of ten pounds sterling. The Indian laborer was in debt beyond his ability to pay before he had killed a single whale. The Montauk whale hunter found himself suspended in a kind of unfreedom, nominally an independent worker, but in fact bound to a specific Englishman for a period of years. In the nineteenth-century South such labor agreements have been characterized as debt peonage, an improvement over slavery to be sure, but by the same token, not a product of an open labor market.

In any case, no one ever wrote a whale contract for the benefit of the Indians. The agreements protected the private companies from other private companies which often attempted to steal Montauk laborers just as the hunting season commenced. Able-bodied Indians were in short supply, and it was a financial blow to have a crew member suddenly show up on a competitor's boat. In April 1678, the Reverend Thomas James lost his temper, warning the representatives of other companies to keep away from his Indians. Indeed, he and his partners entered into the town records "a solemn protest against any person or persons who have or shall contrary to all law of God or man, justice or equity, go about to violate or infringe the above mentioned contracts or agreements without our consent." James was not given to sociological analysis. He might have observed, however, that a sudden new source of wealth—whale oil—had created fault lines in East Hampton, dividing neighbors who so recently had journeyed to the New World to establish a covenanted community.

Be that as it may, on such occasions the Indians were frequently blamed for unfaithfulness. In 1680, one local official reported to the governor of New York that he had received many complaints from East Hampton:

> that they are like to be much disappointed and damnified in
> their business of whaling by the deceits and unfaithfulness of
> the Indians with whom they did contract the last spring for
> their service in whaling this present season, who notwith-
> standing said contracts under hand and seal do now betake
> themselves to the service of other men, who do gladly except
> them . . . so that the Indians having received goods of one man
> in the spring upon account of whaling and now again of an-
> other to fit them for sea, leave their masters to quarrel.

It was a short step from accusations of deceit in the job market to harsher judgments against a body of Native American laborers who seemed to have flunked what was in fact a crash course in Western capitalism. The eighteenth-century local historian John Lion Gardiner, for example, protested that the Montauks had brought their problems upon themselves, for in Gardiner's words, the Indians' "idle dispositions and savage manners prevent the most of them from living comfortable."

Although the means to "living comfortable" may have eluded the Native Americans, the families who profited from the Whale Design prospered in the New World. They did not, of course, live in the man-

ner of Spanish Conquistadores. But in comparison to other seventeenth-century New Englanders, they experienced a notable improvement in the material culture of everyday life. The vessels that sailed
out of the protected waters of Northwest Harbor, filled with barrels of
oil and other local products such as hides and meat, wool and feath-
ers, returned from Boston and New York laden with consumer goods.
These manufactured items originated for the most part in England.
They flowed through the stores that Abraham Schellinger and other
East Hampton merchant-traders operated near the large warehouses
where employees busily processed whale products. An inventory
prepared by Schellinger lists practical household items such as guns,
nails, and skillets. His shelves also contained imports that reveal
how far the villagers had distanced themselves from notions of self-
sufficiency. They purchased everything from colorful textiles to fine
pewter ware.

These English manufactures traveled the roads of East Hampton to
individual homes where they were lovingly possessed, finding their
way eventually into probate records. In these documents we once
again encounter imported cloth and ceramics, brass pots, and in the
case of Thomas Diament who died in 1682, a "great looking glass." Such
a range of goods appeared at this time in the port cities of Boston and
Salem, but in terms of physical well-being the colonists of East Hampton seem to have participated fully in a vast new consumer economy
some decades before the residents of other country towns throughout
New England. Indeed, consumer desire was the engine that drove the
Whale Design, for as the members of the private whale companies
fully understood, without consumer opportunity large-scale oil production made no economic sense.

During the period of rapid commercial expansion, men and
women of African background first appeared in East Hampton. About
their own life histories, we know very little. They were mentioned in
community documents from time to time without surnames, as Bess,
Jack, Peter, Rose, Bristo, and Hannah. They sat in the back of the Reverend Nathaniel Huntting's church. And, almost without exception,
they were slaves. A crude census complied in 1687 lists twenty-five
bondsmen, eleven males and fourteen females. That figure represented
just under five percent of the town's population. Like other categories
of property, local blacks were listed in probate inventories that leave
no doubt about the existence of slavery in early East Hampton. In John
Stratton's will, for example, we find described along with a table,
blankets, and pewter plates two blacks and their child, humans val-

ued officially at fifty pounds sterling. This figure represented a very large expenditure. Since East Hampton did not define itself around a plantation economy, and since the local Indians served as whalers, the community would seem to have had no reason to purchase so many slaves. One can only speculate about such matters. At a moment of giddy prosperity the white people of East Hampton aggressively entered a burgeoning consumer economy, and among the imported goods they acquired were black slaves. In this curious environment African-Americans were at once a personal indulgence and a solid investment.

The consumer engine that propelled the local economy soon overheated. The town's resource base simply could not sustain such a high level of market participation. Like the great tobacco planters of the Chesapeake colonies who depleted virgin fields in only seven years, the East Hampton settlers asked too much of the land and the sea, and by the early decades of the eighteenth century a scene of almost limitless bounty—a place where men fearful of being "stinted" by competitors could possess all the land they desired—had begun to collapse in upon itself.

At first, no one in the community comprehended what was happening. The herds of cattle and sheep continued to expand without any thought given to the grass needed to sustain them. Between 1678 and 1688 the number of sheep in East Hampton rose from about a thousand animals to over 15,000 head. In economic terms, explosive growth made good sense. After all, the livestock provided the meat and hides which merchants sold in robust markets as far away as the West Indies. And to make room for the new animals, the villagers cut down the trees, opening up pasture lands so quickly that soon local farmers began to protest that they did not have enough wood even to build proper fences. Deforestation accelerated the decline of fur-bearing animals such as fox, otter, and wildcat, all of which had appeared in the export ledgers as marketable furs.

The most dramatic transformation, however, involved the disappearance of the right whales. In 1718 an alarmed Samuel Mulford wrote to London that "there [sic] is very little [whale oil] gott to go any where: and the people are become miserable poor." Mulford was given to exaggeration, but a respected eighteenth-century historian of New York, William Smith, confirmed Mulford's observation. "The whale fishery, on the south side of the island," Smith explained, "has declined of late years, through the scarcity of whales, and is now almost entirely neglected." Like the famed striped bass of modern times, the oil-bearing mammals that had once migrated in such impressive numbers to the waters off East Hampton failed year after year to reappear.

Mulford had a ready explanation for what had occurred. He blamed meddling colonial bureaucrats for the problem, claiming loudly that if the New York government would just get off the backs of the local whalers, dropping its demand for expensive licenses and repealing intrusive regulations, then the good times would soon return. "The imports of whale oil and bone from New York have greatly decreased," Mulford announced, "owing to disputes with the Governor as to a duty for whales catched there. We propose that the inhabitants have free liberty to kill whales." Free enterprise was the answer to an environmental crisis. "I say," protested East Hampton's most successful entrepreneur, "that there was more people went a whale fishing on Long Island twenty or thirty years ago when they were undisturbed [by government regulations], than hath done of late, which if they had not been discouraged might have been now double that number." But Mulford's demand for "free liberty" in the marketplace was off the mark. Even contemporaries knew that state regulations had not strangled the whale industry in East Hampton. The problem was over-fishing. As one commentator noted laconically, "whalebone and whale oil ... will soon grow less plentiful as the people increase."

Sometime during the first third of the eighteenth century East Hampton entered into a long period of inanition. The community closed in on itself; contacts with the outside world became less frequent. Visitors came to the eastern end of the Island not so much as deal-makers, but rather as primitive anthropologists, searching for a small pocket of settlement seemingly untouched by the corrosive force of commerce, a place that time forgot. In 1768 John Gardiner sounded almost like a romantic poet, claiming that in East Hampton "nothing more than usual for all country towns has taken place ... for this century past. Remote from their Capitol, they have lived plain Agricultural lives & generally happy." Gardiner celebrated a sturdy population of pious "grazers." And another curious traveler, Timothy Dwight, the president of Yale College, described late eighteenth-century East Hampton as if it were a kind of living museum. "A general air of equality, simplicity, and quiet is visible here in a degree singular," the scholar observed in his journal. "Sequestered in a great measure from the world, they exhibit scarcely a trace of that activity which everywhere meets the eye in New England." Perhaps the locals who gawked at Yale's president remembered an earlier period when East Hampton had exhibited a level of "activity" exceeding that encountered in almost all of New England. But then again, perhaps they had forgotten how the Whale Design had transformed the lives of men and women of three different races.

In the gathering light of the twentieth century, we might inquire with Kublai Kahn just what it is that we have been discussing. Perhaps Marco Polo has told of a strange anomaly, a community quite unlike any other that existed at the dawn of time, one consumed by the heat of its own commercial ambition and then returned to a bucolic state that masked its original character. Or perhaps Polo only meant to remind us that in the earliest records of colonial East Hampton one recovers stories that in a more modern age we dare not ignore.

Sections of this essay were taken from T.H. Breen, *Imagining The Past: East Hampton Histories* (Addison-Wesley Publishing Company, Inc., Reading, 1989). Copyright 1989 by T.H. Breen. Used by permission.

A TRADITION OF
CRAFTSMEN

Dean Failey

E AST HAMPTON HAS secured a permanent and prominent role in the study of furniture-making in America because of the fortuitous survival of not only documentary written records concerning three generations of the Dominy family's woodworking craft practice but also the remarkable existence of the actual shops where they worked and the tools with which they worked. Their specific detailed story is told here by Charles Hummel and it is not my intention to cover the same ground. Rather, I hope to place the Dominys in a broader context of a craft tradition specific to East Hampton and which attempts to explain why the furniture that was made in this community over a period of 150 years looks the way it does.

The study of decorative arts and material culture today had progressed from an antiquarian approach that stressed a hierarchial, elitist, and identification-oriented methodology to a more inclusive analysis which desires to encompass social, political, economic and even religious issues which might impact the objects, the craftsmen who produced them and even the consumers who bought them. The conclusions I have reached may conflict with or contradict some of the other presentations you have heard in this series but history, particularly social and cultural history, is comprised of many layers which lead scholars to a variety of interpretations. In my case, I have tried to let the objects speak for themself.

The relative ease with which we travel today, not to mention our ability to span hundreds and even thousands of miles with telephones, faxes, radios and televisions, dulls our senses to what it meant to be liv-

284

ing in East Hampton in 1650, 1750, or 1850. A letter written by a visitor to East Hampton, Aaron Carter of Newark, New Jersey, to his brother Horace in July, 1858 states, "I will try and tell you what kind of a place I am at. It is 5 miles from Sag Harbor, 15 from Greenport, and about 100 from New York. But from the way they are behind the times, should think they were about 5000."[1]

Some fifty years earlier, Yale president Timothy Dwight had a similar impression when he visited Eastern Long Island:

> The passion for appearance, so far at least as far as building is concerned, seems, hitherto, to have fastened very little on the inhabitants of East Hampton. A general air of equality, simplicity and quiet is visible here in a degree perhaps singular. . . . Living by themselves more than the people of most other places, they have become more attentive to whatever is their own, and less to the concerns of others. Hence their own customs, especially those which have come down from their ancestors, have a commanding influence on their conduct.[2]

And just over a decade earlier, in 1798, John Lyon Gardiner writing to Reverend Samuel Miller in New York stated, "One might suppose that East Hampton might have been settled from Southampton but the method of pronunciation is quite different altho the towns join. An East Hampton man may be known from a Southampton man as well as a native of Kent in England may be distinguished from a Yorkshire man."[3]

These three observations suggest that East Hampton might accurately be described as a somewhat isolated and discrete entity, similar in fact to the thirteen distinctive areas of early New England identified by linguist Hans Kurath in his study, *Linguistic Geography of New England*.[4] Each of the regions he identified, ranging from York County, Maine to eastern Connecticut, are separated by physical barriers such as mountains, valleys or rivers and were approximately a day's travel from the adjacent regions. Within each area the inhabitants shared a commonality of speech patterns and cultural values including preferences for specific types of furniture and the manner in which it was ornamented.[5] Clearly East Hampton fits the description of physical separation given by Kurath and the descriptions of the community quoted above suggest a place where the majority of the population had more in common than not. Just as they shared a single church and religion for nearly two centuries, the people of East Hampton shared a common way of life and similar values when it came to a matter of taste and fashion. As we will see, the relative physical isolation of East

Hampton combined with related factors would determine both the pattern of woodworking craft practice and the appearance of the furniture produced in this village for over 150 years.

Following the initial settlement in 1649, East Hampton experienced a brief period of rapid growth followed by a sharp decline in the number of new settlers when land within the town was completely accounted for. David Gardiner, in his *Chronicles of the Town of Easthampton*, indicates that by 1653 "almost all of the arable land around the first place of settlement, and in the western and eastern plains, comprising a circuit of two miles, was under some degree of cultivation. The division of the land continued to be made among the original purchasers of their heirs and assigns, in proportion to their interests as tenants in common."[6] It is critical to understand the importance of land ownership, particularly to these initial settlers, all transplants to the new world. In their native England, the ownership of land was the most important determinant of social and economic status.[7] This was especially true for the artisan class, whether they were woodworkers, blacksmiths or weavers. Practicing their specialized trades under guild and town regulations, the ownership of a farm or land was almost impossible to dream of for the average craftsman. The yeoman, or basic farmer who owned his land, was by the far the rural artisan's superior in terms of security of livelihood. The best of worlds therefore for the rural craftsman was to own land which he could farm to supplement his craft earnings. It was this possibility of self-sufficiency that farming as well as a craft practice offered that attracted many of the early settlers to America, not the promise of religious freedom.

In East Hampton, within fifty years of settlement, it was almost impossible to obtain land unless you were a descendant of an original family or were fairly wealthy. The result was that at a very early date there was no incentive, in fact no reason for new craftsmen bringing with them new fashions and skills to migrate to the very end of Long Island. The pattern of craft practice that was therefore established relied on the transferal of tools and skills from master to apprentice, meaning in most cases from father to son or other member of the family. Joshua Garlick, who died in 1677 and was the husband of accused witch Goody Garlick, provided in his will to "give my tools to my sons Joshua and John equally to bee Devided betweene them when they are capable to use them." These tools included joyner's tools, turning tools, cooper's tools and carpenter's tools.[8]

The father to son transferral of the knowledge and equipment to earn a living forms a clear pattern in East Hampton. Among the families with multi-generational woodworking craftsmen, many traceable to the seventeenth century, are the Bakers, Dominys, Fithians, Hedges, Mulfords and Schellingers. We cannot forget that other craftsmen appear early in the records and then disappear, such as Alexander Willmott, originally from New Haven, possibly having died without heirs or who moved on, unable to compete against the several family dynasties.[9]

The first generation of craftsmen who settled in East Hampton and other Long Island and New England towns probably had rather specialized skills. For example, a woodworker who was termed a carpenter in England would have been assumed to possess only the tools and skills needed to build houses, not furniture. Joyners were a step above carpenters in both skills and the type of tools they owned. They were trained to do finer finishing work and furniture-making. Other woodworkers specialized in turning, coopering, wheelwrighting, and ship-carpentry. The large urban centers in the Colonies, such as New York and Boston, could support such specialized branches of the craft but the realities and needs of the small rural towns dictated that woodworking craftsmen were forced to take on a variety of woodworking tasks, hence the diversity of tools Joshua Garlick left to his two sons.

Cultural historian Robert St. George, in his article "Fathers, Sons, and Identity: Woodworking Artisans in Southeastern New England, 1620–1700," poses another intriguing idea related to the development of multi-task woodworkers.[10] In his study of the relationships between the first three generations of craftsmen and their sons in the early settlements, he suggests that family craft units or dynasties encouraged diversification of skills to enable the younger members of the family to remain in their home village and compete economically both within and outside the family. In other words, there was a limit to how much new furniture was needed in a demographically stable community like East Hampton and a newly trained artisan might find himself either in competition with his own father or forced to consider moving away. But if the craftsman could also make shingles and clapboard, build houses and mills, produce barrels for whale oil and flour, or build boats, his chances of earning a sufficient living were greatly enhanced.

There were, however consequences to generalization versus specialization. On the one hand families tended to remain as a unit and within their original community, but the trade-off was that the roles and skills of the local craftsman, once distinct, now began to blur together and become more homogenous. Taking on many tasks rather than concentrating on one tended to reduce each to a formulaic process more than a creative one. This was particularly true where furniture-making was involved and which we will look at shortly.

Having a diversity of skills was actually a necessity in a rural community dominated by an agrarian economy. Since ownership of land was of primary importance the practice of a craft took on a different character in East Hampton and surrounding areas than it would have in an urban center. To begin with, lack of enough business and the need to raise crops and animals made woodworking a part-time rather than full-time enterprise. The typical Long Island craftsman owned his house and had his shop within or adjacent to it, as did the Dominys and their contemporary Timothy Mulford. He owned approximately 100 acres of land, usually a few acres adjacent to his house and the rest in fields a short distance away. Agrarian economies depended heavily upon barter rather than cash transactions and labor was a common means of paying for goods and services. With his own farm providing much of the family's basic needs, the craftsman could use his special skills to provide products and services in exchange for any other items he needed.

An active imagination helps to comprehend the variety of tasks a woodworking craftsman might be called upon to perform in a town like East Hampton. There were houses to be built, houses to be moved and houses to be torn down. The meeting house might need repairs, the jail a new door. Barns, sheep sheds and chicken coops were required not to mention work on the fulling mill, pecking mill and grist mill. For the farm the craftsman might provide an ox yoke; a wheel barrow; rake, hoe or ax handle; feed troughs; or even a wagon. Household needs had to be accommodated and might include bread trays, knife boxes, butter molds, salt boxes, rolling pins, curtain rods, shelves, dough troughs, dry sinks, mortars and pestles, pressing boards, ink stands, cartridge boxes, foot stoves and hat boxes. There was also a need for looms, spinning wheels, hetchel boards and swifts. Among the more unusual items were crutches, writing slate frames, rulers and wig boxes. The craftsman literally provided a cradle to grave service, with his products including coffins.

We tend to think of craftsmen as those who were creating and making brand new items, but a look through any woodworker's account books indicate that a great deal of his time was spent repairing or fixing furniture, farm equipment and household articles. In fact, entries for "mending" appear so frequently it would appear that no broken furniture was ever discarded. Farm equipment received hard use as did spinning wheels and replacement parts were constantly needed.

Chair posts, stretchers and splats as well as table tops and leaves were replaced. In 1831, East Hampton cabinetmaker Septimus Osborne mended twenty-four desks at Clinton Academy.[11] Furthering my belief that nothing was thrown away even if it did go out of style, Osborne also altered old style chests with one or two drawers into more fashionable four drawer bureaus.[12]

Another important determinant in the pattern of craft practice for the woodworker in a rural environment was the change of seasons. The rhythm of daily life, the tasks to be performed and when, were all dictated by the calendar. As Philip Zea has said in his essay "Rural Craftsman and Design," "In rural America, cyclical patterns of production, exchange and consumption define the life of the people."[13] Charles Hummel noted that both Nathaniel Dominy IV and Felix Dominy showed "a preoccupation with the passage of time" and the seasons with Felix even keeping a "Journal of Weather and Heat."[14] It only makes sense that as a part-time craftsman with a need to work his farm the rural woodworker would prefer, if possible, to concentrate on making furniture during the winter months. Of course he would take on work in the summer if necessary and especially if he had sons to help out or could barter his services for labor in the fields. The importance of maintaining a balance between his craft and the source of food for his family and livestock is nowhere better illustrated than in the accounts of Bridgehampton woodworker Nathan Topping Cook. In the midst of a series of entries dated 1797 involving the building of a house for David Hedges, Cook simply noted, "this Day quit to harvest."[15]

Let us quickly summarize several key points which will help us place these objects in context. The rural and essentially agrarian environment of East Hampton dictated a pattern of woodworking craft practice that was part-time rather than full-time in nature and which quickly evolved, shortly after initial settlement, into a craft characterized by diversified rather than specialized skills. The relative physical isolation of East Hampton and the lack of land or other inducements to attract new settlers and particularly new craftsmen, until the late eighteenth-century development of nearby Sag Harbor, meant that the community was dependant upon a group of craftsmen who were part of locally trained family craft dynasties. Skills, tools and patterns, not to mention shared values and attitudes, were passed from one generation to the next establishing a continuity in craft practice and in deed—that is, the physical shape and form of the furniture produced—which remained almost unchanged and only rarely challenged for 150 years.

The story of East Hampton is embodied in its furniture. Yes, the story could be more complete and detailed but it does at least provide an outline. Founded in 1649 by a small group of settlers who were apparently unhappy in their original landing point of Lynn, Massachusetts, East Hampton actually found itself under the jurisdiction of the New Haven Colony and subsequently Connecticut. Despite years of political dispute and wrangling which ended with all of Long Island becoming part of New York, the eastern end of Long Island became a virtual annex of Connecticut through its family and commercial connections. Many of the early settlers on both the north and south forks of Long Island came from the New Haven Colony. Among the earliest surviving pieces of furniture which have a history of ownership in East Hampton are those with a New Haven Colony connection.

The carved chest originally owned by Thomas Osborne, a tanner who moved to East Hampton from New Haven about 1650, is one of the most important pieces of American seventeenth-century furniture and possibly the earliest documented example since it would have to have been made before Osborne's cross-Sound move. In the collection of Home Sweet Home, it is believed to have been made by Thomas Mulliner, a craftsman who learned his trade in Ipswich, England.[16] The most elaborate of seven related examples it represents the transition from medieval to classical design in both furniture and architecture. The chest displays the overall repetitive designs associated with medieval art but it is organized within a classical framework of architectural arches. Interestingly, four of the seven chests have a history of ownership in East Hampton and three of them were possibly made there.

The chest now in the Metropolitan Museum of Art descended in the Stratton family and purportedly was originally owned by John Stratton (d. 1685). Although its design follows the same format of the Mulliner-Osborne chest, there is a flattening of the facade with the arches incise-carved on the flat panels. Another chest owned by the Society for the Preservation of Long Island Antiquities was, in all likelihood, made in East Hampton for the Hedges family from whom it was obtained. The carving is quite linear and appears to be copied from similar carving on the end panels of the Osborne chest. One gets a sense from this chest of what other joined furniture in East Hampton looked like. Apparently the chest was originally painted, the stiles and rails in red, the panels possibly ochre and the channel moldings and abstract flower stems in black or a dark green. Supporting an attribution to an East Hampton craftsman, albeit an anonymous one, is yet another locally owned chest with similar carved motifs, associated with the Sherrill family.

Small seventeenth-century lidded boxes have traditionally been called Bible boxes although they were probably used to store other books and papers and even small articles of clothing and jewelry. Two examples in the collections of the East Hampton Historical Society, one carved with foliated S-scrolls, the other with stylized flowers and the date 1703, may have been brought to East Hampton from the Guilford area of Connecticut. A similar small box-like cupboard which descended until recently in the Hedges family served a similar purpose of storing valuables. The interior contains small drawers which could be secured by locking the paneled door. Apparently someone lost the key at some point and had to resort to forcing open the lock, hence the patch on the door.

Sadly, our study of and knowledge about the furnishing of seventeenth- and eighteenth-century Long Island homes has been severely hampered by the loss of the vast majority of the probate records and inventories through a series of fires, including the 1911 fire at the New York State Library in Albany. The surviving 1682 will of Thomas Diament of East Hampton gives us a glimpse, however, of what one of the more substantial members of the community owned:

> To my eldest sone James Diament . . . {I leave) my best fether
> bed that I usually lie upon and all the furniture belonging to it
> as Curtains boulsters vallainces pellows Coverled blankets pil-
> low beers and a paire of my best sheets together with my bed-
> stead . . . my long table In the bigger Roome with ye forme
> {bench} belonging to it and my greater looking glass and the
> coboard in the room aforesaid and one of my great chests and
> three of my best chayres and my great wicker chayre, also a
> Chest of Drawers.[17]

We can only imagine what a grand statement that bed with its curtains, valances and pillows must have made. For those with a desire to see a close approximation of what a fully dressed bed of this type might have looked like, the American Wing at the Metropolitan Museum of Art has recently installed a wonderful reproduction fully-hung seventeenth-century bedstead. Diament's reference to his "great wicker chayre" probably referred to the material the seat was fashioned from. A great chair otherwise indicated a large armchair reserved for the head of the house. Such a chair might have been similar to the example in the Wheelock collection of the East Hampton Historical Society. Even with the loss of its finials and handgrips and with the addition of rockers it is still an impressive chair. An even better understanding of the power that such a chair could convey can been seen in a great chair owned by Barnabas Horton, just across the Bay in Southold, and which is now in the Winterthur Museum collections. Benches and stools were probably the most common form of early seating furniture but are exceedingly rare survivals.

While I have stressed the isolation of East Hampton, I have not intended to imply that communication, trade and commercial intercourse with the outside world did not exist. A great deal of trade occurred, but my guess is that a very limited number of people from East Hampton actually traveled outside the town and conversely, since East Hampton was not at the crossroads of a major trade route, that few outside visitors came to East Hampton until late in the eighteenth century. This situation would have had a considerable effect on consumer tastes. After all, if you could not actually see the latest fashions or styles how would you know you wanted them?

We can only guess at this point that an occasional individual who did travel or who had family or business contacts in New York, New Haven or other outside locations either ordered or brought back to East Hampton an item of furniture that struck their fancy. The other possibility is that an enterprising merchant, and there were many of them during this period, simply took a chance and sent items to an agent who would sell them in the community. For example, in 1735, the schooner *Hannah*, out of the port of Boston and bound for Long Island, carried a cargo that included "twenty hundreds of Isle of May salt, three thousand and five hundred feet of Boards & plank, one chaise, two dozen chairs & a parcel of Earthen ware here made also two barrels of nails, a parcel of Brasiery wire, Sundry Loose Shopgoods & one Trunk & one box cont. Sundry European goods here openly bought & all here legally imported."[18] We don't know if this schooner was headed to eastern Long Island but certainly similar ships did trade regularly along the length of the Sound.

All of this detour to try to explain the existence of this leather upholstered chair in East Hampton. Of New York origin, it is similar to hundreds of chairs made in the second-half of the seventeenth century both in New York and Boston and which were staples of a coastal trade up and down the eastern seaboard. The chair is an urban and sophisticated statement. Its ownership in East Hampton either conferred status upon the owner or raised a few eyebrows.

Let us look at one more seventeenth-century piece of furniture before moving on. Collected locally at the end of the nineteenth century by William Efner Wheelock and gifted twenty years ago with many other examples of East Hampton furniture to the East Hampton Historical Society, this square table, as it may contemporarily have been referred to, also relates to New Haven Colony furniture design. The vigorous disc or spool turnings of the legs and stretchers are similar to turned supports on a great cupboard in the Metropolitan Museum of Art believed to have been owned by Connecticut Governor Robert Treat of Milford and a second cupboard probably owned by Milford minister Samuel Andrew. While undoubtedly owned in East Hampton, we do not know whether this Jacobean style piece was made in Connecticut or here in East Hampton.

A major stylistic change occurred at the end of the seventeenth and beginning of the eighteenth century in furniture design, which involved significant innovations in the way furniture was conceived, constructed and used. Most significantly for the woodworking craftsman, joinery gave way to cabinetmaking. Mortise-and-tenon pegged stiles and rails fitted with panels were replaced by dovetailed case and drawer construction and carved surfaces were banished in favor of burled or otherwise figured shimmering facades of veneer. New skills and new tools were required to make furniture in the William and Mary and subsequent Queen Anne styles. In urban areas this happened seemingly overnight as European-trained craftsmen flooded into the cities of Philadelphia, New York and Boston. Within a generation their trained apprentices were producing furniture in the latest fashion. But what about rural areas such as East Hampton?

The simple answer is that they couldn't compete and couldn't change, at least not overnight. Fortunately for them, their customers walked to the beat of the same drummer. Change, when it came, came slowly and was modified to accommodate the skills that the local craftsmen possessed. Over time they would acquire a few new tools and learn to make rough dovetails. They would adopt a number of new furniture forms and they would attempt to update them even if only superficially. Occasionally they would be challenged to attempt to replicate a piece of furniture from outside their world. They did their best with the tools they possessed but, eventually, they would find that they were left behind.

A tall-case clock in the Winterthur Museum which was found in East Hampton exemplifies the new William and Mary style. While it may have been owned in East Hampton it was certainly not made there since no local craftsman possessed the ability to make a veneered case. It is much more likely to have been made in New York or one of the western Long island towns. It may have served, however, as a model for the clock in the Wheelock Collection which is possibly the earliest tall-case clock made here. Its simple case reflects the abilities of an East Hampton carpenter-joiner to emulate urban styles. The works are not complex and appear original to the case.

East Hampton's response to the new style of chairs was a relatively easy one. Rural versions could be produced using the same tools and techniques that had been used previously. Whether using vertical moulded bannisters, as on the armchair said to have been owned by Reverend Nathaniel Huntting (1675–1753), or a slat-back armchair, both in the East Hampton Historical Society collections, the compo-nent parts could be turned on a lathe or shaped simply by hand.

Another new seating form in the early eighteenth century was the corner chair. Tales abound that it was created for a gentleman to be able to sit in while accommodating his broad-coat and sword. Regard-less of its purpose, other than a piece of seating furniture, it appears to have been a popular form on eastern Long Island judging from the number of surviving examples. One, owned by Samuel Miller of Fire-place in East Hampton is the only example of Long Island furniture known to have had a Spanish or paintbrush foot. Again, the chair is composed of turned or simply cut-out elements. A second corner or roundabout chair in the East Hampton Historical Society collections amplifies the rural joiner's approach to duplicating a high-style design.

The desk was one of the important new furniture forms, necessary for any man who claimed a pretense to business. Certainly East Hamp-ton craftsman had to have seen or had access to a desk in the new style to be able to copy one. Their version was without veneers but it was credible nonetheless. The slant-front desk in the collection of the Soci-ety for the Preservation of Long Island Antiquities, made for a member of the Tallmadge family around 1720, is in the full-blown style, sans ve-neer; but with ball-turned feet and William and Mary style brasses it is a fashionable item. Both the Tallmadge and the Timothy Mulford desk, owned by the East Hampton Historical Society, represent a significant step up in the skills of the local craftsman. Not only is dove-tailing em-ployed, but part patterns are being employed to make, in the case of the Mulford desk, bracket feet.

The Mulford desk is a monument in itself because it proves that East Hampton had at least one other eighteenth-century craftsman ca-pable of making substantial furniture. The desk which otherwise might easily have been attributed to the Dominy family of craftsmen, bears an inscription on the interior document drawer, "Made att East Hampton / By Timothy Mulford / Bridgehampton may ye 24 1749 / John Cook His Box." Mulford is identified as a joiner in a land indenture of 1754, and he was one of at least six other Mulford family woodworkers.[19] His shop, like the Dominy's was adjacent to his house on the corner of Main Street and Buell's Lane. Deacon John Cook, for whom the desk was made, lived in Mecox, part of present-day Bridgehampton.

There is no question that the Dominy family was, to put it as a pun, the dominant craft family dynasty in East Hampton. Their mechanical genius seems to have been in their genes and they are one of very few craft families in Colonial America able to work both with wood and metal. Yet it is clear that other woodworking craftsmen were able to hold their own and earn a living in East Hampton. During the same period that the Dominys were most active, David Baker, Mordecai Homan, Reuben Hedges, William Huntting, Obadiah Jones and several other craftsmen were also working.[20] Nearby, Southampton also had several woodworking family dynasties including the Sanfords, Coopers, and Jaggers, and it was inevitable that their territories and potential customers would overlap in the middle ground between them. Undoubtedly there were feelings of competition, but in a rural small town environment there was also a realistic evaluation of how much one could depend on craft practice versus other means of earning a living.

Probably the most common form of case furniture in a rural town was the chest with drawer or drawers. Its simple construction was perfectly suited to the carpenter-joiners skills. Essentially these chests are large boxes constructed from six boards. The sides are cut out at the base to provide boot-jack feet, the top is hinged to provide access to the deep compartment and a drawer is inserted in the front. Finishing decorative touches consist of a simple plane-run moulding around the lid and base and the application of a coat of paint, or "cullering" as account book entries called it. Red, or vermillion, blue and black seem to have been the most frequently used colors. Charles Hummel, in discussing the products from the Dominy shop, refers to the timeless quality they seem to possess.[21] Indeed, the local craftsmen repeated the same design concepts over and over again distilling forms like these chests to their basic elements and without additional ornament or decoration which might have dated them more closely to a particular style or fashion. One of the few clues to dating these chests with drawers, all of which were found in East Hampton, is to study the brass hardware and follow the progression from the early eighteenth century William and Mary tear-drop pulls to late-eighteenth century Chippendale backplates with bail handles.

The acceptance of these simple, utilitarian and timeless, almost styleless pieces by the vast majority of the community reinforces our sense of communally-shared sets of values. If someone wanted to really make a statement they could always turn to a source outside of the town or they could indulge in a piece that more subtlety said fashion through choice of more expensive materials, such as the imported mahogany used in a chest with drawers owned by Southampton silversmith, Elias Pelletreau.

If any single object, including buildings, could be said to represent the identity of the town of East Hampton during the colonial period, it was the Meetinghouse. Serving as both the ecclesiastical and secular center of the community, it was here that most of the town would have gathered together. Interestingly, therefore, it was the Meetinghouse that served as the public stage or showcase for tradition, values and even fashion. A turned post that is a surviving relic from the 1717 Meetinghouse speaks as eloquently as any piece of furniture can of East Hampton's craft tradition. The prominent baluster-turned vase is the basic decorative element found on chairs, tables and stair-balusters throughout the eighteenth century. It is the common vocabulary of all East Hampton's craftsmen, whether they were Dominys, Bakers or Schellingers.

Several other architectural remains from the Meetinghouse are also in the East Hampton Historical Society's collections. Dating from a remodeling project in the 1750s, the boldly modeled pulpit with distinctive meandering vine-and-berry carving and polychrome-paint is derived directly from architectural work found in Hartford and surrounding areas of the Connecticut River Valley. The architectural capital is strikingly similar to those on a doorway from a Westfield, Massachusetts house now in the Metropolitan Museum of Art. Sherry Foster in her article entitled "The Reverend Buell of East Hampton: Tastemaker in the Connecticut Valley Tradition" makes a cogent case for Buell being responsible for importing Connecticut craftsmen to undertake this work.[22] Indeed, it would have taken a personality as strong and influential as Buell to push this project through. Assuming this was the case, just what did the local craftsmen think of being usurped?

Perhaps it was Buell's influence, perhaps it was the upset of the Revolution and enforced contact with Connecticut, or perhaps it was plain chance but breezes and hints of outside fashion occasionally blew across East Hampton. Tea-drinking and the social ceremony accompanying it called for specialized furniture forms. Clearly the model for a locally made tea table came from Connecticut. Another variant of the tea table had a circular top and turned pedestal base supported on tripod cabriole legs.

The high chest of drawers was not a popular form in New York after 1730 but numerous examples from eastern Long Island are known and which indicate the cross-Sound influence of New England and particularly Connecticut. The terminology is somewhat confusing since the Dominys referred to this form as a chest-on-chest while Caleb Cooper in Southampton apparently called them high chests and his contemporary Daniel Sandford seems to have termed them a case of drawers and frame. Certainly more stylish than the chest with drawer and significantly more expensive, anywhere from four to ten times the cost of a simple chest, I am struck yet again at how little variation exists between the numerous surviving examples despite the fact that they were made by at least three, and maybe more, different craftsmen. The similarity of these chests may indicate a particular prototype but more likely speaks to the issue of tradition and shared taste. The first example is in the Wheelock collection. The second was found in Bridgehampton and bears an inscription, "O.B. Lucas." Lucas was a nineteenth century Sag Harbor cabinetmaker who must have repaired this piece. The third, also in the Wheelock collection, is attributed to Caleb Cooper of Southampton.

The most ambitious piece of furniture made in East Hampton was probably the desk and bookcase Nathaniel Dominy V made for John Lyon Gardiner in 1800. Charles Hummel will be sure to discuss it in his lecture so I mention it only as a culminating and aberrational example of a rural East Hampton craftsman using all of his skills and ingenuity to produce an object that really was foreign to his experience. Gardiner was clearly one of the most worldly inhabitants of East Hampton and was affluent enough to buy and order fashionable items such as a pair of Liverpool ceramic pitchers from England, decorated with his name and family coat-of-arms.[23] When remodeling and furnishing his house in 1796, he acquired numerous articles from New York including a sideboard, looking glass, sofa, carpet and mahogany bedstead. His instructions for the latter were that it be "plain neat and fashionable."[24]

Gardiner owned other furniture indicative of his wide-ranging tastes including a Hartford, Connecticut area desk-and-bookcase, yet he frequently and constantly patronized local craftsmen and accepted their vision of taste and fashion. Lest we conclude that Gardiner was a singular exception, we do know that other examples of outside fashion and different style were owned in eighteenth century East Hampton. But, in the final analysis, we must conclude that for most members of the East Hampton community the traditional values and objects created and shaped over a 150 year period of time were more acceptable and desired than the choices available elsewhere.

NOTES

1. Letter, Aaron Carter to Horace Carter, July 27, 1858, East Hampton Free Library, East Hampton, New York.

2. Timothy Dwight, *Travels in New England and New York* (4 vols.; London: Printed for William Baynes and Son et. al), 1823, 111,297.

3. John Lyon Gardiner, "Gardiner's East Hampton," *Collections of the New York Historical Society* (New York: Printed for the Society, 1869), 233.

4. Hans Kurath, *Handbook of the Linguistic Geography of New England*. 2nd ed. (New York: AMS Press, 1973), 1-18.

5. Philip Zea, "Rural Craftsman and Design." *New England Furniture: The Colonial Era*. By Brock Jobe and Myrna Kaye (Boston: Houghton Mifflin Company, 1984), 49.

6. David Gardiner, *Chronicles of the Town of Easthampton, County of Suffolk, New York* (Sag Harbor: William Ewers, Printers, 1973), 18.

7. Robert Blair St. George, "Father, Sons, and Identity: Woodworking Artisans in Southeastern New England, 1620-1700." *The Craftsman in Early America*. Ed. Ian M. G. Quimby (New York: W.W. Norton & Company 1984), 95.

8. Dean F. Failey, *Long Island Is My Nation: The Decorative Arts & Craftsmen, 1640-1840* (Setauket, N.Y. : Society for the Preservation of Long Island Antiquities, 1976), 276.

9. Ibid., 291.

10. St. George, 120-125.

11. Failey, 196.

12. Ibid.

13. Zea, 47.

14. Charles F. Hummel, *With Hammer In Hand: The Dominy Craftsmen of East Hampton, New York* (Charlottesville, Va. : The University Press of Virginia, 1968), 21.

15. Failey, 196.

16. Patricia E. Kane, *Furniture of the New Haven Colony: The Seventeenth Century* (New Haven: The New Haven Colony Historical Society, 1973), 10-11.

17. Failey, 15.

18. Document Book 15, 1737, p.17, East Hampton Free Library, East Hampton, New York.

19. Failey, 249, 280.

20. Failey, 269, 276-278.

21. Charles F. Hummel, "The Dominys of East Hampton, Long Island, And Their Furniture," *Country Cabinetwork and Simple City Furniture*. Ed. John D. Morse. (Charlottesville, Va.: The University Press of Virginia, 1970), 64-66.

22. Sherrill Foster, "The Reverend Samuel Buell of East Hampton: Tastemaker in the Connecticut Valley Tradition, " *The Connecticut Historical Society Bulletin*, 54 (Summer / Fall 1989), 189-211.

23. Failey, 160.

24. Failey, 160.

ACTUALLY EARNING
A LIVING

The Dominy Craftsmen of East Hampton

~~~

Charles F. Hummel

FOR MORE THAN 100 YEARS, craftsmen represented by four generations of the Dominy family were able to support themselves and
their families with the products of their craft activity. Because virtually
no records or products documented to Nathaniel Dominy III (1714-
1778), a carpenter and surveyor, have survived, my studies have focused on a father, son and grandson active between 1760 and about
1850. They are Nathaniel Dominy IV (1737-1812), Nathaniel V (1770-
1852), and Felix Dominy (1800-1868).

In the twentieth century, many individuals are called to become
craftsmen (probably craftspersons would be a more politically correct
term). Many actually practice a craft, but very, very few are able to earn
a living as craftsmen. Why then, were the Dominy craftsmen able to
function successfully as craftsmen throughout most of the eighteenth
century and for almost fifty years of the nineteenth century? The answers to that question can be found in the unique survival of more
than 200 manuscript items, approximately 2,000 craft tools and heavy
equipment, and well over 100 objects made in their shops.

Being in "the right place at the right time" has always been a partial
explanation for success stories. In the Dominys' case, that phrase is applicable. By the time that Nathaniel Dominy IV began to function as a
craftsman, his family had lived in East Hampton for almost 100 years.
The first Nathaniel Dominy settled in East Hampton about 1669, only
twenty-one years after the founding of the town. The home in which
Nathaniel IV lived had been built about 1715, forty-five years before he

became active as a craftsman, on the North Main Street site on the road that led from the town to Three Mile Harbor and Long Island Sound. Dominy males had also married into local families such as Edwards, Baker and Miller. In short, they were a known and trusted family.

The Dominy craftsmen were also fortunate to have been born into a rural, agricultural region. They were, like most craftsmen producing goods in the eighteenth and early nineteenth centuries, the vast majority of whom lived and worked in rural areas. The United States Census of 1790 counted a rural population of over 3,700,000 individuals while only 202,000 people lived in "urban" communities. In all thirteen states, there were only twenty-four towns or cities that had more than 2,500 people residing in them. East Hampton, for example, had only 1,250 inhabitants in 1776 and had grown to a population of only 2,076 by the 1840 Census.

In describing the state of American manufactures in 1794, Tench Coxe defined rural tradesmen as

> that part of the tradesmen and manufacturers, who live in the country, generally reside on small lots and farms of one acre to twenty, and not a few upon farms of twenty to one hundred and fifty acres, which they cultivate at leisure times, with their own hands, their wives, children, servants and apprentices and sometimes by hired laborers, or by letting out fields for a part of the produce, to some neighbor, who has time or farm hands not fully employed.

The Assessment Roll of the Town of East Hampton for 1814 notes that the Dominys owned 100 acres of land. By 1770, Nathaniel IV rented some of his land in exchange for a portion of the wheat, flax, corn, and rye grown on it. At the start of his career, Nathaniel IV had performed agricultural labor for others, earning for example, four shillings for cradling, bundling, and storing one-half acre of oats in 1765. As late as 1830, Felix Dominy purchased twelve sheep to graze on Dominy acreage and obtained sweet potato seed for his garden. City craftsmen in Colonial America generally were forced to purchase food and other basic necessities of living. Thus, their overhead costs were higher than their craftsmen counterparts working in rural areas.

Not only were the Dominy craftsmen a known quantity as a family with a long history of residence in East Hampton, they were also a known quantity as producers of goods. Nathaniel Dominy II (1684-1768) was a weaver and a surveyor, the latter always an important service skill in an agricultural community. He supervised the building of the town's first poorhouse and was a partner in a local sawmill. It's already been noted that Nathaniel Dominy III was a carpenter and a surveyor. Nathaniel Dominy IV functioned as a joiner, house and barn carpenter, turner, millwright, coffinmaker, clockmaker, and a repairer of guns, jewelry and watches. His son, Nathaniel V was a cabinetmaker, joiner, turner, millwright, wheelwright, coffinmaker, and repairer of small boats. His son, Felix, worked as a clockmaker, jewelry and watch repairer, and general metalworker.

What the local community needed in the way of woodwork or metalwork—furniture, house and mill carpentry, clocks, watch repair, agricultural tools, spinning wheels, dry cooperage, coffins, and more—the Dominys provided for well over 100 years. In short, they were a well-known, respected local family of full-service craftsmen whose craft activity was also supported by a 100-acre farm.This recipe for success in earning a living as craftsmen is confirmed by the fact that one Dominy account book alone contains the names of over 1,600 different customers while the names of customers who gave their watches to Nathaniel IV and Felix Dominy total almost 2,000.

In addition to East Hampton Village and Township customers, the Dominys provided services to individuals living in Flushing, Huntington, Islip, Moriches, Patchogue, Quogue, Riverhead, Smithtown, Southold, and at least eight other towns on Long Island. A short sail across Gardiners Bay and Long Island, they had customers in Haddam, Hartford, Lyme, Moodus, New Haven, Saybrook, Stonington, and Wethersfield, Connecticut. Sometimes, the Dominys would travel to seek additional work. In 1795, Nathaniel IV credited Nathan Dayton with twelve shillings for the use of Dayton's mare "on a clock-tour to Mastick." Several years later, in 1809, he advertised in the *Suffolk Gazette*,"... a tour to the western parts of this county," for the purpose of repairing clocks.

Another key to the Dominys' success in supporting themselves as craftsmen, is the fact that there were always a substantial number of years during which father and son could work together. This enabled them to specialize in their craft activity and increase their production. Nathaniel Dominy IV had received sufficient training to begin working on his own by 1758. His father did not die until 1778, thus enabling Nathaniel IV to concentrate on making clocks and repairing both watches and clocks as well as other metalwork while his father focused on woodwork. When "young Nat," Nathaniel V, started his craft activity about 1789, his father was able to concentrate, again, on metalwork, clockwork and repairing of watches and clocks until his death in

1812. Nathaniel V focused on woodwork until his father's death, adding metalwork until his son, Felix, took on metalwork, clockwork and watch repair in 1817.

Raised in a rural, agricultural area, the Dominys knew their customers' tastes—their likes and dislikes. As one looks at the surviving products of their handiwork, one might question the degree of craft skill posessed by the Dominys. My assessment of the superlative skills of the Dominy craftsmen, made thirty years ago, has not changed. Indeed, an excellent article by Phillip Zea, "Diversity and Regionalism in Rural New England Furniture," published in *American Furniture* in 1995, reinforces my earlier conclusions. Zea notes that rural design doesn't reflect ignorance and eccentricity. He observed that provincial objects can have elements of high style and command an expensive price. In general, agricultural economies demand conservative, solid, functional, time-tested objects unlike the demand for changing, "mutable fashion" in urban economies. The Dominys' customers demanded "neat" goods. According to the *Oxford English Dictionary*, in the eighteenth and early nineteenth centuries, "neat" meant "elegance of form or arrangement with freedom from all unnecessary additions or embellishment; of agreeable but simple appearance; nicely made or proportioned." That is a perfect summary of Dominy craft products. The importance of a large number of customers who trusted the Dominy craftsmen to make objects for them which they liked and with which they were comfortable cannot be overemphasized. As businessmen needing to support their families and themselves, the Dominys functioned in a barter economy involving the exchange of goods and services and the extension of credit over long periods of time. In exchange for their products the Dominys received household goods such as woven coverlets, "Sundries of Earthenware," linen cloth, shoes, skeins of wool, indigo, spoons, hats and blanketing. Customers paid them with foodstuffs—bushels of wheat, corn, rye, oats, spices, rice, beef, mutton, fish, salt pork, vinegar, apples, tea, molasses, rum and tobacco. They were also paid with business supplies and services such as tools, lumber, paint, varnish and the carting of products.

Because their names appear prominently on the dials of clocks made in their house and shops on North Main Street, the Dominy craftsmen had been primarily known as clockmakers. But close examination of their records and surviving products indicates that they earned more from furniture production and watch repair than they did from clockmaking. At least 936 pieces of furniture were made in the Dominy Woodworking Shop between 1760 and 1840. Of that number, almost eighty percent were made of wholly or partially turned parts.

Both pole and great wheel lathes were used by the Dominys to make parts for more than 350 chairs recorded in their accounts. Armchairs and side chairs were made in splat-back, fiddle-back, slat-back and Windsor types usually for adults, but occasionally for children as well. After 1804, rocking chairs were also produced by Nathaniel Dominy V. A pole lathe was very useful in a small shop because it required only one person to operate it, thus eliminating the need for an apprentice. Using green wood, that is, wood with a high moisture content, not only furniture parts but pump—box pipe for wells, mill shafts, wagon hubs, workbench screws and hubs for spinning wheels or winding reels, could also be turned by the Dominys on their pole lathe. Five, six-foot tall sections for columns used on the portico of Clinton Academy in East Hampton, were turned on this lathe by Nathaniel V in 1802.

When Nathaniel IV was training his son as an apprentice, or when their other apprentices or journeymen were available, they must have preferred using their great wheel lathe. The differential between the large wheel's diameter of five and one-half feet and the smaller pulleys set into the lathe bed, provided a choice of speeds and continuous cutting motion, resulting in greater productivity. We know that the great wheel lathe also provided rental income to the Dominys. In 1776, for example, Abraham Mulford, Jr. paid Nathaniel IV one shilling threepence for the use of a "gun bit and great wheel."

Patterns or templates for furniture parts were used by all cabinetmakers and joiners from the seventeenth century to the present day. Those used by the Dominys have survived in greater numbers than is the case for any American woodworker of the Colonial or early-Republic periods. These patterns for splats and crest rails helped to speed production of chairs made in the Dominy woodworking shop. By outlining the shape of these patterns on boards, with a scratch awl or pencil, the Dominys and other craftsmen could produce objects in quantity.

Amateur woodworkers and even some hand-craft professionals often scoff at statements relating to the speed with which the Dominy craftsmen produced furniture and other objects. But like today, for those who are self-employed, time is money. When the Dominys were productive craftsmen, materials were expensive and labor was cheap. That, of course, is the reverse of today. Yes, labor-saving devices, like templates for the parts of furniture, hastened the process of cutting, shaping and assembling pieces made in their shop. But more important was the speed with which the Dominys and their contemporaries used their tools and equipment. Long years served as apprentices, journeymen and master craftsmen gave men like the Dominys a sure touch in the use of tools and manipulation of wood. These craftsmen also worked ten to twelve hours each day, six days a week. So it is a romantic notion that craftsmen like the Dominys didn't care about time and took as long as perfection required to complete an object.

Using the traditional division of the price of an object into thirds, one-third each for labor, materials and profit, the number of days or hours spent by the Dominys to produce various objects can be calculated. For example, side chairs like the one owned by the Halsey House in Southampton, the gift of Mr. and Mrs. Paul Fordham, were made by Nathaniel Dominy V at a price of five to six shillings between 1790 and 1830. Given his wages of seven shillings per day, the labor cost for this type of chair never exceeded two shillings or thirty percent of a twelve-hour day. Such chairs could be completed in one- third of his workday. Obviously that time would be spread over more than one day.

From 1790 to 1810, at least thirty-one "fiddle back" chairs are entered into Dominy accounts. They all had a Chippendale style crest rail and were sold for eight shillings each for the side chairs and twelve to fourteen shillings for the armchairs. Time required for completion of the side chair—a little over four and one half hours.

Slat-back chairs were probably the most common type made by the Dominys. Sixty-one are listed in accounts between 1796 and 1818 at prices selling from four to six shillimgs apiece. A "great" slat-back armchair, like one made for Abraham Sherrill, Jr. in 1822, cost fourteen shillings. and eight hours of labor to complete. Nathaniel V made two slat-back rocking armchairs for his own use in 1796 and 1809; a "great" slat-back rocking armchair was made for Thomas Baker at a cost of fourteen shillings.. The pattern for the slats has survived as has a slat-bending clamp used by Nathaniel V to bend a curve into slats that had been immersed in warm water. Slat-back chairs, then, could be had with straight, curved, or arched slats.

At least 206 "chairs" were made for Dominy customers without a description of the type. Included in that group is a set of mahogany Windsor chairs made in 1794 for Captain William J. Rysam of Sag Harbor, at a cost of ten shillings each. That price probably doesn't include the materials because Captain Rysam was the owner of a mahogany grove in Honduras. Very few American Windsor chairs were made of mahogany and it is likely, therefore, that Captain Rysam supplied Nathaniel Dominy V with the material for his chairs.

Rysam was a man of means who had acquired a shipyard, a pier at the foot of Bay Street in Sag Harbor, and a ropewalk by 1799. He was the sole owner of the 200-ton brig, *Merchant*. The Dominys supplied Rysam with other furniture and Nathaniel Dominy V also constructed for him a double-geared sawmill on Studley Hill. The mill was dismantled and shipped on an armed vessel to Honduras where it was re-erected in Rysam's mahogany grove. For work on the sawmill, Nathaniel V and his "Boy", Asa, received £23–2–0 for forty-two days work. That breaks down to seven shillings per day for Nathaniel V and three shillings sixpence per day for Asa.

A direct descendent of the Dominy craftsmen, Phoebe Dominy Mason, rescued a Windsor side chair from the Dominy House in East Hampton, just before that building was torn down in 1946. Dating between 1815 and 1825, the chair, and a related child's fancy rocking chair, resemble Windsors made in the metropolitan New York City area. The child's chair may have been made for a grandson of Nathaniel V. It, too, was rescued from the Dominy House by Phoebe Dominy Mason. These chairs also lend credence to the supposition that some of the undesignated chairs in Dominy accounts were Windsor or Windsor types.

Turned stands were a very useful furniture form in demand from the Dominys. At least seventy-nine stands and three tea-tables were listed in their accounts between 1789 and 1833. Using lathes and patterns for legs, Nathaniel V could produce stands so quickly that his prices for them ranged between seven shillings sixpence to £1, an indication that even the largest stand could be finished in ten or eleven hours of work. Often, the difference in price lay in the wood selected by his customer, mahogany being the most expensive choice, followed in cost by cherry, maple and pine.

The conservative nature of his customers is well illustrated by a maple stand with a cherry top probably made for Thomas Baker between 1800 and 1815. With its pendant drop, the stand resembles those made in the early eighteenth century, rather than a fashionable stand made in the Federal period. By contrast is a cherry stand, made between 1790 and 1820, also with a dished top, but with a plain, baluster-turned shaft. It has a tilt-top without a latch, indicating that only objects light in weight were placed on its top. Its original owner is not known, but it was purchased in Sag Harbor in 1920 by its recent owner when research for *With Hammer in Hand* was underway. It is quite similar to a mahogany stand made for John Lyon Gardiner by Nathaniel V in 1799.

A maple stand with a rectangular top and "swept" corners displayed at the Halsey House in Southampton is similar to one made for Abraham Sherrill (1754-1844) with the exception of curved corners on the latter example. Both were made between 1810 and 1830 and both made use of the same "spider-leg" pattern that survives in the Dominy tool collection at Winterthur. Relatively speaking, that type of leg was up-to-date because it wasn't in popular use by American cabinetmakers until about 1800.

An earlier cherry stand, made by Nathaniel V for Abraham Sherrill, Jr. between 1790 and 1815, uses the cabriole leg with a so-called "snake" foot. It stands out in the group made by the Dominys because its elongated, tapered, columnar shaft springs from an urn. It is a good example of how the Dominys could use variety in their turned work to provide similar, but unique, objects to each of their customers.

Much larger is the mahogany, tilt-top tea table made by Nathaniel V in 1796, for his own use. Like the Sherrill family stand, it, too, has a plain, Doric column for its shaft but the diameter of its dished top is over two feet and its tripod-base, cabriole legs are larger and sturdier. A Dominy family genealogy has an old photograph illustrating this tea table in the parlor of the Dominy House. Only three other tea tables are listed in Dominy accounts. All were made in 1792 at prices ranging from £1-4 shillings. to £1-14 shillings.

All of the plain or dished circular tops for stands and tables were made using the most important piece of lathe equipment to survive in the Dominy Tool Collection. No eighteenth-or-nineteenth century source on tools and craft technology illustrates an "arbor and cross." Responding to a growing demand for these furniture forms, in 1795 Nathaniel V had a local blacksmith, Deacon David Talmage, make "an Arbor and Cross for Turning Stands" at a cost of six shillings, nine pence. Nathaniel V then fitted it to a soft maple pulley and dogwood and hickory screws on a hickory puppet in order to set it in the great wheel lathe bed. The tops were turned in a vertical position.

Turned legs and joinery fashioned the mahogany breakfast table that Nathaniel V made for his son Felix, probably at the time of Felix's marriage to Phoebe Miller in 1826. Its late-Sheraton design would not have been out-of-place in New York City but, then, Felix had received his clock-and-watch training in that city. Presumably, he would have expected a fashionable table for his family's use. Thirteen breakfast tables are listed in Dominy accounts between 1794 and 1823. One made for Abraham Hand in 1803, described as mahogany, fetched £2-16 shillings, almost double the price of a mahogany, tilt-top tea table.

During their productive years, the Dominys used their joinery skills to produce at least 127 case pieces of various types. Patterns for the bracket feet, pad feet and legs for case furniture have survived in the Dominy Tool Collection along with the templates for the legs of stands and tables. In conducting research for *With Hammer in Hand*, only one example of a "chest-on-chest," Nathaniel V's term for a "highboy" was found, although thirteen or fourteen of them were listed in their accounts between 1791 and 1806. Subsequently, the example now on the screen was acquired by Winterthur from a dealer in Ohio. Its history was unknown but it matched in virtually every detail, including the template used for its feet and legs, the chest-on-chest made

"Chest-on-Chest" (High Chest of Drawers), Nathaniel Dominy V, 1791-1806. (Courtesy The Winterthur Museum)

in 1796 by Nathaniel V for his own family's use. Only this year, a third example, undoubtedly, made for John Parsons III in 1791, at a cost of £7-12 shillings-sixpence, was called to my attention. In keeping with the Dominy's practice, all three are, for all intents and purposes, identical.

As just noted, case furniture with drawers was quite expensive, the cost ranging from that made for the Parsons to £12 charged by Nathaniel V for the one he made for Daniel Conkling, Jr. in 1797. Like much of the furniture produced in the eastern end of Long Island, there is a close relationship to cabinetwork produced across Long Island sound in Connecticut and Rhode Island.

By far, the most ambitious and expensive piece of furniture made in the Dominy's woodworking shop was a maple desk and bookcase made for John Lyon Gardiner in 1800 at a cost of £20-8 shillings. That price included carting it to Fireplace, an area just opposite to Gardiner's Island. Much of the cost was due to making thirteen cherry and white pine drawers in the desk section. Showing the Dominys' recognition of the speed with which they could produce lathe work, the elaborate molding on the pediment was first turned on the arbor and cross described earlier, and then sawn into quarter sections that were attached to the pediment. All told, Nathaniel V spent about twenty days to make this piece of furniture. It was inherited by Winthrop Gardiner, Jr. around 1933 and is now owned by Winterthur, installed near the Dominy Shops on the second floor of its new Galleries building. The desk's feet have been correctly restored and its present finish is based on matching segments of the original finish discovered after Winterthur had acquired it.

A cherry desk and bookcase, one of two made by the Dominys for their own use, is a good illustration of why researchers must be cautious in relying solely on a craftsman's accounts. Only one desk and bookcase is recorded in Dominy records but the family's examples, and another made for John Lyon Gardiner are not listed. The desk and bookcase had been owned by Washington Tyson Dominy, but was sold to a Long Island dealer in recent years. Its whereabouts are unknown at this time. Clearly, the practical, straightforward design of the family's desks and bookcases were intended to handle the needs of a flourishing business. Like many other modern owners of antiques, however, the Dominy descendant was in the process of removing the desk's original finish in order to savor the color and grain of its natural wood. But most of the Dominy's cherry, maple and pine furniture had been stained to give surfaces an appearance of more costly woods such as walnut or mahogany.

John Lyon Gardiner, born in the same year as Nathaniel Dominy V (1770), was one of the best customers for Dominy-made objects. A piece of case furniture in point is a mahogany, fall-front desk, made in 1802. Another example of expensive furniture, Gardiner paid £11 or $27.50 for it, but the price certainly doesn't reflect its decoration or lack thereof. It is, again, a plain or "neat," utilitarian object almost devoid of any surface treatment other than moldings or sawn decoration. In addition to the template for the desk's bracket feet surviving in the Dominy Tool Collection, a rare pencil inscription in Nathaniel V's hand on the back of the desk's upper left-hand drawer states, "Nathaniel Domine Junr fecit Jan 1802 / For John Lyon Gardiner Esqr—Price 27$—50 cts."

From 1769 through 1835, the Dominys made at least thirty-four pieces of furniture for nine separate members of the Sherrill family. A looking glass frame, made for Abraham Sherrill about 1820, is one example from that group purchased by Winterthur from Sherrill Foster in 1992. In return for furniture and other goods received from the Dominys, the Sherrill family supplied the craftsmen with shoes for the daughters of Nathaniel IV, work performed in the Dominy's woodworking shop, field work, carting of wood, rental of a horse, butchering of animals to supply meat, and even hammering out the iron triangle that Nathaniel IV used to support his clock-gear cutting engine.

Gun repair and the stocking of guns were always a source of income for the Dominys. It's not surprising, therefore, that a pattern for making a rough cut gunstock has survived in the Dominy Tool Collection. Made of birch, it probably dates about 1820. Its length is very close to a breech-loading flintlock rifle adopted by the United States Army for production on a large scale in 1819. Felix Dominy was active in the militia from 1817 to 1835. It's been suggested, therefore, that this object is actually a training device for militia drills. Dominy records don't help to unravel that mystery. In 1800, for example, the Dominys were paid for "stocking a gun" and also for "2 Rifles at 6 pence." The latter could only be mock toy or training rifles at that price.

Although the Dominy craftsmen's claim to fame initially rested on the products of their clock shop, there can be no doubt that they would not have prospered solely from the sale of their clocks. They made only ninety clocks over a sixty year period. Clocks were expensive and Nathaniel Dominy IV's watchpapers and engraved copperplate for printing them are forthright in describing him as a clockmaker and *repairer* of watches [emphasis mine]. Felix Dominy's watchpaper stretches the truth by describing him as a clock-and-watchmaker. He never made any watches. My current research on the Dominy craftsmen is focused on their business of repairing watches. From 1769 through 1827, Nathaniel IV and Felix kept a record of all watches coming into their shop for repair, including the names of their owners, and makers, and their serial numbers. In that period, 4,600 entries for watch repair occur, representing 1,983 owners and 1,108 different watchmakers. It was an incredibly lucrative business that accounted for a significant portion of the Dominys' annual income.

But I have still to locate any of the watches repaired by the Dominys, although I hope to do so. A couple of examples of their clocks I will describe will have to suffice, therefore, to illustrate their earning a living from clock-and-watchwork. The timepieces made by Nathaniel IV are wonderfully simple mechanisms. One example was made around 1788 or 1790, possibly for William Huntting at a cost of £6. Its hood is the same shape as the pewter dial and only one hand is used to mark the hour and minutes past the hour. Although the narrow case makes the clock appear to be tall, it is only six and one-half feet in height and only twelve inches wide. Ever practical, the Dominys scooped the interior surface of the case's side boards in order to provide enough space for pendulum sway. The original, applied molding brackets for feet are missing from the base of this clock.

Stick-like brass plates to support the clock gears and winding drum for the weight are unique to Dominy clocks. They were designed to save brass, an expensive metal in the eighteenth and early-nineteenth centuries.

One of the most expensive of the Dominy clocks was made for David Gardiner of Flushing, Long Island in 1799. Described in Nathaniel IV's bill as "an Horologiographical, Repeating, alarm, monition clock," it cost ninety dollars or £36. Its mahogany case, silvered bell, alarm and repeater functions account for its high cost. The painted, enamel dial, like most used by American clockmakers in this period, was manufactured in England; in this case, at "Osborne's Manufactory / Birmingham." David Gardiner purchased the dial in New York City and was credited by Nathaniel IV for its cost. Its alarm dial reveals the engraved, script name of "N. Dominy" in East Hampton and the date, 1799. Its complex works are confined to skeleton plates to save brass. The casting pattern for this type of plate survives in the Dominy Tool Collection.

Felix Dominy made a silent clock in 1824 or 1825, probably for Jonathan Osborn III. It came as a gift to Winterthur in 1986. It has a pine case and, in an attempt to hold down costs, its dial is made of painted cherry. It had no strike mechanism but still cost twenty-five dollars, or slightly more than a master craftsman's monthly wage. The dial is from a one-stroke clock made by Felix in 1828 for S. Hedges Miller. It is to illustrate that time was running out for the makers of hand-crafted clocks in 1828. In that year, Sarah Nicoll of Islip canceled an order for a clock by writing to Felix Dominy that "some of my friends think it such a piece of folly for me to have an expensive clock made." In other words, "I can get a cheaper clock of Connecticut manufacture that will serve my purpose."

Printed on Nathaniel IV's watchpaper is the warning, "time flies." It makes sense to move swiftly to a conclusion by describing a mahogany and whalebone swift made by Nathaniel V for his wife Temperance, about 1800. Used to wind wool yarn into skeins of wool, it reveals the craftsman's knowledge of the neo-classical revival underway in fashion centers of the new Republic.

By the late 1820s or early 1830s, for the Dominys to try to earn a living as craftsmen was like tilting at the windmills they had built on the eastern end of Long Island. I have often wondered whether or not Felix Dominy was being somewhat cynical when, in 1822, he paraphrased the New York Mechanics Society motto in his weatherbook by writing:

>With Hammer in Hand
>All Arts Do Stand
>All Arts Do Stand
>With Hammer in Hand

As noted by Pavel Svinin, a Russian artist in America during the early nineteenth century, steampower had been applied to moving boats. It had also been applied to moving railroad trains and machinery. Goods could be produced cheaper, in greater quantity, and much faster than was possible by the Dominys in their handcraft shops. Convinced that the days of being able to earn a living as a craftsmen were severely numbered, Felix Dominy moved to Babylon by 1835 in order to become the keeper of the Fire Island lighthouse and by 1847 was operating a hotel on Fire Island during the summer and in Bay Shore during the winter. A seal on a letter from Felix to his son Nathaniel VII in 1847, advertises his Fire Island Hotel. His son, Nathaniel VII had been left to the care and training of Felix's father, Nathaniel V.

What is probably the most beautiful "make do" tool to survive in the Dominy Collection is a fourteen-inch-long turning chisel made by Nathaniel III or IV from the fine steel of a sword. A flower and leaf design and the date *1660* are inlaid in brass on its blade. This tool bears witness as a reminder of the long period of time when hand craftsmen, like the Dominys, produced all of the structures and objects used by consumers. It also provides sad testimony to the change in the Dominys ability to earn a living from their skills. In 1883, Charles Burr Todd described East Hampton as the new playground of the Barbizon School of artists. He mentioned, "An old weather-beaten dwelling at the upper end of village street." It was sketched and painted so often that an in-joke on new artists arriving in town was "that Dominys is going onto the canvas." After describing the run-down condition of the house, the author noted further,

> Two workshops, one flanking each side of the cottage, present curious interiors, low ceilings, dusty, cobwebbed windows, tools of various callings, disposed on the walls or cribs in the ceiling, and a medley of articles scattered about—old fashioned clocks in long cases, a photographer's camera, a Damascus blade, with gold inlaid hilt, fashioned into a chisel.

Clearly, the Dominy family could no longer earn a living as craftsmen. But the activity of their heyday and the surviving examples of their legacy provide us with ample evidence of what it was like to earn a living in the centuries when With Hammer in Hand all arts did stand.

Winterthur is proud to be the custodian of the major collection of material related to the Dominy craftsmen. In the museum and in its library, this collection offers the best evidence of what it was like to earn your living as a craftsman. A time when "With Hammer in Hand," all arts did stand.

THE *AMISTAD*

Quentin Snediker

THE IDEA OF THE *AMISTAD*—the rebirth of interest in *Amistad*—really goes back quite far. While Mr. Spielberg's efforts in recent years really brought it to public focus, the main impact of the story of the *Amistad* is highlighting concern the concern for human rights in this country. *Amistad* has really never vanished from the awareness or the conscience of the American people. The *Amistad* and its influence on the America never had any hiatus; it never stopped influencing this country.

From 1839 to 1841, fifty-three Africans who wound up on these shores—literally, on the beach right outside at Culloden Point—brought a great deal of national focus to the issue of slavery, and the issues of race to date still continue to concern the American people. From the time of the Constitution to the present, it has been one of the fundamental problems we face as a society. How do we deal with all of these issues that are sort of the legacy of the horrors of slavery?

The *Amistad* as a moment in time really helped to galvanize this nation's attitudes towards the institution of slavery—helped to give a face to an otherwise nameless and faceless institution to many northeners. To be an abolitionist in 1839 was sort of a radical ambition. *Amistad* is the incident that really served to galvanize the American people against the institution of slavery. That opposition really didn't boil until the Civil War, of course, but the *Amistad* trial served to bring the many disparate interests together in opposition to the institution of slavery. As I said, to be an abolitionist in 1839 was sort of very radical. But by 1860, certainly, it was no longer considered radical to be ab-

Quentin Sneidker

solutely against slavery. And it's the *Amistad* incident that served to really bring this to the fore.

Had the *Amistad* incident occurred in New York, it wouldn't have had the influence that it had on the American people. In fact, the *Amistad* were only fifteen rods off the Montauk beach. Why didn't the case get tried in the New York court system? In 1797, New York State had completely abolished slavery. But by fate and the winds, the *Amistad* pasengers wound up back in Connecticut where slavery had not been banned. We've got a little bit of insight we would like to shed on that as we go forward.

The *Amistad* was a freedom vessel. In fact, it was really quite different from a slave ship. It was so ingrained in the American economy that we can think of *Amistad* as a slave ship but, in fact, it was simply a cargo vessel.

The central character of our story is the gentleman who was about twenty-three at the time and really is a biblical character in the *Amistad* incident. Singbe—given the name "Cinque" by the Spanish in their subterfuge to try and cover his identity as an illegal captive—was being sold as a legal slave under Spanish law. So his captors gave him a false passport and called him "Cinque" and that's the name that he was known by during the court trial. But, in fact, Singbe was his name in Mendeland presently within the country of Sierra Leone. Recently, we have come in contact with three men who are the great-grandsons of Singbe and they like to make it very clear that he should known as "Singbe" and not as "Cinque."

Singbe was, as I say, about twenty-three at the time and I don't think that we can really appreciate the leadership abilities that this young man had considering the circumstances that he found himself under. He and about 450 other individuals, kidnapped on the west coast of Africa, was loaded aboard what is in classic terms today described as a slave ship. This was a vessel on which we can't imagine the horror that these people endured; literally, 450 people stuffed into a vessel that was only about 110 feet long. About forty percent was the usual rate of mortality for people making this middle passage; the voyage lasted about two months.

Anyway, Singbe and fifty-three of his fellow Mende survived this passage, wound up in Cuba, and there were sold to plantation owners from another part of Cuba—eastern Cuba—and put aboard the *Amistad*. Again, the *Amistad* was not one of these classic middle-passage slave ships. My point about the slave ship issue versus cargo ship—it's important to put in context the history of the legalities of the slave trade.

Beginning in the fifteenth century really, Europeans began to kidnap Africans for enslavement—both in Europe and with the development of the sugar economy in the New World, for labor in the New World. The first Africans were brought to the United States shores to be sold as slaves in 1619 in Virginia, but really, the Spanish and Portuguese had a thriving economy based on Africans' labor in the New World long before that.

By about 1808, numerous European nations began to increasingly restrict the slave trade. After 1808, the United States and Great Britain signed a treaty which forbade the importation of newly kidnapped Africans for enslavement in any British Colony or in the United States. By 1820, the British had persuaded the Spanish to sign on into these international agreements as well. It did nothing to address the plight of people who were born into slavery in the New World. You could be born, live and die a slave after 1808 in the United States and any British Colony, but it did prohibit the importation of newly kidnapped people for enslavement. That's an important thing to understand in context to the *Amistad* incident because in 1820, some of the people that were aboard the *Amistad* weren't yet born so they could not have been born in the New World before the importation of new Africans for enslavement became illegal. That was one of the pivotal points that allowed them to be given their freedom by the court system.

We refer to this horrible trade as the middle-passage and this kind of has its maritime roots in thinking of things in the triangle trade—remember sixth-grade history about the triangle trade where not every vessel made a three-legged voyage. A voyage is a round trip; if you start in Sag Harbor, go around the world and come back, you have completed your "voyage." But any stop that you've made along the way, let's say, the trip between Sag Harbor and that stop is a "passage." So, in the triangle trade, manufactured goods might have started typically in Liverpool, England, loaded aboard a ship, taken to the west coast of Africa, there sold or traded for human beings. These purchased people were put aboard these ships, the ships would make the passage across the Atlantic, ending up in the New World at Havana which was the principal port for this slave trade. This finished the second leg, or second passage. Then, from Havana, sugar products would have been brought back to Liverpool, completing the voyage of three legs, the middle passage being that which carried Africans from the west coast of Africa to the New World for enslavement. So, this is where we get the term "middle passage"; it's a very specific maritime connotation. But, today, we just think of it to mean the slave trade as a whole.

After about two weeks in Havana, these people were sold to plantation owners from eastern Cuba and put aboard a vessel that I like to think of as sort of the tractor trailer of its day—certainly not a comfortable accommodation. But in 1839, no accommodation was really comfortable. The *Amistad* might have carried Spanish gentlemen or ladies on one voyage and then, on the next voyage, people bound for a life of enslavement on sugar plantations. So, the vessel didn't have the character of the middle-passage slave ships.

A woodcut is based on the words that Singbe used himself when he described to a newspaper man in New Haven the slave ship on the middle passage from Africa. It describes the experience that they had aboard the *Tecora*. Only three feet three inches of headroom—just absolutely, unimaginably crowded conditions, no sanitation, poor food. Literally forty percent of the people on board such vessels would perish on the voyage. But the economics were such that for the capital involved in sponsoring these voyages and the people involved in making profits, there was still plenty of profit to be made. A vessel would literally be paid for in one successful trip. So this is what inspired people, despite the international agreements to continue in this nefarious trade. So, again, it's quite rare to have the graphic description based on the experience of an individual in this trade, so it's really a remarkable document. It was published in 1840 by this man named John Barber in his work called *The History of the Amistad Captives* which goes into a lot more and is one of the primary documents connected to the case.

The bottom line is that the *Tecora* came into Havana with Singbe and his fellow *Amistad* passengers on board. I mentioned that after 1820, it was illegal even under Spanish law to bring newly captive Africans into Spanish colonies in the New World. However, the British were estimating conservatively that 25,000 individuals every year were still being smuggled into the Island of Cuba. So, it wasn't a very effective treaty. The Spanish government really took no steps to enforce these laws whatsoever. In fact, for a fee of what equated to $10 U.S. at the time, you could obtain one of these false passports for someone who was smuggled into the country. You could get a legal Spanish document that said this person was born legally a slave on the Island of Cuba. This is where Cinque got his title "Cinque" rather than Singbe; it was on such a phony document. The document exists now in the National Archives. It was part of the court testimony and part of the court evidence for the case, so it's pretty interesting to track it that far.

In Havana, these people were put aboard this small vessel called the *Amistad* that did the work that tractor trailers do for us today, carrying every commodity of household life. Additionally, aboard the

Amistad, in addition to the fifty-three Africans, there were literally tons of cargo—barrels of olive oil, boxes of property, hardware of many descriptions, umbrellas, looking glasses, books, charts, maps, as well as two cases of sugar cane knives that Singbe and his fellows made good use of, as we now know. The voyage was supposed to last about four days; it was only 310 miles, but it is all to windward, and about two days out—actually, it was midnight between the second and third day, so you'll hear it described differently, because it was after midnight and before 3:00 A.M., as best we can decide—that the Africans took the vessel.

This is a painting that was painted by a WPA artist by the name of Hale Woodruff in 1939 to commemorate the 100th anniversary of the *Amistad* incident. This has always been very much part of the history of the struggle for human rights in this country. Many people have been very well aware of it for many years. The painting takes a lot of artistic license. It depicts the scene in daylight instead of at night, and I think that it really depicts far more violence than occurred aboard the deck of the *Amistad* in 1839—it was June 22nd, that, in fact, only three people lost their lives. The Africans knew that they didn't know how to navigate a sailing vessel. This is like putting me in the cockpit of a 747; I wouldn't know how to get the thing going at all—it is just a completely different technology than works with my background. So they really weren't out to commit mass murder by any means. They knew that there was this dependence on some knowledge on the part of their Spanish captors to navigate the vessel. The first man killed was Silistino, who was the legal slave, property under Spanish law, of the captain and owner of the vessel. He was the cook, not treated very well himself. But earlier in the voyage, he had taunted Singbe and the other Africans that when they got to their destination they would be cooked and eaten. And that threat, while to Silistino was in jest, actually, to someone born on the coast of west Africa who, for many generations had witnessed millions of people being kidnapped by this insatiable appetite of the white man in the New World, there was a very strong tradition that the Caucasian race was consuming Africans. So when Silistino made this jest, it was taken quite seriously. And this is what we think inspired Cinque to risk all and take the vessel.

So, the first man they killed was Silistino, who was going to cook them when they got to their destination. The next man killed was one of the captains themselves. They came up with their sugar cane knives, they killed Silistino, and when they went after the captain, the captain took his single-shot pistol—which was the only technology he had—

and shot one of the captives dead and when that captive was shot, then the other captives fell on the captain with the sugar cane knives. That was the end of the carnage.

Because of this mutual dependence, certainly, the few Spanish on board were easily overwhelmed by fifty-three Africans, or now fifty-two Africans. But the Africans recognized fully that they needed the knowledge of the Europeans to navigate the ship. Two crewmen actually escaped. They got out in a small boat—they were only about fourteen miles off the coast of Cuba—they got back to Havana and sent out word and a Spanish gunboat went out after the *Amistad*, but never did catch up.

They took the *Amistad* about fourteen miles off the Cuban coast and they began to try and navigate back to their homeland which the vessel was really not equipped to do; she didn't have enough food or stores on board. They fell into the Bahamas, spent about two or three weeks sailing around the Bahama Islands, going ashore trying to trade for more food and water. Afraid to communicate with anybody, they foraged wherever they could, but, in fact, had they turned themselves over to British authorities in the Bahamas in 1839, they would have been immediately set free because the British emancipated all people held in enslavement in their New World colonies after 1833.

Again, not trusting what authority might do with them, they continued on their voyage. After about a little more than two and a half weeks, they found their way clear of the Bahama Islands and now they were in the open sea, and at that point, things were getting pretty desperate on board. They were running low on food and water, and after about two months, more by the influence of the Gulf Stream than any real and tangent navigation, they wound up right here, at Culloden Point. They wound up anchored here on the 24th of August, 1839, anchored just—according to the court testimony—fifteen rods off the beach, less than a quarter of a mile, and about twenty of them went ashore and spread out all over what is now very close to where we're sitting, looking for more food and water with the intention of continuing their voyage further to the east.

Chances are they wouldn't have made it, even if they got the food and water; *Amistad* really wasn't big enough or well-equipped enough to make a trans-Atlantic voyage, especially with only two competent and experienced seamen on board. One of the reasons they survived as long as they did, I think, is this man Pedro Montez, who was fifty-three at the time, and Luiz, who was twenty-eight; Montez, in an earlier part of his career, had been captain of coasting vessels and had sailed all around the Caribbean and the east coast of the United States as captain, So he knew the waters, he knew how to navigate and were it not for his individual maritime expertise, I think they probably would have been lost at sea long before they wound up in Montauk. In fact, the night before they saw the Montauk lighthouse, and in desperation, Montez was trying to run the ship ashore because he knew that if they get set out much further, they would probably perish at sea. So, they were trying to run the ship up on the beach, but the tide sent them around the island, and the next morning, they wound up anchoring right off the point.

While they were anchored, they did have quite a bit of contact with some of the locals. The court testimony, again, says that there were only four houses out here at that time—quite different from today. But they did have some interaction with the local people, traded for some potatoes, for some gin, water, and, of course, the locals exploited them to no end. For instance, they paid $17—or one gold doubloon, which in 1839, was worth $17 U.S.—for a barrel of water. You wouldn't pay that for a barrel of water today. So, again, they had some gold on board and it was being rapidly taken from them by the local citizenry. They bought some dogs—certainly not for accompaniment, but as livestock to take with them.

Captain Henry Green was a whaling master, who sailed a vessel out of Sag Harbor. He was out on the East End gunning with a couple of friends, one by the name of Conklin, another by the name of Fordham, and there was a fourth man in there—and I'm not sure what his role was—but he's given the name of Fisher in the court deposition. Captain Green saw the opportunity. There was no ability to communicate at all with these Africans, but in fact, one of them spoke a few words of English, a couple of them spoke some Spanish. There was another crewman aboard the vessel by the name of Antonio. Antonio was a sixteen-year-old-again, he was a slave of the captain, born in Africa suffered this middle passage—but he was sixteen and he spoke fluent Spanish. So, there was some exchange between Fordham, Conklin, and Green about what was going on.

And Green was given to understand that they really wanted to continue their voyage to Africa. He, of course, being a mariner, saw a great salvage opportunity because the vessel wasn't under command by any traditional sense. There was no authority figure on board that would be recognized by courts of law. The vessel was insured for $40,000 when she departed Havana, $22,000 of which was the value of the captives. So, Captain Green thought that there was a good opportunity there if he were to take the vessel. So he promised that he would return the next morning and sail the vessel to Sag Harbor where they could prepare for this extended voyage—a promise he made to the Africans that he had no intention of keeping. Meanwhile, while he was on the beach making this negotiation, the U.S. Navy brig, *Washington*, came over the horizon. She had been out in Block Island Sound sounding the depths.

The *Washington* was operating out of New London for the summer. It was on survey duty adding depth measurements to an navigation chart. And she sees this ship anchored off Culloden Point, which is not a very safe anchorage. So, first of all, the captain of the Washington must have thought, what's a ship doing there? They get a little closer; they see a bunch of half-clad, dark-skinned men running around on the beach; they see Captain Green and his horse and carriage, and a few others; and they think that there may be some smuggling activity going on.

So, the *Washington* felt perfectly justified in coming closer and sending an armed party of four to investigate. They board the vessel, and with that, Luiz Montez falls at the feet of the young officer who's in charge, and immediately begins communicating the Spanish side of the story. The Africans don't have an opportunity to communicate their side of the story in the least.

Captain Green is left somewhat chagrined because the *Washington* tows the *Amistad* back to New London. A lot of controversy as to why that happened. As I mentioned earlier, I think it was 1797 slavery was completely abolished in the State of New York. So modern readers say that, in fact, Lieutenant Gegney on the *Washington* towed the *Amistad* back to New London because he would have an opportunity to claim salvage on the value of the captives in Connecticut courts because Connecticut didn't abolish slavery until 1848. In fact, that's kind of erroneous because it really is the federal court system that decides maritime cases.

I think that the wind we know from the logs of various vessels involved, was light from the southwest, as it usually is in August; it was getting late in the day; the tide was ebbing. He had a square-rigged vessel, the brig *Washington*, and he had to tow another sailing vessel. So, if he decided to go to Sag Harbor as the port of entry for this area at that time, it was about twenty-two miles. He would have had to come here through the tide; it would've been a horrendous thing to do in a sailing ship, just from a navigation point of view. Whereas, all he had to do was fall off the wind and run home into his home port, New London. I am quite confident that that's why he wound up in New London—not to give him advantage one way or the other in the salvage plans.

But, of course, what that did is it made it very difficult for Captain Green to pursue his salvage plan on the other side of the sound, but he pursued it to some extent anyway. At the New London customs house, the vessel was consigned for care and keeping. Then the captives themselves were transported to New Haven. And this is why New Haven had such an interest in this. And for their entire time of incarceration during the court trials, the Africans were kept in jail in New Haven.

The vessel stayed in New London, but Captain Green did make his appearance before the court in New Haven. His claim was dismissed by the judge because Captain Green really hadn't taken charge of the situation; he had arranged to make some future deal, but it hadn't really been consummated, so the court just threw out the claim by Green, Fordham, and Conklin's and we lose their involvement in the case from that point. Captain Green got into farming after whaling, and I really don't know much about his life beyond that.

In 1839, the Africans went through their trials. There was a group of New Haven citizens and prominent abolitionists who rallied to their support, both financially, spiritually and educationally. Mostly centered around Yale, but Louis Tappan was one of the principal financiers, the founder of the New York Mercantile Exchange, now known as Dun & Bradstreet—very prominent citizen, very dedicated to abolition. There was so much energy created around this; as I say, it served to galvanize the abolitionist movement.

Abolitionists in 1839 were a disparate bunch. Some called for immediate abolition with no reparation of the property rights of the individuals who claimed to own other individuals; others wanted gradual elimination of slavery. But the *Amistad* case really served to put a face on this institution, if you will. It was the media event of 1839. Every newspaper up and down the coast covered it; they interviewed the Africans once they could speak English. To many Americans who stood on the fence on the issue of slavery, when they began to see these individuals as individuals—not just as nameless laborers in another part of the country—it served to galvanize the abolitionist movement and give it energy. So, when the Africans found their way home after the Supreme Court case and raising initial funds to charter a vessel to return home, that energy didn't dissipate.

In 1846, the smaller groups that had rallied to support the Africans organized into a larger group called "The American Missionary Association," which became the principal voice for abolition in this country until the time of the Civil War. In fact, immediately upon Lincoln signing the Emancipation Proclamation, the Association sent 400 missionaries into the south to establish schools for the recently freed African-Americans and any whites that would attend these schools. During Reconstruction, a lot of these schools were turned over to the municipal governments and became the infrastructure for the public school system in many rural parts of the southern states. Not only that, some of the schools continue today as what we think of as historically black colleges which find their legacy directly in the *Amistad* incident. This is why a mural stands in the library at Talledega. Another very interesting part of Talledaga's involvement: not only did they put up that mural in 1939, but when they built this library, they put a mosaic on the floor and that mosaic is an image of the *Amistad*, very much like that painting. The tradition at Talledaga is that when you walk across the rotunda in this library, you do not tread on the image of the *Amistad*; you walk around it, because the *Amistad* is a real icon for the struggle of human rights in this country; again, it's not something that Spielberg or Mystic Seaport are partners in the project we discovered—this is a living part of the educational opportunity for people of African descent in the south, and it was really brought home to me.

I've been talking about this at quite a few places. Out in Chicago, I met a man who graduated from Talledaga in the late '40s, and his personal connection to *Amistad*, because he's an alumni of one of these schools, is really quite moving and he said, "You got to remember: Growing up in Mississippi and Alabama after and during the war," he said, "For a black man, the only way I could get an education and become a professional was to go to one of these historically black colleges, and that these schools would not have existed were it not for the *Amistad* incident." And I think that to many Americans, *Amistad* is a very significant part of our history; not only did it occur in 1839, but it has a lasting, living legacy to this very day.

EAST HAMPTON
AND THE CIVIL WAR

Harrison Hunt

THE STORY OF EAST HAMPTON'S role in the American Civil War may seem an unusual topic for this lecture series celebrating the major events of the Town's history. No battles were fought here, and no events which had their inception here had a decisive effect on the war. There are some peripheral connections with several well-known figures of the war, however, chief among them the Beecher family. The Reverend Lyman Beecher served as pastor of the church here from 1799 until 1809, when he move to a new charge at Litchfield, Connecticut. There, he and his wife had two children who were to have significant roles in the Civil War: the Reverend Henry Ward Beecher, outspoken abolitionist and wartime pastor of Brooklyn's Plymouth Church, and Harriet Beecher Stowe, the author of *Uncle Tom's Cabin*. The book's moving depiction of slave life in the South so galvanized Northern public opinion against the institution that Abraham Lincoln, on being introduced to her in 1861, said, "So this is the little lady who started the war."

Other major wartime leaders touched upon locally relate to the Montauk Point Lighthouse. The Light was renovated shortly before the war began, and inside the tower is a plaque installed at that time listing the members of the U. S. Lighthouse Committee in 1860. In a telling reflection of how the war was to split the United States military, the plaque includes two future Union Generals, A. A. Humphreys and Joseph Totten, Confederate General Howell Cobb, and Confederate Admiral Raphael Semmes, remembered as commander of the Southern raider *Alabama*.

The real significance of the war to East Hampton lies not in these connections to well-known figures, but in the effect the struggle had on the lives of the everyday people who lived here. The war was one of the watershed events in American history, and affected the men and women of East Hampton just as it did families across the nation. Virtually everyone here would have known someone serving in the Army or Navy and have been touched by the war in many ways. I will examine some of these local connections, bringing the events of 135 years ago a little closer to home.

East Hampton during the war was a town of 2,300 souls which had changed very little since the turn of the nineteenth century. The population was homogeneous, with only 140 residents foreign-born. With the exception of Sag Harbor, the town was quite rural. The vast majority of citizens made their livings as farmers or farm laborers, raising wheat, oats, rye, Indian corn and turnips (the potato, later to become a staple crop on Long Island, was not yet widely raised). Many other men made their livings from the sea as baymen, whalers or merchant seamen, and most women worked for themselves or others keeping house, according to the 1865 New York State census abstract.

Traditionally, the Town voted for the Democratic Party, to the extent that, in 1860, the editor of the *Sag Harbor Express* wrote that "years ago, scarcely a vote was cast except a Democratic one, and we are credibly informed that the time has been when a unanimous Democratic vote would be polled." However, by the time of the Presidential election in November of 1860 the Republican Party of Abraham Lincoln had made significant inroads in the Democratic bastion of East Hampton. The reasons behind this are unclear, but judging from the rest of Eastern Suffolk they probably have less to do with a deep-seated anti-slavery feeling among the voters of East Hampton than their belief that the South was getting more than its fair share of power under the Democratic Party and that it was time for a change.

The Republicans of the area took up the challenge with enthusiasm in 1860, organizing Lincoln and Hamlin clubs in several locations an holding rallies and processions in Sag Harbor and Amagansett in early November—rallies which far outstripped one held by local Democrats in Sag Harbor in October, if the editor of the *Express* is to be believed (he was, after all, a Lincoln man). Mary Mulford Miller described one of the local electioneering sessions in her autobiographical book *An East Hampton Childhood*:

> I remember a meeting at the church just before Lincoln's election. A row of us school girls sat across the middle of the

church, an if anything was said against Abe Lincoln we would hiss. We must have disturbed the speaker more than we anticipated. Suddenly he stopped speaking and looked down on us and said, 'The hissing of geese once saved Rome, but the hissing of these East Hampton geese will never elect Abraham Lincoln president.'

When the votes were counted, East Hampton had gone for Lincoln by twenty-six votes, and Sag for Lincoln by six. "For the first time the Town of East Hampton has given a majority against the Democratic ticket," the editor of the *Express* crowed on November 15th. "We have carried the Town by a majority of Twenty-six.... Who says the world don't move?" A few days after their victory, area Republicans celebrated their triumph with a "grand jollification" in Sag Harbor. Mary Mulford Miller recalled the excitement of the moment:

Of course when Lincoln was elected president we were all jubilant, girls and boys.... Zebulon Field, a gentle soul who went everywhere with us and was treated as a sort of court jester, used to sing a rhyme in those days which ran like this,
'Solomon they say was a man of great sense
But Uncle Abraham, he could build a rail fence,
And we're hoping he'll build it
So high and so stout
Neither traitor nor rebel won't never get out!'

Following Lincoln's election, Southern states started to secede from the Union and events started the course which led to the firing on Fort Sumter in April 1861, beginning the War Between the States. Local reaction was swift and, unlike that on some other parts of Long Island, decidedly pro-Union. "When the war came there was no division of feeling," Mary Mulford Miller chronicled. "Everyone was for the North...." To show its loyalty, East Hampton organized a rally on May 17 at which a liberty pole—a large flagpole—was raised in the middle of the street in front of Nathaniel Huntting's house. Four days later, crowds gathered there for the first raising of the flag to speeches by the Rev. Stephen Mershon, John Wallace and Lawton Parsons. Sag Harbor, too, showed its support for the Union with a liberty pole raising and rally in early May. An American flag was also placed at the top of the steeple of the Whaler's Church, which was the charge of one of Sag's most outspoken Unionists, the Rev. Edward Hopper. Hopper, now most widely remembered as the author of the sailor's hymn, "Jesus, Savior, Pilot Me," quickly wrote a song in support of the Union entitled "The Old Flag" and sung to the tune "America":

Flag of the Brave and Free
Flag of Our Liberty
Of Thee we sing!
Flag of our father's pride;
With their pure heart's-blood dyed.
When fighting side by side
Our pledge we bring!
We love each tattered rag
Of that old war-rent flag
Of Liberty!
Flag of great Washington!
Flag of brave Anderson!
Flag of each mother's son
Who dare be free!

The Anderson referred to was Major Robert Anderson, commander of the Union garrison at Sumter.

As often happens in wartime, there was a little panic. Jeanette Rattray, in *Montauk: Three Centuries of Romance, Sport and Adventure*, quotes a reminiscence by Thomas Edwards of East Hampton that "when Fort Sumter was fired upon . . . a man came here selling maps, who was suspected of being a Southerner and a spy. It was said he was down to Fort Pond Bay, Montauk, looking up a landing place for the rebels, so they might march straight through to New York. We children imagined how they would look marching through Pantigo. . . ."

As mentioned previously, not all of Long Island was enthusiastic in its support of the war. According to Everett Rattray's book *The South Fork*, Southern sympathizers were found as close to East Hampton as Sagaponack, "just . . . over the line in Southampton Town." "Some of its Democrats were said to have flown the *Stars and Bars* during the late Rebellion," he recorded, "although then as now Washington hardly trembled when Sagaponack grumbled." And while East Hampton residents were solidly in support of the war, some former locals were not. Most notable of these was Julia Gardiner Tyler, the Gardiner's Island native who was married to former United States President John Tyler, a Virginian. She supported the South during the war and, as a result, was unable to inherit from her mother's estate upon the lady's death during the war. Perhaps the most unusual example of a local person siding with the South was that of John H. Hobart, a former resident of Sag Harbor who had moved South. Hobart wrote the editor of the *Sag Harbor Corrector* from Vicksburg, Mississippi on May 11, 1861, to cancel his subscription, telling the publisher to 'keep your infamous abolition newspaper at home. You ... can go to Hell. I belong to the Mississippi 7th Regiment and shall be most happy to meet men who [support your anti-Southern sentiments] on the Battle Field."

Many of the young men of East Hampton were more than willing to take up Mr. Hobart's challenge. Although the numbers who served in the Army and Navy are not fully documented, it appears that around 150 of approximately 400 men of service age in East Hampton did their part during the war. Following the attack on Fort Sumter, several enlisted for 90 days service in the 13th and 71st New York Militia Regiments, in the widely-held but naive belief that the war would be over and done with in that time. Following the rude awakening the nation got at the First Battle of Bull Run in July 1861, the Army quickly began recruiting new regiments to serve for three years or the duration. These regiments were organized under state aegis, and East Hampton boys served in several. Most significant locally was the 81st New York Infantry. Although largely raised upstate in Oswego County, its command had been assigned to Colonel Edwin Rose of Bridgehampton, a former regular Army officer. A number of recruits from the South Fork decided to enlist under his command, forming Company H of his regiment. Among them were 16 men from East Hampton and 35 from Sag Harbor. One, Lieutenant James Wallace Burke, sent a series of letters to the *Sag Harbor Express* under the byline "Wallace" detailing his experiences; his wartime diary was subsequently printed by the same newspaper ninety years later, in 1951. In it, he summed up the local recruits' view of Army service, typical of that throughout the Union at that early stage of the war: "we ... consoled ourselves with the reflections that we had left our excellent homes for a great purpose, had enlisted in service of our beloved country and in that service might expect to see hardships before unknown, and endure trials as yet unthought of."

Burke and the boys of Company H underwent a typical training at camps in New York and Virginia before going off to their baptism of fire during the Peninsular Campaign in Virginia in the spring of 1862. Following this, they had a fairly quiet time of things until June of 1864, when many, including Lieutenant Burke, were killed at the Battle of Col Harbor, Virginia. After this battle, the regiment was engaged in the siege of Petersburg, Virginia, until the end of the war.

The largest number of area residents volunteered to serve in "The Monitors"—the 127th Regiment, New York Infantry, which was almost entirely raised on Long Island. Some thirty-three men from East Hampton and thirty from Sag enlisted in Companies G and K of this regiment. The unit was mustered into service in 1862 and spent most of its time on occupation duty in South Carolina—not a bad billet. The members of the Monitors were particularly proud that, at the end of the war, they took part in the ceremonies at Fort Sumter when the American flag was once again raised over the place where the war began.

Other local men served in a variety of different units. Eleven joined the 11th New York Cavalry; nine, including Captain Henry Garagher of Sag Harbor, enlisted in the 48th New York Infantry; and sixteen young churchgoers from Amagansett followed their pastor, the Reverend Alanson Haines, when he signed up as chaplain of the 15th New Jersey Infantry.

All of the units mentioned above were white regiments, as the Army did not permit African-Americans to serve until 1863. When segregated "Colored Troops" were finally allowed that year, several local African-Americans and Native Americans enlisted, among them the Montauk Stephen Pharaoh, who served in the 29th Connecticut Regiment, and Shinnecocks Warren Cuffee (20th U.S. Colored Regiment) and Stephen Cuffee (14th Rhode Island Artillery). Significantly, due to tribal intermarriage with African-Americans, Shinnecock and Montauk men were forced to serve in Colored units, while members of upstate tribes such as the Senecas were allowed in white regiments.

Even in the colored regiments, African-Americans were not allowed to serve as officers until the very end of the war, so the units had white officers. One Sag resident, George Sherman, transferred from the 81st Regiment to become an officer in the 7th U.S. Colored Infantry, finishing his tour of duty as a major.

As befits an area with such a rich maritime history, there were a good number of local men in the Navy and Revenue Service (the forerunner of the Coast Guard). In 1861, forty-six men volunteered to serve on the Revenue Cutter Crawford in the Port of Sag Harbor, and the following year more signed up for duty on the cutter *Agassiz*, which was headquartered at the Long Wharf. Some twenty East Hampton tars and twenty-one more from Sag Harbor enlisted in the Navy during the war as well. Most notable among them was Oscar Stanton, a career Navy officer who finished his service years after the war as a Rear Admiral.

In addition to Naval service, local sailors did their part in the war effort by serving on civilian troop transports and the merchant ships which were essential to the Union's supply lines. Among these was the steamer *Massachusetts* of Sag Harbor, which was chartered by the U.S. government in 1861 to carry troops and supplies between Fortress Monroe, Virginia and Annapolis, Maryland.

Still other able-bodied seamen from the area took part in an historic effort to block Charleston, South Carolina, to Southern shipping. In December 1861, the U.S. government bought several old whaling vessels from Sag Harbor and New England, filled them with rocks and had them scuttled in Charleston Harbor. Two Sag Harbor ships, *Timor* and *Emerald*, comprised part of this "Stone Fleet." Although the innovative plan worked for a brief time, tides soon cut new new channels into Charleston and the Union abandoned the idea of using Stone Fleets in other Southern harbors.

In many ways, the war at sea hit closer to home than the war on land did for East Hampton area families. Confederate raiders approached as close as 90 miles off Montauk in their relentless pursuit of Northern merchant shipping. Once, the ship *Mary Gardiner* of Sag narrowly evaded capture by a Rebel ship by raising the British flag on her signal gaff. Whalers were especially attractive targets for the Confederates. The Sag Harbor ship *Myra* was pursued by the famed Southern raider *Alabama* off Cuba in 1862, and *Jirah Perry*, another Sag whaler, avoided capture by the C.S.S. *Shenandoah* in the Pacific in 1865. The Sag Harbor fleet can even claim a tie to the enemy side: The steamer *Borosco*, formerly of Sag, became a Confederate blockade runner. She never returned to Long Island, having foundered off the coast of Florida on April 10, 1863.

The effects of the Civil War were felt far beyond its fleets and armies, of course. Throughout the nation, citizens did their part for the war effort. As soon as the hostilities began, women North and South organized Aid Societies to help the soldiers serving their cause. Sag Harbor had a Women's Relief Society raising money for the wounded as early as July 1861. In East Hampton, the Ladies Aid Society succeeded in getting $324.53 worth of clothing for soldiers in hospitals by February 1862. In the months and years which followed they ran ice cream festivals and other fundraisers to ease the sufferings of the wounded boys in blue. And at least one local woman, Adelaide Renken of Sag Harbor, went beyond mere fundraising to volunteer as a nurse with the 127th New York Volunteers. The war was also felt locally in its effect on supplies. Many consumer goods were scarce, preempted by the government's vast needs or unavailable because of blockades and embargoes. "A shortage of luxuries was felt here, as everywhere," Jeanette Rattray recorded in *Montauk: Three Centuries of Romance, Sport and Adventure.* "Cook books of the 1860s advise that 'clean-chopt meadow hay' from Napeague makes a very acceptable substitute for tea; and old people [in a leftover from Civil War times] still maintain that roasted wheat kernels make very good coffee." In response to the shortage of lightweight cotton,"probably the last flax to be raised and dressed in East Hampton was on the Filer [farm] during the Civil War," according to Mrs. Rattray's book *Up and Down Main Street.*

The most dramatic example of the war's effect on the home front occurred in Sag Harbor in October 1862. During that month, Gen. Charles James of the Rhode Island Militia was testing a new type of rifled cannon he had designed. He had three of these guns set up near Conklin's Point for target practice, and attracted quite an audience whenever he fired them. Unfortunately, on October 16, an explosive projectile got jammed in his largest cannon, and the twenty-four-pound shell exploded while being disarmed. The accident killed General James, two of his staff and a French Army observer. Nine local residents were wounded, including former Sag Harbor artillery officer Philander Jennings, Capt. Jeremiah Hedges and Orlando Bears; Bears later died from his injuries.

As the years went on, the U.S. government had a harder and harder time attracting volunteers for the Army. Many men who were willing to serve had families to support and feared leaving them destitute if they enlisted. In response, many towns raised funds to offer a cash bounty to enlistees. East Hampton offered up to $400 to each man who volunteered plus $3.00 per month to his wife and $1.00 for each child. By the end of the war, the Town had spent $35,000 to meet its service quotas.

Not every town was able to meet its quotas, however, and in 1863 the Federal government instituted the draft to get soldiers. The first selection of conscripts in New York, in July 1863, resulted in tremendous draft riots which threatened to spill over onto Long Island. As described in Lisa Donneson's *Guide to Sag Harbor Landmarks*, when Sag Harbor resident Oliver Wade heard that some anti-draft men had made threats against the African-Americans of Eastville (much of the rioters anger was directed toward blacks, who they blamed for the war), he took it upon himself to secure rifles and distribute them among the Eastville residents for protection. When word of this leaked out, Wade himself was threatened. Not one to take chances, he had four harpoon guns loaded with iron slugs positioned in his home on Main Street so as to protect it from all angles. Fortunately, no riots occurred locally and within a week life returned to normal.

The year after the draft riots, the men of the North had a more peaceful way to express their opinions about the war: the Presidential election. The campaign of 1864 was essentially a referendum on the war, pitting Abraham Lincoln and his policies against Democratic candidate George McClellan, the former commanding general of Lincoln's army who was ironically running on a platform offering compromise with the South. McClellan was well-known in the area, having vacationed in Sag Harbor and East Hampton in August 1863. Despite his warm reception at that time and the Town's longstanding support for Democrats, when the votes were finally cast in 1864 Lincoln carried East Hampton by the narrow margin of eight votes.

With Lincoln's reelection, the war continued on to a Northern victory, and its surviving soldiers and sailors finally came home. The local men who returned were saluted by their fellow townsmen at a dinner at Sag Harbor's Washington Hall on July 4, 1865. In the years which followed, these proud veterans kept the memory of their service alive by organizing a chapter of the Grand Army of the Republic, which was the largest Union veterans' group in the country. The members of the Edwin Rose Post, as it was known, organized Memorial Day parades in Sag Harbor for many years and spearheaded the erection of Sag Harbor's striking Civil War memorial statue, which was dedicated on October 24, 1896. The last of their number in East Hampton, George C. King of Springs, died on April 3, 1928 at the age of eighty-five.

EAST HAMPTON:

The Nineteenth-Century Artists' Paradise

Katharine T. Cameron

THE EARLY EAST HAMPTON art colony played a unique role in the formation of this town as a summer resort. I researched this topic in preparing my Master's Thesis in the History Department at New York University so that I came to this work through the history mode, not the art history one. I accepted the fact that there were handsome pictures done here by good professional artists. What interested me more was why such a large and influential art colony developed in East Hampton and what were the connections between the art colony and the citizens of this tiny village on eastern Long Island. I wanted to show how the artists facilitated the growth of East Hampton into a summer resort with a strong artistic component. I did a good deal of my research in that wonderful repository, the Long Island Collection in the East Hampton Library.

There were two very interesting things about the East Hampton art colony—one that it was the most popular art colony in America for almost 15 years—from 1878 to 1890, which corresponds to the town's "Boarding House" era. The other is that it was unique in character among the many art colonies established at the end of the last century in that it was spontaneous and self-generating. Once discovered by illustrators and painters such as Harry Fenn, Winslow Homer, Sanford Gifford, and then the Tile Club, the growth of East Hampton as an art colony grew naturally. Other art colonies such as Newport, Old Lyme and Southampton were formed around a single dominant figure—such as William Merritt Chase at the Shinnecock Summer School of Art in

Southampton. East Hampton had only itself and by its own charm and beauty dominated the art colony era for over a decade.

There are several reasons why East Hampton was so popular with the young artists returning to America after study abroad in the post-Civil War era which has been called "The Era of the American Renaissance." Its popularity was due to a confluence of factors:

1. Proximity to New York City, the acknowledged art capital of the United States.

2. American collectors wanted to buy either European art or American paintings that looked like European art—which at that time was dominated by the pastoral scenes of the Barbizon school. East Hampton's agricultural landscape and the unsophisticated lifestyle of its citizens met these tastes perfectly. Also, painting "en plein aire" was the vogue and the area's clear, bright light met the artist's criteria for painting outdoors.

3. Town was inexpensive. In the late 1870s and early 1880s the boarding houses charged from $6 to $12 a week, including meals.

4. Artists liked to be together. In the New York art world of that time everyone knew everyone else. There was a filigree of relationships that enveloped these young artists through their studies in Paris or Munich, sharing studio space together in New York, working together as illustrators for the many magazines of the time, and, most importantly, through memberships in organizations such as the National Academy of Design, the Society of American Artists, the New York Etching Club, and the American Watercolor Society.

A genuine camaraderie was the mark of the tiny summer art colony in the early days. The artists liked each other's company, especially during the one period a year away from the battle for recognition and the struggle to make ends meet.

A few marine artists had visited eastern Long Island as early as the 1860s. However, the area's attraction to artists was spurred by three events in the 1870s. The first was Winslow Homer's visit to East Hampton in July of 1874. He was already well-known for his illustrations of the Civil War for *Harper's Weekly*. He was charmed by the seaside village and his depiction of beach buggies and a windmill was printed in the September 1874 issue of that magazine. Interestingly enough, he did the preliminary studies for his famous painting *Snap the Whip* while he was in East Hampton.[1] The painting was exhibited at the Centennial Exhibition in Philadelphia in 1876.

Hook Windmill—where North End Cemetery is.

The second catalyst was William Cullen Bryant's publication of a two-volume work titled *Picturesque America* in 1876 which celebrated the beauties of the American landscape. Artist Harry Fenn was chosen to illustrate the chapter "Scenes on Eastern Long Island". The article stated 'Perhaps no town in America retains so nearly the primitive habits, tastes and ideas of our forefathers as East Hampton."

However, the third and pivotal event in attracting artists to East Hampton was the visit of the Tile Club to the area in July 1878. A group of young artists in New York had formed this loosely-knit "club," with an eye to weekly get-togethers. During their evening get-togethers they painted eight inch square tiles with a variety of whimisical pictures, more to poke fun at the current craze for "decorative arts" than for any serious artistic purpose. They named their club accordingly. *Scribners Monthly Magazine* agreed to publish four illustrated articles about the antics of this band of young artists.

This organization has assumed mythic proportions in art history, mainly due to its membership which included William Merritt Chase, Winslow Homer, John Twachtman, Stanford White, Alden Wier and Augustus Saint-Gaudens. However, its purpose was conviviality and good talk about art.

Several of the Tile Club artists had told Thomas Moran what a perfect place the area was for an artist. Moran brought his family to the town later in the summerof 1878. They stayed at "Aunt Phebe" Huntting's boarding house on Main Street. He was the pivotal figure in the development of the East Hampton art colony. Moran's reputation was already established. He was known as the "artist/explorer of the American West" for his work sketching areas being surveyed by the United States government. He had also illustrated chapters about these regions for *Picturesque America*.

Scribner's Monthly Magazine published an article in February 1879 on the group's visit to the area written by a "Tiler." In it East Hampton was referred to as an "artist's gold mine." From that time on artists came to eastern L.I. in increasing numbers.

Moran and his family returned every summer after their original visit and in 1884 Moran built a home overlooking Goose Pond at the entrance to the village. He designed it himself, copying the "Queen Anne" style favored in the current "aesthetic" movement. There were bay windows on all levels, hanging gables, detailed wood trim, and panels carved with sunflower motifs. A two-story livingroom/studio occupied almost the entire ground floor.

The Morans always referred to their home as "The Studio" as did everyone else in the village. A native commented, not unkindly, "The Moran place is about such a dwelling as one might expect to find belonging to an artist." Townspeople and artist alike loved to be invited to the Morans' open house on Saturday afternoons. The Studio became the center for artistic and intellectual life of the town. The evening gatherings there were the highlight of visiting artists' days. The house was always full of guests and the evenings were spent discussing art or in impromtu musicales for all the Morans either sang or played an instrument.

Another reason for the area's popularity was its appropriateness in terms of mood and scenery for the current craze for etching. A common thread among etchers was an interest in landscape studies. Quiet pastoral scenes, tranquil dawn and twilight studies rendered in soft tints of monochrome, and poetic mood studies were the rage. Almost every artist visiting East Hampton in the early 1880s did work in this medium.

Moran taught his wife Mary to etch and she became internationally famous for her work. She submitted her etching "The Goose Pond" to the Royal Society of Painters and Etchers in London for membership and was accepted. They did not know she was a woman and she remained the only woman member of that organization for years.

Her etching "Twixt the Gloaming and the Mirk" is indicative of the boldness and energy of her style. She went directly to nature and drew straight on the plate. She was experimental in technique, utilizing line etching, drypoint, mezzotint, and routette to create coloristic effects. In East Hampton she found the pastoral scenes she loved to draw: the windmills, gardens, ponds, gnarled apple trees, and old houses. Ruskin said that in her "New York possesses the best woman etcher of the day."

Clinton Academy was a gathering place for artists during the 1880s and 90s. The mornings were spent painting out-of-doors. Sketching classes set out for scenic points in great farm wagons, passing at every vantage point an artist working at his easel. Farmers complained they could not get into their own barnyards to milk cows, as the easels and umbrellas were so thick. The artists also found the farmers, fishermen and assorted "characters" of the village interesting subjects for their "genre" paintings. In the evening, the artists would repair to Clinton Academy to critique each other's work.

East Hampton's appeal to artists was becoming better known. Journalists visited the village and wrote for the many magazines of the era about the happy juxtaposition of artists and farmers. *Lippincott's Magazine* referred to the village as the "American Barbizon" and the *Century Magazine* said that East Hampton was the most popular of the adjacent sketching grounds and was a "true artist colony."

The young artists, largely male, stayed in local boarding houses. The best known and most popular was "Rowdy Hall" situated on Main Street facing the Presbyterian Church. Here they played cards, drank beer, and smoked pipes, all considered very daring in those days. When the village elders brought their families to church on Sunday mornings, they watched in disapproving horror as these youthful boarders would "open all the windows, put their feet on the window sills, wave their beer mugs (beer was considered the road to ruin in those days) and sing their most ribald French songs to the pious churchgoers."

One of the most virtuous pillars of the church was shocked to the depths of his Puritan soul by this display and cried out: "Look at Annie Huntting, she's running a Rowdy Hall." Miss Annie took in only male boarders as she did not want to be bothered with women in her kitchen. The house, moved twice since those happy days, now stands on the corner of Egypt and David's Lanes.

The Dominy house, built in 1715, was painted over and over again. It was the homestead of a family renowned for generations for their craftsmanship. Dominys made clocks, furniture, boats and windmills. They also owned and operated the Hook Windmill at the northern end of the village. The current occupant, Nathaniel Dominy VII jokingly complained to the young artists "You fellers git a thousand dollars in York for a picture of my back door and I git nothin'."

Clinton Academy and the Moran studio may have been focal points for the artists' lives but to the townspeople, the Presbyterian Church was the social and moral center of their lives. The disparity between the lifestyles of the artists and the townspeople can be seen in the reply an elderly native gave to an artist one Sunday when he was asked if a drawing might be made of his house. "No, I God no! There can't no-body paint pictures around my house, no on the Sabaday. I God no!" My research of church records showed that no artist rented a pew for the summer season.

"Aunt Fanny" Huntting, a sister-in-law to "Aunt Phebe" of boarding house fame, kept a dairy from 1855 until her death in 1887. She never married, living in a boarding house on the town's Main Street. The combination of her window observations and the tidbits of gossip visitors brought were recorded daily, along with her tart comments. She was painted by the noted artist Edward Lamson Henry amidst her possessions. She too was, as she put it "borne down in mind in consequence of the low estate of relition in this community. The summer visitors leave their religion at home. Surely such things ought not so to be."

However, her worries were not borne out by the facts.

Starting in 1884, the collections at the Presbyterian Church were compiled as a block for the months from June through August. The collections were double the amount collected during the off-season months. The church also began to ask vacationing clergy to preach, augmenting both the attendance and the collections.

A weekly newspaper, the *East Hampton Star*, began publishing in

The Dominy House on North Main Street. Built in 1713.
Many artists painted it. 'You fellers get a thousand dollars
up in York for a picture of my front door and I get nothin.'

December 1885. Almost every issue carried news of the art colony, either their activities in East Hampton or word of their successes at New York exhibitions and sales. During the 1880s and 1890s the number of East Hampton scenes exhibited in the city tripled from the previous years. These landscape artists were caught in a paradoxical dilemna: their paintings were an irresistible advertisement to city dwellers who then descended upon this rural retreat, changing it by their very presence into a fashionable spa with all the trappings of modern society.

The artists were viewed as an exotic branch of the summer colony by the townspeople. The account books of local businesses listed the resident painters by name, but with the appellation "artist" after it. This distinction was not made for the other summer residents. However, the local citizens were proud to pose for the artists. By the same token, the artists took part in local picture exhibitions and musicales to raise money for community projects such as the enlargement of Clinton Academy and for wagons to sprinkle water on the dusty streets.

The *Star* chronicled the artists' social and professional doings weekly. When the Morans held a large costume party in 1890, it merited columns of print in the paper.

The Moran's purchase of a Venetian gondola on a visit to Venice in 1891 was considered a "seven-day wonder" by the villagers and the *Star* wrote weekly reports on its acquisition and shipment to East Hampton. The purchase of this exotic plaything convinced the sober East Hamptonites that artists were truly different from other folks. How could anyone spend $2,000 on an essentially frivolous item! The paper wrote of the boat's voyage to America lashed to the lifeboat deck of a steamship. It was brought by steamer to Sag Harbor, "hung to the davits, it being so long, some 36 feet, that it could not be taken on deck." The Town Pond facing Moran's home was too shallow and inadequate for the boat so he moored it on Hook Pond. George Fowler, a Montauk Indian, who already worked for the Morans as gardener and caretaker, became "quite proficient in the art of propelling the curious craft."

The vacation industry had become the biggest business in the village by 1890. The art colony was as large as ever, but by 1890 relatively few artists rented houses in the village itself as "it has of late become too fashionable and the country around possesses superior attractions and fewer distractions."

Ruger Donoho was one of the greatest artists to live and paint here. He settled here permanently in 1891, living on Egypt Lane. The following year he participated in a torchlight parade during the presidential election of 1892. He and a friend made a huge banner, sixteen feet long and seven feet high, on which was drawn a picture of Teddy Roosevelt, with the slogan "The People's Choice" printed under it. He became active in the community, serving for several years as Chairman and Clerk of the board for the Town Trustees.

Donoho convinced Childe Hassam to come to East Hampton. He first came to visit in 1898, visited each summer after that and finally bought a house next to Donohos in 1919. Hassam would paint many scenes of the old cottages, the beaches and dunes and would love the town the way the Morans had forty years earlier. He said "It has a character all its own, may it never be changed!"

In discussing the early East Hampton art colony and the town's growth as a summer resort, we would be remiss in omitting the enduring contributions of the remarkable Woodhouse family. Lorenzo and Emma Woodhouse and later his nephew and his wife Mary established a legacy of support for the institutions that make up this unique community.

In the late 1890s Emma Woodhouse installed the earliest documented Japanese water garden for a private home in this country.

Open to the public and nationally known, local artists such as Donoho and Hassam made many studies of these famed gardens. They formed the nucleus of the area now known as the Nature Trail.

A later generation of the Woodhouse family was responsible for the building of the East Hampton Library and Guild Hall Museum. Guild Hall itself was the natural evolution of the town's acceptance of and living with artists for fifty years by the time it was built in 1931.

At the opening reception Childe Hassam gave a speech dedicating the Moran Gallery. It was a particularly appropriate gesture as he and Moran were the "bookends" around the most vital period in the art colony's history. Moran was a disciple of the grand, panoramic landscape era of American painting. Hassam was the quintessential Impressionist painter with sunlight, broken brush strokes and fleeting shadows sketched on his canvas. Between them a generation of young American painters had visited this little town. Here they perfected their skills in the Barbizon mode, in a village uniquely suited for their endeavors.

NOTE

1. "Reminiscences of Bruce Crane." Account of a conversation between Bruce Crane and William Whittemore at the Salmagundi Club, NYC on Nov. 17, 1933. Long Island Collection, East Hampton Library.

WRITERS OF THE EAST END:
Responses to a Special Place

—❧—

Constance Ayers Denne

W HEN I WAS INVITED to give this lecture on the writers of the East End, I wondered for a long time how it would be possible to make a selection from among the hundreds of writers associated with this area. Finally, narrowing my focus, I decided to talk about those writers for whom the eastern end of Long Island was a special place. I wanted to emphasize those writers whose art conjured up a vision of the particular character of the East End and who, through their work, provided a record of this unique American place. And the order of presentation? That was easy. I would use the order of time. After all, this lecture is a part of the celebration of the tricentquinquagenary of the town of East Hampton, so an historical approach seemed appropriate.

We begin, then, not at the very beginning, but in 1723, with the birth in Connecticut of a Mohegan Indian who later came to Montauk, Samson Occum. Samson Occum, a preacher and a poet and writer, although a great respecter of tribal culture, was converted to Christianity in 1741, at the age of eighteen. His early years were spent as a teacher in Connecticut, his birthplace, but in 1749 he became a schoolmaster to the Montauk tribe, marrying Mary Fowler, a Montauk Indian. He was ordained by the Long Island Presbytery in 1759. A few years after his ordination, he wrote an "Account of the Montauks," an appreciative consideration of the customs, values, and beliefs of the Montaukets. Occum describes the conventions surrounding marriage and the naming of children; the tribal Gods; the group's perspective on death, burial, and mourning; and their perceptions concerning the future state of the soul. It is altogether sympathetic and, at the same time, a fine piece

341

of writing. Nowadays, one might consider Occum an activist in the cause of Indian rights, for he was adamantly opposed to white encroachment on Indian territory. This had made him extremely unpopular in Connecticut, but he was more effective in New York and succeeded in preserving Indian possessions here. Among his many accomplishments, Occum also wrote a widely-anthologized hymn that is familiar to church-goers of his persuasion: "Awaked by Sinai's Awful Sound" (Niles 7).

A review of his life, which Nathaniel Niles published anonymously, reveals a very interesting incident and an achievement for which Occum gets little credit, for it is not generally known. As a young man, when he was teaching the Indians of Connecticut, he developed the idea for a charity school for Indians. The idea caught on with his superiors among the clergy, and he was sent to England in 1765 to collect funds for this school. He was wildly successful, collecting more than $40,000 from various sources but not from the English clergy. However, it was never used to create the school that Occum had envisioned for the Indians. It was used instead to found a college, Dartmouth College. Niles writes that he was "virtually the founder of Dartmouth College" (3–4). Occum must have been disappointed, but one gets the sense that he probably was not too surprised. In one of his letters from England he had written: "I waited on a number of bishops and represented to them the miserable and wretched situation of the poor Indians. . . . But they never gave us *one single brass farthing*" (4–5). The bishops did not seem interested in evangelizing the Indians. Occum found them "very indifferent whether the poor Indians go to heaven or hell" (5). Despite a slight pang of conscience ("I can't help my thoughts"), he asserts: "I am apt to think that they don't want the Indians to go to heaven with them," and imagining the salvation of some of his brethren, he manages a slight dig: "I believe they will be as welcome there as the bishops" (5).

One year before Samson Occum died, John Howard Payne—poet, playwright, and actor—was born, in 1791. He was not born in East Hampton, for his family had moved to New York City eight months before his birth; but his maternal ancestors, the Isaacs family, had resided in the village for generations, and he was a frequent visitor as a child (Overmyer 19 and 26). His grandfather, Aaron Isaacs, until he was converted by the Presbyterians, was East Hampton's only Jewish citizen. His daughter Sarah had married William Payne of Massachusetts, and their first home was in East Hampton (Overmyer 20–21). It is, therefore, altogether fitting that the small, colonial, salt-box house on Main

Street should have become a shrine to Payne. Now, of course, it is known by the name of the song Payne wrote for the operetta "Clari or the Maid of Milan," which premiered at Covent Garden in the spring of 1823: "Home, Sweet Home" (Overmyer 211). Payne's collaborator was Henry Rowley Bishop, who wrote the music. Clari, a simple maid, is the character who sings the song in the palace of the Duke who is to become her husband, and when she is asked by her maid where she learned it, Clari tells her: "It is the song of my native village" (Overmyer 212). In case there is anyone in the world who does not know the lyrics to this famous song, let me repeat one verse here:

> 'Mid pleasures and palaces, though we may roam,
> Be it ever so humble, there's no place like home!
> A charm from the sky seems to hallow us there,
> Which, seek through the world, is ne'er met with elsewhere.

This and the additional verses are followed by the well-known refrain:

> Home, home, sweet, sweet home—
> There's no place like home, there's no place like home!

Clearly, Payne identified with and had warm memories of East Hampton. When he was nearly fifty and writing to his sister-in-law from Georgia, where he was furthering the interests of the Cherokees, who were being forced to cede their territory and faced removal, he referred to himself as "a staid East Hamptoner" (Overmyer 327). The last papers that Payne prepared for the Cherokees were, he wrote in 1838 to his brother Thatcher: "sealed with the seal given me by Aunt Esther—her father's seal." Her father was, of course, Payne's East Hampton grandfather, Aaron Isaacs. The seal must have contained a Jewish symbol, perhaps a Star of David, for Payne added: "if they [the American Indians] were part of the Ten Tribes . . . the stamp would be a part of the family arms—an omen of our all coming together at last." (Overmyer 322). This gesture speaks well of the influence of his East Hampton heritage on John Howard Payne's later life.

We turn now to another East End village, Sag Harbor. Sag Harbor has a long history of an interest in writing. A Literary Society was organized there, on February 9, 1807. Its constitution stated that all members were to treat each other with decency and respect. The group was "to consist of disputation, composition, declamation and examination upon geography, astronomy, and such other exercise as a majority shall appoint." The treasurer's duties, along with handling the dues and other financial matters, included providing stationery, fuel, and candles. (Members would also be tried for gambling or intoxication and fined for each) (Zaykowski 56).The Literary Society was still in existence in the 1850s and met in the Bethel Baptist Church (Zaykowski 174).

Whether James Fenimore Cooper knew about the Literary Society or not in 1819 there is no way of knowing.We do know, however, that at that time he was in Sag Harbor about to begin a whaling enterprise. He had just purchased a whaling ship, the *Union*, which had been "fitted out for three voyages to Brazilian waters in the next three years" (Beard I. 24). He "owned the ship and two-thirds of her outfit " (Beard I. 43).The system of shareholding was his original idea, but he alone took charge of all the details of the business. Cooper had had a lengthy association with ships. In 1806 his father had "arranged for him to sail before the mast aboard a merchant vessel, *The Stirling*, which carried him to London ... [and] Spain, and back to London." (Beard I. 5–6). He received a warrant as a midshipman in 1808 and was assigned first to the *Vesuvius* and later to the Sloop *Wasp 18*. The latter kept him ashore in New York City. There, in 1810, he met Susan Augusta De Lancey and after a year's furlough "left the Navy forever, though his heart never forsook it" and married (Beard I. 6).

By 1819, Cooper, now thirty and with a wife and children, had settled down on Angevine Farm near Scarsdale in Westchester County, a De Lancey family property. Susan De Lancey also had many relatives in Sag Harbor and on Shelter Island, among them the Derings, Floyds, Nicolls, and Sylvesters, and the young couple were frequent visitors to the East End (Berbrick 6–7). In 1819, Sag Harbor was a major American whaling port. Understandably the ambitious young ex-sailor saw the possibilities and answered again "the call of the running tide" (Walker 10). He enlisted one of the Dering relatives, sold a portion of the shares, hired Captain Jonathan Osborne of Wainscott, purchased outfittings from the Hommedieu family, organized the maiden voyage, and literally waited for his ship to come in. His letters from Angevine Farm reveal that he would set out for Sag Harbor as soon as he heard of the *Union*'s arrival.The results were disappointing, however, and he eventually abandoned the business. He was soon to achieve far greater success as a writer than as a whaler.

The career of the novelist came about as the result of a challenge by his wife. One evening, while reading a novel to her, he threw it aside in disgust saying: "I could write you a better book than that myself." Susan encouraged him to do it (S. F. Cooper 38).The rest, as they say, is history. *Precaution*, his first novel, was published in 1820. *The Spy* followed in a year. In 1823, he launched *The Leather-Stocking* series with *The Pioneers*. Many of his novels have nautical themes, subjects, and settings known to East Enders. *The Water-Witch* (1830), *Miles Wallingford* (1844) and *Jack Tier* (1848), use the Montauk area. Whaling or references to it occur in *The Pioneers* (1823), *The Pilot* (1824), *The Water-Witch*, *Home as Found* (1838), *The Pathfinder* (1840), *Afloat and Ashore* (1844) and *Jack Tier* (Berbrick 15–25; Ringe 11–13).

In 1849, just two years before his death, Cooper wrote *The Sea Lions*. Although it is about sealing, it is set in 1820 and incorporates many of Cooper's memories of his whaling days in Sag Harbor. Melville reviewed the novel when it came out, found it to be one of Cooper's "happiest" and warmly recommended it (Grossman 235). For East Enders, it is of interest for what it tells us about Sag Harbor in Cooper's day:

> The eastern end of Long Island lies so much out of the track of the rest of the world, that even the new railroad cannot make much impression on its inhabitants, who get their pigs and poultry, butter and eggs, a little earlier to market than in the days of the stage-wagons, it is true, but they fortunately, as yet, bring little back.... *The Sea-Lions* (19)

Cooper bemoaned so-called progress:

> It is to us ever a painful sight to see the rustic virtues rudely thrown aside by the intrusion of what are termed improvements. A railroad is certainly a capital invention for the traveller, but it may be questioned if it is of any other benefit than that pecuniary convenience to the places through which it passes. How many delightful hamlets, pleasant villages, and even tranquil country towns, are losing their primitive characters for simplicity and contentment, by the passage of these fiery trains, that drag after them a sort of bastard elegance.... (*The Sea-Lions* 16)

The Sea Lions reveals a little human interest information as well. Through Cooper, we learn something of the local female view of the sailors:

> It may be a little lessened of late, but at the time of which we are writing, or about the year 1820, there was scarcely an individual who followed this particular calling out of the port of Sag Harbor, whose general standing on board ship was not as

well known to all the women and girls of the place, as it was to
his shipmates. (*The Sea-Lions* 14)

There is an additional bit of information about Cooper's association with Sag Harbor that has tantalized scholars for years. It has been
speculated that Captain David Hand is the prototype for Natty
Bumppo of *The Leatherstocking Tales*. Sag Harbor residents thought
so when they read *The Pioneers*, especially because of his peculiar
laugh. Cooper declared him to be fictional. I, however, incline toward
the view that there is a good bit of David Hand in *Leatherstocking*.
Cooper regularly used his experiences in his art, and it is not beyond
imagining that the author recollected and used several aspects of this
colorful old captain in his portrait. It is possible today to visit David
Hand's house in Sag Harbor as well as his grave in Oakland Cemetery.
Captain Hand outlived five wives. His epitaph, which he wrote himself
reads:

> Behold ye living mortals passing by
> How thick the partners of one husband lie.
> (Berbrick 42–43)

East Hampton's first important woman writer was Cornelia Huntington, who lived from 1803 to 1890. To read the introduction to her
Odes and Poems is to agree that she was indeed a marvel. She more
than shone in an East Hampton that during her youth "sparkled with
learning and genuis," according to Henry P. Hedges (9). Hedges himself,
in addition to being an attorney and judge, was a writer with a scholarly bent. He had written *A History of the Town of East-Hampton* in
1897. A lifelong friend of Huntington, he provided the introduction to
this collection of her poetry, which was also a memorial to the re-
cently-deceased author. The poems are various: patriotic, celebratory of
special events (she wrote an ode to commemorate the 200th anniversary of the settlement of East Hampton), lyric, elegiac, and humorous.
One amusing poem, "Woe, Woe, To Thee, Sea Spray" was occasioned by
her reading a rather severe criticism of her novel in a church paper. In
the poem, she defends "that wicked old woman, down on the 'East
End'" (88). Especially delightful are her letters in rhyme, for they contain news of East Hampton in a light-hearted vein and reveal her bright-
ness and wit.

Huntingon was persuaded when she was fifty-four, to publish the
novel she had written, entitled *Sea-spray: A Long Island Village* (1857).
Sea-spray was the village of East Hampton. She published it pseudony-

mously, using the name Martha Wickham, the family name of former residents of her home. *Sea-spray* is a typical nineteenth-century novel of manners. It has a seasonal structure, allowing her to include in her narrative the various activities associated with particular months. For example, in June, the summer people arrived. In winter "Sea-spray was a sad, dull place ... it afforded no resources ... no place for amusement ... no lectures ... no pleasant reading room. ... The great temperence reform had put a dead stop to all roystering games. ... The last great revival had dealt the death-blow to dancing ... and whist was voted out of the village" (*Sea-spray* 148). If one were lucky and Town Pond froze, there was ice skating! The novel describes representative village events, such as holidays, family problems, shipwrecks, politics and elections, and town meetings. Huntington reproduces the speech of the different classes and of Dury, an Indian cook, who serves as a kind of Greek chorus of experience and common sense. Thus, the reader can actually *hear* the residents of Sea-spray.

Early in the novel, Huntington provides a description of *Sea-spray* and its year-round residents in the nineteenth century, after the summer season has ended:

> There was nothing remarkable in the simple, unpretending village of Sea-spray, which stretched itself about a mile from the Atlantic shore, on the eastern extremity of Long Island: the main street lying in a little miniature valley, the rise on either side being so slight as to be scarcely perceptible. There was nothing picturesque in the surrounding scenery: the fields lay in one flat, unbroken level, and there was neither a brook nor a rock within an hour's travel of the street; but the dash of the eternal wave was always sounding amid its solitudes, and the solemn and monotonous roar had, perchance, had its influence in subduing and sobering the spirits of the inhabitants, and imparting to their characters that quiet, unimpulsive sluggishness, for which, more than anything else, they were distinguished.
>
> Stretched far away into the ocean, shut out by their isolated position from any entangling or exciting relations with the busy, bustling world around them, the villagers pursued quietly and contentedly their own usual avocations, and dreamed away a harmless and noiseless existence; dwelling soberly where their fathers had dwelt, treading patiently the paths their fathers' steps had beaten, tilling the same fields, sheltered by the same roofs, believing in the same stern creed, worshipping in the same gray old temple, and finally lying down in

death almost in the same green graves. Still there was a beauty
and a charm in their unobtrusive simplicity, in their perfect innocence of all new-fangled improvements, in their pertina-
cious faith in windmills, and devout abhorrence of steam and
all its noisy abominations.

There was fear now, however, that the spirit of innovation
had begun to creep stealthily among them; the "brushing up"
mania had broken out here and there, and in several places
along the street snug little edifices might be seen, in all the
gloss and glory of fresh paint and side-lights, staring pertly at
their grim gray old neighbors across the way, and turning up
their puggish little portico noses in defiant scorn of the long,
low, rickety roofs that confronted them; barns had marched
sullenly back from the front line, and wood-piles had retired indignantly to the rear, to give place to painted pickets and ornamental shrubbery.

Steamboats, railroads and turnpikes had brought the world
nearer, and the restless, itinerating tendency of the times had
brought troops of seekers after change to explore all the sweet
secluded nooks and shady retreats of Sea-spray, and to claim
and take possession by right of discovery. But those who came
to rusticate and rest—to breathe the pure sea air—to forget
the stifling city heats in the blessed ocean breeze, and bathe
the fevered brow and the languid limb in the dashing ocean
wave, had fled with the flowers and the singing summer birds;
and the deserted haunts of the summer loungers were silent
now, save when the fallen leaves rustled along the paths, or the
wintry wind moaned through the bare branches of the trees. It
was evening, calm and serene, and no sound disturbed the silence, except the sharp stroke of an axe in the distance, busy in
thrifty forecast for to-morrow's fuel, or the slow groaning
wheel of a loaded wagon, late on its homeward way. (9–11)

Interesting as the many descriptive and topical aspects of the
novel are, the modern reader will undoubtedly find herself following
the story line that concerns Mr. and Mrs. Copperly and their two children, Sike and Godwin. Huntington had read the English feminist Mary
Wollstonecraft's *A Vindiction of the Rights of Woman*, and she satirizes
the misuse of her ideas through the character of Mrs. Copperly, who
has "the spirit of Mary Woolstonecraft [sic] in . . . [her] heart" (182). She
is a rabid feminist, neglects her husband and children, talks a great deal,
and she is a writer. She is one of those "scribbling women" of the nineteenth century who received so much ridicule. Her husband is required to take care of the baby while she writes, and he is perpetually

exhausted. Even when guests arrive, she will not interrupt her writing, justifying her behavior firmly: "Those lovely visions of fancy ... are so airy and evanescent—if they are not caught on the wing, gentlemen ... we are so liable to lose them" (171). She is preparing a lecture for the "Association for the Assertion and Vindication of Woman's Rights." Even though her husband is not well, the "shackles of domestic cares" will not deter her (172). Emancipation is her sacred cause. If her husband coughs, she shoves the spittoon closer to him with her foot. Even the suggestion that her husband is dying cannot take her attention from such issues as equal civil rights, political privileges for women as opposed to subjugation, and the evils of male supremacy. Poor Mr. Copperly is an object of sympathy. His wife is no longer what she was when he married her: "The wild notions of the day have ruined her" (176). All he wants to do is die. At the end of the novel, when the author ties up all the loose strings, the reader learns that Mr. Copperly has "laid down the weary burden of life ... only praying to be permitted to sleep and be at rest" (459). The zealous Mrs. Copperly has left him to die, while she attends conventions and carries out "measures for amelioration and reform" (459).

Huntington is satirizing the extremist, the zealot, who neglects family to pursue a cause. She herself seems to have a balanced view of the burdens of keeping house. Her diary entry of December 18, 1826 reveals her pleasure in tasks completed: "I have been busily employed ... in various domestic duties—such as making sausages, candles and mince pies, etc. etc—and now having plenty of beef, port, lard, and tallow laid up for many days I intend to 'eat, drink, and be merry' that is so far as I can do so and sin not." She shows a little more spirit in her diary entry of December 23, 1826: "I have had a party this week and heaven deliver me from ever being doomed to linger through another such a miserable evening. I had rather reap an acre of barley, than to be condemned to be 'Lady Hostess' to people, who will neither afford nor receive entertainment, and I am now fully resolved never to give another party until I am married." Huntington never married. (Although it is not clear whether Huntington was a feminist or not, she undoubtedly would have enjoyed reading Betty Friedan's *The Feminine Mystique*.)

Herman Melville has a tangential connection with the East End. His short story "Benito Cereno," about a slave revolt at sea, was serialized in the October, November, and December 1855, issues of *Putnam's Monthly*. His main source, as Horace Scudder has shown, was Chapter 18 of Captain Amasa Delano's *Narrative of Voyages and Travels, in the*

Northern and Southern Hemispheres. (1817) (Lauter 2454). However, three significant events took place which furnished Melville with additional material for his tale: The Santo Domingo uprising of 1791-1804, led by Touissant L'Ouverture; the slave revolt on board the American domestic slave-trading brig *Creole* in 1841; and the revolt which impinges on the East End—the slave revolt on board the Spanish slave-trading schooner *Amistad* in 1839. Jean Fagan Yellin has demonstrated how this uprising supplied Melville with details for his story. Thanks to Steven Spielberg's 1997 film *Amistad*, the narrative is now well known: fifty-three kidnapped Africans, led by the West African Cinque, mutinied near Cuba, killed the Captain and some members of the crew, and demanded that their Spanish owner, a former captain, return them to Africa, under pain of death. He deceived them by changing course at night and sailing north instead of east. Two months later the *Amistad* landed on Long Island, at Culloden Point, to be exact. Officers from the American brig of war *Washington* arrested the rebels. They remained in jail until the Supreme Court freed them two years later, after John Quincy Adams, former President and abolitionist, had argued successfully that rather than being guilty of the charge of piracy, the Africans themselves had been illegally kidnapped from Africa and the slave-trading captain was therefore a pirate (2500-01).

The East Hampton Star reported on August 6, 1998, that on Saturday, the first of August, "members of the Eastville Community Historical Society and Mayor Pierce Hance of Sag Harbor dedicated a plaque honoring the men of the slave ship *Amistad*" (Hewitt 17). The brass plaque now overlooks Block Island Sound from the lawn of the Montauk Lighthouse, where, according to Jo Anne Carter, the Society's president, more people will see it. Someday, however, it may be moved to Culloden Point off which Cinque and his men anchored almost one hundred and sixty years ago. Culloden Point, Montauk was the site of an event that touched the feelings and the imagination of one of America's greatest writers, and he immortalized the experience in "Benito Cereno."

In 1819, the year that James Fenimore Cooper had purchased the whaling ship *Union*, Walt Whitman, "America's epic poet," was born on Long Island on a farm near Huntington (Miller 65). He had a life-long love for the place of his birth. More than that, he felt that this rural world had shaped him, and he in turn mythologized it as Paumanok. As Whitman's most recent biographer has pointed out: "Paumanake (land of tribute) was the name used by some of the east end tribes. The original deed to the Easthampton [sic] settlers assigned this name to the island, and the chiefs of the Montauk and Shelter Island tribes were styled Sachems of Paumanacke" (Reynolds 19). Of Paumanok, Whitman wrote, in his poem of the same name:

> Sea-beauty! stretch'd and basking!
> One side thy inland ocean laving, broad, with copious
>   commerce, steamers, sails,
> And one the Atlantic's wind caressing, fierce or gentle—
>   mighty hulls dark-gliding in the distance.
> Isle of sweet brooks of drinking-water—healthy air and soil!
> Isle of the salty shore and breeze and brine!
> (*Leaves of Grass* 507)

Whitman is, of course, associated with the entire island but he knew eastern Long Island, for his sister Mary lived in Greenport, and he used it poetically in important and meaningful ways throughout his entire life. Just four years before his death in 1892 he included, in a later edition of *Leaves of Grass*, the poem "From Montauk Point":

> I stand as on some mighty eagle's beak,
> Eastward the sea absorbing, viewing, (nothing but sea
>   and sky,)
> The tossing waves, the foam, the ships in the distance,
> The wild unrest, the snowy, curling caps—that inbound urge
> and urge of waves,
> Seeking the shores forever. (508)

He was no longer living on Long Island, and had settled in Camden, New Jersey, but he still recalled the excursions he had taken on eastern Long Island as a young man and had written about in the New York Sunday Dispatch in the '40s (Reynolds 127). Later there had been other summers in Greenport with his sister, in 1855 and 1861, when he was able to relive his boyhood wandering the beaches and farms, fishing, and sailing (Reynolds 342 and 407).

When Whitman was 70 "in the early candle-light of old age," he wrote a "Backward Glance O'er Travel'd Roads" (*Leaves of Grass* 561). He devotes a section to his early reading. After his sixteenth year he liked to do his reading out in the country or at the seashore. The Bible, Shakespeare, Homer, Aeschylus, Sophocles, and Dante, for example, he read in the woods. "*The Iliad*," he writes, "I read first thoroughly on the peninsula of Orient, . . . in a shelter'd hollow of rocks and sand, with the sea on each side." He was not overwhelmed by these "mighty masters" he concludes, "because I read them . . . in the full presence of Nature, under the sun, with the far-spreading landscape and vistas, or the sea rolling in" (*Leaves of Grass* 569).

The sea always had a fascination for Whitman. In "Specimen Days," an autobiographical work, Whitman describes his boyish wish to write about the seashore: "that curious, lurking something, . . . which means far more than its mere first sight, grand as that is—blending the real and ideal." He writes about haunting the "shores of Rockaway or Coney Island, or away east to the Hamptons or Montauk." He remembers that once "by the old lighthouse, nothing but sea-tossings in sight in every direction as far as the eye could reach, . . . I felt that I must one day write a book expressing this liquid, mystic theme" (Berbrick 150). The Montauk Lighthouse, then, can be said to have given Whitman a seminal poetic epiphany. But he never forgot the real joy of seashore life— swimming, lobstering, eeling, and clamming, and, of course, eating the fruits of the sea. Like Cooper, Whitman also had absorbed the unique people, from relatives to farmers and fisherman he had met during his rambles on Long Island as a boy and in his early manhood. These people became prototypes of the universal characters who populated his future poetry.

It is impossible to read the section of *Leaves of Grass* entitled "Sea-Drift" without feeling the enormous impact that the imagery of Long Island had on the poet's imagination: bird, sands, fields, briers and blackberries, yellow half-moon, waves, lilac, grass, seashore, sun, sea, moon, stars, beach, moonbeams, breakers, woods, spray, leaves, moonlight—all of these appear in the opening poem "Out of the Cradle Endlessly Rocking," (246–63). Elsewhere in *Leaves of Grass*, in "A Paumanok Picture," he creates a poetic painting of ten fishermen haul, seining in the sea, a scene that might have been captured in oil or watercolor by an artist painting on an East End beach (461).

In June 1846, Whitman made a one-day round-trip by railroad to Greenport, from Brooklyn, and in addition to praising the town, the fishing, and the farmers, he complimented the L.I.R.R. and its dining car. (Whitman's may be the last compliment that the L.I.R.R has received). Whitman marveled at the mechanical achievements that enabled him to take "'a flying picnic' a hundred miles away and return the same day" (Allen 77). He made a lengthier visit to Greenport in the summer of 1851. Two articles in which he wrote about summer resort life around Greenport as well as his own vacation pleasures, "swimming, eating bluefish (his favorite dish), and talking and rambling with the country folk, especially unsophisticated ones," grew out of this stay (Allen 111). On one of his stays in Greenport, he had visited Montauk

Point by boat (Allen 77). He knew Shelter Island and Orient, but Montauk Point "was one of Whitman's favorite places" (Berbrick 190). In fact, he could be lyrical about it in his writing, enumerating its beauties:"the soil was rich, the grass green and plentiful, and it had 'the best patches of Indian corn and vegetables I saw last summer' all 'within gun shot of the salt waves of the Atlantic'" (Berbrick 190). Montauk Point, with its lighthouse on Turtle Hill, was a setting that elicited a special response from Whitman, and it comes as no surprise to learn that it is "the only Long Island town honored by its own poem, 'From Montauk Point,'" mentioned earlier (Berbrick 191).

In his "Brooklyniana" Whitman looks to Long Island's past. He recounts the history of Gardiner's Island with its patriarch Lion Gardiner and his Dutch wife. He was especially fascinated by the friendship between the royal Montauk Indian Wyandanch and Gardiner, and he tells the now well-known story of Gardiner's facilitating the ransom of Wyandanch's daughter, a story given a date, 1654, by Morton Pennypacker, whose library is the nucleus of the Long Island Collection. This friendship between a white engineer, Gardiner, and the ruler of thirteen Long Island tribes captured the great democratic poet. Whitman laments the loss of the old settlements, all gone save for Shinnecock and Montauk, the latter of which was in Whitman's day merely a shell of its old situation, when it "was the center of Indian civilization . . . and . . . included the holiest of their burial places." Whitman also describes in detail "the remains of aboriginal fortifications, now called Fort Hill" (Berbrick 179–82). The East End owes Whitman a debt of gratitude for his role as an historian of the area.

Whitman's magnanimous & democratic imagination comprehended all of Long Island, recreated it poetically as Paumanok, and, in so doing, created an epic of America. Real and literary experiences today still resonate with the poetic insights of one of our greatest poets. Those of us who live on the East End pass our lives in the presence of those images catalogued in his poetry and made visible and universal through his art.

The next writer I wish to discuss, Olivia Ward Bush-Banks (1869–1944), a poet, playwright, and journalist, lived here very briefly. She was born in Sag Harbor to Abraham and Eliza Draper Ward. Both parents were free blacks residing in Southampton Township. The Ward family had been free since 1810, the Drapers since 1830. Both of her parents were also descendants of the Montauk tribe. Her mother died when she was nine months old, and her father moved to Rhode Island, where he placed her in the care of her mother's sister. It was she who kept their Montauk Indian and African-American heritage alive (Guillaume, "Olivia Ward Bush" 32). From this "ethnic combination on eastern Long Island . . . emerged an extraordinary woman and writer" (Guillaume, "Introduction" 3).

Throughout her life, in Rhode Island, Chicago, and New York, Bush-Banks revealed her pride in her dual heritage. Although not a resident of Long Island, she was, at one time, "tribal historian" to the Montauk tribe, and, as an adult, she regularly "attended pow-wows and other native gatherings on Long Island" (Guillaume, "Introduction" 7). She was photographed in tribal dress at the 1931 Indian meeting in Sag Harbor (Guillaume, "Introduction" 7). Bush-Banks' play *Indian Trails; or, Trail of the Montauk* reflects her Native American background and raises several issues relating to the extinct Montauk language and to the survival of Montauk culture (Guillaume, Summary). Her poem "Morning on Shinnecock" expresses the nostalgia, yearning, and apprehension evoked by her "African-Indian duality" (Guillaume, "Introduction" 11).

Bush-Banks' work bears a relationship to the best work of the Harlem Renaissance. The character Aunt Viney, in Bush-Banks' twelve *Aunt Viney's Sketches*, recalls but predates Langston Hughes' Jesse B. Simple as she "upholds the validity of traditional (black) values [political, cultural, and religious] in an urban world" (Guillaume, "Introduction" 18). Bush-Banks, like Claude McKay, celebrates the purity of primitivism. Like Charles W. Chesnutt, she records vanishing agrarian folkways; and like Zora Neale Hurston, she courageously preserves in her work regional dialect that might otherwise have been lost.

Charles de Kay, novelist, translator and critic, writing almost a half century after Cornelia Huntington published *Sea-spray*, paints an exceedingly well-rounded portrait of the East End's "restful" resort, East Hampton, in two of his essays. Both articulate his fears of future change.

De Kay had both an East Hampton and a New York City home, and thus was the first of the second-home literary celebrities now so common here. He had been known as the "Charmer of New York" in the 1870s, when he was in his twenties and had newly arrived to make his way socially and in literary circles. Educated in Europe and a Yale graduate, he ornamented salons both abroad and in New York. He knew Henry James, Whistler, and Robert Browning in Venice. In 1876, he took over the post of literary and art editor of the *New York Times* until 1894. In 1899, he founded the National Arts Club and was elected a member of the Institute of Arts and Letters in 1906. He was also art editor of the *New York Evening Post* during 1907 and associate editor of *Art World* from 1915–1917. His obituary quotes an admirer, Robert Underwood Johnson, who thought de Kay was "the master of more branches of knowledge than any man I have ever met—art, science, philosophy, Oriental lore, to general literature. . . . He was not only intellectual but the master of half a dozen languages and of a rare scholarly precision of statement. I doubt if he was ever caught in an error of fact." This is high praise indeed.

De Kay's wife was an interesting person in her own right. Four years after her husband's death, Cholly Knickerbocker chose her as one of his subjects for a series of articles entitled "These Fascinating Ladies," which appeared in *The New York Journal American*. Known as a great hostess, traveler, actress, and an accomplished amateur in all the arts, she was also, according to Knickerbocker, a "live wire." She made her mark in East Hampton as well. She both designed and supervised the construction of the first concrete house in East Hampton for her family of eight lively children. It is believed that Frances Hodgson Burnett wrote *Racketty-Packetty House* about the deKay family. The eight fun-loving dolls who live in the house correspond to the eight deKay children, one of whom married the poet John Hall Wheelock, and Burnett had known the family in East Hampton. It has been speculated that she might have seen the garden that inspired *The Secret Garden* here, but there is no definitive corroboration of that.

De Kay's earliest piece on East Hampton appeared in 1898. It was entitled "East Hampton the Restful." Why is the village restful? Because, de Kay writes: "[P]eople have so far avoided the absurdity of repeating in Summer the same things they do in Winter" ([1]). There are other reasons too: "The law as to the sale of liquor has been enforced; the one man in the township who is charged with selling it in secret has failed and his store is closed" ([1]). And an active game society has discouraged boys with guns, so that at the time de Kay is writing, "robins and catbirds are capable of perching on the cord of your hammock as you lie in the ocean breeze" ([1]). East Hampton is now "peaceful, sleepy, bucolic" ([1]). But de Kay wonders how long East Hampton will retain this soothing atmosphere: "The railway now gives access to thousands, whereas in former years only hundreds cared to brave the tiresome six miles of dust to and from Bridgehampton station" ([1]).

The thought of the "thousands" making their way to his village stirs fear in de Kay's soul.

He knows that East Hampton is the most appealing resort:

> None of the old towns that dot the seaward side of Long Island has quite the same air of quiet and picturesqueness that East Hampton presents.

> Southampton is too crowded and fashionable, West Hampton and Quoque too monotonously flat, Amagansett too straggling and unkempt, Bridgehampton commonplace by comparison. ([2])

Even East Hampton's beach, which is not fashionable, has appeal, for it is a place where "men, women, and children go to bathe without caring for looks or asking what is the correct thing in bathing suits" ([1]). He fears large numbers of tourists. If "large hotels" and "very costly country places" are built, de Kay foresees that "the quiet, home-like, easy-going air of the place will be destroyed and those who know and love East Hampton will regretfully turn their backs and seek some other place where there is a chance for rest and pensive sojourn among country sounds and picturesque views of shore and sea" ([2]).

There is another threat. While the settlers of two centuries earlier, knowing the "severity of nature" did not plant their homes close to the sea, city folks "cannot get close enough" and they are building summer houses "near or directly on the dunes" ([2]). De Kay regrets the "trend of villa building," that is invading both the bathing beach and Georgia Lake and Wainscot" ([2]). Nevertheless, he includes in his essay a lovely image of East Hampton's wide Main Street with its "elms, chestnuts, catalpas and ailanthus trees," its old mills, and its pond, "fringed with willows" ([1]). When he mentions Home Sweet Home, incorrectly citing it as the place where John Howard Payne spent his last years, he foreshadows the subject he will address in another essay five years hence: the emerging architecture of East Hampton. He describes the "very bare, small and simple" salt box and in a challenging tone, adds: "there is no reason to suppose that bay windows, balconies, loggias, turrets, and fancy finials would have made his own home sweeter" ([1]).

Despite the passage of time and the inevitable growth and changes, de Kay still loves East Hampton in 1903. Primarily a paean to the unpretentious cottages of East Hampton, "Summer Homes at East Hampton," which was published in the *Architectural Record*, says a great deal about the life as well as the landscape of the area. Noting the expansive heavens of East Hampton and the ever-present and eye-catching clouds, he provides a loving portrait of the landscape: "A line of wooded hills on the one hand, a low undulation of dunes on the other; here a glimpse of lake or pond, there the blue of ocean served up between two sand hills, as in a bowl; here a wedge of wind-clipped trees hiding a village street, and yonder a long vista of arable lands, pastures and salt marshes—there is the landscape in and near East Hampton!" (21-22). De Kay compares the village to the ocean itself: "so surrounded is it by salt water, so gentle are the fogs and insinuating rain veils that come and go, so constant the breezes right off the sea. Its climate makes one very sleepy the first day and ravenously hungry the second" (28-29). He writes about the "very un-American absence of snap and restlessness in the air" (22). He notes that the individual "walks slower instinctively and turns contemplative" (22). Many different types of people respond to the scenic charms of East Hampton, he asserts: It "is a place where the pressure of anxiety relaxes and the most strenuous begins to dream, where ... people neither labor to entertain nor ask for the excitements of fashionable or merely vulgar seaside resorts" (22). "Writers," he says, have chosen this end of Long Island, owing to its remoteness and beauty, a beauty that does not challenge instant admiration by scenery on a colossal scale, but on the contrary, wins its way to one's heart quietly. . . ." (21).

Finally, de Kay applauds the collective wish of the summer visitors not to build the more costly homes they could have afforded but rather to conform to "the spirit of the place" and "simple living" (22). It is interesting that in 1903 de Kay finds that "the only fear that seems to haunt the summer folk in the old camping ground of the Montauks is a speculation whether the time may come for the advent of those who build great places and try to out-do their neighbors in luxury, thus gradually destroying the informal, easy-going life by the sea which still puts East Hampton apart from many other less fortunate watering places" (22-23). How contemporary that fear sounds and how prescient the warning.

In the mid-nineteen seventies John Hall Wheelock, the son-in-law of Charles de Kay, and an award-winning poet, died. He was ninety-one and had spent part of almost eighty-six summers in East Hampton in "the house in Bonac," the title of one of his poems. He had written that he did his best work in East Hampton. In all, he published eleven volumes of verse, a collection of criticism entitled *What is Poetry?* and, as an editor at Scribner's, numerous collections of the poetry of young unpublished poets. He discovered and was the first to publish in the *Poets of Today* series May Swenson, Louis Simpson, and James Dickey. *What Is Poetry?* includes the essays that served as introductions to these volumes. Together they show the range of Wheelock's interests and his knowledge of the poets of his own day: T.S. Eliot, Dylan Thomas, Marianne Moore, Wallace Stevens, W. H. Auden, Ezra Pound, and William Butler Yeats, as well as the classic poets.

Wheelock was a highly respected editor. He retired from Scribner's as a senior editor after forty-six years there. During his last fifteen years at Scribner's he wrote no poetry, taking up that vocation again only after he retired. He revealed his thoughts about the editing life in an introduction he wrote to his own edition of the letters of Maxwell Perkins, a co-worker at Scribner's and an editor who was "generally regarded as the most far-sighted and creative . . . of his time." Wheelock admired the fact that Perkins was able instantly to recognize "work of a high order." In his introduction he takes the reader behind the scenes and shows just why "Max" (and undoubledly Wheelock himself) was so good as an editor:

> The job of editor in a publishing house is the dullest, hardest, most exciting, exasperating and rewarding of perhaps any job in the world. Most writers are in a state of gloom a good deal of the time; they need perpetual reassurance. When a writer has written his masterpiece he will often be certain that the whole thing is worthless. The perpetrator of the dimmest literary effort, on the other hand, is apt to be invincibly cocksure and combative about it. No book gets enough advertising, . . . or it is the wrong kind. And, obviously, almost every writer needs money and needs it before, not after, delivery of the goods. . . . Through it all Max kept his countenance. (3)

Poets and critics alike valued Wheelock's work. In a tribute to him, which appeared in the *Long Pond Review*, the poet Vince Clemente quotes from a letter of Alan Tate's written on June 17, 1975: "John Hall Wheelock is one of the best poets in English" (Clemente 12). A later tribute, published in *Paumanok Rising* three years after Wheelock's death, reveals the great respect that a number of his contemporaries had not only for his work but also for the man (Clemente 81–113). Wheelock is very much a poet of the East End. In the "Foreword" to *Afternoon:Amagansett Beach* (the book, not the poem) he states: "Much of my work reflects the countryside of Long Island's South Fork and, more especially, of the area comprising Montauk, Springs, Amagansett, Wainscott, and East Hampton, an area affectionately nicknamed 'Bonac' by its native inhabitants" (7). Although Wheelock felt he was not entitled to call himself a "Bonacker," he confessed to being one "at heart" (7). Many of his poems are intimately related to his East Hampton home and the local area "its birds, and insects, its woodlands, dunes, and beaches" as well as to the shaping experiences of his life there (7). For example, "House in Bonac" resurrects his childhood in the old

house that "lay there like a great ship foundered / At the bottom of
green sea-water" (*The Gardener* 69).

He recalls:

> . . . the sound of his father's French horn
> From the little upstairs room, and his mother's gentle
> Irish voice reading aloud to them
>
> from The Golden Treasury or some story book,
> On rainy mornings in the first green of May—"
> (*The Gardener* 76)

"Bonac" celebrates this "enchanted country" (*Afternoon: Amagansett Beach* 12). "Sunday Morning Moment" captures the welcome
silence that comes at the end of the week:"It is Sunday morning,/ From
Montauk Highway no murmur" (*Afternoon:Amagansett Beach* 23).

"Afternoon:Amagansett Beach" describes in loving and perceptive
detail a particular place with a special meaning for the poet:

> The broad beach,
> Sea-wind and the sea's irregular rhythm,
> Great dunes with their pale grass, and on the beach
> Driftwood, tangle of bones, an occasional shell,
> Now coarse, now carven and delicate—whorls of time
> Stranded in space, deaf ears listening
> To lost time, old oceanic secrets.
> Along the water's edge, in pattern casual
> As the pattern of the stars, the pin-point air-holes,
> Left by the sand-flea under the receding spume,
> Wink and blink out again.A gull drifts over,
> Wide wings crucified against the sky—
> His shadow travels the shore, upon its margins
> You will find his signature: one long line,
> Two shorter lines curving out from it, a nearly
> Perfect graph of the bird himself in flight.
> His footprint is his image fallen from heaven.
> (*Afternoon:Amagansett Beach* 21)

Here Wheelock had had his "first glimpse of the young girl
who is now my wife, then Phyllis deKay, as she came toward me
out of the surf" ("Letter to Mrs. Faster"). Their actual meeting is
commemorated in "Aphrodite, 1906," composed in 1974. (*This
Blessed Earth* 18).

Wheelock could be whimsical as well. In "The Beetle In The Coun-

try Bathtub," he describes what is a universal experience for the
dweller in the country:

> After one more grandiloquent effort he slips back—
> Slumping? Oh no, he may be down but he's never out
> (Probably wishes he were); now, pondering a fresh attack,
> He wheels his slender, simonized bulk about,
>
> Fumbles at the slippery surface until he has come to grips,
> Mounts, very slowly, with ever-increasing hope, and then
>
> Mounts, more slowly, with ever-increasing hope—and slips
> All the way down to the bottom of the tub again;
>
> Lies there, motionless, pretty discouraged perhaps? not he—
> It's dogged as does it, keep you chin up, don't take
> No for an answer, etc.—he plots a new strategy,
> The oblique approach. This, too, turns out to be a mistake.
>
> The enamelled surface of his predicament
> Resembles those pockets in time and space that hold
> Sick minds in torture, his struggle is a long argument
> With a fact that refuses to be persuaded or cajoled.
>
> Midnight finds him still confident. I slink to bed,
> Worn out with watching. The suave heavens turn
> Blandly upon their axis, overhead
> The constellations glitter their polite unconcern.
>
> Toward morning, hounded by anxiety, slumberless,
> I post to the scene. Where is he? The enamelled slopes below,
> Vacant—the uplands, vacant—a bathtub full of emptiness,
> The insoluble problem solved! But how? Something no
> one of us, perhaps, will ever know.
>
> Unless he went down the drain?
> (*Poems Old and New* 152–53).

All in all, Wheelock, according to the poet Dorothy Quick, combined "poetic genius, business ability, a warm sympathetic understanding of humanity with a real desire to help and an utter simplicity about
himself and his work" (165).

An East Hampton writer very different from Wheelock was Kip
Farrington, Jr., a Hemingwayesque figure, who published prolifically on
a variety of subjects. In the early 1930s he contributed an essay to

American Big Game Fishing, a fifty-six dollar deluxe edition that proclaimed itself to be a "comprehensive, up-to-date, and lavishly illustrated work of unquestioned authority on all branches of the sport." It
included a contribution by Ernest Hemingway as well, which suggests
something of Farrington's status as a fisherman. Indeed, his *Atlantic
Game Fishing*, which appeared a few years later, had an introduction
by Hemingway. In addition to his love of fishing, Farrington was a great
railroad buff. He traveled widely by rail and wrote at least eight books
on the subject. This great outdoorsman was a keen conservationist, and
on his trips throughout the United States on passenger and freight
trains he observed bird life, ultimately producing *Interesting Birds of
Our Country* in the mid-forties. During that same period he wrote *The
Ducks Came Back*, the story of what he considered to be a "conservation miracle": a non-profit organization, Ducks Unlimited, had increased a declining duck population from 38 to 140 million. Farrington
himself was something of a miracle. He was one of the world's leading
fishermen and held a number of world records, he was salt water editor of *Field and Stream*, and he was called Mister Hockey for his skill
at the game. He wrote a book on the subject entitled *Skates, Sticks,
and Men*.

What about the East End and the writing career of Farrington? He
wrote two delightful books for children with local settings: *Tony the
Tuna* and *Bill the Broadbill Swordfish*. Tony's story, about the danger
of the long-lining and heavy haul-seining of Atlantic bluefish tuna is
somewhat sad and might not do for sensitive children. Tony's sisters
and brothers do not fare too well during the time Tony's large family
spends swimming between Montauk Point and Ambrose Light, feeding
on Menhaden. Bill's story is much more cheerful. In fact it's a romance.
Bill bears a striking resemblance to Fred Astaire. One day, as he swam in
to shore off the Maidstone Club, he hears music, South American
music. (This book was published in 1942. Think of the films of that vintage.) He falls in love with the rhumba, and every time he hears that
music he's "gotta dance." Farrington, in all of his books, is very careful
about the facts, but in *Bill The Broadbill Swordfish* he exercises poetic—or maybe maritime—license. When he charts Bill's migrations, he
has him transit the Panama Canal, which swordfish do not do. However, the author has been seduced by his own aquatic hero and wants
to give him a happy and romantic ending. Bill makes his way to Chile
where he meets Senorita Albacore, another swordfish, and after she exercises her feminine wiles and gets rid of Ronald Remora, the sucker-
fish that has been clinging to Bill's back all his life, they enjoy a

Hollywood ending—they marry and live happily ever after. Bill is still alive at the end of the story, now 1,300 pounds but still enjoying listening to the music from the Grace Line ships that sail off the coast of South America. In both of these books, Farrington expresses his own love of the sea. In fact, in all of his books he communicates a great *joie de vivre.*

Other East End writers who have made the sea their subject are John Cole and Peter Matthiessen. Cole's memoirs *Fishing Came First* and *Away All Boats* have many settings familiar to East Enders. His book *Striper*, which is about fishing for striped bass, is concerned entirely with the East End. Peter Matthiessen's *Men's Lives* gives voice to the East End's beleaguered haul-seining fishermen and their families while at the same time giving life to the saga of the sea. *Men's Lives* was dramatized sensitively by Joe Pintauro and enjoyed enormous success when it was produced at the Bay Street Theatre in Sag Harbor.

Now we leave these male authors and turn to a prolific and cultivated woman, Jeannette Edwards Rattray. If Nettie Edwards (1893–1974) had not been such a willful young woman, the *East Hampton Star* would not be presided over by someone by the name of Rattray. According to Lucinda Mayo, "When Edwards decided in the summer of 1924, to accompany her friend Margaret Arnold to join her businessman husband in China, her father [probably not really wanting her to go at all] told her that the trip was fine as long as she paid for it herself" (71–72). She had just returned from a six-month visit to her brother, who was stationed with the navy in Constantinople. During this time she had visited Egypt and the Holy Land. "The [China] trip seemed out of reach; she was making only five dollars a column for the *Star*. Edwards quickly lined up work as an East End 'stringer' and social correspondent for six Manhattan and three Brooklyn newspapers, and by November 6, she was sailing for the Orient" (Mayo 72). It was on this trip that she met Arnold Rattray. Continuing the practice that she had begun during the earlier trip to Turkey and the Middle East, she sent letters back home to her family and these were published in the *Star*: "Her *Star* letters were full of sights, sounds, and flavors; some of her contemporaries still remember her evocative worldwide menus" (73). The letter that probably created the greatest stir in the Edwards family was the one in which she announced her intention to marry Arnold Rattray. At her father's insistence, she brought him home for family approval, and they married on Christmas 1925. They eventually bought the *Star* from the Broughton family in 1935. Rattray had been writing a column for the newspaper each week, "Looking Them Over," and she signed it "One of Ours," the title of one of Willa Cather's novels. She continued to write her column for fifty years in all, even when she took over the paper as editor and publisher upon her husband's death in 1954.

Rattray's columns are still a delight to read. She was a great traveler and her bylines over the years reflect that. She wrote from Japan, Ireland, Italy, Cuba, the Philippines, Scotland, and Wales, and her columns were often accompanied by photographs of her enjoying herself in some exotic place. Light, humorous, and anecdotal, her writing revealed both the writer and her life in great detail. She once wrote:"East Hampton people who read our paper know every move I make" (Mayo 66).

Rattray was an extraordinarily productive writer quite apart from her contributions to the *Star*. She loved the sea. Descended from whalers, she published a number of maritime works. She collaborated with her father in *Whale Off* to tell the story of how her grandfather and uncle captured "the last right whale on the eastern seaboard in 1907," the whale whose skeleton is in the American Museum of Natural History" (Mayo 66). Both *Ship Ashore!:A Record of Maritime Disasters off Montauk and Eastern Long Island, 1640-1955*, and *The Perils of the Port of New York:Maritime Disasters from Sandy Hook to Execution Rocks* have received high praise. Lloyd Becker has called them "two essential studies of Long Island maritime history ... [but] ... not history in the traditional sense. Rather she has left us a series of facts, myths, eye-witness accounts, passages from old journals and diaries, ships manifests, family legends, rosters of forgotten life-saving stations, reminiscences of retired seamen and excerpts from old newspapers.... [T]hey reaffirm the mythical presence of Paumanok" (39). Becker credits Rattray with revealing the "living soil of Long Island" in a poetic way, as did Walt Whitman, with preserving the "actual voices of people who lived the events," and with "keeping essential human events alive" (40).

As a local historian she is unsurpassed. Her *East Hampton History, Including Genealogies of Early Families*, which she dedicated to Judge Henry P. Hedges, her inspiration, is an invaluable synthesis of earlier histories, town records, and a variety of memoirs. It brings the history of East Hampton up to date (1953) in a definitive way. It also contains some evocative and poetic writing: "The wild geese flying over in a V against the moon, and their lonesome honking over by Hook Pond in the early spring; the peepers' sleighbells ringing from the swamp 'down Egypt'; the first fragrant arbutus hidden away under the dead leaves at Northwest; the salty smell of the ocean and the roar of waves when the wind is east—all these mean East Hampton and home" (Mayo 68). Her earlier *Three Centuries in East Hampton*, while briefer, has fine illustrations. Rattray's eye for interesting illustrations serves her well in *Fifty Years of the Maidstone Club, (1891-1941)*. (There is an eye-catching photograph of the dapper John Drew, after whom this theatre is named, at the 1914 Village Fair.) *Up and Down Main Street* is the product of formidable research. Again, beautifully illustrated, it tells the lore of every house and family, and it is replete with anecdotes and quotations—"an informal history of East Hampton and its old houses," according to Rattray (5). She once wrote in a "Looking Them Over" column: "We must not let East Hampton change too rapidly. We who have known it always appreciate its permanence all the more" (Mayo 67-68). In *Up and Down Main Street*, Rattray gives the street a literary permanence.

In a work titled *East Hampton Literary Group* Rattray writes about five distinguished writers, all newspapermen, who summered in East Hampton in the 1920s: Ring Lardner, Grantland Rice, Percy Hammond, Irvin S. Cobb and John N. Wheeler. She manages to bring them to vivid life through her humorous anecdotes. One story she tells concerns Ring Lardner. In one of his books he "took a crack at the Long Island Lighting Co." or its 1920 equivalent in Great Neck. Asked why he had chosen that particular town as his home, he explained that his wife "had lived all her life ... at the corner of Broadway and 42nd Street and she was sick of the bright lights. ... So I asked a prominent realtor to recommend a town where there would be no danger of being blinded by electricity." Lardner was told by the realtor, in effect, not to worry: "If the weather report reads Cloudy, or Light southwest winds, the current becomes so affected" that one does not have to worry about light (2).

Both of Rattray's sons became writers. Everett T. Rattray was editor of the *Star* from 1958 to 1980 and both editor and publisher from 1974 to 1980. His book *The South Fork* carries on the Rattray tradition of informal but thorough and informed history. After his death, at the age of 47, his novel, *The Adventures of Jeremiah Dimon: A Novel of Old East Hampton*, was published, allowing the reader to see the town of 100 years ago through the eyes of one who had the gift to transport the reader back in time. David Rattray did not make East Hampton his permanent home, nor did he write about it. However, at his mother's death, he wrote a poem about that event in the spring of 1974 and describes a picture she kept at the head of her bed. It was of the Summer

Palace near Peking, which she had visited fifty years before on the trip during which she had met her husband (Mayo 66). A daughter-in-law, Helen Seldon Rattray, today carries on the family tradition, delighting readers with her weekly column "Connections," about her life in East Hampton.

If Everett and Helen Rattray were famous locally, another writing couple living in East Hampton at the time had national reputations: A. J. Liebling and Jean Stafford. Their house in Springs, at 929 Fireplace Road, belonged to Liebling. He had purchased it in 1952 during an earlier marriage. There were thirty-one acres around the house, and Liebling loved both the house and the land: "One of his favorite self-indulgences was to lie on his back in the field behind the house savoring his property" (Roberts 336). When they met in 1956, Liebling was "five-foot-nine-and-a half and 243 pounds" (Roberts 319). This is significant because his obesity would lead to his premature death, in 1962, and it also highlighted the contrast between Stafford's and some of her friends' attitudes toward her new love. Her friends found him very unattractive. Eve Auchincloss describes Liebling as wearing "his pants below the belly" (Roberts 326). But Stafford was attracted by his lack of good looks. Another friend, Eileen Simpson, recalls Stafford's delighting in his being "positively ugly" (Roberts 327).

It is true that Liebling loved food. Janet Malcolm once said: "He was not an epicure. He just ate. He'd go to a French restaurant and eat a great meal, then, on his way back to the office, have a Boston cream pie" (Roberts 337). He really did not believe in denying his body. Quite the reverse. His biographer Raymond Sokolov wrote: "To eat and overeat was . . . a badge of freedom. His belly was the outward and visible sign of an inward and manly grace" (Roberts 337). Significantly, his last book, "a memoir of a great eater's best times in Paris before the war," is entitled *Between Meals: An Appetite for Paris* (Sokolov x). In it, Liebling defines eating: "I use the verb 'to eat' here to denote a selective activity, as opposed to the passive acceptance and regular renewal of nourishment, learned in infancy. An automobile receiving fuel at a filling station or an infant at the breast cannot be said to eat, nor can a number of people at any time in their lives" (Liebling 632).

Liebling was delightful company, courted Stafford lavishly, and she fell deeply in love with him. Each had a great admiration for the other's work, but each had problems of addiction. Stafford was drinking at the time and found in this man of gargantuan appetite a mate who would not deter her from her own indulgences. They courted for three years and married on April 3, 1959 (Goodman 267). A few years later the long

honeymoon was definitely over. He began to think that she was drinking too much; she thought he was eating too much. Both were correct.
He developed a life-threatening obesity along with depression, and it
was no surprise when he died in New York City, December 28, 1963, at
the age of fifty-nine. Liebling and Stafford had been married only three
years. Stafford buried Liebling's ashes in Green River Cemetery in
Springs under a black slate headstone carved with a fleur-de-lis
(Roberts 346).

Stafford made Fireplace Road her residence until her death fifteen
years later. She worked on improving the livability of the very plain
house and property. She once rented a renovated outbuilding to Wilfred Sheed. Domestic life appealed to her: "I'm a compulsive house-
keeper. I even go into corners with Q-tips" (Hulbert 345). However,
that was really an escape, for she was drinking, depressed, and reclu-
sive. One of her neighbors, Eleanor Hempstead, noticed that although
Stafford played at living the country life, she stayed inside the house
most of the time. She did not drive and had to use Schaefer's Taxi to go
shopping. Her few friends included her *New Yorker* colleagues
Howard Moss, Berton Roueche, and Saul Steinberg as well as Jeannette
Rattray, but she especially cultivated a number of her neighbors, especially those she felt were real Bonackers. Reflective of her lack of productivity at this time, one of her wall decorations was a quote from
Thomas DeQuincy: "If once a man indulges himself in murder, very
soon he comes to think little of robbery, and from robbing he next
comes to drinking and Sabbath-breaking, and from that to incivility and
procrastination" (Roberts 351).This seems an especially apt apothegm
for a writer who was not writing.

Some of you may recall the tragic balloon incident that took place
in the fall of 1970 and began in a field near Stafford's house. As the
three adventurers who planned to cross the Atlantic waited for acceptable weather, they were invited to join Stafford each evening for
drinks. In fact, before the launch on September 20, they had been
drinking brandy with Stafford all night. Little more than a day after finally leaving Springs, the balloon went down off Newfoundland, and
the crew was never heard from again (Roberts 376–77).

In poor health for much of the time she lived in Springs, Stafford
once described herself in a summer letter to the *East Hampton Star* as
"cross as a bear" and annoyed by the influx of summer people (Goodman 294).The life of the community though was supportive during the
70s. She lunched at Bobby Van's. She spoke at a commencement at
Southhampton College. She gave readings at the Guild Hall (Roberts

384). Despite her insistence on privacy, once she even opened her house for a Guild Hall-sponsored house tour (Goodman 300). During all these years, as Stafford was becoming more and more difficult and alienating her friends, her faithful, cheerful and uncritical cleaning lady, a pure Bonacker by the name of Josephine Monsell, was especially caring. When Stafford died, in 1979, she left her entire estate to Mrs. Monsell. Stafford's ashes are also buried in Green River Cemetery, next to Liebling's. She has a snowflake on her black slate slab (Roberts 413). If one makes the pilgrimage to their graves, one should bring: "bittersweet and holly in the autumn, roses and daisies in the summer," which the "Widow Liebling" used to bring to her husband's grave (Roberts 351).

Of course, one cannot survey the subject of the literary Hamptons without describing Bobby Van's of the 1960s, the watering hole for many famous writers of our own time. In the July 1998 issue of *Hamptons Country*, Elaine Benson reports on a gathering that was held at the second incarnation of Bobby Van's, right across the street from the legendary Bobby Van's, which had hosted the group of writers that formed the "Hamptons' version of the Algonquin in the early 70s" (61). It was the day of annual John Steinbeck Book Fair, the 21st held for the benefit of Southhampton College. Incidentally, the Nobel Prize winner John Steinbeck is intimately associated with Sag Harbor. *The Winter of Our Discontent*, which is about the Hawley family of New England, is a veiled rendition of Sag Harbor life. The protagonist of *Travels with Charlie* leaves Sag Harbor and finally comes home to it. In a memoir that Benson wrote a few years ago for *Whelks Walk Review* about how her gallery in Bridgehampton came about, she notes that the Book Fair, which she created and has been hosting for over two decades," has been called "the start of the summer season" by the *New York Times*, and adds modestly: "I think that is an exaggeration, but who am I to correct the *New York Times*?" (58).

The spring 1998 lunch at Bobby Van's included James Salter, who was to be given the annual award that day for *Burning the Days*, Peter Matthiessen, Joseph Heller, Shana Alexander, and Wilfred Sheed. Leaving the party to their privacy and laughter (Mattiessen had broken them up with a saying of his father's: "Halitosis is better than no breath at all.") before they later joined the other writers at the gallery, "90 area writers, all of whom had published within the past year," Benson begins to reflect on when it all began—"this concentration of creative people drawn, as if magnetized, to an ocean-bordered strip of land 100 miles from New York City?" (61). She notes that the "heyday" began after World War II. The names she mentions, of course, are a roster of familiar celebrities, among them George Plimpton, Patsy Southgate, Peter Mattiessen, Irwin Shaw, James Jones, all newly arrived from Paris. She speculates that the "'writers' club' may have found its inception through the gregarious Willie Morris," who had moved to Bridgehampton around the same time that Bobby Van opened his restaurant (62). It was the 70s and many writers found a home in the inviting saloon: Truman Capote; Wilfred Sheed; Miriam Ungerer, Sheed's wife and a food writer for the *New York Times*; and Gloria and James Jones, to name just a few. Fortunately, we have *New York Days*, a memoir by Morris, which gives us a glimpse of those heady days.

New York Days reveals that a significant part of Morris' life was spent on the East End. He first knew it when it was "on the precipice of becoming riotous" (292). The riotous times took place in the 70s, the Bobby Van era that Elaine Benson refers to, when Morris would "come to know and spend time with some of the nation's finest writers who would choose out of love for this land to live here" (292). Morris lists these writers and they are a stellar group indeed: Peter Matthiessen, Joseph Heller, Jean Stafford, Shana Alexander, Kurt Vonnegut, Jr., Wilfred Sheed, Betty Friedan, Budd Schulberg, John Knowles, Craig Claiborne," as well as Truman Capote, and James Jones (292). This luminous group more than outnumbered the celebrities he had known earlier, among them Scottie Fitzgerald, whom he had driven around the East End as she searched for Sayre family connections, her mother having been born Zelda Sayre. Together they had found Sayre's Path in East Hampton, which they believed was named for her mother's forebears, early settlers in the vicinity (292).

Morris tells some wonderful stories about George Plimpton but they are, for the most part, set, not on the East End, but in Paris or Manhattan or in Plimpton's east Seventy-second Street apartment on the East River. However, Morris spent a great deal of time on the East End with his closest friend, James Jones, in their favorite meeting place, Bobby Van's. The Jones family actually lived in Paris on the Ile St.-Louis, but they came to the East End each summer and rented a "ranch-style extravaganza" near Three Mile Harbor (295). Before Jones' death, however, they bought a place in Sagaponack, which he christened Spud Farm.

Morris tells us that Jones had been searching all his life for a "nice quiet dimly lit old infantry-man's dream of a bar somewhere" (299). He found it in Bobby Van's. Morris describes that extinct saloon and it should be on the record: Bobby Van's was "an angular structure on

Main Street in Bridgehampton with dark paneling, Tiffany lamps, and old fans suspended from an undistinguished ceiling, a long mahogany bar, and from the back the flickering of candles on small booths and tables covered with red tablecloths" (299). Jones, who had only a few years left, loved the bar and he would sit at it "stirring vinegar and a dab of mustard for his hamburger and taking books and writers and passing the time of day with his admirers" (299).

When Morris resigned the editorship of *Harper's Magazine*, which had been a difficult and traumatic decision, he moved to the East End. He was thirty-seven years old, facing the question of what to do with the rest of his life. In great pain, he sought the place he "had grown to love, and settled in a wing of a sprawling old house on an inlet of the ocean" (365). It was winter. There was snow on the ground. Nights were long and silent. Morris writes: "I gazed interminably out the window upon the hushed landscapes, the frozen inlet, the Canada geese in V formation, trying to put things into some larger piece" (365-66). He describes his mood as "bereft" (366). In his loneliness he "took long walks in that sequestered terrain, past a derelict concrete pillbox or two built against the Nazis in the previous war, to the sand dunes in the snow and the desolate winter beach, the gulls and scurrying little terns, and as far as the eye could see the gray wintry Atlantic breakers" (366). The landscape seems to mirror his spiritual state. Finally, he finds hope and begins to heal.

It is always interesting to see a writer from the perspective of another writer. In *New York Days*, Willie Morris, who got to know him well, writes about running into Truman Capote on the East End: "One day I am strolling up the sidewalk on the main street of Bridgehampton on a Saturday afternoon. An enormous Buick with a small man, so small that his nose barely rises above the dashboard, as in the 'Kilroy Was Here' drawings of World War II, stops before me. 'Hop in and let's ride around and *gossip*" (292-93). Morris jumps in. "We are around the block and toward the ocean. Finally we are traveling in long widening circles about the dunes and potato fields" (293). All this time gesturing, "dramatically" and paying "little attention to the road," Capote is talking about lunching in La Cote Basque, the Four Seasons, and the Plaza and who was there and what famous person is having an extramarital affair. It is a harrowing experience. The reader can almost feel Morris' relief when Capote "negotiates the turn at Church Lane" (293).

Capote was not always this exhilarated. There was his other side. Sadly, Morris says that Capote "often seemed lost and afraid" and adds that he "drove him home from Bobby Van's saloon in Bridgehampton a number of times," as much out of a feeling of protectiveness as of friendship (295). Morris notes a feature of Capote's residence that one hopes gave this increasingly frail writer a measure of distraction: "One heard the roar of the ocean from his house" (295).

There *were* happy times, however. Capote wrote a delightful "Foreword" to *The Potato Book*, by Myrna Davis, a book of potato lore and recipes. This foreword captures Capote's delight in his home in Sagaponack, but, interestingly, is prophetic of the future:

> I live in Sagaponack by the sea [which he did, for twenty years]. The house, which I love, sits smack in the middle of potato fields. In Fall, when harvesting is done and the tractors are gone from the fields, I amble out through the empty rows collecting small, sweet, leftover potatoes for my larder.
>
> Imagine a cold October morning. I fill my basket with found potatoes in the field and race to the kitchen to create my one and only most delicious ever potato lunch. The Russian Vodka—it must be 80 proof—goes into the icebox to chill. The potatoes into the oven to bake. My breathless friend arrives to share the feast. Out comes the icy vodka. Out comes a bowl of sour cream. Likewise the potatoes, piping hot.
>
> We sit down to sip our drinks. We split open steaming potatoes and put on some sour cream. *Now* I whisk out the big tin of caviar, which I have forgotten to tell you is the only way I can bear to eat a potato. Then caviar—the freshest, the grayest, the biggest Beluga—is heaped in mounds on the potato. My friend and I set to. This simple tribute to the fruit of Eastern Long Island farming makes an exhilarating country lunch, fuels the heart and soul and empties the pocketbook.
>
> Some of the potato fields, so beautiful, flat and still, may not be here next year. And fewer the year after that. New houses are steadily popping up to mar the long line where the land ends and the sky begins (7).

Like so many other East End writers, Capote injects an elegiac note into his celebration of this special world.

In 1986, Robert Long published *Long Island Poets*, an anthology of poets of the South Fork. Each poet was asked to submit some poems and "to contribute a statement on the relationship of his or her work to the immediate environment" (6). The comments as well as the poetry of some of these distinguished poets reveal the vitality of the East End as a source of inspiration. For example, James Schuyler, who lived there in the sixties, wrote a great deal of his work "in the Fairfield Porters' house on South Main Street in Southampton" (157). The poems he selected for *Long Island Poets* focus on the view he had from different windows of the house. "In January" offers a winter scene, an unusual subject for the poets of the East End:

> The yard has sopped into its green-grizzled self its new year
> whiteness.
> A dog stirs the noon-blue dark with a running shadow and
> dirt smells cold and doggy
> As though the one thing never seen were its frozen coupling
> with the air that brings the flowers of grasses.
> And a leafless beech stands wrinkled, gray and sexless—all
> bone and loosened sinew—in silver glory
> And the sun falls on all one side of it in a running glance,
>   a licking gaze, an eye-kiss
> And ancient silver struck by gold emerges mossy, pinkly
>   lichened where the sun fondles it
> And starlings of the anthracite march into the east with rapid
> jerky steps pecking at their shadows. (161–62)

When Harvey Shapiro was looking through his work to choose a few poems for *Long Island Poets*, he was surprised to find how much the eastern shore of Long Island had inspired him. He "started coming out to the east end [in 1960], and ... spent more vacations either on the north or south forks than anywhere else in my adult life (177). However, for fifteen years he vacationed in the dunes of Amagansett and many of his poems suggest that source. "At the Shore" creates a familiar experience: "The bugs batting against the lamp, the midges,/ in an old house, in summer" (178). In "July," he describes the "eastern sky . . . streaked with red" where "[l]inkages of bird song make a floating chain/ In a corner of the world, walled in by ocean and sky" (179). Poetically he finds humor in the to-and-fro situation of the second-home owner in his poem "Montauk Highway:" "Murderous middle age is my engine" (181). In "Riding Westward" he confronts traffic and death:

> It's holiday night
> And crazy Jews are on the road,
> Finished with fasting and high on prayer.
> On either side of the Long Island Expressway
> The lights go spinning
> Like the twin ends of my tallis.
> I hope I can make it to Utopia Parkway
> Where my father lies at the end of his road. (180)

And dual elegiac notes creep into "Battlements" a poem on the death of a friend and set at Louse Point. He writes: "Summer eternal, though after we go,/ it may all be paved over" (179). In an earlier poem, published elsewhere, Shapiro celebrates a beach in Montauk in "Ditch Plains Poem":

> To be there when day breaks on the sea's reaches,
> The full moon still hung there. At Ditch Plains,
> For example, before the surfers appear,
> Water over rock and gravel. Shingle sound.
> Beautiful enough in this end of July
> Drought of fish to make me stand there,
> Hungry for a text—in the water, on the sand.
> Something to bring back to my desk like
> Beach glass or polished stone. I want
> My happiness to be visible.
> I want to bless this day with meaning.
> Let the rest of my life take care of itself
> So long as it can hover there. (*Street Magazine* 49)

George Bradley contributed a poem entitled "Walking Sag Beach" to *Long Island Poets*. It is a thoughtful and lengthy poem on the metamorphosis of the poet in communion with the ocean. Stanza Five is the final one:

> Walk to the step-off on Sag Beach and you
> Have reached a place where you cannot proceed,
> Where you are offered endless evasions
> On each hand, but of progress make no more
> Than you could make walking the ocean floor
> Or waving your arms to fly off to Spain.
> There comes the point where you go no further,
> Where you reach the end of your world, alone
> As the last man must someday be, with space
> Soaring off to the distant horizon
> And all that color floating in your brain—
> Azure, cerulean, gun-metal blue—
> As if the sea and sky sluiced right through you,
> Poured into your eyes with a pounding sound
> Like breakers crashing in over the bar,
> As if you could feel an ocean sweeping
> Your mind as the sea does this crumbling shore,
> Shifting your configuration, bearing
> You away and adding chance accretions,
> Changing you once and forever and yet
> Leaving you recognizably the same,
> The way the beach seems the same one morning
> When you come to see what the night has done,

Come to stand awhile in the undertow
And gaze again off into nothingness,
Left with hardly a thought to call your own,
With the breeze and cries of the birds, filled
As if with waves by ideas of the sea. (25-26)

Grace Schulman of Manhattan and Springs sees "things of the natural world as metaphors for human deeds and principles" (150). Her remarks in *Long Island Poets* reveal an imagination that abstracts and invests meaning as it encounters and contemplates the local landscape: "From my studio window . . . I see trees whose names speak of life (*arbor vitae*) and death (hemlock). Their gestures recall human actions: branches of the Norwegian spruce are extended majestically, in command; those of the blue spruce hold votive candles, as in prayer. As strangers exchange greetings, hickories touch branches across the road" (150). Her poem "The Marsh" "deals with the disintegration of a marriage, portrayed in vines that are hooked into elms for survival" (150-51).

For years nothing grew
in acid soil
near my house
that stood on scant legs.
Then, year by year, I saw
sassafras and glassiwort;
creepers curled around
bayberry trees,
tall stalks hunted soil
to live. Nearby, shadblow trees
with striated, gunmetal bark
lifted wiry branches.
Then fires of wind and water
burned the marsh;
only bare vines,
hooked into elms,
survived,
as we had, joined
together, in the house
on bulldozed sandy ground,
draggled, storm-blown,
still holding fast
to memories of dense grasses
and green vines
as if we knew life's law
was cleave or die. (152-53)

Paris Review published Schulman's most recent poem about the East End. "American Solitude" is set in Springs and focuses on the three derelict gas tanks in front of the Springs General Store:

Hopper never painted this, but here
on a snaky path his vision lingers:

Three white tombs, robots with glassed-in faces
and meters for eyes, grim mouths, flat noses,

lean forward on a platform like strangers
with identical frowns scanning a blur,

far off, that might be their train.
Gas tanks broken for decades fact Parson's

smithy, planked shut now. Both relics must stay.
The pumps have roots in gas pools, and the smithy

stores memories of hammers forging scythes
to cut spartina grass for dry salt-hay.

The tanks have the remove of local clammers
who sink buckets and stand, never in pairs,

but one and one and one, blank-eyed, alone,
more serene than lonely. Today a woman

rakes in the shallows, then bends to receive
last rays in shimmering water, her long shadow

knifing the bay. She slides into her truck
to watch the sky flame over sand flats, a hawk's

wind arabesque, an island risen brown
Atlantis, at low tide; she probes the shoreline

and beyond grassy dunes for where the land
might slope off into night. Hers is no common

emptiness, but a vaster silence filled
with terns' cries, an abundant solitude.

Nearby, the three dry gas pumps, worn
survivors of clam-digging generations,

are luminous, and have an exile's grandeur
that says: in perfect solitude, there's fire.

One day I approached the vessels
and wanted to drive on, the road ablaze

with dogwood in full bloom, but the contraptions
outdazzled the road's white, even outshone

a bleached shirt flapping alone
on a laundry line, arms pointed down.

High noon. Three urns, ironic in their outcast
dignity—as though, like some pine chests,

they might be prized in disue—cast rays,
spun leaf-covered numbers, clanked, then wheezed

and stopped again. Shadows cut the road
before I drove off into the dark woods. (283-84)

Read her poem at that place, and you will never see those gas tanks in the same way again.

In his introduction to the selection of poems he provided to *Long Island Poets*, Howard Moss catalogues the images of the East End: "cows, barns, horses, a silo, and small mountains in the distance (the Shinnecock Hills) . . . fishing boats . . . strung out in a line . . . trees and the illusion . . . of deep woods" (98-99). He laments the loss of acres of oaks and the encroachment of the boutique and the shopping mall on the Main Streets of East Hampton and Sag Harbor, "each a testimonial to a distinct way of life and an aesthetic notion—the studied elegance of a New England village green, the bustling life of a port" (99). Sadly, he sees that "[t]he sedate and the maritime are both struggling to hang on to the authentic, to ward off the increasing threat of the suburban" (99). What Moss says he owes to "the stars, the birds, to random drives through the countryside, to the bays and the beaches" is eminently clear in his poetry (99). One stanza of his "Bay Days" charts the disappointment of a would-be florist:

I tried today to make of the wild roses
An untimely bouquet. Opening, falling,
They never last long—in short, they're dying.
Now I am thinking of taking to drinking
Earlier than usual. Gin. And something.
A potion of petals. They're thorns by evening.
Wild roses in the trash can in the morning. (101)

Another poem, "In Traffic," describes so well the impatience of the returnee to the East End, stalled in traffic on a "narrow trap of a road adorned with / a diner, a garage, and a nursery" (101). Forced to stop, the riders have time for a brief reflection:

We're stymied, as usual, by the unknown—
A broken-down truck up ahead, an accident,

A Harvester dragging gigantic claws
too wide for one lane, or an animal
refusing to budge—and we begin to wonder
who we all are: the anonymous
taking on interest, the way a tree
stands out suddenly, exempt from its species.

Nothing is really dancing except
an insect or two, whose lives will be smashed
against a windshield once we begin
to move, which we're beginning to do;
a truck full of trees is carting its garden
away toward somebody's landscaped Eden,
and we're picking up speed, single file,
driving past ponds displaying their steadfast
green, through towns too pretty to be. (101–02)

Moss is able to take the most mundane of situations and make it meaningful.

Kenneth Koch has written a poem entitled "The Boiling Water" which he tells us he "began writing . . . in 1975, in early summer, when I was living in a house I rented on Millstone Road . . . down from . . . Scuttlehole Road . . . next door to the house I later bought and spend summers in now" (80). It is about the drama of the boil, after the water has been watched and waited for. The poem was finally finished on Millstone Road a long time later. The Long Island details, Koch tells us, include: "the tree waving in the wind, the hurricane (of 1976), the fly, and the bee; and the tree, full of pink and whitish blossoms, which was an apple tree in the yard between my house and the fields" (81).

Although David Ignatow confesses an ambivalence about East Hampton, for he must often resist "the calm and quiet" and "the wonder of the trees, bays, and ocean" to keep in mind "the tension, turmoil, and slaughter of people in the cities and in the Third World," he admits to the pleasure in the relief he finds here "in small doses" (68–69). In "Little Friend," the narrator watches first one bird and then another. The first he sees:

... standing as though idly
in the grass, your head turning
slowly in one direction, then in another
without alarm when, suddenly, you crouch,
flutter your wings and leap into the air
as though to escape an attack

or as if in memory of one to which
you still respond, so deep has been your fear.
And now you're safe upon a branch
above my head from which I sit
secluded, not to trouble you again.

The bird sails off and disappears from view. A second bird:

... lands close
to where you stood and looks
in both directions first, before it bends
its head to feed. Off it flies
with something in its beak. I step out
from hiding, reminded of my hunger.

The narrator then synthesizes the demands of the world and the calming distraction of nature:

Later, I turn to read the news of state
and individuals and wonder what
the bird is doing at this moment,
now that it has eaten. (74)

The peace that David Ignatow often found in East Hampton is mirrored fully in "The Bay," which appeared in the 1997 issue of *Hampton Shorts*:

So much of something lying calm,
self-possessed, taking the sun,
the ships, the wind and the gulls,
not letting itself be troubled
or turn upon itself. It is the bay
in its place on the map
and in the world, and it has its work,
to uphold ships and to let the eye
roam across a wide expanse
for a moment of release and calm. (103)

Having looked back over almost 250 years, what conclusions can we come to about the writers of the East End? It is astonishing how many of the best American writers of the nineteenth and twentieth centuries lived and wrote here: poets, novelists, essayists, biographers, journalists, historians, and dramatists. They all uniformly recognized the East End as a special place, and all allowed this place to work on their sensibilities in a profound way. All were happy here, but sounded an elegiac note about the future, fearing change in this unique place. Upon reflection or after long lives, all felt nostalgia for an almost idyllic past.

An overview also reveals the tremendous intellectual vitality of the East End. It has been, and still is, a stimulating environment for both mind and body and is enormously encouraging to writers. The presence of the Bay Street Theatre means that resident playwrights have a forum—now playing: *House*, by Terence McNally and Jon Robin Baitz, set in Noyac in the present. Roger Rosenblatt is creating an exciting program at Southhampton College. Organized by Sherrill Foster, members of the American Association of University Women are transcribing original and primary materials in the Long Island Collection of the East Hampton Library, under the direction of Dorothy T. King and Diana Dayton, Librarians. At present they are transcribing the diaries of Fanny Huntting, her brother James Madison Huntting, Cornelia Huntington, and Morgan Dix. Pushcart Press and Canio are searching out and publishing new talent. Barbara Stone's *Hampton Shorts* is a showcase for local writers. *The East Hampton Star* and all the free papers—in English and Spanish—invite anyone with a BiC pen to try his or her hand at writing. Wilford Sheed has noted: "It might be taken as a general principle that if you see someone in particularly shabby work clothes— and I don't mean designer work clothes, either—it just might be a writer and not necessarily a famous one" (ix).

I regret having had to leave out great writers who have not yet written about the East End. If only Doctorow had written *Summertime* instead of *Ragtime*. Or Edward Albee had written, not *Who's Afraid of Virginia Woolf?* but *Who's Afraid of Martha Stewart?* Or Kurt Vonnegut a collection of commencement addresses for Southhampton College. And then there's Joseph Heller. His latest memoir *Now and Then: From Coney Island to Here* is not about here!

To conclude, the East End has either birthed, bred, nourished, housed, published, comforted, or buried an impressive number of the best American writers for many, many years. It has been, therefore, a special place for them. However, because of them, the East End now holds a very special place in the history of American letters.

THE CANNONBALL

and the

Long Island Railroad

—⁓⁓—

Vincent Seyfried

I AM HAPPY TO PRESENT this very interesting story about how the Long Island Railroad got out to Eastern Long Island.

Most of the effort out here was in the 1890s, and a lot of it grew out of one man's dream, Austin Corbin, who was a very wealthy banker in New York. He became President of the Long Island Railroad in 1881. As soon as he got onto this job, he had a lot of problems because he inherited a railroad that was bankrupt and actually had been formerly three different railroads. Once he put those together after about a year or so, he turned to the fulfillment of his dream and that was, not necessarily to build a railroad to the end of Long Island. His objective was to shorten the distance by water, over the ocean, between England and New York. Now you probably know at the time that people usually took almost a week by steamship at that time to come from England over to this harbor. It occurred to him that as long as he had the railroad on Long Island, why not become a link in this chain of transportation. If he could build his railroad eastward from its terminus in Bridgehampton, at that time, and if he could continue it the rest of the way out to Montauk Point, it would be that much less travel time for both mail and people to come to New York. The statistics are kind of interesting on that. Apparently, if you mailed a letter at that time from Southampton or Liverpool or one of those places, it took ten days to get to New York. Obviously, there wasn't any airmail at that time, so if you wanted real speed, you had to depend, of course, on a very, very vast way of getting it through. The other big thing, of course, that was

Leaving East Hampton, 1899.

very attractive at the time was the possibility of getting people just as quickly as mail and to cut down the travel time to only five days across the Atlantic Ocean, rather than the usual seven. And the way he could do that was to build a big depot at Fort Pond Bay. Today, when we look at it, it seems a very placid and certainly uncommercial body of water. But he visualized it in turns of a great trans-Atlantic port that would be full of custom houses, it would be full of ocean liners and, of course, everybody would immediately transfer to his Long Island Railroad and to be whisked through the island to Brooklyn where they would have a large terminus, and he picked Brooklyn because Brooklyn, as he saw it, had more space to work with than the crowded west side of Manhattan. He was anxious, too, to help the United States in terms of boats. He wanted it possible to have five luxurious steamships that would carry people back and forth. The cost would be very high for these steamships; it would be $10 million which, of course, at that time, was a great deal of money. They would make something like eighteen knots on the water, which was an unheard of speed at that time, and I guess even today to some extent. Each boat would have 7,000 horsepower; each vessel alone would cost $1,250,000. This was certainly a very, very ambitious venture that he was proposing. Naturally, if he was a banker, he had money himself. Of course, he had a great many wealthy friends and acquaintances that he wanted to bring into this process and in order to make the thing go even faster. He called a book on his project, *Quick Transit Between New York and London*, and he published this in 1896, just about at the time when the railroad was actually built out to Montauk Point.

He began with this idea very seriously about 1882, as near as I've been able to figure out. He sent some of his surveyors from Bridgehampton which, at that time, was the end of the railroad before the railroad turned up into Sag Harbor, the actual end. The rails had reached Sag Harbor in 1869, and his idea was simply to continue another twenty miles. The problem was, of course, to get out here, get the land, and to put a railroad through. It was not too easy, as it worked out. He first sent some of his surveyors out here to see what the land looked like and, of course, in his day, there wasn't the development that there is today. Once you got beyond East Hampton, there was nothing at all. The entire East End of Long Island—it's difficult for us to believe that today—was owned by the Town of East Hampton, and it was used entirely as a pasturage during the summer time. The sheep, particularly— 7,000 head of sheep—roamed the whole area here, and the people who owned the cattle and the horses and the sheep paid the Town three dollars per animal for this whole summer pasturage. If you owned a horse, they paid the Town five dollars a piece, and they led them out here through the streets of East Hampton—it must've been an interesting sight to see—something like a western mining town, I guess. All these animals would go the street and then they would drive them out through Amagansett and out to the hills, and then leave them on Hither Hill all summer long. And then, when Labor Day came along, the opposite would happen. The owners would gather all their own animals and they usually were able to tell them by the earmarks that they had pinched into the earlobes of each of the animal and they would drive them all the way back and, again, you had this great big western scene of all the animals coming through Main Street, East Hampton, and then being distributed to their various owners. So, that's what his survey people reported back to him.

There would be no great problem really; there were a few hills in the way, there were a few valleys in the way, but nothing really seemed difficult. It took quite a while to do this. In 1884, he took his next small step and that was to purchase all of the hills—the Shinnecock Hills, as they were called at the time. And he first got that into his control and got a lot of other of his wealthy friends to also put in money and buy it. The idea was for them to have a kind of private, personal summer residence and it worked out fairly well. He bought what land he could get hold of and he spent quite a few years—apparently, 1884, 1885, 1886, and so on—getting these various cottages built and trying to develop a road that would lead up to it. Meanwhile, he kept working on this idea of getting the land. The land situation was very interesting at that time. It's hard for us to believe today that the entire East End—all the land beyond East Hampton—was in the ownership of one man—a man who gave his name to Bensonhurst in Brooklyn. Arthur W. Benson had bought the whole of this Montauk area in 1879, and he paid only $11,000 for it—the entire area. The problem was, of course, was to get Benson to sell a right-of-way for the railroad and to go in with the scheme, if possible. So they worked on this. It turned out that Benson was perfectly willing to do it. Before they could really get started too well on it, the man who had originally bought it died in 1889 and the land passed to his three children: Frank, Mary, and Jane Benson. And they, too, were willing to sell the land, but as so often happens in the real world, the lawyers decided that there was some ambiguity in the will that might prevent them from selling the land in small sections. They could sell the whole thing and there would be no legal objection, but to sell a small amount to the railroad, and perhaps to other people, might be challenged in court. It took them something like three or four years by the time this thing slowly made its way through the courts. Finally, they got permission in 1893. So, even in those days, any legal entanglements was something to be avoided.

The immediate problem now was to build 9.78 miles from Bridgehampton to Amagansett and then, from there on, 11.5 miles from Amagansett out to Montauk. So, the whole extension was really not tremendously long, in terms of distance, but there were problems all the way through. In 1893, he decided the first thing to do was to get permission. If you want to build a railroad in the United States, you have to go to the railroad commission of your state and get permission to do it. Well, with his money and with his reputation, he had no difficulty in getting Albany to agree, so he incorporated the Montauk Extension Railroad, as it was called, and everything seemed very good in that respect. In 1893, he and his friends took the train out during April and they decided the best thing to do would be to get everybody out in the Township of East Hampton to get behind this project. So, one fine day, he went out in his parlor car and had the train run all the way out to Bridgehampton, which was as far as the rails went, and thereafter, he went by carriage all the way out here to East Hampton. They seemed to have made three successive pitches to the various people out here. The first time, they gathered together all the citizens that were around here and told them what a good idea would be if they could get the railroad, how it would benefit their property values; it

A 8169 Scene at Montauk, L. I.

Montauk, Long Island.
(Courtesy William J. Madden)

would make a great kind of summer residence; it would open up a wonderful new area of the island to everybody; and everyone would prosper from it. So, he came out here and he gave these talks. Apparently, he did very well. On April 5th, he brought Mr. Benson, who owned all the property, along with him, and they went out and they gave this talk to the East Hampton people. The people liked what they heard. I guess Corbin was a fairly persuasive speaker. Two weeks later, on April 19th, again, there was a mass meeting of the citizens here in East Hampton and, again, he talked to the people and, again, after they had had two weeks to think this project over, they applauded it this time, and it seemed like a very good idea. The final meeting, apparently, was in May, and they agreed to give him one important thing and that was to give him the land for nothing. Corbin was a very shrewd businessman in those days and whenever he built a new section to his railroad, he tried to get people to donate the right-of-way. It wasn't a very princely gift when you think about it because the right-of-way was only sixty-six feet wide for two tracks of the railroad. Even today, we don't think that's a lot of land. But, of course, it may be only sixty-six feet wide, but remember, it was miles long. The people decided it's not a bad investment; they were willing to donate that much of their property to give him what he needed. So, he got legal permission from the people who liked the idea; for people who had their hesitations about the whole thing, he was able to persuade them to sell their property and as often happens in projects like this, there are always a few obstructionists who don't want to go into something at all. So, again, he lost time because he had to take a handful of people through the courts. Finally, he was able to condemn small, little chunks of property here and there and he was able to string himself out a complete railroad. Now, all this while, this big Benson lawsuit was going on, and it wasn't until June 1, 1893 that the courts finally turned to the Benson heirs and said, okay, you can sell your father's property, and that was really the beginning of the whole railroad project. Once Austin Corbin had this permission and these deeds in his pocket, finally, he was able to get out the shovels and begin to build the railroad. This really, I guess, is the cornerstone and really the beginning of the development—June 1st, 1893—that was when the green light finally came on. So, with the railroad legally incorporated and with everybody apparently happy, they got going.

The original intention was to build the railroad not only to where it ends today—which is right below that hotel that's up on the little mountain there—but to run it along the lakeside and up to Culloden

Point. Later on, because of the little Indian cemetery up there and the fact that this had formerly been the site of an Indian raid, they decided not to take that part and to terminate it where you see it today. So, that was really the only change between then and now. During the rest of 1893, he was able to clear away any other little problems. The man who operated the Sag Harbor Turnpike tried to stop them because the railroad crossed his turnpike at two points, and he didn't like the idea of having a grade crossing where he operated his stagecoaches. So, they had to take him to court and the judges threw out the whole thing for him, so he was alright on that problem. They cut the land in three pieces. The Fort Pond Bay area, which is where the railroad terminates today, was the part sold to the Long Island Railroad. The Hither Hills section—that very beautiful forest there that is now a state park—the Bensons kept that in their own property, and it wasn't until years afterwards that New York State bought the whole of Hither Hills—the nice forest park there—and made it the state park it is today. The extreme tip—the third piece of land out there—also remained with the Benson Heirs and that's the place now where we have a little village in Montauk and where you have Montauk Point. So, this whole vast area—and, incidentally, I'm speaking of 5,500 acres, a lot of ground, and it's hard for us to believe that all of that in 1896 had only three houses on it, and those are still on the map today; if you go along the Montauk Highway, they still tell you where the first house, second house, and third house existed at that time. Today, with all the settlement and with all the development, it seems incredible that on the whole 5,500 acres, that only three houses could have been occupants of this great, great area.

Starting with 1894—one year now we move on in our story—a great deal of preparation was necessary on the part of Corbin and his railroad. He had to get all kinds of people out there to do the building; he had to get all kinds of material out there; he had to get all kinds of material out there; he had to build all kinds of freight cars, and so on, to bring this out and this was a great problem for him. In New York, luckily, for him, there was a vast labor pool at the time, and he was able to get a large group of men willingly to come out to what they regarded as a desolate waste out here. Many of them were Italian, there were a small number of Germans, and a sprinkling of many other groups. One of the things that they comment on in these days is that if you went to the construction camp, you will hear three or four foreign languages spoken all day in addition not only to the supervisory personnel, who were usually white men and well educated, but you also had a large group of African-Americans who had come from the south, who were not well-educated, and of course, they spoke a dialect of their own. But they were very happy to get this employment that lasted all year long. Since there was no place to live, what do you do with all these men? So, this is one of his early problems. He took a lot of broken-down, old freight cars—box cars, as we call them today—and he moved them out here, took them off their wheels, and just put them along the potential railroad track there, and the men lived in those cars all during the rest of the year. As you can imagine, since they were cars that were no longer serviceable for railroad use, they were not too serviceable either for living in. So he simply fitted them out with bunks and I daresay it must have been very, very uncomfortable because many of the men—particularly, the Italians—wanted to bring their home life with them and they brought out their wives and children, so you can imagine if there were something like forty men in one box car, in addition, maybe, to a couple of wives and children besides, how crowded and how uncomfortable it might have been. I guess it's a tribute to the fact that in the nineteenth century, people were used to not having any luxury at their fingertips and were more willing to compromise than we are today for our comfort. But, apparently, it worked out all right. The papers of the day gave a very vivid idea of what the construction was at that time and what an effort it was to put it through. There were no steam shovels invented at that time yet, so all of this work had to be done with horses and oxcarts, and things like that—everything had to be done by hand, so it was a slow process. Most of the area they went through, of course, were sand hills and that made it a little bit easier to do a lot of digging. But the ground was very irregular, particularly, through Hither Hills, and that meant, of course, that you had to have deep cuts through the woods, you had to clear away all kinds of growth all through it, and it took a long time, considering that this was all hand work, to go through this area. Once the original clearing was done, they were able to bring in the ties, and once the ties had been laid, the next step would be to put down the rails, but there were still some problems. You had to have a perfectly flat roadbed at this time. Remember, all movement on the railroad in these days was done by steam locomotives, and the steam locomotive has one big disadvantage: it cannot climb. The steam locomotive can only take a grade, at the most, of two percent which, of course, is two feet in every hundred feet. Anything more than that can't climb, so it was very important in the beginning for them to do grading, to have a perfectly smooth roadbed, if possible, and once you achieved that by means of any bridging, or ditch-digging in, or filling in whatever you needed, once you had a level plain to work with, then you could bring in your ties and, finally, your rails. So, it took most of the summer of 1895 to get this work done. It was, as you can imagine, a slow and difficult business. One advantage, I guess, for the people at the time was that they could walk along with it and pretty well follow what they were doing. I think one of the most interesting scenes—and I wish I had been there to see it— was the arrival of the first locomotive in East Hampton. Remember, there were no tracks laid yet; yet, they brought a locomotive to East Hampton. Now what they did was to hitch up a small locomotive—a contractor's locomotive, really—and it was put on a flatbed trailer and eight oxen were attached to it, and they pulled this thing all the way from East Hampton, which was the last carrier, and this had to go all the way through this new construction before it finally arrived here in town. I wonder what this must have looked like coming along the Montauk Highway, such as it was in that day and age. It worked. So, when it finally came in, of course, it was the sensation of East Hampton at the time it arrived. We know its name; it was called "The F. H. Clement"—no one knows who he is—and it arrived here and was set up on Newton Lane, and the reason for that termination was the fact that they had determined that that would be the site of the station and that it would be the site where the railroad would come through. So they began their track-laying, not from Bridgehampton where the tracks ended, but they started a new railroad right here on Newtown Lane, put the locomotive on it. Of course, once they had this assistance of the railroad, after that, it was no great problem to get the use of the railroad. Naturally, the were able to put their freight cars and so-on on it, their locomotive would go up and down, it would jump ties, it would pick up all kinds of stuff for them, and it certainly accelerated the speed of the road. Things went much faster in the middle of summer after this engine had been delivered. Once the track got close to East Hampton, Austin Corbin came out in his private car. He had a luxurious parlor car called "The Manhattan" and "elegant" would certainly be the word—beautifully painted, leathered on the outside, the interior was four or five different rooms: kitchen, bedroom, bathroom—everything you needed on wheels. Behind that, there would be two or three parlor cars for the officials and anyone else—like newspaper reporters— would ride in the coaches in the back. So he would come out and try to follow the locomotive from time to time in his own private car.

When the courts finally gave permission to continue the road, he was able to get the deed that he wanted to get to Montauk. You might be interested to know that the whole right-of-way all the way out to

Montauk Point sold for $200,000—5,500 acres of land to the railroad for $200,000. Now, in 1895, people were earning $6 a week if they were ordinary workers. If they had a college education and could be a superintendent or whatever, they might make $8 a week. The locomotive engineer who had a lot of responsibility, he took home ten dollars, and if he was on a big railroad, like the Pennsylvania, he might get as much as twelve dollars. But that was the salary that people made in those days. So, you can imagine a sum like $200,000 was something astronomical in that day and age.

Things went through very, very well. The three Benson heirs signed off on the right-of-way, and everything seemed absolutely perfect for going through. By June 28th, the tracks had reached almost through to the Hither Hills area and, surprisingly, they were able to run the first train as far as Amagansett—that is through East Hampton and up to Amagansett—on June 1st. This was a big source of satisfaction and a little bit of celebration on the part of the railroad. I found from the timetables of the day that the first service was with two trains; they ran a train leaving at 6:50 in the morning—a God-awful hour certainly, but, remember, to get all the way to New York was a long journey in those days, and then there was one afternoon train at 3:00. So that was the beginning of service from Amagansett. Meanwhile, work continued on the Montauk section as much as possible. During July and August, they had 250 men and thirty-four teams at work through the hills and down into the main part of Montauk today. They worked like beavers, of course, all during that period. Finally, when the thing was ready, the first train that pulled into Montauk was on December 17, 1895. So, both Amagansett and Montauk both finished not too far away from each other—the one on June 1st and the other on December 17th. To celebrate this, of course, there wasn't anybody who lived out there, so it was really the railroad that celebrated its accomplishment. The first train that came out again with Corbin and all of his officials was "The Manhattan", the private car, and a mail car behind it, and a parlor car, and then two coaches. So it was a five-car train on the first run pulled into town. The mail, by the way, was changed starting with this day. Formerly, if there was any kind of mail to be sent, it went by stagecoach from here over to Sag Harbor and then from Sag Harbor, it would continue by rail into New York. So, starting with this day, it was possible to mail a letter from Amagansett and from Montauk and, for the first time, of course, it would be in New York the same day and not a long, slow journey through Long Island.

Once the service opened, the big problem was, of course, to get anybody to ride the trains. Now East Hampton, as you well know, is an old village and long-settled and there was a fair amount of service at the time and, rightly so, because a fair number of people lived here. But Amagansett was still a very, very small place and, of course, originated almost no traffic. Nobody at all lived in Montauk; there were something like, as near as I can tell on the map, perhaps, twelve or fourteen bungalows—summer-only bungalows—along Montauk there and, of course, these men would come out once and then they stayed there maybe for the whole summer. So, there wasn't any traffic or any revenue from them either. So, they didn't run the train to Montauk at all. The early timetable that we have—and this is true right down to 1900, 1902, and so on—the trains didn't go to Montauk even though the track was laid. All the trains turned back at Amagansett and that was the end of the run. If you wanted to go, if you were one of these wealthy men who had a cottage out at the end of the line, they would accommodate you for an extra charge of ten dollars, and you had to notify the conductor and then he would run you in one coach and one locomotive and go the remaining distance out to the end of the track in Montauk.

As the years went by, two other things that became familiar later on began to come out and this was special trains—trains that were distinguished because of their speed or because of what they meant. I think you've heard, of course, probably of the Long Island Railroad *Cannonball*. Many people have said that this really started when the tracks reached Montauk. Well, that's not true, apparently. I checked on the timetables and the first appearance of the *Cannonball*—and this, by the way, means no stops; that's why it's called the *Cannonball*—there was no bridge in those days, there was no tunnel. All the trains began in Long Island City—that was the terminus right on the East River. The train would stop only at Jamaica, and the next stop was Southampton. So, you can see that's a pretty fast run. Now, if you have nothing in your way and the tracks are clear, you can make pretty good time. The locomotives that they generally ran forty-five miles an hour. Once in awhile, with real testing, they might go up to fifty and fifty-five, but the engine, remember, in the beginning, was small, and the track was not that solid either. So, they made the trip in two hours. Now this was considered like a meteor in those days—fantastic speed; the whole length of the island in two hours. Well, you might smile to yourself now because sometimes it still takes two hours to get out here. They thought it was wonderful speed, and that's how the train came to be named The *Cannonball*. It had a little higher fare at the time and to distinguish the fact that the train was very special, all the cars were painted white. When we think about it, of all the colors they could've used, considering that they were operating speed trains which were full of soot, of course, white?! How do you ever keep the trains clean? Now, I suppose the answer was manpower was cheap in those days and they were able to give it a good wash once it made a round-trip. So, beginning in 1891, you were able to get speed, if you wanted it. The other service that they frequently offered was the parlor car service. Of course, they built a special car with carpet on the floor, all the seats were loose (they weren't screwed to the floor or anything like that), you had over-stuffed chairs and you could move them the way you wanted to, there was usually a bar at the end of the car and you could be served with anything you liked; they had beautiful chandeliers overhead. They tried as far as possible to duplicate a drawing room or a parlor that you would find in a wealthy, New York home. And this was available for the traffic out here because very early, East Hampton, Amagansett and Montauk attracted a wealthy, summer clientele. This was the beginning really of what you have out here now—an affluent group of people for whom money was no great object. They want to be catered to, they're use to being catered to, and they're willing to pay the money to get it. So, starting really at this time, in 1895, we begin to have this luxury of parlor cars for the first time. While I think it's astonishing the way time has changed, the Long Island Railroad up to this year is the last railroad in the United States that still offers any kind of parlor car service. It's astonishing to realize how the quality of the railroad has gone down with the tremendous competition of the airlines, the jitney buses, and so on, and it's a shadow of what it used to be.

The other interesting thing that they had over the years were the fishermen's trains. This gained reknown very early because of the idea of being able to go out all day on a fishing journey and this was particularly true for Southampton where you had a special fishermen's train leaving New York and Jamaica very early in the morning—6:30 in the morning—and getting out here very quickly and, of course, you would change to the boat very quickly and spend the rest of the day fishing. It became very popular. It lasted until very, very recently. They would also take care of your catch by icing it for you and having all kinds of large containers to bring back your catch if you had been successful. So, the railroad over the years has tried to accommodate that type of service as far as possible.

COL. THEODORE ROOSEVELT,

The Rough Riders

& Camp Wikoff

———

Jeff Heatley

O N AUGUST 7TH, 1898, the transport *Miami*, with Gen. Joseph
Wheeler, Col. Theodore Roosevelt, the Rough Riders and members of the Third Cavalry on board, pulled away from the dock at Santiago, Cuba to begin its voyage north. Anxious that his men not miss the
sights, Col. Roosevelt urged them to stay on deck. As the ship approached Morro Castle, the Third Cavalry band began to play John
Howard Payne's "Home, Sweet Home.". The American soldiers stationed
at the castle cheered wildly as the homeward-bound troops passed by.

The *Gate City*, the first transport to start north, had left Santiago
two days earlier. Over the next five weeks, nearly forty ships would
bring a total of 22,500 soldiers of Gen. Shafter's Fifth Army Corps from
Santiago de Cuba to Montauk, where a 4,200-acre military encampment had been hastily prepared for their rest and recuperation.

The 2,000-mile, eight-day journey would prove a further test for
the heroes of the Spanish-American War. Many suffered the ill effects of
tropical diseases like malaria, typhoid, dysentery and, in a few cases,
yellow fever. The ships were over-crowded and lacked adequate supplies for healthy men, let alone fever-stricken ones.

Both the *Mobile* and *Allegheny* transports were called "death
ships" on arrival at Fort Pond Bay. Thirteen soldiers had died on board
the *Mobile* and been buried at sea; fourteen on the *Allegheny* suffered
the same fate. These were men who had embarked for Cuba in top
physical condition only a few months before, men who had survived
the Spanish Mausers and the hazards of war, but who had been weak-

end by scarce and poor army rations, by virulent tropical fevers, by the extreme conditions of the Cuban chapparel in mid-summer, then subjected to overcrowded, poorly equipped transports that were to take them home.

Many of those who survived the voyage were in frightful condition on arrival at Montauk. Exhausted, emaciated, unable to walk without assistance, they virtually staggered off the transports onto the railroad pier at Fort Pond Bay. Some were carried off by their "bunkies," others in litters, then transported by army ambulances to the quarantine camp. Those who had come to cheer the victorious troops were shocked by the debilitated condition of their heroes.

The Round Robin petition and Roosevelt letter, both published nationally on August 4th, had warned of these conditions. If not for the Round Robin protest, many of these soldiers would not have made it home. On August 3rd, a despatch from Secretary of War Alger ordered Gen. Shafter and his Fifth Army Corps to move twenty-five miles inland to a higher elevation. This order enraged the commanding generals at Santiago. They knew that order could not be executed without great hardship, and decided to protest the order from the Secretary of War. Gen. Leonard Wood, Roosevelt's good friend and commander of the Rough Riders until his promotion, wrote the Round Robin protest, in which he stated that "the army must be moved at once or perish." Col. Roosevelt's accompanying letter was printed on the front page of William Randolph Hearst's *New York Evening Journal*:

> Major-General Shafter:
>
> "...All of us are certain, as soon as the authorities at Washington fully appreciate the conditions of the army, to be sent home. If we are kept here, it will in all human possibility mean an appalling disaster, for the surgeons estimate that over half the army...will die. This is not only terrible from the standpoint of the individual lives lost, but it means ruin from the standpoint of the military efficiency of the flower of the American army, for the great bulk of the regulars are here with you ...
>
> "I write only because I cannot see our men, who have fought so bravely, and who have endured extreme hardship and danger so uncomplainingly, go to destruction without striving, so far as lies in me, to avert a doom as fearful as it is unnecessary and undeserved." (Bully, 13/14)

The Round Robin protest, unpredecented in U.S. military history, shocked President McKinley and Secretary of War Alger, who first read the documents in the Washington dailies. Secretary of War Alger quickly blamed Colonel Roosevelt for the documents' release to the press and rebuked him publicly. The news, however, had been published, and the order for the immediate return of the entire Fifth Army Corps had to be issued. Americans were jubilant at the news: the victorious troops were coming home!

To the returning troops, the first sight of Long Island's profile on the horizon brought renewed hope of recovery. From the decks of the transports, Montauk was a green, undulating point of land with high bluffs rising from the sea. Its rolling hills, barren of trees, were dotted with hundreds of white army tents in well-ordered rows. Army wagons racing across the landscape and troops marching to camp could be seen in what appeared to be a healthy, vibrant military encampment. To the returning troops, Camp Wikoff, as the camp had been named, was to be Camp Paradise—or so it seemed.

A reporter for the *Brooklyn Daily Eagle* described the natural beauty of Montauk in these words:

> Everybody ... who visits Montauk Point [says]...
>
> "What air they get out here!" Of course, they do. Montauk is a mere spit of land running out into the Atlantic deeps, and the wind has to wriggle itself out of shape to get to the end of it without crossing open sea ... The wind seems to be always blowing, and it comes with a tang of salt in it, yet strangely and deliciously blended with a wholesome country smell. Everything larger than a bush has been blown from the earth. There is not a tree on the hills. From the great rolling waves of earth you look out over miles of sea. You have the transports in view as they come up from the southwest, you follow their smoke as they turn the point where the lighthouse lifts against the sky ...
>
> It is in this wide viewing land of clear skies...of genial, not oppressive sunshine, of soft, life-giving air and of flowers and sand, that [the] men of the United States Army will come to rest ... (*Bully*, 83, 85)

Not only were the troops returning to a land of extraordinary natural beauty, but to a land of extraordinary people as well. on the night of August 25th, the auxiliary cruiser *Prairie*, with 520 soldiers on board, including members of the famed Seventh Infantry, ran aground off Napeague Beach. By next morning, news of the grounded steamer had reached Amagansett and hundreds of people came to offer their help. Surf boats carried the soldiers from the transport to shore, where the Long Islanders came to their rescue. The *New York Sun* described the scene in these words:

> There were about ten soldiers in the first boatload, and the biggest crowd that ever lined Napeague Beach was gathered on the shore to welcome them. There were even women and children, and as the boat approached they sent up cheer after cheer. When the boat was about twenty yards off shore, fully twenty men rushed into the surf...and one by one the sick men were lifted gently out of the boat and carried up to the soft sand, where blankets had been laid down for them ...

> The second boatload was unloaded in the same fashion. Even soldiers who were able to get ashore themselves were not allowed to walk. The Long Islanders just took them in their arms and carried them through the surf. They fought for the privilege, and in the rush two or three of them were knocked clear over in the water and drenched to the skin ... This enthusiasm was of the greatest assistance to those in charge of landing the men. It made the trips shorter and made it unnecessary to take the boatloads of sick through the surf ...

> The sight was certainly a strange one. Boatload after boatload of sick solders being brought ashore from a stranded war vessel to a strip of beach usually abandoned, but now crowded with people, who cheered and cheered each time a man was brought ashore ..."(*Bully*, 135/136).

On Monday, August 15th, under clear blue skies, hundreds of soldiers and citizens gathered near the railroad dock at Fort Pond Bay. They cheered as the transport Miami was being escorted by tug to the iron pier, where the soldiers were to debark. Rough riders and the troops of the Third Cavalry lined the decks of the Miami and cheered wildly in return as the ship approached. John Hunt, editor of *The Sag Harbor Express*, described the scene in these words:

> The foxes on Montauk must have thought Wyandank and his whooping braves were back again ... in their ancient home! ... There arose such a shout along the hills of Fort Pond Bay, cheer on cheer resounding, as has not been heard there since the Montaukets gathered to repel the Pequot invasion. The [Rough Riders] already here came from Tampa and had never been within range of Spanish guns, but their disappointment only made them all the more eager to greet with royal welcome their returning comrades on whose tattered garments was the

dust of heroic battle, and on their brows, the laurel of match-
less victory. So waits a mighty nation to greet those who come
back from the field of duty done, the shortest and swiftest war
in the annals of the great States . . . (*Bully*, 75).

The gallant Rough Riders, whose heroics in battle exceeded the
wildest of expectations, were home from war. An officer on the pier
shouted to Colonel Roosevelt who stood on the ship's deck next to
Gen. Wheeler:

"How are you, Col. Roosevelt?"

"I am feeling disgracefully well . . .I feel positively ashamed of
my appearance when I see how badly off some of my brave fellows are—Oh, but we have had a bully fight!" ("New York Herald," *Bully*, 62).

Among the Rough Riders who followed Colonel Roosevelt and General Wheeler off the transport were Color Sergeant Albert Wright, the
"goliath" of the regiment; Lieutenant John Greenway, the Yale football
player; Privates Charlie Bull and Bob Wrenn, Harvard oarsman and quar-
terback, respectively; Bill Larned, the tennis champion; Knickerbocker
Club members Craig Wadsworth, Reginal Ronalds and Woodbury Kane.
Troop L, the last to debark the *Miami*, silenced the crowd, as those gathered on the shores of Fort Pond Bay remembered the two fallen heroes
of Troop L, Captain Allyn Capron and Sergeant Hamilton Fish.

Later that afternoon, Colonel Roosevelt praised his men:

Of course, I am proud of my regiment. There was never such
another. In fifty days, it was raised, organized, equipped, armed,
mounted, put into transports, caarried through two victorious
fights. That's the record that I think will be hard to beat . . .

The groundwork of the regiment is the cowpuncher, the man
who has herded cattle on the great plains for a living, and next
to him comes the Rocky Mountain miner . . .then the professional hunter, the mining engineer and civil engineer, and the
packer, and mixed with them the college athlete and the man
who has always been fond of rough out-of-doors sport. They all
go in together without a hitch . . . ("New York Sun," *Bully*,
68/69).

General Joseph Wheeler, known among the soldiers as "Fighting
Joe" since his Civil War days as a Confederate General, had traveled
back with Colonel Roosevelt on the transport *Miami* and had this to
say about the gallant Rough Rider:

I had a good chance of observing Roosevelt during the week we were at sea from another point of view than that offered by the camp. He is a charming fellow. The thing that impressed me most about him is his absolute integrity. Some men have integrity about money, others about their personal conduct. Roosevelt has both; and, more than either, the official integrity that makes him the rare man he is.

The people of New York want him for their Governor. . . The people of the United States will want him to govern them next, and they will have him for their President. I told him so on the ship and he laughed a good deal. . . Certainly, it would be hard for them to make a better choice. Roosevelt is able, energetic and most loyal.

Whether in the camp or in the field, Roosevelt was to be depended on always. He is perfectly fearless, and his men follow him with absolute devotion . . . (*Bully*, 79/80).

At the Long Island Railroad terminus in Montauk, next to the piers at Fort Pond Bay, a small village of buildings had been constructed in a matter of ten days. Montauk Station, as it was known, became the focus of activity of the military encampment. Seven thousand soldiers arrived by train from the southern camps; thousands of visitors arrived by train from points west; and virtually all of the 22,500 soldiers brought to Camp Wikoff by transport left by train. Roughly constructed buildings lined the main street alongisde the railroad station, including a post office, express package building, general store, information bureau, telegraph office, printing facility, electric light and powerhouse, and two restaurants, one of which was just a shanty known as Hungry Joe's. Following the arrival of a train, four- and six-mule team wagons, loaded with passengers, fanned out across the 4,200-acre camp.

After debarking at Fort Pond Bay, the Rough Riders marched to the Detention Camp, located on Observatory Hill across from Montauk Station, where they were required to stay for four days in quarantine. The two-square-mile Detention Camp had its own hospital. Originally planned as a 250-bed facility, it had grown to accommodate 520 fever-stricken soldiers by the third week in August. The day after the Rough Riders returned to Montauk, one of their own, J. Knox Green, died of malaria. He was the first to die at Camp Wikoff of more than 350 soldiers of the Fifty Army Corp.

On the 18th of August, Colonel Roosevelt received permission to stay at Third House, Montauk's only inn. The next day, Colonel Roosevelt said that for the first time in a good many weeks, he had slept in a "civilized bed."

Troops arrived by train and by ship faster than the camp could accommodate them. For a time, there were shortages of tents, cots, even army rations. The press published shocking reports about the soldiers' misfortunes after they reached camp. The people of Long Island, and elsewhere, came to their aid, personally delivering food delicacies to the troops. Ships arrived at Fort Pond Bay from Greenport and New Suffolk on the North Fork; Newport, Rhode Island; Old Stonington, Connecticut; and New York City. These ships brought thousands of pounds of fresh eggs, vegetables, fruits, cakes and pies, canned meats, jellies, preserves, chickens, soups, wine, champagne, brandy, mineral water and even reading materials.

Tragically, more and more soldiers arrived debilitated by tropical fevers. The General Hospital, designed as a 500-bed facility, had to be expanded to serve the needs of 1,620 patients by the third week in August. More and more soldiers lost their individual battles with malaria, typhoid, dysentery, even yellow fever. Visitors to Camp Wikoff witnessed the appearance of "camp ghosts," men who were not ill enough to be admitted to the General Hospital but too ill to care for themselves. These "ghosts" wandered over the camp, collapsing when strength gave out. Devitalized by the hardships of war, by repeated bouts of fever, by poor nourishment, they did make it to the hospital again, but invariably to die. The cause of death was listed as exhaustion.

Five of Gen. Joseph Wheeler's sons and daughters offered their assistance at Camp Wikoff. Lieutenant Joseph Wheeler, Jr. and Naval Cadet Thomas H. Wheeler were aides-de-camp at their father's headquarters. Three daughters worked as nurses in the General Hospital one of whom, Annie Laurie Early Wheeler, had volunteered her services as a nurse for the Red Cross in Cuba. Interviewed shortly after her arrival at Montauk, she related her experiences in Cuba, words that applied as well to the work she did in the General Hospital at Camp Wikoff:

> When I [arrived], I found the men without any of the comforts which belong to the ill. Cots they had none; blankets had been long since cast aside and lost. There was nothing for them to eat, poor fellows, but the scantiest of army rations, hardtack and the like ...
>
> In a few days, the Red Cross supplies began to come in and I got cots for my men. They were remarkably fine cots. Each cot

had four pillow cases, sheets, rubber blankets, woolen blankets and mosquito netting. We also received many delicacies.

I think the happiest hour of my life was when I got my patients off the floor and into these comfortable cots. You ought to (have seen) their eyes shine. Many a man alive today owes his life to the Red Cross ...

My boys were the private soldiers. I found the officers had servants to wait on them and plenty of attention. But the privates were alone and helpless and neglected. That was the sort I had come to help. And oh, they were so grateful, so uncomplaining, so heroic! It was beautiful to see the gratitude shining in their faces over the smallest things that I could do for them. They used to follow me with their eyes ... (*The World, Bully*, 120).

Press accounts described Camp Wikoff as a "pest hole" with fever-stricken troops slowly starving to death. Public anger at their plight was directed at Secretary of War Alger, whom they accused of mismanagement. Editorials called for his resignation, but President McKinldy refused to remove him from office or ask that he resign. Alarmed, however, by the press accounts of conditions at Camp Wikoff, President McKinley decided to tour the camp himself.

The presidential party arrived at Montauk Station on Saturday, September 3rd, after spending the night in five Pullman Palace cars on a sidetrack in Amagansett. General Wheeler greeted the presidential party which included, besides McKinley, Vice-President Hobart, Secretary of War Alger, Attorney General Griggs, and Senator Proctor of Vermont. As they prepared to leave the station in the Victoria carriages that Gen. Wheeler had brought to Montauk for the occasion, President McKinley spotted Colonel Roosevelt a short distance away on horseback.

"Why, there's Col. Roosevelt! Colonel! I'm glad to see you."

The commander of the Rough Riders executed a remarkable maneuver. He forgot to make a formal dismount, but sort of fell off his animal in the way he does at the end of a race across the hills with a squad of his cowpounchers. At the same time, the President did a remarkable thing for a president to do. He stood up in his carriage, pushed open the door and, jumping out, started toward Col. Roosevelt, who was coming toward him as fast as he could. The President held out his hand; Col. Roosevelt struggled to pull off his right glove. He yanked at it desperately and finally inserted the ends of the fingers in his teeth and gave a mighty tug. Off came the glove and a beatific smile came over the Colonel's face as he grasped the President's hand ...

"Col. Roosevelt, I'm glad to see you looking so well."

"Thank you, Mr. President. There isn't a healthier man in camp than I am. I am delighted to see you down here, sir, and hope you will enjoy the trip. I do want you to see my boys while you're here."

"Oh, I will, Colonel, I will." ("New York Sun," Bully, 235/236).

When the column of carriages reached a hilltop, the entire encampment spread out before the presidential party. McKinley remarked that he had never seen a handsomer camp.

The President was deeply moved by the sight of the fever-stricken soldiers in both the General and Detention Hospitals. He spoke to Sgt. John A. Alexander of the First Illinois Volunteers.

"Won't you tell me how you feel and whether there's anything I can do for you?"

"The President of the United States is talking to you," said Gen. Wheeler to the soldier.

It was like an electric shock to the man. He straightened up and by a superhuman effort raised his head up on his left hand and saluted with his right. Immediately he fell in a heap on his cot and, with tears in his eyes, said:

"I didn't know you, sir; I am very weak."

"Yes, poor fellow. This is not the time for you to salute me. I'm here to see how you are and what I can do for you."

"Thank you, but I only want my strength back so that I can go home again. I suppose I'll have to wait for that."

"I hope you won't have to wait long."

"I want you to tell the President whether you have wanted for anything since you have been here," [said Gen. Wheeler.]

"I have had every care and attention." ("New York Sun," Bully, 241.)

Following its inspection of the hospitals, the presidential party made its way to the Great Plain of Montauk where President McKinley addressed 5,000 cheering soldiers of the Fifth Army Corps for the first time since their triumphant return from Cuba.

"GEN. WHEELER, SOLDIERS OF CAMP WIKOFF, SOLDIERS OF
THE FIFTH ARMY CORPS:

"...I am honored to meet the brave men who stand before me
today. I bring you the gratitude of the nation, to whose history
you have added by your valor a new and glorious page. You
have come home after two months of severe campaigning,
which has embraced assault, siege and battle—so brilliant in
achievement, so far—reaching in results as to earn the un-
stinted praise of all your countrymen.

"You had the brunt of the battle on land. You bore yourselves
with supreme courage, and your personal bravery, never before
excelled anywhere, has won the admiration of your fellow citizens and the genuine respect of all mankind, while your en-
durance under peculiar trial and suffering has given added
meaning to American heroism ..." ("New York Sun," *Bully*, 245).

Not everyone found President McKinley's visit to Camp Wikoff in-
spiring. E.S. Boughton, editor of The East Hampton Star, expressed a dissenting opinion the following week:

President McKinley's famous visit to the camp was a farce.
While he shook hands with officers and was shown through
the hospitals, men were dying out in the tents of the Regulars,
without care and proper medical attention. The one person
who succeeded in getting the ear of the President on behalf of
the neglected soldiers in the camp was explained away as 'an
hysterical woman'. If the women whom we saw rescue the neglected invalid soldier from his tent in the Third Regular Infantry care for him and administer restoratives to him during
the journey from the camp to this village, take him to an improvised hospital, procure a nurse and physician for him and
then anxiously watch his slow recovery are hysterical, we wish
some of the heartless officials might become hysterical ...

If there is anyone who thinks the stories of the camp are over-
drawn, we would say go there and do a little investigating on
your own account. Do not ask questions of the officers, but go
into the tents of the privates. (*Bully*, 304/305).

At Montauk Station, a young lieutenant was heard to remark to a
visitor, "We have everything. We have life and we have death." The men
President McKinley praised on the Great Plain that Saturday afternoon
were in "disgracefully" good health. Camp regulations and confinement
did not prevent them from having a rollicking good time in what, for
them, was Uncle Sam's Seaside Park.

Regimental bands played on the hillsides and in the hollows throughout the camp. Visitors and soldiers were treated to enthused renditions of "Tramp, Tramp, Tramp, The Boys Are Marching," "The Girl I Left Behind Me," "Home, Sweet Home," "Marching Through Georgia," and "Yankee Doodle". Expert buglers and beginners practiced to perfect "Taps" and "Reveille" in an informal bugler school on a high bluff at Ditch Plains. One expert bugler, standing on the bluff at sunset, sent "the golden notes in peal on peal over the darkening ocean in a good-night song to the setting sun." ("New York Sun," *Bully,* 320).

> "Whoopee! Hang on to him, Bud! All our dust's on yer. Kick the breeze, yer blankety son of a mule! Yer can't t'row him! Stick to him or we all go broke!"

Roosevelt's Rough Riders vented their joy one afternoon during a bronco busting competition between Troop I and Troop H.

> "We've got an old bronco over in our troop and there ain't a guy of yer that can straddle him. He's old and lame and as gentle as a lamb, but we've got tin that says not a guy of yer can throw his leg over him."

This contemptuous message from Troop I was delivered by The Nipper, so nicknamed because he had cut through three of the barbed-wire fences in front of Santiago. Bets were placed and Troop I's bronco was brought out and appeared to be as "peaceful as a lamb."

> But the bronco wasn't lame and he wasn't blind. . . . As the sergeant of Troop H cautiously approached, the bronco watched him with a vicious look, then suddenly wheeled and kicked.

> "Pick up yer dead!" exultantly yelled the troopers of Troop I.

> But they were almost as much surprised as the bronco. When he kicked, its champion dodged his hoofs, jumped at his bridle and, while the bronco's heels were still in the air, the sergeant was astride him.

> The bronco plunged, reared, pirouetted on one leg, humped himself, sprang into the air, landed with four hoofs together—[but] the sergeant stuck to his back like a plaster, while the opposing troopers yelled encouragement to man or horse.

> Suddenly, the bronco started across the sand dunes, bucking at every jump and disappeared in a little valley. In ten minutes, Troop H's sergeant rode him back, truly gentle as a lamb . . .

"If you've got a live bronco about you, bring him on," remarked the sergeant, as he swung out of the saddle.'" ("The World," *Bully*, 215-7).

All the Rough Riders were excellent horsemen, as well as marksmen, but those who excelled at Bronco Busting were A.C. Fletcher, Newton Stewart, C.T. Owens, Thomas Darnell, Alvin Ash and William Woods. Colonel Roosevelt knew all the riders in the regiment, of course, and said that he had never seen a "bronco buster" in the same class as William Woods of Ratone, New Mexico.

The camp of the Second Cavalry offered soldiers the only canteen and casino in camp. The canteen sold a "hoot" of draught beer at five cents a glass. Individual orders ran as high as fifteen glasses. For some, glasses just couldn't hold enough beer: tin pails, kettles, even a wash boiler, served the purpose. The casino, dubbed Montauk's Monte Carlo, regularly drew as boisterous a crowd as the canteen. Crap shooting and triple dice were the only games played. The crowd waited for a gambler to make a "run" on some number, then placed their bets, inevitably losing to the casino's bank. But they returned the next night to bet again.

The ocean waters were expected to "soak" fevers out of the convalescents' muscles and to drive rheumatism from their bones. As the men's health improved, more and more soldiers ventured to the "splendid" ocean beach; by the first week in September, nearly one thousand bathers could been seen enjoying the surf near the Ditch Plains Life Saving Station. Each afternoon, Colonel Roosevelt would lead a charge of Rough Riders on horseback to the ocean beach for a quick plunge in the sea.

> There was a thunder of hoofs along the level behind Newspaper Row like the sound of a stampede. Everybody ran out and beheld Col. Roosevelt on his big horse tearing across the plain at top speed with a squad of Rough Riders in hot pursuit . . . He was leaning forward in his saddle, his hat jammed far down on his head, his stocky, supple body giving easily to every motion of the powerful animal he rode. He ploughed through a marsh, lifted his mount over a gully in a flying leap, sped over the weedy stretch beyond, plunged down five feet to the sand beach, and pulled up close to the water's edge with his men still behind him. Three minutes later the head of Col. Roosevelt could be seen bobbing just outside the line of breakers . . . Presently, a large and somewhat premature wave broke out beyond the line, caught the cavalry leader unawares, and he disappeared from the scene of action in a swirl of seething water,

to reappear a second later a rod in spluttering and laughing.

"Phew! That makes a man feel alive," he said as he trotted out of the water . . .

A few minutes afterward, he was again leading his squad in a race across the landscape. ("New York Sun," *Bully*, 163).

The ocean held dangers, however, for accomplished and novice swimmers. One week after two Rough Riders were nearly swept out to sea, General Wheeler's youngest son, Naval Cadet Thomas H. Wheeler, and his friend, Lieutenant Newton Kirkpatrick of the First Cavalry, drowned in the waters off Ditch Plains. No incidence of suffering or of death at Camp Wikoff caused greater heartache than the loss of Fighting Joe's youngest son. When Gen. Wheeler reached the spot where his son's body had been found, he knelt there and wept. He said that he wished both he and his son had been killed in Cuba then to have lost his son at Montauk.

As time passed at Camp Wikoff, soldiers were more willing to recall their experiences in the recent war. One night in August, some Rough Riders gathered around the campfire.

"In the city, we all knew that Teddy had moral courage to burn, but since I've seen him in action, I've found out the reason for his independence. I tell you, boys, the trouble with Teddy is that he hasn't got it in him to be afraid. I don't believe even the first bullet scared him," [said Mac] . . .

"Whew! Wasn't he a wild Indian in that charge up the hill!" exclaimed the Spider. "I wouldn't have taken 20-to-1 on his chances of getting to the top alive. He was way ahead of the line all the time."

"Tell you what broke me up," remarked the gambler. 'Just behind him, the boys faltered for a minute, and he turned around and said in that surprised, reproachful sort of way, "Why, boys, you aren't going back on me?' Why, I felt as if my mother had accused me of striking her. There was a lump in my throat like a walnut, and if hell had yawned in front of me, I'd have made a jump to get across rather than not follow after that."

"An' that's the feller that we Western cowpunchers was sort o' dubious about. I'd like to find the man now that would call him a college-bred dude." ("New York Sun," *Bully*, 148/150).

On the afternoon of September 13th, the day mustering out of the famed regiment began, Colonel Roosevelt was asked by a committee of officers to come with them to a flat near his tent, where 500 Rough Riders, 200 men of the Ninth and Tenth Cavalries, and a great number of visitors had gathered. Speaking for the Rough Riders, Private Murphy presented Colonel Roosevelt with Frederick Remington's Bronco Buster statue as an expression of the "admiration, love and esteem" that the Rough had for their fearless leader.

Surprised and visibly affected by this gift from his Rough Riders, Colonel Roosevelt spoke to his regiment for the final time.

> "It gives me extreme pleasure to look around among you and see men of every occupation, men of means and men who work with their hands for a livelihood, and at the same time know that I have you for friends. You are men of widely different pursuits, yet you stand here side-by-side, you fought shoulder-to-shoulder. No man asked quarter for himself, and each one went in to show that he was as good as his neighbor. That is the American spirit. You cannot imagine how proud I am of your friendship and regard.

> "I have also a profound respect for you because you have fighting qualities, and because you had the qualities which enabled us to get you into the fight . . .I realized when I took charge of you that I was taking upon myself a great responsibility. I cared for you as individuals, but did not forget that at any moment it might be necessary to sacrifice the individual for the whole. You would have scorned a commander who would have hesitated to expose you to any risk. I was bound that no other regiment should get any nearer to the Spanish lines than you got, and I do not think any did.

> "I want to say just a word more to some of the men I see standing around not of your number. I refer to the regiments, cavalry regiments, who occupied the right and left flanks of us at Las Guasimas, the Ninth and Tenth Cavalry regiments. The Spaniards called them 'Smoked Yankess,' but we found them to be an excellent breed of Yankee. I am sure that I speak the sentiments of men and officials in the assemblage when I say that between you and the other cavalry regiments there is a tie which we trust will never be broken." ("New York Sun," *Bully*, 324/326).

At 5 P.M. the next day, Colonel Roosevelt, as the commanding officer of his regiment, was the first of the officers to be mustered out of service.

"This ends it, eh?" he remarked with emotion to Lieutenant

Colonel Brodie upon his discharge. The next morning, September 15th, he left Camp Wikoff by train with Lieutenants. Greenway, McIlhenny, Ballard and Sayre, Jr., bound for Sagamore Hill, Oyster Bay.

Within two weeks, he was nominated as the Republican Gubernatorial Candidate at the Republican State Convention in Saratoga. On November 8th, he was elected governor of the state of New York, completing the transition from national war hero to political leader in less than two months.

On October 9th, Secretary of War Alger issued an order directing that the Seventh Infantry, still quartered at Camp Wikoff, proceed to Fort Wayne, thus bringing an end to the military encampment at Montauk.

Following a visit to Montauk later in the month, E.S. Boughton, editor of *The East Hampton Star*, wrote the following:

> There is a weird gloominess about the place from which one cannot escape as he walks around and sees the buildings, which a month since were fairly alive with human beings, now boarded up and left as sad reminders of the scenes of pleasure, joy, delight, sadness, sorrow and misery, which were alternately presented there during the existence of Camp Wikoff ...

> Up on the camp ground, from the tops of the hills, one can look off on sea and sound and imagine Montauk to be what it was before its invasion by the army, but when the eye drops, brown and seared hilltops, gullied and muddy valleys, with hundreds of tall poles scattered far and near and standing as solemn sentinels, picture the transition from past to present.

> With the exception of the wooden hospital buildings which stand in a group over the hill, about a mile east of the station, all that remains of the military grandeur of Camp Wikoff is the little enclosed half-acre on the summit of Rocky Ridge where lie the fever-stricken heroes of the Cuban War. (*Bully*, 448).

Cowpuncher to college athlete, marksmen, horsemen, eleven hundred volunteers hailing from all parts of the country, the First United States Volunteer Cavalry, forever known as Roosevelt's Rough Riders, inspired the nation in the summer of 1898, one hundred years ago.

Much was expected of the Rough Riders that spring and they exceeded those expectations that summer. Just how good were the Rough Riders?

Shortly after his return to Montauk on August 31st, General William

Shafter, commanding general of the Fifth Army Corps, a man in a position to know, said this about the Rough Riders:

> Nobody need make any mistake about that being a good regiment. The Western men were as good as soldiers before they enlisted. . . .The Eastern men were fellows whose nerve and pride carried them along neck-and-neck with the cowboys. Yes, that's a splendid regiment. ("New York Sun," *Bully*, 327).

I would like to thank Tom Twomey and The East Hampton 350th Anniversary Committee, Dr. John Gable of the Theodore Roosevelt Association, the Montauk Historical Society, and the readers who gave dimension to his lecture.

Virgil and Elaine Conway as President and Mrs. McKinley; Jim Foote as Colonel Theodore Roosevelt; Pat Falci as Gen. "Fighting Joe" Wheeler; Anita Brown as Annie Laurie Early Wheeler; Bill Brown for reading "The East Hampton Star" and "Sag Harbor Express" editorials, as well as Roosevelt's charge to the sea; Russell Drumm for reading the descriptions of Montauk and the bronco-busting competition; Jonathan Peters for reading the account of the Prairie, Roosevelt's greeting of President McKinley, and the cowboys in the bronco-busting competition and at the campfire; George Larson for reading the General Hospital narration and the bronco buster; and, finally, Dick White, as the patient in the General Hospital.

FROM BARBIZON TO BONAC

East Hampton as an Art Colony

Helen A. Harrison

A BOUT FORTY MILES southeast of Paris, at the edge of the Fontaine-bleau forest, the rural hamlet of Barbizon began to attract artists as early as the 1820s. Within two decades it had become a mecca for French landscape painters fleeing the city's notoriously disagreeable summers, and for their European and American colleagues searching for picturesque subject matter. Ready access via the railway line from Paris that came to Fontainebleau in 1849 further opened the area to both tourism and artistic colonization. But even when Barbizon was an hour's carriage ride from the nearest railroad station, the rustic village and its wooded surroundings were providing motifs for notable painters such as Camille Corot, Theodore Rousseau, and Diaz de la Pena, who formed the nucleus of the so-called Barbizon School.

By the late nineteenth century, the numerous parallels between the East Hampton art colony and its French predecessor prompted journalists to dub our village the "American Barbizon." Admittedly there were other locales vying for the title—notably Cape Ann in Massachu-setts, where several American veterans of Barbizon set up summer camp in the 1870s, and Old Lyme, Connecticut, which was colonized at the turn of the century by artists who, like their Barbizon forerunners, painted out of doors and aimed to capture the changing effects of light and weather on a domesticated landscape still tinged with wildness. The colonies organized around art schools—for example, the Art Stu-dents League's outpost at Woodstock, New York, William Merritt Chase's Shinnecock Summer School of Art and its offshoot, Provincetown's Cape Cod School of Art, founded by Chase's disciple Charles Hawthorne—were not considered comparable to Barbizon, where established artists congregated in a spirit of collegial enthusiasm and shared creative goals.

Describing the Barbizon phenomenon in *The Good and Simple Life*, his comprehensive and entertaining study of European art colonies, Michael Jacobs mentions various aspects that, if the place names and dates were changed, are also true of East Hampton. Both locations boasted a quaint village peopled by equally quaint inhabitants, many of whom turned out to be remarkably enterprising. Jacobs' account of the Barbizon natives' reaction to the inrush of eager landscapists might well be applicable to East Hampton's villagers:

> They were often initially suspicious, bewildered, amused, and sometimes even antagonistic. However, they were also sensible enough to realize the financial advantages to be gained by having large numbers of artists around: easy money could be had from providing food, accommodation, and studio space, posing for the artists, and even charging them (often illegally) for painting on their land. Moreover, in places where photographers hardly came, it flattered their vanity to have likenesses made of themselves. (pp. 13–14)

The area's legendary character, celebrated in stories and songs, was another of Barbizon's prime attractions for artists. The forest itself had long ago been romanticized by poets, in whose sixteenth-century odes, according to Jacobs, "the real world of Fontainebleau and the world of classical mythology were curiously intermingled." (p. 17) Even the American writer James Fenimore Cooper, who visited in 1827, was surprisingly captivated by the place, declaring that it exceeded in "savage variety" anything he had encountered at home. Cooper's paean to an unspoiled Fontainebleau—pointedly ignoring the nearby royal hunting lodge and convenient thoroughfares developed under Louis XIV—is echoed in Walt Whitman's 1849 treatise on the "wonders and beauties" of Montauk's wilderness in his *Letters from a Traveling Bachelor*, and the laudatory chapter on East Hampton in William Cullen Bryant's popular and liberally illustrated *Picturesque America*, published in 1872–74.

As their French forebears had been drawn to rural peasant life as a symbol of the values missing from modern industrialized society, the idyllic character of John Howard Payne's "Home, Sweet Home," immortalized in a very popular ballad, would make East Hampton a similar focus of sentimental questing. In 1878 the Payne site provided artists with a convenient target at which to aim a well-publicized expedition to eastern Long Island. As one of their number wrote in a lighthearted account of the trip (published in *Scribner's* magazine the following February), the humble cottage was amply endowed with picturesque features, most notably the ancient hearth, which they considered to be "the vital center of the whole Payne legend." Actually the question of whether the artists had indeed discovered the fabled hearth was a subject of some conjecture. "Payne was born in two or three houses of Easthampton," they observed dryly, "besides Boston and No. 33 Broad Street, New York." Despite the initial confusion—during which several competing local guides offered to take them, for a fee, to the genuine property—they reached a consensus on one dwelling and "went on to make it their own, artist-fashion."

Here again the parallel between East Hampton and Barbizon is revealing, for artists responded to both locations selectively, ignoring the aspects that did not suit their aesthetic and ideological purposes. The squalor and poverty that often characterized rural life was glossed over in favor of its bucolic appeal and pre-industrial symbolism. At the same time, the surrounding countryside—whether Barbizon's forest or East Hampton's farmland and coastline—was coming under increasing pressure from the commercial development and tourism made possible by the railroad's advent. The vehicle that embodied the Industrial Revolution's relentless motive power was, according to a French journalist quoted by Jacobs, responsible for making Fontainebleau "seem little more than a suburb of Paris, and bringing (much to the regret of the many artists in the neighborhood) vast crowds of day-trippers to the place at the weekends." (p. 19) That account described Barbizon in 1849, but it is just as relevant to East Hampton after 1895, when the Long Island Rail Road line was extended through from Bridgehampton to Montauk and the whole region became far more accessible to tourists from New York City and its eastern suburbs.

Proximity to the nation's art capital is another of the striking analogies between Barbizon and East Hampton, although in physical distance the parallel is not accurate. Nevertheless, in spite of being more than twice as far from New York City as Barbizon is from Paris, East Hampton's art colony from its inception was similarly linked to the acknowledged urban center of artistic activity. Measured in terms of miles, the Cape Ann-Boston connection is a better match to Barbizon-Paris, but by the 1880s, when Gloucester and Rockport became artistic destinations, New York was ascendant over Boston as the American art world's premier professional training ground and marketplace. In terms of scenery if not distance, one might consider Barbizon closer to the wooded, inland environs of New Hope or Woodstock than to the maritime landscape of eastern Long Island. New Hope, a charming town on the New Jersey-Pennsylvania border, was more allied to Philadelphia's art community than to Manhattan's. Woodstock, which has certainly attracted its share of prominent artists since its advent as an art colony in the early twentieth century, is even farther from Manhattan than is East Hampton, and the village is several miles inland from the New York Central rail line that serves the Hudson Valley. Moreover, and perhaps decisively to its detriment as an artists' retreat, Woodstock suffers from long, hard winters that shorten the season for outdoor work and make travel to and from the city inconvenient, even perilous.

As the real estate agents are fond of repeating, "location, location, location." This indeed seems to have been the factor that tipped the balance in East Hampton's favor during the late nineteenth century and accounts for our continuing vitality as an artists' community. But, like the region itself, the art colony has undergone profound changes since its beginnings as a Barbizon-inspired enclave of plein-air painters in search of scenic vistas and unspoiled rustic motifs. One of the most consequential was the shift in emphasis from representational painting to abstraction. The influx of landscape and genre painters that began in the late 1870s lasted for thirty years, during which many New York-based artists established seasonal residences and some moved here full time. That period of the colony's development will be the subject of Kate Cameron's talk later in this series, so I will focus instead on East Hampton's transition from its "Barbizon" phase to what I have dubbed its "Bonac" incarnation, heralded by the Surrealists' temporary occupation during World War II and fully realized in the following decade with the arrival of New York's vanguard, the Abstract Expressionists.

In spite of its earlier reputation as an art colony, East Hampton was not attracting a new generation in the twentieth century. Although a few artists continued to arrive in the 1920s and '30s—highlighted by the establishment of Hilton Leech's Amagansett Art School in 1933—an aura of complacency and tradition discouraged bohemian aspirations. And, in terms one often hears repeated today, there were complaints that well-heeled summer residents had pushed property prices beyond the reach of all but the most affluent artists. Turning their attention to enclaves that, while more remote, were both affordable and welcoming, the avant-garde summered in Provincetown and Woodstock, leaving East Hampton to established landscape painters like Childe Hassam, William J. Whittemore, Francis Newton, and Arthur T. Hill. These artists and their conservative colleagues provided the regular bill of fare at Guild Hall, which opened in 1931 as the community's cultural center. At the building's inauguration, Hassam dedicated the main gallery to the memory of Thomas Moran, the distinguished landscape painter who, with his wife, the etcher Mary Nimmo, had erected the first purpose-built artists' residence in the village in 1884. But when Hassam held forth eloquently on the Morans' pivotal role in attracting fellow artists to East Hampton, he was essentially speaking in the past tense.

During the following decade, however, that situation was to change in ways that not everyone agreed were for the better. With the outbreak of World War II, New York became a haven for European artists, writers, and intellectuals fleeing Nazi persecution. Their contributions to the city's postwar emergence as the international capital of contemporary art have long been acknowledged, but it was not until Phyllis Braff's 1996 exhibition at Guild Hall that their significance to East Hampton's artistic revitalization was fully examined. In her catalogue for *The Surrealists and their Friends on Eastern Long Island at Mid-Century*, Braff outlined the influences that led the emerging American vanguard to consider the region as a suitable retreat. Like previous migrations to this and other locales, this one was spearheaded by a few individuals whose accounts prompted others to join them.

Among the first to arrive were the abstractionist Fernand Leger and his companion Lucia Christofanetti, who used her first name professionally and was associated with the Surrealist circle in Paris. The couple left Europe under the auspices of Gerald and Sara Murphy, a wealthy expatriate couple who in the 1920s had entertained Picasso, Hemingway, Scott and Zelda Fitzgerald, and other artistic and literary notables at their Mediterranean estate, which they dubbed Villa America. After their return to the United States, the Murphys' country retreat was *The Dunes*, Sara's family property on East Hampton's oceanfront, where they offered hospitality to their refugee friends. As the Murphys' daughter, Honoria Donnelly, recalled in her 1982 memoir, *Sara & Gerald*:

> Villa America and After, her father loved to discuss painting with Leger. Although Murphy had abandoned his own brief career as an artist in 1929, he identified strongly with creative people and relished their company. "It's always great to back up once a year and take on a load of [Leger]," Murphy once told

his friend John Dos Passos. "He's very exciting on the subject of surrealiste direction." (p. 227)

For several summers Leger and Lucia were given the use of cottages at The Dunes, and Lucia was so smitten with the area that she eventually settled here. Her enthusiasm was also responsible for attracting other expatriates. According to Braff, Lucia "urged the Surrealists, now waiting out the war in New York, to join her on Long Island. According to family legend, there was always a room ready in her home for André Breton and for Marcel Duchamp. . . . Many members of the extended Surrealist community shared accommodations with her in East Hampton and Amagansett," where the gregarious Lucia "regularly mixed American and European artists at her gatherings." (pp. 6, 32)

In a vignette from his engrossing 1984 memoir, *A Not-So-Still Life*, Max Ernst's son Jimmy remembered visiting his father in Amagansett during the summer of 1945, when many of the Surrealists and their coterie were in residence there. With Lucia as hostess, "friends like Breton, Ernst, Duchamp, Leger, [Roberto] Matta, David Hare and [Robert] Motherwell . . . shared the potluck of her Syrian cuisine, played chess and engaged in severely regimented intellectual party games on the beach, much to the annoyance of the local Bonackers." (pp. 250–51) Not only were the high-jinks (which also featured bathing beauties in improvised Continental-style bikinis) exotic by neighborhood standards, but the cast of characters was decidedly polyglot and therefore doubly suspect. In addition to the French contingent, it included the German Ernst; Matta, who hailed from Chile; Romanian-born architect Frederick Kiesler; the Cuban Wifredo Lam; Japanese-American sculptor Isamu Noguchi; and Sonia Sekula, a native of Switzerland.

If the foreign interlopers received a predictably cool reception from area residents, they in turn were unexpectedly tolerant of the young American artists who fraternized with them in the relaxed atmosphere of country summers. In New York City, the Surrealists were generally aloof, their air of natural superiority compounded by the language barrier. But with French-speakers like the Murphys and Motherwell and the English-speaking Duchamp and Matta as go-betweens, social tensions were eased and professional guards lowered if not dropped. The pivotal bilingual intermediary was Stanley William Hayter, an English-born printmaker whose Paris workshop, Atelier 17, had been a hotbed of graphic experimentation before the outbreak of war forced it to close. In 1940 Hayter transferred his workshop to New

York, where he soon was joined by many of his former associates, among them Max Ernst, André Masson, Joan Miro, and Ives Tanguy. Hayter's experimental approach, which stressed Surrealist-inspired iconoclasm, improvisation, and technical innovation, also attracted young New York-based artists eager for first-hand contact with the European vanguard.

Hayter and his American wife, the sculptor Helen Phillips, first visited eastern Long Island in 1944. As Phillips later told the author Jeffrey Potter: "There were so many Surrealists there in summer that a pair of women all dressed up stopped me on Amagansett Main Street and said, 'We're from Southampton. Can you tell us where we'll find the Surrealists?' The Europeans did stick together actually, and none of us had much money, which is why we were there. That and Provincetown's being too far from New York." (p. 86) Again location was a crucial factor, but one based on economics and convenience rather than aesthetic imperatives. For unlike their nineteenth-century counterparts, art colonists who sought creative inspiration in the unconscious mind did not look outward to the beautiful seaside scenery and charming villages as sources of subject matter. Still, those assets were highly desirable in a vacation spot, especially if the price was right, and they found that inexpensive rentals were available outside the established summer resort sections. One summer the Hayters rented a fisherman's shack at Louse Point—a decision that, in retrospect, had far-reaching consequences for the art colony.

In his 1985 book, *To a Violent Grave: An Oral Biography of Jackson Pollock*, Potter tells the tale of that fateful summer rental, an economical if somewhat primitive structure "with a leaky roof, a hand pump, and no electricity." (p. 80) Unfortunately, although its position on the shore of Gardiner's Bay was sublime, it was too remote for Hayter, who had to bike to the train station for his regular trips into the city, where Atelier 17 demanded his supervision. At the workshop, Hayter's assistant was a young sculptor named Reuben Kadish, one of Jackson Pollock's closest friends. When Hayter learned that Kadish, short of funds, was stuck in the city for the summer, he offered him the use of the shack, which was paid up for the season. Kadish accepted gladly, and invited Pollock and Lee Krasner, who were then living together, to share the place with him and his wife. Thus it happened that by chance Pollock and Krasner, who had been summering in Provincetown but were too broke to afford the trip that year, found themselves in East Hampton in August 1945.

The Kadishes remembered the vacation as a carefree time, the days filled with bike rides, clamming, and good-natured horseplay, although Krasner was worried, as always, that Pollock's beer drinking would get out of hand. (pp. 80–81) But compared to the city, where liquor and like-minded companions were plentiful, East Hampton offered a respite from the social and professional pressures that literally drove Pollock to drink and caused Krasner such anxiety. The couple even speculated about subletting their city apartment and finding a cheap winter rental where they could concentrate on work. They did a little house-hunting with the Kadishes in Amagansett, but it wasn't until they returned to the city after Labor Day that Pollock suddenly decided their pipe dream would become a reality. Their friends, the writers Harold Rosenberg and May Tabak, had bought an old house on Neck Path in The Springs, a hamlet that had previously attracted few people "from away." If the Rosenbergs could manage it, so could Pollock and Krasner. They contacted the realtor Edward Cook, who showed them a rundown homestead on Fireplace Road that was on the market for $5,000. As Cook explained to Potter, the property was also available for rent, but Pollock was looking to purchase and move to the area permanently. "Pollock had no money at all but access to some, I guess," Cook remarked. "Anyway, he knew enough about money to want to own instead of paying it out in rent with nothing to show." (p. 86)

The money to which Pollock had "access" was a loan from his dealer and patron Peggy Guggenheim. With her $2,000 as down payment and a local bank mortgage for the balance, Pollock took title to the property in November 1945. He and Krasner had been married the previous month, with May Rosenberg as witness. According to a 1973 videotaped interview with Krasner, in the Pollock-Krasner House and Study Center's oral history collection, she wanted to formalize their relationship now that they were settling down, especially in a community she believed was conservative and would not accept an unmarried couple. Their honeymoon was spent cleaning out the house, which was an improvement on the Louse Point shack but nevertheless lacked hot water and a bathroom, and had only coal stoves downstairs for heat. Notwithstanding the initial hardships, the couple felt confident enough to invite the family for Thanksgiving and were soon issuing eager invitations to their artist friends.

Like the Morans sixty years earlier, the Pollocks were a magnet for their contemporaries and were soon acting as unofficial real estate agents for colleagues who could scrape together the price of a fixer-upper in the neighborhood. In his anecdotal account of the Bonac art colony's rapid growth, written for the 1984 book, *Springs: A Celebra-*

tion, David Myers noted (p. 58) that Pollock found houses for David Porter, Conrad Marca-Relli, John Little, and Wilfrid Zogbaum, who in turn sold parcels of his land to Willem de Kooning and John Ferren. The Pollocks were also responsible for notifying Alfonso Ossorio that The Creeks—the spectacular Georgica estate built in 1899 for the artists Albert and Adele Herter—was on the market, and it became Ossorio's permanent home in 1952. By that time the Surrealists were long gone, but in their wake had developed something like an artistic tidal wave that included many members of the burgeoning Abstract Expressionist movement.

The transition from Old Guard to vanguard was not greeted with universal approval, however. Motherwell had already caused consternation among his Georgica Road neighbors in 1946 with his audacious home and studio, designed by the French architect Pierre Chareau using war surplus Quonset huts, and the presence of other modernists threatened the equilibrium of East Hampton's cultural establishment. When Guild Hall's art committee elected to invite several of the newcomers to participate in the 1949 annual invitational exhibition of regional artists, the latent animosity between conservative and progressive factions escalated into open conflict. The *East Hampton Star*'s reviewer (as quoted by Enez Whipple in her invaluable 1993 history, *Guild Hall of East Hampton: An Adventure in the Arts*), found the artists' vision "sordid and scrambled," but conceded that not everyone shared that opinion. "It was our happy experience to hear an art lover exclaim again and again what he found in gazing upon a combination of colors that to us did not seem to hold possibilities for even a fourth-rate linoleum pattern," the balanced editorial voice advised, concluding that a visitor to the show "will either go home a raving enthusiast for the new expression, or leave the galleries perplexed and disappointed." (p. 241) Eight years later the confrontational mood was still evident, but as Gerald Sykes wrote of the "art wars" in a checklist essay for the 1957 invitational at Guild Hall, "so far at least, all the bloodshed has been verbal. . . . There will be violence, but it will exhaust itself in a few well-worn phrases, such as every museum guard knows by heart."

No amount of negative rhetoric could stem the tide of change, as more and more of the vanguard generation made their own transition from young tyros to modern masters. By the late 1950s quite a few of them were under the guidance of respected New York dealers, but there was no commercial gallery in East Hampton to market the work locally. Ad hoc exhibitions at the House of Music and Books lasted only two years, and came to an end when the bookshop moved. In 1957 three artists—Ossorio, Little, and Elizabeth Parker—took on the task of showing and selling advanced art as a labor of love. Their venture, known as the Signa Gallery to indicate its status as a "sign of the times," mixed the work of area residents with that of outsiders, including a sizeable foreign contingent. In keeping with the philosophy that contemporary art is international in character, Signa exhibited European, Asian, and American artists—more than 120 of them during its four seasons of operation. The gallery's emphasis was on abstraction and its image cosmopolitan, two qualities that did not contribute to audience cultivation in a community already ambivalent over the new art's merits. As Ossorio told me in a 1990 interview, excerpts of which were published in my Guild Hall exhibition catalogue, *East Hampton Avant-Garde: A Salute to the Signa Gallery*, most of the gallery's sales were to "established collectors ... who knew a good thing when they saw it," not to the converts he had hoped the gallery would attract. (p. 15)

According to Ossorio, the Signa Gallery "more or less broke even," but the fact that it failed to accomplish its ideological purpose made it a disappointment for the three partners, whose involvement was increasingly time-consuming and burdensome. As Little's wife, Josephine, pointed out, there came a moment when each "had to decide either to run a gallery or be a painter." (p. 18) They all decided in favor of their own art, and the gallery closed after the 1960 season. By then, however, other commercial galleries had appeared in the area, and Guild Hall's policy of including advanced artists in regional invitationals was no longer controversial. And the local art community—comprising property owners (some of whom were full-time residents), seasonal renters, and occasional visitors—had grown exponentially, representing numerous aesthetic viewpoints, from traditional landscape painting to Pop Art.

While East Hampton, especially the Bonac neighborhood, remained its undisputed hub, the South Fork's loosely knit confederation of artist-residents extended throughout the region, and as the decades wore on the growth rate showed no signs of slackening. Southampton had attracted the figurative painter Fairfield Porter as a full-time resident in 1949, after which several of his friends migrated there and prompted others to follow. Even earlier, the Russian emigrant David Burliuk had transferred from New York City to Hampton Bays, where he established an artistic enclave that included the painter George Constant and the sculptor Michael Lekakis. In Sag Harbor, Alexander Brook and Niles Spencer were among the postwar colonists, while far-flung Montauk, once home to Balcomb Greene and Andy Warhol, continues to attract the younger generation through seasonal artists' residencies offered by the Edward Albee Foundation. Today even the idea of listing all the artists active in the region is too daunting to contemplate seriously, although I have toyed with it in delusional moments.

Unlike Barbizon, in fact unlike most art colonies, East Hampton maintained its appeal even after its original artist population died or migrated elsewhere and its raison d'etre, plein-air landscape and genre painting, fell out of fashion. After a fallow period that might have proved fatal, it was revitalized by a group that fortunately had no interest in pursuing a moribund aesthetic. Looking for recreation rather than inspiration, the Surrealists found a convenient, affordable rural retreat where they could both work and play. The psychological effect was to shatter the stereotype of an art colony as a Barbizon-style source of motifs and to reinvent it as a place of spiritual and creative sustenance. This radical rethinking of such a community's function—coupled with the obvious advantage of its easy access to and from New York City—virtually guaranteed that this would become a permanent destination for artists, regardless of their work's medium or style. And, paradoxically perhaps, many of those who came and continue to come as the century draws to a close are landscape painters, who are reinvigorating what once seemed to be an outmoded tradition by investing it with subjectivity and originality.

Also in contrast to the Fontainebleau area, eastern Long Island can boast a significant contingent of native artists. As I wrote in a 1989 article for the annual magazine, *Provincetown Arts*, "for those born and raised here, the existence of an active art community has provided both validation of their artistic impulses and a sympathetic milieu in which to develop. Unlike most artists who come from areas outside the urban centers of artistic activity, they are able to find stimulation and support right in their own back yard." (p. 137) To my mind, the true test of an art colony's vitality is its contribution to the community at large, as exemplified by the South Fork's artist immigrants, who nurture indigenous talent through teaching, mentoring, and personal encouragement, and participate in civic life as active and responsible residents. This is the spirit that will ensure the artistic future of East Hampton, and indeed the region, for generations to come.

EAST HAMPTON
ARCHITECTURE:

Plain and Fancy

―⁓⁓―

Paul Goldberger

I AM DELIGHTED TO BE HERE, for all kinds of reasons. It is a great pleasure to speak at Guild Hall at any occasion, but particularly as part of
this celebration. Not that many towns get to mark this kind of an anniversary, and fewer still mark it in this way—with a kind of introspec-
tive look at the town's past and the town's present, and with an eye to
figuring out what all of this will mean to the town's future.

The seriousness of conception of this entire lecture series is really
unusual; I would tend to think that most towns, upon reaching a significant anniversary, would mark it with some sort of celebration or party
or whatever. If I did not have some experience with East Hampton I
would have to conclude that this must obviously be a town that does
not think much of parties, and tends to avoid any kind of merriment in
favor of constant sobriety. After all, tell me in what other beach community in the country are people spending the Fourth of July weekend
inside a lecture hall? If my only introduction to East Hampton were the
program of this lecture series, I would think this would be the worst
place in the world to locate a catering business. In any event I congratulate Tom Twomey on turning East Hampton, at least for the 350th, into
the most Calvinist of summer resorts.

In truth, however, there is a long history of connecting summer resorts to learning, and study, and reflection. There are the religious retreats like Ocean Grove, New Jersey and Oak Bluffs, Martha's Vineyard.
There is also Chautauqua near Jamestown in upstate New York, the
world capital of summer lecturing. And of course even right here,
Guild Hall has a long and honorable tradition of reminding people that

thinking hard, being entertained, and relaxing by the sea are not incompatible objectives.

I'm starting off with these general thoughts because my real subject this afternoon is not so much architecture in terms of individual buildings, though I will say something about several of them, as it is the way in which architecture relates to the whole idea of spirit of community, and sense of place. What is it that makes East Hampton East Hampton? What gives it its extraordinary character? How much of its character is a matter of history, coming from the past, and how much of it is made by the present? And—the crucial question—how much does the future of East Hampton depend upon the past?

I hope in the next few minutes to be able to address these questions, since they are more on everyone's mind these days than ever before, I think—in large part because so many of us feel that the character of East Hampton, so secure for so long, is now in danger. Since I want to talk more about these general issues than about individual buildings, I ask your indulgence so far as slides are concerned— I've decided not to show any, since it would force us back to focusing on this building and that building, and I want to talk more about the wholeness of this place, and where it is going. Another way to put this would be to say that if there is any reason to devote one of the lectures in this important series to the subject of architecture, it is not because of the individual buildings of East Hampton, important though many of them may be, but because of the connections between architecture and sense of place. That is the key issue right now. The specific architectural differences between, say, the Schuyler Quackenbush House by Cyrus Eidlitz on Lee Avenue—one of the greatest Shingle Style houses of all, in many ways the Platonic Shingle Style house from the first great wave of resort construction here—and a neo-Shingle Style house built five years ago down Georgica Road matter less to me than looking at both of these buildings to think about the question about how old and new relate together to affect a sense of place, and whether the best way to preserve those qualities of East Hampton that we value is by making more Shingle Style houses that resemble the great and beloved originals, or whether it is by doing something else.

I will warn you at the outset that no matter how carefully you listen you will not find a simple, formulaic answer to this question, because there is none. There are a million specific instances, and formulas do not help get us through them. This is too complex a town, and its architectural and urbanistic fabric too richly multilayered, for any neat and pat formula to get us through.

There is no place like East Hampton, anywhere—not even that town, whatever it is, you know, the one a few miles to the west where they have a lot of car dealerships—even Southampton, for all its might, does not have precisely the combination of qualities that gives East Hampton its extraordinary, gentle and powerful aura. This is a remarkable anniversary, the 350th birthday, and before I say anything else I should state, emphatically and absolutely, how strong this town remains as both an architectural and a natural environment, whatever criticisms and fears about its changes and its losses all of us may have. It is astonishing to me that fifteen years have passed since I wrote a long article in the *New York Times Magazine* entitled "The Strangling of a Resort," an article that was among the first to sound an alarm about what is happening here, and I am about to say something which will sound on its face very contradictory, which is that things were bad then, and they have gotten considerably worse since then—and yet they are still not nearly as bad as they could have been, or as other places are.

East Hampton was among the first towns anywhere in this country to recognize the urgency of preservation, but you know from experience how firmly and absolutely it is possible to say that the work of preservation is never done—that it is impossible to sit back in confidence, congratulating yourselves on being the distinguished and beautiful place that you are, certain that your work is done and the task is over. The task is never over; the work is never done. There are always new threats, new dangers to the historic integrity of a city. But it is not merely a matter of being the police force for architectural integrity. If it were just that, the job would be simple. There is the much more complex task of land use, since one of the things I have been saying is that land use—issues of zoning and planning—cannot be separated from issues of architecture. That is one of the things I was trying to say back in that 1983 article, when architecture critics were not supposed to think in these terms. But now more than ever, we have to look at architecture in terms of land use, and not simply esthetics. Once East Hampton had the luxury of simply building, of building what seemed to make sense, and not thinking very deeply of the effect of each building on the whole. Each building could be a thing unto itself. Now we have no such luxury, and every building, every project, every possible building and project has to be looked at in terms of what it will mean for the community at large. That is why, at this moment in East Hampton's history, I think it is fair to say that our planning boards may mean more for the future of our architecture than any architect. So, too, with organizations such as the Peconic Land Trust, the Group for the South Fork, and the Nature Conservancy—they will make this community safe for architecture, and without them it will not matter whether we make decent buildings or not, because we will not have a decent community.

And frankly, if we want to be brutally honest, if we look at what makes the village of East Hampton the extraordinary place that it is, the good architecture is only a part of it. The landscape, the trees, the presence of the town pond and cemetery as both symbol and visual amenity, the beaches, the exquisite eclecticism of Main Street and Newtown Lane, and the magnificent way in which Route 27 passes through the heart of the village, democratically revealing its beauties for all, the precise opposite of that other town—all of these things define East Hampton. It may be heresy for an architecture critic to say that these things are more important than architecture, but the truth is—they are. Land matters more than buildings. If we preserve the land, then we can afford to start worrying about what buildings we build. If we do not preserve the land, it will not matter what buildings we build, because the East Hampton we love and cherish will be gone.

We often want our favorite places, like cherished friends, to be frozen in time, their images precisely as we remembered them when we last saw them, whether it is a year ago or five years ago or yesterday. Who has ever gone to Venice in search of change, happy to find things different? Who, even, goes to Paris looking for new things, restaurants, I suppose, excepted?

But of course time does not freeze for people, and it does not do so with towns and cities, either. East Hampton has not changed as much as some of you may think it has, but it has changed plenty over the last decade, as it had changed over the decade before that, and as it will change over the decade to come. It is painful to accept, but it is real and necessary. You cannot freeze a city in time any more than you can freeze a human being. You cannot, that is, unless what you want is a kind of Colonial Williamsburg, a town that is really a museum, and if that is what you want, I am the wrong person to be talking to you today, since that route—the Williamsburg route—in my opinion is death for any real city. Perhaps Venice is an exception, but then again, perhaps not, since Venice is not a real city either in the terms by which we define real cities today—it is an extraordinary place, dazzlingly potent in a way that is like no other place in the world, but not, for all its power and glory, truly a living city. But East Hampton, I think, has the mission of being more of a living community, and thus raises all kinds of other issues.

Towns and cities—at least the real kind, the category I believe East Hampton must be in—change to stay alive, as people change to stay alive. They go through phases, and periods, and in the very fact of change is a kind of affirmation of life. Yet I have to say that there is something faulty in my metaphor, since in the end, towns and cities are not like people. Yes, they change continually, and cities cannot be frozen in time just as people cannot be frozen in time, but towns and cities have one great advantage over people: change in towns does not have to be a series of steps toward inevitable decline. When we see change in the faces of our friends there is a kind of sadness because the process of aging reminds us that they are one step toward leaving us, one step closer, alas, to death, but it is not so at all for cities. Indeed, in cities, change is not merely a reminder of continued life, it is a step toward assuring it. The city that evolves healthily lives, perhaps forever. The city that does not change is more often the city that dies. It is the opposite of the natural cycle we experience as people.

All well and good, to speak in such generalities. But what does this mean in real life of towns—towns that, like East Hampton, are faced with pressures for change that are enormous, and are full of citizens who, like many in this room I suspect, know that to give in to these pressures is to watch the disappearance of the town as they have known and loved it. Change has been a horror in the recent history of many towns and cities, and it has not always been a friend to East Hampton, as I need hardly tell any of you. Let me make it perfectly clear that by advocating change at the outset I am not here to say that I advocate a laissez-faire approach to cities, or anything remotely resembling that. Don't take anything I've said in favor of change as a general principle as even remotely suggesting that I believe that change is right for its own sake, just because it is change. No, no, a thousand times no. Probably ninety percent of the changes that have been proposed for East Hampton over the last generation are wrong, and destructive, and those of you who have been trying to stop them are probably right. I mean to say only that I hope you are not stopping them because you want to stop all change, and freeze this city in time. I do not want you to stand in the way of the ten percent of changes that are positive, that are healthy for the future of East Hampton. I do not believe that cities survive when they are completely frozen in time. All I am trying to say is that cities are not meant to be embalmed—not that they should ever let down their guard about negative and destructive change.

Let me say another general word or two about the meaning of change in cities right now, about how it affects our sensibility, our sense of where we are and our relationship to a place. Perhaps it is better thought of as a kind of parable. Some years ago the late Anatole Broyard, who for many years was a book reviewer at the *New York Times*, wrote a column in which he recalled a visit to New York by the novelist Francoise Sagan and her friend Florence Malraux, daughter of the great writer Andre Malraux. It was the first visit to the United States for both women, and they were entranced, like many Europeans, by the sense of freedom they felt here. Miss Malraux noted that New York had no past, that it was improvised every moment. She called the French the spoiled children of history, the Americans its resourceful orphans. Miss Sagan observed that the French are made tired by their past, for it surrounds them too tightly; "we can never be unfaithful to it," she said. And then she noted that history, ideally, should be "not a continued presence but a series of passionate interludes."

Well, it is hard not to like the metaphor of history and passion— the French, of course, can make anything into a metaphor involving passion, but in this case it is particularly appealing. History should not surround us so tightly we cannot breathe. That is oppressive in every aspect of culture, and not just architecture. But the opposite—the sense of being without a past altogether—is equally oppressive, in its way. It may be initially exhilarating, especially to a visitor to whom it connotes escape from too much history. But it is also formless, lonely, empty—a culture of shifting sands.

As in all things, balance is the key. A place that changes not at all will die, and a place that changes too much, though it will live, will live an existence empty of meaning. Francoise Sagan was not speaking of architecture when she talked of history as a series of passionate interludes, but she could have been. For a physical environment with the right mix of time in the past and time in the present, with the right mix of things that can change and things that cannot and will not change, is what we have always needed. For all things are not permanent and should not be. But one of the hardest things to learn is where we should have those passionate interludes, where they will do the most for us and for the quality of life and the place we care about.

It goes without saying, of course, that the parable of Francoise Sagan's observations about history in this country could well apply to East Hampton. This is a town in which we run the risk, continually, of being somewhat like Francoise Sagan found France, or indeed all of Europe, to be—spoiled by history, surrounded by too much of it, glorious though it may be, and in the end, despite its glory not uplifted by it but instead oppressed by it. Now, in an age in which historic preservation is an accepted good, an age in which we no longer have to fight the battles in favor of the basic idea of preservation, there is a terrible danger of having history be too present, a danger of pressure to make this place one in which change is no longer valued. To those of you who fight the good fight to keep East Hampton from turning into Ronkonkoma, this may seem an odd problem to raise—after all, with every possible danger that faces a this town, how could there be anything wrong with too much preservation, how could there even be such a thing as too much preservation? In fact, as I've been saying for the last couple of minutes, there can be something very wrong about too much preservation, about a city preserved in amber, cut off from the change that is urban lifeblood. The "passionate interludes" that Francoise Sagan spoke of—and that is a wonderful phrase—become harder and harder to achieve when a place is frozen in time. Is there passion in Williamsburg? Not much to my mind.

The incredibly difficult goal is to keep the passion in East Hampton, to keep it from becoming bloodless, like Williamsburg, but retain a sense of the real. Now I don't think that a loss of passionate interludes, a loss of a sense of history as something intense enough to inspire passion rather than as so routine nobody cares about it, is the primary risk East Hampton faces at this moment in history, but it is still something to keep in mind. A town as rich in history as East Hampton, and with a quality as unique, runs the genuine risk of taking its history so for granted that it loses all sense of perspective about it, loses the ability to think of it as something to inspire wonderful emotional connections, and constant surprise. History must never be thought so routine, so ordinary, so omnipresent, that we cease to feel it. And the other side of that same coin—we must never fall so in love with history that we lose all desire to live in the present—is an equal danger. The beauty of the East Hampton we imagine from the turn of the last century is magically, wonderfully, seductive. How easy it is to look around these streets and think that the more we wrap ourselves in the illusion that it is 1900, the better off we will be!

And yet that never works. The only true, valid, lasting gift the preservation movement can give us is to integrate history into the normal, everyday life of a city and its citizens, to make it not just an occasional occurrence but part of the lifeblood: to help us live better today, not to create the illusion that we are living in yesterday. History should not confine us, it should not take us away from reality, and neither should it be kept to the periphery of our lives. It should liberate us, free us, to define a place on our own terms, with our own perceptions. We preserve not just to defer to the past, but to make a richer present.

Of course it's only fair and proper to ask at this point just what I am talking about when I say history in East Hampton. Whose history? The settlers' East Hampton of the eighteenth century? The first summer colonists' East Hampton of the late nineteenth century? The East Hampton of fishermen, the East Hampton of artists, the East Hampton of teachers and firemen and policemen and storekeepers who live every day of the year here, the East Hampton of investment bankers who stop here in between Manhattan and Aspen? The East Hampton of Childe Hassam or the East Hampton of Jackson Pollock? To a certain extent I am talking about all of these groups, and a key issue East Hampton has faced for a long time, as all of you know, is the tension between its different layers of history. This is not a pure New England village, and it is not just a fishing community, and it is not just a cultural center and it is not just a well-to-do summer resort, and it is most certainly not just a World's Fair of elegant architecture in various styles. It is a most astonishing hybrid of all of these things, and it is in the dynamic between all of these layers of history that much of East Hampton's uniqueness lies.

By that I mean to say that the presence of late twentieth-century East Hampton, far from compromising the integrity of eighteenth- and nineteenth-century and early twentieth-century East Hampton, enriches it, for it takes it out of the realm of a make-believe place, and into the realm of a city that exists over time. The same is true the other way around—the presence of eighteenth-century East Hampton makes the newer buildings here something different from what they might otherwise have been. It shows us that they spring out of a community, however little architectural connection some of them they may have to that community, and we cannot but think of them, at least in part, as saying something about their context, if only to reject it.

Is there an East Hampton style? Now we get down to the real business of the afternoon. The answer to that question is almost, but not totally, and I am very grateful for the "not totally" part of this equation, for the buildings that make this place less purebred, that show it to be of complicated and mixed architectural ancestry, are especially important to my vision of East Hampton. This town is not only eighteenth- and nineteenth-century architecture, rich though our inventory of such buildings is, and it is certainly not just Shingle Style, for all that East Hampton has some essential works of American architecture in this style, and it is not nineteenth-century industrial, or Gothic Revival, or

English cottage, or mid-twentieth-century modern, or late twentieth-century post-modern. It is something of all of these things, but no one kind of architecture controls all, and that is an essential fact of East Hampton architecture. New England farmhouses and saltboxes and cottages play as major a role in East Hampton's architectural heritage as the great mansions of the Shingle Style; so do the commercial buildings of the nineteenth and twentieth centuries, and so do the important monuments of twentieth-century domestic architecture, which flourished here as in few other places in the country. This mixture prevents East Hampton from falling prey to the disease of a place like, say, Santa Barbara, where everything either is Spanish Mission or is presumed to be; or Santa Fe, where a kind of hybrid of Spanish Colonial and Pueblo architecture is all but mandated; or Aspen and Vail, where increasingly a kind of Swiss Alps or neo-Adirondack Lodge style is considered the only proper way to honor the place's history.

There are times when this is forgotten, of course, and one of the more troubling aspects of the current day is the extent to which the Shingle Style, for all its wonders and glories—and this is one of the great civilizing architectural styles in American history—has been taken up as a kind of automatic vernacular style of this area today. Well, better a piece of imitation Shingle Style architecture than a piece of second-rate modernism, or strip mall architecture, or whatever. But still—this is not an answer. Not long ago I saw a local architect—I will not use his name—quoted in one of the slick Hamptons magazines as saying that the Shingle Style was the true style of this area, that nothing else was authentic, and that therefore it was right and proper to build everything now in that style.

To me this is a sign not of the strength of East Hampton's commitment to good architecture, but of the weakness of it. For by doing every last thing in the Shingle Style, for all the good intentions this may represent, we are denying our town the most precious gift its historic architecture can give it, which is authenticity. When everything is done in one style, and all new buildings are ordered to imitate a certain style of the past, we begin to lose the very thing architecture is supposed to give you in a real town or city, which is a sense of time. Strangely enough, we destroy the very idea of continuity that we are trying to preserve.

This is not to deny the seriousness and beauty of much of the neo-Shingle Style work that has been produced in the last generation, or to deny the reason that it came about—that so much modern architecture was so woefully second-rate, so wretchedly indifferent to the needs of its occupants. I know that the idea of authenticity is a poor substitute for comfort and visual pleasure, and one of the great failings of the postwar era was the inability of contemporary architects to create the degree of comfort and visual pleasure that their predecessors had done all the time. It is not surprising, then, that the post-modern movement arose in the 1970s, bringing us more and more revival of historical styles. Modernism's failings pushed us into that.

My problem is not with historical revival per se, since there are plenty of times when it is altogether appropriate, even wonderful, to work in past styles. My problem is with mandating it across the board—and with building almost everything new in a single style, and declaring it to be the style of the town. I worry sometimes that East Hampton might be tempted to go the route of Santa Fe, where after World War II the city, concerned about the creeping presence of modern architecture, decided that it would be necessary to mandate the so-called "Santa Fe Style" for almost all architecture in the center of the city. What had been thought desirable suddenly became legally required, and design controls began to become the rule in the city. And at that moment, it began to become less spontaneous, more forced, less gracefully integrated into the wholeness of the city. As the tourist boom increased the profile of the city through the 1960s and 1970s and then, heaven help us, into the 1980s, "Santa Fe Style" became ever more prevalent, and ever more distant from whatever roots it had had. What did all these flat roofs and adobe walls, or adobe-like walls, and wooden details have to do with the life that was being lived there? Not always a lot. More and more the city was beginning to feel like an adobe theme park—a make-believe creation whose architectural form existed for marketing purposes more than anything else.

So that people with lots of money who found the whole idea of Santa Fe quaint and appealing could play in this adult theme park, whether permanently by building houses of their own or temporarily as tourists, it was necessary to keep the marketing image up, to be as strict about it as Disney might be at Disneyland. But there is tremendous risk to a city thinking itself so special that it tries to bottle itself, turn itself into something that is not real at all, but make-believe.

And that, of course, is what I am fearful of—that we begin to think of East Hampton as something that can be bottled, essence of East Hampton, falling prey to the worldview, so indicative of our time, where the notion of the theme park and the notion of the real city are increasingly becoming confused. East Hampton, like Santa Fe, is lucky enough to be one of those "trophy towns," as a colleague of mine calls them, places that are believed to have special qualities and that are deeply attractive to people of great wealth, who come in such high numbers that they throw the balance of everything off for everyone else. Indeed, East Hampton was one of the very first trophy towns, for it reached this status back when Aspen was but a tiny mining village. And today, it is that early trophy-town status that underwrites so much of East Hampton's wealth today—so many people want to come to be part of this beauty that they risk destroying it. It is sort of like the problems of the national parks, only here it is harder to regulate, because you are talking about private property and peoples' homes, not about something that everyone agrees is a public resource. But of course the civic qualities of East Hampton, and their natural ones, together do make up a kind of public resource. Main Street, Newtown Lane, the beaches, the bays, Northwest Woods, Barcelona Neck, Cedar Point, Georgica Pond—I could go on and on and on. I would even include such technically private things as the Maidstone Club, whose golf course is a public resource in the sense that it provides blessed public open space, light, vistas and a sense of calm in the heart of the village. How to hold onto all this, how to keep it from destroyed by the pressures that act upon it?

Ninety-nine percent of the communities in this country would give anything to have such problems as this, of course, but that makes it no less real a problem when you have to face it yourselves. In this sense East Hampton is not entirely different from Aspen, or Vail, or Carmel, or Santa Barbara, or Nantucket, or Martha's Vineyard, or Charleston, or a handful of other places that have remarkable natural and architectural qualities that they now manage, just barely, to hold onto. Too many people love these places, and flock to them like moths to a flame, and in their sheer numbers they run the risk of destroying the very thing that they loved. And even when they manage to save it, they save it at a price—the price of turning what had been authentic into something vaguely inauthentic, vaguely ersatz—something forced, self-conscious, precious. We see it with all the cutesy shingled architecture in East Hampton, architecture that, like Santa Fe's adobe, is based on some of the greatest architecture of the American past, but now is often turned into something facile, superficial, too easy and glib, to serve an eager audience wanting to play in the spirit of a place for a few brief moments. A stage-set version of East Hampton suits their needs, just like a stage-set version of Santa Fe suits the needs of many of that city's visitors.

But does it suit the long-term health of the town? Paradoxically, given that all of this latter-day Shingle Style architecture in East Hampton or the new adobe in Santa Fe were done in the name of giving these cities an "authentic" feeling, we squeeze out a sense of authenticity, too. And does anybody think that the A&P got any better when it re-did its Newtown Lane building some years ago into what I call the Arches & Pilasters? The A&P has other problems, of course, since it is now threatening to destroy a key piece of open space at the edge of East Hampton village in what I consider a dangerously misguided move. We should have known from the building on Newtown Lane that their architectural judgments were suspect.

Now, let me make one thing very clear. I am not trying to hide behind the old modernist argument about the spirit of the age, and saying that any architecture that resembles anything traditional, anything old, is automatically invalid, and that everything has to be modern to be real. Not at all. That was something of a fallacy, this claim the modern architects made in the '20s and '30s that this was a new age requiring new architecture, and that anything that looked like anything that had been done before was in some way untrue to its time, almost immoral. Nonsense. Simply not true, and not only because people love what has come before, and cherish it, and seek it in what they build now. They seek it now, and they always have. But the spirit-of-the-age argument is untrue also because it is not the way architecture has ever worked—everything has always built on what has come before, taken from it and reinterpreted it, revised it, built upon it. Architecture has never had to completely reinvent the wheel to express the needs and feelings of its time.

Today most people—architects and clients alike—understand this, and of course we have seen in the last generation a tremendous revival of traditional architectural styles. Unfortunately, however, as the 80s went on, we saw more and more traditional architecture being churned out, faster and faster, getting more and more glib and simple and facile, and less and less connected to anything about the real spirit of architecture, or of place. Traditional architecture was becoming more and more an architecture of appearances only, done to satisfy a marketing instinct more than anything else. If those people churning out Shingle Style houses all over the Sagaponack fields were really concerned about the "spirit of place," they would be building silos and potato barns, not shingled mansions for the newly rich. It is a glib attempt to knock off the spirit of East Hampton village in the old potato fields, and it is patently false, made worse, in my opinion, by the way in which it is masked in all of this "spirit of place" rhetoric.

For what is missing in the overwhelming amount of traditional architecture that has been sweeping across the landscape is a quality we can best call authenticity. I increasingly think that authenticity is the rarest and most precious quality a community of any kind can have. We don't see a lot of it in this day and age. Indeed, I sometimes think we are in an age when artifice well executed is often considered to pass for authenticity—it is the authenticity of our time. In an era of malls, of theme parks, of festival marketplaces, of virtual reality; an age in which the private realm has so often triumphed over the public realm—an age when a kind of ersatz, contained, privatized quasi-urban entertainment passes for real urban life—this is an age that has come to devalue authenticity considerably.

East Hampton's greatest danger is not destruction, but caricature. The economy will not destroy this city by tearing it down—the real risk is that it will destroy this city by building it up, by making it replicate itself over and over until it becomes a caricature of itself, horrendously overcrowded and jammed together so that the very things that made it attractive in the first place are impossible any longer to find. Never forget that once Sayville and Ronkonoma were pretty attractive places, too.

And yet—what is the alternative? You do not want to cut off your nose to spite your face; you do not want to reject those people who come out of goodwill, if sometimes out of innocence, seeking a different and better kind of experience from that which they will find in any other American oceanfront town. After all, almost all of us were once newcomers, too, and there is nothing more unattractive than the sight of the last people in pulling up the ladder and slamming the door in the face of newcomers.

This is a real, and genuine dilemma, and I have no simple answers. The one thing I can say is that East Hampton is doing a vastly better job than Southampton, or almost any other community I know in this region. Nothing in East Hampton, however troubling it may be, looks like County Road 39 in Southampton, and I hope it never will. The tightness of the zoning regulations in this town helps everyone, even if it makes it difficult to build. And the deep commitment to building additional publicly assisted housing to help those who are squeezed out of the market economy is key to East Hampton's quality—for it makes clear that we recognize that the marketplace alone cannot create the civilized community we all crave, that more has to be done.

I have been talking about what we might call the dark underside of preservation so far this evening—about some of the risks inherent in what all of us surely consider fundamentally a good thing, which is saving your architectural heritage, and basing the future of a community on it. The point I am trying to make is that preservation alone does not bring a city to the promised land, right though it obviously is as a starting point. The culture and economy we live in at the end of the twentieth century poses risks and dangers that were never dreamed of in the days of Grosvenor Atterbury or Joseph Greanleaf Thorp, when the translation of the city's history into contemporary built form was a relatively new concept, one that could be pursued with a certain earnestness.

So when we talk about preservation, and about the saving of a community, it is necessary, I think, to talk about authenticity—about the valuing of what is authentic, and about the elevating of that over all other things. And that brings us, inevitably, to the deeper questions of what East Hampton wants to be.

Let me say another word on another aspect of the struggle between preservation and everyday life, and it is an issue that goes far beyond East Hampton. Far too much preservation goes on not because we value what is being preserved, but because we fear what will replace it. This is sort of the dark underside of preservation, the reason behind it that we rarely like to talk about, but it is true—that often we preserve not to honor the general usefulness of knowing what our ancestors did and seeing how they lived, and not for the sense of continuity that this inspires, anchoring us in the larger sea of time, but only because we are terrified that if we allow something to disappear, our time will be unable to replace it with anything equal in stature.

Alas, that is all too often true, and East Hampton has more than a few pieces of evidence of the truth of this remark. But remember, again, that the builders of this city in the nineteenth century had no such fears. And if we are ever going to produce a valid and authentic architecture in our own time, we have to overcome that fear ourselves.

We cannot, in the end, preserve to deny a sense of time. We must preserve to enhance a sense of time, to richen and deepen our sense of time, to place ourselves in a larger continuum, to remind ourselves that we came from somewhere and are going somewhere, too. We preserve, we save our landmarks, to create resonance.

It is a subtle process. If we preserve too little, we have no sense of history, and we are lost, adrift in the shifting sands of time. If we preserve too much, too rigidly, we can stifle a community, cut out all fresh air, become the spoiled children of history, as Florence Malraux put it.

East Hampton, of course, has this risk. Like Europe, its legacy is great—incomparably great, I would even say—but with so great an architectural legacy lies a challenge. The challenge is not to be stifled by that legacy, not to be inhibited by it, and to keep in mind that the way to respect its spirit is often not to precisely replicate its forms. For if we want this place to remain real, to feel like a true and living community rather than a theme park, it is essential that there be some sense of continued fresh air within its creative realms.

That does not mean that anything that is new and different is okay, and that anything traditional is wrong. Let me say one more time that my point is more subtle than that. I would even go farther and say that a mediocre traditional building will do less harm to East Hampton than a mediocre modern one, since there is a kind of architectural safety net that sits under traditional, or historicist, architecture in a place like this. But while it is safe, it is not always ambitious, and it does not always offer us the chance to aim highest so far as creativity and a sense of continued energy is concerned.

Indeed, if I may come back to a phrase I used much earlier, "passionate interludes," I think that is the goal when you build a new building in this town: to create a passionate interlude. So that, in the end, is what preservation at its best can mean: a chance to renew and restore cities in the most meaningful way, to bring back that sense of authenticity that modern culture has so often taken away from us. It is not easy, for all the reasons I've mentioned, and often, paradoxically, there is greater authenticity in allowing architecture to reflect the difficult, messy realities of life, and not be as neat and prim and tied up with a pretty bow as the theme-park culture would have it.

In East Hampton, that can sometimes mean not doing everything by the book, not making every last thing a picture-perfect reflection of a past that never was. The Ralph Laurenization of American cities is a phenomenon more or less similar to the Disneyfication of our culture; in each case there is a loss of authenticity, a determination to remake the world in the image of a past more perfect than it ever was.

The real history of East Hampton is vibrant, layered, and often contradictory. This is a real place, with its own qualities that make it different from other places—but never forget, please, that its history was not a history of cuteness or primness. And never forget, too, that the greatest mission of preservation is not to deny us a chance to perceive time, but to enhance it—to make time more visible, in all its scope: the East Hampton of the past, the East Hampton of the present, and the East Hampton of the future, presenting it with authenticity, glory and power.

Biographies

JOHN T. AMES is the nineteenth minister of the First Presbyterian Church of East Hampton. He is a graduate of the University of Mississippi, Union Theological Seminary in Virginia, and received a Ph.D. in American Church History from Duke University.

T.H. BREEN is the William Smith Mason Professor of American History at Northwestern University. He is former director of the Kaplan Center for Humanities at Northwestern and currently holds the chairmanship of the Department of History. Breen earned a Ph.D. from Yale University. In addition to grants from the Guggenheim Foundation, the Mellon Foundation, and the National Endowment for the Humanities, he held research fellowships at Oxford University, Cambridge University, the Institute for Advanced Study (Princeton), The National Humanities Center (North Carolina), and the Huntington Library (San Marino, California). Breen is completing a book for Oxford University Press entitled, The Baubles of Britain: Revolutionary Consumers on the Eve of American Independence.

KATE CAMERON is a graduate of Fordham University and received a Master's Degree in History from New York University in 1988. Her Master's thesis was on the subject of the East Hampton art colony from 1875–1900. She was the guest curator for the Guild Hall exhibitions "East Hampton: The Nineteenth Century Artists' Paradise" in 1991, "The Artist as Teacher: William Merritt Chase and Irving Wiles" in 1994, and "The Moran Family Legacy" in 1997–1998. She has lectured on Long Island artists and East Hampton's historic gardens at the Florence Griswold Museum, Old Lyme, Conn., the East Hampton Historical Society and the Sotheby's Institute Series on Historic Gardens of the East End.

PETER R. CHRISTOPHE is editor of the Dongan Papers, 1683–1688, two volumes of documents from the administration of New York Governor Thomas Dongan, as well as ten other volumes of colonial, state, and regional records. He has written more than forty historical articles and given over a hundred talks on history, genealogy, and records research. He was curator of manuscripts and special collections at the New York State Library in Albany for twenty years, during which time he served for ten years as director of a project to translate New York's colonial Dutch records, and is currently director and senior editor of the New York Historical Manuscripts publications project.

CHRISTOPHER COLLIER is Professor of History at the University of Connecticut at Storrs and Connecticut State Historian. He has written extensively about the history of Connecticut for both scholarly and popular readers. Among his works are Roger Sherman's Connecticut: Yankee Politics and the American Revolution and The Literature of Connecticut History, an annotated bibliography of some four thousand published works. Collier is perhaps best known for the eight historical novels he has written with his brother, James Lincoln Collier, several of which have Connecticut and New York settings, most notably, My Brother Sam is Dead. Collier, who was born in New York City and lived the first eight years of his life on Long Island, has three grown children and now lives in Orange, Connecticut with his wife, Bonnie.

CONSTANCE AYERS DENNE is Professor of English at Baruch College, The City University of New York. Specializing in nineteenth-century American literature, she received her Ph.D. from the University of Pittsburgh. A textual editor, she has prepared definitive editions of several works by James Fenimore Cooper, all published by the State University of New York Press. Her articles on American writers have appeared in Nineteenth-Century Fiction, the Nation, and Women's Studies, among other journals.

RICHARD DUNN is the Nichols Professor Emeritus of History at the University of Pennsylvania and Director of the Philadelphia Center for Early American Studies. He has published numerous books on American colonial history, including Puritans and Yankees: The Winthrop Dynasty of New England, 1630–1717 (1962) and a new edition (1996) of the famous journal written in the 1630's and 1640's by John Winthrop, the first governor of Massachusetts and the father of John Winthrop, Jr.

DEAN FAILEY serves as Senior Vice President of Christie's, and Senior Director of its American Furniture and Decorative Arts Department. Mr. Failey was a Winterthur fellow, earning his Master of Arts degree from the University of Delaware. After graduating from Winterthur, Mr. Failey assumed the position of Associate Curator of the Museum of Fine Arts in Houston, a major American decorative arts collection. Prior to joining Christie's, Mr. Failey was curator of the Society for the Preservation of Long

Island Antiquities and the author of the important bicentennial exhibition catalogue, Long Island is My Nation. Mr. Failey has written numerous articles in American decorative arts for such publications as the magazine Antiques and American Art Journal. He served as executive director of the East Hampton Historical Society and wrote a regular byline column in regional editions of the Sunday New York Times. He has lectured extensively at museums such as the Museum of Fine Arts in Boston, the Smithsonian Institute, Historic Deerfield, and Colonial Williamsburg.

SHERRIL FOSTER is a descendant of numerous East Hampton first families and was born and grew up in East Hampton the daughter of a businessman, Ed Sherrill of Sherrill's Dairy. After graduation from East Hampton High School and Brown University, where she majored in Art History, she worked in New York City. During the war, she joined the Air WAC, becoming a control tower operator. She received an M.A. degree in Art History from the Villa Schiafanoia in 1972, where she attended classes in Florence, Italy. Her Master's thesis was in "Boarders to Builders: the Beginnings of Resort Architecture in East Hampton, L.I. 1870–1892." She worked at Guild Hall under Enez Whipple where she organized exhibitions including the 1976 exhibit, "Life Styles." She then directed the cataloguing project for the East Hampton Historical Society. She became the Village Historian and attended various meetings of N.Y.S. Municipal Historians organization. In 1992, she conducted a symposium about East Hampton in honor of 200 years of ownership of her property in one family. She presently writes for the East Hampton Independent.

NOEL GISH is an instructor of history at Hauppauge High School. He is on the Board of Trustees for both the Suffolk County and Smithtown Historical Societies. He is Chairperson for the Historic Advisory Board for the Town of Smithtown, and in 1996, authored Smithtown, 1660–1929, Looking Back Through the Lens.

PAUL GOLDBERGER, one of the best-known writers in the world in the field of architecture, design and urbanism, joined the New Yorker magazine in July of 1997 as a staff writer. His arrival at the New Yorker, where he writes about a wide range of cultural subjects, including architecture, art and cities, follows a twenty-nine-year career at the New York Times, where, in 1984, he won the Pulitzer Prize, the highest award in journalism, for his architecture criticism. He is married to Susan Solomon, Chairman and CEO of Lancit Media Entertainment Corporation, an award-winning producer of children's television programming, and they are the parents of three sons, Adam, Ben, and Alex. They live on the Upper West Side of Manhattan and in East Hampton, New York.

HELEN A. HARRISON, Director of the Pollock-Krasner House and Study Center in the Springs, is an art historian who specializes in modern American art. She is also an art reviewer and feature writer for the Long Island Weekly section of the New York Times.

JEFF HEATLEY is a freelance architectural photographer. His book, Colonel Theodore Roosevelt, the Rough Riders & Camp Wikoff, Montauk Point, New York–1898, a selected and edited compilation of news reports, feature articles, editorials, illustrations and photographs from seventeen major dailies and seven local news weeklies. It will be published this spring by Pushcart Press in cooperation with the Montauk Historical Society as part of Suffolk County's Centennial Celebration of Col. Roosevelt and the Rough Riders.

CHARLES F. HUMMEL'S entire professional career was spent at Winterthur where he served in various capacities for the museum from 1955 through 1991. He has served on the National Museum Services Board as a trustee of the Chipstone Foundation, Landmarks Society of Philadelphia, and the Wood Turning Center of Philadelphia. Mr. Hummel's numerous publications include With Hammer in Hand: the Dominy Craftsmen of East Hampton, New York and A Winterthur Guide to American Chippendale Furniture. He is listed in Who's Who in America, Who's Who in the East, and the Dictionary of International Biography. Although retired from the Winterthur Museum as Senior Deputy Director, Mr. Hummel continues to work there as Curator Emeritus and Adjunct Professor. He teaches a course on the Colonial craftsmen in the Winterthur Program in Early American Culture.

HARRISON HUNT has a B.A. in History from Hofstra University and an M.A. in History Museum Studies from the Cooperstown Graduate Program. He is currently Supervisor of Collections and Historic Sites with the Nassau County Department of Recreation and Parks. Mr. Hunt has done extensive research on Long Island's role in the Civil War.

HUGH R. KING, East Hampton's officially appointed Town Cryer, leads historical walking tours of East Hampton's Main Street and South End Burying Ground for the East Hampton Historical Society. He writes a column on local history for the East Hampton Independent newspaper.

LORETTA ORION teaches anthropology and sociology at Hofstra University. She is the author of Never Again the Burning Times; Paganism Revived. Her play, The Siberian Shaman's Dress, received first prize for anthropological fiction writing from the Society for Humanistic Anthropology.

DAVID E. MULFORD, a native of East Hampton and a descendant of one of East Hampton's founding families, is a Presbyterian minister, now retired, who lives with his wife, Nancy, in Black Mountain, N.C. With degrees from Colgate University, Princeton Theological Seminary and Drew University, he served churches in Albany, New York and Chatham, New Jersey, and retired as pastor of First Presbyterian Church in Vero Beach, Florida in 1994. In his retirement, Dr. Mulford, a history buff, lectures on the lives of the U.S. Presidents and continues his interest in East Hampton history.

JOHN M. MURRIN, Professor of History at Princeton University, received his B.A. from the College of St. Thomas in St. Paul, Minnesota; his M.A. from the University of Notre Dame; and his Ph.D. from Yale University. Before moving to Princeton in 1973, he taught for ten years at Washington University, St. Louis. A specialist in early American history, he has co-edited five books, including Colonial America: Essays in Politics and Social Development (1983, 1992) and Saints and Revolutionaries: Essays in Early American History (1984). He has written the section on colonial and revolutionary America in Liberty, Equality, Power: a History of the American People (1996; 2d ed., summer, 1998). He will serve as president of the Society of Historians of the Early American Republic in 1998-99.

ROBERT C. RITCHIE received his B.A. from Occidental College and his Ph.D. in History from the University of California Los Angeles, specializing in Early American History, especially the seventeenth century. At present, he is the W.M. Keck Foundation Director of Research at the Huntington Library. He has received a number of awards and fellowships, and among his major publications are The Duke's Province: a Study of Politics and Society in New York, 1664-1691 and Captain Kidd and the War Against the Pirates. He is currently working on a history of beach culture.

VINCENT SEYFRIED, a native of Queens, obtained his M.A. from Fordham University and thereafter taught in Queens from 1946 to 1979. He is currently a historian of the Long Island Railroad.

DONALD G. SHOMETTE is a retired staff member of the Library of Congress, a maritime historian and underwater archaeologist. He is a 1965 graduate of Pratt Institute, and was awarded an Honorary Doctor of Humane Letters by the University of Baltimore in 1998. He has published thirteen books, including Raid on America: the Dutch Naval Campaign of 1672-1674, and numerous scientific papers. His writings have appeared in such publications as National Geographic Magazine, American Neptune, and American Heritage of History & Technology.

QUENTIN SNEDIKER was named the Mystic Seaport Amistad Project Coordinator in January, 1995. Snediker has spent the past three years researching the appearance and construction details of the ship Amistad and working with Amistad America, Inc. developing program planning and vessel design. Construction of the freedom schooner Amistad will be fully underway by summer of 1998 and is scheduled to be completed in 2000. Amistad is not the first ship Snediker has built. Snediker led Mystic Seaport's efforts to historically furnish the Charles W. Morgan during the museum's 1991 anniversary celebration of the 150-year-old whale ship, the last survivor of the once great Yankee fleet. From 1993–1994, Snediker was associate director of programs at the Chesapeake Bay Maritime Museum. He supervised museum programming and coordinated cooperative work for young people through other educational institutions and the Job Training Partnership Act.

GAYNELL STONE is Museum Director of the Suffolk County Archaeological Association and editor of the eight volumes of its series, Readings in Long Island Archaeology & Ethnohistory. She teaches at Stony Brook University and Suffolk Community College and is a New York Council for the Humanities Speaker on the Native peoples of coastal New York.

JOHN A. STRONG is a professor of history at the Southampton College of Long Island University. He holds a Ph.D. from Syracuse University. He has written extensively on the Algonquian peoples of Long Island. His most recent publications include The Algonquin Peoples of Long Island from Earliest Times to 1700 (1997), We Are Still Here: The Algonquian Peoples of Long Island Today (1996, 2nd edition, 1998), and articles in Ethnohistory (1994), The Long Island Historical Journal (1997), The Encyclopedia of American Indian Biography, edited by Fred Hoxie (1995), and Northeastern Indian Lives, edited by Robert Grumet (1996).

TOM TWOMEY is the East Hampton Town Historian and President of the East Hampton Library. He also serves as an officer of the Guild Hall Cultural Center of East Hampton. Recently, he served as Vice-Chair of the 350th Anniversary Celebration of the Town of East Hampton Committee and Chair of its Lecture Series Committee. Throughout the last twenty years, he has held governmental appointments to state agencies, including the Energy Council, the Freshwater Wetlands Appeals Board, the Long Island Power Authority, and the East End Economic & Environmental Task Force. He founded his law firm in 1973 and is included in Who's Who in American Law. He holds a Bachelor's Degree from Manhattan College and he attended University of Virginia Law School and Columbia Law School from which he received his Juris Doctor in 1970.

STUART VORPAHL is a native of Amagansett and a lifelong commercial fisherman working at ocean seining and bay pound traps, and a builder of steel fishing vessels. He is a past president of the Long Island Fisherman's Association and the East Hampton Town Baymen's Association. His interest in local history has led him to read all Town and Trustee records since 1650, and the East Hampton Star since 1885. First elected Town Trustee in 1977, he served five terms and is still reading the Town Records.

LANGDON WRIGHT received a B.A. degree in History from Harvard and M.A. and Ph.D. degrees from Cornell. His dissertation was on "Local Government in Colonial New York, 1640 to 1710." Since 1974, he has taught American Social History, History Research, and other subjects at the Cooperstown Graduate Program in History Museum Studies, cosponsored by the State University College at Oneonta and the New York State Historical Association.

ROGER WUNDERLICH is professor of Long Island History at the State University at Stony Brook, where he also serves as editor of the Long Island Historical Journal. As a scholar absorbed in the study of "Long Island as America," Dr. Wunderlich presents Lion Gardiner, New York's first English settler, as the "prototypical pioneer, who helped to fashion the building blocks of American independence."

Selected Bibliography

THIS SECTION ORIGINATED with recommended readings by each of the 27 lecturers in The 350th Lecture Series. Dorothy King, former East Hampton Town Historian, and Tom Twomey, President of The East Hampton Library, and current Town Historian, added other books and materials to the list to provide the reader with a comprehensive bibliography on East End and Long Island history.

Many of the items can be found in The Long Island Collection at The East Hampton Library. Although virtually all of these books and materials are out of print, many—but not all—of these books and materials can be found from time to time by the collector in rare book stores or on the Internet.

However, readers are welcome to use these books and materials for research purposes at The Long Island Collection. In these comfortable surroundings, professional and amateur historians, family genealogists, writers and journalists can use these items, without cost, to their heart's content. Librarians Diana Dayton and Dorothy King stand by to assist with your research. Please stop by for a visit at 159 Main Street, East Hampton, or call (516) 324-0222 for further information.

Abbott, Wilbur C. *Colonel John Scott of Long Island*, 1634(?) -1696. New Haven, Connecticut: Yale University Press, 1918.

Adams, James Truslow. *History of the Town of Southampton*. Bridgehampton, New York: Hampton Press, 1918.

—— *Memorials of Old Bridgehampton*. Bridgehampton, New York, by the author, 1916.

Allen, Gay Wilson. *The Solitary Singer*. New York: Grove Press Inc., 1955.

Andrews, Charles M. *The Colonial Period of American History*. 4 vols. New Haven, Connecticut: Yale University Press, 1934-1938.

Bailyn, Bernard. *The New England Merchants in the Seventeenth Century*. Cambridge, Massachusetts: Harvard University Press, 1955.

Bayles, Richard. *Historical and Descriptive Sketches of Suffolk County, and Its Towns, Villages, Hamlets, Scenery, Institutions and Important Enterprises; with a Historical Outline of Long Island, from Its First Settlement.* Port Jefferson, New York: Richard M. Bayles, 1874, 1873.

Beard, James F. *The Letters and Journals of James Fenimore Cooper.* Cambridge, Massachusetts: The Belknap Press, vols. I and VI, 1960 and 1968.

Becker, Lloyd. "Two Local Studies by Jeannette Edwards Rattray." *Street Magazine II*, no. 2 (1976): 39-42.

Beecher, Lyman. *Autobiography.* 2 vols. Edited by Barbara M. Cross. Cambridge, Massachusetts: Belknap Press of Harvard University Press, 1864, [c1961].

———. *A Sermon, Containing a General History of the Town of East Hampton.* Sag Harbor, New York: Alden Spooner, 1806.

Benson, Elaine. "Group Portrait." *Hampton Country*, (July 1998): 61-62.

———. "How an Art Galley Came to Be: A Memoir." *Whelks Walk Review*, I, no. 1 (1998): 56-68.

Berbrich, Joan D. *Three Voices from Paumanok.* Port Washington, New York: Ira J. Friedman, Inc., 1969.

Black, Robert C. *The Younger John Winthrop.* New York: Columbia University Press, 1966.

Boughton, E. S., ed. *Historic East Hampton, Long Island; the Celebration of Its Two Hundred and Fiftieth Anniversary.* East Hampton, New York: E. S. Boughton, 1899.

Boxer, C. R. *The Dutch Seaborne Empire, 1600-1800.* New York: Knopf, 1965.

Breen, T. H. *Imagining the Past: East Hampton Histories.* Reading, Massachusetts: Addison-Wesley, 1989.

———. *Puritans and Adventurers: Change and Persistence in Early America.* New York: Oxford University Press, 1980.

Bridenbaugh, Carl. *The Colonial Craftsman.* Chicago: University of Chicago Press, 1950.

Brodhead, John Romeyn. *History of the State of New York.* 2 vols. New York: Harper & Bros., 1853-1871.

Burnett, Frances Hodgson. *Racketty-Packetty House.* New York: J.B. Lippincott Company, 1975.

Bushman, Richard L. *The Refinement of America: Persons, Houses, Cities.* New York: Alfred A. Knopf, 1992.

Capote, Truman. Foreword in *The Potato Book* by Myrna Davis. Bridgehampton, New York: The Hampton Day SchoolPress, 1972.

Cave, Alfred A. *The Pequot War.* Amherst, Massachusetts: University of Massachusetts Press, 1996.

Ceci, Lynn. "The Effect of European Contact and Trade on the Settlement Pattern of Indians in Coastal New York, 1524-1665: The Archaeological and Documentary Evidence." Ph.D. diss., University of New York, 1977.

"Charles de Kay Dies: Novelist, Poet and Critic." Obituary, *Herald Tribune*, 24 May 1935.

Clarke, Gerald. *Capote.* New York: Simon and Schuster, 1988.

Clemente, Vince, ed. "John Hall Wheelock." *Paumanok Rising.* Port Jefferson, New York: Street Press, 1981, 81-113.

———. "John Hall Wheelock: Poet of Death and Honeysuckle." *Long Pond Review* (Jan. 1976). 10-18.

———. "Walt Whitmen in the Hamptons." *Street Magazine II*, no. 1 (1975).

Clowes, Ernest S. *The Hurricane of 1938 on Eastern Long Island*. Bridgehampton, New York: Hampton Press, 1939.

Cole, John N. *Away All Boats*. New York: Henry Holt and Company, 1994.

———. *Fishing Came First*. New York: Lyons & Burford, Pub., 1989.

———. *Striper*. Boston: Little, Brown and Company, 1978.

Cooper, James Fenimore. *Correspondence of James Fenimore Cooper*. 2 vols. New Haven, Connecticut: Yale University Press, 1922.

———. *The Sea-Lions: or The Lost Sealers*. New York: D. Appleton and Company, 1873.

Daniels, Bruce Colin. *The Connecticut Town: Growth and Development, 1635-1790*. Middletown, Connecticut: Wesleyan University Press, 1979.

Davis, Myrna. *The Potato Book*. Bridgehampton, New York: The Hampton Day School, 1972.

DeForest, Bartholomew S. *Random Sketches and Wandering Thoughts, or, What I Saw in Camp, on the March, the Bivouac, the Battlefield and Hospital While with the Army in Virginia, North and South Carolina, During the Late Rebellion Microform: With a Historical Sketch of the Second Oswego Regiment* Enlisted Men. Albany: Avery Herrick, 1866.

de Kay, Charles. "East Hampton the Restful." *The New York Times Illustrated Magazine*. 30 October 1898: 40-43.

———. "Summer Homes at East Hampton, L.I." *The Architectural Record*, XII. no. 1 (Jan. 1903). 21-29.

Demos, John. *Entertaining Satan: Witchcraft and the Culture of Early New England*. New York: Oxford University Press, 1982.

Dunn, Richard S. *Puritans and Yankees: the Winthrop Dynasty of New England, 1630-1717*. New York: Norton, 1962.

Duvall, Ralph G. and Jean L. Schladermundt. *History of Shelter Island, 1652-1932; with a Supplement 1932-1952*. Second Edition. Shelter Island Heights, New York, n.p., 1952.

East Hampton, New York (Town). *Journal of the Trustees of the Freeholders and Commonalty of the Town of East Hampton, 1725-1960*. 10 vols. [East Hampton: Town of East Hampton, 1926-1976].

East Hampton, New York (Town). *Records of the Town of East Hampton, Long Island, Suffolk Co., New York, with Other Historic Documents of Ancient Value*. vols. 1 and 3. Sag Harbor, New York: J. H. Hunt, Printer, 1887-1905.

Edwards, Everett Joshua and Jeannette Edwards Rattray. "Whale Off!": *The Story of American Shore Whaling*. New York: Frederick A. Stokes Company, 1932.

En Plein Air: the Art Colonies at East Hampton and Old Lyme, 1880-1930. East Hampton, New York: Guild Hall Museum, 1989.

Epstein, Jason and Elizabeth Barlow. *East Hampton: A History and Guide*. Wainscott and Sag Harbor: Medway Press, 1975.

Esten, John and Rose Bennett Gilbert. *Hampton Style*. Boston: Little, Brown and Company, 1993.

Farrington, S. Kip, Jr. *American Big Game Fishing*. New York: The Derrydale Press, 1935.

Fernow, Berthold, (ed.). *The Records of New Amsterdam from 1653 to 1674 Anno Domini*. 7 vols. New York: Knickerbocker Press, 1897.

Flint, Martha. *Early Long Island: A Colonial Study*. New York: G. P. Putnam's Sons, 1896.

Fiske, John. *The Dutch and Quaker Colonies in America*. 2 vols. Boston: Houghton, Mifflin, 1902.

Force, Peter. *American Archives, Fourth Series: Containing a Documentary History of the English Colonies in North America, from the King's Message to Parliament, of March 7, 1774, to the Declaration of Independence by the United States*. 11 vols. Washington, D.C.: M. St. Clair Clarke and Peter Force, 1837-1853.

Foster, Stephen. *Their Solitary Way, the Puritan Social Ethic in the First Century of Settlement in New England*. New Haven, Connecticut: Yale University Press, 1971.

Foy, Jessica H. and Thomas J. Schlereth, eds. *American Home Life, 1880-1930: A Social History of Spaces and Services*. Knoxville: University of Tennessee Press, 1992.

Friedan, Betty. *The Feminine Mystique*. New York: Norton, 1963.

Fryxell, Fritiof. *Thomas Moran, Explorer in Search of Beauty*. East Hampton, N.Y.: East Hampton Free Library, 1958.

Furman, Gabriel. *Antiquities of Long Island*. New York: J.W. Bouton, 1874.

Gabriel, Ralph Henry. *The Evolution of Long Island: a Story of Land and Sea*. Port Washington, New York: I. J. Friedman, 1960, 1921.

Gaines, Steven. *Philistines at the Hedgerow*. Boston: Little, Brown and Company, 1998.

Gardiner, Curtiss Crane. *Lion Gardiner and His Descendants*. St. Louis: A. Whipple, 1890.

Gardiner, David. *Chronicles of the Town of East Hampton, County of Suffolk, New York*. New York: [Bowne Printers], [1840, 1871].

Gardiner, John Lyon. *Gardiners of Gardiner's Island*. East Hampton, New York: Star Press, 1927.

Gardiner, Lion. "Leift Lion Gardiner, His Relation of the Pequot Warres". Chap. in *Collections of the Massachusetts Historical Society*, Vol. 3, 3rd, Series, 131-160. Cambridge, 1833.

Gardiner, Sara Diodati. *Early Memories of Gardiner's Island*; (The Isle of Wight, New York). East Hampton, New York: East Hampton Star, 1947.

Gaynor, James M. and Nancy L. Hagedorn. *Tools: Working Wood in Eighteenth-century America*. Williamsburg, Va.: Colonial Williamsburg Foundation, 1993.

Godbeer, Richard. *The Devil's Dominion: Magic and Religion in Early New England*. New York: Cambridge University Press, 1992.

Goodman, Charlotte Margolis. *The Savage Heart*. Austin: University of Texas Press, 1990.

Grossman, James. *James Fenimore Cooper*. Stanford, Calif.: Stanford University Press, 1949.

Guillaume, Bernice F. "Ethnic Duality and the Harlem Renaissance in the Work of Olivia Bush (Banks)." Presented at the 1982 Meeting of the Organization of American Historians: Philadelphia. 2 April 1982.

———. "Olivia Ward Bush: Factors Shaping the Social and Cultural Outlook of a Nineteenth-Century Writer." *Negro History Bulletin*. 43, no. 2 (April, May June 1980): 32–34.

Hauptman, Laurence M. and James D. Wherry, eds. *The Pequots in Southern New England: The Fall and Rise of an American Indian Nation*. Norman: University of Oklahoma Press, 1990.

Heatley, Jeff, ed. *Bully!: Colonel Theodore Roosevelt, The Rough Riders & Camp Wikoff, Montauk Point, New York 1898, a Newspaper Chronicle with Roosevelt's Letters*. Montauk, New York: Montauk Historical Society; Pushcart Press, 1998.

Hedges, Henry Parsons. *A History of the Town of East-Hampton, New York: Including an Address Delivered at the Celebration of the Bi-Centennial Anniversary of Its Settlement in 1849, Introductions to the Four Printed Volumes of Its Records, with Other Historic Material, an Appendix and Genealogical Notes*. Sag Harbor, New York: John H. Hunt, Printer, 1897.

Heller, Joseph. *Now and Then: From Coney Island to Here*. New York: Alfred A. Knopf, 1998.

Hewitt, Janis. "Amistad Plaque Dedicated." *The East Hampton Star*. 6 August 1998: I, 7.

Heyman, Christine Leigh. *Commerce and Culture: The Maritime Communities of Colonial Massachusetts, 1690–1750*. New York: Norton, 1984.

Hassle, Kathleen L. *The Letter Kills But the Spirit Gives Life: the Smith— Abolitionists, Suffragists, Bible Translators*. Glastonbury, Connecticut: Historical Society of Glastonbury, 1993.

Howell, George Rogers. *The Early History of Southampton, L.I., New York*. Albany: Weed, Parsons & Company, 1987.

Hulbert, Ann. "The Interior Castle: The Art and Life of Jean Stafford." New York: Alfred A. Knopf, 1992.

Hummel, Charles F. "The Business of Woodworking, 1700–1840." Chap. in *Tools and Technologies: America's Wooden Age*. eds. Paul Kebabian and William Lipke, 1979.

———. *With Hammer in Hand: The Dominy Craftsmen of East Hampton, New York*. Charlottesville, Virginia: University Press of Virginia, 1968.

Huntington, Cornelia. *Odes and Poems and Fragmentary Verses*. New York: A. Huntington, 1891.

———. *Sea-Spray: A Long Island Village*. New York: Derby & Jackson, 1857

Ignatow, David. "The Bay." *Hampton Shorts* (1997): 103.

Innes, John H. *New Amsterdam and Its People; Studies, Social and Topographical, of the Town under Dutch and Early English Rule*. 2 vols. 1909. Reprint, Port Washington, New York, I. J. Friedman, [1969].

Innes, Stephen. *Creating the Commonwealth: The Economic Culture of Puritan New England*. New York: W. W. Norton, 1995.

Jameson, J. Franklin, ed. *Narratives of New Netherland, 1609-1664*. 1909. Reprint, n.p., Barnes & Noble, [1959].

Jennings, Francis. *The Invasion of America: Indians, Colonialism, and the Cant of Conquest*. New York: Norton, 1976, 1975.

Jones, Mary Jeanne Anderson. *Congregational Commonwealth Connecticut, 1636-1662*. Middletown, Connecticut: Wesleyan University Press, 1968.

Karlsen, Carol F. *The Devil in the Shape of a Woman: Witchcraft in Colonial New England*. New York: Norton, 1987.

Kelsey, Carleton. *Amagansett, a Pictorial History, 1680-1940*. Amagansett, New York: Amagansett Historical Association, 1986.

Kennedy, John Harold. *Thomas Dongan, Governor of New York (1682-1688)*. New York: AMS Press, 1974.

Knickerbocker, Cholly. "These Fascinating Ladies." *New York Journal-American*, 8 June 1939.

Kupperman, Karen Ordahl. *Providence Island, 1630-1641: The Other Puritan Colony*. Cambridge, Massachusetts: Cambridge University Press, 1993.

Lancaster, Clay, Robert A. M. Stern. *East Hampton's Heritage*. Second Edition. East Hampton, New York: Ladies Village Improvement Society, 1996.

Lockridge, Kenneth A. *A New England Town: The First Hundred Years: Dedham, Massachusetts, 1636-1737*. New York: Norton, 1985.

Long, Robert, ed. *Long Island Poets*. Sag Harbor, New York: The Permanent Press, 1986.

Love, William DeLoss. *The Colonial History of Hartford; Gathered from Original Sources*. [Chester, Connecticut]: Centinel Hill Press, [1974].

———. *Samson Occom and the Christian Indians of New England*. Boston: Pilgrim Press, 1899. Syracuse, New York: Syracuse University Press, 1998.

Marhoefer, Barbara. *Witches, Whales, Petticoats & Sails: Adventures and Misadventures from Three Centuries of Long Island History*. Port Washington, New York: Associated Faculty Press, 1983.

Martin, John Frederick. *Profits in the Wilderness: Entrepreneurship and the Founding of New England Towns in the Seventeenth Century*. Chapel Hill, N.C.: North Carolina Press for the Institute of Early American History and Culture, Williamsburgh, Virginia, 1991.

Mather, Frederick G. *The Refugees of 1776 from Long Island to Connecticut*. Albany: J. B. Lyon Company, 1913.

Matthiessen, Peter. *Men's Lives*. New York: Vintage Books, 1988, 1986.

Mayo, Lucinda A. "'One of Ours': The World of Jeannette Edwards Rattray." In *Long Island Women: Activists and Innovators*. ed. Natalie A. Naylor and Maureen O. Murphy. New York: Empire State Books, 1998.

McGrath, Franklin, ed. The History of the 127th New York Volunteers, "Monitors," in the War for the Preservation of the Union—September 8th, 1862, June 30th, 1865. n.p.: ca. 1898.

McIntyre, Ruth A. William Pynchon; *Merchant and Colonizer, 1590-1662*. n.p.: Connecticut. Valley Historical Museum, 1961.

McMurry, Sally Ann. *Families and Farmhouses in Nineteenth-Century America: Vernacular Design and Social Change*. New York: Oxford University Press, 1988.

Melville, Herman. "Benito Cereno." In *The Heath Anthology of American Literature*. vol. 1, 3rd ed., ed. Paul Lauter, et al. 2454-2509. Boston: Houghton Mifflin Company, 1998.

Miller, James, Jr. "America's Epic." In *Whitman*. ed. Roy Harvey Pearce, 60-65. Englewood Cliffs, New Jersey: Prentice-Hall, Inc., 1962.

Miller, Mary Esther Mulford. *An East Hampton Childhood*. East Hampton: Star Press, 1938.

Miller, Perry. *Errand into the Wilderness*. Cambridge, Massachusetts: Belknap Press of Harvard University Press, 1956.

———. *Nature's Nation*. Cambridge, Massachusetts: Belknap Press of Harvard University Press, 1967.

———. *The New England Mind: from Colony to Province*. Cambridge, Massachusetts: Harvard University Press, 1953.

Miller, Perry and Thomas H. Johnson, eds. *The Puritans: A Source book of Writings*. 2 vols. New York: Harper & Row, 1963.

Morris, Willie. *New York Days*. Boston: Little, Brown and Company, 1993.

Mowrer, Lilian T. *The Indomitable John Scott: Citizen of Long Island*, 162?-1704. New York: Farrar, 1960.

Munsell, W. W., ed. *History of Suffolk County, New York, with Illustrations, Portraits and Sketches of Prominent Families and Individuals*. New York: W. W. Munsell & Company, 1882.

New York Historical Society. *Collections of the New York Historical Society for the Year 1809*. New York: I. Riley, 1811.

Niles, Nath. *Samson Occum. The Mohegan Indian Teacher, Preacher and Poet, with a Short Sketch of His Life*. Madison, New Jersey: [Privately printed anonymously], 1888.

Novak, Barbara. *American Painting of the Nineteenth Century; Realism, Idealism, and the American Experience*. New York: Praeger, [1969].

Nylander, Jane C. Our *Own Snug Fireside: Images of the New England Home, 1760-1860*. New York: Knopf, 1993.

O'Callaghan, E. B., ed. *Documents Relative to the Colonial History of the State of New York*. 11 vols. Albany: Weed, Parsons and Company, 1853-1861.

———. *History of New Netherland; or, New York under the Dutch*. New York: D. Appleton, 1848.

Occum, Samson. "Account of the Montauks." In *Collections of the Massachusetts Historical Society*. 106–111. Boston: The Massachusetts Historical Society, vol. X, 1809.

Onderdonk, Henry. *Revolutionary Incidents of Suffolk and Kings Counties: With an Account of the Battle of Long Island, and the British Prisons and Prison Ships of New York*. New York: Leavitt, 1849.

Osgood, Herbert L. *The American Colonies in the Seventeenth Century.* 3 vols. Glouchester, Massachusetts: P. Smith, [1904], 1957.

Overmyer, Grace. *America's First Hamlet*. Washington Square: New York University Press, 1957.

Palfrey, John Gorman. *History of New England*. 5 vols. Boston: Little, Brown & Company, 1858–1890.

Pena, Elizabeth S. *Wampum Production in New Netherland and Colonial New York: The Historical and Archaeological Context*. Boston: Boston University, 1990.

Pennypacker, Morton. *General Washington's Spies on Long Island and in New York*. 2 vols. Brooklyn: The Long Island Historical Society. East Hampton, New York: East Hampton Free Library, 1939, 1948.

Phelan, Thomas Patrick. *Thomas Dongan, Colonial Governor of New York, 1683–1688*. n.p, 1933.

Pisano, Ronald G. *Long Island Landscape Painting*. 2 vols. Boston: Little, Brown, 1985, 1990.

Prince, Henry W. *Civil War Letters & Diary of Henry W. Prince, 1862–1865*, compiled by Helen Wright Prince. Riverhead, New York: Suffolk County Historical Society, 1979.

Quick, Dorothy. "Long Island Poet." *The Long Island Forum 3*, no. 8 (Aug. 1949): 165–66 and 168.

Rattray, Everett T. *The Adventures of Jeremiah Dimon*. Wainscott, New York: Pushcart Press, 1985.

———. *The South Fork, the Land and the People of Eastern Long Island*. New York: Random House, 1979.

Rattray, Helen. "Connections." *The East Hampton Star*. (1980–1998).

Rattray, Jeannette Edwards. *East Hampton History, Including Genealogies of Early Families*. Garden City: Country Life Press, 1953.

———. *Montauk: Three Centuries of Romance, Sport and Adventure*. East Hampton: The Star Press, 1938.

———. *Ship Ashore!: A Record of Maritime Disasters Off Montauk and Eastern Long Island*. New York: Coward-McCann, 1955, 1962.

———. *Up and Down Main Street: An Informal History of East Hampton and Its Old Houses*. East Hampton: East Hampton Star, 1968.

Reynolds, David. *Walt Whitman's America*. New York: Alfred A. Knopf, 1995.

Ringe, Donald A. *James Fenimore Cooper*. New Haven: College and University Press., 1962.

Ritchie, Robert. *Captain Kidd and the War Against the Pirates*. Cambridge, Massachusetts, 1986.

———. *The Duke's Province: A Study of New York Politics and Society,*

1664-1691. Chapel Hill: University of North Carolina Press, 1977.

Roberts, David. *Jean Stafford: A Biography*. Boston: Little, Brown and Company, 1988.

Roosevelt, Theodore. *The Rough Riders*. New York: Scribner, 1902; reprint, Da Capo Press, 1990.

Seabury, Samuel. *Two Hundred and Seventy-five Years of East Hampton, Long Island, New York: A Historical Sketch*. East Hampton, New York: privately printed, 1926.

Seyfried, Vincent F. *The Long Island Rail Road: a Comprehensive History*. 7 vol. Garden City, N.Y.: Seyfried., 1961.

Shammas, Carole. *The Pre-industrial Consumer in England and America*. New York: Oxford University Press, 1990.

Shapiro, Harvey. "Ditch Plains Poem," *Street Magazine II*, no. 2 (1976) 49.

Sleight, Harry D. *Sag Harbor in Earlier Days*. Bridgehampton, New York: Hampton Press, 1930.

Steinbeck, John *Travels with Charley*. New York: Viking Press, 1962.

———. *The Winter of Our Discontent*. New York: Penguin Books, 1996.

Stone, Gaynell. "Long Island As America: A New Look at the First Inhabitants." *Long Island Historical Journal 1*, no. 2 (Spring 1988): 159–169.

———. "Long Island Before the Europeans." *In Between Ocean and Empire: An Illustrated History of Long Island*. ed. Robert MacKay, Geoffrey L. Rossano, and Carol A. Traynor, 10–29. Northridge, Calif.: Windsor Publications, 1985.

———. *The History & Archaeology of the Montauk*. 2d ed., rev. Stony Brook, New York: Suffolk County Archaeological Association, 1993.

———, ed. *The Montauk Native Americans of Eastern Long Island*. East Hampton, New York: Guild Hall, 1991.

———, ed. *The Shinnecock Indians: A Culture History*. Stony Brook, New York: Suffolk County Archaeological Association, 1983.

Stone, Gaynell and Nancy Bonvillain, eds. *Languages and Lore of the Long Island Indians*. Stony Brook, New York: Suffolk County Archaeological Association, 1980.

Strong, John A. *The Algonquian Peoples of Long Island from Earliest Times to 1700*. Interlaken, New York: Empire State Books, 1997.

Taylor, Robert Joseph. *Colonial Connecticut: A History*. Millwood, New York: KTO Press, 1979.

Thompson, Benjamin F. *History of Long Island from Its Discovery and Settlement to the Present Time*. Third Edition. New York: Robert H. Dodd, 1918.

Tooker, William Wallace. *Early Sag-Harbor Printers and Their Imprints*. Evanston, Ill., 1943.

Trelease, Allen W. *Indian Affairs in Colonial New York: The Seventeenth Century*. Ithaca, New York: Cornell University Press, 1960. Reprint, Lincoln, Nebr.: University of Nebraska Press, 1997.

Underhill, Lois Beachy. *The Woman Who Ran for President: The Many Lives of Victoria Woodhull*. Bridgehampton, New York: Bridge Works

Pub.; distributed by, Lanham, Md.: National Book Network, 1995.

Van der Zee, Henri and Barbara van der Zee. *A Sweet and Alien Land:The Story of Dutch New York*. New York:Viking Press, 1978.

Van Rensselaer, Schuyler, Mrs. *History of the City of New York in the Seventeenth Century.* N.Y.: Macmillan, 1909.

Van Wyck, Frederick. *Select Patents of New York Towns*. Boston: A.A. Beauchamp, 1938.

Waard, C. de, jr., ed. *De Zeeuwsche Expeditie Naar de West onder Cornelis Evertsen den Jonge, 1672-1674, Nieuw Nederland een jaar onder Nederlandsch Bestuur.* 's-Gravenhage, M. Nijhoff, 1928.

Walker,Warren S. *James Fenimore Cooper*. New York: Barnes & Noble, Inc. 1961.

Weeden, William B. *Economic and Social History of New England, 1620-1789*: 2 vols. n.p.: Houghton, Mifflin & Company, 1890. Reprint. N.Y. Hillary House Publishers, 1963.

Wheelock, John Hall. *Afternoon:Amagansett Beach*. New York: Dandelion Press, 1978.

——. *The Gardener and Other Poems*. New York: Charles Scribner's Sons, 1961.

——. *Poems Old and New*. New York: Charles Scribner's Sons, 1956.

——. *This Blessed Earth*. New York: Charles Scribner's Sons, 1978.

——. *What Is Poetry?* New York: Charles Scribner's Sons, 1963

——, ed. *Editor to Author:The Letters of Maxwell E. Perkins*. New York: Charles Scribner's Sons, 1950.

Wheelock, John Hall, New York, letter to Mrs. [N. Sherrill] Foster, East Hampton, 6 Feb. 1976. [X FG 86], Long Island Collection, East Hampton Library, East Hampton, New York.

Whitaker, Epher. *History of Southold, Long Island, Its First Century.* Southold, New York: by the author, 1881.

Whitman, Walt. "From Montauk Point." *Complete Poetry and Selected Prose*, ed. James E. Miller, Jr. Boston: Houghton Mifflin Company, 1959.

——. *Leaves of Grass*. New York:W.W. Norton & Company, Inc., 1973.

Winthrop, John. *The Journal of John Winthrop, 1630-1649.* ed. Richard S. Dunn and Laetitia Yeandle. Abridged ed. Cambridge, Mass: Belknap Press of Harvard University Press, 1996.

Wollstonecraft, Mary. *A Vindication of the Rights of Woman*. New York:W. W. Norton & Company, 1988.

Wood, Silas. *A Sketch of the First Settlement of the Several Towns on Long Island with Their Political Condition to the End of the American Revolution*. Brooklyn:Alden Spooner, 1828.

"Writers Talk: George Plimpton, James Salter, Daniel Stern." *Hampton Shorts* (1977): 252-76.

Zaykowski, Dorothy. *Sag Harbor: The Story of an American Beauty*. Sag Harbor, New York: Sag Harbor Historical Society, 1991.

Ziel, Ron and George H. Foster. *Steel Rails to the Sunrise*. New York: Hawthorn Books, 1965.

Additional Notes

The following notes pertain to the lecture "By Choice or by Chance: Single Women's Lives in Nineteenth-Century Suffolk County, N.Y." by Sherrill Foster on pp. 221–240.

1. Jeannette Edwards Rattray, *East Hampton History and Genealogies* (Garden City Press, 1952), passim; hereinafter JER, *EHH&G*. Information on all the women discussed, except Eliza Jane Glover, can be found in JER, *EHH&G*, and in *ibid, Up and Down Main Street*. It is only when tracing the female lines do these cousinships emerge. For the genealogist, it is interesting to note that some of these women, with their extensive New England ancestry, were distant cousins. Abigail Kimble and the Huntingtons were descendants of a first settler of Windsor, Ct., Christopher Huntington. Adelia Anna Parsons and the husband of Abbey Kimble were eighth cousins, descendants of Robert Parsons of Lynn, Mass. and East Hampton. Phebe van Scoy and the Glovers have a common van Scoy/van Schaick ancestor. The Hicks and the van Scoys have a Sherrill ancestor. Pre-revolutionary ancestors for Eliza Jane Fisk have not been found. Her husband's family, the Glovers, are New Englanders who moved to Southold, L.I., where they intermarried with the Southold early families. Documented family group sheets are on file with the Connecticut Society of Genealogists, P.O. Box 435, Glastonbury, CT 06033.

2. *East Hampton Star*, December 1901 (microfilm p. 403).

3. Christine Stansell, "Women, Children and the Uses of the Streets: Class and Gender Conflict in New York City, 1850-1860" in *Unequal Sisters*, p. 121.

4. David S. Reynolds, *Walt Whitman's America, A Cultural Biography* (New York, Alfred A. Knopf, 1995), p. 31.

5. Richard L. Bushman, *The Refinement of America: Persons, Houses, Cities* (New York, Alfred A. Knopf, 1992), passim.

6. David S. Reynolds, *op. cit.*, p. 141.

7. Will of Cornelia Huntington, written 31 August 1858, gives all her

451

real and personal property to her sister and her brother, not knowing she would outlive them both. East Hampton Library [X DG–101].

8. Cornelia Huntington, diary 1826-27. [Not transcribed.] East Hampton Library [OG 25].

9. Robert Hefner, *Windmills of Long Island* (New York, W.W. Norton, 1983), passim.

10. William D. Halsey, *Sketches from Local History* (Southampton, N.Y., 1934), pp. 96, 98.

11. Photograph of marker in William T. Griffith, *Nature Preserves in East Hampton* (Nature Conservancy, Sag Harbor, N.Y., 1190), p. 5, with map.

12. James Truslow Adams, *Memorials of Old Bridgehampton* (New York, 1916), p. 97.

13. Cedar Point County Park, several hundred acres; The Grace Estate of 516 acres.

14. Halsey, *Sketches...*, pp. 145-146.

15. Arnold van Scoy house in Sag Harbor, *AIA Architectural Guide to Nassau and Suffolk Counties, Long Island* (AIA and SPLIA, Dover, 1992), #210. Daguerre (1787-1851) had invented his photographic process by 1837.

16. Many of Isaac, Sr.'s, siblings were dead by this time. His sister, Mercy Edwards, died in Sag Harbor in the 1830's; Elizabeth Bennett died a widow at Northwest in 1858; Hetty Osborne died there in 1840; David died in Amagansett in 1854; Patience Payne lived in North Haven; and Polly Ranger died in 1833 at Northwest. Isaac's cousin, Abraham van Scoy, ran a store in Sag Harbor. Zaykowski, *Sag Harbor*, pp. 84 and 132. It is probable that Charlotte van Scoy was brought up by her mother's family in East Hampton.

17. This voyage is discussed in *Prentice Mulford, His Story* (The White Cross Library, ca. 1885), passim.

18. The population of The Springs is not listed separately and, therefore, it is probably included in the East Hampton count.

19. The census reads 80 acres unimproved land, 8 acres "improved," 3 acres plowed. Eight acres of meadow in 1864 had been reduced to 5 acres in 1865. Four tons of hay had been produced, 3 acres planted in Indian corn for grain. Her two cows of 1864 had become one in 1865. In 1864, Phebe Scoy had made 70 lbs. of butter and 200 lbs. of pork. She sold 5 cords of wood in 1864 for $25.

20. JER *EHH&G*, p. 603.

21. The samplers are owned by the East Hampton Historical Society.

22. "Wickham, Martha" Pseud. [Cornelia Huntington], *Sea-Spray: A Long Island Village* (Derby & Jackson, 119 Nassau Street, New York, 1857), pp. 9-10.

23. Reynolds, *Walt Whitman's America*, p. 85.

24. "Wickham, Martha" Pseud. [Cornelia Huntington], *Sea-Spray: A Long Island Village* (Derby & Jackson, 119 Nassau Street, New York, 1857), pp. 9-10.

25. Stowe's tetrology of New England stories begins with *The Minister's Wooing* (1850), *Pearl of Orr's Island* (1862), *Oldtown Folks* (1869), and *Poganuck People* (1878).

26. Dr. Abel Huntington, ed., C. Huntington, *Odes and Poems* (New York, 1891), p. 59.

27. Huntington's Disease was pinpointed by the pioneering work of the Drs. Huntington. It is a genetic disease, the gene of which has now been isolated.

28. *Odes & Poems*, p. 10, Introduction by Henry P. Hedges (1891) in which he describes Cornelia's enrollment at Clinton Academy. Some records of Clinton Academy, which operated as an education institution for almost 100 years, are in the East Hampton Library. Lists of students seem to be missing. They were possibly burned in the New York State Library fire of 1911.

29. Cornelia Huntington's diary 1826-1827, unpaginated.

30. *Ibid*.

31. Lydia Sigourney (1791-1865) is discussed in Elsworth Grant, ed., *The Miracle of Connecticut* (c. 1992), pp. 248-251, and in David M. Roth, ed., *Connecticut History and Culture* (1985, Hartford, Ct.), p. 133.

32. John Wallace presented the Sag Harbor Episcopal Church, Christ Church, with paired marble plaques with the Lord's Prayer and the Apostle's Creed sculpted on them. Dorothy Ingersoll Zaykowsky, *Sag Harbor: The Story of an American Beauty* (Sag Harbor, N.Y., 1991). Throughout the summer of 1858, Wallace spearheaded a construction fund for an Episcopal Church building in East Hampton for which he raised $1,600 with most donations coming from the summer visitors.

33. Dr. Abel Huntington, ed., C. Huntington, *Odes and Poems* (New York, 1891), p. 59.

34. 1870 Diary, Delia Sherrill, entry for Sunday, March 13. Original and transcript in East Hampton Library [HI 23 Envelope 1].

35. Diary, 1875-1903, Delia Sherrill. Entry for January 1, 1875. Original and transcript East Hampton Library [HI 23 Envelope 2].

36. *Ibid*. Rag party, June 10, 1875; purchase of chairs, June 18, 1875.

37. Diary entry for May 11, 1875.

38. *Ibid*. Entry for April 29, 1875.

39. *Ibid*. Entry for January 17 and 23, 1878.

40. *East Hampton Star*, December, 1901 (microfilm p. 403).

41. George J. Fluhr, *A Generation of Suffering on the Upper Delaware Frontier: 1742-1782* (Shohola, Penn., 1976). Map on p. 9.

42. Interview with Mrs. Rickert of Dyberry, Penn., October, 1988. Abbey's relatives ran this until the 1920's, when the area was denuded for a "dry dam" for the State of Pennsylvania Flood Control project.

43. Jane and Dency Ross were sisters. Dency married a Jacks, and Jane married a Mulford, related to the East Hampton Mulfords. They were daughters of William and Hannah Ross of Poquannock, Morris Co., N.J.

The recent research genealogy is entitled *George Ross and Constance Little* (1990).

44. Gwendolyn Wright, *Moralism and the Model Home* (Univ. of Chicago Press, 1980), p. 26. The house, much altered, is at 824 Springs-Fireplace Road.

45. Woodward, *East Hampton...*, p. 175.

46. JER, *EHH&G*, p. 493.

47. Abram Parsons Sherrill first moved to L.I. towns as a schoolteacher, but then moved to Pike, N.Y., as a storekeeper. F.W. Beers & Co. *History of Wyoming Co., N.Y.* (N.Y. 1880), Town of Pike, p. 262. Nathaniel Huntting Sherrill moved to LeRoy, becoming a carpenter. 1850 Federal Census (New York, microfilm reel 507, Genesee Co., Town of LeRoy) lists N.H. Sherrill, 43, carpenter; Harriet A. Sherrill, 36, b. Vt.; Harriet A. Sherrill, 13, f. NY, attended school; and S.A. Higgins, 40, f. VT, apparently a sister of Mrs. Sherrill. They had a 33-year-old male laborer, born in New York, living with them. 1850 Federal Census (New York, microfilm reel 617, Wyoming Co., Town of Pike) lists Abram P. Sherrill, 46, merchant with real estate valued at $800; wife Elizabeth, 39; children Mary E., 9, John S., 6, Eleanor W., 3, and Abram P., Jr., $6^{1}/_{2}$. They had a 20-year-old female live-in helper, a native-born New Yorker.

48. Diary, William Henry Hobart Glover, 1877. Diary and transcription, East Hampton Library. [Diary XMD 27; Transcription vf 9292 Glover].

49. *Ibid.* Entry for June 20 and 22, 1877.

50. Diary, WHH Glover, 1877 entries, 25, 1 November.

51. *New York Times*, August 1, 1890, p. 8, col. 5.

52. I am indebted to Patricia (White) Wroten whose mother was a Glover and knew the family gossip.

53. Diary of Eliza Jane (Fisk) Glover, 1905-1909. Original and transcription at East Hampton Library [LIC HI 112, Env. 1-2].

54. *Ibid.* Entries for July 22, 1907, to August 13, 1907.

Index

Gratitude

THE 350TH ANNIVERSARY LECTURE SERIES of the Town of East Hampton could not have been possible without the vision and wisdom of Bruce Collins, Chair of the Anniversary Committee. His dedication to providing the town with a meaningful and thoughtful anniversary celebration provided the necessary and continuing support for the success of this series.

Fred Yardley, Averill Geus, Carolyn Snyder, and Carolyn Preische, all members of the Executive Committee, provided the backbone of support and organization, which made the series possible. Averill Geus and John Strong as Vice-Chairs of the lecture committee provided invaluable assistance in securing many of the nationally renowned lecturers. Stuart Epstein as Publicity Chair, Sheila Rogers as Finance Vice-Chair, Ann Roberts as Deputy Events Coordinator, Janice Olsen, Gekee Wickham, and Adrienne Kataeoff worked tirelessly in pulling it all together.

Henry Korn, President of Guild Hall, and the rest of his staff hosted 24 of the 27 lectures, absorbing all of the cost as one of its contributions to the Anniversary of the Town. Fraser Dougherty of LTV and his wonderful staff of volunteers taped each of the lectures to broadcast them throughout the Town and preserve them for all posterity.

Dorothy King, Town Historian, and Diana Dayton Librarian of East Hampton Library's Long Island Collection provided many of the lecturers with much-needed resource material and helped to prepare the very valuable bibliography included in this book.

And this anthology would not have been possible without the commitment of Esther Margolis, the owner of Newmarket Press, who, with her staff, dedicated themselves to making this book the beautiful edition that you hold in your hand.

EAST HAMPTON TOWN AND VILLAGE OFFICIALS

DONORS TO THE 350TH ANNIVERSARY CELEBRATION

GOLDEN BENEFACTOR
Suffolk County National Bank

BENEFACTORS

Anonymous
Emmie and William C.
Heppenheimer III
in memory of Blanche
Miller Heppenheimer

Mary Ellen Kay —
Prudential Securities
East Hampton

Dorothy Herman —
Prudential Long Island.
Realty of East Hampton

Bicky and George Kellne
Susan and Alan Patricof
Riverhead Building
Supply Corp.

PATRONS

Bank of New York
Christopher H. Browne
Mrs. Thomas R. Burns,
Kathleen Burns Buddenhagen
and Madeleine D. Burns

Cook Pony Farm Real Estate
Joan and Joseph F. Cullman, 3rd
Ian Cumming
Mr. and Mrs. Robert Goelet

Hampton Jitney
Alexander Jackson
John R. Kennedy
McCarver & Moser Jewelers
North Fork Bank and Trust

Franci and Joe Rice
William E. Simon
Sharon and Fred Stein
Twomey Latham Shea & Ke
Volk's Disposal Service

UNDERWRITERS

Allan M. Schneider Associates
Amaden Gay Agencies
Amagansett Building Materials
Alixandra and Stuart Baker
Bistrian Gravel Corp.
Patrick Bistrian, Jr.
Bridgehampton National Bank
Veronica & James Carbone
Charde Computers
Faith Chase
Jane and Bruce Collins
Dayton and Osborne Insurance
Carol and Disque Deane
DeLalio-South Fork Asphalt
Devlin-McNiff Real Estate
Dreesen's Excelsior Market
William A. Dreher
Dunemere Associates
East End Hardware Corp.

East Hampton Lions Club
Edward F. Cook Agency
Edwards and Duggan, P.C.
Robert D.L. Gardiner
Golden Eagle
Gosman's Restaurant and Bar
H.M. Trenching
H.O. Penn Machinery
Robert and Lynn Hanke
Home Sweet Home
Moving and Storage Co.
Billy Joel
Nancy Mette and Barnet Kellman
C.E. King and Sons and Dorothy T. King
JoCarol and Ronald S. Lauder
Gayle and Frederick W. Lester
Dr. Marjorie Lewisohn
The Kenneth and Evelyn Lipper Foundation
The Maidstone Arms Inn and Restaurant
Manhattan Mortgage Co.

Charles and Kathleen Marder of Marc
Markowitz, Preische and Stevens, P
Peter Marino, Architect
Ethel and William Marran
Harold McMahon
Joyce and Robert Menschel
Patricia and Douglas Mercer
Brooke and Daniel Neidich
Nick and Toni's
PaineWebber of East Hampton
Amy and Joseph Perella
Plitt Ford Lincoln Mercury, Inc.
Sheila Johnson Robbins
Mr. and Mrs. Arthur Ross
Round Swamp Farm Families
Sabin Metal Corp.
Sotheby's International Realty
Village Hardware
Jeanette S. and Paul A. Wagner
Whitmore's

SUPPORTERS

Jane Bayard
Karl and Elaine Behr
Mr. and Mrs. Peter Berley
Bermuda Bikes Plus
Robert L. Burch, III
Mr. and Mrs. Marshall Clark
Confetti of East Hampton, Ltd.

Arthur Dubow Foundation
Mary and James Evans
Frederic J. Fuller, Jr.
Mrs. Gianluigi Gabetti
Mr. and Mrs. G. S. Beckwith Gilbert
Barbara Lubin Goldsmith
Zuzana and Dan Justman
Alexandra and Joseph Kazickas

Mr. and Mrs. Theodore W. Kheel
Leah and Alain Lebec
Cheryl and Michael Minikes
Lee Radziwill and Herbert Ross
Perdita Schaffner
Mr. and Mrs. Paul R. Scheerer, J
Joel M. Stern

350th SOCIETY MEMBERSHIP

Jane and Bruce Collins		
Harold and Carolyn Lester Snyder		
Rose Tuthill White and Richard F. White, Jr.		
Albert J. and Dianna Lester Catozzi		
Gayle D. and Frederick W. Lester		
Henry and Martha Murray		
Carolyn and Walter Preische		
Herbert Cohen and Mark Zimmerman		
Sherrill Foster		
Hugh R. King		
Eleanor and Ilmar Ratsep		
Irene Silverman		
Judith Hope and Tom Twomey		
James M. and Mary Ella Parsons Moeller		
Edwin and Averill Geus		
Lynn and Stuart A. Epstein		
Ann Williams Chapman		
Doreen A. Niggles		
Peter Rana		
Norman and Carol Mercer		
Clayton and Frances Morey		
Bill and Charlotte Bennett		
Richard E. Whalen		
David W. Collins		
Lisa and Charles Niggles		
Mrs. Samuel Davis		
Guida and John West		
Carol Kroupa		
Sheila Rogers and Van Ellman		
Mary Louise E. Dodge		
Donna Stein and Henry Korn		
Mary Ella Reutershan		
Richard T. and Allene Talmage		
Elbert, Hedwig, and Pember Edward		
Donald and Marilyn Hunting		
Dorothy V. Osborn		
Harriet L. Edwards		
Mr. and Mrs. Henry C. Clifford		
Mr. and Mrs. E. L. Sherrill, Jr.		
John and Eunice Juckett Meeker		
Lisa and Thomas Grenci		
David and Merolyn Parker		
Carol Morrison		
Joan M. Lycke		
Frederick W. and Edna Yardley		
Christopher and Nancy Kelley		
Edward Gorman		
John and Beverley DiSunno		
Jean and Paul Rickenbach, Jr.		
Richard W. Smith		
James and Olivia Brooks		
Constance Ayers Denne and C. J. Denne, Jr.		
Richard Quaranto		
Arlene Bujese		
Randall and Patricia Parsons		
Diane S. Wilner		
Richard and Ann A. Roberts		
Vincent and Susan D'Angelo		
Thomas and Catherine Peacock		
Charles and Joy Squires		
Mrs. Robin Guldi		
Carol A. Morgan		
Dr. Michael R. Laspia		
Mrs. Edward H. Jewett, Jr.		
Joseph and Claire Lester Olszewski		
Peter Diefendorf and Floyd Diefendorf		
Shelly C. Snyder		
Virginia S. and Kennell I. Schenck		
William A. Babinski		
Gary L. and Sue Grant		
Richard and Susan Herrlin		
John and Judy Caramagna		
Frank and Barbara Borth		
Joy and Richard Lupoletti		
Rev. William J. Chase		
in memory of Jean Lowry Davis		
Edith B. and Vincent B. Schuman		
Dorothy T. King		
Mr. and Mrs. James D. Dana		
Mary Ellen Kay		
Curt and Angel Schade		
Mr. and Mrs. James C. McCrea, Jr.		
James and Sandy Conklin		
Russell H. Card		
Dan and Bev Grimes		
Joseph and Carol Macdonald Nye		
Tom and Irene Scott		
Dr. and Mrs. David C. Baker		
Robert D. Uher		

#	Name	#	Name	#	Name
89	Brian J. Lester	179	Marie-Therese Duryea and Perry B. Duryea	266	Harold M. Wit
90	Ted and Jean Tillinghast	180	Fred and Sharon Stein	267	Marillyn B. Wilson
91	Norman Altstedter	181	Jan L. Bernstein	268	Michael and Kate DeSario
92	Pintchik/Mofenson	182	Richard and Susan Davies	269	Richard and Dianne Balnis
93	Eric and Ericha Oberg	183	Alice and Richard Netter	270	Annamaria and Greg Ajemian
94	Laura and James J. Ross	184	Kate and Bill Cameron	271	Courtney Sale Ross
95	Mary Ann and Matty Savarese	185	Kenneth I. Greenstein	272	Arthur and Betsy Frank Strauss
96	Steven and Sharon Rabinovici	186	Mrs. R. Thomas Strong,	273	Richard N. Dunn and Lawrence Hayd
97	Richard McKenna		in memory of R. Thomas Strong	274	Barbara and Arthur Dubow
98	Carl S. and Jo Ann Quinn	187	Therese Van Went Furst	275	Janet and Gerald Gutterman
99	Nancy K. Quinn	188	Chris and Paul Amaden	276	Mrs. James C. Edwards
100	Robert Rattenni	189	Mary Ann and Bruce Bozzi	277	Ms. Patricia M. Weeks & Mr. Stuart B. Rel
101	Mr. and Mrs. Seymour C. Kaback	190	John C. and Barbara O. Nelson	278	Alice Sydney Minkoff
102	Thomas E. and Frances L. Gaines	191	Mr. and Mrs. Morris Z. Hocherman	279	Richard N. and Dorothy L. Bennett
103	Dr. and Mrs. Thomas P. Magill	192	William F. Trinkle	280	Eleanor Pam
104	Carla Caccamise Ash	193	William Hawxhurst Wheelock	281	Mrs. Edward F. Cook
105	Dr. and Mrs. William E. McManus	194	Carl and Cordelia Menges	282	Stephen and Antonia Bellanca Mahon
106	Holly and Jack Whitmore	195	Judith S. Teller	283	Robert F. Stein
107	Barbara O. and Henry Von L. Meyer, Jr.	196	Marion L. Parsons	284	Mary K. Villa
108	George E. Mallouk	197	Ruth B. Terry	285	Philip J. and Sharon N. Lester
109	Margaret Hedges Schneider	198	Chip Rae and Mark Olives	286	Leen and Stephen D. Gould
110	David L. and Jane P. Talmage	199	Maureen and David Egen	287	Hedy and Bruce Collins, Jr.
111	John and Olga Collins	200	Henri and Catherine Talerman	288	Dennis and Leslie Collins Curles
112	Ruth Mueller	201	Horst Decker	289	W. Russell G. Byers, Jr.
113	Elizabeth L. White	202	William J. Fleming	290	Joan Ward
114	Lisa and Michael Schultz	203	Betsy and Bob DeVecchi	291	Luly and Tony Duke
115	Leonard and Marian Harmon	204	Jane Overman	292	Michael Davis and Nancy Berger
116	Terrence and Saskia Keeley	205	James L. Weimar	293	Ann C. and Dan Kolb
117	W.R. Grant	206	Mary Busch	294	Minerva Taylor
118	Mr. and Mrs. Timothy P. Sullivan	207	Alexander and Deborah Walter	295	Anne Hollister
119	Beth Conrad Aery	208	Joel M. Stern	296	Robert L. Plancher
120	Barnet Kellman and Nancy Mette	209	James D'Auria	297	William S. and Mary B. Jenkins
121	Job Potter	210	Jane and Michael London	298	Dr. and Mrs. David Paton
122	Barbara McClancy	211	Allen and Deborah Grubman	299	Walter J. Fried
123	Helene Blank and Marc Dittenhoefer	212	Jean Claude Baker	300	Elizabeth Schiff
124	Mr. and Mrs. Alexander M. Laughlin	213	Mary Ann Eddy	301	Isabel and Richard Furlaud
125	Medina Marasca	214	Henry and Katherine Parsons Schwatzman	302	Theodora DiSunno and Carmine DiSu
126	Mrs. Carolyn P. Williams	215	Robert and Simone Marshall	303	Debbie and Fred Goldstein
127	Phyllis and Sheldon Estey	216	Wanda Dworman	304	Robert Luzzi
128	Barbara Phillips	217	David W. Lewing	305	Mr. & Mrs. George W. Gowen
129	Evelene and Robert Wechsler	218	Jerome J. DeCosse	306	Mr. and Mrs. Stanley M. Rumbough, .
130	Capt. Joe McBride	219	Pam and John Cataletto	307	Mary Jane and Charles Brock
131	Mary Lou Barnes Mayo	220	Donald L. Norton	308	Helen S. Rattray
132	Bruce and Nancy Nagel	221	Helen and Claus Hoie	309	Albert Frederick Lester
133	Ernest Clark, Jr.	222	Mr. and Mrs. Stanley R. Becker	310	Sheila L. Birnbaum and Barbara Wrul
134	Mr. and Mrs. C. Lewis Johnson	223	Barbara and Kirk White	311	Virginia and Alfred Morgan
135	Susan W. Stachelberg	224	JoAnn M. Goldberg	312	Patrick Corser
136	James G. and Kathleen A. Morris	225	Mr. and Mrs. Robert C. Osborne	313	Dr. James A. Underberg
137	Dorothy Rouse-Bottom	226	Mr. and Mrs. Leander Arnold	314	David and Alice Jurist
138	Denise DeShane and Alan Gelband	227	Peter and Patricia Handal	315	Brenda M. Landrum
139	Bob and Min Hefner	228	Carmen and Paul Arbia	316	Jacqueline W. Vogelstein and
140	Charles C. Savage	229	Madeleine I. E. Meehan		Charles M. Kinsolving, Jr.
141	Jack and Jane Rivkin	230	Beverly Bond	317	The Chanos Family
142	Diane Ingalls Astorr	231	Freeman Fairchild	318	Joyce and Robert Menschel
143	Beverly Dash and Debra Lobel	232	Georgia R. and Michael H. de Havenon	319	Rick, Liz and Richard Holub
144	Barbara B. Chase	233	Dr. Michael and Arlene Hinkemeyer	320	Mark W. McGorry
145	Ennius E. and Judy A. Bergsma	234	Raymond A. Bernabo	321	Robert and Enid Kay
146	Yves-Andre Istel	235	C.G.B. Garrett/Jack H. Peltier	322	Ronald, Marcy and Alexx Balcuns
147	Elizabeth STRONG-CUEVAS	236	Mr. and Mrs. Ira H. Washburn, Jr.	323	Mary Struk Niggles and
148	James B. Jeffrey	237	Mr. and Mrs. Sheldon M. Harnick		Albert A. Niggles, Jr.
149	Jane E. Lappin	238	Mr. and Mrs. Samuel Rotrosen	324	Barbara J. Lester in memory of
150	Tina S. Fredericks	239	Alfred and Bonnie Devendorf		Albert C. Lester
151	Mr. and Mrs. William Tintle, Jr.	240	C. Jay Moorhead	325	East Hampton Kiwanis Club
152	Sara and Robert Coe	241	Mr. Seton Shanley	326	David and Carolyn Clark
153	David and Sarah Toren	242	Ms. Roslyn S. Teicher	327	Frances K. Levine
154	Patrica and Richard Flach	243	Richard Pollak	328	Mr. and Mrs. Ken Schenck, Jr.
155	Blair Oakley Rogers, M.D.	244	Peter D. McCann, M.D.& Deborah L. Berke	329	Elizabeth K. and Charles Callahan
156	Barbara and Ted Borsack	245	Barbara and Harry Kamen	330	Roger Sherman and Dorothy Kalins
157	Everit Albert Herter VFW Post 550	246	Marjorie Loggia	331	Jim, Pat and Jaclyn Zaborski
158	Janet and C. Sherrill Dayton	247	Carroll L. and Nina Wainwright	332	Arthur and Millicent Kaliski
159	Paula G. Hopping	248	Edward R. Roberts	333	Gerald and Stephanie Brody Lederma
160	Mary and David Solomon	249	Mr. and Mrs. Marc Roberts	334	Kristen Lester Tuma, Rebecca Lester
161	Karla K. Bergeson	250	Cynthia Osborn and Paul Shellman		DeBiase and Katherine Ann Lester
162	Wayne and Pat Isom	251	Jack and Maureen O'Leary	335	Richard C. Hoadley
163	Lalitte and Howell Scott	252	Warren and Virginia Schwerin	336	Mr. and Mrs. Norborne Berkeley, Jr.
164/165	Mr. and Mrs. Ernest J. Dayton	253	The Village Preservation Society of E. H.	337	Susanne and Charles Bullock
166	Kay Delaney Bring	254	Bill Rosenthal and Jerry Gebo	338	Ralph and Sherry Wolfe
167	Andrew Goldstein and Gillian Jolis	255	Linda and Seldon James, Jr.	339	Pat Tsien and Tom Cleveland
168	Ben and Bonnie Krupinski	256	Abby Abrams	340	David and Mary Jane Lifson
169	George Polychronopoulos	257	Fayette Alberta Rost Parsons	341	Mr. and Mrs. Pierre Casimir-Lambert
170	Audrey and John Nagel	258	Dorothy E. Cumby and David G. Virgil	342	Mr. and Mrs. Michael W. Hedges, Jr.
171	Matthew and Mary Laspia	259	Joseph L. Aversano, III and	343	Garden Club of East Hampton
172	Bicky and George Kellner		Robert D. Caruso	344	Philip and Annamae Freedman
173	Catherine H. Lester and Della Ann Lester	260	Mark and Lynne Mapes	345	Kenneth H. and Linda W. Brown
174	Mr. and Mrs. John P. Ecker	261	Betty and Robert Loughead	346	Ellen and Martin Goldman
175	Daniel and Joanna S. Rose	262	Malcolm P. Aldrich, Jr.	347	Henrika Hadjipopov and John Conner
176	Donald Zucker	263	Walter A. and Grace Dominy Renkens	348	Cornelia and Lawrence H. Randolph
177	Cynthia Cook Bognolo and Sally Cook	264	Michael McCully	349	Duck Creek Farm Association, Inc.
178	Mr. and Mrs. Joseph A. Hren	265	Stanley J. Arkin	350	The East Hampton Library

FRIENDS

George and Christine Alexio
Apple Bank for Savings
The Artists Alliance of East Hampton
Leonard Barkan
Arthur Beckenstein
Marjory L. Bellefountaine
Katherine E. Bennett
Lois B. Bernstein
Bermuda Parties
Heinz and Rosemarie Binggeli
Susan L. Blair and Robert R. Metz
Edward and Magda Palacci Bleier
Stephanie Bonsignore and
  Eileen Bonsignore
Bookhampton, Inc.
Judith Borakove and Marvin Wolfe
Bill Bortree
Mr. Darl Bower
John and Elizabeth Breslin
Anita and Bill Brown
Gloria and Lawrence Brown
Michael and Lynne Brown
Dorothy J. Bunim
Miriam E. Burstein
Betty and George Cafiso
Gordon J. Campbell
Clark and Marshall
Margaret M. Kane
  and Sedgwick A. Clark
Shirley and Jarvis Collins
Suzie and Eckley B. Coxe
Richard C. Cucci
Kate Rabinowitz & Rameshwar Das
Michelle Davitt, M.D.
Althea Debellis
Dorothy M. and Lillian T. Disken
Mike DiSunno and Sons, Inc.
Elizabeth Dow
East End Dunes Resident Association
East Hampton Cleaners
East Hampton Veterinary Group, P.C.
Mary Ann Eddy
James N. and Helen P. Edwards
Mr. and Mrs. Frederick Einsidler
Todd Elliott
Marilyn and Stephen Engel
Katherine and David Epstein
MaryJean Erario
Gloria Euben
Mr. and Mrs. Lex Federbush
Kenneth and Patti Ferrin
Barbara and Andrew Fisher
Murray Fishman
Ronald Fleitman
Karl G. Fossum
Tom and Evelyn Frankel
Mr. and Mrs. Gerald J. Gargiulo
Dr. and Mrs. James M. Garvey
Harvey Ginsberg
Milly and Arne Glimcher

Mr. and Mrs. Robert S. Goldman
Marilyn Goldstein
Daniel J. and Joan A. Gorman
Suzanne Koch Gosman
Mary and Jack Graves
Mr. and Mrs. Robert S. Greenbaum
Roy E. Greenberg, Esq.
Griffith's Carpet and Upholstery Cleaning
Keith Grimes, Inc.
Mr. and Mrs. Bernard Grob
Janet and Gerald Gutterman
Mr. and Mrs. Richard Haagen
Carolyn Buhai Haas
William and Wendy Hall
Pamela Hanson
Harold E. and Jeanne Harris
Douglas P. Herrlin
Roseann and Barry Hirsch
Laura and Robert Hoguet III
Edward W. Horne
InsideOut
Robert W. Jackson
Andrew E. Jacoby
Mrs. Helene CR Jenkins
Mr. and Mrs. Martin Joffe
Mr. and Mrs. James L. Johnson
Jane and Christopher Johnson
David R. Jones and Valerie King
Susan and Rees Jones
Pamela Keen
Dr. Victoria Kingsley
Mr. and Mrs. Gerald Kissler
Mr. and Mrs. Timothy W. Knipe
Arthur and Virginia Kwarta
Mrs. Condie Lamb Agency
Elizabeth W. Lazzara, M.D.
Melvin C. Levine
Florence Levitt
Debra Lobel, Esq.
Lobster Roll, Inc.
Mr. and Mrs. Norman Lowenstein
Maria Lubinska
Pamela S. Luchansky
Lloyd and Barbara Macklowe
Charles and Theresa Magistro
Christian Malige
Mr. and Mrs. Frank Mansell
Charlotte and Irving Markowitz
Greg McCarthy and Peter Bickford
Sean McCarthy
Mr. and Mrs. James J. McCourt
Donald and Alice McDonald
Mr. and Mrs. John McGuirk, Jr.
Donald and Frances McLoughlin
David and Elizabeth McMaster
Ruth Ann and Jack McSpadden
Jackie and George Metzger
Dr. and Mrs. Joseph Mirman
Mr. and Mrs. Norman L. Morton
Frances B. and Wendelyn L. Mott
Albert Nalaboff
Michelle Napoli

Julia S. Neagle
Roy and Helen Nicholson
Anne and John Oliver
William H. Ostertag
Jeffrey L. Parker
Ed and Barbara Peller
Dr. Fred Pescatore and Steven Feldma
Donald and Mary Petrie
Judith Pfister and Nancy Skean
Mr. and Mrs. Howard W. Phillips
Diana and Norman Plitt
Mrs. Dana M. Raymond
Mr. and Mrs. William Rayner
Denyse E. Reid
Margaret and Conor Reilly
Camille and Mauro Romita
Pamela Rosenthal
Enid Roth
Mr. and Mrs. Kenneth W. Rousell
Mary Bayes Ryan
Santa Fe Junction Restaurant
Saskas Surveying Co.
Barbara and Arthur Sawitsky
Schenck Fuels
Robert E. Schmitz
Jill and Judd Shanker
Ivanette G. Shinsato
Mr. and Mrs. William C. Shopsin
George and Sarah Shuttleworth
Vincent Frezzo & Brendan Skislock
Martin Slater
Joan and Don Sourras
Dr. and Mrs. Robert H. Stackpole
Joanna Steichen
Laura Stein and Gene Wolsk
Julie S. Steitz
Michael and Ruby Steklacci
Robert A.M. Stern
Bruce Stevens
Martha Stewart Living
Jonda C. Stilwell
Ralph and Sarah Stout
Betsy Frank and Arthur M. Strauss
Eileen O. Strauss
Stuart and Vicki Match Suna
Jamie and Julie Sykes
Mrs. Christine Theodoratos
Lois B. Underhill
Laura VanBinsbergen
Victoria and Jose Vega
Johanna E. Veiga
Janet P. Wainwright
Alan Washkowitz
David Webb
Sally and Harold Weisman
Joan Werbel
Ann M. Wilson
Anna Wingfield
Jessica Wolf
Marian Zucker